The Geological Society of America, Inc.
Memoir 158

Contributions to
the Tectonics and Geophysics
of Mountain Chains

Edited by
Robert D. Hatcher, Jr.
Harold Williams
Isidore Zietz

1983
Reprinted 1984

Published by The Geological Society of America, Inc.
3300 Penrose Place, P.O. Box 9140, Boulder, Colorado 80301
Printed in U.S.A.

Library of Congress Cataloging in Publication Data
Main entry under title:

Contributions to the tectonics and geophysics of
    mountain chains.

    (Memoir / Geological Society of America ; 158)
    "Volume grew out of a Geological Society of America
Penrose Conference held in Helen, Georgia, in May 1980"
—Introd.
    Includes bibliographies.
    1. Orogeny—Congresses. I. Hatcher, Robert D.,
1940–   . II. Williams, Harold, 1934–
III. Zietz, Isidore, 1919–   . IV. Series: Memoir
(Geological Society of America) ; 158.
QE621.C66   1983   551.4'32   83-5670
ISBN 0-8137-1158-4

Contents

Geological Society of America
Memoir 158
1983

Introduction

Robert D. Hatcher, Jr.
Department of Geology
University of South Carolina
Columbia, South Carolina 29208

Harold Williams
Department of Earth Sciences
Memorial University of Newfoundland
St. John's, Newfoundland A1B 3X5
Canada

Isidore Zietz
Phoenix Corporation
1700 Old Meadow Road
McLean, Virginia 22102

Capability of integrating the multitude of data from geologic and geophysical investigations in orogenic belts is essential to arriving at solutions to some of the great problems related to the development of mountain chains. This volume grew out of a Geological Society of America Penrose Conference held in Helen, Georgia, in May 1980, where geologists and geophysicists from academic institutions, government, and industry addressed some of the complex problems of orogenic terranes. Geologic and geophysical data that were either proprietary or of a preliminary nature were displayed and openly discussed at this meeting. The stimulating discussions coupled with the continuously changing displays of new data made for a most exciting conference. Participants are listed at the end of this introduction.

The papers presented herein develop ideas either generated by the conference or presented there. It is through such interdisciplinary efforts that solutions to the difficult and complex problems of the origin and evolution of mountain chains will eventually be produced. We attempt to make a small contribution in this volume toward a solution to some of these problems.

The subjects covered in this volume include regional geology and tectonics of the Appalachian orogen; comparisons with the Caledonides, Mauritanides, Alps, and the North American Cordillera; the application of mechanical principles to the solution of structural problems; and the utilization of the technique of reflection seismology, as well as data from aeromagnetic and gravity studies, to interpret large-scale problems in the tectonics of mountain chains.

The concept of suspect terranes has been successfully applied and developed most extensively in studies of the North American Cordillera (Coney and others, 1980). It had been applied earlier to the Alps (Dewey and others, 1973) and probably to other orogenic terranes in a less rigorous sense. In this volume, papers by Williams and Hatcher and by Zen attempt to apply the concept to the Appalachians. A technique that is extremely important in identifying and restoring suspect terranes is paleomagnetic reconstruction. Van der Voo deals with this subject and the reconstruction of Pangea in his paper.

Paired gravity anomalies in the southern and central Appalachians have led several geologists and geophysicists to conclude that these reflect the buried edge of Grenville crust. M. D. Thomas addresses this question and makes comparisons of the Appalachian gravity anomaly to examples from Precambrian crust. The paired gravity anomaly is an attribute of mountain chains, occurring in the Alps and in other modern orogens as well as in Paleozoic and Precambrian mountain chains. Thomas points out herein that in Precambrian mountain chains the paired anomaly is definitely present where topographic relief is not a problem for correction of gravity data. Therefore, the anomalies are real. The paper comparing the similarities of the Appalachians and the Canadian Cordillera by Price and Hatcher likewise brings out this point.

The papers by Haworth and Jacobi and by Lefort suggesting geophysical and geologic correlations between the Paleozoic orogens of North America and western Europe provide new information to suggest similarities between the respective orogenic terranes which have been subsequently broken apart via the present episode of continental separation. Higgins and Zietz offer a new interpretation of the geology beneath the Coastal Plain in the southeastern United States based upon gravity and magnetic data. This interpretation has a significant bearing upon the relationships between the Appalachians and buried segments of other continents to the south and east.

The papers by Wiltschko and Eastman and by Laubscher dealing with specific aspects of thrust and compressional tectonics contain additional new ideas on thrust tectonics and the nature of large thrust sheets. Rathbone, Coward, and Harris discuss the nature and contrasts in style between Caledonides cover and basement rocks, furnishing an additional study of the tectonics of deformation of the core of an orogenic terrane.

St. Julien and others and Ando and others present additional interpretations of the SOQUIP and COCORP seismic reflection profiles through different parts of the Appalachians. These sets of data have provided us with new insights into the structure of the internal parts of the Appalachian orogen and opportunities for additional studies as well as more exact comparisons to other orogens. Geiser and Engelder attempt herein to subdivide the Alleghanian orogeny in the Appalachians into two distinct phases, something which has not been done before but which has been suggested in several studies. This investigation is the result of a long-continued study into the nature of incremented strain associated with the Acadian and Alleghanian orogenies.

REFERENCES CITED

Coney, P. J., Jones, D. L., and Monger, J.W.H., 1980, Cordilleran suspect terranes: Nature, v. 288, p. 329–333.
Dewey, J. F., Pitman, W. C., III, Ryan, W.B.F., and Bonnin, Jean, 1973, Plate tectonics and the evolution of the Alpine system: Geological Society of America Bulletin, v. 84, p. 3137–3180.

MANUSCRIPT ACCEPTED BY THE SOCIETY SEPTEMBER 10, 1982

PENROSE CONFERENCE PARTICIPANTS

Charlotte Abrams
M. J. Aldrich
Richard Allenby
Clifford J. Ando
Arild Andreasen
John Armbruster
Robert Atkins
Albert W. Bally
James E. Barkdell
Noel Barstow
Colleen Barton
Chris Beaumont
Kenneth W. Bramlett
Laurie Brown
W. G. Brown
J. Robert Butler
Frederick A. Cook
John K. Costain
Marc Daignieres
David L. Daniels
Edward Davin
George H. Davis
Jelle De Boer
William Diment
Avery Drake

Brooks B. Ellwood
James F. Farley
Stewart Farrar
David G. Gee
Peter Geiser
Lynn Glover, III
Bernard Granger
Leo M. Hall
Allan Hansen
A. L. Harris
Leonard D. Harris
Richard T. Haworth
William H. Hazlett
Norman Herz
Richard A. Hopkins
Gregory Horne
J. Wright Horton, Jr.
Robert D. Jacobi
Leonard Johnson
Dennis Kent
J. Duncan Keppie
C. K. Kim
H. P. Laubscher
Jean-Pierre LeFort
J. W. Lindemann

Leland T. Long
Peter Lyttle
David B. MacLachlan
Stephen Marshak
Michael D. Max
Keith I. McConnell
J. Gregory McHone
Floyd C. Moulton
Stefan Mueller
Daniel Murray
Arthur E. Nelson
Robert B. Neuman
Stuart Nishenko
Jack E. Oliver
Neil D. Opdyke
Frank Owings
Richard J. Page
William J. Perry
Lucian B. Platt
Howard A. Pohn
Raymond A. Price
Douglas Rankin
Nicholas Rast
Mitchell W. Reynolds
Donald A. Rodgers

Jacques Roussel
Pierre St. Julien
Donald T. Secor, Jr.
Maurice Seguin
James Skehan, S. J.
Douglas L. Smith
Arthur Snoke
Jean Sougy
John H. Spang
Ian Stewart
Harold Stowell
Pradeep Talwani
Michael Thomas
William A. Thomas
James F. Tull
Rob Van der Voo
David Wenner
Russell L. Wheeler
Charles C. Wielchowsky
David Wiltschko
Fredrik Wolff
James A. Wright
Thomas O. Wright
Jeffrey Wynn
E-an Zen

Geological Society of America
Memoir 158
1983

A new geophysical criterion to correlate the Acadian and Hercynian orogenies of western Europe and eastern America

Jean-Pierre Lefort

CNRS—Centre Armoricain d'Etude Structurale des Socles
Institut de Géologie de l'Université de Rennes
Beaulieu—35042 RENNES Cedex
France

ABSTRACT

The evolution of the middle Paleozoic subduction in the South Armorican Massif (southern Brittany, France) is compared with that of the Petite Sole–Cordoba fault (western Spain and Portugal). This comparison suggests that this fault acted as a transform fault during Ordovician and Devonian times.

The gravity and magnetic data compiled on both sides of the North Atlantic indicate that the southern end of the Cordoba fault links with a 2,400-km-long mafic body which extended from the South Portuguese zone to New England (U.S.A.) before the opening of the present Atlantic Ocean. The mafic body may be considered as the suture of the Theic Ocean. However, the closing of the South Armorican and Theic oceans did not occur at the same time; the South Armorican subduction ended in Late Devonian time, whereas the Theic closed in early Carboniferous time. This diachronous evolution could be explained by the existence of an Iberian (Spanish) microplate.

INTRODUCTION

Recent studies of magmatic and metamorphic events between Hadrynian and Carboniferous time in southern Brittany suggest that the Hercynian mountain building should be separated in two cycles (Cogné, 1977). An earlier cycle from Silurian to Late Devonian time was probably the result of a northward subduction beneath South Armorica (southern Brittany); a latter cycle from Dinantian to Westphalian time involved an ensialic evolution cycle of the whole area.

The tectonometamorphic events related to subduction are therefore more or less contemporaneous with phases recognized in the Appalachian-Caledonian orogenic belt. However, the term "Acadian" is not yet accepted in Brittany, mainly because it has not been demonstrated that the deformations recognized in the Armorican Massif are really cogenetic with the phases known in the Appalachian Mountains. One of the purposes of this paper is to show that such a correlation exists.

ACADIAN EVENTS IN AND NEAR WESTERN EUROPE

Some of the Acadian events are localized onshore in Brittany (Armorican Massif) and in the Massif Central (France). However, the conclusive data supporting the existence of a suture are based mainly on marine geology and offshore geophysical interpretations.

Evidence for a Devonian Suture South of Brittany

The discovery of blueschists and the existence of a linear cordilleran orogeny in southern Brittany are responsible for several geodynamic models for the development of that area (Nicolas, 1972; Riding, 1974; Badham, 1975; Carpenter, 1976; Leeder, 1976).

It is only recently however that a high-temperature belt of migmatites has been clearly recognized, its age ranging between 370 and 460 m.y. (Peucat and others, 1978); in the more northern zone it exhibits Ordovician

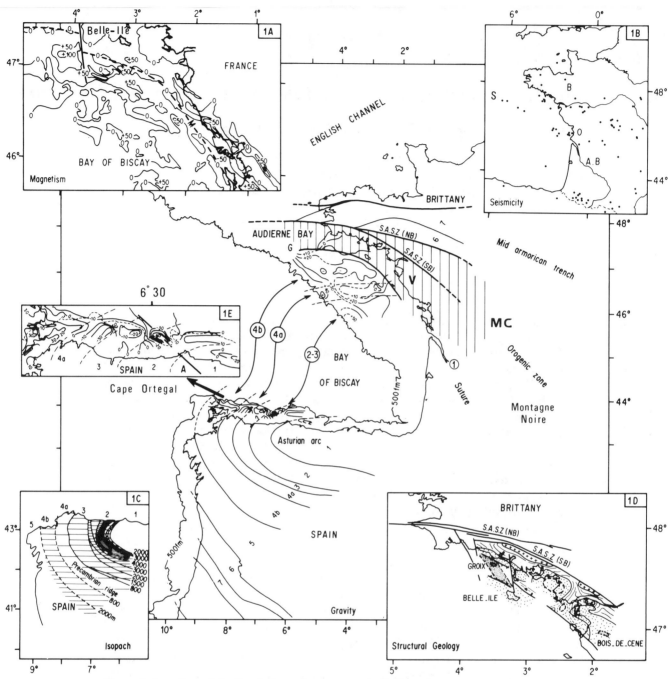

Figure 1. Location of the South Armorican suture. A, B, E, and central maps display geophysical data: A, Aviles fault; A. B., Aquitaine Basin; B, Brittany; G, gravity boundary; M, magnetic trend; M. C., Massif Central; O, Oleron Island; S, seismic alignement; S.A.S.Z., South Armorican Shear Zone; NB, northern branch; SB, southern branch; V, Vendée. C shows isopachs of the lower middle Paleozoic cover in northwest Spain. D displays geological data (for clarity, post-Devonian granites are not shown in the structural inset) with heavy lines, faults; thin lines, observed foliation trends (S2) in migmatites; heavy dashed lines, hidden diapirs; spaced dot pattern, epimetamorphic envelopes; close-dot pattern, blueschists; crosses, anatectic granites.

alkaline granites transformed into orthogneiss by the "Acadian" deformations. Southward, blueschists have been dated between 375 and 420 m.y. (Peucat and Cogné, 1977), but they were rejuvenated in Carboniferous time between 295 and 320 m.y. (Maluski, 1976; Carpenter and Civetta, 1976). The results quoted above were used by Cogné (1977) when he constructed his geodynamic model for southern Brittany. This model is oversimplified, mainly because it did not take into account the structural relationship which exists between the offshore geology and the blueschists, now isolated on the little island of Groix, 8 km south of mainland Brittany.

The marine geophysical and marine geological data now available (Audren and Lefort, 1977; Lefort and Segoufin, 1978; Lefort and others, 1981) allow a more accurate understanding and support the following points:

1. The blueschist outcrop is probably not the ancient location of the South Armorican suture; the whole of the blueschist belt is now regarded as a flat-lying obduction sole or a klippe which was emplaced northward during Silurian or Early Devonian time (Quinquis, 1980).

2. The suture must be looked for approximately 60 km to the south of Groix, where gravity and magnetic discontinuities display an arcuate belt which parallels the present coastline beneath the Mesozoic and Cenozoic cover (Lefort, 1979a).

3. This belt separates two different structural domains: the southwesternmost domain is characterized by east-west-trending gravity highs and lows (Sibuet, 1972a); these represent a remnant of the Ibero-Armorican arc that links with the Galician arc when the Bay of Biscay is closed (Fig. 1). The airborne magnetic data show, after a second derivative calculation (Horn and others, 1974), the same structural trends, which in places are cut by a late set of faults, oriented N 130° E (Lefort, 1975). To the north and east, the same magnetic data reveal the existence of structures that are parallel to the South Armorican orogen. Gravity data are sparse in this area, but they are dense enough to show that the alternation of "highs" and "lows" disappears to the east of line G (Fig. 1).

All of these data have been discussed in greater detail recently in two papers (Lefort, 1979; Lefort and Haworth, 1979). In general, the inferred suture is characterized by a small volume of magnetic rocks; to the southwest of Groix some of these rocks seem to overlap locally the northernmost gravity high (Lefort and Segoufin, 1978).

The Western Extension of the South Armorican Suture

The proposed suture and associated mafic bodies detected in places (47° N, 4° W) can be extended westward by an elongated magnetic anomaly (amplitude 120 nT) mapped between 6° and 10° W (Fig. 2); this anomaly ends close to Meriadzec Terrace (10° 30′ W). It is locally cut at 47° N, 5° 15′ W by a linear fault which trends N 130° to 140° E and which has been accurately identified by seismic reflection, seismic refraction, and magnetics. Most faults with this orientation in the Armorican margin are dextral (Lefort, 1973); this one makes a similar displacement of the magnetic body.

Even though it is at times parallel to the continental margin, this magnetic body cannot be considered as an edge-effect between the oceanic and continental crusts for the following reasons:

1. The magnetic structure extends a continental structure of the inner shelf.

2. There is no equivalent edge-effect south of Brittany.

3. The boundary between the oceanic and continental crusts is located 90 km to the south (Guennoc, 1978) (Fig. 2).

Unfortunately, the seismic refraction shots to the south of the Meriadzec Terrace (Avedik and Howard, 1979) were not powerful enough to determine whether the mafic intrusions are deeper or shallower than the Paleozoic basement.

The Westernmost End of the South Armorican Suture

Westward, the magnetic anomaly of the Meriadzec Terrace is interrupted by two faults oriented N 40° E, which are recognized in seismic reflection data (Guennoc, 1978). These faults are considered to be old features, rejuvenated during the present north Atlantic opening. They separate two sets of fractures: the earlier ones occur in the eastern part of the area and trend approximately east-west as everywhere in Brittany (II, Fig. 2), while the others in the western part trend N 130° (I, Fig. 2) and are parallel to the "proto-Atlantic" dyke swarm (Lefort, 1975). The N 40° E faults acted as transform directions for the contact between the present-day oceanic crust and continental crust (Fig. 2), confirming that they were preexisting (Lefort, 1979b).

The interruption of the South Armorican Paleozoic suture, which ends in the Shamrock Canyon (SH, Fig. 2), by two major faults near 10° 30′ W now explains why the Precambrian and lower Paleozoic magnetic arcs previously described on the Grand Banks of Newfoundland (Haworth and Lefort, 1979) are still intact along the 47th parallel (Fig. 3). In the following text, the faults that terminate the South Armorican trends, and whose transform origin will be discussed later, will be called the Petite Sole lineament after the name of a bank located north of the Meriadzec Terrace.

Acadian and Pre-Acadian Events to the Southeast of Brittany

In this section only a few major points will be outlined. Southeastward of Brittany the earliest pre-Hercynian events are located in the region of the Vendée, where a post-Ludlovian/pre-Givetian deformation exists (Ters, 1976); this is usually characterized by large recumbent folds facing south. In the Massif Central, four to five superimposed phases have been recognized which fold the entire Silurian series. Phases P1 and P2 are contempo-

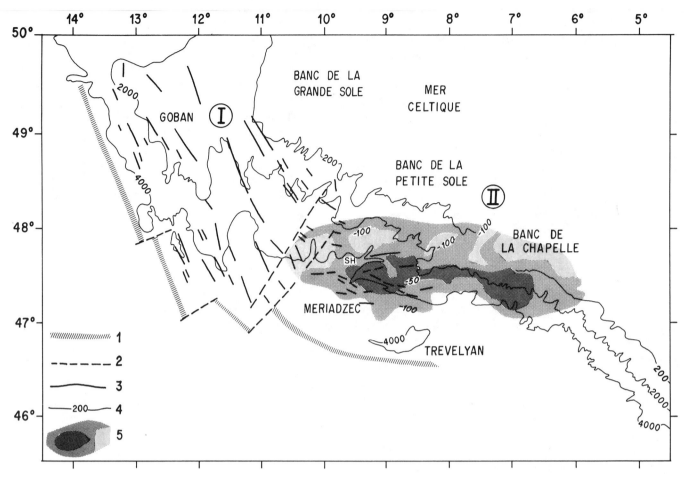

Figure 2. The western extension of the South Armorican suture from geophysical data: 1, oceanic crust boundary; 2, transform directions; 3, faults (1-2-3 after seismic data); 4, water depth in meters; 5, magnetic anomaly; Zone I, pre-opening trends; Zone II, Armorican trends; S. H., Shamrock Canyon.

raneous with a regional metamorphism which began everywhere under high-pressure/high-temperature conditions and are dated between 362 and 400 m.y. (Autran, 1978). In the same area, many alkaline granites, now transformed into orthogneiss, are dated between 520 and 420 m.y. (Bernard-Griffiths, 1976). The position of the Acadian suture is not accurately known beneath the Aquitain Basin (Fig. 1).

In summary, there exists a large crescent-shaped feature, 700 km long and 100 to 250 km wide, where at different structural levels one can recognize the effect of an Acadian subduction. However, the place of the proposed suture is clearly marked only between Shamrock Canyon and Oleron Island, probably because the volume of the mafic rocks now preserved steadily decreases eastward.

The Southern Extension of the Petite Sole Lineament

As noted above, the Petite Sole lineament cuts the

South Armorican "Suture" near 10° 30′ W; this lineament may be extended southward to the Iberian block.

Several geophysical markers have already been correlated between Europe and the Grand Banks of Newfoundland (Lefort and Haworth, 1978); others have been identified between Europe and Spain (Lefort, 1979a). These correlations have been used to fit the continents around the North Atlantic (Lefort, 1980), improving in latitude the pre-Triassic reconstitution proposed by Le Pichon and others (1977).

When using such a "fit," one can see the clear extension of the Petite Sole lineament into the Spanish shelf. Just in front of the N 40° faults mapped on the Armorican margin, a deep furrow occurs, which is filled by Mesozoic and Cenozoic sediments. This inner basin (Fig. 3), separating Spain from Galicia Bank, has been interpreted to be the result of Mesozoic rifting which developed along an old line of weakness (Auxietre and Dunand, 1978).

Such an interpretation is reenforced by the study of

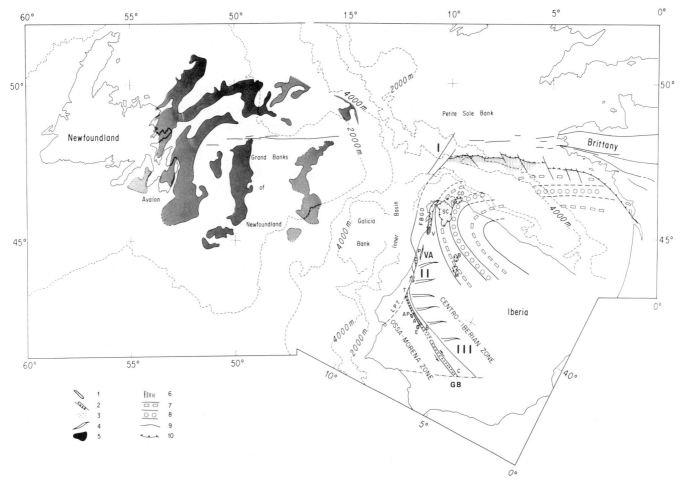

Figure 3. The relationship between the South Armorican suture and the Petite Sole–Cordoba transform fault: 1, peralkalic igneous rocks (A, Arronches; AP, Alter Pedroso; E, Elvas; V, Vigo); 2, blastomylonitic belt of Porto-Badajoz-Cordoba; I, Petite Sole lineament; II, Porto-Coimbra-Tomar fault; III, Cordoba-Badajoz-Tomar fault; 3, obducted rocks (B, Bragança; CO, Cape Ortegal; FBGO, blastomylonitic furrow of western Galicia; M, Morais; SC, Santiago de Compostela); 4, Sardic phase fold axes; 5, gravity and magnetic ridges of the Grand Banks of Newfoundland; 6, mafic rocks of the South Armorican suture; 7, pre-Carboniferous basins in Spain and "gravity" basins South of Brittany; 8, Precambrian ridge in Spain and "gravity" ridge south of Brittany; 9, faults; 10, South Armorican suture. B, Badajoz; C, Cordoba; GB, Guadalquivir Basin; P, Porto; T, Tomar; LPT, Porto-Tomar lineament; VA, Valongo.

magnetic data; the eastern limit of the Galician Basin links with the submerged end of the Porto-Badajoz-Cordoba fault (Lefort and others, 1981). This fault, which extends between Porto and the Guadalquivir basin (Fig. 3) acted as a major structure during the entire Paleozoic history of Iberia. It is considered as an important boundary for the early Paleozoic faunas (Paris and Robardet, 1977) and separates the Centro-Iberian domain (with Armorican likeness) from the South Iberian domain (Ossa Morena Zone). Other studies suggest that this fault acted as a deep shear zone between Late Proterozoic and late Paleozoic time (Blachere and others, 1977; Crouzilles and Dixsaut, 1977). Because of the major role played by this fault in

Iberia, and because its extension cuts the inferred Acadian suture west of Brittany, the structural evolution of both structures will be compared next.

The Evolution of the Petite Sole-Porto-Badajoz-Cordoba Lineament

Onshore, the Porto-Cordoba consists of two different faults: the Porto-Coimbra-Tomar fault and the Cordoba-Badajoz-Tomar fault (Fig. 3).

1. The Porto-Coimbra-Tomar fault is a submeridian fracture, 180 km long, which extends from Porto to Tomar. It cuts the older lineament of Cordoba north of

Tomar; to the South it is covered beneath Mesozoic and Cenozoic sediments. This fracture had a complex history which could be summarized as follows: Several tens of kilometers of dextral shear occurred in Westphalian time, followed by a few meters of sinistral shear during the Stephanian; today the lineament has a steep inverted dip toward the west. The subvertical foliation observed in the granitic rims of the fault exhibits sigmoidal features, which indicate dextral shear. The total amount of displacement is considered to be 100 km (Pereira and others, 1979).

2. The Cordoba-Badajoz-Tomar lineament is 350 km in length and 1 to 5 km in width; it is marked by blastomylonites that originated in a Precambrian basement or in peralkaline intrusions dated between 460 and 430 m.y. (Late Ordovician). In the inner part of the blastomylonitic belt the fabric is completely metamorphic, whereas close to the lineament Hercynian deformation increases rapidly, suggesting the existence of a major shear zone. The subvertical foliation and characteristics of the fabric imply a sinistral movement during the Hercynian orogeny (Burg and others, 1981).

It is possible to restore the pre-Hercynian evolution of the Cordoba-Badajoz-Tomar lineament through the Carboniferous events; this reconstruction is supported by the following points:

Ordovician rocks of the Centro-Iberian zone rest with angular unconformity on Cambrian strata. This unconformity originated in the Sardic phase, the significance of which is now better understood (Lefort and Ribeiro, 1980). The angle of the unconformity between the two formations increases toward the Ossa Morena Zone, where the lineament is located. The Sardic folds can be distinguished from later Hercynian *sensu stricto* folds because the former do not have axial plane cleavage. The fold axes usually trend northeastward, but also northward in some places; for example, the Valongo anticline of east Portugal. The general distribution of the "en echelon" Sardic folds suggests that the Cordoba lineament may have undergone dextral displacements in Cambrian-Ordovician time. The Valongo anticline (VA in Fig. 3) is related to a sinistral conjugated movement associated with the main displacement. Identical patterns exist today, in many places, for example close to the San Andreas transform fault, south of Malacca strait, or between Aquaba Gulf and Dead Sea (Wilcox and others, 1973). Other faults parallel to the lineament in the Centro-Iberian zone (such as the Portuguese coalbearing furrow), separate blocks where the effects of the Sardic phase are different (Schermerhorn, 1956).

b. In the Ossa Morena Zone, the Upper Ordovician Series includes a long hiatus, widespread volcanism, and peralkaline intrusions associated with ultramafic, mafic, and acidic suites. The peralkaline rocks are differentiated into granites, syenites, and nepheline syenites (with sodalite), some of which are rich in riebeckite or acmite. Alkaline intrusions with ferrohastingsite exist in some places. All of these rocks suggest an environment of continental rifting and crustal thinning. These associations are known elsewhere as bounding transform faults. During the Late Ordovician, the Cordoba lineament was probably a sinistral feature (B, Fig. 4). According to this interpretation, crustal distension began during Middle Ordovician time, and Portugal was an area of relaxation with no orogenic events. Possibly this was the time when the direction of shear movements reversed (from dextral during Late Cambrian time to sinistral during Late Ordovician time) Lefort and Ribeiro, 1980).

c. There are no field data to reveal Silurian to Middle Devonian history.

d. The polymetamorphic klippen of northern Portugal and northwestern Spain result from Late Devonian obduction (Ribeiro, 1976; Bayer and Matte, 1979; Ribeiro and Ribeiro, 1979). The klippen are restricted to the area north of Porto, but the true extension of the obducted nappe may be restored (even where eroded) owing to the deformation recognized in the deep Paleozoic parautochtonous series known in the same area (Pereira and Ribeiro, 1979). Obducted oceanic slices are preserved in places in the lowest part of the klippen. The ocean was probably located to the northwest. The displacement trajectories generated by the obducted slabs suggest that the Cordoba-Badajoz-Tomar lineament was sinistral when the obduction occurred. Figure 4 summarizes all of these.

Comparative Evolution between the South Armorican Suture and the Petite-Sole-Cordoba-Lineament

Two lines of evidence suggest that the South Armorican Ocean and the Petite Sole–Cordoba lineament were related. The first is given by the timing of the South Armorican subduction, and the second depends on shear movements along the Iberian lineament:

1. The anatectic diapirs related to the subduction process (Audren, 1976) indicate that the convergence period probably began in Late Ordovician time and ceased in Late Devonian time (Vidal, 1976); therefore, the South Armorican Ocean was open before Late Ordovician time.

2. As discussed above, the Cordoba lineament was dextral during the Sardic phase, whereas it reversed just when the subduction began: it is the reason why the Petite Sole–Cordoba lineament will be considered here as a fossil transform fault.

But the true movement may have been much more complex, and limited spreading may have taken place between the Avalon domain (e.g., Grand Banks of Newfoundland, Galicia Bank, and West Portuguese Zone) and the Centro-Iberian zone. Furthermore, the Petite Sole–

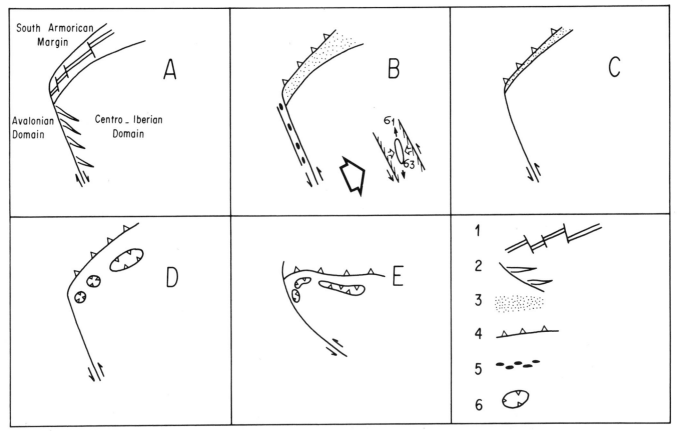

Figure 4. The geodynamic evolution of the Centro-Iberian domain is shown for the time between Cambrian and late Paleozoic (Hercynian): A, Late Cambrian; B, Late Ordovician; C, Silurian; D, Late Devonian; E, Carboniferous. 1, oceanic ridge; 2, Sardic phase fold axe; 3, oceanic crust; 4, subduction zone; 5, peralkaline rocks; 6, klippen.

Cordoba lineament was possibly not the only fracture involved in the inferred transform movement, and many faults, now assumed to be Hercynian, could have been associated with the major lineament in a wide transform belt.

GEOPHYSICAL CORRELATION BETWEEN WESTERN EUROPE AND EASTERN AMERICA

Since the South Armorican suture shows a definite orientation and typical geophysical characteristics, an equivalent structure has been sought on the western Atlantic margin. For this reason gravity and magnetic data from both continental shelves of the North Atlantic between 35° and 50° latitude have been compiled.

Magnetic Data

Data (Fig. 5) have been established as total field values from airborne surveys (G, Fig. 5) (Serviços Geológicos de Portugal, 1979), as a first-derivative map of the anomalies reduced to the actual pole (A and C, Fig. 5) (Gérard, 1975; Horn and others, 1974), or as anomalies from aeromagnetic data (E, Fig. 5) (in Sibuet, 1972b) or from sea-towed magnetometer data (B, D, and F, Fig. 5) (Segoufin, 1975; Guennoc, 1978; Groupe Galice, 1976). Syntheses already published in Canada (H, Fig. 5) (Haworth and McIntyre, 1975) as well in the United States (I, Fig. 5) (Kane and others, 1972) have also been used.

For an easier reading of the map (Fig. 5), only the magnetic highs have been drawn. There are two clearly independent sets, one trending roughly east-west and the other oriented north-south or N 50° to 60° E; the former cuts the latter.

Gravity Data

The data (Fig. 6) have been published either as free-air anomalies (A, C, D, and H, Fig. 6) (Sibuet, 1972b; Groupe Galice, 1978; Roberts, 1970) or as Bouguer anomalies (F, G, I, J, and K, Fig. 6) (Instituto Geographico y Cadastral, 1972; Instituto Geografico e Cadastral, 1958; Haworth and McIntyre, 1975, 1977; Kane and others, 1972). Locally the gravity edge-effect has been removed in

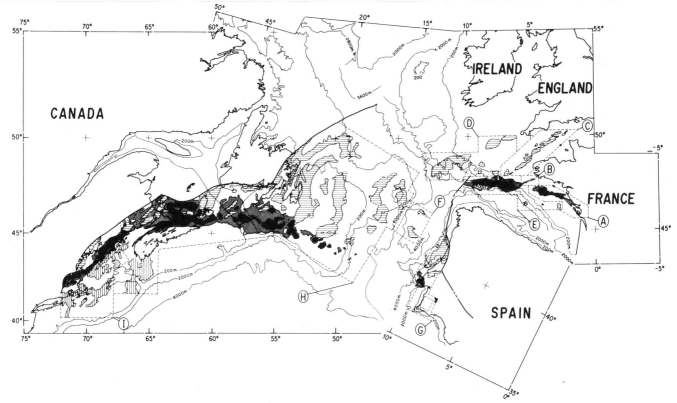

Figure 5. Magnetic data after: A, Horn and others, 1974; B, Ségoufin, 1975; C, Gérard, 1975; D, Guennoc, 1978; E, Sibuet, 1972b; F, Groupe Galice, 1976; G, Serviços Geológicos de Portugal, 1979; H, Haworth and McIntyre, 1975, 1977; I, Kane and others, 1972 (Triassic fit). Horizontal ruling, magnetic highs recognized in the Avalonian domain; vertical ruling, magnetic highs recognized north of Gondwanaland; black and interlaced lines, magnetic highs recognized south of the Avalon Prong.

order to assist the interpretation (Sibuet, 1972a). Data from the oil industry have been used, but their publication is not allowed (E, Fig. 6). Although more complicated because of the contouring of the anomalies, one can see, as in magnetics, two sets of gravity highs.

All the data, slightly smoothed, have been compiled on the same map (Fig. 7). Interpretation is restricted to the areas located south and east of the Northern Appalachian axis (Osberg, 1978; Haworth and Lefort, 1979; Williams, 1979). The two different orientations already noticed are clearly separated, and most of the gravity highs are superimposed on the magnetic highs; this suggests that they are related either to mafic bodies or to the morphology of the top of the basement.

Significance of the Arcuate Structures Recognized South of Brittany and between Massachusetts and the South Portuguese Zone

As discussed above, the mafic elongated body recognized south of Brittany is considered to be an Acadian suture (Lefort, 1979a). Although this body never crops out

and stays buried beneath the Mesozoic and Cenozoic cover, calculated magnetic susceptibilities suggest that it consists of either gabbro or basalt (Lefort and Segoufin, 1978).

Despite the gap that exists (as in every transatlantic "fit") between the Tail of the Banks and the South Portuguese Zone, it is possible to connect the gravity and magnetic anomalies existing in these two areas. In southern Portugal, magnetic data that are missing eastward do not preclude this connection, since the geophysical data stop just where the Iberian mafic belt begins. This belt is constituted by the gabbro-dioritic zone of Beja (inset B, Fig. 7) and by the Aracena complex (inset A, Fig. 7). The former contains gabbros, basalts, and serpentinites with ophiolitic composition (Andrade, 1979), whereas the latter has felsic and mafic tuffs associated with layered amphibolites identical to abyssal tholeiites (Bard, 1977; Bard and Moine, 1977). Both exposures occur in a narrow line which has been interpreted as a "geosuture" (Tamain, 1978). The mafic belt tends to link, beneath the Guadalquivir Basin, with the southern end of the Petite Sole–Cordoba transform fault. Near Beja, the intrusions are

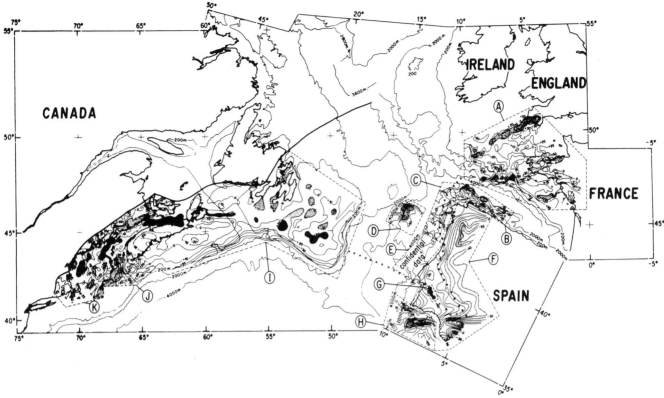

Figure 6. Gravity data after: A, Sibuet, 1972b; B, Sibuet, 1972a; C and D, Groupe Galice, 1978; E, Oil industry (confidential); F, Instituto Geografico y Cadastral, 1972; G, Instituto Geografico e Cadastral, 1958; H, Roberts, 1970; I, Haworth and McIntyre, 1975, 1977; J, Kane and others, 1972. Close-dot pattern, gravity trends recognized in the Avalonian domain, Spain and Gondwanaland; black, gravity highs recognized south of the Avalon Prong (Triassic fit).

Devonian in age (Ribeiro, personnal communication), whereas the volcanics of Aracena are pre-Silurian (Bard, 1977). However, none of these rocks are considered as true ophiolites, and they do not show tectonites in their lowest part.

The entire South Portuguese Zone has been interpreted as the location of a Devonian-Carboniferous subduction zone dipping northeast (Bard, 1971; Carvalho, 1972; Bard and others, 1973; Vegas and Munoz, 1976). Although broadly convincing, this model has to be modified in order to take into account recent geochemical analyses (Munha, 1979). In this new interpretation, the Iberian mafic belt probably resulted from crustal extensions behind a volcanic arc (Bard and Moine, 1977); the true suture must be looked for a few kilometers to the south, beneath the Carboniferous cover of the south Portuguese zone.

The linear magnetic anomaly that faces the Portuguese mafic belt on the Grand Banks of Newfoundland has been called the Collector Anomaly (Haworth and McIntyre, 1975). This structure extends into Nova Scotia where it has been interpreted as a suture (Poole, 1976).

The mafic body that exists at depth never crops out, and is probably not related to the Ordovician, Silurian, and Devonian volcanics of the Cobequid Mountains and Antigonish Highlands (Keppie, 1979, Keppie and Dostal, 1979) (inset C, Fig. 7). Westward, the Collector Anomaly disappears beneath the Bay of Fundy, perhaps because of the thick sediments existing there (Belt, 1968). Moreover, Keppie (1977) thought that the graben was the place of an old subduction zone.

Near Passamaquoddy Bay the thickness of the sediments decreases (Ballard and Uchupi, 1975), and mafic rocks of the Collector Anomaly are again exposed; farther south down to Cape Ann, superimposed magnetic and gravity highs indicate a continuance of mafic rocks (Kane and others, 1972). This body is called the Bay of Maine igneous complex (Chapman, 1962): it is composed of volcanics (old andesites and rhyolites) of Early Silurian to Early Devonian age, and gabbroic rocks of Devonian age (Gates, 1969). The same body appears again north of Cape Ann (insets D and E, Fig. 7), but slightly offset by late-Hercynian dextral faults (Lefort and Haworth, 1981). The Bay of Maine mafic complex is probably adjacent to a

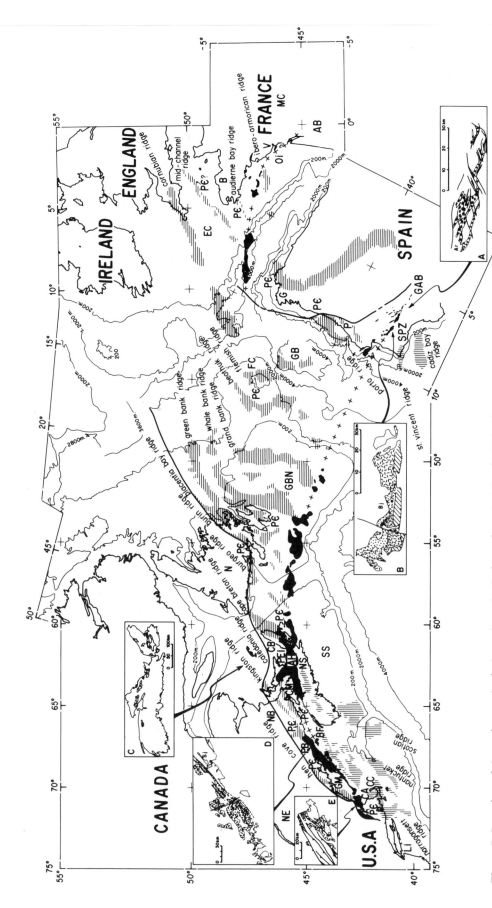

Figure 7. Location of the main geophysical trends on both sides of north Atlantic (Triassic fit): AB, Aquitaine Basin; AH, Antigonish Highlands; AR, Aracena; B, Brittany; BF, Bay of Fundy; BJ, Beja; CA, Cape Ann; CB, Cape Breton; CC, Cape Cod; CM, Cobequid Mountains; EC, English Channel; FC, Flemish Cap; G, Galicia; GAB, Guadalquivir Basin; GB, Galicia Bank; GBN, Grand Banks of Newfoundland; GM, Gulf of Maine; MC, Massif Central; N, Newfoundland; NB, New Brunswick; NS, Nova Scotia; OI, Oleron Island; P, Portugal; PB, Passamaquoddy Bay; PEI, Prince Edwards Island; SS, Scotian Shelf; SPZ, South Portuguese Zone; V, Vendée. Horizontal ruling, basement ridges recognized in the Avalon Prong and Iberia (mainly Precambrian); vertical ruling, basement ridges recognized in Gondwanaland. Inset A, Aracena zone (open circle, basaltic tuffs; V, metamorphosed amphibolites). Inset B, Beja zone (random slashes, gabbros; fine stippled, basalts; right inclined ruling, serpentinites). Inset C, Nova Scotian Zone, V, volcanic rocks. Inset D, Passamaquoddy Bay Zone (random slashes, gabbroic rocks; fine stippled, volcanic rocks). Inset E, Cape Ann Zone (random slashes, gabbroic rocks). Black, Acadian suture; crosses, extension of the Acadian suture; PE, Precambrian outcrops.

suture (Osberg, 1978); the geochemical relationships of some associated ultramafic-mafic rocks strongly suggest an oceanic crustal affinity and origin (Gaudette, 1980). Onshore all these rocks are faulted and show recumbent folds or thrusts facing west. In the Boston area the position of the suture is less clear; the mafic compositions of some of the rocks west of Cape Ann are compatible with those of the suture, but their probable pre-middle Paleozoic age may preclude this correlation.

Thus, the same geophysical marker may be followed from south of Brittany to south of Iberia and south of the Maritimes. Apparently it is composed everywhere of Silurian or Ordovician volcanics associated with Devonian gabbros and diorites. True obducted ophiolites are not found in America, but the presence of a Paleozoic volcanic arc developed on or adjacent to oceanic crust is very possible. Subsequently, this belt has been rejuvenated in some places in Triassic time, since the old volcanics and intrusives are in places bounded by younger basalts, as at the Bay of Fundy and west of Lisbon.

Significance of the Ridges Oriented from North-South to North 60°

In order to facilitate the following discussion, the north-trending ridges have been named on Figure 7. Most of these ridges show a gravity high superimposed on a magnetic high, and their amplitudes suggest that most of them are related to mafic rocks at depth. In addition, several ridges display mafic volcanics or gabbro-dioritic intrusions where they crop out, such as in the Audierne Bay (Peucat and Cogné, 1974), on the Flemish Cap (Pelletier, 1971), on the Grand Banks of Newfoundland, in New Brunswick, and in Newfoundland (Haworth and Lefort, 1979). North of the Collector Anomaly, only two ridges show a more acidic composition when they crop out; nevertheless it is remarkable that the entire structures are Late Proterozoic or Precambrian in age when they rise to the surface. The Cornubian ridge is, among them, the only trend that can be related to a morphological effect caused by hercynian granites beneath the Mesozoic and Cenozoic cover (Day and Williams, 1970). Nevertheless, Figure 7 includes it because parallel Precambrian structures exist in South Wales (Edmonds and others, 1975), and because granitic intrusions of Carboniferous age, controlled by Precambrian structures, are known elsewhere (such as in northwest Spain; Matte, 1968).

The geophysical and geochemical arguments that support the existence of an Upper Proterozoic mafic belt in the middle of the Channel are discussed in Lefort (1975) and Auvray and Lefort (1980), and will not be repeated here. The Narragansett ridge is probably the only structure among those located south of the east-west mafic belts that could be Precambrian in age, since the rocks crop out near Providence (Rhode Island); its extension into the Gulf of Maine is considered to be Precambrian by Kane and others (1972). The Nova Scotian high, on the other hand, is not Late Proterozoic in age, but arises from the magnetic effect of pyrrhotite in the Cambrian-Ordovician Meguma Group (McGrath and others, 1973). Finally, the origin of the Cape Saint Vincent and Cadiz Bay ridges is not known, since they are buried offshore as well as onshore beneath Carboniferous thrusts or Cenozoic cover.

The Massachusetts–South Portuguese Mafic Body and Paleozoic Geodynamic Evolution

The major structural trends of the eastern Appalachian margin have been followed onshore by Williams (1979) and offshore by Jacobi and Kristoffersen (1976) and Haworth and others (1976) for the northern part of Newfoundland (Fig. 8). South of the Gulf of St. Lawrence the structural zoning has been interpreted from gravity and magnetic data collected by Haworth and McIntyre (1977).

Three zones are recognized: (1) The Dunnage Zone, which represents the suture of the Iapetus Ocean, is cryptic (Dewey, 1977) near the St. Lawrence and New York promontories. (2) The Gander Zone, which has been interpreted as an Andean type margin of Iapetus (Williams, 1979), is narrower near the St. Lawrence promontory than elsewhere (Rankin, 1976). (3) The Avalon Zone, which shows typical Precambrian ridges, represents the continental crust which was underthrust by the Iapetus oceanic crust (Osberg, 1978; Haworth and others, 1978). It has been named the Avalon Prong or Avalon Apron (Rast, 1979). The mafic body discussed above, trending between New England and South Portugal, is the southern limit of the Avalon Prong.

The interpretation of the Massachusetts–South Portuguese mafic body as a Paleozoic plate boundary is based on the following points: (1) The Precambrian ridges are everywhere interrupted by the inferred suture. (2) Some of the mafic bodies show oceanic affinities where they crop out, and a volcanic arc is highly possible. (3) Volcanic and intrusive rocks range between Ordovician and Devonian in age. (4) South of the suture in Atlantic Canada, deep-sea fan facies of Cambrian-Ordovician age exist as the Meguma Group (Schenk, 1971). Rocks of the same age, dispersal, and provenance facies as found in the Meguma have also been found in northern Morocco (Schenk, 1978); geophysical data suggest that they may underlie the Tail of the Banks (Haworth and Keen, 1979); it is even possible that the Meguma extends into the South Portuguese zone, where a thick series of schists, characterized by a 5.3-km/s velocity (Sousa Moreira and others, 1977), has been found underneath the Carboniferous thrusts, 5.4

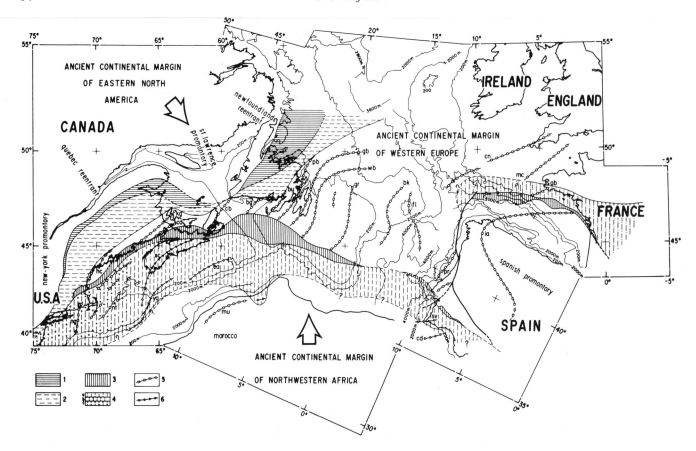

Figure 8. Arrangement of Iapetus and Theic sutures during Late Carboniferous time: 1, vestiges of Iapetus Ocean; 2, Andean margin of Iapetus; 3, structures related to the subduction of the Theic and South Armorican oceans; 4, African margin to the south of the Avalon Prong, or margin of Southern Brittany (a, Meguma facies; b, unknown basement; c, African basement); 5, Precambrian trends; 6, trends beneath or in Meguma facies (initials refer to the geophysical ridges named in Fig. 7).

km/s being the velocity of Meguma facies in Nova Scotia (Dainty and others, 1966). (5) The crust known south of the "suture" is dissimilar to that known to the north. In the South Portuguese zone (south of Beja), gravity data indicate that the continental crust thins (Gaibar-Puertas, 1976). In southern Nova Scotia a highly conductive structure of the crust is indicated by magnetotelluric measurements, which suggest a quasi-oceanic crust at depth (Schenk, 1971; Cochrane and Wright, 1977), whereas in the Gulf of Maine the same crust is intruded by a huge volume of mafic rocks (Kane and others, 1972) and is considered to be "different" from the onshore crust. (6) In addition, Middle Devonian paleomagnetic poles found in rocks of southern New England differ from those of North America (Schutts and others, 1976); they suggest that eastern Massachusetts was close to North Africa at that time.

All these arguments imply that the inferred suture was really a plate boundary in middle Paleozoic time. The entire length of this boundary has been associated with

Acadian and Hercynian orogenic events, well known in New England (Osberg, 1978; Skehan and Murray, 1979), in Canada (Poole, 1976; Keppie, 1977; Schenk, 1978), or south of Spain and Portugal (Bard, 1969; Bard and others, 1973).

The nature of the terranes involved in the suture changes from place to place and may include pre-opening rifting volcanics (e.g., in Nova Scotia), slabs of oceanic crust (e.g., in northeastern New England), remnants of back-arc basins (e.g., in Portugal), or dismembered volcanic arcs (e.g., in New England). The zoning found today in most active subduction zones has obviously not been preserved in these terranes, and if a truly ophiolitic layer of roughly the same age once existed along the entire suture, it has certainly been dismembered depending on the extent of the collisional forces.

It is very difficult, however, to recognize the dip of the subduction; according to Portuguese data this subduction dipped northeast (Bard and others, 1973), but Keppie (1977), based on the geochronological zoning of granitic

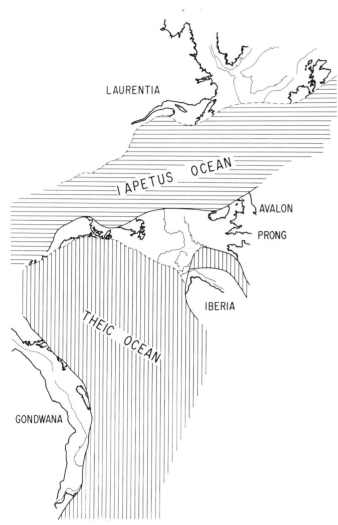

Figure 9. Relative positions of the Iapetus, Theic, and South Armorican oceans during Early Silurian time.

vician stratigraphical and paleontological similarities between Spain and Brittany (Paris and Robardet, 1977; Henry, 1980), just when the South Armorican Ocean was at its widest, suggest that Iberia did not drift a long distance away from the Avalon Prong.

CONCLUSIONS ABOUT THE FINAL EVOLUTION OF THE THEIC AND SOUTH ARMORICAN OCEANS

Figure 9 corresponds to the closing of the Iapetus, Theic, and South Armorican oceans in Early Silurian time; during that time, Gondwanaland approached the Avalon Prong, Iberia (Centro-Iberian zone), and Laurentia. The Iapetus Ocean closed first (Scotese and others, 1979), uniting the Laurentian plate with the Avalon Prong to produce the Laurussian plate.

The subduction of the Theic and South Armorican oceans probably ended at a different time.

This diachroneity is supported by the interpreted narrow belt of oceanic crust that was still present north of Gondwanaland (Van der Voo and others, 1980) when the South Armorican subduction ceased (Cogné, 1977). Finally, both sutures were affected by Hercynian events which represent the end of the closing cycle.

The huge volume of mafic rocks contained in the suture south of the Grand Banks of Newfoundland and the existence of the very thick and widespread abyssal fan system (the Meguma Group) to the south of it suggest that this old margin is a sheared margin rather than a collision margin. This could be the reason why there are no true obducted ophiolites in Nova Scotia, since an incomplete suturing should not develop obduction (Dewey, 1977); east of New England the suture is probably cryptic (Osberg, 1978). It is not known whether the southern torsion of the Precambrian ridges, which is obviously the result of

rocks in Nova Scotia, suggested an inverted polarity between Late Ordovician and Late Devonian time, which is in good agreement with the data gathered by Piqué (1979) in Morocco.

The sutures recognized in Europe and America limit, therefore, the Avalon Prong in the South, although there is not sufficient proof that they represent everywhere the northern boundary of Gondwanaland or whether microcontinents existed between these two main plates.

The Centro-Iberian Plate and the Paleozoic Geodynamic Story

Notwithstanding the absence of accurate paleomagnetic data from Mid-Paleozoic rocks of Iberia, different models exist to connect the South Armorican and Collector subductions, depending on the distance Iberia drifted away from Europe during spreading of the Theic Ocean (Hagstrum and others, 1980). However, good Late Ordo-

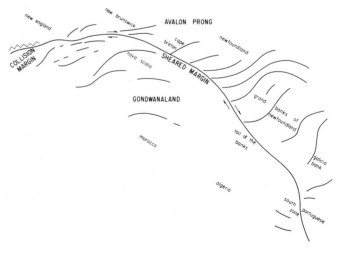

Figure 10. Deformation of preexisting trends along the northern boundary of Gondwanaland.

a dextral shear movement south of the Grand Banks of Newfoundland (Fig. 10), resulted from a counterclockwise rotation of Gondwanaland against the southern margin of the Avalon Prong or whether this deformation developed during the final tightening in Carboniferous time.

The first hypothesis, which is in good agreement with the sinistral movement of Gondwanaland already proposed by paleomagnetism (French, 1976), implies again that the southern boundary of the Avalon Prong behaved as a transform or sheared margin during Late Devonian or Early lower Carboniferous time.

ACKNOWLEDGMENTS

I thank R. T. Haworth, P. E. Schenk, and R. Van der Voo for useful suggestions.

REFERENCES CITED

Andrade, A.A.S., 1979, Aspectos geoquimicos do Ofiolitoide de Beja: Communicações dos Serviços Geologicos de Portugal, T. LXIV, p. 39–48.

Audren, C., 1976, Modèle structural de la mise en place des massifs anatectiques en Bretagne méridionale: Paris, 4ème Réunion Annuelle des Sciences de la Terre, p. 23.

Audren, C., and Lefort, J. P., 1977, Géologie du plateau continental sud armoricain entre les îles de Glénan et de Noirmoutier: Implications géodynamiques: Bulletin de la Société géologique de France, v. 7, T. 19, p. 395–404.

Autran, A., 1978, Synthèse provisoire des événements orogéniques calédoniens en France: I.G.C.P. 27, Geological Survey of Canada Paper 78-13, p. 159–175.

Auvray, B., and Lefort, J. P., 1980, Evolution géodynamique du Nord du Massif armoricain au Protérozoïque supérieur. Tectonic studies group abstract: Journal of the Geological Society of London, v. 137, p. 213.

Auxietre, J. G., and Dunand, J. P., 1978, Géologie de la marge ouest ibérique (au Nord de 40° N) [thesis]: University of Paris, 215 p.

Avedik, F., and Howard, D., 1979, Preliminary results of seismic refraction study in the Meriadzek-Trevelyan area, Bay of Biscay: Initial Reports of the Deep Sea Drilling Project Leg 48, U.S. Government Printing Office, v. XLVIII, no. 53, p. 1015–1023.

Badham, J.P.N., 1975, Microplate tectonics oblique collision and evolution of the hercynian orogenic systems: Geology, v. 2, p. 373–376.

Ballard, R. D., and Uchupi, E., 1975, Triassic rift structures in the Gulf of Maine: American Association of Petroleum Geologists Bulletin, v. 59, p. 1041–1072.

Bard, J. P., 1969, Le métamorphisme régional progressif des Sierras d'Aracena en Andalousie occidentale (Espagne), sa place dans le segment hercynien sud-ibérique [thesis]: University of Montpellier, 397 p.

——1971, Sur l'alternance des zones métamorphiques et granitiques dans le segment hercynien sud-ibérique; comparaison de la variabilité des caractères géotectoniques de ces zones avec les orogènes "orthotectoniques": Boletín geológico y minero, T. LXXXII, v. 3 and 4, p. 324–345.

——1977, Signification tectonique des métatholéites d'affinité abyssale de la ceinture métamorphique de basse pression d'Aracena (Huelva, Espagne): Bulletin de la Société Géologique de France, v. 7, T. XIX, no. 2, p. 385–393.

Bard, J. P., and Moine, B., 1977, Variations géochimiques et affinités tholéïtiques abyssales des orthoamphibolites d'Acebuches dans la ceinture métamorphique de basse pression d'Aracena (Huelva), Espagne: Rennes, Réunion Annuelle des Sciences de la Terre, p. 41.

Bard, J. P., Capdevila, R., Matte, P., and Ribeiro, A., 1973, Geotectonic model for the Iberian Variscan orogen: Nature, Physical Science, v. 241, p. 50–52.

Bayer, R., and Matte, Ph., 1979, Is the mafic/ultramafic massif of cabo Ortegal (Northwest Spain) a nappe emplaced during a Variscan obduction? A new gravity interpretation: Tectonophysics, v. 57, p. 9–18.

Belt, E. S., 1968, Post-Acadian rifts and related facies, eastern Canada, *in* Studies in Appalachian geology—Northern and Maritime: Zen, E-an, ed., New York, Interscience, p. 95–113.

Bernard-Griffiths, J., 1976, Essai sur la signification des âges au strontium dans une série métamorphique du Bas Limousin [thesis]: University of Clermont, v. 55, no. 27, 243 p.

Blachere, H., Crouzilles, M., Deloche, Ch., Dixsaut, Ch., Hertrich, B., Prostdame, V., Simon, D., and Tamain, G., 1977, Le "linéament de Cordoue" et la mégatectonique de la partie sud-Hespérique de l'arc ibéro-armoricain: Rennes, Réunion Annuelle des Sciences de la Terre, p. 80.

Burg, J. P., Iglesias, Ph., Laurent, Ph., Matte, Ph., and Ribeiro, A., 1981, Variscan intracontinental deformation, the Porto-Tomar-Cordoba shear zone: Tectonophysics, v. 78, p. 161–177.

Carpenter, M.S.N., 1976, Petrographic study of the glaucophane schists and associated rocks from île de Groix, France [Ph.D. thesis]: Oxford, 271 p.

Carpenter, M.S.N., and Civetta, L., 1976. Hercynian high pressure/low temperature metamorphism in the île de Groix blue-schists: Nature, v. 262, p. 276–277.

Carvalho, D., 1972, The metallogenic consequences of plate tectonics and the upper Paleozoic evolution of southern Portugal: Estudos Notas e Trabalhos do Serviços de Fomento Mineiro, v. 20, p. 297–320.

Chapman, C. A., 1962, Bays-of-Maine Igneous Complex: Geological Society of America Bulletin, v. 73, p. 883–888.

Cochrane, N. A., and Wright, J. A., 1977, Geomagnetic sounding near the northern termination of the Appalachian system: Canadian Journal of Earth Sciences, v. 14, p. 2858–2864.

Cogné, J., 1977, La chaîne hercynienne ouest-européenne correspond-elle à un orogène par collision? Propositions pour une interprétation géodynamique globale: CNRS International Symposium, no. 268, p. 111–129.

Crouzilles, M., and Dixsaut, Ch., 1977, L'association ophiolitique varisque du Varas-Guadalbarbo (Cordoue, Espagne). Aspect structural et métallogénique, [thesis]: University of Paris-Sud, 289 p.

Dainty, A. M., Keen, C. E., Keen, M. J., and Blanchard, J. E., 1966, Review of geophysical evidence on crust and upper mantle structure on the eastern seaboard of Canada, *in* The earth beneath the continents: American Geophysical Union Monograph 10, p. 349–369.

Day, G. A., and Williams, C. A., 1970, Gravity compilation in the N.E. Atlantic and interpretation of gravity in the Celtic sea: Earth and Planetary Science Letters, v. 8, p. 205–213.

Dewey, J. F., 1977, Suture zone complexities: A review: Tectonophysics, v. 40, no. 6, 1-2, p. 53–68.

Edmonds, E. A., McKeown, M. C., and Williams, M., 1975, South-west England. (fourth edition): London, National Environment Research Council, p. 1–136.

French, R. B., 1976, Lower Paleozoic paleomagnetism of the North American Craton [Ph.D. thesis]: University of Michigan, 159 p.

Gaibar-Puertas, C., 1976, Variaciones del espesor crustal y grado de equilibro isostatico associables a las anomalias de Bouguer en la Espana Peninsular: Boletín Geológico y Minero, 87/84, p. 371–401.

Gates, O., 1969, Lower Silurian–Lower Devonian volcanic rocks of New England coast and Southern New Brunswick, *in* Kay, M., ed., North Atlantic geology and continental drift: American Association of Petroleum Geologists, Memoir 12, p. 484–503.

Gaudette, H. E., 1980, Zircon isotopic age from the Union ultramafic complex, Maine: Canadian Journal of Earth Sciences, v. 18, p. 405, 409.

Gérard, A., 1975, La tectonique du socle sous la Manche occidentale d'après les données du magnétisme aéroporté: Royal Society of London Philosophical Transactions, v. 279, ser. A, p. 55–68.

Groupe Galice, 1976, Les anomalies magnétiques du champ terrestre dans la région des bancs de Galice: Paris, 4ème Réunion Annuelle des Sciences de la Terre, p. 181.

——1978, The continental margin off Galicia and Portugal: Acoustical stratigraphy, dredge stratigraphy and structural evolution: Initial Reports of the Deep-sea Drilling Project Leg 47B, v. 47, no. 2, p. 633–662.

Guennoc, P., 1978, Structure et évolution géologique de la pente continentale d'un secteur de l'Atlantique nord-est: de la terrasse de Meriadzec à l'éperon de Goban [thesis]: University of Brest, 95 p.

Hagstrum, J. T., Van der Voo, R., Auvray, B., and Bonhommet, N., 1980, Eocambrian-Cambrian palaeomagnetism of the Armorican Massif, France: Geophysical Journal of the Royal Astronomical Society, v. 61, p. 489–517.

Haworth, R. T., and Keen, C. E., 1979, The Canadian Atlantic margin: A passive continental margin encompassing an active part: Tectonophysics, v. 59, no. 1-4, p. 83–126.

Haworth, R. T., and Lefort, J. P., 1979, Geophysical evidence for the extent of the Avalon zone, in Atlantic Canada: Canadian Journal of Earth Sciences, v. 16, p. 552–567.

Haworth, R. T., and McIntyre, J. B., 1975, The gravity and magnetic field of Atlantic offshore Canada: Geological Survey of Canada Paper 75-9, 22 p.

——1977, The gravity and magnetic fields of the Gulf of St. Lawrence, Canada: Geological Survey of Canada Paper 75-42, 11 p.

Haworth, R. T., Poole, W. H., Grant, A. C., and Sandford, B. V., 1976, Marine geoscience survey northeast of Newfoundland: Geological Survey of Canada Paper 76-1 A, p. 7–15.

Haworth, R. T., Lefort, J. P., and Miller, H. G., 1978, Geophysical evidence for an east-dipping Appalachian subduction zone beneath Newfoundland: Geology, v. 6, p. 522–526.

Henry, J. L., 1980, Trilobites ordoviciens du Massif armoricain [thesis]: University of Rennes, 250 p.

Horn, R., Munck, F., and Muraour, P., 1974, Quelques remarques sur la tectonique du socle sous la plateforme continentale atlantique d'après le magnétisme: Bordeaux, Colloque internatinal sur l'exploitation des Océans, p. 1–6.

Instituto Geográfico e Cadastral, 1958, Carta gravimetrica de Portugal, escala 1/1,000,000.

Instituto Geographico y Cadastral, 1972, Avance del mapa gravimetrico de la peninsula Iberica, escala 1/2,000,000, p. 1–30.

Jacobi, R., and Kristoffersen, Y., 1976, Geophysical and geological trends on the continental shelf off northeastern Newfoundland: Canadian Journal of Earth Sciences, v. 13, p. 1039–1051.

Kane, M. F., Yellin, M. J., Bell, K. G., and Zietz, I., 1972, Gravity and magnetic evidence of lithology and structures in the Gulf of Maine region: U.S. Geological Survey Professional Paper 726B, p. 1–22.

Keppie, J. D., 1977, Tectonics of southern Nova Scotia: Nova Scotia Department of Mines Paper 77-1, p. 1–34.

——1979, Geological map of the Province of Nova Scotia: Department of Mines and Energy, Nova Scotia, scale 1/500,000.

Keppie, J. D., and Dostal, J., 1979, Paleozoic volcanic rocks of Nova Scotia, Proceedings of the Caledonides in the USA: Virginia Polytechnic Institute and State University, Department of Geological Sciences, Memoir 2, p. 249–259.

Leeder, M. R., 1976, Sedimentary facies and the origins of basin subsidence along the northern margin of the supposed Hercynian Ocean: Tectonophysics, v. 36, p. 167–179.

Lefort, J. P., 1973, La "zonale" Biscaye-Labrador: mise en évidence de cisaillements dextres antérieurs à l'ouverture de l'Atlantique Nord: Marine Geology, v. 14, p. M33–M38.

——1975, Le socle péri-armoricain: étude géologique et géophysique du socle submergé à l'Ouest de la France [thesis]: University of Rennes, 250 p.

——1979a, Iberian-Armorican arc and Hercynian orogeny in Western Europe: Geology, v. 7, p. 384–388.

——1979b, Failles de socle et directions transformantes en Atlantique Nord: Lyon, 7ème Réunion Annuelle des Sciences de la Terre, p. 287.

——1980, Un "fit" structural de l'Atlantique Nord: Arguments géologiques pour corréler les marqueurs géophysiques reconnus sur les deux marges: Marine Geology, v. 37, p. 355–369.

Lefort, J. P., and Haworth, R. T., 1978, Geophysical study of basement fractures, on the western European and Eastern Canadian shelves: Transatlantic correlations and late Hercynian movements: Canadian Journal of Earth Sciences, v. 15, p. 397–404.

——1979, The age and origin of the deepest correlative structures recognized off Canada and Europe. Tectonophysics, v. 59, p. 139–150.

——1981, Geophysical correlation between basement features in North West Africa and North America, and their control over structural evolution: Société Géologique et Minéralogique de Bretagne, T. (C), v. XIII, no. 2, p. 103–116.

Lefort, J. P., and Ribeiro, A., 1980, La faille Porto-Badajoz-Cordoue a-t-elle contrôlé l'évolution de l'océan paléozoïque sud-armoricain?: Bulletin de la Société Géologique de France, T. XXII, no. 3, p. 455–462.

Lefort, J. P., and Segoufin, J., 1978, Etude géologique de quelques structures magnétiques reconnues dans le socle péri-armoricain: Bulletin de la Société Géologique de France, T. XX, no. 2, p. 185–192.

Lefort, J. P., Alverhinho-Dias, J., Monteiro, H., and Ribeiro, A., 1981, Les structures profondes du socle Portugais à l'ouest de la Faille Porto-Badajoz: Comunicações dos Serviços Geológicos de Portugal, T. 67, ser. 1, p. 57–63.

Lefort, J. P., Audren, C., Jegouzo, P., Max, M. D., Grant, P., and Rattey, P., 1981, Disposition of structures in the South of Brittany (France). Belt of high pressure metamorphism: Edinburgh, The Sixth International Scientific Symposium of the World, Underwater Federation (in press).

Le Pichon, X, Francheteau, J., and Sibuet, J. C., 1977, The fit of continents around the North Atlantic Ocean: Tectonophysics, v. 38, p. 169–209.

Maluski, H., 1976, Intérêt de la méthode $^{40}Ar/^{39}Ar$ pour la datation des glaucophanes: Exemple des glaucophanes de l'île de Groix (France): Paris, Comptes-rendus de l'Académie des Sciences, T. 283, ser. D, p. 223–225.

Matte, Ph., 1968, La structure de la virgation hercynienne de Galice (Espagne): Revue de Géologie Alpine, v. 44, 128 p.

McGrath, P. H., Hood, P. J., and Cameroun, G. W., 1973, Magnetic surveys of the gulf of St. Lawrence and the Scotian shelf: Geological Survey of Canada Paper 71-23, p. 339–358.

Munhá, 1979, Blue amphiboles, Metamorphic Regime and plate tectonic modelling in the Iberian Pyrite Belt: Contributions to Mineralogy and Petrology, v. 69, p. 279–289.

Nicolas, A., 1972, Was the hercynian orogenic belt of Europe the Andean type?: Nature, v. 236, p. 221–223.

Osberg, P. H., 1978, Synthesis of the geology of the northeastern Appalachians, U.S.A.: I.G.C.P. 27, Geological Survey of Canada Paper 78-13, p. 137–148.

Paris, F., and Robardet, M., 1977, Paléogéographie et relations ibéro-armoricaines au Paléozoïque anté-carbonifère: Bulletin de la Société Géologique de France, T. XIX, no. 5, p. 1121–1126.

Pelletier, B. R., 1971, A granodiorite drill core from the Flemish Cap, eastern Canada continental margin: Canadian Journal of Earth

Sciences, v. 8, no. 11, p. 1499–1503.

Pereira, E., and Ribeiro, A., 1979, Tectonica do sector NW da Serra do Marao: Lisbonne, Encontro de Geosciencias.

Pereira, E., Ribeiro, A., and Severo, L., 1979, Analise da deformacao da zona de cisalhamento Porto-Coimbra-Tomar, na transversal de Oliveira de Azémeis: Lisbonne, Encontro de Geociencias.

Peucat, J. J., and Cogné, J., 1974, Les schistes cristallins de la Baie d'Audierne (sud-Finistère): un jalon intermédiaire dans le socle antécambrien entre la Meseta ibérique et les régions sud-armoricaines: Paris, Comptes-rendus de l'Académie des Sciences, T. 278, ser. D, p. 1809–1811.

—— 1977, Geochronology of some blueschists from île de Groix, France: Nature, v. 268, p. 131–132.

Peucat, J. J., Audren, Cl., and Le Métour, J., 1978, Arguments géochronologiques en faveur de l'existence d'une double ceinture métamorphique d'âge siluro-dévonien en Bretagne méridionale: Bulletin de la Société Géologique de France, T. XX, no. 2, p. 163–167.

Piqué, A., 1979, Evolution structurale d'un segment de la chaîne hercynienne: la meseta marocaine nord-occidentale [thesis]: University of Strasbourg, 242 p.

Poole, W. H., 1976, Plate tectonic evolution of the Canadian Appalachian Region: Geological Survey of Canada Paper 76-1B, p. 113–126.

Quinquis, H., 1980, Schistes bleus et déformation progressive: l'exemple de l'île de Groix (Massif Armoricain) [thesis]: University of Rennes, 145 p.

Rankin, D. W., 1976, Appalachian salients and recesses: Late Precambrian continental break up and the opening of the Iapetus Ocean: Journal of Geophysical Research, v. 81, no. 32, p. 5605–5619.

Rast, N., 1979, The Avalonian plate in the Northern Appalachians and Caledonides, *in* Wones, D. R., ed., The Caledonides in the U.S.A.: Department of Geological Sciences, Virginia Polytechnic Institute and State University, Memoir 2, p. 63–63.

Ribeiro, M. L., 1976. Consideracoés sobre una ocoriencia de crossite em Tras-os-Montes oriental: Publication of the University of Coimbra, v. 82, p. 1–16.

Ribeiro, A., and Ribeiro, M. L., 1979, Obduccao no cadeia, Hercinica da Peninsula Iberica: Lisbonne, Encontro de Geociencias.

Riding, R., 1974, Model of the Hercynian fold belt: Earth and Planetary Science Letters, v. 24, p. 125–135.

Roberts, D. G., 1970, The Rif-Betic orogen in the Gulf of Cadiz: Marine Geology, v. 9, p. 31–37.

Schenk, P. E., 1971, Southeastern Atlantic Canada, northwestern Africa and continental drift: Canadian Journal of Earth Sciences, v. 8, p. 1218–1251.

—— 1978, Synthesis of the Canadian Appalachians. Caledonian Appalachian Orogen of the North Atlantic Region: I.G.C.P. 27, Geological Survey of Canada Paper 78-13, p. 111–136.

Schermerhorn, L.J.G., 1956, Igneous, metamorphic and ore geology of the Castro-Daire-Sao Pedro do Sul-Satao region (N. Portugal): Comunicaçòes dos Serviços Geológicos de Portugal, v. 37, 617 p.

Schutts, L. D., Brecher, A., Hurley, P. M., and Montgomery, C. W., 1976, A case study of the time and nature of paleomagnetic resetting in a mafic complex in New England: Canadian Journal of Earth Sciences, v. 13, p. 898–907.

Scotese, C. R., Bambach, R. K., Barton, C., Van der Voo, R., and Ziegler, A., 1979, Paleozoic base maps: Journal of Geology, v. 87, no. 3, p. 217–277.

Segoufin, J., 1975, Structure du plateau continental armoricain: Royal Society of London Philosophical Transactions, v. 279, no. 1288, p. 109–121.

Serviços Geológicos de Portugal, 1979. Intensidade Total do campo magnético (cópia provisoria).

Sibuet, J. C., 1972a, Histoire structurale du Golfe de Gascogne [thesis]: University of Strasbourg, 174 p.

—— 1972b, Contribution de la gravimétrie à l'étude de la Bretagne et du plateau continental adjacent: Comptes-rendus de la Société Géologique de France, no. 3, p. 124–127.

Skehan, J. W., and Murray, D. P., 1979, A model for the evolution of the eastern margin (EM) of the Northern Appalachian, *in* Wones, D. R., ed., The Caledonides in the U.S.A.: Department of Geological Sciences, Virginia Polytechnic Institute and State University, Memoir 2, p. 67–72.

Sousa Moreira, J., Mueller, St., Mendes, A. S., and Prodehl, Cl., 1977, Crustal structure of Southern Portugal: Publication of the Institut of Geophysics of Poland, v. A4, no. (115), p. 413–426.

Tamain, G., 1978, L'évolution calédono-varisque des Hespérides: P.I.C.G. Project 27.23, Geological Survey of Canada Paper 78-10, p. 183–241.

Ters, M., 1976, Notice explicative de la 2ème édition de la feuille Pallueau-île d'Yeu, de la carte géologique de France à l'échelle du 1/80,000: B.R.G.M., Orléans.

Van der Voo, R., Briden, J. C., and Duff, B. A., 1980, Late Precambrian and Paleozoic paleomagnetism of the Atlantic-Bordering continents: International Geological Congress, Paris, Colloque C 6, p. 203–212.

Végas, R., and Munoz, M., 1976, El contacto entre las zonas Surportuguesa y Ossa Morena en SW Espana. Una nueva interpretacion: Comunicações dos Serviços Geológicos de Portugal, T. LX, p. 31–51.

Vidal, Ph., 1976, L'évolution polyorogénique du Massif armoricain: apport de la géochronologie et de la géochimie isotopique du strontium [thesis] University of Rennes, 142 p.

Wilcox, R. E., Harding, T. P., and Seely, D. R., 1973, Basic wrench tectonics: American Association of Petroleum Geologists Bulletin, v. 17, p. 74–96.

Williams, H., 1979, Appalachian Orogen in Canada: Canadian Journal of Earth Sciences, v. 16, no. 3, Part 2, p. 792–807.

MANUSCRIPT ACCEPTED BY THE SOCIETY SEPTEMBER 10, 1982

Geological Society of America
Memoir 158
1983

A plate-tectonics model for the Paleozoic assembly of Pangea based on paleomagnetic data

Rob Van der Voo
Department of Geological Sciences
The University of Michigan
Ann Arbor, Michigan 48109

ABSTRACT

Paleomagnetic data have become available in the past decade that enable us to constrain better the motions of the continental blocks involved in the Paleozoic assembly of Pangea. Drawing upon various aspects of earlier models for this assembly, this paper briefly outlines a new model that is fully compatible with the currently available paleomagnetic poles. In this new model, the last two major collisions are between Gondwana and the northern continents in the Carboniferous and between the more northerly cratonic blocks of Asia (Siberia and Kazakhstan) and the combined Atlantic-bordering continents in the Permian. Earlier, the northern continents (the North American craton, the Baltic Shield–Russian Platform, and Hercynian Europe, herein called Armorica) assembled. The timing of this coalescing of the northern continents cannot be precisely identified by the available paleopoles, but the orogenic belts that mark the collision zones formed during the time between the Late Ordovician (Taconic orogeny) and the Middle Devonian (Acadian orogeny), that is, between 440 and 380 Ma. It should be noted, furthermore, that the northern continents assembled in a configuration different from that of the fit by Bullard and coworkers; the paleomagnetic data argue for a Carboniferous megashear between the North American craton, on the one hand, and the Baltic Shield, Russian platform and Armorica, on the other hand.

Since Wilson (1966) queried, "Did the Atlantic close and then reopen?" much research in Paleozoic tectonics and paleomagnetism has been directed toward the documentation of the proto-Atlantic oceans, such as Iapetus (McKerrow and Ziegler, 1972). A multitude of models, paleogeographic maps, and paleotectonic analyses have been published, and it is impossible here to review all the syntheses of the past decade, which are often conflicting with each other. Moreover, recent paleomagnetic data have been obtained for North America and western Europe, which modify or constrain many of these models. In this paper, I will briefly review the new paleomagnetic developments. A more detailed review (Van der Voo, 1982) has been prepared at the time of writing.

The final assembly of Pangea incorporated the following cratons: Laurentia (the North American craton and Greenland in pre-drift position), Baltica (the Baltic Shield and the Russian Platform), Siberia, and Gondwana (in the assembly of Smith and Hallam, 1970). By Permian-Triassic times Pangea is thought to have been assembled in a Wegener-type configuration. Although Morel and Irving (1981) have argued for a major dextral shear of up to 3,500 km between Gondwana and the northern continents in the Permian-Triassic, the paleomagnetic data do not require this, in my opinion, whereas geological arguments may also be found that argue against it. The final welding of Siberia to Baltica probably occurred during Permian time, although the two may have been roughly adjacent since Devonian time (Irving, 1977).

Probably the most dramatic event in the assembly of Pangea has been the collision of Gondwana and Laurussia (i.e., Laurentia and Baltica). Late Devonian and early and late Carboniferous paleopoles provide evidence for this collision. Whereas in Late Devonian time a wide ocean

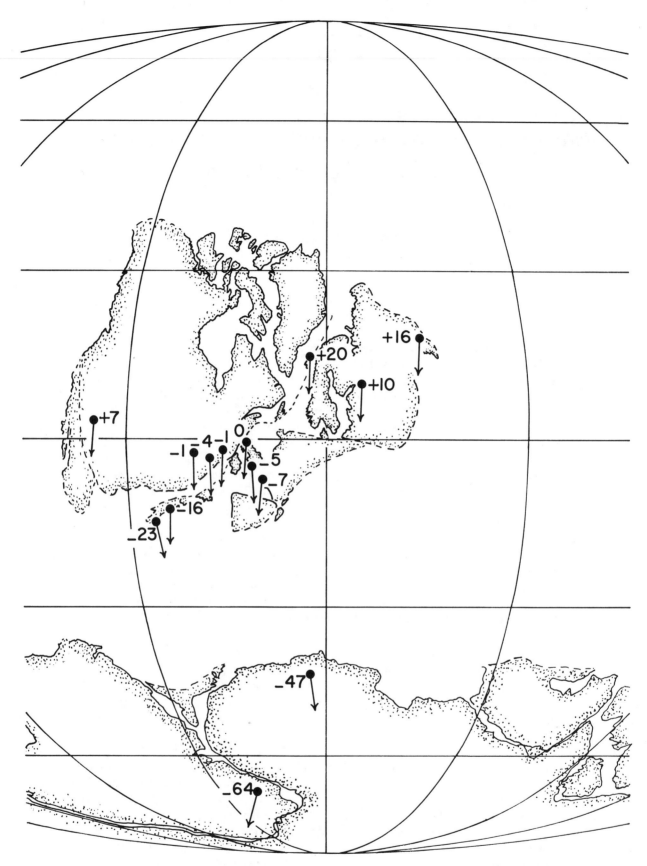

Figure 1. Paleogeographic map in Mollweide projection for the Middle to Late Devonian of the Atlantic-bordering continents, compiled on paleomagnetic data (from Van der Voo, 1982). Each plotted point represents the average declination (arrow) and paleolatitude for a given region.

(~3,000 km) still existed between the two (Fig. 1), this ocean had narrowed significantly by Visean time. The Hercynian, late Mauritanide, Alleghanian, and Ouachita orogenies resulted from the collision, which may have had a fairly prolonged history between Visean and Stephano-Autunian time. Lefort and Van der Voo (1981) have argued that the impact of Gondwana caused an extensive rearrangement of Laurussia, including an ~2,000-km megashear between North America and Europe. On the basis of paleomagnetic data from these two continents, the megashear occurred mostly between Visean and Stephanian times (Van der Voo, 1983). The location of the megashear is not precisely known, paleomagnetic data suggest that the Scottish Highlands north of the Great Glen fault belonged to the American side (Van der Voo and Scotese, 1982), whereas eastern coastal New England, the coastal Canadian Maritimes, and eastern Newfoundland (the "Acadia" displaced terrane of Kent and Opdyke, 1978, 1979) belonged to the European side.

Late Devonian paleopoles from the Armorican Massif, France (Fig. 1), and Middle Devonian through early Carboniferous results from Germany, France, and northern Spain suggest that these areas belonged to Laurussia in the Late Devonian, rather than to Gondwana (e.g., Perroud and Bonhommet, 1981; Bachtadse and others, 1983). The major ocean between Gondwana and Laurussia must therefore have been to the south of most of Hercynian Europe, although narrow (oceanic?) basins may have existed farther north, as suggested for instance for the Kulm Basins in England and Germany (Johnson, 1973).

As will be discussed below, Van der Voo (1979) has proposed that a major part of Hercynian Europe together with Wales and southern England constituted an early Paleozoic "Armorica" plate. It is conceivable that eastern Newfoundland and the Canadian Maritimes (the Avalonian terrane) belonged to Armorica as well, although there are no paleomagnetic data from these areas to test this idea. However, it is well known that the Precambrian basement of the Avalon terrane and the (Cadomian) basement of large areas in Hercynian Europe and southern England have remarkable similarities, in support of this contention. Latest Precambrian and Cambrian paleomagnetic data from Armorica agree with those from Gondwana (Hagstrum and others, 1980), whereas they are very different from Laurentia's poles, which suggests that Armorica broke off from Gondwana and collided (as a unity or as several segments) with Laurentia and Baltica before Late Devonian time. Three orogenies are therefore likely candidates for this collision: the Taconic (~440 to 480 Ma), the Caledonian (~415 Ma), or the Acadian (~380 Ma) orogenies. There are insufficient paleomagnetic or geologic data to make a definite choice between these three events for specific collisions. I note, however, that the location of Armorica in the Late Devonian configura-

tion of Figure 1 argues for a choice between the Taconic and the Acadian orogenies insofar as the coalescence of Armorica and Laurentia is concerned. If Baltica and Armorica are to have collided as well (which is not entirely clear because few reliable paleopoles exist for the early Paleozoic of Baltica), then only the Caledonian mobile belt between Scotland and the North Sea to northern Germany and Poland (Zwart and Dornsiepen, 1978; Ziegler, 1978) is a candidate. Finally, there is a consensus that the collision between Laurentia and Baltica closed the Iapetus Ocean in

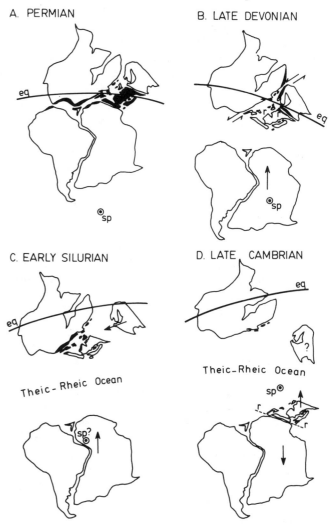

Figure 2. Cartoon of four stages in the assembly of Pangea. A. A Permian configuration of the final assembly, with recently formed (Hercynian-Appalachian) mountain belts in black. The equator and South-Pole location are indicated. B. A Late Devonian schematic map, similar to Figure 1, with the recently formed Caledonian mountain belts in black. The arrows indicate the post-Late Devonian megashear between Europe and North America, and 'r' indicates intracontinental(?) rifting. C. Early Silurian schematic map showing the Taconic orogenic belt formed in preceding times in black and the inferred relative motion of Baltica which will produce the Late Silurian Caledonides. D. Late Cambrian map with Armorica and Gondwana about to break apart.

Late Silurian time, thus producing the main Caledonian belt between Great Britain, Norway, northeastern Greenland, and Spitsbergen.

I have favored the scheme of Figure 2 for the pre-Late Devonian collisions for the following reasons. First, Baltica's northwest and southwest margins are both marked by Caledonian (*sensu stricto,* ~415 Ma) mobile belts (shown in black in Fig. 2B), and the simplest pattern of the coalescence of Laurentia, Baltica, and Armorica argues for a Caledonian collision between Baltica and the combined Laurentia-Armorica continent. Second, if southern England and Wales were part of Armorica (a contention that needs firmer paleomagnetic substantiation), then its paleomagnetic results indicate that it was in the same paleolatitudes throughout Late Ordovician, Silurian and Devonian times as the central Appalachians in the United States (Van der Voo, 1982, 1983). This would argue in favor of a Taconic collision between Laurentia and all or parts of Armorica, so that the two are adjacent in the Silurian (Fig. 2C). Ordovician paleomagnetic work is planned for the near future in the Armorican Massif in order to test this idea.

This scheme, of course, leaves the Acadian orogeny unexplained insofar as continent-continent collisions are concerned. An ad-hoc hypothesis for the Acadian orogeny, occurring in Acadia as well as along that part of the (Ibero-) Armorican Arc facing the interior of the arc (Peucat and others, 1978), could be that it was due to northward subduction of the ocean between Laurussia and Gondwana as the latter moved northward toward Laurussia during Silurian and Early Devonian time (Fig. 2B, 2C). Alternatively, the Acadian orogeny may have been due to a collision with southern parts of what we have called Armorica, arriving more than 60 Ma later than the first Armorica fragments, such as southern England. Before any substantial progress can be made in resolving such questions, many more Paleozoic paleomagnetic data are needed for the various tectonic elements located within the Hercynian and Appalachian belts themselves. Although results are now emerging for the northern Appalachians (e.g., Spariosu and Kent, 1980) and Hercynian Europe (Bachtadse and others, 1983; Perroud and Bonhommet, 1981) that suggest relative rotations for Devonian and Carboniferous time of some of these elements, the critical time of the earlier Paleozoic lacks data altogether.

The late Precambrian and Early to Middle Cambrian apparent polar wander paths of Gondwana and Armorica have been compared by Hagstrum and others (1980). They have interpreted the remarkable similarity between the two paths as suggesting coherence of these areas in approximately the configuration of Figure 2D. This proposal then led in turn to the development of the idea of an Armorica plate (Van der Voo, 1979). During late Precambrian and Cambrian time, Laurentia straddled the equa-tor, whereas near-equatorial paleolatitudes are indicated by the few paleopoles for Baltica as well (McElhinny, 1973; Prasad and Sharma, 1978). Thus, all continental elements of Pangea were dispersed at the beginning of the Paleozoic Era.

An interesting final question is whether a Pangea-type or other supercontinental assembly existed before Middle Cambrian time. A paucity of Hadrynian paleopoles leaves this question thus far unanswered; in particular for Laurentia, paleomagnetic data with ages between 900 and 650 Ma are badly needed.

ACKNOWLEDGMENTS

This research was supported by the Division of Earth Sciences, the National Science Foundation, grant EAR 81-03130.

REFERENCES CITED

Bachtadse, V., Heller, F., and Kröner, A., 1983, Paleomagnetic investigations in the Hercynian mountain belt of Middle Europe: Tectonophysics, 91, p. 285–299.

Hagstrum, J. T., Van der Voo, R., Auvray, B., and Bonhommet, N., 1980, Eocambrian-Cambrian paleomagnetism of the Armorican Massif, France: Geophysical Journal of the Royal Astronomical Society, 61, p. 489–517.

Irving, E., 1977, Drift of the major continental blocks since the Devonian: Nature, 270, p. 304–309.

Johnson, G.A.L., 1973, Closing of the Carboniferous sea in western Europe, *in* Tarling, D. H., Implications of continental drift to the earth sciences: and Runcorn, S. K., eds., New York and London, Academic Press, v. 2, p. 845–850.

Kent, D. V., and Opdyke, N. D., 1978, Paleomagnetism of the Devonian Catskill red beds: Evidence for motion of the coastal New England–Canadian Maritime region relative to cratonic North America: Journal of Geophysical Research, 83, p. 4441–4450.

——1979, The Early Carboniferous paleomagnetic field for North America and its bearing on the tectonics of the northern Appalachians: Earth and Planetary Science Letters, 44, p. 365–372.

Lefort, J. P., and Van der Voo, R., 1981, A kinematic model for the collision and complete suturing between Gondwanaland and Laurussia in the Carboniferous: Journal of Geology, 89, p. 537–550.

McElhinny, M. W., 1973, Paleomagnetism and plate tectonics: Cambridge University Press, 358 p.

McKerrow, W. S., and Ziegler, A. M., 1972. Paleozoic oceans: Nature Physical Science, 240, p. 92–94.

Morel, P., and Irving, E., 1981, Paleomagnetism and the evolution of Pangea: Journal of Geophysical Research, 86, p. 1858–1872.

Perroud, H., and Bonhommet, N., 1981, Paleomagnetism of the Ibero-Armorican arc and the Hercynian orogeny in Western Europe: Nature, 292, p. 445–448.

Peucat, J. L., Le Métour, J., and Audren, C., 1978, Argument géochronologique en faveur de l'existence d'une double ceinture métamorphique d'âge siluro-dévonien en Bretagne méridionale: Bulletin Societé Géologique de France, 7 (20-2), 163–167.

Prasad, S. N., and Sharma, P. V., 1978, Paleomagnetism of the Nexø sandstone from Bornholm Island, Denmark: Geophysical Journal of the Royal Astronomical Society, 54, p. 669–680.

Smith, A. G., and Hallam, A., 1970, A fit of the southern continents: Nature, 225, p. 139–144.

Spariosu, D. J., and Kent, D. V., 1980, Paleomagnetic results from northern Maine and their bearing on displaced terrains [abs.]: EOS (American Geophysical Union Transactions) v. 61, p. 220.

Van der Voo, R., 1979, Paleozoic assembly of Pangea: A new plate tectonic model for the Taconic, Caledonian and Hercynian orogenies [abs.]: EOS (American Geophysical Union Transactions) v. 60, p. 241.

—— 1982, Pre-Mesozoic paleomagnetism and plate tectonics: Annual Reviews Earth and Planetary Science Letters, 10, p. 191–220.

—— 1983, Paleomagnetic constraints on the assembly of the old Red continent: Tectonophysics, 91, p. 271–283.

Van der Voo, R., and Scotese, C. R., 1981, Paleomagnetic evidence for a large (~2000 km) sinistral offset along the Great Glen fault during Carboniferous time: Geology, 9, p. 583–589.

Wilson, J. T., 1966, Did the Atlantic close and then reopen? Nature, 211, p. 676–681.

Ziegler, P., 1978, Northwestern Europe: Tectonics and basement development: Geologie en Mijnbouw, 57, p. 589–626.

Zwart, H. J., and Dornsiepen, V. F., 1978, The tectonic framework of central and Western Europe: Geologie en Mijnbouw, 57, p. 627–654.

MANUSCRIPT ACCEPTED BY THE SOCIETY SEPTEMBER 10, 1982

Geological Society of America
Memoir 158
1983

Geophysical correlation between the geological zonation of Newfoundland and the British Isles

R. T. Haworth
Atlantic Geoscience Centre
Geological Survey of Canada
Bedford Institute of Oceanography
P.O. Box 1006, Dartmouth, Nova Scotia B2Y 4A2
Canada

R. D. Jacobi
Department of Geological Sciences
State University of New York at Buffalo
4240 Ridge Lea Road
Amherst, New York 14226

ABSTRACT

All available gravity and magnetic data for Newfoundland, the British Isles, and their adjacent continental margins are compiled on an early Mesozoic, pre–continental drift reconstruction of the North Atlantic. These data support geological correlation between the southern termination of the Caledonides and the northern termination of the Appalachians. Geological zones southeast of the postulated early Paleozoic suture in both Newfoundland and the British Isles have distinctive geophysical signatures, and these may be extrapolated to locations at the edge of the continental shelf that were in close proximity in early Mesozoic time. Geological zones northwest of the suture also have associated distinctive geophysical anomalies, but their correlations on the early Mesozoic reconstruction are more tenuous because (1) off Ireland the zones converge and trend toward a low-angle intersection with the continental margin, (2) off Newfoundland the zones diverge and trend perpendicular to the margin, and (3) the Mesozoic location of Rockall Plateau, the intervening continental fragment, is poorly defined.

INTRODUCTION

Both of us have for several years attempted to interpret and correlate the offshore extension of the Appalachian and Caledonide structures on opposite sides of the Atlantic (Fig. 1) based primarily on geophysical data collected on the Canadian, British, Irish, and French continental margins, and geological/geophysical correlations observed on land (Haworth, 1975; Jacobi and Kristoffersen, 1976; Lefort and Haworth, 1978; Haworth and Keen, 1979; Haworth, 1980, 1981; Jacobi and Kristoffer-son, 1981). With the dearth of geological samples offshore, such interpretations tend to be speculative, and our opinions have occasionally differed. This paper presents an up-to-date synthesis of the gravity and magnetic data available (Figs. 2, 3, in pocket inside back cover) and summarizes those aspects of the interpretation of the data upon which we can agree. Further details of any specific correlation may be found elsewhere (Haworth, 1981; Jacobi and Kristoffersen, 1981). All three figures will need to

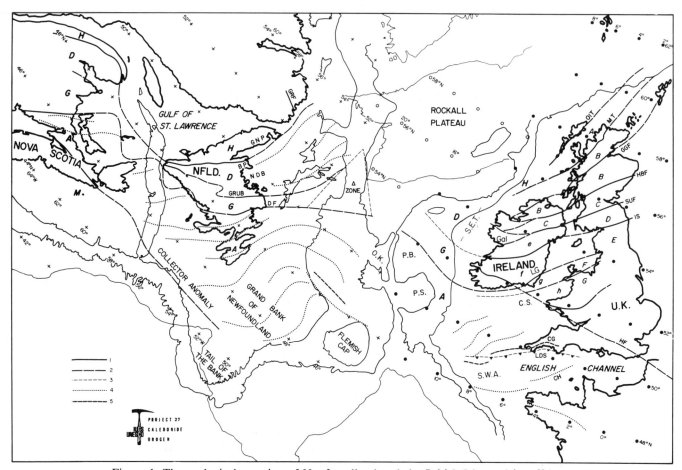

Figure 1. The geological zonation of Newfoundland and the British Isles and its offshore extension as defined geophysically (see text). The bold letters, **H, D, G, A,** and **M** on the Canadian margin denote the Humber, Dunnage, Gander, Avalon, and Meguma zones, respectively, and on the British margin the Hebrides, Dundee, Greenore, and Anglesey zones, respectively (Williams, 1978b). Within the British Isles, the upper case letters A through G denote the geological zones of Dewey (1974) and the lower case letters e through h those of Phillips and others (1976). Other abbreviations are as follows: BP = Burlington Peninsula, CG = Cornubian Granites, CH = Channel High, C.S. = Celtic Sea, DF = Dover fault, Gal = Galway, GGF = Great Glen fault, GNP = Great Northern Peninsula, GRF = Gilbert River fault, GRUB = Gander River Ultrabasics, HBF = Highland Boundary fault, HF = Hercynian Front, IS = Iapetus suture, LDS = Lizard-Dodman-Start thrust, LG = Leinster Granite, MT = Moine thrust, NDB = Notre Dame Bay, NFLD = Newfoundland, OIT = Outer Isles thrust, O.K. = Orphan Knoll, P.B. = Porcupine Bank, P.S. = Porcupine Seabight, S.E.T. = Slyne Eris Trough, SUF = Southern Uplands fault, and S.W.A. = Southwest Approaches. Lineament patterns are as follows: (1) Well-defined boundaries between geological zones on land, (2) less well defined or offshore extensions of those geological zone boundaries, (3) poorly defined zone boundaries, (4) linear magnetic highs within geological zones, and (5) linear gravity lows within geological zones. Paleogeographic reconstruction from Sclater and others (1977) and Srivastava (1978); see text.

be referred to continuously while reading the paper; therefore, individual reference to them within the text has been avoided.

GEOLOGICAL ZONATION OF NEWFOUNDLAND AND ITS OFFSHORE EXTENSION

Newfoundland geology has been subdivided into characteristic zones since Williams (1964) first recognized a bilateral symmetry to the island's geology. Williams and others (1972, 1974) developed a detailed zonation which, although applicable to Newfoundland, had characteristics that were not generally applicable to the Appalachians as a whole. A more simple zonation was therefore developed (Fig. 1) which Williams (1978a) believed could be recognized throughout much of the Appalachians. This zonation is based on tectono-stratigraphic units that are generically related to the elements of a Paleozoic ocean, Iapetus, and its margins.

The Humber zone, the westernmost zone in Newfoundland, represents the continental margin on the western side of Iapetus and is underlain by Grenvillian rocks. These are well exposed in the Long Range Mountains of the Great Northern Peninsula and represent the basement upon which a sequence of lower Paleozoic platform sedimentary rocks were deposited in a typical passive margin environment. The dominant geophysical characteristics of this zone are negative Bouguer gravity anomalies bordered on the east by a prominent gravity gradient, positive to the east. This set of anomalies is observed along the entire length of the western margin of the Appalachian orogen, and the gradient generally marks the eastern extent of Grenvillian crust that has not been greatly deformed or metamorphosed by younger events. The regional gravity field is perturbed by local geological features, such as ophiolite thrust slices forming the White Hills at the tip of the Great Northern Peninsula, where the gravity gradient is displaced westward. Despite such local divergences, continuity of the gravity gradient indicates that the Grenville margin lies close to the eastern edge of the Great Northern Peninsula and trends only slightly east of north close to the Labrador Coast. A major break in the characteristic gravity gradient at $52\frac{1}{2}°$ N off Labrador marks its oblique junction with gabbroic rocks north of the Gilbert River fault zone, but thereafter the zone continues north to approximately $53\frac{1}{2}°$ N. Magnetic anomalies in the Humber zone have long wavelengths and low amplitudes over the Paleozoic cover rocks and have short wavelengths and high amplitudes where Grenvillian basement is exposed. Their variable trend and nature make the magnetic anomalies an unreliable indicator of the offshore continuation of the Humber zone.

The Dunnage zone represents the vestiges of Iapetus (Williams, 1978a). It contains all the volcanic, sedimentary, and oceanic crustal rocks that were characteristic of the Paleozoic ocean or created by its closing. The most definitive evidence for the association of this area with Paleozoic oceanic crust comes from the ophiolites on the western side of Notre Dame Bay at Betts Cove. These ophiolites have high magnetic and gravity anomalies associated with them and can readily be traced offshore. The ultramafic rocks at the western margin of the Dunnage zone are generally marked by a narrow zone of high magnetic and gravity anomalies superimposed on a broad regional high. The narrow zone of highs is truncated abruptly at the seaward end of the Gilbert River fault zone (which also interrupts the high gravity gradient correlative with the Humber/Dunnage boundary), but the broad regional magnetic high continues northward to about 53°N, $54\frac{1}{2}°$ W. No complete ophiolite suites are observed in

southern Notre Dame Bay, but the sequence of rocks is such that dismembered ophiolites or complete ophiolites with their ultramafic members unexposed are interpreted to be present. A zone of high gravity and magnetic anomalies associated with these ophiolites parallels the southern and eastern edges of Notre Dame Bay and then swings northeastward toward the present continental margin. We believe that the area between the two gravity highs that bound Notre Dame Bay is underlain by an extension of the Dunnage zone. Where these gravity highs begin to decrease in amplitude halfway between Notre Dame Bay and the continental margin, our confidence in their extrapolation decreases, but the pattern of magnetic anomalies, their gradual synchronized eastward swing just before intersecting the present margin, and their high amplitude at the margin suggest that the remnants of Paleozoic oceanic crust extend all the way to the margin.

The Gander zone is an enigmatic zone which has been interpreted as the eastern margin of Iapetus (Williams, 1978b). Its eastern boundary is the Dover fault, while between the Dunnage and Gander zones lies the Gander River Ultrabasic Belt (GRUB line). This line has been interpreted as the edge of an ophiolite thrust sheet similar to the Baie Verte lineament in the west. The linear zone of high amplitude magnetic anomalies characteristic of the GRUB line has, however, a more variable signature than that of the Baie Verte lineament whose offshore extension helped define the extent of the Dunnage zone. The GRUB line does, however, mark the change from the high magnetic and gravity anomalies in the Dunnage zone to low gravity and generally low magnetic anomalies over the Gander zone. Much of the gravity low may be caused by granitic intrusions, but modeling shows that an entirely plutonic source for the anomaly is unlikely; a fundamental change in type of, or depth to, basement is also indicated. The Dover fault is intruded by granites which disrupt the gravity correlation with the zone. Offshore, the zone of low gravity anomalies is well defined so that it can be traced two-thirds of the way across the shelf paralleling the anomalies associated with the eastern edge of the Dunnage zone. Farther northeast, the anomalies are dominantly parallel to the present continental margin in an area referred to as the Delta zone which might have correlatives off Rockall Bank (Haworth, 1980).

The Avalon zone (Rast and others, 1976) is composed predominantly of Precambrian volcanic and metasedimentary rocks. The metasedimentary rocks fill northeast-southwest-trending basins that are fault-bounded between volcanic structural highs. The volcanic "horsts" are well correlated with magnetic and gravity highs that can be extrapolated offshore (Haworth and Lefort, 1979). The gravity signature is not as well developed as the magnetic, except for that associated with the 10-km-deep basin along the southern and eastern edges of the Avalon Peninsula (King, 1980). Offshore and parallel to these Avalon lineaments are similar magnetic and gravity lineations that we consequently interpret as indicating the location of Avalonian crust. Intersecting these lineations at 48½°N (between 45° and 50°W) is another band of magnetic highs that might appear to be an extension of the easternmost "Avalonian" zone on the Grand Banks. However, within that band, the magnetic and gravity highs are *inversely* correlated, so the band of anomalies appears to have a different source. The extent of the "Avalonian anomalies," which swing consistently eastward north of the island and westward south of the island, indicates that much of the Grand Banks is underlain by Avalon-type crust. A major eastward-trending magnetic and gravity high, the Collector Anomaly, appears to mark the southern limit of the Avalon zone. The Tail of the Bank may therefore be an isolated extension of the Meguma zone, which is exposed in the southern half of Nova Scotia.

SEAWARD EXTENSION OF THE ZONATION OF THE BRITISH ISLES

The British Isles have also been divided into various tectonostratigraphic zones (Fig. 1). Upper case lettered zones in the British Isles are from Dewey (1974) and the lower case lettered zones correspond to those of Phillips and others (1976). The approximate correlation between these zones and those recognized in Newfoundland by Williams (1978b) is also indicated in Figure 1. The seaward extension of each of these zones will be discussed in the following sections.

The Moine thrust marks the boundary between Zone A and Zone B. A prominent gravity gradient follows the boundary, with gravity values in Zone A generally higher than in Zone B. The boundary is also marked by a discontinuous magnetic gradient. The most distinctive regional anomalies within Zone A are a northeast-trending, linear, high-amplitude gravity and magnetic "high" located over the Outer Isles thrust of the Outer Hebrides (McQuillin and Binns, 1973) and northeast-trending gravity and magnetic lows over sedimentary basins related to Mesozoic and Tertiary continental breakup. The most distinctive localized gravity and magnetic anomalies are highs that occur over Tertiary intrusive centres. In addition, a northeast-trending discontinuous band of positive magnetic anomalies occurs over Scourian pyroxene granulites on the mainland. The distinct magnetic and gravity high coincident with the Outer Isles thrust allows a well-constrained southwestward offshore extension to 56½°N. Similarly, the magnetic highs over the Scourian granulites may be extended southwestward to 56½°N. However, south of 56½°N the extensions become more problematical. The distinct gravity gradient over the A/B boundary

can be extended southwestward along the southeastern edge of gravity highs to 56°N, 8°W. Southwest of this location, two northeast trending magnetic highs between 9° and 10°W, 55½° and 56°N might be correlative with the two magnetic highs over the Outer Isles thrust and the Scourian granulites, in which case we can extend the A/B boundary southwest to 55°N 9½°W. We recognize that this extension of the fault is west of that proposed on some geological evidence, but we see no geophysical evidence for such suggestions. Riddihough and Max (1976) have proposed a further continuation of the A/B boundary on a similar trend to 54°N.

In contrast to the region immediately northwest of the Moine thrust and immediately southeast of the Highland Boundary fault, Zone B is characterized by two northeast-trending, long wavelength magnetic and gravity lows separated by a central magnetic and gravity high. The source of the northwestern gravity and magnetic lows is the Moinian sedimentary sequence (Powell, 1970). The central magnetic and gravity high occurs over the Great Glen fault. The source of the southeastern magnetic and gravity lows is the nonmagnetic upper Dalradian sedimentary section (Powell, 1970; Hall and Dagley, 1970). In the northeastern part of Zone B between the Highland Boundary fault and the Great Glen fault, isolated magnetic and gravity highs are related to mafic-ultramafic complexes such as the Belhelvie intrusion near the northeast coast (Ashcroft and Boyd, 1976; McGregor and Wilson, 1967).

Numerous possible routes for the offshore extension of the Great Glen fault have been proposed, but the paths of the most prominent gravity and magnetic anomalies offshore would favour extension of the Great Glen fault to the Leannan fault. Obviously, splays of the fault are possible, but they have less prominent geophysical anomalies. The magnetic low corresponding with the Dalradian on the southeastern side of Zone B can be followed across northern Ireland to County Mayo.

Zone C is characterized by relatively high gravity and magnetic anomalies. The C/D (C/e) boundary is characterized by a change from gravity highs to gravity lows and from short to long wavelength magnetic anomalies. This boundary can be followed from Scotland across northwest Ireland to Galway. Gravity and magnetic anomalies suggest that the Galway Granite/Conemara Complex which straddles the C/e boundary in Ireland appears to continue offshore to 11½°W where it intersects the Slyne Eris Trough. All zone boundaries north of Zone e appear to converge in the vicinity of the Slyne Eris Trough, west of which their individual continuity is problematical.

The present geologically defined boundary between Zones e and f is not consistently correlative with any distinct geophysical signatures. It is therefore impossible at this time to define this boundary offshore. The only possible indication of its path (as shown in Fig. 1) is given by the *minimum* width of zone f as shown by that zone's geophysical signature.

The geophysical signature characteristic of Zone f is the most dominant gravity anomaly in Ireland: a linear, large-amplitude gravity low that occurs over the Leinster massif and its hypothesized southwest extension beneath the Carboniferous in southwest Ireland. The pattern of magnetic anomalies, although subdued, follows the gravity trend. Offshore a linear gravity low on either side of the Porcupine Seabight occurs on strike with the Leinster massif low. This provides evidence for the western extension of Zone f to the edge of the continental margin at 52° N, 15° W.

In the Celtic Sea area, Zone F(g) is characterized by a gravity high and short-wavelength magnetic anomalies. The source of the anomalies is the metamorphic basement of the Irish Sea horst. The anomalies can be traced easily from Anglesey to the Rosslare Complex in southeast Ireland. West of Rosslare the linear, short-wavelength gravity high can be traced at most to 9½° W. The F/G (g/h) boundary is exposed between Anglesey and mainland Wales where it is characterized by a short-wavelength gravity low to the south. The offshore extension of the g/h boundary is problematic because the gravity field of the Celtic Sea is dominated by the gravity lows of Permian-Triassic rift basins. However, the northwestern edge of the gravity low is on strike from the g/h boundary onshore and may represent reactivation of faults marking the g/h boundary. The g/h boundary is also characterized by a positive magnetic gradient. Offshore this gradient is somewhat oblique to the gravity trend. A reduction in quality of data west of 5½° W limits our ability to assess the importance of this conflict.

The effect of the Hercynian Front on the gravity and magnetic fields is commonly minimal and very inconsistent; therefore, it is impossible to select a seaward extension of the Hercynian Front on the basis of gravity and magnetic anomalies.

The packet of northeast-striking magnetic and gravity anomalies in the Celtic Sea is interpreted to be caused by horst blocks of Precambrian volcanic, intrusive, and metamorphic rocks because of their similarity in trend and character with possible onshore equivalents along strike. These northeast-trending anomalies extend westward to about 10° W.

The Cornubian granites are characterized by a distinct gravity low in southwest England, which can be recognized as far southwest as 8° W. The Lizard-Dodman-Start thrust crops out in southwestern England and is characterized by short-wavelength, relatively high amplitude, magnetic anomalies and an increase in gravity to the south. These distinct anomalies allow the thrust to be traced southwest to 8° W, with a possible extension to the continental margin.

The very distinctive, linear magnetic high and discontinuous gravity high with a Caledonide trend in the English Channel (the Channel High) has been considered by Allan (1961), Hill and Vine (1965), Day and Williams (1970), and Avedik (1975) to be caused by a continuous, basic intrusion along the faulted boundary of the Mesozoic-Tertiary basin. However, Lefort (1977) suggested that the magnetic anomaly is related to an ophiolite involved in a Caledonian, south-dipping subduction zone complex. Neither interpretation can be confirmed.

TRANS-ATLANTIC GEOPHYSICAL CORRELATIONS ON AN EARLY MESOZOIC RECONSTRUCTION

The gravity and magnetic data have been compiled on a reconstruction of the Atlantic borderlands that is a combination of the paleogeographic interpretations of Sclater and others (1977) and Srivastava (1978). Rotations between South America and Africa, their subsequent rotation with respect to North America, and the rotation of Iberia with respect to Europe are from Sclater and others (1977), while the rotations of Greenland and Europe (including Iberia) with respect to North America are from Srivastava (1978). Both paleogeographic interpretations were deduced from the correlation of magnetic lineations produced after initial rifting and therefore do not take into account any effects of shearing or deformation during break-up. It should be noted that the reconstruction used here is far superior to that of Bullard and others (1965), which is still mistakenly used by many geologists. The existence of continental crust several hundred kilometres seaward of the isobath chosen by Bullard and others (1965) as the continental margin to be used in their best-fit procedure makes inferences based on their incorrect reconstruction misleading. Refinement to produce even better Mesozoic reconstructions than the one used here will follow from trans-Atlantic correlation of geological and geophysical features as described in this paper or, for example, LePichon and others (1977).

Because of (1) the lack of geophysical information on Rockall Plateau, (2) the extreme complexity of data in the vicinity of Porcupine Bank, and (3) the great separation between the northwestern sides of the two orogens, correlation between the southeastern zones of the Caledonides and Apalachians is more definitive than between the more northwesterly zones. Our greatest confidence lies in the correlation between the Gander zone gravity low in Newfoundland and the Leinster massif gravity low in Ireland (Jacobi and Kristoffersen, 1981), since (1) in each case the gravity anomaly can be extended to the present shelf edge, and (2) their shelf edge locations correlate well on reliable early Mesozoic reconstructions of the North Atlantic. This geophysical correlation is supported quite strongly by the known geology: both gravity lows are caused by Acadian/Caledonian metamorphic infrastructure and related granitic rocks. Furthermore, some of the country rocks adjacent to the infrastructure in Newfoundland and Ireland have been correlated from Newfoundland to Ireland by independent means (e.g., Bray Series in Ireland with the Gander Lake Group in Newfoundland, by Rast and others, 1976). The geophysical correlation provided a point of reference that influenced our correlation of the other zones.

The magnetic and gravity lineations east of the Gander zone in the Avalon zone of Newfoundland have an offshore arcuate extension following a trend that could be continuous with the zones of magnetic and gravity lineations in the southwest Celtic Sea (Jacobi and Kristoffersen, 1981). This possible continuity is consistent with the hypothesized sources of the anomalies; both are probably fault blocks (horsts) of late Precambrian volcanic rocks. It should be noted, however, that the magnetic anomalies are not nearly as pronounced in the Celtic Sea as they are in the Avalon zone of Newfoundland, whereas the gravity anomalies are perhaps more pronounced. These differences may be due to differences in Mesozoic reactivation and overprinting. The geophysical signature of Zone F (g), which separates the Gander and Avalon equivalents in the Celtic Sea, narrows westward and its geological source is not observed in Newfoundland.

Having correlated the Gander-Leinster gravity low and the Avalon geophysical lineations, one could suspect a correlation between the magnetic high in the Southwest Approaches (the Channel High) and that occurring along the northern margin of the Flemish Cap. Both of these lie on the same trend, but the Channel High has a variable correlation between the gravity and magnetic fields, and that north of Flemish Cap has an inverse correlation between gravity and magnetic anomalies. Since we have no control on the source of the anomalies, it is improper to speculate about their tectonic significance.

If one accepts the correlation of the Gander/Leinster low, then the correlation between the geophysical characteristics of the neighbouring zones to the southeast is consistent with the interpretation of this area on both sides of the Atlantic as the eastern margin of the Caledonide/Acadian suture (Phillips and others, 1976; Williams, 1978b; Kennedy, 1979).

Although geological correlations between zones north of the suture have been proposed (Phillips and others, 1976; Williams, 1978b; Kennedy, 1979), geophysical identification of such zones across the continental shelves on both sides of the Atlantic is speculative at best. Any such correlations must invoke as much (if not more) sinuosity in their connecting boundaries as that of the traceable boundaries on the southeastern side of the orogen.

Extensive transcurrent movement has been postulated along a shear zone roughly following the axis of the Appalachian-Caledonide system (e.g., Morris, 1976; Kent and Opdyke, 1978; Piper, 1979). The geophysical correlation between, and continuity of, geological zones east of the early Paleozoic suture would indicate that the shear zone always lies along or northwest of that suture, as is indeed implied geologically, in Newfoundland, by Hanmer (1981). Unfortunately, few geophysical anomalies intersect that shear zone to provide markers by which the validity of the paleomagnetically inferred motion might be tested.

Only gravity and magnetic data have been analyzed here as a means of testing the continuity of the hypothesized geological correlation between the Appalachians and the Caledonides. Seismic reflection and refraction data may also be compared (Haworth, 1981), but their results are perhaps less conclusive. This may be due both to the location of the lines with respect to structural boundaries on the Canadian margin and to the lack of detail in the structural interpretation of the trans-Britain seismic line. It is evident that considerably more seismic reflection and refraction work in particular must be carried out to determine the degree of structural continuity across the zones of postulated Paleozoic subduction and transcurrent shear and therefore test their validity.

ACKNOWLEDGEMENTS

The compilation of data presented here from a variety of published sources was facilitated by the cooperation fostered through the International Geological Correlation Program's Project 27: The Caledonide Orogen. In particular, we would like to thank our principal collaborators Yngve Kristoffersen and Jean Pierre Lefort. This paper was initially submitted 4 January 1982.

REFERENCES CITED

Allan, T. D., 1961, A magnetic survey in the western English Channel: Quarterly Journal of the Geological Society of London, v. 117, p. 157–171.

Anonymous, 1:250,000 Bouguer gravity anomaly maps (of the United Kingdom): Published by the Institute of Geological Sciences, London, England.

—— 1965, Aeromagnetic map of Great Britain: England and Wales: Geological Survey of Great Britain, sheet 2.

—— 1972, Aeromagnetic map of Great Britain: England, Scotland and Northern Ireland: Institute of Geological Sciences, sheet 1.

—— 1974, Gravity anomaly map of Ireland: Communications of the Dublin Institute for Advanced Studies, series D, no. 32.

Ashcroft, W. A., and Boyd, R., 1976, The Belhelvie mafic igneous intrusion, Aberdeenshire—a re-investigation: Scottish Journal of Geology, v. 12, p. 1–14.

Avedik, F., 1975, The seismic structure of the Western Approaches and the South Armorica continental shelf and its geological interpretation, in Woodland, A. W., ed., Petroleum and the continental shelf of northwest Europe, Volume 1, Geology: New York, John Wiley and Sons, p. 29–43.

Bailey, R. J., Buckley, J. S., and Kielmas, M. M., 1975, Geomagnetic reconnaissance on the continental margin of the British Isles between 54° and 57°N: Journal of the Geological Society of London, v. 131, p. 275–282.

Blundell, D. J., 1975, The geology of the Celtic Sea and Southwestern Approaches, *in* Yorath, C. J., Parker, E. R., and Glass, D. J., eds., Canada's continental margins and offshore petroleum exploration: Canadian Society of Petroleum Geologists, Memoir 4, p. 341–362.

Bott, M.H.P., and Young, D.G.G., 1971, Gravity measurements in the North Irish Sea: Quarterly Journal of the Geological Society of London, v. 126, p. 413–434.

Buckley, J. S., and Bailey, R. J., 1975, A free-air gravity anomaly contour map of the Irish continental margin: Marine Geophysical Researches, v. 2, p. 184–195.

Bullard, E. C., Everett, J., and Smith, A. G., 1965, The fit of the continents around the Atlantic, *in* Blackett, P.M.S., Bullard, E. C., and Runcorn, S. K., ed., A symposium on continental drift: Philosophical Transactions of the Royal Society of London, series A, v. 258, p. 41–51.

Day, G. A., and Williams, C. A., 1970, Gravity compilation in the N.E. Atlantic and interpretation of gravity in the Celtic Sea: Earth and Planetary Science Letters, v. 8, p. 205–213.

Dewey, J. F., 1974, The geology of the southern termination of the Caledonides, *in* Nairn, A.E.M., and Stehli, F. G., eds., The ocean basins and margins, Volume 2, The North Atlantic: New York, Plenum Press, p, 205–231.

Hall, D. H., and Dagley, P., 1970, Regional magnetic anomalies: An analysis of the smoothed aeromagnetic map of Great Britain and Northern Ireland: Institute of Geological Sciences, report 70/10, 8 p.

Hanmer, S., 1981, Tectonic significance of the northeastern Gander zone, Newfoundland: An Acadian ductile shear zone: Canadian Journal of Earth Sciences, v. 18, p. 120–135.

Haworth, R. T., 1975, The development of Atlantic Canada as a result of continental collision-evidence from offshore gravity and magnetic data, *in* Yorath, C. J., Parker, E. R., and Glass, D. J., eds., Canada's continental margins and offshore petroleum exploration: Canadian Society of Petroleum Geologists Memoir 4, p. 59–77.

—— 1980, Appalachian structural trends northeast of Newfoundland and their trans Atlantic correlation: Tectonophysics, v. 64, p. 111–130.

—— 1981, Geophysical expression of Appalachian-Caledonide structures on the continental margins of the North Atlantic, *in* Kerr, J. Wm., and Fergusson, A. J., eds., Geology of the North Atlantic borderlands: Canadian Society of Petroleum Geologists Memoir 7, p. 429–446.

Haworth, R. T., and Keen, C. E., 1979, The Canadian Atlantic margin: A passive continental margin encompassing an active past: Tectonophysics, v. 59, p. 83–126.

Haworth, R. T., and Lefort, J. P., 1979, Geophysical evidence for the extent of the Avalon zone in Atlantic Canada: Canadian Journal of Earth Sciences, v. 16, p. 552–567.

Hill, M. N., and Vine, F. J., 1965, A preliminary magnetic survey of the Western Approaches to the English Channel: Quarterly Journal of the Geological Society of London, v. 121, p.463–475.

Jacobi, R., and Kristoffersen, Y., 1976, Geophysical and geological trends on the continental shelf off northeastern Newfoundland: Canadian Journal of Earth Sciences, v. 13, p. 1039–1051.

—— 1981, Transatlantic correlations of geophysical anomalies of Newfoundland, British Isles, France and adjacent continental shelves, *in* Kerr, J. Wm., and Fergusson, A. J., eds., Geology of the North Atlantic borderlands: Canadian Society of Petroleum Geologists Memoir 7, p. 197–229.

Kennedy, M. J., 1979, The continuation of the Canadian Appalachians into the Caledonides of Britain and Ireland, *in* Harris, A. L., Holland, C. H., and Leake, B. E., eds., The Caledonides of the British Isles—reviewed: Scottish Academic Press, p. 33–64.

Kent, D. V., and Opdyke, N. D., 1978, Paleomagnetism of the Devonian Catskill red beds: Evidence for motion of the coastal New England—Canadian Maritime region relative to cratonic North America: Journal of Geophysical Research, v. 83, p. 4441–4450.

King, A. F., 1980, The birth of the Caledonides: Late Precambrian rocks of the Avalon Peninsula, Newfoundland and their correlatives in the Appalachian orogen, *in* Wones, D. R., ed., The Caledonides in the U.S.A.: Virginia Polytechnic Institute and State University Memoir 2, p. 3–8.

Lefort, J. P., 1977, Possible "Caledonian" subduction under the Domnonean Domain in North Armorican area: Geology, v. 5, p. 523–526.

Lefort, J. P., and Haworth, R. T., 1978, Geophysical study of basement features on the western European and eastern Canadian shelves: Transatlantic correlations and late Hercynian movements: Canadian Journal of Earth Sciences, v. 15, p. 397–404.

LePichon, X., Sibuet, J.-C., and Francheteau, J., 1977, The fit of the continents around the North Atlantic Ocean: Tectonophysics, v. 38, p. 169–209.

Maroof, Sabah U., 1974, A Bouguer anomaly map of southern Great Britain and the Irish Sea: Journal of the Geological Society of London, v. 130, p. 471–474.

Max, M. D., 1981, Magnetic measurements in Ireland and the adjacent continental shelf: Geological Survey of Ireland Open File.

Max, M. D., and Riddihough, R. P., 1975, Continuation of the Highland Boundary fault in Ireland: Geology, v. 3, p. 206–210.

McGregor, D. M., and Wilson, C.D.V., 1967, Gravity and magnetic surveys of the younger gabbros of Aberdeenshire: Quarterly Journal of the Geological Society of London, v. 123, p. 99–123.

McQuillin, R., and Binns, P. E., 1973, Geological structure in the Sea of the Hebrides: Nature Physical Sciences, v. 241, p. 1–4.

McQuillin, R., and Watson, J., 1973, Large-scale basement structures of the Outer Hebrides in light of geophysical evidence: Nature Physical Sciences, v. 245, p. 1–3.

Morris, W. A., 1976, Transcurrent motion determined paleomagnetically in the Northern Appalachians and Caledonides and the Acadian orogeny: Canadian Journal of Earth Sciences, v. 13, p. 1236–1243.

Phillips, W.E.A., Stillman, C. J., and Murphy, T., 1976, A Caledonian plate tectonic model: Journal of the Geological Society of London, v. 132, p. 579–609.

Piper, J.D.A., 1979, Aspects of Caledonian palaeomagnetism and their tectonic implications: Earth and Planetary Science Letters, v. 44, p. 176–192.

Powell, D. W., 1970, Magnetized rocks within the Lewisian of western Scotland and under the Southern Uplands: Scottish Journal of Geology, v. 6, p. 353–369.

Rast, N., O'Brien, B. H., and Wardle, R. J., 1976, Relationships between Precambrian and lower Palaeozoic rocks of the "Avalon Platform" in New Brunswick, the Northeast Appalachians and the British Isles: Tectonophysics, v. 30, p. 315–338.

Riddihough, R. P., 1975, A magnetic anomaly map of the area 51°-55°N, 10°-16°W: Communications of the Dublin Institute for Advanced Studies, Series D, Geophysical Bulletin, No. 34.

Riddihough, R. P., and Max, M. D., 1976, A geological framework for the continental margin to the west of Ireland: Geological Journal, v. 11, p. 109–120.

Riddihough, R. P., and Young, D.G.G., 1970, Gravity and magnetic surveys of Inishowen and adjoining sea areas off the coast of Ireland: Proceedings of the Geological Society of London, n. 1664, p. 215–220.

Sclater, J. C., Hellinger, S., and Tapscott, C., 1977, The paleobathymetry of the Atlantic Ocean from the Jurassic to the Present: Journal of Geology, v. 85, p. 509–552.

Srivastava, S. P., 1978, Evolution of the Labrador Sea and its bearing on the early evolution of the North Atlantic: Geophysical Journal of the Royal Astronomical Society, v. 52, p. 313–357.

Watts, A. B., 1971, Geophysical investigations on the continental shelf and slope north of Scotland: Scottish Journal of Geology, v. 7, p. 189–218.

Williams, H., 1964, The Appalachians in northeastern Newfoundland. A two-sided symmetrical system: American Journal of Science, v. 262, p. 1137–1158.

—— 1978a, Tectonic-lithofacies map of the Appalachian Orogen: Memorial University of Newfoundland Map No. 1.

—— 1978b, Geological development of the northern Appalachians and its bearing on the evolution of the British Isles, *in* Bowes, D. R., and Leake, B. E., eds., Crustal evolution in northwestern Britain and adjacent regions: Geological Journal Special Issue 10, p. 1–22.

Williams, H., Kennedy, M. J., and Neale, E. R., 1972, The Appalachian structural province, *in* Price, R. A., and Douglas, R.J.W., eds., Variations in tectonic styles in Canada: Geological Association of Canada Special Paper 11, p. 181–261.

—— 1974, The northwestward termination of the Appalachian orogen, *in* Nairn, A.E.M., and Stehli, F. G., eds., The ocean basins and margins, Vol. 2: New York, Plenum Press, p. 79–123.

MANUSCRIPT ACCEPTED BY THE SOCIETY SEPTEMBER 10, 1982

Geological Society of America
Memoir 158
1983

Appalachian suspect terranes

Harold Williams
Department of Earth Sciences
Memorial University of Newfoundland
St. John's, Newfoundland
Canada, A1B 3X5

Robert D. Hatcher, Jr.
Department of Geology
University of South Carolina
Columbia, South Carolina 29208

ABSTRACT

Since the advent of plate tectonics, the widely accepted model for the development of the Appalachian orogen has involved the opening and closing of a late Precambrian–Paleozoic Iapetus Ocean. Only a few of a growing number of geologically distinctive terranes are easily explained by this model. Vestiges of Iapetus are nowhere coupled to the ancient North American margin. Furthermore, it cannot be demonstrated that any of the extensive Appalachian terranes, now east of the Iapetus tract or its suture, were once connected to the North American miogeocline. All are therefore suspect.

The major suspect terranes of the Appalachian orogen are in most respects analogous to previously recognized zones or tectonic lithofacies belts. In the north, these are the Dunnage, Gander, Avalon, and Meguma terranes. In the south, they include easterly parts of the Blue Ridge, the Piedmont, Slate Belt, and the geophysically distinctive Brunswick and Tallahassee-Suwannee terranes beneath the Atlantic Coastal Plain. Most of these are composite and include smaller terranes of uncertain paleogeography. Taconic allochthons are included because they fit the definition of suspect terranes.

Stratigraphic and sedimentologic analyses indicate that the Appalachian orogen built up during three major Paleozoic accretionary events. Their timing coincides with the times of structural, metamorphic, and plutonic effects assigned to the Taconian, Acadian, and Alleghanian orogenies.

Accretion of the Appalachian orogen progressed from the North American miogeocline outward. The boundaries of the earliest accreted western terranes are marked by melange zones and ophiolite complexes, implying head-on collisions. Later boundaries between eastern terranes are steep mylonite zones and brittle faults, implying oblique movements.

The suspect terrane concept, first developed for the North American Cordilleran, provides new insights into the evolution of the Appalachian orogen and solves several enigmas. It is a surgically clean analytical approach and a superior framework in which to view the anatomy of any complex orogen.

INTRODUCTION

Preamble

Before the advent of plate tectonics, failure to recognize and emphasize major tectonic junctions between contrasting geologic provinces led to gross oversimplifications and major misconceptions in analyses of the Appalachian orogen (e.g., Williams, 1964). Even now, many plate models assume proximity of contrasting terranes or imply known paleogeography. Few emphasize the stratigraphic and sedimentologic relationships that bear upon accretionary history or attempt to relate the timing and styles of accretion to structural, metamorphic, and plutonic development of the orogen.

Since the wide acceptance of plate tectonics, models for the evolution of the Appalachian orogen have involved the opening and closing of a late Precambrian–Paleozoic Iapetus Ocean following the lead of Wilson (1966) and Dewey (1969). However, some terranes along the east flank of the orogen are not easily incorporated into these models. This paper analyzes the Appalachian orogen from the viewpoint that the North American connection, or that part of North America that was separated during the initiation of Iapetus, is ill defined within the present orogen. Furthermore, ophiolitic vestiges of Iapetus are nowhere coupled to the North American margin. There is no assurance therefore that terranes now east of the North American miogeocline were ever previously connected to or evolved in sight of the North American continent. The orogen is viewed therefore as a mosaic of accreted terranes, all of unknown paleogeography.

This viewpoint encourages the delineation and close scrutiny of contrasting terranes of the Appalachian orogen and provides an opportunity to reassess previous subdivisions. It neither negates the concept of a simple Wilson Cycle (Wilson, 1966) nor casts aspersions on attempts to devise models for the orogen that assume or presuppose a certain paleogeography for its component parts. It does, however, emphasize the complexities inherent in accretionary processes and stresses an unbiased view of orogenic development. Conveniently, it alleviates the immediate necessity of incorporating every facet of geologic development in a single all encompassing model.

Definition and Concept

The definition and concept of suspect terranes have been clearly expressed for the Cordilleran orogen of western North America (Coney and others, 1980). There, over 70 percent of the orogen is regarded as suspect and made up of a multitude of terranes, 50 in Alaska alone (Jones and others, 1981), all accreted to the ancient continental margin of western North America during Mesozoic and Cenozoic time. The following account of definition and concepts is partly recast from Coney and others (1980) and included here for purposes of completeness and clarity.

Suspect terranes (Coney, 1978; Coney and others, 1980) of orogenic belts are internally homogeneous geologic provinces, with features that contrast sharply with those of nearby provinces. They are recognized by contrasts in any or all of the following: stratigraphy, structure, metamorphic and plutonic histories, faunas, mineral deposits, and paleomagnetic signatures. Their boundaries are sharp structural junctions marking discontinuities that cannot be explained by normal gradations in structural style, conventional facies changes, or standard unconformities.

Terranes are suspect because they are of unknown paleogeography with respect to nearby miogeoclines and stable cratons. Their time of accretion or docking, either at an ancient continental margin or against one another, can be gleaned from the age of similar cover rocks (overlap assemblages), the depositional age of detritus shed from one upon another (sedimentologic linkage), or similar postdocking intrusive, metamorphic, structural, paleontologic, or paleomagnetic histories.

Dimensions and form of suspect terranes vary from those of small allochthons to major geologic provinces. The number of terranes recognized in any orogen is conditioned somewhat by the scale and resolution of a particular study. It is also dependent upon the basic philosophies of current workers. Those inclined to emphasize similarities among rock groups in large areas are likely to define fewer terranes than those who emphasize differences in local areas. Our approach in this analysis is a regional one for the entire orogen. Thus, the number of terranes is minimal (see also Rowley, 1981; Zen, 1983, and Keppie, 1983).

We are impressed by the number of our colleagues, peers, and associates who reiterate that the suspect terrane approach to the analysis of an orogen is not entirely new; for example, see papers by Wilson (1968), Coney and others (1972), Monger and others (1972), Williams and others (1972), and Helwig (1974). However, sharp and clear expressions of the concept are more recent (Jones and others, 1978; Coney and others, 1980; Jones and others, 1981; Monger and others, 1982; and Williams and Hatcher, 1982). Unlike the judicial system of presuming innocence until guilt is proven, the suspect terrane concept invokes suspicion from the outset. Once the miogeocline, or cratonic margin, of an orogen is identified, all geologic terranes outside it are inherently suspect. This approach is a first step toward the analysis of any complex orogen.

APPALACHIAN SUSPECT TERRANES

Suspect terranes of the Appalachian orogen are

named and outlined in Figure 1. Almost all are defined on their early Paleozoic or older rocks. A few are recognized beneath the Atlantic Coastal Plain by distinct magnetic signatures and limited drill-hole data. In the north, some boundaries are extended offshore, based on underwater sampling and geophysical data. The largest terranes, the Piedmont, Dunnage, Gander, Avalon, and Meguma, coincide with lithofacies belts defined in earlier analyses (Williams, 1978, 1979). Most of these are composite or superterranes (Coney and others, 1980) and contain smaller geologic divisions of uncertain relationships (Rowley, 1981; Keppie, 1981; Zen and Palmer, 1981; Zen, 1981, 1983). The familiar Taconic allochthons, lying above the miogeocline, are also included because they fit the suspect terrane definition. Several terranes have faunas that contrast with those of the North American miogeocline, and some have distinct volcanic, plutonic, and metallogenic characteristics.

Silurian and younger rocks are not shown in Figure 1 because they are mainly overlap (postdocking) assemblages, except for Devonian rocks of the Talladega terrane and Silurian rocks of the Avalon and more easterly terranes. In eastern Maine, a mid-Paleozoic suture zone is suggested by the occurrence of an ophiolitic complex dated at 410 m.y. (Gaudette, 1981), and paleomagnetic evidence indicates major offsets that affected rocks as young as Early Carboniferous (Kent and Opdyke, 1978, 1979, 1980; Irving, 1979; Van der Voo and others, 1979). However, there are few other contrasts on which to define suspect terranes in the Silurian or younger stratigraphic record, with the exception of the Talladega terrane. This may mean that the chief accretionary phase in the development of the Appalachian orogen took place in Ordovician time, except for accretion of some terranes exposed in the east and others buried beneath the Atlantic Coastal Plain and continental shelf.

Brief descriptions of Appalachian suspect terranes, the natures of their boundaries, times of accretion, and some problems concerning their setting and possible significance form the basis for the discussion that follows.

Suspect Terranes Above the North American Miogeocline

Taconic Allochthons. Taconic allochthons that occur above the carbonate rocks of the miogeocline are regarded as suspect, since they have been transported great distances to their present positions and some include volcanic and plutonic complexes of uncertain paleogeography. From north to south, these are designated the Hare Bay, Humber Arm, St. Lawrence, Taconic Ranges, and Hamburg terranes. Several others are too small to depict at the scale of Figure 1. These terranes occur in a set position with respect to the miogeocline, their mid-Ordovician age of final emplacement is roughly similar, and their in-

ternal order of structural stacking is predictable (Zen, 1967, 1972; Williams, 1975; St. Julien and Hubert, 1975; Rowley and Kidd, 1981).

The allochthons are composite, and those that are complete consist of lower structural slices of sedimentary rocks and upper slices of volcanic rocks, igneous rocks, and ophiolitic suites. The contacts of latest emplacement, either between different structural slices or beneath the assembled allochthons, are marked by thin chaotic melanges with exotic blocks. Although laterally extensive, the allochthons rarely exceed a few kilometres in overall structural thickness.

Stratigraphic analyses of the transported sedimentary rocks indicate that deposition was coeval with westerly parts of the miogeocline, and sedimentologic studies imply that they lay at the ancient continental slope and rise (Stevens, 1970; Williams and Stevens, 1974). Some volcanic rocks in upper structural slices may represent oceanic seamounts (Baker, 1978), and the ophiolitic suites are interpreted as oceanic crust and mantle (Stevens, 1970; Williams, 1975).

Sedimentologic linkages and overlap relationships provide tight control on the accretionary history of these displaced terranes. Ophiolite detritus in Lower Ordovician sedimentary rocks of the allochthons and in Middle Ordovician clastics shed across the miogeocline indicate a progressive westward transgression from the continental edge across the subsiding continental shelf. The oldest overlap assemblage upon any Taconic allochthon is the Middle Ordovician (Caradocian) Long Point Group that links the Humber Arm terrane and miogeocline in western Newfoundland (Rodgers, 1965; Bergström and others, 1974). In Quebec, Silurian and Devonian rocks of the Gaspé synclinorium overlap the St. Lawrence terrane (St. Julien and Hubert, 1975) and link it with the more outboard Dunnage and Gander terranes (Williams, 1978). Similarly, in New York the Helderberg Formation at Becraft Mountain is a Devonian overlap assemblage upon the Taconic Ranges terrane (Zen, 1967).

The most logical model for accretion relates the westward transport of the allochthons to eastward subduction and an attempt to submerge the North American margin beneath an overriding oceanic plate (Church and Stevens, 1971). This model of an accretionary prism is supported by the stacking order within the allochthons and facies relationships that indicate that the structural pile was assembled from the east. Earliest movements detached ophiolite suites at mantle depths, and these traveled as hot masses that acquired thin dynamothermal aureoles (Williams and Smyth, 1973; Malpas, 1979; Jamieson, 1980; Feininger, 1981). Assembly of lower sedimentary slices possibly progressed through peeling of successively landward sections by overriding oceanic lithosphere. Chaotic melanges at the lowest structural surfaces of latest

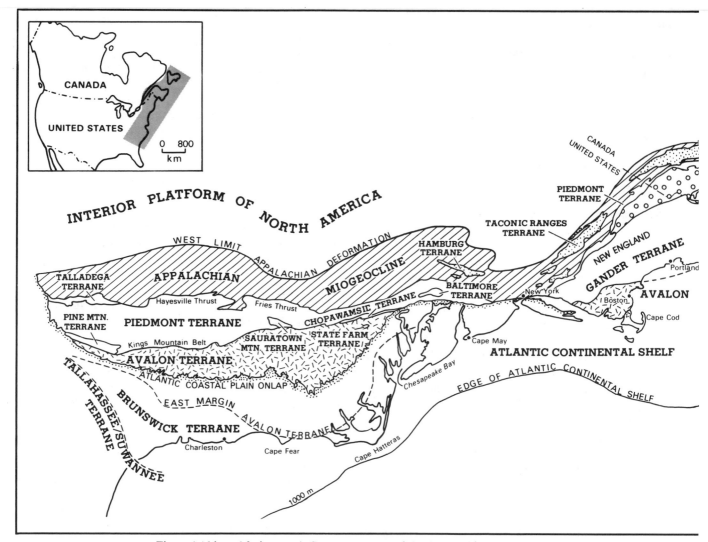

Figure 1 (this and facing page). Suspect terranes of the Appalachian orogen.

emplacement are interpreted as the result of mass wastage and tectonic mixing associated with surficial sliding.

The initiation of Iapetus is dated stratigraphically as late Precambrian to earliest Cambrian, while some isotopic studies suggest much earlier initiation (Williams and Stevens, 1974; Rankin, 1975). However, the oldest preserved Appalachian ophiolites barely exceed 500 m.y. (Mattinson, 1975, 1976), and most seem to have formed in the vicinity of island arcs (Upadhyay and Neale, 1979). Since there is no contemporary volcanism or plutonism to suggest subduction beneath the North American miogeocline, then the island arcs and coeval ophiolites must have evolved elsewhere. Similarly, uncoupled volcanic assemblages that form integral components of the Hare Bay and Humber Arm terranes may have formed in regions far removed from the North American margin. Attempts to relate the geometry of west Newfoundland ophiolite complexes to the position and form of marginal oceans at the east edge of North America should therefore be viewed with caution.

The stratigraphic and structural analyses of the sedimentary parts of Taconic terranes, and analyses of their overlap assemblages and sedimentologic linkages, are the most sophisticated and best known for any suspect terrane within the Appalachian orogen.

Talladega Terrane. The Talladega terrane is a small, narrow, suspect terrane in Alabama and Georgia of the southern Appalachians. Its rocks are thrust westward across early Paleozoic carbonates of the miogeocline, and it is structurally overlain to the east by crystalline rocks of the Piedmont terrane.

The oldest rocks of the Talladega terrane are early Paleozoic (possibly including late Precambrian) metaclastics, marbles, and quartzites that are overlain by conglomerates and local coarse diamictite (Ordovician Lay Dam Formation). These are succeeded by mid-Paleozoic clastic

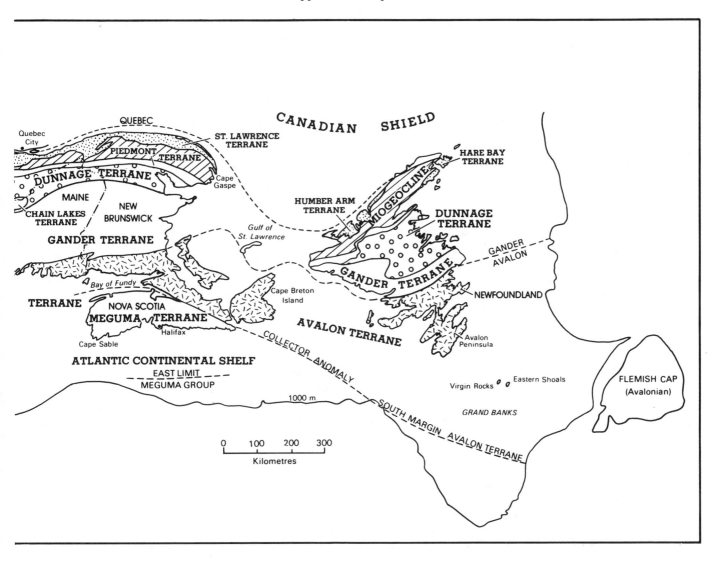

sedimentary rocks and fossiliferous Devonian (Jemison) chert. A continuous unit of mafic volcanic rocks (Hillabee Greenstone) occurs at the top of the section. All of the rocks are highly deformed, and some are metamorphosed to greenschist facies (Tull and Stow, 1980a).

The Talladega terrane is suspect because of its stratigraphic contrasts with the nearby miogeocline. The lithology and age of its upper units and the position it occupies in the southern Appalachians between the miogeocline and Piedmont terrane are also worthy of note. Elsewhere in the south, crystalline rocks of the Piedmont terrane are thrust directly upon continuous early Paleozoic or older units of the miogeocline.

The oldest metaclastic rocks of the Talladega terrane may be equivalents of basal clastics of the miogeocline, that is, Ocoee Series of nearby Georgia, although the Talladega metaclastics are thinner and much less extensive. Similarly, its marbles and quartzites may correlate with early Paleozoic, less deformed equivalents of the miogeocline (Tull, 1978). These correlations indicate an early linkage with the North American margin, and probably deposition as offshore slope and rise equivalents of platform assemblages.

Deformation of the Talladega terrane is attributed to Acadian orogeny (Tull, 1978), and it was emplaced onto the miogeocline during Alleghanian orogenesis. Its western boundary, with less deformed rocks of the miogeocline, is a major Alleghanian thrust (the Talladega thrust). Its eastern boundary, with much higher grade metamorphic rocks of the Piedmont terrane (Ashland nappes), is also interpreted (Tull, 1978) as a major Alleghanian thrust (Hollins line).

The Hillabee Greenstone has been interpreted as a distal product of island arc volcanism, mainly because of its chemical characteristics (Tull and Stow, 1980a, 1980b). As no earlier deformation is recognized in the Talladega sequence beneath the Hillabee, it is implied that the Devonian Hillabee arc stood at or near an undisturbed North American miogeocline. Contrasts between this model and that for the development of the ancient continental margin of eastern North America elsewhere in the Appalachian orogen are further reasons for suspicion.

Piedmont Terrane. The Piedmont terrane is defined in the southern Appalachians, but its rocks are traceable along the full length of the orogen from Alabama to Newfoundland. In the south, the terrane is wide and extensive, bounded by the Hayesville fault and possibly the Martic line to the west, and by mylonites of the Goat Rock and Towaliga fault zones and premetamorphic faults within the Kings Mountain belt to the east. It includes the eastern Blue Ridge, Brevard zone, Chauga belt, Inner Piedmont, much of the Kings Mountain belt, and smaller diverse elements such as the Alto and Smith River allochthons.

Piedmont terrane assemblages are less distinct in the central Appalachians. The western boundary here is shown as the Martic line, but it may be that this terrane is discontinuous and consists of a series of disconnected klippen resting upon the miogeocline east of the Martic line. Drake and Morgan (1981) suggested that all the mafic/ultramafic complexes of northern Virginia and nearby Maryland are transported. The Martic line is, however, a significant lithotectonic boundary with contrasting assemblages on either side.

In the northern U.S. Appalachians and in Canada, the Piedmont terrane is uniformly narrow. Its western boundary there is either faulted or defined by a sharp increase in deformation and metamorphism in clastic rocks of the miogeocline. Its western boundary in New England is defined by Cameron's line (Hatcher, 1981). Throughout the Canadian Appalachians, its eastern boundary is defined by a steep zone of discontinuous ophiolite complexes, the Baie Verte–Brompton line (Williams and St. Julien, 1982) that separates the Piedmont terrane from the oceanic Dunnage terrane to the east.

Rocks of the Piedmont terrane are of late Precambrian to early Paleozoic age, except for small areas of Grenvillian rocks, some of which are separated in Figure 1, for example, the Pine Mountain, Sauratown Mountain, and Baltimore terranes. However, it is possible that the Grenvillian terranes are exposures in windows through the overthrust portions of the Piedmont terrane. Basement rocks exist only as small detached massifs in the southern portions of the Piedmont terrane (Tallulah Falls and Toxaway domes). Farther north, basement massifs may be all within the western (North American) margin.

The rocks of the Piedmont terrane are mainly pelitic to quartzofeldspathic metasedimentary rocks and mafic volcanics that are everywhere polydeformed and regionally metamorphosed from upper greenschist to upper amphibolite facies. Structures within the deformed rocks are generally directed toward the miogeocline. Granitic and mafic intrusions, mainly of Ordovician and Devonian age, are common in the Piedmont terrane of the southern Appalachians, and they occur locally in western Newfoundland in the north.

Mafic-ultramafic bodies are characteristic of the Piedmont terrane along its full length (Williams and Talkington, 1977; Misra and Keller, 1978; Hatcher and others, 1981). Most are small and in the southern Appalachians they are concentrated along the western margin of the terrane. Several larger complexes occur in Maryland, including the Baltimore Gabbro Complex, which is interpreted as ophiolitic (Morgan, 1977). Most of those in the southern and central Appalachians appear to have late Precambrian or Early Cambrian ages, whereas those in Canada appear to have Ordovician ages. Problems of distinguishing ophiolitic from intrusive or arc-related mafic-ultramafic complexes have been outlined by Hatcher and others (1981). Mafic-ultramafic complexes of the western Piedmont terrane probably are dismembered ophiolites (Williams and Talkington, 1977; Drake and Morgan, 1981).

The Piedmont terrane is viewed as suspect because of its contrasts in stratigraphy with the North American margin immediately to the west, the presence of ultramafic rocks within it (and lack of them to the west), and the paucity of Grenville basement rocks within the New England, central, and southern Appalachians. One model interprets the Piedmont terrane as a micro-continent that was rifted from the North American margin during the initiation of Iapetus (Hatcher, 1978; Cook and others, 1979; Hatcher and Odom, 1980; Cook and Oliver, 1981). This implies that the boundaries of the Piedmont terrane at the Hayesville-Fries faults and Kings Mountain belt are major suture zones. Another model interprets part of the Piedmont terrane of the southern Appalachians as composite and including the opposite sides of an ocean that is sutured at the Brevard zone (Rankin, 1975). According to this model, the smaller Grenvillian terranes at Pine Mountain and Sauratown Mountain represent North American windows through overlying African crust which extends westward to a surface suture at the Brevard zone. This interpretation conflicts with stratigraphic and structural data of Hatcher (1978, 1981) and Hatcher and others (1980).

Seismic reflection studies across the Piedmont terrane in the southern Appalachians indicate that it is underlain by a continuous shallow décollement (Cook and others, 1979; Harris and Bayer, 1979). The same reflector coincides with a major sole thrust beneath the imbricated rocks of the miogeocline farther west. This implies that the entire Piedmont terrane of the south is contained in a major subhorizontal crystalline slice that was emplaced above the North American miogeocline. Magnetic signatures and a sharp gradient in the Bouguer anomaly field suggest that the subsurface eastern limit of the North American miogeocline is roughly coincident with the eastern margin of the Piedmont terrane near the Kings Mountain belt (Hatcher and Zietz, 1978, 1980; Zietz and others, 1980; Haworth and others, 1980; Hatcher, 1981; Cook and Oliver, 1981; Thomas, 1983). The geometry and timing of Piedmont thrusting, combined with timing of Piedmont plutonism and metamorphism, require that its final emplacement above the miogeocline was a late event related to Alleghanian orogenesis. Hatcher (1981), Price and Hatcher (1983), and Iverson and Smithson (1982) have presented alternative interpretations of geologic and geophysical data which bear on several of the problems implicit in assuming that a master décollement exists beneath the entire southern Appalachians.

In the northern Appalachians from New York to Newfoundland, correlatives of the southern Appalachians Piedmont terrane are interpreted as the deformed and metamorphosed rocks at the eastern edge of the North American miogeocline. Furthermore, small mafic/ultramafic complexes throughout its length are viewed as olistoliths and dismembered slices of oceanic crust and mantle, now structurally commingled with surrounding sedimentary rocks (Williams and Talkington, 1977). The main phase of deformation and metamorphism occurred during the Ordovician Taconic orogeny, and it was possibly coeval with or it immediately followed the accretion of Taconic terranes above the miogeocline to the west. An Ordovician age of metamorphism and deformation is especially clear in Quebec, where the deformed Piedmont rocks are overlapped by Silurian and Devonian rocks of the Gaspé synclinorium.

Applied to the southern Appalachians, relationships in the north suggest that at least westerly parts of the southern Piedmont terrane, if not all, consist of rocks derived from the North American margin and adjacent oceanic crust. They were subsequently transported westward as a series of nappes and imbricate thrust slices. Major differences between the northern and southern Appalachians are the timing of final accretion of the Piedmont rocks, and the far greater width of the terrane in the south.

Suspect Terranes Outboard of the North American Miogeocline

Dunnage Terrane. The Dunnage terrane is defined in the well-exposed cross-section of the Appalachian orogen in northeast Newfoundland (Williams, 1979). Its early Paleozoic oceanic rocks can be traced southwestward into the New England Appalachians, but they are absent in the southern Appalachians. Throughout its length, the Dunnage terrane is bounded by the Piedmont terrane to the west and the Gander terrane to the east.

The Dunnage terrane is widest (150 km), and its rocks are best preserved in northeast Newfoundland. An offshore seismic refraction profile indicates a thick (45 km) dense crust beneath the Dunnage compared to that of adjacent terranes (Dainty and others, 1966). The nature of the crust is also expressed in a positive Bouguer anomaly (Haworth and others, 1980). Nearby in southwest Newfoundland, the Dunnage terrane is absent at the Cape Ray suture (Williams, 1978). These local swells and constrictions of the Dunnage terrane may relate to the geometry of the bordering miogeocline and Gander terrane. Thus, its widest segments of least deformed rocks occur at matching reentrants, whereas the terrane is obliterated at colliding promontories (Williams, 1979).

Early Paleozoic rocks of the Dunnage terrane are mafic pillow lavas, volcanic breccias, volcaniclastic rocks, graywackes, slates, cherts, and minor limestones. Melange units are prominent in northeast Newfoundland (Dunnage and Carmanville melanges), and similar chaotic rocks occur locally in New Brunswick. Ophiolitic complexes of the Dunnage terrane include the Advocate, Point Rousse, Betts Cove, South Pond, and Annieopsquotch complexes in Newfoundland, the Fournier complex of New Brunswick, and the numerous mafic/ultramafic complexes of the Quebec Serpentinite belt. All are interpreted as oceanic crust and mantle. Thick overlying volcanic sequences are interpreted as the products of Early Ordovician island arc volcanism.

The western boundary of the Dunnage terrane is the Baie Verte–Brompton line (Williams and St. Julien, 1982). It is a steep structural zone, marked by numerous occurrences of ophiolitic rocks that separate polydeformed metaclastic rocks of the Piedmont terrane from volcanic sequences of the Dunnage terrane. The eastern boundary of the Dunnage terrane is largely covered by Silurian strata, except in Newfoundland where the boundary is marked by discontinuous ophiolite occurrences and shale melanges (Blackwood, 1978; Pajari and others, 1979). These are followed eastward by metaclastic rocks of the Gander terrane.

Deformation across the Dunnage terrane is uniformly mild compared to that in the bordering Piedmont and Gander terranes. In central parts of the Dunnage terrane the Lower Ordovician volcanic sequences and melanges are overlain by Caradocian black shales, graywackes, and Silurian conglomerates. Along its western margin, imbricated ophiolitic complexes are steeply dipping to overturned, but the sequences of units face eastward. At the Baie Verte–Brompton line, ophiolite complexes are overlain by olistostromes and coarse conglomerates. Farther west the ophiolitic complexes are structurally and metamorphically gradational with ophiolitic melanges and metaclastic rocks that are an integral part of the Piedmont terrane. Structures and metamorphism here are interpreted as Ordovician and related to westward transport of ophiolitic complexes, such as the Bay of Islands, from a Dunnage root zone to their present positions above the miogeocline.

Locally in northeast Newfoundland, Dunnage ophiolitic rocks are thrust eastward upon clastic rocks of the Gander terrane. The ophiolitic rocks are overlain by polymictic conglomerates and Caradocian shales, implying a Middle Ordovician disturbance. Nearby olistostromes contain huge rafts of volcanic rocks surrounded by Caradocian shales, and these are interpreted as marine slides that slumped westward and back toward the basin from which the ophiolitic rocks originated (Pajari and others, 1979). These relationships are somewhat analogous to those of the Baie Verte–Brompton line, where olistostromes and coarse conglomerates above the ophiolite complexes there are thought to have slid eastward.

The boundaries of the Dunnage terrane, where unmodified by later faulting, were therefore established during Ordovician time. Unassailable evidence for an Ordovician linkage between the Dunnage terrane and the deformed North American miogeocline to the west and between the Dunnage terrane and the Gander terrane to the east is provided by a continuous belt of Middle to Upper Ordovician and Silurian rocks of the Aroostook-Metapedia Groups that form an overlap assemblage extending from the deformed miogeocline of Quebec to the Gander terrane of New Brunswick and Maine.

The age and chemistry of volcanic rocks in the Dunnage terrane indicate that an island arc was active there during the passive development of the North American miogeocline to the west (Kean and Strong, 1975). A cover of Caradocian shales above the island arc volcanic rocks indicates that the evolution of the volcanic arc ceased at the time of destruction of the North American miogeocline and final emplacement of Taconic terranes across the miogeocline (Dean, 1978). The relationships also imply that the North American margin was destroyed by collision with an island arc and that the Dunnage terrane was juxtaposed with the North American margin in Early to Middle Ordovician time.

The coincidence of the Dunnage terrane in Newfoundland with a dense overthickened substrate and positive Bouguer anomaly implies that the terrane is rooted with respect to the North American miogeocline. It appears to have been caught in an Ordovician vice whose jaws are represented by the North American miogeocline to the west and the Gander terrane to the east. Subsequent Acadian (Devonian) deformation reflects this local Ordovician model with westward polarity of structures across the North American miogeocline and eastward polarity across the Newfoundland Gander terrane. Palinspastic restoration of the widest segment of the Dunnage terrane in northeast Newfoundland indicates an original ocean having a minimal width of 1,000 km (Williams, 1980).

The position of the Dunnage terrane in the northern Appalachians, and its apparent interplay with the emplacement of Taconic allochthons and the destruction of the North American miogeocline, implies that it represents the vestiges of an ocean that bordered the ancient continental margin of eastern North America. This further implies that the Piedmont terrane of the northern Appalachians represents rocks at the deformed precarious edge of eastern North America, rather than a far-traveled alien terrane. These relationships, applied to the central and southern Appalachians, imply a North American origin for the Piedmont terrane there and an oceanic suture between it and the bordering Avalon terrane. Such a suture would be equivalent to the Baie Verte–Brompton line of the northern Appalachians, and it may have been the root zone and source of ophiolitic fragments that occur throughout the Piedmont terrane to the west.

Chain Lakes Terrane. The Chain Lakes terrane is a relatively small area of crystalline rocks located at the United States–Canada international border in Maine and Quebec. Zircons from quartz-feldspar gneisses of the terrane have been dated at 1,600 m.y. (Naylor and others, 1973), and its rocks contrast in metamorphic grade and structural style with surrounding Paleozoic rocks.

The Chain Lakes terrane is bordered by a steeply dipping Upper Cambrian or Ordovician ophiolite complex to the south; it is intruded by Paleozoic granite to the east, and it is faulted against or unconformably overlain by Silurian sedimentary rocks to the north (Boudette and Boone, 1976, 1982).

Rocks of the Chain Lakes terrane are at least 3 km thick normal to layering. The lower 2 km consist of massive to poorly stratified diamictite with abundant gabbroic clasts, and this is overlain by metavolcanic and metasedimentary rocks. All of the rocks have been metamorphosed to upper amphibolite and granulite facies and have been variably retrograded. The zircon age of 1,600 m.y. is tentatively considered the age of metamorphism, and indirect evidence suggests an original Archean age (Boudette and Boone, 1982). The unusual fragmental textures of the diamictite facies, the age of the rocks, and complex strain lamellae in quartz all suggest an impact origin (Boudette and Boone, 1982).

A large slab of metamorphic rock in an olistostrome of the Dunnage terrane near Beauceville, Quebec, resembles metamorphic rocks of the Chain Lakes terrane (Williams and St. Julien, 1982). Since the olistostromal rocks (St. Daniel Formation) are overlain by Middle Ordovician shales (Beauceville Formation), the relationship implies proximity of the Chain Lakes terrane and west flank of the Dunnage terrane in Middle Ordovician time.

This sedimentologic linkage, combined with the occurrence of a Dunnage-type ophiolite complex along its southern flank, suggests that the ancient crystalline rocks of the Chain Lakes terrane lie structurally beneath or within the younger ophiolitic Dunnage terrane.

Another example of a small suspect terrane within the Dunnage terrane is afforded by the Twillingate Granite and surrounding volcanic rocks in northeast Newfoundland. The Twillingate Granite is dated at 510 m.y., and its metamorphic grade and structural style locally contrast with surrounding Ordovician rocks. As well, the mylonitic phase along its southern border is cut by mafic dikes dated at 470 m.y. and interpreted to relate to nearby Ordovician volcanic rocks. The timing of intrusion, metamorphism, and deformation in the Twillingate terrane is enigmatic, for it coincides with the time of ophiolite generation and extension in the surrounding Dunnage terrane. The Twillingate terrane is viewed therefore as suspect.

Chopawamsic Terrane. The Chopawamsic is a small elongate terrane in the interior part of the southern Appalachians of Virginia. Its oldest rocks are mixed volcanics of the Chopawamsic Formation that are cut by a granite pluton dated at 560 m.y. (Pavlides and others, 1980; Pavlides, 1981). The granite, in turn, is nonconformably overlain by Middle to Late Ordovician slates of the Quantico Formation.

Volcanic rocks of the James Run Formation in eastern Maryland may be Chopawamsic equivalents. Sedimentary rocks of the Arvonia syncline toward the south are possible Quantico correlatives and part of the cover sequence. The Arvonia rocks contain a Middle to Late Ordovician brachiopod fauna that has diverse elements compared to faunas of similar age in rocks of the North American miogeocline.

The Chopawamsic terrane is bounded to the east by the Spotsylvania Lineament, and its volcanic rocks contrast with those of the nearby Avalon terrane. An ophiolitic melange zone 8 km northwest of the Chopawamsic Formation may mark another major tectonic boundary, and its presence implies that the Chopawamsic terrane is allochthonous (Pavlides, 1981).

Gander Terrane. The Gander terrane is traceable from Newfoundland to Long Island Sound, New York. It is defined on its Middle Ordovician and older rocks, although throughout much of its length in Atlantic Canada and New England these are hidden by Silurian and younger rocks. In Canada, the Gander terrane is characterized by a thick sequence of pre-Middle Ordovician arenaceous rocks that are in most places polydeformed and metamorphosed. Their relationship with underlying migmatites and granitic gneisses has been variously interpreted as unconformable to gradational (Kennedy, 1976; Blackwood, 1978). In Newfoundland, the clastic rocks are overlain by Middle Ordovician shales and chaotic olisto-stromes that include ophiolitic components. In New Brunswick, the clastic rocks are overlain by a thick Middle Ordovician volcanic sequence.

Gneiss dome complexes of New England have been equated with metamorphic rocks of the Gander terrane in Canada, and these can be traced from Bronson Hill, Massachusetts, to Boundary Mountain at the Canadian border (Robinson and Hall, 1980). Metamorphic rocks of the New England dome complexes are overlain by volcanics (Ammonoosuc) and Ordovician shales (Partridge), and the prominent clastic unit of Canada is absent.

Granitic intrusions, mainly megacrystic biotite granites and garnetiferous muscovite leucogranites and associated pegmatites, are everywhere common throughout metamorphosed parts of the Gander terrane. This main phase of plutonism and metamorphism is mainly Devonian (Bell and others, 1977). The significance of older plutonic rocks in the Gander terrane of New England (Fitchburg Pluton and Massabesic Gneiss) are unknown, and these can be viewed either as basement inliers or smaller suspect terranes within the larger composite Gander terrane. Earliest deformation in the Gander terrane was pre-Silurian and locally pre-Middle Ordovician.

Discontinuous ophiolite occurrences along the eastern edge of the Dunnage terrane in Newfoundland and nearby Gander terrane psammites are overlain by the Middle Ordovician Davidsville Group, thus providing a Middle Ordovician Dunnage-Gander overlap relationship. Recent mapping and new fossil discoveries in the interior part of the Newfoundland Gander terrane (P. F. Wonderley, personal commun., 1982) suggest that Davidsville rocks once extended much farther east, possibly as an overlap assemblage.

In New Brunswick and southward, the western margin of the Gander terrane is marked by faults or hidden by younger cover rocks (Rast and Stringer, 1980). In a few places where volcanic rocks like those of the Dunnage terrane occur above clastic rocks of the Gander terrane, the real Dunnage-Gander distinction can only be made at deeper stratigraphic levels. The exposed eastern margin of the Gander terrane is marked by important faults along its length (Dover, Frediction, Norumbega, Clinton-Newbury, Lake Char, and Honey Hill).

Because its clastic rocks are overlain in places by thick volcanic units, all above a sialic gneissic substrate, the Gander terrane has been interpreted locally as an Andean continental margin (Williams and Doolan, 1978). Its position with respect to the Dunnage terrane implies that it developed at a great distance from the North American miogeocline on the opposite side of a major ocean.

The Gander terrane, like the North American miogeocline, interacted with the Dunnage terrane through ophiolite obduction and melange formation in Early to Middle Ordovician time. Its clastic rocks have been equated with similar rocks of the North American miogeocline, and its structures are diametrically opposed and face southeastward. This symmetry of rocks and structures has been interpreted to indicate similar margins, deformed by similar processes on opposite sides of the oceanic Dunnage terrane (Kennedy, 1976; Colman-Sadd, 1980). However, the Gander terrane lacks many of the following features so necessary for a stratigraphic analysis like that available for the North American miogeocline: (a) it has no proven Grenvillian basement; (b) it lacks mafic dikes, volcanic rocks, and coarse clastics, normally associated with rifting and initiation of a continental margin; (c) it does not have a long history as a passive margin; (d) thickness, age, facies variations, and provenance of its clastic rocks are unknown; (e) its Ordovician volcanic rocks and profuse granitic intrusions are lacking at the North American margin; and (f) relationships to more easterly terranes are unknown.

A long history of deformation and intrusion in the Gander terrane has been related to large horizontal displacements along a megashear (Hanmer, 1981).

Avalon Terrane. The Avalon terrane is the largest of all Appalachian suspect terranes. It extends along the entire length of the orogen and can be traced offshore to Virgin Rocks and Flemish Cap in the north (Fig. 1). Its width in the north is at least twice that for the rest of the orogen, and its width in the south equals the combined widths of the miogeocline and Piedmont terranes. Similar rocks of the same age occur in Wales, Brittany, Spain, and Morocco. Cambrian strata of the Avalon terrane have distinctive Atlantic realm trilobite faunas, and this was recently confirmed by the discovery of a new trilobite locality in South Carolina (Sampson and others, 1982).

Rocks of the Avalon terrane are mainly late Precambrian and Cambrian volcanic and sedimentary rocks that are relatively unmetamorphosed and undeformed compared to nearby parts of the Gander terrane in the north and the Piedmont terrane in the south. However, the Charlotte belt of the Carolinas and equivalents in Georgia are considered to be a high-grade (upper amphibolite facies) portion of the Avalon terrane in the south. In some places, the late Precambrian rocks pass upward with structural conformity into Cambrian shales. In other places, there are unconformities in the late Precambrian successions, and late Precambrian intrusions are common throughout the length of the Avalon terrane. These late Precambrian structural and intrusive events define the Avalonian orogeny.

The oldest Precambrian rocks of the Canadian Avalon terrane are marbles and quartzites in New Brunswick and Nova Scotia. These are interpreted to underlie the late Precambrian volcanic and sedimentary rocks with structural unconformity. Preliminary isotopic studies in

Cape Breton Island, Nova Scotia, suggest a still older basement at about 1,000 m.y. (Sandra Barr, personal commun., 1981). Similarly in the southern Avalon terrane, 1,000-m.y. ages have been obtained from the State Farm gneisses of northeast Virginia (Glover and others, 1978). These reports suggest a local Grenvillian basement to the Avalon terrane. However, Grenville basement rocks in Virginia may occur as structural windows within overthrust Avalon rocks.

The Avalon terrane encompasses a variety of diverse geologic elements; some of its Precambrian volcanic rocks are calc-alkaline, others are alkalic or bimodal, and still others are mafic with ocean-floor chemical affinities (Strong, 1979; Bland and Blackburn, 1980; Black, 1980; Papezik, 1980); Precambrian melanges occur locally in Rhode Island (Rast and Skehan, 1981); Precambrian intrusions are common in some areas of the Avalon but not in others; effects of Precambrian deformation and metamorphism are variable throughout the terrane, and Precambrian tillite and fossiliferous Precambrian rocks are present in some places. This variety of features suggests a composite makeup of the Avalon terrane and the likelihood of smaller terranes that are just as suspect as the larger Avalon terrane itself (Keppie, 1983).

If composite, the Avalon terrane was assembled during late Precambrian time, as its Cambrian rocks have similar faunas and stratigraphy throughout the orogen. In fact, this continuity of Cambrian stratigraphic units and faunas in the north led to the concept of an Avalon platform or shelf. However, the nature of this platform, its polarity with respect to bounding elements, and the thickness and facies variations of its rocks are not well known.

The Avalon terrane is everywhere bounded by faults in the northern Appalachians. In the southern Appalachians, low-grade Carolina slate belt rocks grade westward into high-grade Charlotte belt assemblages and are probably faulted farther west.

There are no confirmed pre-Silurian linkages between the Avalon terrane and bounding terranes. In addition, the Avalon terrane in the north is unaffected by Ordovician (Taconic) orogeny, which is evident in more westerly terranes. This negative evidence suggests that the time of docking of the Avalon terrane was later than the accretion of the Dunnage and Gander terranes. In the south, isotopic ages indicate Ordovician plutonism (Lynn Glover III, personal commun., 1981); however, like late Precambrian plutonism, this need not relate to North American accretion.

In Newfoundland, a previous report of Gander terrane plutonic clasts in late Precambrian Avalonian conglomerates has not been supported by recent studies (Blackwood and O'Driscoll, 1976). Similarly, the report of a 500-m.y.-old pluton (Straddling Granite of Blackwood and O'Driscoll, 1976) that intruded both the Gander and

Avalon terranes at Hermitage Bay, Newfoundland, has been modified, and the pluton is interpreted now as being confined to the Avalon terrane (P. Elias, personal commun., 1981). Devonian plutons clearly cut the Avalon-Gander terrane boundary, and the most recent geochronological studies in northeast Newfoundland indicate an Early Devonian (400 to 420 m.y.) age for mylonite development and first movement of the Dover fault (Dallmeyer and others, 1981). Coarse conglomerates that contain a sampling of metamorphic and plutonic rocks of the Gander terrane occur on the east side of the Hermitage Bay fault at Belle Bay, Newfoundland (Williams, 1971). The conglomerates are interpreted as Silurian or Devonian and provide the first clear sedimentologic linkage between the Gander and Avalon terranes at this locality.

In New Brunswick and Maine, the Avalon and Gander terranes are linked by a similar Devonian plutonic history. Silurian marine graywackes of New Brunswick (Fredericton Trough) have been interpreted to mark the site of a Silurian ocean (McKerrow and Ziegler, 1971) at or near the Gander-Avalon boundary, but this interpretation is equivocal (Rast and others, 1976a; Williams, 1979). The interpretation of the Union Complex of Maine as ophiolitic and a recent 420-m.y. isotopic age for its gabbros (Gaudette, 1981) have been used as evidence of a mid-Paleozoic oceanic suture zone at or near the Gander-Avalon terrane boundary in southern Maine. Here too there is some doubt as to whether these rocks are true ophiolites and if this zone successfully separates Silurian rocks of the Vassalboro Formation (Osberg, 1981).

The absence of dated Paleozoic rocks in the southern Appalachian Piedmont terrane negates the possibility of establishing stratigraphic or sedimentologic linkages between the Avalon and Piedmont terranes. However, in most existing models (e.g., Hatcher and Odom, 1980), their junction is interpreted as a Devonian suture that marks the site of an earlier ocean whose closing provided a mechanism for Acadian orogeny.

The overall geochronologic and stratigraphic evidence suggests, therefore, a mid-Paleozoic docking of the Avalon terrane that followed an early Paleozoic assembly of more westerly terranes.

Although the geology of the Avalon terrane is clear locally, the controlling features of its late Precambrian development are still largely unknown. The Avalon terrane did not directly face or abut the Dunnage oceanic tract, except possibly in the south where the intervening Gander terrane may be absent. But the Dunnage terrane may be absent here also. Relationships in the northern Avalon terrane have been interpreted to suggest late Precambrian subduction and island arc evolution that were unrelated to an Iapetus cycle (Rast and others, 1976b) or else rifting and the initiation of the Iapetus cycle (Strong, 1979). In the southern Appalachians the same terrane has been

viewed as an island arc that developed at the North American margin (Hatcher, 1972). This interpretation has also been questioned (Hatcher, 1978; Hatcher and Odom, 1980), and a North American arc seems especially incongruous for the south since the Avalon terrane lies outboard of the Dunnage and Gander terranes in the north.

The Raleigh and Kiokee belts in the southern Appalachians could conceivably be considered additional terranes. However, they appear to be little more than linear Alleghanian high-grade metamorphic zones which occur within the Avalon terrane. They consist of amphibolite facies equivalents of lower grade rocks and contain deformed Carboniferous plutons (Snoke and others, 1980). However, the presence of a probable ophiolite sequence (Kite and Stoddard, 1981) in the Raleigh belt raises the possibility of a pre-Alleghanian cryptic suture there.

Meguma Terrane. The Meguma terrane occurs in mainland Nova Scotia, and its geophysical expression suggests that it underlies a large part of the nearby Atlantic continental shelf (Haworth and Lefort, 1979). Its onland boundary with the Avalon terrane is marked by the Glooscap fault, which apparently extends eastward across the tail of the Grand Banks as implied by a linear zone of magnetic and Bouguer anomalies (Haworth and MacIntyre, 1976).

The Meguma terrane (Schenk, 1978) consists mainly of a conformable succession of graywackes and shales up to 13 km thick (Meguma Group). Its uppermost shales contain Early Ordovician graptolites; lower parts of the thick succession are interpreted as Cambrian. The Meguma Group is overlain conformably by undated sedimentary and volcanic rocks that include a possible Ordovician tillite unit at its base (Schenk, 1972; Lane, 1976). This sequence is in turn overlain by Devonian sediments, mainly terrestrial.

The Meguma terrane was first deformed by Acadian orogeny, and its folded rocks are cut by Devonian intrusions (Clark and others, 1980). Carboniferous deformation is important only along the Glooscap fault.

Provenance studies of the Meguma Group indicate that its source was a low-lying metamorphic area to the southeast, and the volume of sediments suggests a source area of continental dimensions. Accordingly, the Meguma Group is interpreted as the offshore remnant of an ancient continental embankment (Schenk, 1978). Isotopic ages of 2,500 m.y. for detrital zircons in the Meguma Group suggest its source area was exceedingly old (J. D. Keppie, personal commun., 1981). In addition, quartz-feldspar gneisses in southeastern Nova Scotia are interpreted now as basement to the Meguma Group (J. D. Keppie, personal commun., 1982).

An eastern limit of the Meguma Group is suggested by a change in magnetic anomaly patterns near the edge of the Nova Scotia continental shelf. The Meguma terrane, therefore, may be followed outward by still another terrane, or the geophysical change may represent the edge of the Meguma Group sedimentary rocks where they may be followed eastward by basement rocks of the same terrane.

The Meguma terrane has no apparent linkage with the Avalon terrane, or any other Appalachian terrane, except that both share a similar Carboniferous overlap assemblage. Even the large batholithic intrusions of the Meguma terrane are distinct from those of the nearby Avalon terrane (Clark and others, 1980). This suggests a late Paleozoic docking of the Meguma with the Avalon terrane.

Present models imply an oceanic tract to the west of the Meguma terrane, but there is no evidence for such a feature at the Meguma-Avalon contact now. The provenance, sedimentology, and thickness of the Meguma Group imply that it bordered an ocean in early Paleozoic time, but there is nothing in the Silurian or later stratigraphic record of either the Avalon or Meguma terranes to suggest an ocean between the two during mid-Paleozoic time. The mechanism of accretion of the Meguma terrane was most likely by transcurrent faulting.

Subsurface Suspect Terranes in the Southeastern United States

Brunswick and Tallahassee/Suwannee Terranes.
Magnetic and gravity data (Wollard and Joesting, 1964; Zietz and Gilbert, 1980) provide strong evidence for exotic rocks beneath the Coastal Plain of the Carolinas, south Georgia, and north Florida. The suggested east boundary of the Avalon terrane, which continues for some distance beneath the Coastal Plain to the east, is quite evident in the magnetic signatures in the area beneath the Coastal Plain east of the Raleigh belt. Frequencies and wavelengths of anomalies in this area are similar to those of the Avalon terrane which is exposed to the west of the Raleigh belt in the southern Appalachians. However, there is an abrupt termination farther to the southeast where the high frequency, short wavelength anomalies typical of the Avalon terrane give way abruptly to much lower frequency, much more symmetrical long wavelength anomalies, which define the Brunswick terrane. Dampening of the magnetic field intensity may mean that the Brunswick terrane constitutes a series of successor basins or an aulacogen that is filled by extensive late Paleozoic sedimentary rocks, possibly superseded by Triassic-Jurassic sediments (Popenoe and Zietz, 1977). The Brunswick terrane also contains evidence of a number of plutons, some of which must be mafic because they are expressed both by gravity and magnetic highs. Other plutons are probably granites (see, for example, Zietz and Gilbert, 1980).

South of the Brunswick terrane, there is a sudden change to a more high amplitude, high frequency magnetic pattern which probably corresponds to a different crustal type. We propose to call this area the Tallahassee-Suwannee terrane. Gravity signature here is likewise somewhat different from that to the north (Wollard and Joesting, 1964). There is a transition from a gravity low in the Brunswick area to a gravity high or intermediate intensity gravity field farther to the south. Drill-hole data indicate the presence of mildly deformed and unmetamorphosed lower and middle Paleozoic shelf clastics, and fossils in lower parts of the section are akin to African forms. Granites of probable late Paleozoic age are also present (Milton and Hurst, 1965; McLaughlin, 1974; Arden, 1974; Pojeta and others, 1976). The Tallahassee-Suwannee terrane probably once belonged to either Africa or South America, depending upon which paleomagnetic reconstruction of the late Paleozoic continents one wishes to accept (Kent and Opdyke, 1978; Irving, 1979).

The boundary between the Brunswick and Tallahassee-Suwannee terranes trends almost due west of the Georgia coast, then northwest, then more westerly at the Alabama-Georgia state line. The Brunswick terrane narrows rapidly across Georgia and terminates farther west in Alabama. At that point the magnetically distinct Tallahassee-Suwannee terrane is very close to the exposed rocks of the Avalon and Piedmont terranes. Farther west, the entire Appalachian orogen is truncated in subsurface by an abrupt northwest-trending structure. This may represent a transform fault, linking the Appalachians and Ouachitas, and bordering an ancient crustal block in the Mississippi embayment (Cebull and others, 1976; Thomas, 1977). Recent compilations of gravity and magnetic data support this model (Thomas and others, in preparation), and separation along a transform may explain the contrasts in coeval stratigraphic sequences in the Ouachitas and Appalachians.

ACCRETIONARY HISTORY OF THE APPALACHIAN OROGEN

The accretionary history of the Appalachian orogen is emphasized by the suspect terrane concept. Time of accretion of various terranes, both with respect to the North American miogeocline and with respect to one another, is essential to tectonic analyses. Likewise, the duration and mechanisms of accretion and comparisons between accretionary history and structural, metamorphic, plutonic, and metallogenic development are all important parameters in the study of any orogen.

Early Paleozoic rocks that define the large first-order suspect terranes of the Appalachian orogen occur in a regular and predictable manner (Fig. 1). Thus, the miogeocline is followed outward by the Piedmont terrane, interpreted, at least in part, as the deformed and metamorphosed edge of the ancient North American continent.

In the north, the Piedmont terrane is followed outward by the Dunnage terrane or vestiges of the ancient Iapetus Ocean. The Dunnage is, in turn, followed outward by the ensialic Gander, Avalon, and Meguma terranes, respectively. In the south, the Piedmont terrane is followed outward by the Avalon terrane, in turn followed by the Brunswick and Tallahassee-Suwannee terranes. The absence of the Dunnage terrane in the south may mean complete suturing and a total destruction of Iapetus there. Apparent absence of the Gander terrane in the south may mean structural truncation at accretionary boundaries or that it did not span the full length of the orogen at the time of accretion. Similarly, the Meguma, Brunswick, and Tallahassee-Suwannee terranes may have only local significance. The geometry and disparate widths of some terranes and the apparent truncation of lithofacies belts in others, for example, the Avalon, suggest segmentation at accretionary boundaries rather than original shapes.

Therefore, while there are omissions of some terranes, reversals or repetitions of the broad subdivisions are unknown. This implies an orderly and relatively simple accretionary history and an existing geometry that is not confused by major transcurrent faults that cross terrane boundaries.

Time of Accretion

The presence of a full time range of Paleozoic rocks in the northern Appalachians provides the stratigraphic basis for an accretionary analysis there. In the south, this analysis is based necessarily on relative times of intrusion, metamorphism, and deformation. Geochronological studies also provide an important adjunct to this analysis.

The stratigraphic analysis of accretionary history of the Canadian Appalachians compared to time of deformation, plutonism, and metamorphism is summarized in Figure 2. The same analysis for the southern Appalachians, based mainly on the age of plutonism and metamorphism, is summarized in Figure 3. Triassic sedimentary and volcanic rocks are omitted from these analyses as they are an obvious overlap assemblage across the Appalachian orogen and relate to the initiation of the modern Atlantic Ocean.

In the northern Appalachians, the Dunnage and Gander terranes were juxtaposed with the North American miogeocline and with one another during Middle Ordovician time (Fig. 2A, 2B). The presence of the Avalon terrane cannot be clearly demonstrated until Silurian or Devonian time (though it may have been accreted earlier), and the Meguma terrane appears to have maintained a distinct plutonic history during much of Devonian time. Thus, the accretion of the orogen in the north seems to have progressed from west to east, or from the miogeocline outward.

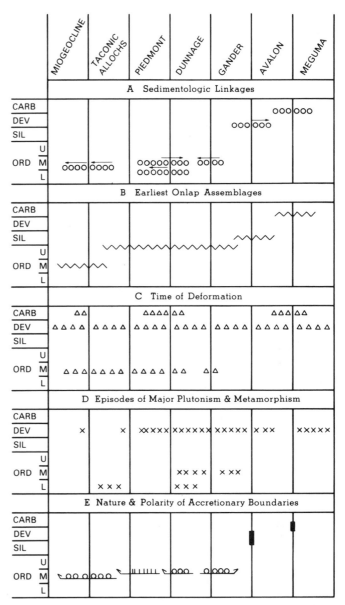

Figure 2. Sedimentologic and stratigraphic analyses of accretionary history of northern (Canadian) Appalachians compared to time of deformation, plutonism, and metamorphism. Arrow in A indicates direction of sedimentary transport. In E, arrow with circles indicates thrust zone marked by melange and ophiolitic rocks, arrow with vertical lines indicates sharp thrust contact, and thick vertical bar indicates steep fault zone, commonly with mylonites.

In the southern Appalachians, the earliest accretionary history is less sharply defined. Geochronological evidence for Taconic and Acadian orogeneses imply early and mid-Paleozoic accretionary events. However, the emplacement of the Talladega and Piedmont terranes across the miogeocline took place during Carboniferous-Permian time. The Brunswick and Tallahassee-Suwannee terranes were accreted last, because their boundaries truncate other terrane boundaries farther west. This last accretionary

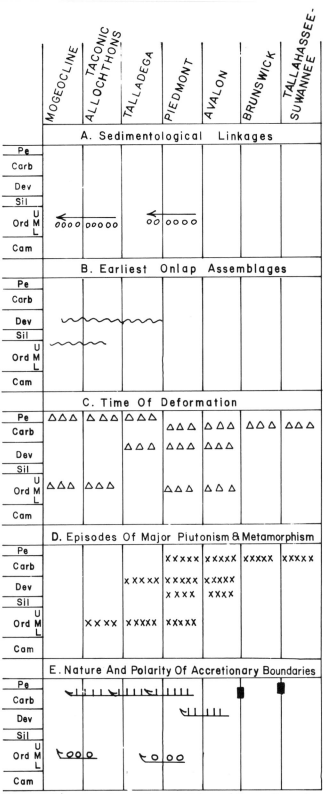

Figure 3. Summary of accretionary history of the southern Appalachians (symbols as per Fig. 2).

event may relate to the evolution of the nearby Ouachita orogen.

The entire accretionary process for the Appalachian orogen endured intermittently for about 200 m.y.

Mechanism and Style of Accretion

The boundaries of the earliest accreted terranes in the northern Appalachians (Taconic terranes, Dunnage and Gander terranes) are marked by broad, soft, melange zones and the emplacement of ophiolite complexes (Fig. 2E). In contrast, the Gander-Avalon boundary and the Avalon-Meguma boundary are marked by steep faults with local wide zones of ductile deformation and the development of mylonitic rocks. Furthermore, whereas the evidence of an oceanic tract between the miogeocline and Gander terrane is virtually unassailable, oceanic vestiges are absent at the boundaries of more outboard terranes, except possibly for the Union Complex at the Gander-Avalon boundary of Maine.

The mechanism of earliest accretion was by obduction of the Dunnage terrane across the miogeocline and by obduction and/or subduction of the Dunnage terrane across-beneath the Gander terrane. Later accretion of the Avalon and more outboard terranes appears to have been controlled by major transcurrent movements. Such movements are suggested also by paleomagnetic disparities between mid-Paleozoic rocks of the eastern Appalachians with respect to coeval rocks of the North American craton.

The emplacement of the crystalline Piedmont terrane across the miogeocline in the southern Appalachians reflects the intensity of Carboniferous deformation there (Fig. 3). Where Alleghanian deformation is absent in the northern Appalachians, there is no indication of profound telescoping and transport of crystalline slices comparable to that in the south.

Accretionary History and Time of Deformation

The spatial distribution of the effects of Taconic, Acadian, and Alleghanian orogeneses is depicted in Figure 4.

The first major orogenic episode to affect the Appalachian orogen was Taconic orogeny mainly during Middle Ordovician time. It affected the eastern margin of the North American miogeocline, all of the Piedmont terrane, marginal zones of the Dunnage terrane, most of the Gander terrane, and the Chopawamsic terrane (Fig. 4A). Evidence of Taconic orogeny is scarce or absent throughout most of the Avalon terrane and entirely absent in the Meguma and outboard terranes of the southern Appalachians. The most intense effects of Taconic orogeny are localized in the Piedmont terrane (Fig. 4A) along the western flank of the orogen.

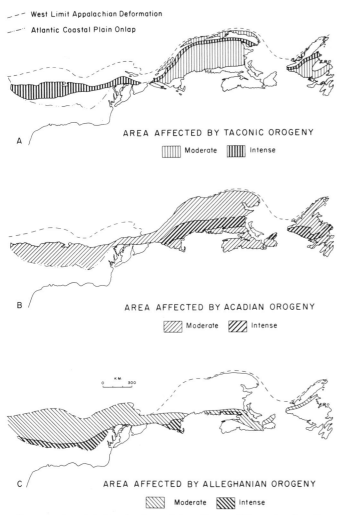

- - - West Limit Appalachian Deformation

-··- Atlantic Coastal Plain Onlap

A

AREA AFFECTED BY TACONIC OROGENY

▥ Moderate ▦ Intense

B

AREA AFFECTED BY ACADIAN OROGENY

▨ Moderate ▨ Intense

KM
0 ——— 300

C

AREA AFFECTED BY ALLEGHANIAN OROGENY

▧ Moderate ▧ Intense

Figure 4. Spatial distribution of the effects of Taconic, Acadian, and Alleghanian orogeneses throughout the Appalachian orogen.

This distribution of Taconic deformation fits well with the stratigraphic analysis for the accretionary history of the orogen. Thus, the most westerly terranes (miogeocline, Piedmont, Dunnage, Gander, and Chopawamsic) that were attached to the miogeocline, or one another, during Middle Ordovician time are the terranes that best exhibit the effects of Taconic orogeny. It seems reasonable, therefore, to equate Taconic deformation and the earliest accretionary phase of the orogen. The lack of Taconic deformation in much of the Avalon and more easterly terranes further supports the stratigraphic evidence for later accretion of more easterly terranes.

Mid-Paleozoic Acadian orogeny affected the entire orogen, except for westerly parts of the miogeocline in the south, local areas of the Avalon terrane in east Newfoundland, and easterly parts of the Avalon terrane and more easterly terranes in the southern Appalachians (Fig. 4B). Its effects are most intense in interior parts of the orogen, especially along the east flank of the Gander terrane in the

north. As well, this phase of orogenesis coincides with the plutonic and metamorphic climaxes in the development of the orogen. It possibly relates to compression and shearing across the orogen in response to the accretion of the Avalon terrane, and perhaps also to accretion of the Meguma terrane in the northern Appalachians.

Late Paleozoic Alleghanian orogeny affected the flanks of the southern Appalachians, but its effects are restricted to a narrow zone in the north through eastern New England, southeast New Brunswick, and along the Avalon-Meguma boundary in Nova Scotia (Fig. 4C). Its effects are also evident in a narrow zone of relatively mild deformation along the east margin of the miogeocline in Newfoundland.

Although Alleghanian thrusting and folding affected the entire miogeocline along the western margin of the southern Appalachians, Alleghanian intrusive and regional metamorphic effects are localized in the Avalon terrane along the eastern margin of the orogen (Uchee, Kiokee, and Raleigh belts). Possibly this phase of orogenesis in the south relates to compressive forces associated with the accretion of the Brunswick and Tallahassee-Suwannee terranes. Farther north, Alleghanian plutonism and regional metamorphism are restricted to the Avalon terrane of New England, and in New Brunswick and Nova Scotia the most intense Alleghanian deformation is localized in the Avalon terrane at the Avalon-Meguma terrane boundary. In the north, these effects may relate to either the initial accretion of the Meguma terrane, or possibly renewed compression or translation at the Avalon-Meguma terrane boundary.

Thus, the times of deformation in the Appalachian orogen coincide with the main phases of accretion of the orogen. Equally important is the distribution of the effects of each episode and the relative positions of the axes of most intense deformation for each event. The effects of Taconic orogeny are restricted to the first accreted western terranes with the axis of most intense deformation along the west flank of the orogen. Acadian orogeny affected central and some eastern terranes, as well as the earlier Taconic deformed zone, and its axis of most intense deformation was outboard of that for Taconic orogeny. Similarly, the effects of Alleghanian orogeny are locally widespread, especially in the south, but its most intense effects are localized in the Avalon terrane along the eastern flank of the orogen. This structural analysis supports the stratigraphy analysis and the interpretation that accretion of the Appalachian orogen progressed from the miogeocline outward by the successive addition of more outboard terranes.

A model for the accretion of the Appalachian orogen is summarized spatially in Figure 5 and diagrammatically in Figure 6. This crude analysis implies a one-to-one relationship between accretionary events and times of defor-

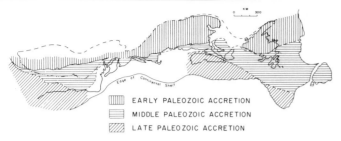

Figure 5. Style of accretion of the Appalachian orogen by the addition of successively outboard terranes.

mation. Furthermore, it explains the episodic nature of orogeny and the sequential nature of the orogenic cycle even though the causes of orogeny are essentially continuous.

Accretionary History Versus Plutonism, Metamorphism, and Metallogeny

The major plutonic episodes to affect rocks of the Appalachian orogen occurred during late Precambrian, Ordovician, Devonian, and Carboniferous times. These compare well with the times of major deformation, that is, Avalonian, Taconic, Acadian, and Alleghanian, respectively. The Taconian, Acadian, and Alleghanian orogenic episodes are also the times of major Paleozoic regional metamorphism. Thus, episodes of deformation, plutonism, and metamorphism are all tied temporally (Figs. 2 and 3).

The intrusion of late Precambrian granitic batholiths is mainly confined to the Avalon terrane. These intrusions relate to the early history of the Avalon terrane, and they were an integral component of that terrane before its mid-Paleozoic accretion.

Ordovician batholithic intrusions are minor in the orogen and are confined mainly to the Piedmont, Dunnage, Gander, and Chopawamsic terranes. Tonalites, diorites, and granodiorites are the common rock types, compared to a preponderance of more potassic granites emplaced during later plutonic phases.

Large Devonian granitic batholiths are numerous throughout the Appalachian orogen, and they are common in all terranes east of the miogeocline. The granitic intrusions bear little similarity to those of modern island arcs and Andean continental margins, and this view has been expressed independently for plutons in Newfoundland (Strong, 1980), New Brunswick (Fyffe and others, 1981), and Maine (Wones, 1980). Thus, a subduction mechanism of generation is not favored. Furthermore, mid-Paleozoic intrusions cut Silurian-Devonian rocks which are overlap assemblages across the earlier accreted terranes. Recent models for the northern Appalachians re-

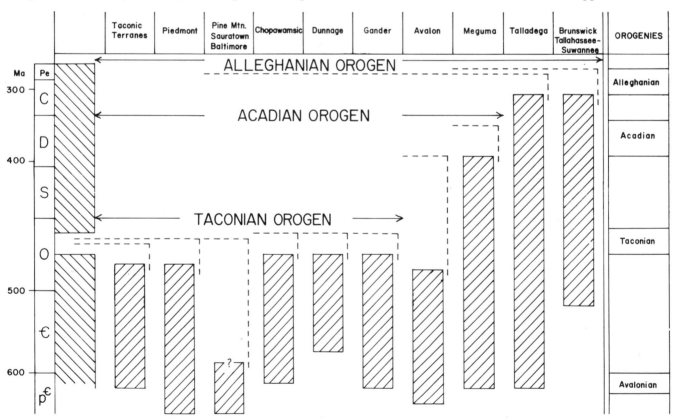

Figure 6. Relationships between timing of accretion, age of rocks in accreted terranes, and orogenic events affecting the Appalachian mountain belt.

late Devonian plutonism to melting of a compressed and overthickened crust (Fyffe and others, 1981) or to generation along major shear zones (Strong, 1980; Hanmer, 1981). A paucity of Ordovician granitic plutons, emplaced at a time when subduction was most in evidence, also supports an alternative mechanism of generation.

Large late Paleozoic granitic plutons are common throughout the Avalon terrane of the southern Appalachians, and deformed Carboniferous plutons are found in the Kiokee and Raleigh belts. Carboniferous granitic plutons also occur in the Avalon terrane of New England. These plutons in the southern and central Appalachians occur in areas affected by Carboniferous regional metamorphism. Farther north, a few smaller Carboniferous plutons occur in unmetamorphosed rocks of the Avalon terrane.

Metamorphism is related to plutonism both spatially and temporally throughout the orogen (Figs. 2 and 3). The main episodes relate to mid-Paleozoic Acadian orogenesis and later Paleozoic Alleghanian orogenesis. Noteworthy is the lack of plutonic rocks within the deformed miogeocline and their abundance in more easterly terranes. This pattern agrees with a west-to-east accretionary model for the orogen. Furthermore, a shearing mechanism for the generation of the middle to late Paleozoic plutonic rocks supports the concept of outboard accretion by major transcurrent movements. Localization of late Paleozoic plutons in the Avalon terrane and a general west-to-east age progression of Paleozoic plutons across the southern Appalachians (Fullagar, 1971; Zartman and Sinha, 1982) favor a model involving later accretion of more outboard terranes. The distribution of Paleozoic intrusions in the Appalachian orogen is depicted in Figure 7.

Mineral deposits that formed during the late Precambrian and early Paleozoic pre-accretionary development of suspect terranes are as distinct across the orogen as the terranes themselves. These vary from Mississippi Valley–type lead-zinc deposits in carbonates of the miogeocline, Cyprus-type copper-pyrite deposits and asbestos occurrences in ophiolitic rocks of the Dunnage terrane, polymetallic deposits of the Gander terrane, local oddities such as pyrophyllite and manganese in the Avalon terrane, and gold and tin in the Meguma terrane. After mid-Paleozoic and late Paleozoic accretionary events, mineral deposits that relate to plutonism and hydrothermal systems, and that occur in overlap assemblages, obviously bear no relationship to suspect terranes as outlined in this paper.

CONCLUDING REMARKS

Since the advent of plate tectonics, models for the evolution of the Appalachian orogen have involved the opening and closing of a late Precambrian–early Paleozoic Iapetus ocean. The western margin of Iapetus, the miogeocline of eastern North America, is well defined, and its stratigraphy and sedimentologic analyses are among the most sophisticated for any ancient continental margin. The eastern margin of Iapetus, the North American connection, is ill defined within the Appalachian orogen. Furthermore, an embarrassing number of outboard terranes along the east flank of the orogen are not easily incorporated in a simple model of a single symmetrical ocean. Prior to the closing of Iapetus and the systematic accretion of outboard terranes, the situation may have been more akin to a modern ocean cluttered with submerged plateaus (Ben-Avraham and others, 1981), as exhibited by the modern western Pacific (Hamilton, 1979).

The suspect terrane concept provides a fresh approach to Appalachian syntheses. Problems of explaining a variety of outboard terranes in a simple Wilson Cycle model are easily rationalized in a suspect terrane model based upon the complexities of modern oceans. Likewise,

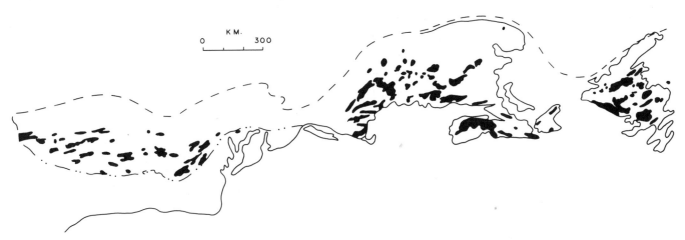

DISTRIBUTION OF PALEOZOIC GRANITIC ROCKS

Figure 7. Distribution of Paleozoic intrusions in the Appalachian orogen.

age-old problems of equating episodic orogenic events to continuous orogenic processes are accommodated with ease (Fig. 6). These freedoms and the actualistic approach provide a superior framework in which to view the anatomy of any complex orogen.

The foregoing analysis of the Appalachian orogen is crude and does not fully consider the composite aspect of some terranes and their internal complexities. Furthermore, any attempt to rationalize the stratigraphic and sedimentologic aspects of accretionary history with structural, plutonic, metamorphic, and metallogenic aspects will require compilation maps that depict each of these parameters for the entire orogen. Definitive analyses therefore await the completion and dissemination of the necessary data base.

ACKNOWLEDGMENTS

The authors wish to acknowledge P. J. Coney, D. L. Jones, and J.W.M. Monger for invaluable advice and discussions of conceptual models. We also wish to acknowledge discussions with E-an Zen, J. D. Keppie, R. T. Haworth, and the 1982 Geology 6000 class of Memorial University. Review by D. T. Secor, Jr., and Louise Quinn of a final draft of the manuscript resulted in further improvements.

The first author wishes to acknowledge financial support for his field work and compilation projects through the National Sciences and Engineering Research Council of Canada and the Department of Energy, Mines and Resources. Research support in the Appalachians has been provided to the second author by the U.S. National Science Foundation.

REFERENCES CITED

Arden, D. D., 1974, A geophysical profile in the Suwannee basin, northwestern Florida: Georgia Geological Survey Bulletin 87, p. 111–222.

Baker, D. F., 1978, Geology and geochemistry of an alkali volcanic suite (Skinner Cove Formation) in the Humber Arm Allochthon, Newfoundland [M.Sc. thesis]: Memorial University of Newfoundland, 314 p.

Bell, K., Blenkinsop, J., and Strong, D. F., 1977, The geochronology of some granitic bodies from eastern Newfoundland and its bearing on Appalachian evolution: Canadian Journal of Earth Sciences, v. 14, p. 456–476.

Ben-Avraham, Nur, A., Jones, D., and Cox, A., 1981, Continental accretion: From oceanic plateaus to allochthonous terranes: Science, v. 213, July 3, p. 47–54.

Bergström, S. M., Riva, J., and Kay, M., 1974, Significance of conodonts, graptolites, and shelly faunas from the Ordovician of western and north-central Newfoundland: Canadian Journal of Earth Sciences, v. 11, p. 1625–1660.

Black, W. W., 1980, Chemical characteristics of metavolcanics in the Carolina slate belt, in Wones, D. R., ed., Proceedings "Caledonides in the U.S.A.": Virginia Polytechnic Institute and State University Memoir 2, p. 271–278.

Blackwood, R. F., 1978, Northeastern Gander zone, in Gibbons, R. V., ed., Report of activities for 1977: Newfoundland Department of Mines and Energy, Mineral Development Division, Report 78-1, p. 72–79.

Blackwood, R. F., and O'Driscoll, C. F., 1976, The Gander-Avalon zone boundary in southeastern Newfoundland: Canadian Journal of Earth Sciences, v. 13, p. 1155–1159.

Bland, A. E., and Blackburn, W. H., 1980, Geochemical studies on the greenstones of the Atlantic seaboard volcanic province, south-central Appalachians, in Wones, D. R., ed., Proceedings "Caledonides in the U.S.A.": Virginia Polytechnic Institute and State University Memoir 2, p. 263–270.

Boudette, E. L., and Boone, G. M., 1976, Pre-Silurian stratigraphic succession in central western Maine, in Page, L. R., ed., Contributions to the Stratigraphy of New England: Geological Society of America Memoir 148, p. 79–96.

——1982, Diamictite of the Chain Lakes Massif of Maine: A possible metasuevite: Geological Society of America Abstracts with Programs, v. 14, no. 7, p. 448.

Cebull, S. E., Shurbet, D. H., Keller, G. R., and Russell, L. R., 1976, Possible role of transform faults in the development of apparent offsets in the Ouachita-southern Appalachian tectonic belt: Journal of Geology, v. 84, p. 107–114.

Church, W. R., and Stevens, R. K., 1971, Early Paleozoic ophiolite complexes of the Newfoundland Appalachians as mantle-oceanic crust sequences: Journal of Geophysical Research, v. 76, no. 5, p. 1460–1466.

Clark, D. B., Barr, S. M., and Donohoe, H. V., 1980, Granitoid and other plutonic rocks of Nova Scotia, in Wones, D. R., ed., Proceedings "Caledonides in the U.S.A.": Virginia Polytechnic Institute and State University Memoir 2, p. 107–116.

Coleman-Sadd, S. P., 1980, Geology of south-central Newfoundland and evolution of the eastern margin of Iapetus: American Journal of Science, v. 280, p. 991–1017.

Coney, P. J., 1978, Mesozoic-Cenozoic Cordilleran plate tectonics: Geological Society of America Memoir 152, p. 38.

Coney, P. J., Powell, R. E., Tennyson, M. E., and Baldwin, B., 1972, The Champlain thrust and related features near Middlebury, Vermont: in Doolan, B. L., and Stanley, R. S., eds.; 64th New England Intercollegiate Geological Conference Guidebook, p. 97–115.

Coney, P. J., Jones, D. L., and Monger, J.W.H., 1980, Cordilleran suspect terranes: Nature, v. 288, November 27, p. 329–333.

Cook, F. A., and Oliver, J. E., 1981, The late Precambrian-early Paleozoic continental edge in the Appalachian orogen: American Journal of Science, v. 281, p. 993–1008.

Cook, F. A., Albaugh, D. S., Brown, L. D., Kaufman, Sidney, Oliver, J. E., and Hatcher, R. D., Jr., 1979, Thin-skinned tectonics in the crystalline southern Appalachians; COCORP seismic reflection profiling of the Blue Ridge and Piedmont: Geology, v. 7, p. 563–567.

Dainty, A. M., Keen, C. E., Keen, M. J., and Blanchard, J. E., 1966, Review of geophysical evidence on crust and upper mantle structure on the eastern seaboard of Canada: American Geophysical Union Monograph 10, p. 349–369.

Dallmeyer, R. D., Blackwood, R. F., and Odom, A. L., 1981, Age and origin of the Dover fault: Tectonic boundary between the Gander and Avalon zones of the northeastern Newfoundland Appalachians: Canadian Journal of Earth Sciences, v. 18, p. 1431–1442.

Dean, P. L., 1978, Volcanic stratigraphy and metallogeny of Notre Dame Bay, Newfoundland: Memorial University of Newfoundland, Geology Report 7, 205 p.

Dewey, J. F., 1969, The evolution of the Appalachian/Caledonian orogen: Nature, v. 222, April 12, p. 124–129.

Drake, A. A., Jr., and Morgan, B. A., 1981, The Piney Branch Complex—A metamorphosed fragment of the central Appalachian ophiolite in northern Virginia: American Journal of Science, v. 281,

p. 484–508.

Feininger, Thomas, 1981, Amphibolite associated with the Thetford Mines ophiolite complex at Belmina Ridge, Quebec: Canadian Journal of Earth Sciences, v. 18, p. 1878–1892.

Fullagar, P. D., 1971, Age and origin of plutonic intrusions in the Piedmont of the southeastern Appalachians: Geological Society of America Bulletin, v. 82, p. 2845–2862.

Fyffe, L. R., Pajari, G. E., and Cherry, M. E., 1981, The Acadian plutonic rocks of New Brunswick: Maritime Sediments and Atlantic Geology, v. 17, p. 23–36.

Gaudette, H. E., 1981, Zircon isotopic age from the Union ultramafic complex, Maine: Canadian Journal of Earth Sciences, v. 18, p. 405–409.

Glover, Lynn III, Mose, D. G., Poland, F. B., Bobyarchick, A. R., and Bourland, W. C., 1978, Grenville basement in the eastern Piedmont of Virginia: Implications for orogenic models: Geological Society of America Abstracts with Programs, v. 10, p. 169.

Hamilton, Warren, 1979, Tectonics of the Indonesian region: U.S. Geological Survey Professional Paper 1078, 345 p.

Hanmer, Simon, 1981, Tectonic significance of the northeastern Gander zone, Newfoundland: An Acadian ductile shear zone: Canadian Journal of Earth Sciences, v. 18, p. 120–135.

Harris, L. D., and Bayer, K. C., 1979, Sequential development of the Appalachian orogen above a master décollement—A hypothesis: Geology, v. 7, p. 568–572.

Hatcher, R. D., Jr., 1972, Developmental model for the southern Appalachians: Geological Society of America Bulletin, v. 83, p. 2735–2760.

——1978, Tectonics of the western Piedmont and Blue Ridge, southern Appalachians: Review and speculation: American Journal of Science, v. 278, p. 276–304.

——1981, Thrusts and thrust nappes in the North American Appalachian orogen, *in* McClay, K. R., and Price, N. J., eds., Thrust and nappe tectonics: Geological Society of London Special Publication no. 9, p. 491–499.

Hatcher, R. D., Jr., and Odom, A. L., 1980, Timing of thrusting in the southern Appalachians, U.S.A.: Model for orogeny?: Journal of Geological Society of London, p. 321–327.

Hatcher, R. D., Jr., and Zietz, Isidore, 1978, Thin crystalline thrust sheets in the southern Appalachian Inner Piedmont and Blue Ridge: Interpretation based upon regional aeromagnetic data: Geological Society of America Abstracts with Programs, v. 10, p. 417.

——1980, Tectonic implications of regional aeromagnetic and gravity data from the southern Appalachians, *in* Wones, D. R., ed., Proceedings, "The Caledonides in the U.S.A.": Virginia Polytechnic Institute and State University Memoir 2, p. 235–244.

Hatcher, R. D., Jr., Butler, J. R., Fullagar, P. D., Secor, D. T., and Snoke, A. W., 1980, Geologic synthesis of the Tennessee-Carolinas-Northeast Georgia: Southern Appalachians, *in* Wones, D. R., ed., Proceedings "The Caledonides in the U.S.A.": Virginia Polytechnic Institute and State University Memoir 2, p. 83–90.

Hatcher, R. D., Jr., Hooper, R. J., Petty, S. S., and Willis, J. D., 1981, Tectonics of emplacement and origin of Appalachian ultramafic bodies: Geological Society of America Abstracts with Programs, v. 13, no. 7, p. 469–470.

Haworth, R. T., and LeFort, J. P., 1979, Geophysical evidence for the extent of the Avalon zone in Atlantic Canada: Canadian Journal of Earth Sciences, v. 16, p. 552–567.

Haworth, R. T., and MacIntyre, J. B., 1976, The gravity and magnetic fields of Atlantic offshore Canada: Geological Survey of Canada Paper 75-9, 22 p.

Haworth, R. T., Daniels, D. L., Williams, Harold, and Zietz, Isidore, 1980, Bouguer gravity anomaly map of the Appalachian orogen: Memorial University of Newfoundland, Map no. 3, scale 1/1,000,000, Map no. 3a, scale 1/2,000,000.

Helwig, James, 1974, Eugeosynclinal basement and a collage concept of orogenic belts: Society of Economic Paleontologists and Mineralogists Special Publication 19, p. 359–376.

Irving, E., 1979, Paleopoles and paleolatitudes of North America and speculations about displaced terrains: Canadian Journal of Earth Sciences, v. 16, p. 669–694.

Iverson, V. P., and Smithson, S. B., 1982, Master decollement root zone beneath the southern Appalachians and crustal balance: Geology, v. 10, p. 241–245.

Jamieson, R. A., 1980, Formation of metamorphic aureoles beneath ophiolites—evidence from the St. Anthony Complex, Newfoundland: Geology, v. 8, p. 150–154.

Jones, D. L., Silberling, N. J., and Hillhouse, J. W., 1978, Microplate tectonics of Alaska—Significance for the Mesozoic history of the Pacific Coast of North America, *in* Howell, D. G., and McDougall, R. A., eds., Mesozoic paleogeography of the Western United States: Pacific Coast Paleogeography Symposium 2, Pacific Coast Section, Society of Economic Paleontologists and Mineralogists, p. 71–74.

Jones, D. L., Silberling, N. J., Berg, H. C., and Plafker, George, 1981, Tectonostratigraphic terrane map of Alaska: U.S. Geological Survey Open File Report 81-792.

Kean, B. F., and Strong, D. F., 1975, Geochemical evolution of an Ordovician island arc of the central Newfoundland Appalachians: American Journal of Science, v. 275, p. 97–118.

Kennedy, M. J., 1976, Southeastern margin of the northeastern Appalachians: Late Precambrian orogeny on a continental margin: Geological Society of America Bulletin, v. 87, p. 1317–1325.

Kent, D. V., and Opdyke, N. D., 1978, Paleomagnetism of the Devonian Catskill redbeds: Evidence for motion of the coastal New England-Canadian Maritime region relative to cratonic North America: Journal of Geophysical Research, v. 83, p. 4441–4450.

——1979, The early Carboniferous paleomagnetic field for North America and its bearing on tectonics of the northern Appalachians: Earth and Planetary Science Letters, v. 44, p. 365–372.

——1980, Paleomagnetism of Siluro-Devonian rocks from eastern Maine: Canadian Journal of Earth Sciences, v. 17, p. 1653–1665.

Keppie, J. D., 1981, The Appalachian collage [abs.]: Terra Cognita, v. 1, no. 1, p. 54.

——1983, The Appalachian collage: Uppsala I.G.C.P. Caledonide Orogen Volume (in press).

Kite, L. E., and Stoddard, E. F., 1981, Whole-rock and primary mineral chemistry of the Halifax County mafic-ultramafic complex, a probable ophiolite in the northeastern North Carolina Piedmont: Geological Society of America Abstracts with Programs, v. 13, p. 11.

Lane, T. E., 1976, Stratigraphy of the White Rock Formation: Maritime Sediments, v. 12, p. 87–106.

Malpas, John, 1979, The dynamothermal aureole of the Bay of Islands ophiolite suite: Canadian Journal of Earth Sciences, v. 16, p. 2086–2101.

Mattinson, J. M., 1975, Early Paleozoic ophiolite complexes of Newfoundland: Isotopic ages of zircons: Geology, v. 3, no. 4, p. 181–183.

——1976, Ages of zircons from the Bay of Islands ophiolite complex, western Newfoundland: Geology, v. 4, p. 393–394.

McKerrow, W. S., and Ziegler, A. M., 1971, The Lower Silurian paleogeography of New Brunswick and adjacent areas: Journal of Geology, v. 79, p. 635–646.

McLaughton, R. E., 1974, Paleozoic geology underlying the southeastern Coastal Plain [abs.]: Georgia Geological Survey Bulletin 87, p. 19.

Milton, C., and Hurst, H. V., 1965, Subsurface "basement" rocks of Georgia: Georgia Geological Survey Bulletin 76, 56 p.

Misra, K. C., and Keller, F. B., 1978, Ultramafic bodies in the southern Appalachians: A review: American Journal of Science, v. 278, p. 389–418.

Monger, J.W.H., Souther, J. G., and Gabrielse, Hugh, 1972, Evolution of the Canadian Cordillera: A plate-tectonic model: American Journal of Science, v. 272, p. 577–602.

Monger, J.W.H., Price, R. A., and Tempelman-Kluit, D. J., 1982, Tectonic accretion and the origin of the two major metamorphic and plutonic welts in the Canadian Cordillera: Geology, v. 10, p. 70–75.

Morgan, B. A., 1977, The Baltimore Complex, Maryland, Pennsylvania, and Virginia, in Coleman, R. G., and Irwin, W. P., eds., North American ophiolites: Oregon Department of Geology and Mineral Industries Bulletin 95, p. 41–49.

Naylor, R. S., Boone, G. M., Boudette, E. L., Ashenden, D. D., and Robinson, P., 1973, Pre-Ordovician rocks in the Bronson Hill and Boundary Mountain anticlinoria, New England, U.S.A. [abs.]: EOS, v. 54, p. 495.

Osberg, P. H., 1981, Stratigraphic and structural relationships in the Silurian turbidite sequence, south-central Maine: Geological Society of America Abstracts with Programs, v. 13, p. 169.

Pajari, G. E., Pickerill, R. K., and Currie, K. L., 1979, The nature, origin and significance of the Carmanville ophiolitic melange, northeastern Newfoundland: Canadian Journal of Earth Sciences, v. 16, p. 1439–1451.

Papezik, V. S., 1980, Volcanic rocks of Newfoundland: A review, in Wones, D. R., ed., Proceedings "The Caledonides in the U.S.A.": Virginia Polytechnic Institute and State University Memoir 2, p. 245–248.

Pavlides, Louis, 1981, The Central Virginia volcanic-plutonic belt: An island arc of Cambrian(?) age: U.S. Geological Survey Professional Paper 1231-A, 34 p.

Pavlides, Louis, Pojeta, J., Jr., Gordon, M., Jr., Parsley, R. L., and Bobyarchick, A. R., 1980, New evidence for the age of the Quantico Formation of Virginia: Geology, v. 8, p. 286–290.

Pojeta, John, Jr., Kriz, Jiri, and Berdan, J. M., 1976, Silurian-Devonian pelecypods and Paleozoic stratigraphy of subsurface rocks in Florida and Georgia and related Silurian pelecypods from Bolivia and Turkey: U.S. Geological Survey Professional Paper 879, p. 1–32.

Popenoe, Peter, and Zietz, Isidore, 1977, The nature of the geophysical basement beneath the Coastal Plain of South Carolina and northeastern Georgia, in Rankin, D. W., ed., Studies related to the Charleston, South Carolina, earthquake of 1886—A preliminary report: U.S. Geological Survey Professional Paper 1028, p. 119–138.

Price, R. A., and Hatcher, R. D., Jr., 1983, Tectonic significance of similarities in the evolution of the Alabama-Pennsylvania Appalachians and the Alberta-British Columbia Canadian Cordillera, in Hatcher, R. D., Jr., and others, eds., Contributions to the tectonics and geophysics of mountain chains: Geological Society of America Memoir 158 (this volume).

Rankin, D. W., 1975, The continental margin of eastern North America in the southern Appalachians: The opening and closing of the Proto-Atlantic Ocean: American Journal of Science, v. 275-A, p. 298–336.

Rast, N., and Skehan, J. W., 1981, Possible correlation of Precambrian rocks of Newport, Rhode Island, with those of Anglesey, Wales: Geology, v. 9, p. 596–601.

Rast, N., and Stringer, P., 1980, A geotraverse across a deformed Ordovician ophiolite and its Silurian cover, Northern New Brunswick, Canada: Tectonophysics, v. 69, p. 221–245.

Rast, N., Kennedy, M. J., and Blackwood, R. F., 1976a, Comparison of some tectonostratigraphic zones in the Appalachians of Newfoundland and New Brunswick: Canadian Journal of Earth Sciences, v. 13, p. 868–875.

Rast, N., O'Brien, B. H., and Wardle, R. J., 1976b, Relationships between Precambrian and Lower Paleozoic rocks of the "Avalon Platform" in New Brunswick, the northeast Appalachians and the British Isles: Tectonophysics, v. 30, p. 315–338.

Robinson, P., and Hall, L. M., 1980, Tectonic significance of southern New England, in Wones, D. R., ed., Proceedings "The Caledonides in the U.S.A.": Virginia Polytechnic Institute and State University Memoir 2, p. 73–82.

Rodgers, J., 1965, Long Point and Clam Bank Formations, western Newfoundland: Proceedings of the Geological Association of Canada, v. 16, p. 83–94.

Rowley, D. B., 1981, Accretionary collage of terrains assembled against eastern North America during the Medial Ordovician Taconic Orogeny: Geological Society of America Abstracts with Programs, v. 13, no. 7, p. 542.

Rowley, D. B., and Kidd, W.S.F., 1981, Stratigraphic relationships and detrital composition of the Medial Ordovician Flysch of Western New England: Implications for the tectonic evolution of the Taconic orogeny: Journal of Geology, v. 89, p. 199–218.

St. Julien, P., and Hubert, C., 1975, Evolution of the Taconian orogen in the Quebec Appalachians, in Tectonics and mountain ranges: American Journal of Science, v. 275-A, p. 337–362.

Sampson, S. L., Secor, D. T., Jr., Snoke, A. W., and Palmer, A. R., 1982, Geological implications of recently discovered Middle Cambrian trilobites in the Carolina slate belt: Geological Society of America Abstracts with Programs, v. 14.

Schenk, P. E., 1972, Possible Late Ordovician glaciation of Nova Scotia: Canadian Journal of Earth Sciences, v. 9, p. 95–107.

—— 1978, Synthesis of the Canadian Appalachians: Geological Survey of Canada Paper 78-13, p. 111–136.

Snoke, A. W., Kish, S. A., and Secor, D. T., Jr., 1980, Deformed Hercynian granitic rocks from the Piedmont of South Carolina: American Journal of Science, v. 280, p. 1018–1034.

Stevens, R. K., 1970, Cambro-Ordovician flysch sedimentation and tectonics in west Newfoundland and their possible bearing on a Proto-Atlantic ocean, in Lajoie, J., ed., Flysch sedimentology in North America: Geological Association of Canada Special Paper 7, p. 165–177.

Strong, D. F., 1979, Proterozoic tectonics of northwestern Gondwanaland: New evidence from eastern Newfoundland: Tectonophysics, v. 54, p. 81–101.

—— 1980, Granitoid rocks and associated mineral deposits of eastern Canada and western Europe, in Strangway, D. W., ed., The continental crust and its mineral deposits: Geological Association of Canada Special Paper 20, p. 741–769.

Thomas, M. D., 1983, Tectonic significance of paired gravity anomalies in the southern Appalachians, in Hatcher, R. D., Jr., and others, eds., Contributions to the tectonics and geophysics of mountain chains: Geological Society of America Memoir 158 (this volume).

Thomas, W. A., 1977, Evolution of Appalachian-Ouachita salients and recesses from reentrants and promontories in the continental margin: American Journal of Science, v. 277, p. 1233–1278.

Tull, J. F., 1978, Structural development of the Alabama Piedmont northwest of the Brevard zone: American Journal of Science, v. 278, p. 442–460.

Tull, J. F., and Stow, S. H., 1980a, Structural and stratigraphic setting of arc volcanism in the Talladega slate belt of Alabama, in Frey, R. W., ed., Excursions in southeastern geology: Geological Society of America Field Trip Guidebook, 1980 Annual Meeting, v. II, p. 545–581.

—— 1980b, The Hillabee Greenstone: A mafic volcanic complex in the Appalachian Piedmont of Alabama: Geological Society of America Bulletin, v. 91, p. 27–36.

Upadhyay, H. D., and Neale, E.R.W., 1979, On the tectonic regimes of ophiolite genesis: Earth and Planetary Science Letters, v. 43, p. 93–102.

Van der Voo, R., French, A. N., and French, R. B., 1979, A paleomagnetic pole position from the unfolded Upper Devonian Catskill red beds, and its tectonic implications: Geology, v. 7, no. 7, p. 345–348.

Williams, Harold, 1964, The Appalachians in Northeastern Newfoundland—A two-sided symmetrical system: American Journal of Science, v. 262, p. 1137–1158.

—— 1971, Geology of Belleoram Map-Area, Newfoundland: Geological

Survey of Canada Paper 70-65, 39 p.

—— 1975, Structural succession, nomenclature, and interpretation of transported rocks in western Newfoundland: Canadian Journal of Earth Sciences, v. 12, p. 1874–1894.

—— (compiler), 1978, Tectonic lithofacies map of the Appalachian orogen: Memorial University of Newfoundland, Map no. 1, scale 1:1,000,000, Map no. la, scale 1:2,000,000.

—— 1979, Appalachian orogen in Canada: Canadian Journal of Earth Sciences, v. 16, p. 792–807.

—— 1980, Structural telescoping across the Appalachian orogen and the minimum width of the Iapetus Ocean, *in* Strangway, D. W., ed., The continental crust and its mineral deposits: Geological Association of Canada Special Paper 20, p. 421–440.

Williams, Harold, and Doolan, B. L., 1978, Margins and vestiges of Iapetus: Geological Society of America and Geological Association of Canada Abstracts with Programs, v. 10, no. 7, p. 517.

Williams, Harold, and Hatcher, R. D., Jr., 1982, Suspect terranes and accretionary history of the Appalachian orogen: Geology, v. 10, p. 530–536.

Williams, Harold, and St. Julien, Pierre, 1982, The Baie Verte-Brompton Line: Early Paleozoic continent-ocean interface in the Canadian Appalachians, *in* St. Julien, P., and Béland, J., eds., Major structural zones and faults of the northern Appalachians: Geological Association of Canada Special Paper 24, p. 177–207.

Williams, Harold, and Smyth, W. R., 1973, Metamorphic aureoles beneath ophiolite suites and Alpine peridotites: Tectonic implications with west Newfoundland examples: American Journal of Science, v. 273, p. 594–621.

Williams, Harold, and Stevens, R. K., 1974, The ancient continental margin of eastern North America, *in* Burk, C. A., and Drake, C. L., eds., The geology of continental margins: New York, Springer-Verlag, p. 781–796.

Williams, Harold, and Talkington, R. W., 1977, Distribution and tectonic setting of ophiolites and ophiolitic melanges in the Appalachian orogen, *in* Coleman, R. G., and Irwin, W. P., eds., North American ophiolites: Oregon Department of Geology and Mineral Industries Bulletin 95, p. 1–11.

Wilson, J. T., 1966, Did the Atlantic close and then re-open?: Nature, v. 211, p. 676–681.

—— 1968, Static or mobile earth: The current scientific revolution:

Proceedings of the American Philosophical Society, v. 112, no. 5, p. 309–320.

Wollard, G. P., and Joesting, H. R., 1964, Bouguer gravity anomaly map of the United States: U.S. Geological Survey, Map G64-121, scale 1:2,500,000.

Wones, D. R., 1980, A comparison between granitic plutons of New England, U.S.A., and the Sierra Nevada batholith, California, *in* Wones, D. R., ed., Proceedings, "The Caledonides in the U.S.A.": Virginia Polytechnic Institute and State University Memoir 2, p. 123–130.

Zartman, R. E., and Sinha, A. K., 1980, Timing of igneous events in the Appalachians and their tectonic implications: Geological Society of America Abstracts with Programs, v. 12, p. 554.

Zen, E-an, 1967, Time and space relationships of the Taconic allochthon and autochthon: Geological Society of America Special Paper 97, 107 p.

—— 1972, The Taconide zone and the Taconic orogeny in the western part of the northern Appalachian orogen: Geological Society of America Special Paper 135, 72 p.

—— 1981, An alternative model for the development of the allochthonous southern Appalachian Piedmont: American Journal of Science, v. 281, p. 1153–1163.

—— 1983, Exotic terranes in the New England Appalachians: Limits, candidates, and ages. A speculative essay, *in* Hatcher, R. D., Jr., and others, eds., Contributions to the tectonics and geophysics of mountain chains: Geological Society of America Memoir 158 (this volume).

Zen, E-an, and Palmer, A. R., 1981, Did Avalonia form the eastern shore of Iapetus Ocean? Geological Society of America Abstracts with Programs, v. 13, no. 7, p. 587.

Zietz, Isidore, and Gilbert, F. P., 1980, Aeromagnetic map of part of the southeastern United States: U.S. Geological Survey, Map GP-936, scale 1:2,000,000.

Zietz, Isidore, Haworth, R. T., Williams, Harold, and Daniels, D. L., 1980, Magnetic anomaly map of the Appalachian orogen: Memorial University of Newfoundland, Map no. 2, scale 1:1,000,000, Map no. 2a, scale 1:2,000,000.

MANUSCRIPT ACCEPTED BY THE SOCIETY SEPTEMBER 10, 1982

Geological Society of America
Memoir 158
1983

Exotic terranes in the New England Appalachians—limits, candidates, and ages: A speculative essay

E-an Zen
U.S. Geological Survey
959 National Center
Reston, Virginia 22092

ABSTRACT

Recent discoveries in the North American Cordillera of composite exotic terranes that had become accreted to the Cordillera during its evolution require reexamination of the older Appalachian mountain systems for evidence of possibly similar history. In the New England segment of the Appalachian orogen, the three Paleozoic orogenies (Taconian, Acadian, Alleghanian) must be separately examined. Evidence for Taconian orogeny supplies the best support for subduction processes at the margin of a continent-ocean plate junction. Definition of ancestral North America prior to the completion of that subduction process is the starting point for a search of Taconian exotic terranes. On the basis of such criteria as age of basement, occurrence of in-place ophiolite, melange, blueschist, continental-margin facies, and island-arc rocks, this margin is proposed to be best preserved in northern Maine, where it runs from the Jim Pond–Boil Mountain ophiolite south of the Chain Lakes massif northeast to the Elmtree ophiolite in New Brunswick. Rocks of the Weeksboro–Lunksoos Lake and Miramichi anticlinoria are southeast of this boundary. In Maine, this boundary, which was the trace of a subduction zone, was marked by a residual marine basin in Late Ordovician and Early Silurian time.

No Taconian accreted terrane has been detected on the North American craton side except for the Chain Lakes massif, which is suggested to be an obducted allochthon derived from the opposite side of Iapetus Ocean; this opposite side is labeled "Craton X" and is otherwise largely unknown. The Merrimack synclinorium is interpreted to have formed on Craton X.

Acadian orogeny probably resulted from a continent-continent collision. The nature and extent of the Silurian and Devonian flysh sequences demand basins of deposition much larger than present geologic relations allow; these sequences may or may not be in mutual sedimentary contact, and may not have been even before their deformation and metamorphism. This fact and the anomalous paleomagnetic pole position for the Merrimack synclinorium suggest possible large-scale tectonic transport during the Acadian orogeny. In that sense, the terrane now occupied by the synclinorium may be exotic, both because its basement was originally Craton X and because the Taconian suture may have been disrupted by younger longitudinal transport of unknown extent.

The coastal belt of Rhode Island, Massachusetts, and Maine contains rocks in distinct lithotectonic blocks. These blocks are best defined in northeast Massachusetts and around Penobscot Bay in Maine, where they are mutually separated and also separated from the Acadian version of North America by large faults. These blocks appear to be exotic; they may have arrived at their present locations since the peak of the Acadian orogeny and thus have been largely unaffected by it. This coastal belt includes the Avalonian terrane; it may have been emplaced during latest Acadian to early Alleghanian deformations. If the Avalonian terrane did arrive late, then it could not have constituted Craton X during the Taconian event.

The three Paleozoic orogenies led to three types of accreted terranes: (1) Taconian, thrust allochthons directly attributable to subduction-induced collision during the closing of Iapetus Ocean; (2) Acadian, continent-continent collision and possible large concomitant transcurrent displacement; (3) Alleghanian, oblique-slip high-angle faulting, the concomitant formation of a sedimentary basin having no immediately identifiable sediment source, and the formation of a microplate collage.

For ancient mountain belts, the detection of microplate accretion is at best difficult. The use of a combination of geological, geochemical, and geophysical methods is necessary. Sedimentologic analysis may furnish the best clue to the arrival of new terranes; criteria to detect root zones of transcurrent faults are needed. Geochemical study may lead to definition of discrete blocks and the nature of sutures between them. Geophysical data are generally corroborative rather than definitive; even paleomagnetic data need geologic confirmation and are best used to sniff out suspect land and eventually to define the extent of motion. The hard middle part of establishing an exotic terrane must remain a geologic task.

INTRODUCTION

Recent studies (Hamilton, 1969, 1970, 1978; Monger and others, 1972; Monger and Irving, 1980, Jones and others, 1977; see also Beck and others, 1980; Coney and others, 1980; Ben-Avraham and others, 1981) of the western Cordillera from California to Alaska have shown that orogenic belt to be composite, consisting of smaller units of crust, each having its own stratigraphic and tectonic integrity but not related in obvious ways to those next to them.[1] To explain these enigmas, the concept of long-distance transport of terranes through plate-tectonic processes has been invented; terms such as "microplates" and "suspect terranes" have been applied to these accreted rock masses. The idea that at least some of these terranes have traveled far is supported by several lines of evidence. The study of the contemporary tectonics of Indonesia (Hamilton, 1979) shows that complex interactions of small plates constitute an actual process and that long-distance transport is real. Environmental implications of fossil assemblages of some of the microplates in the Canadian and Alaskan Cordillera show that some of the fauna evolved in far-removed areas relative to those in their neighboring terranes and/or relative to cratonic North America (Jones and others, 1977, 1980; Churkin and others, 1980). Most persuasive, however, is the evidence afforded by paleomagnetic studies, which show that some of the exotic terranes must have moved many thousands of kilometers

relative to their present locations (Hillhouse, 1977; Monger and Irving, 1980).

If accretion of relatively small terranes can happen to contemporary orogenic belts in Indonesia and seems reasonable for Cenozoic and Mesozoic orogenic belts, including the Tethyan belt of Europe and Turkey (Dewey and Şengör, 1979; Dewey and others, 1973), then the question can be raised whether such processes operated in older orogens, at least in Paleozoic mountain belts. If so, what kind of evidence might be extant to demonstrate or at least make plausible such a process? Existing paleomagnetic studies for the Appalachians, meager as they are, already show that displaced terranes may indeed exist and constitute a significant factor in the makeup of part of the Appalachians (Irving, 1979; Kent and Opdyke, 1978, 1979, 1980; Rao and Van der Roo, 1980; Van der Roo and others, 1979; Morris, 1976, Schutts and others, 1976; Spariosu and Kent, 1980, among others). In an earlier note, I proposed (Zen, 1981) that we need to examine the geology of the southern Appalachian Piedmont with such a possibility in mind. If the concept of exotic terranes is real, then we should not expect to find onstrike continuity or correlation of lithic, stratigraphic, or tectonic units between the northern and southern Appalachian regions, and each region must be examined on its own. The sort of onstrike continuity depicted by generations of Appalachian geologists, summarized most recently by Williams (1978) and Williams and Max (1980), for instance, would have to be looked at with jaundiced eye for fortuity or forced interpretations, especially after one has stepped off

---

[1]Curiously, though, this belt shows a highly coherent pattern of lead-isotope characteristics, much more so than does the North American craton (Zartman, 1974). The implications of this observation must be considerable but have not been explored.

the limits of the early Paleozoic North American craton into debatable terranes. This paper intends to look at parts of the New England Appalachians with such a jaundiced eye and with the intention of placing some limits to possibilities of exotic terranes (see also Williams and Hatcher, 1981, 1983).

EPISODES OF APPALACHIAN DEFORMATION

Excluding the probably complex and so far only sketchily understood events that affected Precambrian rocks of the Appalachians and adjacent areas (*see* McLelland and Isachsen, 1980, for an excellent study of the Adirondack foreland), the only pre-Phanerozoic tectonic event of immediate interest to us is the proposed rifting event (Rankin, 1975, 1976; Rankin and others, 1969; Thomas, 1977; Bird and Dewey, 1970) that has been repeatedly invoked to explain the nature of the oldest Paleozoic sedimentary and volcanic rocks that are part of an integral sequence ending up in paleontologically datable Cambrian and probably Cambrian rocks in the northern Appalachians. I accept in this essay the reality of such an event. The location of the axial region of the rift, however, is not easily proven. The best preserved rocks interpreted as of the rift facies are allochthonous or at best parautochthonous, and known geologic evidence has provided no limit for the amount of transport. Analysis of the facies of these rocks and attempted reconstruction (for instance, Ratcliffe, *in* Zen and others, 1983) can at best give relative dispositions and minimum displacements and not absolute transport distances for displaced terranes. Another related difficulty is the nature of the two sides that define the rift. The North American craton, to the extent that we can define its margins, obviously provides one side of the rift system. It is commonly, though not universally, assumed that rocks of the Avalon "plate" constitute the other side. This assumption tacitly involves three suppositions: (1) that the two "plates," North American and Avalon, share at least some Precambrian rocks and have some geologic history in common (for it would be most unlikely that the rift precisely cut along a geologic boundary over its entire extent); (2) that the Avalonian rocks are or were one large continuous piece, and their present state of discontinuity is a subsequent phenomenon; and (3) that between Avalonian rocks and rocks of the North American craton there are no interposed exotic terranes that might cast doubt on the former continuity of the two plates. As I will argue, the first two suppositions are not provable, and the last is not valid. The opposite shore of the rift, which presumably evolved into Iapetus Ocean, is undetermined (Zen and Palmer, 1981).

Of the Phanerozoic orogenic events, the oldest, the Taconian event (about 480 to 430 Ma ago), will be examined in some detail; it is the only orogeny for which the geologic record contains good evidence of plate-margin processes involving the interaction of oceanic and continental crusts as we know them. The second, the Acadian event (about 360 to 400 Ma ago), is usually considered the principal event in the northern Appalachians in its geographic scope and in its metamorphic and plutonic intensity. The Acadian event, however, shows little or no evidence of involvement of oceanic crust, at least southwest of northern Newfoundland. If the plate-tectonic model is used, this event may have largely involved, at least in the New England segment, continent-continent collision, or could even be intracratonal, but then the motive force for the deformation becomes a problem. The Alleghanian event (about 250 to 300 Ma ago) has received various interpretations; it too lacks evidence of involvement of oceanic material. Its plutonic and metamorphic record is ambiguous at many places, though its local intensity is unchallenged (Mosher, 1981; Farrens and Mosher, 1982). The final event, the Mesozoic rifting, was an intracratonal response to early phases of the opening of the present Atlantic Ocean and will not be specifically dealt with in this paper.

TACONIAN MARGIN OF THE NORTH AMERICAN CRATON

Among the geologic records for the Paleozoic orogenies that affected the Appalachians, that for the Taconian orogeny contains the best indication of active subduction processes akin to those of modern active plate margins (see many references cited in this paper), though the possibility of important strike-slip component of motion, that is, oblique subduction, cannot be excluded. If so, then we need to examine the geologic record for evidence of accreted terranes and possibly of microplates. We will do so in this section.

Ideally, we should begin our examination with the youngest geologic record and try to remove the effects of the later events on their predecessors in order to reconstruct more reliably the older geologic events. To do so, however, requires that we know the nature and extent of these younger processes and their associated paleogeographic arrangements with fair accuracy. This is precisely the information that we do not have and is a principal purpose of this essay. I have, accordingly, adopted the opposite tack; I will proceed from the oldest record to the youngest and from the craton toward the ocean. This procedure is justified on the basis that if we know which parts of the orogen can be shown to have been a coherent part of North America at a given time, then any accretion or removal of exotic terranes must have been confined to the seaward part of this momentary configuration of the craton. These two opposite approaches complement each other, and they should form a mutually iterative pair;

likewise, models and interpretations of field facts need to be tested against each other. My essay is, at best, a modest beginning in the endeavor.

Age and Nature of the Basement

A direct approach to the delineation of the North American craton during early Paleozoic time is to look at the areal distribution of basement rocks of Grenvillian age. This direct approach makes the debatable assumption that there is a one-to-one correspondence between the apparent radiometric age of a rock sequence and its tectonic origin. There is no intrinsic reason that two unrelated cratonic masses might not have the same "age," that is, simultaneous thermal events to the limit of geochronologic resolution; therefore, the use of age to define a craton, particularly in the context of evidence for exotic terranes, is unsound. Within the northern Appalachians, where late Precambrian rifting of a cratonic mass took place, at least in the general vicinity of the rift the two resulting blocks might be expected to contain rocks of the same ages. For North America, we do indeed have evidence of late Precambrian (Proterozoic Z) radiometric ages; for example, the Yonkers Granite in the New York City area, associated with the Grenvillian Fordham Gneiss (Clark and Kulp, 1968; Long, 1969; Mose and others, 1979), the Pound Ridge Granite of Bell (1936) in Westchester County (Mose and Hayes, 1975), and mafic dikes that intrude Grenvillian gneiss of Long Range, Newfoundland (Stukas and Reynolds, 1974), all have Avalonian ages. Clearly, we cannot use the Avalonian ages alone to define an Avalonian craton; by the same token, we are not justified in assuming that all rock sequences having a Grenvillian age were part of the North American craton, for to do so would be circular reasoning. Another problem is that we do not know for sure the identity of the opposite side of the Proterozoic Z rift. Many assume that the opposite side is Avalonia, but I will argue in this paper that this probably is not true (see also Zen and Palmer, 1981). This unidentified cratonic mass will be dubbed "Craton X" in this paper; its establishment beyond reasonable doubt remains an outstanding problem for Appalachian geologists.

Despite all the caveats, I will try nevertheless to determine whether rocks of Grenvillian age can be used to define an internally consistent terrane at least across the New England Appalachians. We will assume that the Grenvillian ages defined by modern lead-isotopic methods of chronology record an event or group of events so intense and pervasive that for all intents and purposes they can be used as the basis for identifying a packet of rocks under one name, whatever the real ages of the rocks may be, recognizing the perils of relying on available techniques of geochronology alone. On this basis, the Long Range, the basement rocks of the Burlington Peninsula

(Neale, 1972; DeWit and Strong, 1975), the Indian Head Range in southwest Newfoundland, the Green Mountains massif, the gneisses of Chester, Athens, and Rayponda domes, the Berkshire Highland, the Housatonic Highland, and the Hudson Highland (northern end of the Reading Prong), most likely were all parts of the North American craton at the inception of the Paleozoic. I will not document their ages here, as they are in the literature, and references to the source material will be made elsewhere in this paper. The small areas of Precambrian rocks in the Notre Dame Mountains of Quebec (Vallières and others, 1978), apparently slivers in thrust slices, are likewise probably part of the North American craton. Recent work by Ratcliffe (1982; Ratcliffe and Hatch, 1979) and Ratcliffe and Harwood (1975) shows that the rocks of the Berkshire Highland were transported; probably this is true also of the gneisses of the Chester, Athens, and Rayponda domes, though the ages of the dome rocks themselves (Faul and others, 1963) require modern confirmation. Even though some of the rocks have been transported unknown distances, the overall direction of Taconian transport seems to be clearly to the west and northwest. The use of the present eastern and southeastern limit of these rocks as a limit of the North American craton is therefore a conservative estimate. Thus, east and southeast of the present outcrop areas of these rocks (Fig. 1), allochthonous or otherwise, no Grenvillian rock is found for some distances. When rocks similarly old or older do reappear, as in eastern Massachusetts (Olszewski, 1980), coastal New Brunswick (Olszewski and Gaudette, 1981), and Cape Breton Island (Olszewski and others, 1981), they are in a different tectonostratigraphic setting, and most of the rocks are not of truly Grenvillian age; therefore, they cannot be readily assigned to a North American craton.

In the area between Newfoundland and a point near the Vermont-Quebec border, no Grenvillian basement rock is known at the surface. Knowledge of its presence at depth comes from seismic extrapolation of the Laurentian highlands southeastward from Quebec City to the Maine border (Beiers, 1976; SOQUIP, 1979a, 1979b); basement rocks have been traced at least as far eastward as the Notre Dame Mountains at a depth of 5 seconds or about 15 km. The Chain Lakes massif of northwestern Maine is a special problem that will be discussed in another section. Thus, in the intervening area from the Gaspé Peninsula to northern Vermont, the problem of definition of the limit of the craton is particularly severe and will be discussed in the following sections.

Ophiolite Suite

The position of ophiolite suites can be a powerful criterion to define the limits of a craton if they can be reasonably interpreted as ocean-floor material brought into place by obduction. The ophiolite suites of the Humber Arm and Hare Bay allochthon in western Newfoundland were transported by thrusting (see Williams, 1978, 1979, for discussion and references). The ophiolites east of White Bay, including Ming's Bight, are more likely part of the "root zone" of the transported masses, albeit deformed. In Quebec, the Baie Verte–Brompton Line (Williams, 1978) includes the ophiolites of the Thetford and Asbestos areas; these are entirely within a transported terrane (St-Julien and Hubert, 1975; Laurent, 1977) of large Taconic thrust sheets. The field-geologic interpretation that much of the Quebec segment of the exposed Appalachians south of Logan's Line has undergone long-distance thrust transport is persuasively confirmed by the recent vibroseismic survey that traversed the area between the St. Lawrence River below Quebec City and the Quebec-Maine boundary (Beiers, 1976; SOQUIP, 1979a, 1979b). The survey shows that the rocks exposed on the surface south of Logan's Line, as far as the Notre Dame Mountains, are underlain by rocks apparently continuous with the Paleozoic carbonate rocks of the platform, judging by the flat-lying nature of the reflectors. Rocks exposed in the area between the Notre Dame Mountains and the southeast end of the survey area, just north of the Chain Lakes massif, can also be best interpreted as allochthonous. Extrapolation of the vibroseismic data southward along the tectonic strike indicates that the ultramafic belt of Vermont, Massachusetts, and Connecticut at least as far south as Long Island Sound (Chidester, 1968) may also have been transported; this point is supported by the preliminary COCORP data (Ando and others, 1982). An additional point is that south of northern Vermont, the ultramafic rocks do not show the typical ophiolite suite, at least in a coherent sequence. An attractive alternative interpretation is that some of the ultramafic blocks are ophiolite olistoliths, derived from the east by rapid in-trench erosion and deposition, possibly retransported by thrusting (Stanley and Roy, 1982) so that the occurrences of these olistoliths again would provide only a western limit to the eastern margin of the North American craton. Such an explanation readily explains the discontinuity of the ultramafic rocks. Means must be devised to test the oceanic crustal affinity of these rocks, or the lack thereof; perhaps use of relative abundances of the platinum elements (N. J. Page, written commun., 1981) or the initial neodymium ratios (e.g., Shaw and others, 1981) will eventually provide such tests.

Boudette (1970, 1981) and Boudette and Boone (1976) reported an intrusive and extrusive ultramafic suite in northwestern Maine, just south of the Chain Lakes massif. The suite apparently contains most of the rock assemblages and structures indicative of an ophiolite suite. The intrusive part is called Boil Mountain Complex; the extrusive part, including some sedimentary rocks, is the Jim Pond Formation (Boudette, 1981). A 515-Ma zircon age has been tentatively given to a rock of the intrusive complex (Eisenberg, 1981). Rocks of the suite were intruded by the 445-Ma Attean Quartz Monzonite (Boudette, 1981; Albee and Boudette, 1972; Boudette and Boone, 1976) after their emplacement. The older age presumably is the age of formation of the crust; the age of emplacement, that is, destruction of the crust, must be somewhat younger. I interpret this ophiolite as an autochthonous part of the Taconian suture at the margin of North America, equivalent to the ophiolites at Elmtree (Rast and Stringer, 1980) in northern New Brunswick. I postulate that the line connecting these two localities roughly defines the seaward edge of the Taconian North American craton and extends into western Newfoundland along the Baie Verte lineament, which was already suggested by Williams (1979) as the margin of North America. The mafic rocks of Caucomgomoc Lake (Pollock, 1982) may be part of this suture. I will cite other kinds of evidence to bolster this argument.

Blueschist and Related Rocks

The presence of blueschist-facies metamorphism has often been cited as evidence of subduction-zone processes. Certainly, the high-pressure low-temperature environment of such rocks suggests conditions consistent with those postulated for subduction of cold sediments in a trench. Blueschist facies and eclogite-facies metamorphic rocks are not widespread in the Appalachian orogen. Church (1969; see also DeWit and Strong, 1975) reported isolated eclogite occurrences in the Fleur de Lys Supergroup of Burlington Peninsula. Jamieson (1977) reported magnesioriebeckite-bearing rocks from the Maiden Point Formation of the Hare Bay Allochthon. Helmstaedt (1971) reported crossite-bearing metamorphic rocks, and Skinner (1974) reported glaucophane(?), from the lower Paleozoic Tetagouche Group of the Miramichi anticlinorium in northern New Brunswick. Trzcienski (1976) reported crossite from southeastern Quebec. The tectonic significance of crossite and magnesioriebeckite is not obvious because the high ferric iron content in the octahedral site probably relaxes the pressure requirement for its formation. However, Doolan and others (1973) and, in much greater detail, Laird and Albee (1981) did report relict glaucophane schist that survived the later Acadian metamorphic imprint in north-central Vermont; Lanphere and Albee (1974) had previously given evidence that the early metamorphism was Taconian. Harwood (1976; name in original reference erroneously given as Hardwood, q.v.) suggested that a retrograde-metamorphosed mafic dike in the allochthonous rocks of the Canaan Mountain Formation near Norfolk in northwestern Connecticut originally was metamorphosed to an eclogitic mineral assemblage

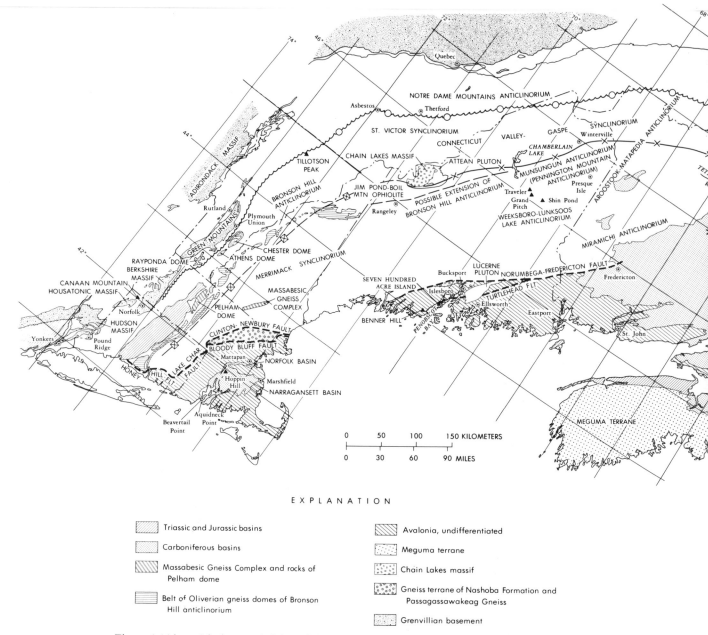

EXPLANATION

Triassic and Jurassic basins		Avalonia, undifferentiated
Carboniferous basins		Meguma terrane
Massabesic Gneiss Complex and rocks of Pelham dome		Chain Lakes massif
Belt of Oliverian gneiss domes of Bronson Hill anticlinorium		Gneiss terrane of Nashoba Formation and Passagassawakeag Gneiss
		Grenvillian basement

Figure 1 (this and facing page). Map of the northern Appalachian region, showing locations of major tectonic and stratigraphic units discussed in the text, and of reference localities. Lithotectonic units are not all shown for Newfoundland, and that part of the map is included for geographic reference only.

during the Taconian event. The Fleur de Lys and Teta-gouche rocks occur within the zone of the postulated *in situ* ophiolite-marked Ordovician suture, so their presence supports a possible determination of the present map trace of the Taconian subduction zone. The other occurrences of blueschist are all in transported rocks and suggest that the relative ages of transportation and metamorphism need reexamination. For example, could the north-central Vermont occurrences of glaucophane schist in mafic rocks be olistoliths of metamorphic rocks in a melange? Taken as a whole, the occurrences of rocks of the eclogite and glaucophane facies of metamorphism at least do not contradict the possible existence of a subduction zone, and thus the cratonic margin, no farther northwest than their present loci.

I suggest that blueschist-facies and eclogite-facies metamorphism might be expected in a subduction melange, on the craton side rather than oceanic side of the final suture. This is so because if the metamorphism was concomitant with subduction, then the deep-seated metamor-

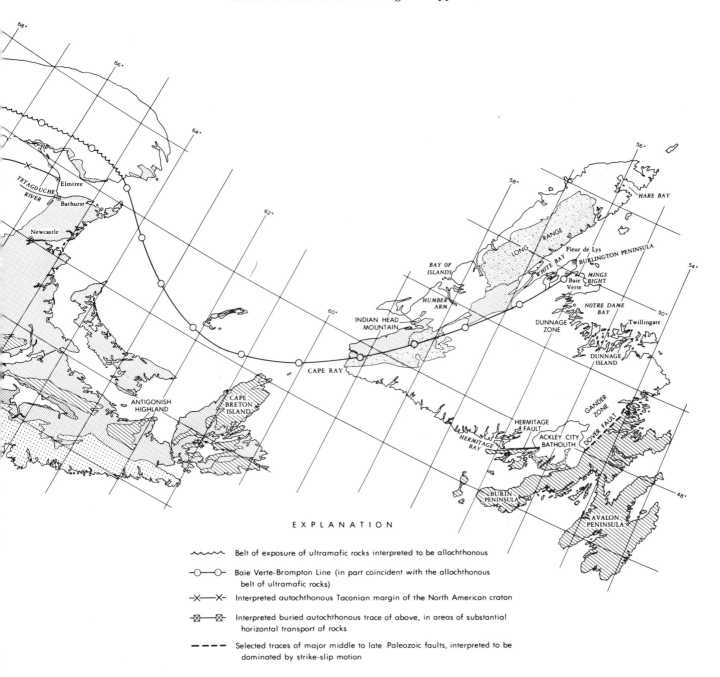

E X P L A N A T I O N

～～～～ Belt of exposure of ultramafic rocks interpreted to be allochthonous

–O––O– Baie Verte-Brompton Line (in part coincident with the allochthonous
belt of ultramafic rocks)

–X––X– Interpreted autochthonous Taconian margin of the North American craton

–⊠––⊠– Interpreted buried autochthonous trace of above, in areas of substantial
horizontal transport of rocks

– – – – Selected traces of major middle to late Paleozoic faults, interpreted to be
dominated by strike-slip motion

phic rocks might be expected to be obducted onto the craton, not away from it. Application of this concept to the model of Osberg (1978) and Robinson and Hall (1980) would then suggest that such rocks ought to occur on the margin of Craton X, on the far shore of Iapetus Ocean. Their presence in non-transported rocks would then help to define the limits of the North American craton; the picture is consistent with that deduced previously.

Melange Zone

Another hallmark of subduction tectonics is the pres-

ence of melanges in the sedimentary sequences of roughly the same age as the proposed subduction event. Two kinds of chaotic rocks deserve separate consideration because they may imply different processes. First are chaotic, wildflysch-like rocks that are part of the autochthonous or parautochthonous shale sequence underlying the Taconic, Humber Arm, and Hare Bay allochthons (see Zen, 1972). Formation of these rocks is indirectly related to subduction, but the rocks were formed on the craton-shelf sequence outside the active zone of subduction. The formative process was largely sedimentary, involving no concomitant local tectonic deformation in a subduction environment (see Bosworth and Vollmer, 1981). Thus, I prefer to distinguish these rocks from subduction melanges.

Information on true subduction melanges associated with the Taconian orogeny comes mostly from the Canadian segment of the Appalachians. Such rocks have been reported from the Dunnage Zone of the Notre Dame Bay area of northern Newfoundland (Kay, 1976; Williams, 1979). In Quebec, rocks interpreted to be subduction melange are found in the Ordovician St. Daniels Formation (St-Julien and Hubert, 1975) in a belt southeast of the Thetford ophiolite complex, in the St. Victor synclinorium. These rocks may have been transported for the same reason that the Thetford ophiolite was probably transported. The relative positions of the two rock sequences, however, may yet record their original dispositions, and they agree with the relations in Newfoundland: the melange is east (and oceanward relative to the North American craton) of the ophiolite. This polarity is consistent with a tectonic model (e.g., Robinson and Hall, 1980) which states that subduction was toward the far shore of Iapetus, that is, between the oceanic plate and Craton X. Harwood (1979a) suggested that the early Paleozoic Hazens Notch Formation and related units of northern Vermont are part of a serpentinite melange; if so, they have clearly been modified by later tectonism (Stanley and Roy, 1982). The Rowe schist in western Massachusetts may enclose additional melanges (Ratcliffe and Hatch, 1979; Harwood, 1979b), but over much of western New England no subduction melange has been reported. Why is it missing? Is it there but not recognized by field workers? Has the increase of the metamorphic grade and Acadian deformation obliterated the evidence? Has the belt been overridden by higher thrust sheets and thus is now hidden? Or are the geologic relations and plate-margin history different in this segment of the orogen? These questions need to be answered by future workers.

Island Arc

Whether island arcs ever were present in the eastern margin of the northern Appalachian orogen prior to the Taconian orogeny is unclear. The gneiss domes of the Bronson Hill anticlinorium, and their core rocks of leucocratic granitic to trondhjemitic gneisses (see, for example, Naylor, 1968; Leo, 1976) and cover rocks of leucogneiss and tholeiitic basalt, including pillow lava of oceanic affinity (Naylor, 1968), have been cited by many workers (e.g., Rodgers, 1981) as possible examples of island arcs. The low initial strontium ratios of the associated rocks, 0.706 and 0.7045 (Naylor, 1968; Foland and Loiselle, 1981, respectively), support derivation of the magma from an oceanic source. The location of the island arc, if that was what the rocks represent, in pre-Taconian time is controversial. Robinson and Hall (1980) have suggested that the

arc may be associated with Craton X across the Iapetus Ocean and that it is now accreted to North America only as the result of subduction that destroyed the intervening ocean. This suggestion would explain the difference in Ordovician rock facies between the East Vermont sequence and the Bronson Hill anticlinorium and would be compatible with an east-facing polarity to the subduction system. It also avoids the need to subduct continental material under oceanic material, which would be true for an east-facing subduction zone fronting North America. I do not propose to discuss the pros and cons of subduction polarity here; Williams (1979) has provided a nice summary. The model of Robinson and Hall (1980) does seem to contain the elements needed to explain the geologic relations without incurring awkward situations.

To the south, the Bronson Hill gneiss domes can be traced to the Honey Hill fault just north of Long Island Sound; a second group of domes south of the fault trends east, has a late Proterozoic Z age (Hills and Dasch, 1968), and may not be the same (see Rodgers, 1981). Despite the tremendous structural complexities in this belt, including structural inversions (Thompson and others, 1968), the location of the Bronson Hill gneiss domes and associated rocks defines the western surface limit to the permissible original location of the island arc, because tectonic transport was from east to west in this belt during Acadian time. This limit agrees extremely well with the limit, previously discussed, for the eastern margin of the North American craton during the Ordovician.

Northward, the structure of the Bronson Hill anticlinorium can be traced across northern New Hampshire into Maine as the Jefferson dome (Milton, 1961), south of the presumed Ordovician subduction-related ophiolite of Jim Pond–Boil Mountain (Boudette, 1981). The continuation of the island arc, if that is what it is, farther northeast is almost totally conjectural. Ordovician volcanic rocks are found at the south end of the Munsungsun anticlinorium (Hall, 1970) in the Chesuncook Lake area and are found in abundance in the Weeksboro–Lunksoos Lake and Pennington Mountain anticlinoria (Pavlides, 1973; Roy and Mencher, 1976). Volcanic rocks are also found in the Tetagouche sequence of the Miramichi anticlinorium (Skinner, 1974; Helmstaedt, 1971; Rast and others, 1976a) in New Brunswick and easternmost Maine. Are these, or parts of these, related to the supposed island arc (see, in this context, Naylor, 1968)? One problem is that the last three named broadly synchronous sequences trend generally northwest, across the trend of the Appalachian belt in this area and across the extrapolated trend of the presumed Bronson Hill island arc. At this point one can only guess at the relations; I will do so in a later section.

Continental Margin Facies

Assemblages of sedimentary rocks showing evidence

of deposition at the margin of a continental block, including turbidite deposits, ribbon chert, and graptolite-bearing shale, are known in the Appalachian orogen. If such a facies interpretation for these sedimentary rocks is accepted, then the associations can be used to help delineate the margin of the North American continental block and, indirectly, of the North American craton.

Rodgers (1968) suggested that the location of sedimentary facies transition between reefy limestone and dark shale, in northwestern Vermont and in southeastern Pennsylvania, is useful to define the edge of the continent in early Paleozoic time. This interesting suggestion has been much quoted. However, the "margin" thus defined probably refers to a rather abrupt topographic change from very shallow tidal zone to deeper water; this contact may not be directly related to the cratonic margin and, in fact, very likely was actually entirely within the North American craton. The same caveat of correlating sedimentary facies (a function of the physiography, land-sea relations, and bathymetry) with a continental margin (a function of the nature of the crustal block) also applies to the hemipelagic sediments and related rocks. However, for very large differences in water depth, and for changes from near-shore to open-ocean environments, such correlations are probably better warranted.

We know little or nothing about such a facies transition in Connecticut, Massachusetts, and Vermont because large tectonic transport of rocks apparently has hidden or destroyed the original sedimentary evidence. Cambrian and Ordovician rocks of the Taconic allochthon perhaps constitute a good candidate for a continental slope-rise type of deep-water hemipelagic deposit (Zen, 1967, 1972; Stevens, 1970; Bird and Dewey, 1970; Rowley and Kidd, 1981a, 1981b). Features in these rocks that are suggestive of their depositional environments include a condensed stratigraphic section (the so-called starved-basin deposits); their general fine grain size except for the well-sorted turbidite conglomerates; and turbidite and, for the Ordovician part of the sequence, graptolitic shale, massive and bedded chert, and manganiferous deposits. As suggested elsewhere (Zen, 1967), the Ordovician Moretown Formation of eastern Vermont and its on-strike equivalent units may also be beds deposited in a slope-rise environment, but if these are transported rocks, then the present locations can only supply the minimum extent of the cratonic margin. Use of the allochthonous rocks for paleogeographic restoration depends on a correct identification of the depositional sites for these rocks. Zen (1967) suggested the Green Mountains, assuming that rocks of east Vermont are by and large in place. Recent geologic studies in Quebec (St-Julien and Hubert, 1975) and Vermont (Stanley and Roy, 1982) including vibroseismic work (SOQUIP, 1979a, 1979b; Ando and others, 1982), and a new interpretation of the geology of Massachusetts (Ratcliffe,

1982; R. S. Stanley and N. M. Ratcliffe, *in* Zen and others, 1983) make it unlikely that the east Vermont rocks are autochthonous. The site of deposition of rocks of the Taconic allochthon, therefore, needs to be resought, farther east. This idea, that the shelf facies once extended farther east than the Green Mountain anticlinorium, is supported by the discovery (Thompson, 1972, p. 227) that rocks virtually identical with the Lower Cambrian carbonate rocks of the shelf facies (Dunham Dolomite of Clark, 1934 near Rutland, Vermont) are found near Plymouth Union, Vermont, in the basal part of the east Vermont sequence.

The east Vermont sequence of rocks includes the Missisquoi Formation as used by Doll and others (1961), assigned to the Middle Ordovician, which includes volcanic-rock–rich beds in the upper part. A major regional unconformity separates the Missisquoi from the post-Taconian rocks of Silurian and Devonian age. The pre-Silurian rock sequence has been correlated with confidence with rocks in northern New Hampshire and northwestern Maine known as the Aziscohos, Albee, and Dixville Formations (Hatch, 1963; Green and Guidotti, 1968; Osberg and others, 1968; Hall, 1970). The time-*plus*-facies correlatives of these units in northern and northeastern Maine are more problematic, and several seemingly plausible candidates exist.

1. In the area near Chamberlain Lake in northern Piscataquis County, at the south end of the Munsungun anticlinorium, Hall (1970) mapped a sequence of Cambrian(?) and pre-Caradocian Ordovician sedimentary rocks that bear strong lithic and time affinity to the rocks of the Aziscohos-Albee (= lower part of Missisquoi)-Dixville sequence. Farther northeast, in the Presque Isle–Winterville area, Roy and Mencher (1976) mapped two separate sequences. One, the Madawaska Lake Formation, consists of green-gray slate and graywacke about 600 m thick, showing turbidite fabric; the other, the Winterville Formation, is mainly volcanic and volcanogenic rocks, black slate, graywacke, and chert. These rocks are Ordovician in age, and Roy and Mencher considered them to be lateral facies equivalents. Are these sequences the on-strike continuation of the rocks mapped by Hall, and the continuation of those in Vermont and New Hampshire?

2. In the area of the Weeksboro–Lunksoos Lake anticlinorium in north-central Maine, Pavlides (1962, 1968; see also Pavlides and others, 1968; Boucot and others, 1964) mapped a complex sequence of interbedded graywacke, thin-bedded carbonate, and volcanic rocks, and some manganiferous beds of Early Ordovician through Silurian age. Radiolarian chert and graptolitic argillite that produced Zone 12 *Climacograptus bicornis*, of Middle Ordovician Normanskill age, have been reported (Pavlides, 1974). One particular unit, the Carys Mills Formation, is thin-bedded limestone that Pavlides (1968) interpreted as a flysch deposit. The Carys Mills, however, is

Middle Ordovician to Early Silurian, younger than the supposed cessation of the Taconian subduction event in the New England Appalachians. If the rocks of north-central Maine constitute a continental-margin facies, and if their lithofacies permits such an interpretation, then the Carys Mills' age would seem to pose a distinct anomaly in its time-space setting within the tectonic regime. A reasonable explanation is that locally a relict deep-water basin continued to receive flysch sediments after the main subduction event. These rocks and their correlative units in northern Maine appear to be reasonable candidates for continental-margin-facies rocks, relict or otherwise, though the craton with which they are associated has not been established—it could be North America, but could conceivably be Craton X. Serpentinite is scattered through the area (Pavlides, 1962), but it has uncertain structural and petrogenetic implications for the tectonic regime.

3. South and west of the area just discussed, a sequence of Proterozoic Z to Lower Cambrian *Oldhamia*-bearing gray to varicolored shale, siltstone, and graywacke, the Grand Pitch Formation (Neuman, 1967), is overlain by mafic volcanic and volcanogenic rocks, including pillow lava and some mafic intrusive rocks, the Shin Brook Formation, of Ordovician age. The succession includes a unit of interbedded ribbon chert and black shale, the Wassataquoik Chert; the interbedded shale has produced Middle Ordovician Zone 12 graptolites (*Climacograptus bicornis*). The facies of the Grand Pitch and the Wassataquoik is very similar to the Proterozoic Z to Lower Cambrian slate and the Middle Ordovician, Zone 12 graptolite-bearing chert in the "Mount Merino Member" of the Normanskill Formation in the Taconic allochthon of Vermont and New York. If the Taconic rocks are a continental-slope-rise, that is, continental-margin, facies, then the Grand Pitch–Wassataquoik combination should similarly qualify. The associated craton for the Grand Pitch–Shin Brook–Wassataquoik formations, however, must be Craton X.

The structural relation between the Grand Pitch and the immediately overlying volcanic rocks is reported to be an unconformity and involves a basal conglomerate in the Shin Brook Formation (Neuman, 1967). The Wassataquoik, however, is everywhere in fault contact (Neuman, 1967), thus further obscuring the interpretation of the original paleogeographic relations of these rocks.

4. Farther east and south, partly in eastern Maine but particularly in northern New Brunswick, rocks occur in the Miramichi anticlinorium that have been correlated with those in the Grand Pitch area. A thick sequence of volcanic and volcanogenic rocks, the Tetagouche, contains Middle Ordovician graptolites in its upper part (Poole and others, 1970, p.247; Rast and Stringer, 1974). Beneath the Tetagouche are older sedimentary rocks that reportedly (Rast and others, 1976a) resemble the Grand Pitch and

thus, presumably, are also of continental-margin facies. Whether the two sequences were once connected as a single depositional system is not known; attempts to correlate units between them by various authors suggest a general inclination among local workers to think so.

Of considerable interest is the reported occurrence of crossite and glaucophane in the Tetagouche rocks of the Bathurst-Newcastle area of northern New Brunswick, cited earlier. If these minerals constitute valid examples of blueschist-facies metamorphism, then the Tetagouche might well have gone down the subduction zone and come back. Combining this occurrence with a hypothesis of a southeast-dipping subduction zone (Robinson and Hall, 1980), I conclude that the Tetagouche sequence was deposited on the eastern side of the Iapetus Ocean, perhaps as part of Craton X and not part of the North American craton. The rocks along the Weeksboro–Lunksoos Lake anticlinorium, including the Grand Pitch area, might have had a similar geologic history if the stratigraphic correlations suggested for them are valid. This would leave the rocks of the Munsungun anticlinorium as the sole remnant of North American rocks among those just discussed.

To summarize: One important factor in determining the pre-Taconian limits of the North American craton in Maine is the correct stratigraphic correlation of pre-Taconian units; presumably, rocks that are firmly correlated with one another did not originate on opposite sides of the Iapetus Ocean. Some proposed correlations are shown in Table 1. Hall (1970) suggested correlating his

TABLE 1. SOME PROPOSED CORRELATIONS OF STRATIGRAPHIC UNITS IN MAINE, NEW HAMPSHIRE, AND VERMONT

Eastern Vermont (Doll and others, 1961)		Western New Hampshire (Billings, 1956)	Northern New Hampshire and western Maine (Green and Guidotti, 1968)	Northern Maine (Hall, 1970)	North-central Maine (Neuman, 1967)
Missisquoi Formation	Cram Hill Member	Partridge and Ammonoosuc Formations	Dixville Formation	Chase Lake Formation	Unnamed volcanic rocks
	Moretown Member	Albee Formation	Albee Formation	Unnamed unit	Shin Brook Formation
Stowe and Ottauquechee Formations		?	Aziscohos Formation	Chase Brook Formation	Grand Pitch Formation

Chase Brook Formation of the Munsungun anticlinorium with at least part of the Grand Pitch (Neuman, 1967) of the Weeksboro–Lunksoos Lake anticlinorium; at the same time, he pointed out that massive quartzite beds of the Grand Pitch do not occur in his Chase Brook. Hall also correlated his Chase Brook with the Aziscohos Formation of westernmost Maine and northern New Hampshire (Green and Guidotti, 1968). In the latter area, the Aziscohos is overlain by the Albee Formation, and the combined sequence extends southwest into western New Hampshire as part of the Bronson Hill anticlinorium sequence. The Albee Formation has been correlated by Doll and others (1961) with the Moretown Member of the Missisquoi Formation (as used by Doll and others, 1961) of eastern Vermont. The Aziscohos is not recognized in the Bronson Hill anticlinorium in west-central New Hampshire, but it was correlated (Hall, 1970) with the Stowe and Ottauquechee Formations that underlie the Moretown (Doll and others, 1961; Green and Guidotti, 1968). If the Ottauquechee-Stowe-Moretown sequence is North American, and if the correlations are all valid, then the presence of the Grand Pitch, which has been identified even in the Miramichi anticlinorium, would indicate that all these tectonic units were part of North America in pre-Taconian time. Here is one of the major dilemmas of northern Appalachian geology. A pre–plate-tectonic model could readily accommodate these correlations, but plate-tectonic reconstructions suggest that things might be wrong somewhere and that one or more of the correlations may be invalid. I suggest that Hall's Chase Brook and Grand Pitch may not truly correlate but merely resemble one another because they are both continental-margin facies; Hall (1970) emphasized that his Chase Brook does not have the quartzite beds of the Grand Pitch but that its resemblance to the Aziscohos is strong. Thus, assuming the legitimacy of the other correlations of Table 1 and assuming that the east Vermont rocks are North American, I conclude that Hall's Chase Brook and associated rocks were part of North America. If the weak link is somewhere else (for instance, the resemblances between the Aziscohos-Albee sequence and the Ottauquechee-Stowe-Moretown sequence may be deceptive and may result from both sequences having been deposited in similar oceanic environments), then the conclusion on the limit of the North American craton might have to be modified. It is even possible that none of the rocks listed in Table 1 are North American but now rest on a North American craton as a result of later tectonic transport.

Because Hall's Chase Brook sequence and related rocks crop out now near the line I draw for the outer limit of pre-Taconian North American craton and do not occupy a large area, they can be delegated to Craton X without drastically changing the proposed locus of the craton edge.

Bird and Dewey (1970) suggested that a suture zone runs through northeastern Maine southeast of the area of the Madawaska and Winterville Formations of Roy and Mencher (1976) near Presque Isle. Roy and Mencher (1976) cautioned against this idea because field relations indicate that no suture exists in this area and that sedimentation was continuous through the Late Ordovician into the Silurian (Neuman, 1967; Roy and Mencher, 1976;

Pavlides and others, 1968).[2] They concluded that a suture, if it exists, must be either northwest of the Winterville area or southeast of the Tetagouche. Clearly, I am coming up against an old and difficult problem. My suggestion of putting the suture northwest of the Winterville has one feature in its favor: It would permit the ophiolite and melange sequence of the Elmtree area (Rast and Stringer, 1980) to be assigned to the suture zone, aligned with the Jim Pond–Boil Mountain ophiolite near Chain Lakes massif and with the possible ophiolite sequence of the Caucomgomoc Lake area (Pollock, 1982). Because the Tetagouche Group is southeast of the Elmtree ophiolite, my solution excludes it from pre-Taconian North America and thus avoids the need for some complicated geometry or multiple Taconian suturing. Thus by assuming a southeast-dipping Taconian subduction zone, by accepting the validity of local stratigraphic correlations in northeastern Maine and adjacent New Brunswick, and by postulating the usefulness of crossite as an indicator of blueschist-facies metamorphism in a trench-subduction environment, I conclude that the edge of the North American craton lies very nearly at the south flank of the present Munsungun anticlinorium (the continuing post-Taconian sedimentation here as well as in the Rangeley, Maine, area [Moench, 1970] is thus a nonproblem beyond the active suture zone). This conclusion is consistent with what we know of the seismic data in Quebec (SOQUIP, 1979a, 1979b), but leaves a perilously narrow strip of this craton southeast of Logan's Line. Clearly, more intensive seismic survey is needed. Perhaps some of the problematic sequences in northeastern Maine are not mutually correlative; perhaps longitudinal transport of crustal blocks and superjacent rocks in Taconian time, which resulted from oblique rather than orthogonal subduction, has confounded the original paleogeography to the extent that, with the added confusion of later cover rocks and deformation, we are following a wrong lead of inquiry. For instance, the Wassataquoik Chert might be itself a small displaced terrane not attached to the Grand Pitch–Shin Brook stratigraphically (in this connection, see Jones and others, 1980, for a possible analog). Some of the sequences might be North American in pedigree but have been displaced out of their original positions; certainly the nearly north-south trend of the Ordovician volcanic rocks along the Maine–New Brunswick border arouses suspicion of later transport. In the complex and puzzling relations here, we have a window into the past not afforded by areas of simple facies dispositions.

The proposed location of the margin of the Taconian North American craton has strong geophysical expres-

---

[2]The Late Ordovician fossils of the Sherbrooke Formation reported from the Taconic allochthon in Quebec (see discussion and references in Cady, 1969, p. 103) could be a displaced part of the same belt of continuous deposition, or could be part of a post-accretion, overlap sequence.

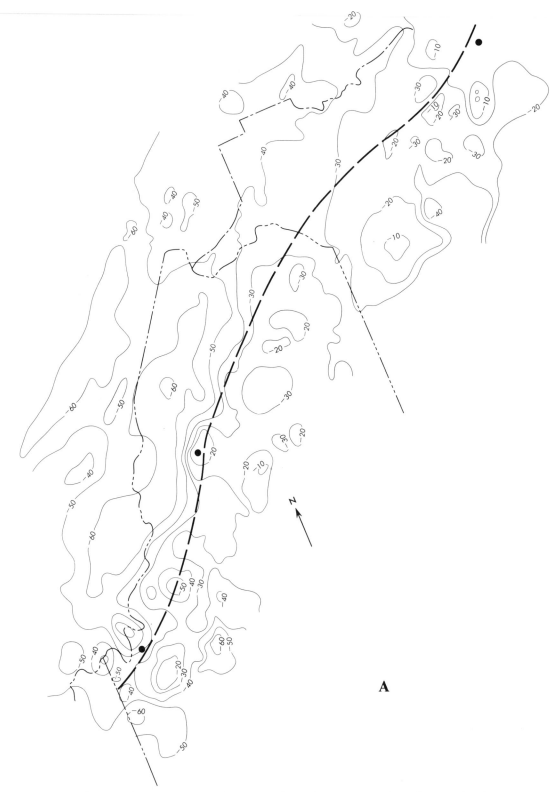

A

Figure 2 (this and facing page). Geophysical expressions of the proposed Taconian margin of the North American craton. A, Bouguer gravity anomaly map (Haworth and others, 1980) with the proposed margin superimposed in heavy broken line. B, aeromagnetic anomaly map (Zietz and others, 1980) with the same proposed cratonal margin superimposed. Point A, the Jim Pond–Boil Mountain ophiolite complex. Point B, the Caucomgomoc Lake complex of Pollock, 1982. Point C, the Elmtree ophiolite complex.

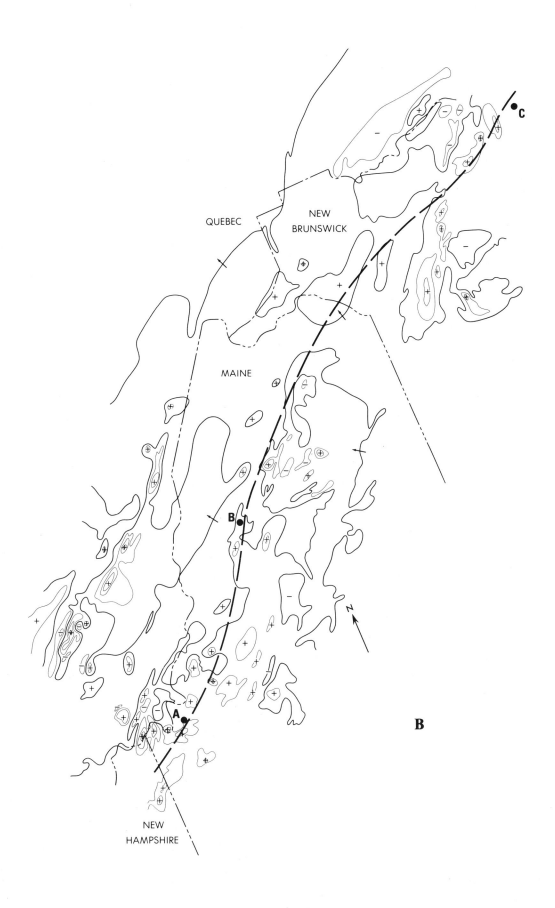

QUEBEC

NEW
BRUNSWICK

MAINE

N

B

NEW
HAMPSHIRE

sions. Figure 2A superimposes the aeromagnetic map of the area (Zietz and others, 1980) on the proposed margin; Figure 2B superimposes the Bouguer gravity map (Haworth and others, 1980) on the same margin. The coincidence of the proposed margin with the strong gravity gradient of Kane and Bromery (1968) is striking. Hildenbrand and others (1982) recently presented a set of wavelength filtered Bouguer gravity maps of northeastern United States; the version that filters out wave lengths over 250 km, thus corresponding approximately to the gravity effects of crustal source, bears an even more pronounced correspondence to the proposed cratonal margin.

Summary of Taconian Exotic Terranes

The presentation in this section was intended to highlight the point that various criteria for continental-margin subduction can be related to known geologic features, and that anomalous relations such as the absence of ophiolite in eastern Vermont can probably be rationalized in terms of subsequent displacements due to thrust faulting. The distribution pattern of these geologic features suggests that the pre-Taconian east edge of the North American craton was somewhere east of the Connecticut River in southern New England, passing northeast to the Rangeley area of western Maine, thence east-northeast through Aroostook County and to the area around Bathurst in northern New Brunswick. It reappears in western Newfoundland from Cape Ray to the Burlington Peninsula.

To the extent that this might be so, no exotic terrane is likely to be found northwest of this line, of any age as old as the Taconian orogeny, except for the well-known "Taconic allochthons" (Zen, 1972). There is, however, one other candidate—the Chain Lakes "massif." Zircon dating of rocks of the massif (Naylor and others, 1973) shows the rocks to be about 1.5 Ga old, significantly older than the conventional age of the Grenvillian basement. The rocks have been severely deformed and probably mylonitized. The massif is not on trend with the belt of Long Range–Green Mountains massifs of Grenvillian basement. The vibroseismic data in Quebec, though stopping just short of the international boundary (SOQUIP, 1979a, 1979b) and thus missing the massif by a scant few kilometers, seem nonetheless to indicate unequivocally that the massif cannot be locally rooted but that it is part of a transported mass having an unknown amount of horizontal displacement, presumably from the southeast, and from beyond the Jim Pond–Boil Mountain ophiolite complex that Boudette (1981) and I suggest to be a more or less in-place limit to the North American craton. Thus, the anomalous age, lithic nature, tectonic location, and probably rootless relation of the rock mass suggest that it is an allochthonous terrane. One possibility (see also Boudette, 1981) is that it is part of Craton X that formed the alien shore

during the Taconian subduction event (debris from this rock is included in the Upper Silurian part of the Hobbstown Formation nearby, so it was in place before that time; see Boucot, 1961, p. 174–175). I suggest that this massif was thrust over the suture and ophiolite as a result of continent-continent collision that succeeded the closing of the Iapetus Ocean. It would be analogous to the interpretation accorded some of the 2-Ga-old gneiss found in the Shuswap terrane in western Canada (Brown, 1980; Read, 1980; Wanless and Reesor, 1975) as an allochthonous terrane overthrust onto the North American craton during a collision at the continental margin.

Exotic terranes of Taconian vintage beyond the limit of the postulated edge of the Taconian North American craton cannot be excluded from existing data. If the Taconian orogeny did result from active plate-margin subduction more or less similar to its modern counterpart and model, then we might turn the argument around and ask why more exotic terranes are not in evidence. The rock sequences of northeastern Main are possible candidates that might be pieces of the major plates caught up in the zone of collision in a manner similar to that postulated for the Alpine-Tethyan system (Dewey and others, 1973); Craton X itself clearly is an exotic terrane from the North American–centric viewpoint. Additional exotic terranes of Taconian vintage could be hidden beneath younger cover rocks. However, I conclude, conservatively, that in the segment of the Appalachians now found in New England, transport of displaced terranes was not piecemeal, or if it was, the process was mainly removal from this area (negative microplates or decreted terranes). Therefore, we need to go elsewhere, for example western Europe, for the preserved positive record.

The absence of definite evidence for large-scale, piecemeal accretion of terranes, especially those composed of continental material, during active Taconian plate-margin subduction is in stark contrast with the relations that obtain in the western Cordillera. A lack of significant oblique motion of plates, with the opportunity for fragmentation and transport of crustal blocks that such motion would offer, may be a reason for this contrast.

POST-TACONIAN CANDIDATES FOR EXOTIC TERRANES

Problems Related to the Acadian Orogeny

Although enough information exists to suggest that the Taconian deformation in the northern Appalachian region had a strong flavor of contemporary plate tectonics, evidence is much less clear for the Acadian orogeny, at least in the New England segment of the Appalachians. For this area, presumably this younger and more intense (at least insofar as plutonism, regional metamorphism, and formation of penninic nappes go) event ultimately also resulted from plate-tectonic processes, but geologic evidence is elusive and fragmentary. Leggett and others (1979) made a strong case for plate tectonics in the Scottish Midland Valley, an event that lasted from the Ordovician into at least Late Silurian time, beginning with the emplacement of the Ballantrae ophiolite complex (see also Bluck and others, 1980). In northern Newfoundland, which was the first landfall of the late Caledonide belt on the west side of the modern Atlantic Ocean, syntectonic Silurian olistostromal rocks occur in the Dunnage Zone (McKerrow and Cocks, 1979, 1981; see also Kay, 1969, 1976; Williams, 1979). In the New England Appalachians, the interpretation, largely based on the absence of oceanic crustal material, is one of continent-continent collision (Robinson and Hall, 1980). Suggestions of anomalously thick crust in the core zone of the Acadian orogen in southern New England (Tracy and Robinson, 1980), as shown by the metamorphic assemblages at the present level of erosion, support this idea.

Thompson and others (1968) and Robinson and Hall (1980), among others, described large penninic nappes of Silurian and Devonian rocks within the Merrimack synclinorium, nappes that were thrust over the Bronson Hill anticlinorium. This anticlinorium has been interpreted as an island arc on the far shore of Iapetus Ocean, which accreted to North America during the Taconian orogeny. Therefore, the depositional basin for these rocks presumably was sited on the continental crust of former Craton X, rather than on oceanic crust, as many have conjectured. If the nappes were deconvoluted, they would require a depositional basin many times wider than the present outcrop belt or available "hinterland," even if allowance is made for stratigraphic stretching due to deformation. Neither such an area of deposition nor a source area for the large volume of sediments is known to exist today, as rocks of the nappes are bounded on the southeast (rootward) side, not by a root zone, into which we can dispose our ignorance, but by a narrow discontinuous zone of gneiss of late Proterozoic Z age (the lower part of the Massabesic Gneiss Complex; Aleinikoff and others, 1979) and by metamorphosed sedimentary rocks of probably Ordovician to Devonian age (the Hebron, Paxton, Oakdale, Eliot, Berwick, Worcester, and related rocks). Areas underlain by the metamorphosed sedimentary rocks cannot have been the root zone out of which the nappes evolved, because rocks of similar ages are still there (see, in this context, Rodgers, 1981). The fact that these rocks on the southeast side also preserve much lower pressure metamorphic assemblages of Acadian age (Thompson and Norton, 1968; Zen and others, 1983) that include andalusite rather than staurolite and kyanite accentuates the problem. This easterly belt in turn is cut off to the south-

east by the Clinton-Newbury fault zone, beyond which yet another and geologically distinct rock assemblage appears.

Although some of the Silurian and Devonian rocks of the Merrimack synclinorium had a northwesterly sedimentary source (Moench, 1970), others (Hall and others, 1976) appear to have had an easterly source. At first sight, the northwest source might be associated with the Somerset Island or geanticline that Boucot (1961) and Cady (1968) postulated for northwestern Maine on the basis of Boucot's study of the stratigraphy of the Moosehead synclinorium. The on-strike continuity of these Silurian and Devonian rocks probably as far south as Massachusetts (Robinson, 1981), however, suggests that an isolated landmass will not suffice. The source areas of much of the relatively mature Silurian and Devonian clastic sedimentary rocks of the core region of the Acadian orogen must be extensive and relatively homogeneous, but their nature, age, and location are unresolved problems.

At least locally in this region, these Silurian and Devonian rocks clearly rest unconformably on older rocks; however, we cannot prove that these rocks everywhere were in their original sedimentary position at the time of their intense metamorphism and nappe formation. Hatch and Stanley (Zen and others, 1983) have postulated a decollement zone near the base of this stratigraphic interval in Massachusetts, but a simple consistent lithostratigraphic restoration for these pelitic rocks to their original facies relations has proved exceedingly difficult. Studies (Hsü, 1960) of Tertiary flysch beds in the region in front of the penninic nappes of the western Alps show that these beds are largely allochthonous. The Devonian flysch deposits of the New England Appalachians also may be already allochthonous prior to the formation of the nappes, and this factor might have to be taken into account in resolving the apparent stratigraphic problems of this area (see also Robinson and others, 1979, p. 108). The location of the source of sediments and sufficient space to properly deconvolute the penninic nappes remain problems that do not seem to permit a ready solution within a frame of discussion that accepts only essentially static crustal blocks involved at most in simple subduction processes.

Conventionally, the direction of tectonic transport in a deformed area is assumed to be within the plane of the cross section, and balanced cross sections are attempted within this frame of reference. The procedure assumes that there is little or no component of transport normal to the plane of section. If that is not true, for example if longitudinal transport along strike-slip and tectonically longitudinal faults was associated with nappe formation, then large apparent widths of sedimentary basins could result from off-section telescoping, through the removal (decretion) of the terrane that was the root zone. This is equivalent to saying that crust might have been lost longitudinally rather than vertically, or that crust might have served as a freight train that offloaded its sedimentary burden at a fixed spot.

I realize that suggesting longitudinal rather than vertical transport of crustal material merely shifts the blame but does not solve the problem. I do suggest, however, that such a possibility needs to be considered and that the consequences of such a solution need to be explored. A crustal block that has been moved out of place ought to be preserved elsewhere (i.e., an accreted terrane microplate must always have its negative, decreted counterpart in the geological record) so that the hypothesis can be tested. More than ever, we need to have some firm information on the nature of the crust underlying the entire Merrimack synclinorium.

One fact that is relevant to this discussion is the occurrence of clasts of rocks of the Chain Lakes massif in the Upper Silurian part of the Hobbstown Formation nearby (Boucot, 1961), already mentioned. This part of the Merrimack synclinorium thus was already in place at that time. If this stratigraphic evidence of welding of the terrane to the North American craton can be extrapolated to the entire Merrimack synclinorium, then longitudinal transport during the Acadian orogeny, as discussed in this section, would not be a viable solution to the "room problem" for the penninic nappes. An alternative possibility is that a more southeast portion of the original Merrimack terrane had been decreted after the emplacement of the nappes but prior to the accretion of the Avalonian terrane (Zen and Palmer, 1981; see also later section). Could such a terrane be identified elsewhere? Could the sharp reduction of the width of the Merrimack terrane in southern New England reflect such a phenomenon?

Existing gravity and aeromagnetic data do not point to a mafic crust in the Merrimack synclinorium (Bothner and others, 1980; Harwood and Zietz, 1976) but do not rule out this possibility. Interestingly, Kane and Bromery's (1968) northern gravity "step" (more positive to the south) in Maine is closely parallel to my proposed Taconian suture and is offset to the north by about 25 km (Fig. 2). The paleomagnetic pole position of the Devonian Traveler Rhyolite in northern Maine, south of the proposed suture, suggests a considerable displacement or rotation with respect to the North American craton (Spariosu and Kent, 1980, 1981). Integration of these geophysical data with geological and geochronological information could help to test the idea of Acadian longitudinal transport and might hold the key to the problem of unscrambling the tectonic role of the Tetagouche–Grand Pitch–Shin Brook–Weeksboro–Lunksoos Lake rock units previously discussed.

Late Acadian and Alleghanian Possibilities

Late Acadian and Alleghanian tectonic events in the northern Appalachians present an aspect altogether different from that of the preceding Paleozoic tectonic events. Again, there is no evidence of subduction-related geologic processes. Juxtaposition of terranes across long faults that show strong cataclasis and mylonitic deformation, however, is a major additional feature for the northern Appalachian orogenic belt. Moreover, the terranes thus placed side by side may show entirely different radiometric ages, metamorphic grades, structural history, stratigraphic ages, and thicknesses. These features suggest the strong possibility of analogy with the displaced terranes of the western North American Cordillera (Monger and others, 1972; Jones and others, 1977, and other references cited at the beginning of this essay). Insofar as accreted terranes go, we have something tangible to examine at last, though whether these terranes extend their roots into the asthenosphere is quite unclear; for many terranes, this extension almost certainly cannot exist, because they are so small.[3]

The first area to be discussed is eastern Massachusetts and adjacent parts of Rhode Island. Rock sequences that can be related to Acadian orogenic events and that are an integral part of the post-Acadian North American craton can be traced as far east as the Clinton-Newbury fault zone in east-central Massachusetts. The Clinton-Newbury fault is an abrupt boundary separating these rocks from those on the opposite side that have a different lithic sequence, metamorphic grade, and probably original as well as metamorphic ages. Probable contrast in crustal constitution across this fault is shown by the data of Hildenbrand and others (1982). The fault probably continues northeastward out to sea somewhere near the Massachusetts–New Hampshire border, but no definite position has been established. Simpson and others (1980) and Arthaud and Matte (1977) suggested connecting this fault with major strike-slip fault systems in Europe. Implicit in these reconstructions is that the Clinton-Newbury fault is a major plate boundary, in accord with the original suggestion of Wilson (1966). The southwest continuation of the fault is commonly attributed to the Lake Chargoggagoggmanchauggagoggchaubunagungamaugg fault in eastern Connecticut, which has an attendant major zone of cataclasis (Dixon and Lundgren, 1968; Rodgers, 1981) that might have formed during the displacement. However, whether the geometry and ages of these faults and their associated cataclastic rocks are mutually compatible remains to be resolved, even though there seems no doubt that both fault systems separate rocks that are part of the Acadian version of North America from those that are strangers.

In northeastern Massachusetts, a block of rocks immediately east of the Clinton-Newbury fault is the "Na-

---

[3] Perhaps accreted terranes typically have low-angle contacts except where they are bounded by transcurrent faults. The bulldozer analogy (Zen, 1981) may not be far wrong. (See also Ben-Avraham and others, 1981).

shoba Zone" (Zen and others, 1983), consisting of high-grade, possibly volcanogenic gneisses and amphibolites and metamorphosed calcareous, aluminous to feldspathic sedimentary rocks. The rocks have undergone several episodes of deformation, are structurally complex, and have an internal stratigraphy very different from the stratigraphy west of the Clinton-Newbury fault. The rocks have not yielded fossils; they may be too old. Zircon crystals from the volcanogenic Fish Brook Gneiss of the terrane (Olszewski, 1980) are slender euhedra, and the lead-isotope ratios plotted on the concordia gave an upper intercept age of 742 ± 91 Ma. Zircon crystals from the Shawsheen Gneiss have detrital cores and euhedral overgrowths. Their upper intercept is at 1.55 ± 0.06 Ga. Olszewski (1980) interpreted the 742-Ma age as that of volcanism that produced the Fish Brook Gneiss. Because the protolith of the Shawsheen is sedimentary, the old intercept implies an even older source terrane from which the detrital zircon was derived. Both members, thus, are supracrustal; the 1.5-Ga age may correspond to the age of an old basement, tantalizingly close to that of the Chain Lakes massif (Naylor and others, 1973). Could the Nashoba Zone and Chain Lakes massif be pieces of the same terrane, Craton X, that somehow managed to collide with North America during the long Paleozoic history—first during Taconian subduction and the closing of Iapetus Ocean and later at the beginning of the Alleghanian (or possibly as early as the late Acadian) event, through largely longitudinal translations of exotic terranes?

The younger of the upper intercept ages, about 750 Ma, is recurrent in the coastal part of the present northern Appalachians. Brookins (1976) reported a Rb-Sr isochron date of 750 ± 100 Ma from gneisses of the Seven Hundred Acre Island in the Penobscot Bay region, Maine. Cormier (1969) reported a Rb-Sr isochron age of 750 ± 80 Ma for the Coldbrook sequence of southern New Brunswick (see also Olszewski and Gaudette, 1981). Though both these reported ages have large uncertainties, the gross lithic similarity of the rocks, as well as those of the Nashoba, would suggest a possible Proterozoic Z thermal event in bits and pieces of the coastal belt. In New Brunswick, the Coldbrook sequence is inferred to rest on the Proterozoic Y Green Head sequence with profound unconformity (Rast and others, 1976a), and one wonders whether the detrital component of the zircon from the Nashoba Zone might have had a Green Head–type source, and also where that source might be today. In this connection, Stewart's suggestion (1974, p. 90) that rocks of Seven Hundred Acre Island resemble the Green Head Formation presents an anomaly that needs to be resolved. Finally, the lack of a recognizable Acadian thermal imprint on the Nashoba zircon fractions shows that the rocks had not participated in the intense Acadian metamorphism and plutonism. It strongly suggests, though does not prove, that the terrane

was not there during the Acadian and has been accreted since then.

East of the Nashoba terrane in Massachusetts, across the Bloody Bluff fault zone, is the terrane of "typical" Avalonian stratigraphy. The Bloody Bluff fault (see Bell and Alvord, 1976, for summary of the relations) not only separates rocks of different stratigraphy and tectonic history and style, but probably also of different ages, and certainly of different metamorphic grades. The fault is thus as fundamental a tectonic line as is the Clinton-Newbury fault. In Massachusetts, the Avalonian terrane includes the intrusive Dedham Granite, dated at 608 ± 17 Ma, a typical Avalonian age (Kovach and others, 1977), and some mafic intrusive rocks. Volcanic rocks are little deformed and metamorphosed; the Mattapan Volcanics Complex south of Boston has an upper intercept age of zircon of 602 ± 3 Ma (Kaye and Zartman, 1980). Thus, the Avalonian ages are all obtained from supracrustal or intrusive rocks and do not date the basement. Olszewski (1980) reported a 2.05-Ga lead age for the detrital zircon from the Westboro Formation from this area, so an old basement is indicated; we do not know, however, whether this unit can be simply related to the pre-Avalonian rocks of the Nashoba Zone across the Bloody Bluff fault.

Cambrian rocks rest on the Dedham rocks east of the Bloody Bluff fault with depositional contact (Dowse, 1950); crossbeds in the Cambrian quartzite just above the granitic rocks at Hoppin Hill (Palmer, 1971; Zen and Richard Goldsmith, unpublished data) strongly corroborate the conclusion that this contact is not a fault. The Cambrian rocks of eastern Massachusetts and Rhode Island bear an Atlantic Province trilobite fauna (Palmer, 1971; Skehan and others, 1978), are only mildly metamorphosed, and, except at the Beavertail Point locality (see below), are little deformed. The Silurian and Devonian sequence of this terrane consists of volcanic and intercalated sedimentary rocks that are locally fossiliferous (Shride, 1976); again, except for some faulting and tilting, these are only mildly metamorphosed and lack penetrative deformation. The rocks are bounded by faults, so their substrate is unknown. Rocks of the Boston Basin, traditionally referred to the Carboniferous and Permian, are now known to be latest Proterozoic Z in age (Lenk and others, 1982), consistent with the Proterozoic Z age of the Mattapan Volcanic Complex (Kaye and Zartman, 1980). These rocks are also little deformed or metamorphosed and do not have features that one might expect of rocks that acted as one side of a "vise" that squeezed the Acadian central mobile belt.

The Carboniferous sedimentary rocks in eastern Massachusetts are in the Narragansett and Norfolk basins. These rocks have been locally deformed and metamorphosed, especially toward the south (Skehan and others, 1976; Grew and Day, 1972; Quinn, 1971; Farrens and

Mosher, 1982), but over large tracts they have been subjected to only low-grade metamorphism and to even less penetrative deformation (see Murray and Skehan, 1979). How did these basins evolve? Belt (1968) proposed a model for the similar-aged and presumably tectonically related basins of the Canadian Maritime Provinces that involved penecontemporaneous extension of the crust. However, penecontemporaneous crustal motions involving a large strike-slip component seems possible, as has been suggested by Webb (1969); the formation of such basins would produce areas of alternating compression and dilatation (see Harland, 1971; also articles *in* Ballance and Reading, 1980). This last prediction appears consistent with the observed tectonic environments of the Carboniferous rocks of the Atlantic seaboard (Mosher, 1981).

If this inference of oblique-slip formation of Carboniferous basins and synchronous sedimentation is correct, it implies that the basement rocks on opposite sides of a given basin, such as the Narragansett, might be entirely different because of significant strike-slip motion. On older geologic maps of eastern Massachusetts (e.g., Emerson, 1917), the east end of the Narragansett basin is shown to end on land, and the granite-gneiss terrane is shown to continue around the end near the town of Marshfield. Such a continuity would deny significant strike-slip movement. Recent drilling for rock record by the U.S. Geological Survey to provide data for the new bedrock geologic map (Zen and others, 1983), however, shows that the Carboniferous rocks continue under glacial cover right to Boston Bay, as Murray and Skehan (1979) have previously independently inferred. Indeed, rocks south of the Narragansett basin are somewhat different from those immediately north of the basin; Richard Goldsmith (*in* Zen and others, 1983) discovered a sequence of metamorphosed mafic volcanic rocks in the southern terrane unlike rocks to the north, and its presence supports the idea that the substrate of Cape Cod and adjacent coastal land may be distinct from the main part of the Avalonian terrane of eastern Massachusetts. The Carboniferous basins may be fault bounded on one or both sides.

Skehan and others (1978) reported a Cambrian trilobite fauna from Beavertail Point on Conanicut Island in Narragansett Bay. To the east across the channel, the metamorphosed sedimentary sequence (Newport Formation of Murray and Skehan, 1979) of Aquidneck Island has been interpreted by Kay and Chapple (1976) as the basement on which the Cambrian rocks of Beavertail Point were laid down. These rocks are intruded by a granodiorite at the Cliffwalk trail that has a Rb-Sr isochron age of 595 Ma according to Smith (1978), quoted by Murray and Skehan (1979). The Cambrian rocks at Beavertail Point are considerably more deformed and metamorphosed than those near Boston, but the deformation may be related to movement along the postulated strike-slip basin-border

fault, as they similarly affect the Carboniferous rocks, which have also been subjected to considerable deformation and metamorphism (Mosher, 1981; Farrens and Mosher, 1982). The multiply deformed and low-grade metamorphosed rocks of Beavertail Point, and possibly also those of Aquidneck Point, might have been brought in from another area along the suggested strike-slip fault, even though they may well be part of the same general Avalonian terrane.

To summarize: In eastern Massachusetts and adjoining Rhode Island, there seem to be at least two recognizable terranes that were not "North American" in their complexion and architecture (stratigraphy, fauna, structure, metamorphism, age) at the time of the Acadian orogeny. These terranes are the Nashoba Block and the Dedham-Milford Block of Zen and others (1983). They are separated from each other and from the Acadian limit of the Appalachian orogen by systems of faults, some of which must have had large movements. The time of arrival of these blocks, if they are indeed exotic, cannot be fixed by local evidence because no dated local intrusive body is known to weld the blocks. The arrival time, however, was probably between Late Devonian and Early Pennsylvanian, bridging the time between the Acadian and Alleghanian orogenies. The geometry and kinematics of the faults separating these blocks need additional study (see Skehan, 1968). Anomalous rocks in the zone associated with the fault systems need to be examined for clues to the history of the tectonic emplacement of the blocks, as these anomalous rocks may themselves be remnant fragments of exotic blocks (a peculiar rock exposed on Wolfpen Hill near Marlborough in Massachusetts, shown to me by A. F. Shride, is an example; for others, such as the Greenleaf Mountain Formation, see Bell and Alvord, 1976).

A second candidate area for exotic terranes is the strip of land along the coast of Maine. The geology of this area was studied by Stewart and Wones (1974), Bickel (1976), Wones and Stewart (1976), Wones and Thompson (1979), Wones (1980), Osberg (1979), and Ludman (1981). A major east-northeast-striking fault, the Norumbega, separates the Silurian and Devonian argillite sequence of central Maine (the Vassalboro, Waterville, and "Sangerville" Formations; Osberg, 1979) from rocks to the southeast, somewhat the way the Clinton-Newbury fault separates the Silurian and Devonian and possibly older shaly rocks of Acadian North America from the strange rocks to the east. The Norumbega fault has apparently undergone extensive ductile deformation, as indicated by a wide mylonite (pseudotacolite) zone (Stewart and Wones, 1974, p. 231). Immediately south of it, feldspathic augen gneiss makes up a large terrane; this unit, the Passagassawakeag Gneiss (Bickel, 1976), of undefined though probable Proterozoic age, is polydeformed. This terrane resembles the Nashoba Block in its tectonic position, apparent age, and rock type. The Passagassawakeag is overlain (Stewart and Wones, 1974; Bickel, 1976) by metamorphosed younger sedimentary rocks assigned to the Cambrian (Wing, 1957) or to the Cambrian or Ordovician (Bickel, 1976) and then intruded by rocks having a 430-Ma zircon age (Stewart and Wones, 1974, p. 232).

Other distinctive rock sequences south of the Norumbega fault include the Bucksport block, in probable fault contact against the Passagassawakeag and showing a decided hiatus in metamorphic grade against the latter. The Bucksport Formation of Wing (1957) was assigned to the Ordovician by Stewart and Wones (1974), but Wones (1980) has correlated it with the Silurian part of the Vassalboro Formation. Wones, (1980, p. 414), however, cautioned that such a correlation does not require that movement on the fault is minor, as "rocks similar to the Vassalboro are known from Long Island Sound in the south to the St. John River in New Brunswick." Wing's Bucksport is overlain by the Appleton Ridge Formation of Bickel (1976) which has an Ordovician (455 ± 25 Ma) Rb-Sr isochron age (Brookins, 1976; Stewart and Wones, 1974).

The Penobscot Formation has been assigned by Stewart and Wones (1974) to yet another block south of the Norumbega fault. They correlated the unit with similar-looking rocks at nearby Benner Hill (Boucot and others, 1972; Osberg and Guidotti, 1974) and in New Brunswick, both of which contain Ordovician fossils. Wones (1980) summarized existing views and problems of its contact relations and of dating the tectonic events associated with it. However that may be, rocks of the Passagassawakeag, Bucksport, and Penobscot blocks do appear to overlap in age but differ in metamorphic grades, rock assemblages, and thicknesses. They are probably exotic, and also exotic with respect to the rocks north of the Norumbega fault that are presumed to have been part of the North American craton at the time of the Acadian orogeny. Both right-lateral and left-lateral fault-movement senses have been suggested for the Norumbega, and right-lateral movements have been demonstrated (Wones and Stewart, 1976; Wones and Thompson, 1979); paleomagnetic data, cited below, suggest that left-lateral movement should have predominated. The Norumbega fault is but one fault and may not be the master fault, in a fault zone, so the cumulative displacement and sense of movement are more important than those on a single fault.

Farther southeast, the rocks just mentioned are separated by another large fault, the Turtlehead, from rocks farther seaward. According to Stewart and Wones (1974), these rocks are in two blocks. The Islesboro block includes the Islesboro Formation of mafic greenstone, gray and green slate, limestone, dolostone, quartzite, and conglomerate, and rocks of the Seven Hundred Acre Island,

consisting of schist, amphibolite, quartzite, and marble. Stewart (1974, p. 90), on the basis of lithologic similarity to "virtual identity," correlated these latter rocks with the Green Head Formation of New Brunswick. Brookins (1976) provided a whole-rock Rb-Sr isochron of 750 ± 100 Ma for rocks of the Seven Hundred Acres Island; crosscutting pegmatite gave a 600 ± 20-Ma, an Avalonian age (possible inconsistencies of various authors' correlations have already been noted). The other, the Ellsworth block, consists of low-grade greenstone and associated feldspathic phyllite. Rocks of the block show lower metamorphic grade, different structural history and lithology from those of the Islesboro block; a 510 ± 15-Ma isochron age, or Cambrian age, has been assigned (Brookins, 1976) to it.

No Cambrian fossil has been found in the coastal belt of Maine. In New Brunswick and in the eastern Massachusetts–Rhode Island area, as we have seen, Cambrian fossil-bearing rocks are associated with schist, gneiss, and carbonate rocks that can be correlated on a lithic basis with rocks of the Islesboro block of Stewart and Wones (1974). The Islesboro is indeed the block that has provided the 600-Ma or Avalonian radiometric ages on intrusive bodies in Maine (see also Rast and others, 1976a, 1976b; Rodgers, 1972).

The possibility seems real that the coastal "Avalonian" belt of Maine and, by extrapolation, of New Brunswick and even Nova Scotia, including the Antigonish Highlands and Cape Breton Island, is made up not of a simple tectonic and stratigraphic unit but a hodgepodge of several units in a tectonic megabreccia, having blocks as large as many tens, or possibly even hundreds, of kilometers. The entire zone may itself be an exotic block relative to the rest of the Appalachian system.

Ludman (1981) suggested that rocks of the coastal belt of Maine have evolved together and share sedimentary as well as tectonic histories. This interpretation is in direct contrast to that of Stewart and Wones (1974), and this conflict must be resolved. Paleomagnetic data may eventually provide the definitive tests. Available data from this area are sparse and enigmatic. Spariosu and Kent (1980) have indicated that the Devonian Traveler Rhyolite in the northern part of the Merrimack synclinorium has an anomalous pole position (29°N, 82°E) compared with either North America or "Acadia" (Kent and Opdyke, 1978, 1979, 1980). The coastal volcanic rocks near Eastport, Maine, in contrast, have a typical "Acadia" orientation (Kent and Opdyke, 1980). The paleomagnetic data are useful because they at least show that things are very complex and that mutually far-traveled rocks probably have become juxtaposed. Blocks may have been assembled at different times and in different parts of the globe. The contrast between the "exotic terrane" interpretation and that of Ludman (1981), quite apart from the paleomagnetic input, is reminiscent of the ongoing discussion of whether the Modoc fault in eastern South Carolina and Georgia, which separates the Kiokee belt from the Carolina slate belt, is a major fault or only a front of deformation and metamorphism (see Snoke and others, 1980a, 1980b; Secor and Snoke, 1978; and Hatcher and Zietz, 1980, for discussions and references). This analogy may be more than a mere coincidence, for the Carolina slate belt has yielded an Atlantic Province Cambrian trilobite and Avalonian magmatic ages, whereas the Kiokee belt (and the Raleigh belt) may correlate with some of the other terranes of coastal Maine.

The age of welding of the blocks, or at least of cessation of major movement on the faults, has not been specifically established. As indicated previously, this age is unknown in Massachusetts, except that it must be post-Middle Devonian. The evolution of the Pennsylvanian rocks of the Narragansett and Norfolk basins, which include conglomerates containing clasts not readily identified with rocks now immediately bordering the basin, suggests possible beheaded source terranes and thus some movement after that time (after Westphalian and Stephanian; Lyons, 1979). There is no record of sedimentary rocks that lap across the boundaries of two exotic terranes that might help to date their mutual welding as in the western Cordillera (e.g., Berg and others, 1978). Information on time of welding is better in Maine. The Turtlehead fault is intruded by the Lucerne pluton, which gives a Pb-Pb radiometric age of 380 ± 3 Ma (Wones, 1980) and cuts Lower Devonian rocks, whereas the Norumbega fault cuts the pluton (Wones and Thompson, 1979). Thus, some amalgamation of blocks within the Avalonian terrane was pre-Carboniferous. The continuation of the Norumbega fault into New Brunswick, there called the Fredericton fault, deforms the lower part of the Carboniferous rocks of the Fredericton basin; thus, this fault must have been active as late as the early part of the Carboniferous, and its movement history spans the time between the Acadian and Alleghanian orogenies. Age of movement, determined on the same basis, across the Dover fault and its southward continuation, the Hermitage Bay fault, which separates the Avalon sequence from rocks of the Gander zone in eastern Newfoundland, is provided by a Rb-Sr isochron of 345 ± 5 Ma for the Ackley City batholith (Bell and others, 1977; see Colman-Sadd, 1980, for details and references). All told, the data, scanty as they are, at least are consistent in the age of welding.

I will not discuss the relations of possible exotic blocks in the Avalonian terrane in the Maritime Provinces of Canada. Among the many and excellent summaries of the geology of these areas in New Brunswick, Nova Scotia, and Newfoundland are those by Rodgers (1972), Rast and others (1976a, 1976b), Colman-Sadd (1980), and Williams (1979). Suffice it to note that the reported relations generally are similar to those of coastal Maine and eastern Massachusetts: Relatively little deformed or metamorphosed lower Paleozoic, particularly Cambrian, sedimentary rocks carrying the *Paradoxides* and *Callavia* faunas (Palmer, 1971) rest unconformably on Proterozoic Z sedimentary rocks and gneisses. These Proterozoic Z rocks are intruded by granitic rocks that have a typical "Avalonian," that is, about 600-Ma age and at places show a 750-Ma thermal geochronologic record, as mentioned previously. Grenvillian ages are generally absent, though Olszewski and others (1981) reported anomalous model Rb/Sr ages of 917 and 973 Ma on Cape Breton Island.

In summary, what is traditionally called the "Avalonian" belt in the eastern part of the present Appalachian orogen appears to be far from uniform. It contains a heterogeneous aggregation of crustal blocks having different sedimentary, tectonic, metamorphic, and probably magmatic histories; some blocks show different but synchronous evolutionary events. The blocks do not everywhere have clear mutual relations, but major fault boundaries seem well documented at some places, such as eastern Massachusetts. Ages of amalgamation of these blocks remain a problem. The important features shared by these rocks are that they are not known to have a Grenvillian basement, that the Cambrian faunas are of the Atlantic Province, and that many of the rocks have undergone a 600-Ma thermal event. Some blocks have a 750-Ma thermal record; this is not known in areas of the Merrimack terrane. The terrane boundaries toward the Taconian or Acadian North American craton cannot be defined unambiguously because of the uncertain evolutionary history of the Merrimack synclinorium. However, within or at the boundary of the east side of the synclinorium—toward the coast today—this boundary seems to be marked by fault systems of first-order importance, and these are probably high-angle faults, some of which show intense shearing. The recent paleomagnetic data from this belt (Kent and Opdyke, 1978, 1979, 1980; Irving, 1979) suggest that the Avalonian terrane moved into place in late Acadian to early Carboniferous time, consistent with radiometric ages that are related to tectonic and plutonic activities, as summarized above.

In contrast, Kirschvink (1979) measured paleomagnetic data for the Cambrian rocks of Burin Peninsula of the Avalon area and suggested that the area was possibly already a part of North America in Late Cambrian time. Though Kirschvink's data can be interpreted in an alternative way, that is, that this part of the Avalon was contiguous with parts of Great Britain in Ordovician time, the results do suggest inconsistency, and they caution against hasty conclusions based on paleomagnetic information.

There is one interesting test that can be applied to the concept that the Avalonian terrane of Maine, Massachusetts, and Rhode Island, as well as those of nearby Canada, is exotic and had been transported for distances indicated by the paleomagnetic data. In eastern Pennsylvania, there exists a sequence of Mississippian and Pennsylvanian sedimentary rocks, aggregating at least 3 km thick and having the coarsest and thickest parts to the southeast (Colton, 1970). Yet a southeasterly source area of the required size is not in sight. One could argue that the source area is buried under the coastal plain sediments and is part of the foundered continental crust that resulted from the opening of the Atlantic Ocean. As an alternative, one wonders whether Avalonia could be the transient source terrane. Could this conjecture be tested by comparing the petrographic, geochemical, or geochronological signatures of the two groups of rocks? Earlier I have summarized information that points to a 750-Ma event that seems to be prevalent in and peculiar to the Avalonian rocks of New England and adjacent Canada. Could evidence for the same event be recovered from the detrital zircon of the Mississippian and Pennsylvanian rocks of eastern Pennsylvania? If so, we would have a direct tie between the sourceless sedimentary rocks and the passage of a docked but not yet welded exotic terrane.

CONCLUSIONS

In this paper, I have indulged in speculations and have tried to show that there are indeed rock sequences in the northern Appalachian orogen that allow possible interpretation as exotic terranes relative to their neighbors and to an undisputed North American craton at that time of the geologic history appropriate to the terrane. These suspect terranes, or at least potentially suspect terranes, ought to be examined more closely. The most obvious, and generally accepted, candidates are the group of terranes collectively known as Avalonia; to this group, the Meguma terrane of Nova Scotia no doubt should be added (Schenk, 1980; Williams, 1979). I have, however, tried to show that, at least in coastal New England, Avalonia is itself complex, that it probably did not have anything to do with the closing of Iapetus Ocean during Paleozoic time, and that it may be totally adventitious as far as a significant role in the evolution of the New England Appalachian fold system is concerned. Rather, it may be a very late comer, arriving only a short time prior to the breakup of Pangea at the beginning of Mesozoic time. The paleomagnetic data of Kent and Opdyke (1978, 1979, 1980) are particularly significant, as they show that Acadia (or, in my usage, Avalonia *sensu lato*) was welded to the rest of North America in early Carboniferous time (roughly corresponding to the time interval between the known age of movement on the Norumbega fault and the age of intrusion of the Lucerne pluton that welded blocks within this terrane). However, the age of welding for a given area should not be extrapolated to all of Acadia;

diachronous welding seems more likely, and local paleomagnetic and radiometric data must be obtained for each segment to work out the details.

Spariosu and Kent (1980) reported paleomagnetic evidence of rotation of terranes in central Maine. This rotation may be related to the Acadian evolution of the Merrimack synclinorium, the tectonic element at the core of Acadian deformation in the New England Appalachians and the site of many enigmatic flysch-type sedimentary rocks. These phenomena may have a significant common thread; a dominant role for Acadian strike-slip motion may be one solution. However, we must eventually solve the younger movement picture before we can begin to deconvolute older motions properly. Solutions to the Acadian problems are in turn the antecedents for completely assessing the closing history of the Iapetus, both in Acadian and in Taconian time, and for assessing possible exotic terranes formed in the Taconian orogeny.

Clearly, many kinds of new data are needed to resolve some of the major puzzles. The gathering of high-quality paleomagnetic data obviously is a first-order demand. Rocks showing good reference horizons rather than massive intrusive rocks probably are less disputable, and there are plenty of candidates to be considered. Sedimentological studies of the rocks involved should furnish important clues to solving the jigsaw puzzle. For instance, the Carboniferous as well as older sedimentary rocks should be studied for evidence of penecontemporaneous tectonic movement, for the nature and location of source areas, for their tectonic-sedimentary facies, and for any evidence of beheaded sedimentary piles. Geochemical evidence and criteria to define different basement blocks and plutonic rocks that intrude them seem a potentially important tool. Thus, for a first cut, we can look for differences in the oldest postorogenic plutonic rocks as samples of the basement; different blocks as defined by paleomagnetic data can be compared. Up to now, in the absence of other evidence, apparent ages of crustal blocks have been used for their correlation. Time of last thermal setting of isotopic clocks may be a useful tool, but hardly definitive. Furthermore, *even rocks of the same craton may become mutually exotic through large-scale relative motion*. However, if two crustal blocks have had different cumulative evolutionary histories, their geochemical evolution, assuming initial homogeneity, should diverge. The plutonic rocks they produce, therefore, should still show important differences that can be useful clues, even with the masking effect of similar last major thermal history.

Criteria for determination of crustal sutures (used in the broad sense, and not confined to subduction sutures) need to be developed and refined. Is there any intrinsic way to estimate the amount of strain in a shear zone that might be used to estimate the amount and direction of motion? Can we unequivocally determine the origin of ultramafic bodies, for example, by their geochemical properties to discover whether a given body is a metamorphic segregation, a remnant of an oceanic ophiolite, or a fragment of a layered intrusion or diapiric intrusion into a sialic crust? Can the use of initial Nd ratios (e.g., Shaw and others, 1981) or relative abundance of the platinum metals (N. J. Page, 1981, written commun.) serve the purpose adequately? Lack of this kind of provenance information has greatly hampered our ability to utilize the ultramafic bodies and belts in the Appalachians for tectonic reconstruction, and we must devise new tools so that we may use the information contained in these rocks more fully, especially as they are obscured by complex metamorphic and deformational history.

A discussion of exotic terranes in the northern Appalachians in any confident way is clearly premature; we have as yet neither definitive evidence nor the necessary tools for a proper evaluation of the evidence. However, the presence of exotic terranes in young and contemporary orogenic belts related to plate margins seems to demand that we give serious consideration to the possible presence of exotic terranes in the Appalachians and other Paleozoic mountain belts, and we need to gear up for this new exciting round of Appalachian tectonic thinking, sort out our assumptions, evaluate their validity, and decide which are fundamental to tectonics and which are merely appendages of particular frames of reference.

ACKNOWLEDGMENTS

Many ideas contained in this study derived from a graduate seminar that I conducted, jointly with John Suppe, at Princeton University in the spring of 1981, while I was Harry H. Hess Visiting Fellow. For the criticisms, contributions, and encouragement by members of that seminar, and for the opportunity afforded by the Department of Geological and Geophysical Sciences, I am grateful. In particular, I want to thank these members of the department and guest lecturers: A. G. Fischer, J. E. Suppe, L. S. Hollister, A. R. Palmer, N. D. Opdyke, R. D. Hatcher, Jr., F. B. van Houten, F. J. Spera, V. B. Sisson, W. J. Morgan, R. A. Phinney, J. L. Kirschvink, Mike Covey, K. S. Deffeyes, and J. B. Evans. Others who have added to my knowledge include N. M. Ratcliffe, D. J. Milton, A. A. Drake, Jr., D. B. Stewart, W. H. Diment, Louis Pavlides, N. L. Hatch, Jr., D. W. Rankin, P. H. Osberg, D. S. Harwood, R. S. Stanley, L. D. Harris, W. S. McKerrow, M. F. Kane, Richard Goldsmith, J. G. Arth, A. G. Harris, Harold Williams, D. R. Wones, D. T. Secor, Jr., A. W. Snoke, R. B. Neuman, and J. F. Dewey. The paper was reviewed by Drake, Stewart, Pavlides, Hatch, Palmer, Hatcher, and Williams; I thank them for their very substantial help. The responsibility for ideas in this paper, fantastic or otherwise, is, however, entirely my own.

REFERENCES CITED

Albee, A. L., and Boudette, E. L., 1972, Geology of the Attean quadrangle, Somerset County, Maine: U.S. Geological Survey Bulletin 1297, 110 p.

Aleinikoff, J. N., Zartman, R. E., and Lyons, J. B., 1979, U-Th-Pb geochronology of the Massabesic Gneiss and the granite near Milford, south-central New Hampshire; new evidence for Avalonian basement and Taconic and Alleghenian [sic] disturbances in eastern New England: Contributions to Mineralogy and Petrology, v. 71, p. 1–11.

Ando, C. J., Cook, F. A., Oliver, J. E., Brown, L. D., and Kaufman, Sidney, 1982, Crustal geometry of the Appalachian orogen from seismic reflection studies: Geological Society of America Abstracts with Programs, v. 14, p. 2.

Arthaud, Francois, and Matte, Phillipe, 1977, Late Paleozoic strike-slip faulting in southern Europe and northern Africa: Result of a right-lateral shear zone between the Appalachians and the Urals: Geological Society of America Bulletin, v. 88, p. 1305–1320.

Ballance, P. F., and Reading, H. G., 1980, Sedimentation in oblique-slip mobile zones: International Association of Sedimentologists Special Publication 4, 265 p.

Beck, M. E., Cox, A. V., and Jones, D. L., 1980, Mesozoic and Cenozoic microplate tectonics of western North America: Penrose Conference Report, Geology, v. 8, p. 454–456.

Beiers, R. J., 1976, Quebec lowlands: Overview and hydrocarbon potential, *in* Shumaker, R. C., and Overbey, W. K., Jr., eds., Devonian shale production and potential: 7th Appalachian Petroleum Geology Symposium, Proceedings, Energy Research and Development Administration—Morgantown Energy Research Center, Sp 7612, p. 142–161.

Bell, G. K., Jr., 1936, Poundridge [sic] [New York] granite [abs.]: Geological Society of America Proceedings, 1935, p. 65–66.

Bell, Keith, Blenkinsop, John, and Strong, D. F., 1977, The geochronology of some granitic bodies from eastern Newfoundland and its bearing on Appalachian evolution: Canadian Journal of Earth Sciences, v. 14, p. 456–476.

Bell, K. G., and Alvord, D. C., 1976, Pre-Silurian stratigraphy of northeastern Massachusetts, *in* Page, L. R., ed., Contributions to the stratigraphy of New England: Geological Society of America Memoir 148, p. 179–216.

Belt, E. S., 1968, Post-Acadian rifts and related facies, Eastern Canada, *in* Zen, E-an, and others, eds., Studies of Appalachian geology: Northern and maritime: New York, Wiley-Interscience, p. 95–113.

Ben-Avraham, Zvi, Nur, Amos, Jones, D. L., and Cox, A. V., 1981, Continental accretion: From oceanic plateaus to allochthonous terranes: Science, v. 213, p. 47–54.

Berg, H. C., Jones, D. L., and Coney, P. J., 1978, Map showing pre-Cenozoic tectonostratigraphic terranes of southeastern Alaska and adjacent areas: U.S. Geological Survey Open-File Report 78-1085, 2 sheets.

Bickel, C. E., 1976, Stratigraphy of the Belfast quadrangle, Maine, *in* Page, L. R., ed., Contributions to the stratigraphy of New England: Geological Society of America Memoir 148, p. 97–128.

Billings, M. P., 1956, The geology of New Hampshire, Pt. II, Bedrock geology: New Hampshire State Planning and Development Commission, 200 p.

Bird, J. M., and Dewey, J. F., 1970, Lithosphere plate—continental margin tectonics and the evolution of the Appalachian orogen: Geological Society of America Bulletin, v. 81, p. 1031–1059.

Bluck, B. J., Halliday, A. N., Aftalion, M., and Macintyre, R. M., 1980, Age and origin of Ballantrae ophiolite and its significance to the Caledonian orogeny and Ordovician time scale: Geology, v. 8, p. 492–495.

Bosworth, William, and Vollmer, F. W., 1981, Formation of melange in a foreland basin overthrust setting: Example from the Taconic orogen: Geological Society of America Abstracts with Programs, v. 13, p. 413.

Bothner, W. A., Simpson, R. W., and Diment, W. H., 1980, Bouguer gravity map of the northeastern United States and adjacent Canada: U.S. Geological Survey Open-File Report 80-2012, scale 1:1,000,000.

Boucot, A. J., 1961, Stratigraphy of the Moose River synclinorium, Maine: U.S. Geological Survey Bulletin 1111E, p. 153–188.

Boucot, A. J., Field, M. T., Fletcher, Raymond, Forbes, W. H., Naylor, R. S. and Pavlides, Louis, 1964, Reconnaissance bedrock geology of the Presque Isle quadrangle, Maine: Maine Geological Survey Quadrangle Mapping ser. no. 2, 123 p.

Boucot, A. J., Brookins, D. G., Forbes, William, and Guidotti, C. V., 1972, Staurolite zone Caradoc (Middle-Late Ordovician) age, Old World Province brachiopods from Penobscot Bay, Maine: Geological Society of America Bulletin, v. 83, p. 1953–1960.

Boudette, E. L., 1970, Pre-Silurian rocks in the Boundary Mountains anticlinorium, northwestern Maine: Excursion C *in* Boone, G. M., ed., New England Intercollegiate Geological Conference Guidebook, 62nd Annual Meeting, Rangeley, Maine: Department of Geology, Syracuse University, p. C1–21.

——1981, Ophiolite assemblage of early Paleozoic age in central western Maine: Geological Association of Canada Special Paper 24, p. 209–230.

Boudette, E. L., and Boone, G. M., 1976, Pre-Silurian stratigraphic succession in central western Maine, *in* Page, L. R., ed., Contributions to the stratigraphy of New England: Geological Society of America Memoir 148, p. 79–96.

Brookins, D. G., 1976, Geochronologic contributions to stratigraphic interpretation and correlation in the Penobscot Bay area, eastern Maine, *in* Page, L. R., ed., Contributions to the stratigraphy of New England: Geological Society of America Memoir 148, p. 129–145.

Brown, R. L., 1980, Frenchman Cap dome, Shuswap Complex, B. C.—a progress report: Geological Survey of Canada Paper 80-1A, p. 47–51.

Cady, W. M., 1968, The lateral transition from the miogeosynclinal to the eugeosynclinal zone in northwestern New England and adjacent Quebec, *in* Zen, E-an, and others, eds., Studies of Appalachian geology: Northern and maritime: New York, Wiley-Interscience, p. 151–161.

Cady, W. M., 1969, Regional tectonic synthesis of northwestern New England and adjacent Quebec: Geological Society of America Memoir 120, 181 p.

Chidester, A. H., 1968, Evolution of the ultramafic complexes of northwestern New England, *in* Zen, E-an, and others, eds., Studies of Appalachian geology: Northern and maritime; New York, Wiley-Interscience, p. 343–354.

Church, W. R., 1969, Metamorphic rocks of Burlington Peninsula and adjoining areas of Newfoundland, and their bearing on continental drift in North Atlantic, *in* Kay, M., ed., North Atlantic: Geology and continental drift: American Association of Petroleum Geologists Memoir 12, p. 212–233.

Churkin, Michael, Jr., Carter, Claire, and Trexler, J. H., Jr., 1980, Collision-deformed Paleozoic continental margin of Alaska—Foundation for microplate accretion: Geological Society of America Bulletin, Part I, v. 91, p. 648–654.

Clark, G. S., and Kulp, J. L., 1968, Isotopic age study of metamorphism and intrusion in western Connecticut and southeastern New York: American Journal of Science, v. 266, p. 865–894.

Clark, T. H., 1934, Structure and stratigraphy of southern Quebec: Geological Society of America Bulletin, v. 45, p. 1–20.

Colman-Sadd, S. P., 1980, Geology of south-central Newfoundland and evolution of the eastern margin of Iapetus: American Journal of Science, v. 280, p. 991–1017.

Colton, G. W., 1970, The Appalachian basin—its depositional sequences and their geologic relationships, *in* Fisher, G. W., and others, eds., Studies of Appalachian geology: Central and southern: New York, Interscience Publishers, p. 5–47.

Coney, P. J., Jones, D. L., and Monger, J.W.H., 1980, Cordilleran suspect terranes: Nature, v. 288, p. 329–333.

Cormier, R. F., 1969, Radiometric dating of the Coldbrook Group of southern New Brunswick, Canada: Canadian Journal of Earth Sciences, v. 6, p. 393–398.

Dewey, J. F., and Şengör, A.M.C., 1979, Aegean and surrounding regions: Complex multiplate and continuum tectonics in a convergent zone: Geological Society of America Bulletin, Part I, v. 90, p. 84–92.

Dewey, J. F., Pitman, W. C. III, Ryan, W.B.F., and Bonnin, Jean, 1973, Plate tectonics and the evolution of the Alpine system: Geological Society of America Bulletin, v. 84, p. 3137–3180.

DeWit, M. J., and Strong, D. F., 1975, Eclogite-bearing amphibolites from the Appalachian mobile belt, northwest Newfoundland: Dry versus wet metamorphism: Journal of Geology, v. 83, p. 609–627.

Dixon, H. R., and Lundgren, L. W., Jr., 1968, Structure of eastern Connecticut, *in* Zen, E-an, and others, eds., Studies of Appalachian geology: Northern and maritime: New York, Wiley-Interscience, p. 219–229.

Doll, C. G., Cady, W. M., Thompson, J. B., Jr., and Billings, M. P., 1961, Centennial geologic map of Vermont: Vermont Geological Survey, scale 1:250,000.

Doolan, B. L., Drake, J. C., and Crocker, David, 1973, Actinolite and subcalcic hornblende from a greenstone of Hazen's Notch Formation, Lincoln Mountain quadrangle, Warren, Vermont: Geological Society of America Abstracts with Programs, v. 5, p. 157.

Dowse, A. M., 1950, New evidence on the Cambrian contact at Hoppin Hill, North Attleboro, Massachusetts: American Journal of Science, v. 248, p. 95–99.

Eisenberg, R. A., 1981, Chronostratigraphy of metavolcanic and associated intrusive rocks of the Boundary Mountains Anticlinorium: Geological Society of America Abstracts with Programs, v. 13, p. 131.

Emerson, B. K., 1917, Geology of Massachusetts and Rhode Island: U.S. Geological Survey Bulletin 597, 289 p.

Farrens, Christine, and Mosher, Sharon, 1982, Alleghenian deformation in southeastern Narragansett basin, R.I.: Geological Society of America Abstracts with Programs, v. 14, p. 17.

Faul, Henry, Stern, T. W., Thomas, H. H., and Elmore, P.L.D., 1963, Ages of intrusion and metamorphism in the northern Appalachians: American Journal of Science, v. 261, p. 1–19.

Foland, K. A., and Loiselle, M. C., 1981, Oliverian syenites of the Pliny region, northern New Hampshire: Geological Society of America Bulletin, Part I, v. 92, p. 179–188.

Green, J. C., and Guidotti, C. V., 1968, The Boundary Mountains anticlinorium in northern New Hampshire and northwestern Maine, *in* Zen, E-an, and others, eds., Studies of Appalachian geology: Northern and maritime: New York, Wiley-Interscience, p. 255–266.

Grew, E. S., and Day, H. W., 1972, Staurolite, kyanite, and sillimanite from the Narragansett basin of Rhode Island: U.S. Geological Survey Professional Paper 800-D, p. D151–D157.

Hall, B. A., 1970, Stratigraphy of the southern end of the Munsungun anticlinorium, Maine: Maine Geological Survey Bulletin 22, 63 p.

Hall, B. A., Pollock, S. G., and Dolan, K. M., 1976, Lower Devonian Seboomook Formation and Matagamon sandstone, northern Maine: A flysch basin-margin delta complex, *in* Page, L. R., ed., Contributions to the stratigraphy of New England: Geological Society of America Memoir 148, p. 57–63.

Hamilton, Warren, 1969, Mesozoic California and the underflow of Pacific mantle: Geological Society of America Bulletin, v. 80, p. 2409–2430.

——1970, The Uralides and the motion of the Russian and Siberian platforms: Geological Society of America Bulletin, v. 81, p. 2553–2576.

——1978, Mesozoic tectonics of the western United States, in Howell, D. G., and McDougall, K. A., eds., Mesozoic paleogeography of the western United States: Pacific Section, Society of Economic Paleontologists and Mineralogists, Pacific Coast Paleogeography Symposium 2, p. 33–70.

——1979, Tectonics of the Indonesian region: U.S. Geological Survey Professional Paper 1078, 345 p.

Harland, W. B., 1971, Tectonic transpression in Caledonian Spitsbergen: Geological Magazine, v. 108, p. 27–42.

Hardwood [sic], D. S., 1976, Clinopyroxene-plagioclase simplectite after omphacite and polymetamorphism of allochthonous rocks in northwestern Connecticut: Geological Society of America Abstracts with Programs, v. 8, p. 189.

Harwood, D. S., Compiler, 1979a, Geologic map of northeastern United States and adjacent Canada: U.S. Geological Survey Open-File Report 79-374, scale 1:1,000,000, 3 sheets.

——1979b, Geologic map of the South Sandisfield quadrangle, Massachusetts and Connecticut: U.S. Geological Survey Geologic Quadrangle Map GQ-1519.

Harwood, D. S., and Zietz, Isidore, 1976, Geologic interpretation of an aeromagnetic map of southern New England: U.S. Geological Survey Geophysical Investigations Map GP 906, scale 1:250,000.

Hatch, N. L., Jr., 1963, The geology of the Dixville quadrangle, New Hampshire: New Hampshire Department of Resources and Economic Development Bulletin 1, 81 p.

Hatcher, R. D., Jr., and Zietz, Isidore, 1980, Tectonic implications of regional aeromagnetic and gravity data from the southern Appalachians, in Wones, D. R., ed., The Caledonides in the U.S.A., IGCP Project 27 Proceedings: Caledonides Orogen, 1979 Meeting, Blacksburg, Virginia: Virginia Polytechnic Institute and State University, Department of Geological Sciences Memoir 2, p. 235–244.

Haworth, R. T., Daniels, D. C., Williams, Harold, and Zietz, Isidore, 1980, Bouguer gravity anomaly map of the Appalachian orogen: St. John's, Memorial University of Newfoundland, Map no. 3, scale 1:1,000,000.

Helmstaedt, Herwart, 1971, Structural geology of Portage Lakes area, Bathurst-Newcastle district, New Brunswick: Geological Survey of Canada Paper 70-28.

Hildenbrand, T. G., Simpson, R. W., Jr., Godson, R. H., and Kane, M. F., 1982, Digital colored residual and regional Bouguer gravity maps of the conterminous United States with cut-off wavelengths of 250 and 1000 Km: U.S. Geological Survey Geophysical Investigations Map GP 953-A.

Hillhouse, J. W., 1977, Paleomagnetism of the Triassic Nikolai Greenstone, McCarthy Quadrangle, Alaska: Canadian Journal of Earth Sciences, v. 14, p. 2578–2592.

Hills, F. A., and Dasch, E. J., 1968, Rb-Sr evidence for metamorphic remobilization of the Stony Creek granite, southeastern Connecticut: Geological Society of America Special Paper 121, p. 136–137.

Hsü, K. J., 1960, Paleocurrent structure and paleogeography of the ultrahelvetic flysch basins, Switzerland: Geological Society of America Bulletin, v. 71, p. 577–610.

Irving, Edward, 1979, Paleopoles and paleolatitudes of North America and speculations about displaced terrains: Canadian Journal of Earth Sciences, v. 16, p. 669–694.

Jamieson, R. A., 1977, The first metamorphic sodic amphibole identified from the Newfoundland Appalachians—its occurrence, composition, and possible tectonic implications: Nature, v. 265, p. 428–430.

Jones, D. L., Silberling, N. J., and Hillhouse, J. W., 1977, Wrangellia—A displaced terrane in northwestern North America: Canadian Journal of Earth Sciences, v. 14, p. 2565–2577.

Jones, D. L., Silberling, N. J., Csejtey, Béla, Jr., Nelson, W. H., and Blome, C. D., 1980, Age and structural significance of ophiolite and adjoining rocks in the Upper Chulitna District, south-central Alaska: U.S. Geological Survey Professional Paper 1121-A, 21 p.

Kane, M. F., and Bromery, R. W., 1968, Gravity anomalies in Maine, in Zen, E-an, and others, eds., Studies of Appalachian geology: Northern and maritime: New York, Wiley-Interscience, p. 415–423.

Kay, Marshall, 1969, Silurian of northeast Newfoundland coast, in Kay, M., ed., North Atlantic: Geology and continental drift: American Association of Petroleum Geologists Memoir 12, p. 414–424.

——1976, Dunnage melange and subduction of the Protacadic ocean, northeast Newfoundland: Geological Society of America Special Paper 175, 49 p.

Kay, S. M., and Chapple, W. M., 1976, Pre-Pennsylvanian rocks of Aquidneck and Conanicut Islands, Rhode Island, in Cameron, Barry, ed., New England Intercollegiate Geological Conference Guidebook, 68th Annual Meeting, Boston: Science Press, Princeton University, p. 428–446.

Kaye, C. A., and Zartman, R. E., 1980, A late Proterozoic Z to Cambrian age for the stratified rocks of the Boston basin, Massachusetts, U.S.A., in Wones, D. R., ed., The Caledonides in the U.S.A.: IGCP Proceedings, Project 27: Department of Geological Sciences Virginia Polytechnics Institute Memoir 2, p. 257–261.

Kent, D. V., and Opdyke, N. D., 1978, Paleomagnetism of the Devonian Catskill Red Beds: Evidence for motion of coastal New England–Canadian maritime region relative to cratonic North America: Journal of Geophysical Research, v. 83, p. 4441–4450.

——1979, The early Carboniferous paleomagnetic field of North America and its bearing on tectonics of the northern Appalachians: Earth and Planetary Science Letters, v. 44, p. 365–372.

——1980, Paleomagnetism of Siluro-Devonian rocks from eastern Maine: Canadian Journal of Earth Sciences, v. 17, p. 1653–1665.

Kirschvink, J. L., 1979, I. A paleomagnetic approach to the Precambrian-Cambrian boundary problem. II. Biogenic magnetite: Its role in the magnetization of sediments and as the basis of magnetic field detection in animals [Ph.D. thesis]: Princeton University, 277 p.

Kovach, Adam, Hurley, P. M., and Fairbairn, H. W., 1977, Rb-Sr whole rock age determinations of the Dedham granodiorite, eastern Massachusetts: American Journal of Science, v. 277, p. 905–911.

Laird, Jo, and Albee, A. L., 1981, High-pressure metamorphism in mafic schist from northern Vermont: American Journal of Science, v. 281, p. 97–126.

Lanphere, M. A., and Albee, A. L., 1974, ^{40}Ar/^{39}Ar age measurements in the Worcester Mountains: Evidence of Ordovician and Devonian metamorphic events in northern Vermont: American Journal of Science, v. 274, p. 545–555.

Laurent, Roger, 1977, Ophiolites from northern Appalachians of Quebec, in Coleman, R. G., and Irwin, W. P., eds., North American ophiolites: Oregon Department of Geology and Mineral Industries Bulletin 95, p. 25–40.

Leggett, J. K., McKerrow, W. S., and Eales, M. H., 1979, The southern Uplands of Scotland: a Lower Paleozoic accretionary prism: Geological Society of London Quarterly Journal, v. 136, p. 755–770.

Lenk, Cecilia, Strother, P. K., Kaye, C. A., and Barghoorn, E. S., 1982, Precambrian age of the Boston Basin: New evidence from microfossils: Science, v. 216, p. 619–620.

Leo, G. W., 1976, Geochemistry, origin, and age of the Glastonbury gneiss body, Massachusetts and Connecticut: A progress report: Geological Society of America Abstracts with Programs, v. 8, p. 217.

Long, L. E., 1969, Whole-rock Rb-Sr age of the Yonkers gneiss, Manhattan Prong: Geological Society of America Bulletin, v. 80, p. 2087–2090.

Ludman, Allan, 1981, Significance of transcurrent faulting in eastern

Maine and location of the suture between Avalonia and North America: American Journal of Science, v. 281, p. 463–483.

Lyons, P. C., 1979, in The Mississippian-Pennsylvanian (Carboniferous) systems in the United States—Massachusetts, Rhode Island, and Maine, by Skehan, J. W., S. J., Murray, D. P., Hepburn, J. C., Billings, M. P., Lyons, P. C., and Doyle, R. G.: U.S. Geological Survey Professional Paper 1110A, 30 p.

McKerrow, W. S., and Cocks, L.R.M., 1979, A lower Paleozoic trench-fill sequence, New World Island, Newfoundland: Geological Society of America Bulletin, v. 89, p. 1121–1132.

——1981, Stratigraphy of eastern Bay of Exploits, Newfoundland: Canadian Journal of Earth Sciences, v. 18, p. 751–764.

McLelland, James, and Isachsen, Yngvar, 1980, Structural synthesis of the southern and central Adirondacks: A model for the Adirondacks as a whole and plate-tectonic interpretations: Geological Society of America Bulletin, Part I, v. 91, p. 68–72; Part II, v. 91, p. 208–292.

Milton, D. J., 1961, Geology of the Old Speck Mountain quadrangle, Maine [Ph.D. thesis]: Harvard University, 190 p.

Moench, R. H., 1970, Premetamorphic down-to-basin faulting, folding, and tectonic dewatering, Rangeley area, western Maine: Geological Society of America Bulletin, v. 81, p. 1463–1496.

Monger, J.W.H., and Irving, Edward, 1980, Northward displacement of north-central British Columbia: Nature, v. 285, p. 289–294.

Monger, J.W.H., Souther, J. G., and Gabrielse, Hubert, 1972, Evolution of the Canadian Cordillera: A plate-tectonic model: American Journal of Science, v. 272, p. 577–602.

Morris, W. A., 1976, Transcurrent motion determined paleomagnetically in the northern Appalachians and Caledonides and the Acadian orogeny: Canadian Journal of Earth Sciences, v. 13, p. 1236–1243.

Mose, D. G., and Hayes, John, 1975, Avalonian igneous activity in the Manhattan Prong, southeastern New York: Geological Society of America Bulletin, v. 86, p. 929–932.

Mose, D. G., Eckelmann, F. D., and Hall, L. M., 1979, Age-determination and zircon morphology studies of the Yonkers and Pound Ridge granite gneisses in the Manhattan Prong, southeastern New York: Geological Society of America Abstracts with Programs, v. 11, p. 45–46.

Mosher, Sharon, 1981, Late Paleozoic deformation of the Narragansett Basin, Rhode Island: Geological Society of America Abstracts with Programs, v. 13, p. 515.

Murray, D. P., and Skehan, J. W., S. J., 1979, A traverse across the eastern margin of the Appalachian-Caledonian orogen, southeastern New England, in Skehan, J. W. S.J., and Osberg, P. H., eds., The Caledonides in the U.S.A., IGCP Project 27, Geological Excursions in the northeast Appalachians: Weston, Massachusetts, Department of Geology and Geophysics, Boston College, p. 1–35.

Naylor, R. S., 1968, Origin and regional relationships of the core-rocks of the Oliverian domes, in Zen, E-an and others, eds., Studies of Appalachian geology: Northern and maritime: New York, Wiley-Interscience, p. 231–240.

Naylor, R. S., Boone, G. M., Boudette, E. L., Ashenden, D. D., and Robinson, Peter, 1973, Pre-Ordovician rocks in the Bronson Hill and Boundary Mountain anticlinoria, New England, U.S.A. [abs.]: EOS, v. 54, p. 495.

Nealé, E.W.R., 1972, A cross section through the Appalachian system in Newfoundland: International Geological Congress, 24th, Montreal, Canada, Excursion A 62.

Neuman, R. B., 1967, Bedrock geology of the Shin Pond and Stacyville quadrangles, Penobscot County, Maine: U.S. Geological Survey Professional Paper 524-I, 37 p.

Olszewski, W. J., Jr., 1980, The geochronology of some stratified rocks in northeastern Massachusetts: Canadian Journal of Earth Sciences, v. 17, p. 1407–1416.

Olszewski, W. J., Jr., and Gaudette, H. E., 1981, The late Precambrian of eastern New England and maritime Canada: A speculative

survey: Geological Society of America Abstracts with Programs, v. 13, p. 169.

Olszewski, W. J., Jr., Gaudette, H. E., Keppie, J. D., and Donohoe, H. V., 1981, Rb-Sr whole rock ages of the Kelly's Mountain basement complex, Cape Breton Island: Geological Society of America Abstracts with Programs, v. 13, p. 169.

Osberg, P. H., 1978, Synthesis of the geology of the northeastern Appalachians, U.S.A., in Caledonian-Appalachian orogen of the North Atlantic region: Geological Survey of Canada Paper 78-13, p. 137–147.

——1979, Geologic relationships in south-central Maine, in Skehan, J. W. S.J., and Osberg, P. H., eds., The Caledonides in the U.S.A., IGCP Project 27, Geological Excursions in the northeast Appalachians: Weston, Massachusetts, Department of Geology and Geophysics, Boston College, p. 37–62.

Osberg, P. H., and Guidotti, C. V., 1974, The geology of the Camden-Rockland area, in Osberg, P. H., ed., New England Intercollegiate Geological Conference Guidebook, 66th Annual Meeting, Orono, Maine: University of Maine, p. 48–60.

Osberg, P. H., Moench, R. H., and Warner, Jeffrey, 1968, Stratigraphy of the Merrimack synclinorium in west-central Maine, in Zen, E-an and others, eds., Studies of Appalachian geology: Northern and maritime: New York, Wiley-Interscience, p. 241–253.

Palmer, A. R., 1971, The Cambrian of the Appalachian and eastern New England regions, eastern United States, in Holland, C. H., ed., Cambrian of the New World: New York, Interscience, p. 169–217.

Pavlides, Louis, 1962, Geology and manganese deposits of the Maple and Hovey Mountains area, Aroostook County, Maine: U.S. Geological Survey Professional Paper 362, 116 p.

——1968, Stratigraphic and facies relationships of the Carys Mills Formation of Ordovician and Silurian age, northeast Maine: U.S. Geological Survey Bulletin, 1264, 40 p.

——1973, Geologic map of the Howe Brook quadrangle, Maine: U.S. Geological Survey Geologic Quadrangle Map GQ 1094.

——1974, General bedrock geology of northeastern Maine, in Osberg, P. H., ed., New England Intercollegiate Geological Conference Guidebook, 66th Annual Meeting, Orono, Maine: University of Maine, p. 61–65.

Pavlides, Louis, Boucot, A. J., and Skidmore, W. B., 1968, Stratigraphic evidence for the Taconic orogeny in the northern Appalachians, in Zen, E-an and others, eds., Studies of Appalachian geology: Northern and maritime: New York, Wiley-Interscience, p. 61–82.

Pollock, S. G., 1982, Stratigraphy of the Caucomgomoc Lake area, northern Maine: Example of an obducted ophiolite-melange complex: Geological Society of America Abstracts with Programs, v. 14, p. 73.

Poole, W. H., Sanford, B. V., Williams, Harold, and Kelley, D. G., 1970, Geology of southeastern Canada, in Douglas, R.J.W., ed., Geology and economic minerals of Canada: Geological Survey of Canada Economic Geology Report no. 1, p. 228–304.

Quinn, A. W., 1971, Bedrock geology of Rhode Island: U.S. Geological Survey Bulletin 1295, 68 p.

Rankin, D. W., 1975, The continental margin of eastern North America in the southern Appalachians: The opening and closing of the proto-Atlantic Ocean: American Journal of Science, v. 275-A (Tectonics and mountain ranges), p. 298–336.

——1976, Appalachian salients and recesses; late Precambrian continental break up and the opening of the Iapetus Ocean: Journal of Geophysical Research, v. 81, p. 5605–5619.

Rankin, D. W., Stern, T. W., Reed, J. C., Jr., and Newell, M. F., 1969, Zircon ages of felsic volcanic rocks in the upper Precambrian of the Blue Ridge Appalachian Mountains: Science, v. 166, p. 741–744.

Rao, K. V., and Van der Roo, Rob, 1980, Paleomagnetism of a Paleozoic anorthosite from the Appalachian piedmont, northern Delaware, possible tectonic implications: Earth and Planetary Science

Letters, v. 47, p. 113–120.

Rast, Nicholas, and Stringer, P., 1974, Recent advances and the interpretation of geological structure of New Brunswick: Geoscience Canada, v. 1, pt. 4, p. 15–25.

——1980, A geotraverse across a deformed Ordovician ophiolite and its Silurian cover, northern New Brunswick, Canada: Tectonophysics, v. 69, p. 221–245.

Rast, Nicholas, Kennedy, M. J., and Blackwood, R. F., 1976a, Comparison of some tectonostratigraphic zones in the Appalachians of Newfoundland and New Brunswick: Canadian Journal of Earth Sciences, v. 13, p. 868–875.

Rast, Nicholas, O'Brien, B. H., and Wardle, R. J., 1976b, Relationships between Pre-cambrian and lower Paleozoic rocks of the "Avalon Platform" in New Brunswick, the northeast Appalachians and the British Isles: Tectonophysics, v. 30, p. 315–338.

Ratcliffe, N. M., 1982, External massifs of western New England: Variously reactivated North American basement: Geological Society of America Abstracts with Programs, v. 14, p. 75.

Ratcliffe, N. M., and Harwood, D. S., 1975, Blastomylonites associated with recumbent folds and overthrusts at the western edge of the Berkshire massif, Connecticut and Massachusetts—A preliminary report, in Tectonic studies of the Berkshire massif, western Massachusetts, Connecticut, and Vermont: U.S. Geological Survey Professional Paper 888. p. 1–19.

Ratcliffe, N. M., and Hatch, N. L., Jr., 1979, A traverse across the Taconide Zone in the area of the Berkshire massif, western Massachusetts, in Skehan, J. W., S.J., and Osberg, P. H., eds., The Caledonides in the U.S.A., IGCP Project 27, Geological Excursions in the northeast Appalachians: Weston, Massachusetts, Department of Geology and Geophysics, Boston College, p. 175–224.

Read, P. B., 1980, Stratigraphy and structure: Thor-Odin to Frenchman Cap "domes," Vernon east-half map area, southern B. C.: Geological Survey of Canada Paper 80-1A, p. 19–25.

Robinson, Peter, 1981, Siluro-Devonian stratigraphy of the Merrimack synclinorium, central Massachusetts—Review based on correlations in Maine: Geological Society of America Abstracts with Programs, v. 13, p. 172.

Robinson, Peter, and Hall, L. M., 1980, Tectonic synthesis of southern New England, in Wones, D. R., ed., The Caledonides in the U.S.A. IGCP Proceedings, Project 27: Department of Geological Science, Virginia Polytechnic Institute Memoir 2, p. 73–82.

Robinson, Peter, Thompson, J. B., Jr., and Rosenfeld, J. L., 1979, Nappes, gneiss domes, and regional metamorphism in western New Hampshire and central Massachusetts, in Skehan, J. W., S.J., and Osberg, P. H., eds., The Caledonides in the U.S.A., IGCP Project 27, Geological Excursions in the northeast Appalachians: Weston, Massachusetts, Department of Geology and Geophysics, Boston College, p. 93–116.

Rodgers, John, 1968, The eastern edge of the North American continent during the Cambrian and early Ordovician, in Zen, E-an, and others, eds., Studies of Appalachian geology: Northern and maritime: New York, Wiley-Interscience, p. 141–149.

——1972, Latest Precambrian (post-Grenville) rocks of the Appalachian region: American Journal of Science, v. 272, p. 507–520.

——1981, The Merrimack synclinorium in northeastern Connecticut: American Journal of Science, v. 281, p. 176–186.

Rowley, D. B., and Kidd, W.S.F., 1981a, Relationship between shelf and rise sedimentation of the early Paleozoic continental margin of western New England: Geological Society of America Abstracts with Programs, v. 13, p. 173.

——1981b, Stratigraphic relationships and detrital composition of the medial Ordovician flysch of western New England: Implications for the tectonic evolution of the Taconic orogeny: Journal of Geology, v. 89, p. 199–218.

Roy, D. C., and Mencher, Ely, 1976, Ordovician and Silurian strati-

graphy of northeastern Aroostook County, Maine, in Page, L. R., ed., Contributions to the stratigraphy of New England: Geological Society of America Memoir 148, p. 25–52.

St-Julien, Pierre, and Hubert, Claude, 1975, Evolution of the Taconian orogen in the Quebec Appalachians: American Journal of Science, v. 275-A, p. 337–362.

Schenk, P. E., 1980, Paleogeographic implications of the Meguma Group, Nova Scotia—a chip of Africa?, in Wones, D. R., ed., The Caledonides in the U.S.A., IGCP Proceedings, Project 27: Department of Geological Science, Virginia Polytechnic Institute Memoir 2, p. 27–30.

Schutts, L. D., Brecher, A., Hurley, P. M., and others, 1976, A case study of the time and nature of paleomagnetic resetting in a mafic complex in New England: Canadian Journal of Earth Sciences, v. 13, p. 898–907.

Secor, D. T., Jr., and Snoke, A. W., 1978, Stratigraphy, structure, and plutonism in the central South Carolina piedmont, in Snoke, A. W., ed., Geological investigations of the eastern Piedmont, southern Appalachians: Carolina Geological Society Field Trip Guidebook, West Columbia, South Carolina, p. 65–99.

Shaw, H. F., Wasserburg, G. J., and Albee, A. L., 1981, Sm-Nd, Rb-Sr systematics of mafic complexes and ophiolites of the Appalachians and western U.S. [abs.]: EOS, v. 62, p. 409.

Shride, A. F., 1976, Stratigraphy and correlation of the Newbury volcanic complex, northeastern Massachusetts, in Page, L. R., ed., Contributions to the stratigraphy of New England: Geological Society of America Memoir 148, p. 147–177.

Simpson, R. W., Bothner, W. A., and Shride, A. F., 1980, Offshore extension of the Clinton-Newbury and Bloody Bluff fault systems of northeastern Massachusetts, in Wones, D. R., ed., The Caledonides in the U.S.A., IGCP Proceedings, Project 27: Department of Geological Science, Virginia Polytechnic Institute Memoir 2, p. 229–233.

Skehan, J. W., S.J., 1968, Fracture tectonics of southeastern New England as illustrated by the Wachusett-Marlborough tunnel, east-central Massachusetts, in Zen, E-an, and others, eds., Studies of Appalachian geology: Northern and maritime: New York, Wiley-Interscience, p. 281–290.

Skehan, J. W., S.J., Murray, D. P., Belt, E. S., Hermes, O. D., Rast, Nicholas, and Dewey, J. F., 1976, Alleghenian deformation, sedimentation, and metamorphism in southeastern Massachusetts and Rhode Island, in Cameron, Barry, ed., New England Intercollegiate Geological Conference Guidebook, 68th Annual Meeting, Boston: Science Press, Princeton University, p. 447–471.

Skehan, J. W., S. J., Murray, D. P., Palmer, A. R., Smith, A. T., and Belt, E. S., 1978, Significance of fossiliferous Middle Cambrian rocks of Rhode Island to the history of the Avalonian microcontinent: Geology, v. 6, p. 694–698.

Skinner, Ralph, 1974, Geology of Tetagouche Lakes, Bathurst, and Nepisiguit Falls map-areas, New Brunswick, with emphasis on the Tetagouche group: Geological Survey of Canada Memoir 371, 133 p.

Smith, B. M., 1978, The geology and Rb-Sr whole rock age of granitic rock of Aquidneck and Conanicut Islands, Rhode Island [M.Sc. thesis]: Providence, Rhode Island, Brown University, 94 p.

Snoke, A. W., Kish, S. A., and Secor, D. T., Jr., 1980a, Deformed Hercynian granitic rocks from the piedmont of South Carolina: American Journal of Science, v. 280, p. 1018–1034.

Snoke, A. W., Secor, D. T., Jr., Bramlett, K. W., and Prowell, D. C., 1980b, Geology of the eastern piedmont fault system in South Carolina and eastern Georgia: Geological Society of America Field Trip Guidebook, trip no. 5, p. 59–100.

SOQUIP (Societe Quebecoise d'Initiative Petroliere), 1979a, Acquisition et traitement de donnees sismiques: Basses-Terres du St. Laurent; lignes sismiques 2001, 2002, et 2003, DP-665: Ministere des Richesses Naturelles du Quebec.

——1979b, Interpretation du profil sismique 2001 par SOQUIP, DP-721:

Ministere des Richesses Naturelles du Quebec.

Spariosu, D. J., and Kent, D. V., 1980, Paleomagnetic results from northern Maine and their bearing on displaced terranes [abs.]: EOS, v. 61, p. 220.

——1981, Paleogeography of the northern Appalachians during the Devonian and the plate tectonic setting of the Acadian orogeny: Implications of paleomagnetic results: Geological Society of America Abstracts with Programs, v. 13, p. 558.

Stanley, R. S., and Roy, D. L., 1982, Tectonic geology of the northern Vermont ultramafic belt: Geological Society of America Abstracts with Programs, v. 14, p. 85.

Stevens, R. K., 1970, Cambro-Ordovician flysch sedimentation and tectonics in west Newfoundland and their possible bearing on a proto-Atlantic Ocean: Geological Association of Canada Special Paper 7, p. 165–177.

Stewart, D. B., 1974, Precambrian rocks of Seven Hundred Acre Island and development of cleavage in the Islesboro Formation, *in* Osberg, P. H., ed., New England Intercollegiate Geological Conference Guidebook, 66th Annual Meeting, Orono, Maine: University of Maine, p. 86–98.

Stewart, D. B., and Wones, D. R., 1974, Bedrock geology of northern Penobscot Bay area; *in* Osberg, P. H., ed., New England Intercollegiate Geological Conference Guidebook, 66th Annual Meeting, Orono, Maine: University of Maine, p. 223–239.

Stukas, Vidas, and Reynolds, P. H., 1974, $^{40}Ar/^{39}Ar$ dating of the Long Range dikes, Newfoundland: Earth and Planetary Science Letters, v. 22, p. 256–266.

Thomas, W. A., 1977, Evolution of Appalachian-Ouachita salients and recesses from reentrants and promontories in the continental margin: American Journal of Science, v. 277, p. 1233–1278.

Thompson, J. B., Jr., 1972, Lower Paleozoic rocks flanking the Green Mountain anticlinorium, *in* Doolan, B. L., and Stanley, R. S., eds., New England Intercollegiate Geological Conference Guidebook, 64th Annual Meeting, Burlington, Vermont: University of Vermont, p. 215–229.

Thompson, J. B., Jr., and Norton, S. A., 1968, Paleozoic regional metamorphism in New England and adjacent areas, *in* Zen, E-an, and others, eds., Studies of Appalachian geology; Northern and maritime: New York, Wiley-Interscience, p. 319–327.

Thompson, J. B., Jr., Robinson, Peter, Clifford, T. N., and Trask, N. J., Jr., 1968, Nappes and gneiss domes in west-central New England, *in* Zen, E-an, and others, eds., Studies of Appalachian geology: Northern and maritime: New York, Wiley-Interscience, p. 203–218.

Tracy, R. J., and Robinson, Peter, 1980, Evolution of metamorphic belts: Information from detailed petrologic studies, *in* Wones, D. R., ed., The Caledonides in the U.S.A., IGCP Proceedings, Project 27: Department of Geological Science, Virginia Polytechnic Institute Memoir 2, p. 189–195.

Trzcienski, W. E., Jr., 1976, Crossitic amphibole and its possible tectonic significance in the Richmond area, southeastern Quebec: Canadian Journal of Earth Sciences, v. 13, p. 711–714.

Vallières, A., Hubert, Claude, and Brooks, C., 1978, A slice of basement in the western margin of the Appalachian orogen, Saint-Malachie, Quebec: Canadian Journal of Earth Sciences, v. 15, p. 1242–1249.

Van der Roo, Rob, French, A. N., and French, R. B., 1979, A paleomagnetic pole position from the folded Upper Devonian Catskill red beds, and its tectonic implications: Geology, v. 7, p. 345–348.

Wanless, R. K., and Reesor, J. E., 1975, Precambrian zircon age of orthogneiss in the Shuswap metamorphic complex, British Columbia: Canadian Journal of Earth Sciences, v. 12, p. 326–332.

Webb, G. W., 1969, Paleozoic wrench faults in Canadian Appalachians, *in* Kay, M., ed., North Atlantic: Geology and continental drift: American Association of Petroleum Geologists Memoir 12, p. 754–786.

Williams, Harold, 1978, Tectonic lithofacies map of the Appalachian orogen: St. John's, Memorial University of Newfoundland, Map no. 1, scale 1:1,000,000.

——1979, Appalachian orogen in Canada: Canadian Journal of Earth Sciences, v. 16, p. 792–807.

Williams, Harold, and Hatcher, R. D., Jr., 1981, Suspect terranes: A new look at the Appalachian orogen: Geological Society of America Abstracts with Programs, v. 13, p. 581.

——1983, Suspect terranes: A new look at the Appalachian orogen; *in* Hatcher, R. D., and others, eds., Contributions to the tectonics and geophysics of mountain chains: Geological Society of America Memoir 158 (this volume).

Williams, Harold, and Max, M. D., 1980, Zonal subdivision and regional correlation in the Appalachian-Caledonian orogen, *in* Wones, D. R., ed., The Caledonides in the U.S.A., IGCP Proceedings, Project 27, Department of Geological Science, Virginia Polytechnic Institute Memoir 2, p. 57–62.

Wilson, J. T., 1966, Did the Atlantic close and then reopen?: Nature, v. 211, p. 676–681.

Wing, L. A., 1957, Aeromagnetic and geologic reconnaissance survey of portions of Hancock and Penobscot Counties, Maine: Maine Geological Survey GP. and G. Survey, no. 1, sheet 1, scale 1:62,500.

Wones, D. R., 1980, Contribution of crystallography, mineralogy, and petrology to the geology of the Lucerne Pluton, Hancock County, Maine: American Mineralogist, v. 65, p. 411–437.

Wones, D. R., and Stewart, D. B., 1976, Middle Paleozoic regional right-lateral strike-slip faults in central coastal Maine: Geological Society of America Abstracts with Programs, v. 8, p. 304.

Wones, D. R., and Thompson, Woodrow, 1979, The Norumbega fault zone: A major regional structure in central eastern Maine: Geological Society of America Abstracts with Programs, v. 11, p. 60.

Zartman, R. E., 1974, Lead isotopic provinces in the Cordillera of the western United States and their geologic significance: Economic Geology, v. 69, p. 792–803.

Zen, E-an, 1967, Time and space relationships of the Taconic allochthon and autochthon: Geological Society of America Special Paper 97, 107 p.

——1972, The Taconide zone and the Taconic orogeny in the western part of the northern Appalachian orogen: Geological Society of America Special Paper 135, 72 p.

——1981, An alternative model for the development of the allochthonous southern Appalachian Piedmont: American Journal of Science, v. 281, p. 1153–1163.

Zen, E-an, and Palmer, A. R., 1981, Did Avalonia form the eastern shore of Iapetus Ocean?: Geological Society of America Abstracts with Programs, v. 13, p. 587.

Zen, E-an, editor, Goldsmith, Richard, Ratcliffe, N. M., Robinson, Peter, and R. S. Stanley, compilers, 1983, Bedrock geologic map of Massachusetts: U.S. Geological Survey and Commonwealth of Massachusetts, scale 1:250,000 (in press).

Zietz, Isidore, Haworth, R. T., Williams, Harold, and Daniels, D. L., 1980, Magnetic anomaly map of the Appalachian orogen: St. John's, Memorial University of Newfoundland, Map no. 2, scale 1:1,000,000.

MANUSCRIPT ACCEPTED BY THE SOCIETY SEPTEMBER 10, 1982

Geological Society of America
Memoir 158
1983

Crustal geometry of the Appalachian orogen from seismic reflection studies

Clifford J. Ando*
Frederick A. Cook
Jack E. Oliver
Larry D. Brown
Sidney Kaufman
Department of Geological Sciences
Cornell University
Ithaca, New York 14853

ABSTRACT

Regional seismic reflection studies in the New England and southern Appalachians by COCORP and in Québec by the Ministére des Richesses Naturelles have provided critical subsurface geological information. The data clearly show considerable horizontal transport of off-shelf metasediments over coeval, relatively undeformed, lower Paleozoic shelf and miogeoclinal rocks. In the southern Appalachians, long distance (>200 km) transport of thin crystalline thrust sheets can be shown as well.

The COCORP data from the Green Mountains of Vermont and a USGS seismic study in the Grandfather Mountain window of North Carolina and Tennessee appear to indicate that Precambrian (ca. 1.0 b.y.) Grenville basement in those areas is allochthonous and underlain either by shelf sediments or detachment horizons. In Québec, allochthonous basinal facies clastics are still preserved over a major anticlinorial structure, and extensive exposures of Precambrian basement are not found in an internal position in this part of the Appalachian mountain belt.

The Bouguer gravity gradient in the central and southern Appalachians and the gravity high in New England and Québec are interpreted to mark a fundamental crustal density change at depth along the mountain chain, perhaps representing a preserved transition from continent to ocean. We infer, in part from the distribution of surface rock units with respect to the locus of the gravity gradient, that allochthonous off-shelf rocks may have been transported farther in the southern than in the northern Appalachians. Perhaps this is true for allochthonous Grenville basement as well, although the question cannot be unequivocally answered at this time.

The seismic data suggest that highly deformed rocks exposed in the Appalachian chain are part of a relatively thin, composite allochthon presently confined to high structural levels and that the deeper part of the crust may constitute a largely undeformed ancient continental margin, perhaps including a transition from continental to rift stage or oceanic crust. Surface geologic relationships similar to those described for the Appalachians exist in a number of other mountain belts, and a modern analog for the subsurface structure of the frontal part of the Appalachians is present in the

*Present address: Shell Development Company, Bellaire Research Center, P.O. Box 481, Houston, Texas 77001.

Banda arc of Indonesia. Regional deep crustal seismic surveys are clearly needed in other ancient deformed mountain belts and their active modern analogs.

INTRODUCTION

Observations from high-angle reflection seismic imaging in deformed mountain belts are adding a critical link in the acquisition of three-dimensional geological information, that of subsurface geometry. In particular, regional seismic profiles (>100 km) in the United States and Québec Appalachians have provided new and critical data bearing on the subsurface structural geometry in more "internal" parts of the deformed mountain chain. Whereas a thin-skinned style of deformation involving sedimentary strata of the Valley and Ridge foreland of the Appalachians has been known and documented for some time (e.g., Rich, 1934; Rodgers, 1949; Gwinn, 1964; Harris, 1976), the extent to which crystalline thrust sheets have played a role in this deformation was not fully appreciated prior to the acquisition of regional, deep seismic reflection data.

The purpose of this paper is to present a comparison of subsurface structure of the New England Appalachians, Québec Appalachians, and southern Appalachians based on regional seismic reflection studies. We will compare geometric aspects of seismic data collected by the Consortium for Continental Reflection Profiling (COCORP) from the New England and southern Appalachians, and by the Société Québecoise d'Initiative Petrolière (SOQUIP) for the Ministère des Richesses Naturelles from the Québec Appalachians. In the ensuing discussion, selected parts of more extensive data sets (see Fig. 1) will be treated. These are the COCORP New England traverse Parts I and II (~175 km; Fig. 2), part of the SOQUIP Québec Appalachian traverse Part 2001 (~124 km; Fig. 4), and the COCORP southern Appalachian traverse Part I (~300 km; Fig. 6). There thus exist at present at least three regional seismic traverses across parts of the Appalachian orogen at different latitudes, and it seems appropriate at this time to attempt comparisons among these.

Because there are fundamental differences in surface geology along strike in the Appalachians, it may be very dangerous to attempt correlation of specific features over large distances. In fact, different parts of the orogen may have evolved very differently, as the complex plate collisions through time which are called upon would seem to suggest. Yet if the structures in the foreland and perhaps more internal parts of the orogen developed as a result of compressional forces generated by collisions or perhaps the subduction process itself, the geometry of subsurface structures in different parts of a complex mountain belt might look very similar because they result from the same basic driving mechanism—the lateral interaction of lithospheric plates. It is in this light that we attempt these geometric comparisons.

At present these data allow us to suggest that transported rocks in the Appalachians may have been thrust for greater distances in the south than in the north and that, in places, Grenville age continental basement is allochthonous as well. We make the inference that the complexly deformed rocks which comprise the Appalachian mountain belt are confined in the vertical dimension to a relatively thin zone at high structural levels and that the deeper part of the ancient continental margin may lie preserved at depth.

Owing to the difficulty in reproducing seismic data, we have chosen to represent the seismic sections by line drawings, showing the most prominent reflection events, with excerpts of the actual data in pertinent places. Accompanying each traverse is a simplified tectonic cross section interpreted from the data. The discussion which follows will focus on large-scale aspects of the various seismic transects, rather than on details of the data.

All of the multichannel seismic data presented in this paper were collected using the Vibroseis (trademark, CONOCO, Inc.) method. Computer processing of the southern Appalachian data was done partly by Geosource, Inc., and partly at Cornell University on the Megaseis (trademark, Seiscom Delta, Inc.) computer system. Processing of the COCORP New England Appalachian data was done at Cornell on the Megaseis, and the Québec Appalachian data were processed by Geodigit of Calgary, Alberta. Recording and processing parameters are not discussed in detail here, but aspects of these are brought in where pertinent to interpretation of the data. Reviews of recording and processing for the southern and New England Appalachian traverses are presented in Cook and others (1983) and Brown and others (1983), respectively. General aspects of COCORP processing of reflection data are discussed in Schilt and others (1979).

NEW ENGLAND APPALACHIANS

The first phase of the COCORP New England Appalachian traverse was completed in the fall of 1980 and extends eastward from near Glens Falls, New York, to Windsor, Vermont. The second phase, completed during the summer of 1981, extends southeastward from south of Claremont, New Hampshire, to Mont Vernon, New Hampshire (Fig. 2). The survey transected the Taconic Mountains of New York and Vermont, the Green Moun-

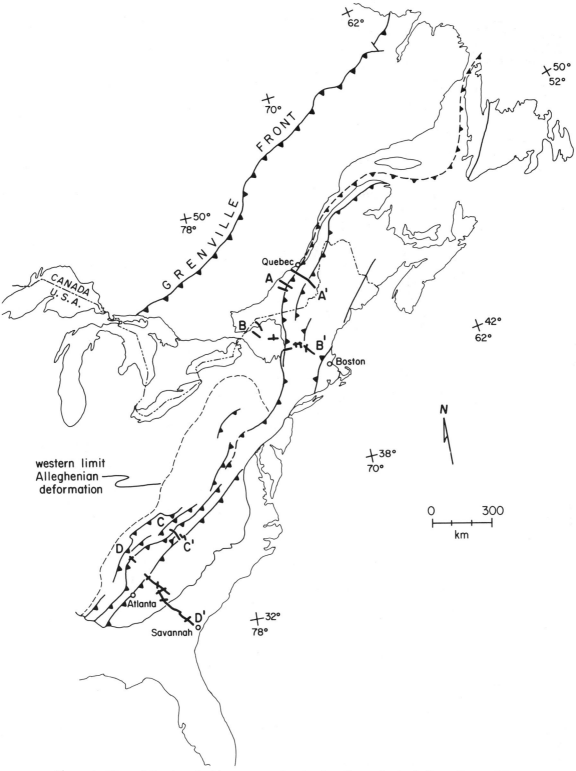

Figure 1. Map of the Appalachian orogen showing locations of seismic lines discussed in text. Select parts of these data sets are treated (see Figs. 2, 4 and 6 for specific parts). A-A′ = Québec Appalachian data from the St. Lawrence lowlands, collected for the Ministère des Richesses Naturelles du Québec; B-B′ = COCORP northeast survey (Adirondack Mountains traverse and New England Appalachian traverse, Parts I and II); C-C′ = USGS Grandfather Mountain survey in North Carolina and Tennessee; D-D′ = COCORP southern Appalachian traverse, Parts I and II.

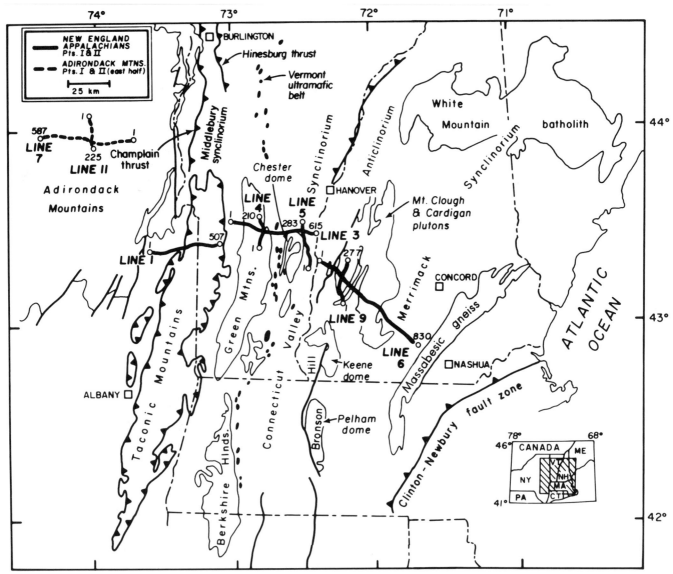

Figure 2. Location map for COCORP New England traverse showing major geographic and tectonic features; geologic contacts are from Williams (1978). Heavy solid lines are seismic lines discussed in text; dashed heavy lines are data that have been collected but not treated in this paper. Numbers along seismic traverses are vibrator stations.

tains and Chester dome of Vermont, and the Bronson Hill anticlinorium/Merrimack synclinorium of New Hampshire. The data that we discuss here are part of a larger COCORP study in the northeast which includes traverses across Grenville-age rocks in the Adirondack Mountains of New York (Brown and others, 1983).

Interpretation of some of the seismic data from the New England Appalachians has been hampered by a low signal-to-noise ratio. Nevertheless, these data are very important in that there are few deep seismic reflection profiles now in the public domain that have crossed exposed Grenville (ca. 1.0 b.y.) basement in the Appalachian orogen.

Taconic Mountains

Rocks exposed in the Taconic Mountains comprise a sequence of imbricate thrust slices (Zen, 1967) of Cambrian(?) to Middle Ordovician, dominantly deep water argillite, wacke and minor carbonate sediments, which lie structurally atop a largely shallow water carbonate platform and flysch sequence. The two suites of rocks are coeval, and the allochthonous deep water materials have been interpreted as the continental rise facies equivalents of the platform and shelf carbonates (Bird and Dewey, 1970). Rocks of the allochthonous slices are preserved in the core of the south-plunging Middlebury synclinorium (Fig. 2);

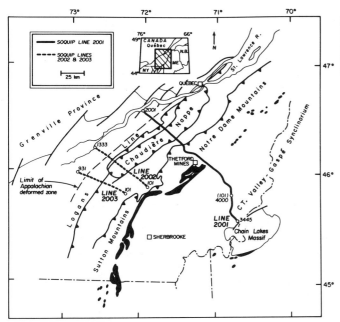

Figure 4. Location map for Québec seismic traverse showing major geographic and tectonic features. Geologic contacts from Williams (1978) and St. Julien and Hubert (1975). The first 124 km of line 2001 (from station 101 in southeast to station 2001 in northeast) are discussed in text. Québec lines 2002 and 2003 (dashed heavy lines) are not treated. Black areas are ophiolites or ultramafic outcrops continuous with Vermont ultramafic belt to south.

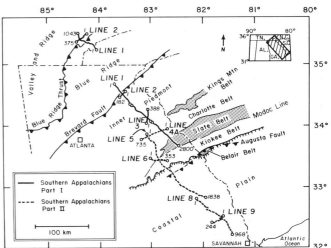

Figure 6. Location map for the COCORP southern Appalachian traverse showing major geographic and tectonic features; Part I shown in heavy solid lines and Part II in heavy dashed lines. Geologic contacts taken from Williams (1978). Part II traverse is not discussed in text.

they are multiply deformed (Zen, 1972; Rowley and others, 1979) and have traditionally been regarded as stacked in order from bottom to top (Zen, 1967; Fisher, 1979). Other interpretations, based on relationships in the Newfoundland and Québec Appalachians (e.g., Stevens, 1970; Hiscott, 1978), and recent work in the Taconic Mountains (Rowley and Kidd, 1981) have suggested that slices of the Taconic allochthon were originally stacked from structurally higher to lower levels, in the manner of modern accretionary prisms (e.g., Karig, 1974; Seely and others, 1974; Hamilton, 1979). A widely accepted model for the Taconian orogeny suggests that the presently observed structural and stratigraphic relationships resulted from collision of an offshore arc with the passive early Paleozoic North American continental margin, above an east-dipping subduction zone (Chapple, 1973; Rowley and Kidd, 1981). In the interpretations of these authors, the allochthonous off-shelf Taconic sequence would have been transported westward by thrust faulting over the coeval carbonate shelf during arc-continent convergence.

COCORP New York line 1 (Fig. 2) began on Grenville gneisses at the southeast flank of the Adirondack Mountains, passed eastward over exposed shelf carbonates and clastics, and transected the Taconic klippe, crossing the basal Giddings Brook fault at about V.P. 260. A number of reflections are visible on the seismic profile

(Fig. 3, in pocket inside back cover). The most prominent of these is a zone of subhorizontal events between V.P.s 200 and 500, at a two-way travel time of 1.5 seconds (about 4.5 km for a velocity of 6 km/s). This zone undoubtedly represents the lower Paleozoic shelf and miogeoclinal sedimentary sequence (Beekmantown, Black River, and Trenton Groups) lying structurally beneath the Taconic klippe. West of V.P. 200, reflected energy at shallow levels is not abundant; here the shelf carbonates and overlying Middle Ordovician flysch are exposed at the surface, and the unconformity between Grenville gneisses and Cambrian shelf clastics is not far west of the beginning of line 1.

The zone of reflections at 1.5 seconds exhibits a disrupted pattern, possibly indicating that the sedimentary section is broken and/or imbricated by faults. Few events are observed beneath the outcrop of the Taconic allochthon (V.P.s 200 to 500) at times less than 1.5 seconds, suggesting that the rocks here are homogeneous with respect to the input seismic signal; this is perhaps due to their internal structural complexity. Those events that are observed above 1.5 seconds are probably reflections from fault surfaces or lithologic boundaries within the Taconic slices. One of these events projects to the surface near the outcrop of the basal Giddings Brook fault (GBF of Fig. 3, about V.P. 260) and is perhaps a reflection from the fault. Most of the very shallow events cannot be interpreted unequivocally because they are discontinuous and do not correlate with obvious geologic features exposed at the surface. However, they very likely represent detail within the allochthonous slices.

At longer travel times, arcuate to dipping events are

present between 6.0 and 12.0 seconds on New York line 1. We suggest these events are due to discontinuities within Grenville basement beneath the Taconic Mountains, but other interpretations are possible. These deep reflections are not treated in detail here but are discussed as part of the first phase COCORP Grenville study in the Adirondack Mountains by Brown and others (1983).

Green Mountains and Chester Dome

Precambrian metamorphic rocks in the Green Mountains and Chester dome of Vermont (Fig. 2) crop out as doubly plunging anticlinorial and subsidiary domal massifs that form part of a chain of similar structures from Newfoundland to Georgia (Rankin, 1976). Gneisses of the Mount Holly complex (Doll and others, 1961) exposed in the cores of the Green Mountain anticlinorium and Chester dome are widely regarded as Grenvillian basement; these rocks have been overprinted by younger deformations but have yielded radiometric ages of about 1.0 b.y. (Tilton and others, 1960; Faul and others, 1963). As such (excluding apparently older rocks such as the Chain Lakes massif in Maine), these massifs constitute the easternmost exposures of Grenville age basement in the New England Appalachians.

Nearby massifs such as the Berkshire Highlands to the south (Fig. 2) have yielded Grenvillian ages (Tyringham gneiss, ca. 1.0 b.y.; Ratcliffe and Zartman, 1976). Significantly, thrust faulting of basement gneisses in the Berkshire massif has been shown to have taken place during the Taconian orogeny (Ratcliffe and Harwood, 1975; Ratcliffe and Mose, 1978; Ratcliffe and Hatch, 1979). Although multiply deformed and metamorphosed, these Precambrian basement massifs may have part of their original shelf sedimentary cover still resting depositionally upon them (e.g., Doll and others, 1961; Ratcliffe, 1975, 1979).

COCORP Vermont line 3 (Fig. 2) is offset slightly northward from New York line 1 across an east-west data gap of about 6 km. The profile started in the Vermont Valley east of the outcrop of the Taconic allochthon, crossing deformed/metamorphosed lower Paleozoic shelf lithologies (Champlain Valley sequence) and the Green Mountain anticlinorium south of the latitude of Rutland, Vermont. Farther east, the survey transected the Townshend-Brownington syncline of Doll and others (1961) and the Chester dome just north of Mount Ascutney.

Because there is a low signal-to-noise ratio, the reflections on Vermont line 3 are not prominent. Nevertheless, a number of interesting events are observable. A zone of subhorizontal, discontinuous reflections is present beneath the Green Mountains between V.P.s 100 and 325, at a time of 1.5 seconds (Fig. 3). It is important to note that the zones of reflections at 1.5 seconds on New York line 1

and Vermont line 3 correlate in time. Figure 3 depicts an interpretation that shelf sedimentary lithologies may underlie basement rocks of the Green Mountains. Alternatively, the reflections at 1.5 seconds could represent lamellar zones of high strain (e.g., ductile faults) entirely within the basement complex, or perhaps layering within the Grenville gneisses. Owing to the relatively poor data quality and because none of the events at 1.5 seconds can be correlated with known features at the surface, one must entertain the suggested alternatives (or perhaps others) as viable interpretations.

In the vicinity of the east flank of the Green Mountain anticlinorium (V.P.s 250 to 450) there is a zone of dipping events which extends to about 4.5 seconds (about 13.5 km for an average velocity of 6 km/s). This zone dips 30° to 35° (unmigrated), and various apparent splays project to the surface both within crystalline rocks of the Green Mountains and within the metasedimentary cover to the east. Hand migration of these events suggests that they could steepen to about 40°. The zone of reflections also appears at about 4.0 seconds as a subhorizontal set of events on the north-south cross line (COCORP Vermont line 5, Fig. 2). Since some of these reflections project to the surface within the Green Mountains, they may thus represent zones of high strain in the Grenville basement; others correlate with the east-dipping layered metasediments at the east flank of the Green Mountains and may reflect lithologic contacts. Owing to the high metamorphic grades which these rocks have attained (e.g., Thompson and Norton, 1968; Downie, 1980), it seems reasonable that these dipping events could represent discrete zones of deformation (i.e., faults) in an otherwise more distributively ductilely deformed sequence of rocks.

Virtually no seismic expression of the Chester dome (Figs. 2, 3) is visible on Vermont line 3. Rocks flanking the dome and rocks within the core of the dome itself are complexly deformed (Thompson, 1950; Rosenfeld, 1968; Nisbet, 1976). There are many effects which could degrade reflection data in this area (e.g., near-surface attenuation, noisy recording conditions, etc.). There is also a notable absence of deep basement reflections on Vermont line 3. Although it could be argued that a low signal-to-noise ratio is obscuring any basement reflections, deep reflections are observed on New York line 1 farther west where noisy recording conditions were encountered for the first half of the survey. This suggests that the lack of strong deep reflections on Vermont line 3 may not be an artifact.

Bronson Hill Anticlinorium and Merrimack Synclinorium

During the time this paper was in review, the second phase of the COCORP New England Appalachian survey was completed across southwestern New Hampshire. Preliminary results and interpretations of the New Hampshire data which are pertinent to the crustal comparisons are presented here. Results of the entire COCORP New England study are being discussed at greater length elsewhere (Ando and others, in prep.).

The Bronson Hill anticlinorium and Merrimack synclinorium comprise the major regional geologic features transected by COCORP New Hampshire line 6 (Fig. 2). The Bronson Hill anticlinorium is the easternmost of two prominent gneiss dome belts described by Thompson and others (1968) in western New England. The belt crops out as a zone of complex domical structures that have been widely regarded as remnants of volcanic islands (Hitchcock, 1883; Kay, 1951) or an island arc assemblage (Rodgers, 1970) that subsequent tectonic syntheses have treated as a basement terrane distinct from the Grenville rocks exposed in the Green Mountains and Chester dome to the west. The arc sequence and its basement were presumably accreted to the proto–North American continent during early Paleozoic convergence, perhaps related to emplacement of the Taconic allochthon (e.g., Bird and Dewey, 1970; Osberg, 1978; Robinson and Hall, 1980; Rowley and Kidd, 1981). Structural relationships between basement and cover rocks of the Bronson Hill domes and neighboring rocks in the Merrimack synclinorium are very complex, the domes themselves apparently being late features which were predated by extensive formation of nappes accompanied by high (as high as sillimanite-K feldspar) grades of metamorphism (Thompson and others, 1968; Thompson and Norton, 1968).

COCORP New Hampshire line 6 began just east of the Connecticut River, southwest of Claremont, New Hampshire. In a southeasterly direction, the survey transected the Unity Dome of the Bronson Hill anticlinorium, exposures of the Devonian Mount Clough and Cardigan plutons, and metasedimentary rocks of the Merrimack synclinorium, ending at the village of Mont Vernon, New Hampshire.

The most obvious feature of the seismic reflection profile is a very prominent zone of east-dipping to subhorizontal events beneath the surface outcrop of the Bronson Hill anticlinorium and Merrimack synclinorium. This zone, which is virtually continuous in the subsurface, dips about 20° to 30° (unmigrated) at the western end of the profile and becomes subhorizontal near the eastern end (Fig. 3). Strong reflections are present to about 10.0 seconds (two-way travel time) or about 30 km for an average velocity of 6.0 km/s. Some of the events within this zone project in the subsurface beneath the Connecticut River Valley to line up with the east-dipping events on Vermont line 3, and may thus correlate with them.

The top of the zone of strong reflections dips eastward from about 1.0 seconds at V.P. 100 (Fig. 3) to 5.0 seconds beneath V.P. 525. This upper boundary is very pronounced and separates the east-dipping reflections below from a more seismically transparent zone above. Weak events are present above the top of this east-dipping zone west of V.P. 525; these dip westward and are discordant with the east-dipping zone. East of V.P. 525, strong reflections are present from about 2.0 seconds down to 10.0 seconds. Most of the events dip eastward, but some, particularly those above about 4.0 seconds, dip westward.

In general, the strong east-dipping to subhorizontal reflections exhibit internal complexity on the unmigrated time section in the form of locally variable dips and crosscutting character. Two roughly vertical panels of apparently poor data quality occur between V.P.s 100 and 175, and 475 and 575 (see line drawing, Fig. 3). The cause of the degraded data quality within these zones is not known at present.

Other Geophysical Data

Other types of geophysical data that bear directly on determining the structure of the crust in western New England are not abundant. Seismological studies, primarily of earthquake travel time residuals, have identified crustal to lithospheric scale velocity anomalies in the northeastern United States (Fletcher and others, 1978; Taylor and Toksöz, 1979; Taylor and others, 1980). Early refraction work by Leet (1941) was interpreted as delineating a three-layer crust with velocities increasing with depth, and a total crustal thickness of 35 to 36 km beneath the northeastern United States. A similar study by Katz (1955) using quarry blasts apparently showed a nonlayered, homogeneous crust beneath New York and Pennsylvania; an average crustal thickness of 34.4 km was reported.

Available information that appears to be most relevant to this discussion is the potential field data. Analyses of gravity measurements from about the same latitude as the COCORP traverse were made by Bean (1953) and Diment (1968). In both cases, a Bouguer gravity high over the Green Mountains was modeled by an uplift of dense crustal to subcrustal layers by warping, high-angle faulting, or both. A corresponding gravity low over the Middlebury synclinorium to the west was modeled by depression of lighter materials to deeper levels of the crust. It is significant that although Bean (1953) modeled the gravity by crustal warping, he entertained the idea that it could also be satisfied in part by thrust faulting, an idea suggested early on by Woollard (1939, 1940). Further discussion of the relationship of the New England gravity interpretations to other parts of the orogen is made later.

Interpretation

The most striking aspect on New York line 1 and Vermont line 3 when taken together as one seismic traverse is the correlation in time of the subhorizontal events at 1.5 seconds. While on New York line 1, this zone almost certainly represents shelf and miogeoclinal sediments below the allochthonous Taconic sequence, its nature beneath the Green Mountains on Vermont line 3 is less clear. We interpret the zone of reflections to mark a subhorizontal detachment beneath crystalline rocks of the Green Mountain anticlinorium, which may or may not have slices of shelf and miogeoclinal sediments in its lower plate (Fig. 3). This detachment appears to continue westward beneath the Taconic Mountains, where its position may be controlled stratigraphically by layering within the shelf sequence. In this respect, thrust faulted (allochthonous) Grenville basement in the Green Mountains bears similarities to structurally interleaved slices of basement and shelf rocks observed in the Berkshire Highlands (e.g., Ratcliffe and Harwood, 1975; Ratcliffe and Hatch, 1979). If the events at 1.5 seconds beneath the Green Mountains do not represent slices of sediments, geometry would suggest that this is where the detachment shown on Figure 3 cuts out of the sedimentary section into basement. Faults at the western flank of the Green Mountains (e.g., Pine Hill fault; Wolff, 1891; Thompson, 1967) may be splays off a detachment zone at 1.5 seconds.

We suggest that the detachment zone near 1.5 seconds beneath the Taconic Mountains involves complex splay faults that structurally imbricate or duplicate parts of the shelf sequence. Structural cross sections of the Taconic klippe near New York line 1 (e.g., Zen, 1961) indicate that the allochthon is probably thin (about 2.0 km). Since the zone of relatively continuous reflections on line 1 begins at 1.5 seconds (4.0 to 4.5 km), there is likely a considerable (structural) thickness of shelf carbonates and overlying flysch beneath the allochthon. Further, between V.P.s 100 and 200, only a few kilometers west of the outcrop of the basal Taconic thrust (Giddings Brook fault), the lowermost units of the shelf sequence (Potsdam sandstone and Beekmantown carbonates) rest depositionally on Grenville basement at the surface. Thus, the sequence must thicken very rapidly to the east. Evidence for tectonic thickening of the shelf beneath the Taconic klippe is not unexpected, for along strike to the north, the Champlain thrust system (e.g., Coney and others, 1972) juxtaposes two different facies and thicknesses of coeval lower Paleozoic shelf and miogeoclinal rocks (Champlain lowland sequence, Welby, 1961, and Middlebury synclinorium sequence, Cady, 1945). Thus, the detachment that we infer is in the same structural position as the Champlain thrust zone, but in the area of the COCORP profile, occurs where allochthonous Taconic rocks are still preserved at higher structural levels in the core of the Middlebury synclinorium.

Farther to the east, the zone of reflections at 1.5 seconds turns downward into or is truncated by the zone of east-dipping events near the east flank of the Green Mountains. An interpretation that is compatible with other data is that this east-dipping zone is one of complex deformation associated with a large thrust ramp which brings Precambrian basement to higher levels. In this context, the Green Mountains can be regarded as a large hanging wall anticlinorial structure. Satellitic outcrops of basement such as the Chester, Athens, and Ray Pond domes may also be thrust-related structures.

A widely accepted explanation for structural relationships in western New England has been that Grenville basement massifs east of the Green Mountains were upthrust or domed due to buoyant forces (Thompson, 1950; Thompson and others, 1968), perhaps with concomitant subsidence in the Taconic region. Previous interpretations suggest that the emplacement of the lowermost Taconic slice (Giddings Brook) was accomplished by gravity-induced sliding, possibly related to the uplift of the basement rocks to the east (e.g., Zen, 1968; Bird, 1969).

The presence of a zone of subhorizontal reflections (our inferred detachment) beneath crystalline rocks of the Green Mountains suggests that uplift of the basement there may have been accomplished largely by thrust faulting rather than vertical doming. The amount of horizontal translation of the basement complex is not known, but if the east-dipping events near the east flank of the Green Mountains do represent thrust ramp structures, the amount of horizontal movement is probably not large. The geometry depicted on the cross section in Figure 3 suggests that basement rocks of the Green Mountains could have ramped up, deforming earlier Taconian structures. Thus, in the present interpretation, this lower level of detachment cuts into basement beneath the Green Mountains; movement on this zone was responsible for deforming an earlier, higher level, once continuous thrust zone which emplaced the off-shelf Taconic sequence onto the shelf. The reflection geometry beneath the locus of the Chester dome strongly suggests that the domal structure itself is detached. The presence of these reflections does not necessarily preclude the possibility of a buoyancy-induced component of uplift for the dome rocks. Rather, it argues that bouyant upwelling did not occur in situ.

The age of thrusting of the basement complex is not known; it could have happened late in the Taconian orogeny as part of a progressive deformation, or it could be related to Acadian deformation and metamorphism as suggested by Thompson (1950) and Rosenfeld (1968). Indeed, the complexities in the reflection pattern beneath the Green Mountains might indicate folding of earlier Taconian structures. In addition, there are Acadian (Devonian) metamorphic ages from many of the rocks in Vermont and New Hampshire (e.g., Faul and others, 1963; Harper, 1967), and there is considerable evidence for synmetamorphic Acadian deformation in the same region (Thompson and others, 1968).

The possible correlation of east-dipping events on Vermont line 3 and similar events deeper in the crust on New Hampshire line 6 (Fig. 3) has important implications.

If the interpretation of the dipping events in Vermont as boundaries between slices of basement and/or high-grade metasediments is correct, such a structural style may extend in the subsurface of New Hampshire for a considerable distance beneath the Bronson Hill anticlinorium and Merrimack synclinorium. Because some of the dipping events project to the surface in Vermont within a zone of pre-Silurian metasediments between the Green Mountains and Chester dome, it may thus be that some of the reflections beneath New Hampshire represent thrust imbricated and/or folded equivalents of the Cambrian-Ordovician sequence seen at the surface farther west.

Also, the contrast in seismic character and discordance in dip of the east-dipping zone and the more seismically transparent zone above it in New Hampshire might be taken to suggest that the rocks represented by the highly reflective zone are detached from those above. Indeed, gravity modeling by Nielson and others (1976) of New Hampshire series plutons within the region transected by the COCORP survey suggests that intrusions such as the Mount Clough and Cardigan bodies are less than 2.5 km thick, and likely transported. The interpretation shown in Figure 3 for the New Hampshire data is meant to depict a possible style that could convey this interpretation.

Alternatively, many of the events beneath New Hampshire may represent layered igneous plutons or sills (possibly related to Late Proterozoic(?) or Triassic(?) rifting or perhaps a pervasive tectonite fabric within the crust. However, the strength of the interpretation of many of these events as thrust imbricated metasediments lies in being able to project some reflections to the surface where such rocks are observable.

Thus, interpretations of seismic reflection profiles in New England suggest that Grenville basement rocks in the Green Mountain anticlinorium and Chester dome are allochthonous. In addition, shelf and miogeoclinal sediments preserved in the Middlebury synclinorium appear to be structurally thickened, probably by thrust faulting. Dipping reflections near the east flank of the Green Mountains could very well represent ductile fault zones which imbricate basement and metamorphosed sediments. Dipping to subhorizontal events beneath New Hampshire may correlate with similar events in Vermont and thus might also represent imbricated high-grade metasediments. The data from New Hampshire also suggest that rocks exposed at the surface in the Bronson Hill anticlinorium and Merrimack synclinorium may lie above a zone of detachment which dips eastward at a low angle.

QUÉBEC APPALACHIANS

Three seismic reflection profiles of the Québec Appalachians are available at present. Data were collected in the fall of 1978 from the St. Lawrence lowlands southwest of Québec City (Fig. 4) by the Québec government (lines 2001, 2002, and 2003; Ministère des Richesses Naturelles, 1979a). Our discussion will revolve around the first 124 km of line 2001 (Ministère des Richesses Naturelles, 1979a) which transected the Québec Appalachians from St. Croix in the northwest to Audet near the Québec-Maine border in the southeast. From northwest to southeast, the traverse sequentially crosses lower Paleozoic platformal sediments, the Chaudière, St. Hénédine and related nappes, Notre Dame Mountains anticlinorium, St. Victor synclinorium, and the Connecticut Valley–Gaspé synclinorium (see Fig. 4 and St. Julien and Hubert, 1975).

The interpretive cross section shown in Figure 5 (in pocket inside back cover) is modified from a published interpretation of seismic line 2001 (Ministère des Richesses Naturelles, 1979a). Detailed accounts of the geologic relationships of the Québec Appalachians have been presented by St. Julien and Hubert (1975). We summarize the relationships that are pertinent to the present discussion. Significantly, the Québec seismic section is processed to a total of 4.0 seconds two-way travel time in the northwest, and 6.0 seconds in the southeast, thus yielding no deep crustal information. In contrast, COCORP data are routinely processed to 20.0 seconds; these differences should be kept in mind when comparing the seismic data sets.

The Québec Appalachians have been subdivided into domains (St. Julien and Hubert, 1975) which include from northwest to southeast: (1) a lower Paleozoic platformal sequence (autochthonous domain); (2) a foreland-style thrust belt which includes imbricate faults and nappes (external domain); and (3) a zone of more metamorphosed sediments and igneous rocks (internal domain). Figure 4 depicts the locations of these domains. The autochthonous domain corresponds to the zone northwest of the "limit of Appalachian deformed zone", the external domain consists of the Chaudière and related nappes, and the internal domain coincides with the Sutton–Notre Dame Mountains anticlinorium (Fig. 4).

Rocks exposed in the Chaudière and other nappes and in the Notre Dame Mountains have experienced at least two phases of Ordovician (Taconian) deformation. Some rocks, in particular those east of the axis of the Notre Dame Mountains, have also been affected by mid-Devonian (Acadian) metamorphism and deformation (St. Julien and Hubert, 1975). The nappes in the Québec foreland are believed by these authors to have slid gravitationally as the continental margin was uplifted, perhaps due to convergence with an arc to the east (now represented by the Ascot and Weedon volcanics). Cambrian and Ordovician rocks of both the nappes and the Notre Dame Mountains anticlinorium were thrust westward during the latest part of the Taconian orogeny (St. Julien and Hubert, 1975).

The seismic reflection profile is generally of very good

quality and shows a large number of events; only a select number of these are shown on Figure 5. Very clearly imaged is a set of eastward downstepping reflections which represent the lower Paleozoic shelf carbonate and clastic sequence (Beekmantown, Chazy, Black River, and Trenton Groups). These units are essentially at the surface near the northwest end of the profile (V.P. 2001, Figs. 4, 5) and have been penetrated in the subsurface by numerous wells (Granger and others, 1980). The zone can be traced eastward to about 4.0 seconds (about 8 km, based on the interpretation by SOQUIP; Ministère des Richesses Naturelles, 1979b) east of V.P. 1200. As shown on Figure 5, this is where the first half of the data ends at 4.0 seconds and the 6.0-second data begin. No obvious continuation of the shelf sedimentary reflections is seen eastward of this point.

Many reflections are visible in the shallow part of the section beneath the Chaudière and other nappes west of the Notre Dame Mountains. Some of these can readily be interpreted as structure within the complexly deformed nappes of flysch and sandstone/shale sequence which have been transported westward over the largely coeval shelf carbonates. Shown in Figure 5 is the Chaudière klippe composed of allochthonous Charny Group (feldspathic sandstones and shales; Rasetti, 1946) which was probably originally deposited east of the shelf sequence during early Paleozoic time. These and other allochthonous assemblages were apparently emplaced and redeformed during a progressive Taconian event that began in late Early Ordovician and continued to Late Ordovician or Early Silurian (St. Julien and Hubert, 1975).

Farther to the east, beneath the Notre Dame Mountains anticlinorium (Fig. 5), there are many strong reflections as well. Most prominent of these are a zone of west-dipping events beneath the west flank of the Notre Dame Mountains and a thick (about 2.5 seconds = 5.0 km) zone of slightly curved to subhorizontal events beneath the central and eastern parts of the mountains. These events have been interpreted in different ways. An interpretation by SOQUIP (Ministère des Richesses Naturelles, 1979b) suggests that stacked thrust slices of Cambrian-Ordovician clastics make up the bulk of the zone beneath the Notre Dame Mountains. Alternatively, Seguin (1982) suggested that higher levels within the anticlinorium are dominated by stacked slices of oceanic crust, with wedges of continental basement perhaps present in structurally lower thrust slices (near 4.0 seconds). Earlier cross sections by St. Julien and Hubert (1975) show more or less wholesale uplift of Precambrian continental basement beneath the Notre Dame Mountains. The layered character of the seismic data from beneath the mountains would perhaps militate against such wholesale uplift, however, and argue more in favor of a series of stacked slices, not necessarily composed entirely of continental basement.

The presence of dense mafic (ophiolitic) material at relatively shallow levels (above 15 km) beneath the Notre Dame Mountains is supported by a gravimetric model of the positive Bouguer anomaly over the mountains (Seguin, 1982). The gravity data are apparently consistent with there being no dense lower crustal material at depth. Since the reflection seismic data do not extend past 6.0 seconds (12 km) and refraction or wide angle reflection data are not available for this area, the eastward extent of Grenville continental basement is not uniquely constrained. Seguin (1982) suggested that the continent–ocean crust transition is located at depth east of the Notre Dame Mountains (about V.P. 500, Fig. 5).

Based on the gravity and magnetic anomalies over the Sutton Mountains (see Zietz and others, 1980; Haworth and others, 1980) and the seismic reflection data (Ministère des Richesses Naturelles, 1979b), Kumarapeli and others (1981) suggested that the Sutton Mountains anticlinorium is underlain by about 8 km of mafic volcanic rocks. These rocks, largely greenstone and chlorite-epidote schists, comprise the Tibbit Hill volcanic sequence, which is the lowermost unit in the Oak Hill sequence of Clark (1934). The Oak Hill sequence can apparently be mapped southward from the Notre Dame Mountains (St. Julien and Hubert, 1975) into Vermont where it rests depositionally on Grenville basement of the Green Mountains (Doll and others, 1961). In contrast to the interpretation of Seguin (1982), Kumarapeli and others (1981) suggested that the observed Bouguer gravity cannot be satisfied entirely by a shallow Tibbit Hill source, but believed that a mid to deep crustal source must also be present to account for part of the observed anomaly.

At the eastern end of the SOQUIP seismic profile (Fig. 5), layered events that are present down to about 10 km have been interpreted as early Paleozoic flysch sediments and volcanics of the St. Victor synclinorium (St. Victor, St. Daniel, Ascot, and Weedon Formations). In addition, relatively low-angle (about 30° unmigrated), east-dipping reflections at the western flanks of both the St. Victor and Gaspé–Connecticut Valley synclinoria have been suggested to be faults (near V.P.s 600 and 300, respectively; Ministère des Richesses Naturelles, 1979b). The faults apparently imbricate the early Paleozoic sequences and, in the case of the Gaspé–Connecticut Valley synclinorium, Silurian-Devonian rocks as well.

Thus, the reflection data on Québec seismic line 2001 very clearly show the lower Paleozoic shelf sedimentary sequence dipping eastward beneath complexly faulted, more basinal facies sediments which have been thrust over the shelf. East of the traceable locus of the shelf sequence in the subsurface (beneath the Notre Dame Mountains and eastward), the interpretations are less well constrained. Layered reflections there suggest that the thick piles of thrust-faulted Cambrian-Ordovician sediments seen at the surface may extend to considerable depths, and slices of oceanic and/or continental crust may be present beneath the Notre Dame Mountains.

SOUTHERN APPALACHIANS

Results of the COCORP southern Appalachian traverse Part I (Figs. 6, 7) have previously been published (Cook and others, 1979), and a detailed account of the COCORP data in their entirety (Parts I and II) is being published (Cook and others, 1983). Data from the southern Appalachians Part I extend from near Madisonville, Tennessee, in the Valley and Ridge province to northwest of Augusta, Georgia, in the Carolina slate belt. The Part I survey crossed the tectonic boundary between the Valley and Ridge and Blue Ridge provinces (Great Smokey or Blue Ridge thrust) and transected high-grade rocks of the Blue Ridge and Piedmont. Rocks comprising these tectonic provinces were variously deformed and metamorphosed during the Taconian, Acadian, and Alleghenian phases of Appalachian tectonism (see Hatcher, 1978, 1981 for reviews).

The major features of this profile, depicted in Figure 7 (in pocket inside back cover), are a series of subhorizontal reflections which can be traced from the Valley and Ridge province beneath the Blue Ridge to the eastern part of the Inner Piedmont, where they merge with a zone of east-dipping reflections which continue beneath the western part of the Charlotte belt. The subhorizontal reflections, which have been interpreted as upper Precambrian or lower Paleozoic sedimentary strata and/or detachment horizons, are virtually continuous beneath the Blue Ridge and Inner Piedmont, indicating that crystalline rocks constituting these provinces are allochthonous (Cook and others, 1979). It appears clear from the data that the composite allochthon consisting of the Blue Ridge and Inner Piedmont nappes has been transported westward along a subhorizontal detachment for a distance of at least 200 km. The east-dipping events beneath the eastern Inner Piedmont and western Charlotte belt (below V.P. 2000; Fig. 7) have been suggested by Cook and others (1979) and Cook and Oliver (1981) to represent basinal facies sediments or metasediments which may be correlative with shelf facies sediments farther west. The reflection pattern and dip of the events could perhaps indicate that the sedimentary prism has been imbricated and disrupted by faulting. The cross section in Figure 7 depicts this interpretation.

A model which is consistent with existing geological and geophysical data (Cook and Oliver, 1981) suggests that the zone beneath the Inner Piedmont–Charlotte belt transition represents a tectonically buried early Paleozoic continent-ocean transition. In particular, the Appalachian Bouguer gravity gradient above this zone (Woollard and Joesting, 1964; Haworth and others, 1980), short wave-

length, high amplitude magnetic anomalies above the Charlotte belt (Hatcher and Zietz, 1980), and low near-surface seismic refraction and reflection velocities (Long, 1979; Cook and others, 1979) taken in combination, are consistent with the interpretation that the crustal transition in this region represents the largely intact late Precambrian/early Paleozoic continental edge. The interpreted overlying allochthon thickens eastward from about 6 km near the northwestern end of the transect to about 15 km near the southeastern end.

Cook and others (1981) believed that the basal detachment zone(s) continues at depth beneath the eastern Piedmont and perhaps the Coastal Plain overlap. The data presently available do not allow a unique interpretation, however, and at least one major alternative has been proposed. Hatcher and Zietz (1980) have suggested that a fundamental tectonic boundary separates the Inner Piedmont and the Charlotte belt/Carolina slate belt (their central Piedmont suture). They imply that the suture zone penetrates the crust and perhaps separates two very different basement terranes.

Some very important geologic relationships which are pertinent to this discussion exist in the Grandfather Mountain area of North Carolina and Tennessee. At this locality, a window in the Blue Ridge thrust sheet exposes Grenville-age gneisses and lower Paleozoic clastic and carbonate rocks (Wilson Creek and Blowing Rock gneisses, Chilhowee Group, and Shady dolomite, respectively; Bryant and Reed, 1970). Recent seismic reflection profiling across the Grandfather Mountain window by the USGS (Harris and others, 1981; C-C′, Fig. 1) reveals a zone of relatively flat-lying reflections beneath the gneisses in the window. The reflections correlate in time and style with the subhorizontal reflections seen on the COCORP seismic traverse about 250 km to the southwest. It thus appears that Grenville basement gneisses and overlying shelf clastics and carbonates in the Grandfather Mountain window are allochthonous and rest tectonically on subhorizontal, relatively in-place sediments.

Although the COCORP southern Appalachian profile did not cross exposed Precambrian Grenville basement, the transect passed very close to the Tallulah Falls dome (Wiley gneiss, ca. 1.0 b.y.; Odom and others, 1976), located a few kilometers to the northeast of COCORP line 1. In view of the relationships in the Grandfather Mountain area, perhaps it can be inferred that the Tallulah Falls basement exposures are allochthonous as well. Such a suggestion has, in fact, been made by Hatcher (1972, his Fig. 4). Thus, in three areas, the Green Mountains, the Grandfather Mountain window, and perhaps the Tallulah Falls dome, subsurface data indicate that Precambrian Grenville basement is allochthonous and overlies either shelf and miogeoclinal sediments or detachment horizons. The significance of this finding will be discussed later.

DISCUSSION

In this comparative discussion it should be pointed out again that we make no attempt to correlate rigorously specific structural features along strike of the Appalachian orogen, for such correlations very likely would not withstand the test of close scrutiny. Correlations of exposed tectonic units have already been made by Williams (1978), and considerable along-strike variations in surface geology do exist. However, insofar as specific structures may have played similar roles in geometric development of the orogen, but are perhaps separated by considerable distances along strike, it may be appropriate to bring such relationships into the discussion.

We feel it is very important that where exposed basement in more "interior" parts of the Appalachian Mountain belt has been surveyed, it is apparently allochthonous. More specifically, by basement we mean 1.0-b.y. Grenville basement of the late Precambrian–early Paleozoic North American continent. A question which one would eventually want to answer is not only whether all such basement massifs presently exposed in the Appalachians are allochthonous, but whether or not they could have been emplaced in a "thin-skinned" or some form of wholesale "thick-skinned" manner. The thrust fault emplacement of relatively thin slices of crystalline basement has certainly been recognized in the field for many years; examples include the Altkristalline complex in the axial zone of the eastern Alps (Oxburgh, 1968), the Winters' Pass thrust plate in the southern U.S. Cordillera (Burchfiel and Davis, 1971), the Offerdfahl and Olden nappes in the Scandinavian Caledonides (Gee, 1975), and basement nappes of the Reading Prong and Berkshire Highlands in the northeastern United States (Drake, 1970; Ratcliffe and Harwood, 1975; Ratcliffe and Hatch, 1979).

An insight gained from the COCORP southern Appalachian data is the geometrical extension of thin-skinned thrusting on a large scale to include crystalline rocks of the Blue Ridge and Inner Piedmont (Cook and others, 1979). A very important result was that one could imply very large amounts of horizontal transport of crystalline thrust sheets. As was mentioned earlier, the COCORP southern Appalachian traverse passed very close to exposed Precambrian Grenville basement but did not actually cross it. The high-grade Blue Ridge metasediments and metavolcanics (Ocoee Supergroup and other rocks) along the COCORP traverse do not represent older Grenville basement of the North American continent. As a result, no firm statements regarding the allochthonous or autochthonous nature of Grenville basement rocks could be made at that time, although it now appears that critical data are at hand.

At present there are several seismic surveys that have crossed exposed Grenville basement in the Appalachians;

these include the COCORP New England traverse of the Green Mountains (Brown and others, 1983), the USGS Grandfather Mountain study (Harris and others, 1981), and a recent transect by the USGS from Charlottesville to Richmond, Virginia (Harris and others, 1982). In each of these cases, the most reasonable interpretation of the data is that the exposed Grenville basement is underlain by a thrust fault or faults and is therefore allochthonous. For example, the USGS Grandfather Mountain data some 250 km northeast of the COCORP southern Appalachian traverse (Fig. 1) and the geologic field relationships there (Bryant and Reed, 1970) appear to indicate that the Wilson Creek/Blowing Rock gneisses and their associated sedimentary cover are allochthonous, detached both from the overlying Blue Ridge thrust sheet and the underlying (autochthonous) shelf sediments, and must have been transported from somewhere east of their present location.

In New England, northward along the trend of the Blue Ridge crystalline uplifts, the Housatonic Highlands–Berkshire Highlands–Green Mountains anticlinoria expose Grenville basement. Farther north in Québec, these anticlinoria continue as the Sutton–Bennett–Notre Dame Mountains but do not contain large tracts of exposed Grenville rocks. It is interesting that where Grenville rocks are exposed at the surface in New England, the autochthonous or parautochthonous sedimentary sequences associated with them indicate a lateral change in depositional environment. Examples from New England include the Green Mountains and Berkshire Highlands where flanking sedimentary rocks on the west are largely shelf carbonates and clastics (e.g., Champlain Valley sequence, Thompson, 1967; Stockbridge and Walloomsac Formations, Ratcliffe and Harwood, 1975), and those on the east are mostly quartzofeldspathic wackes and pelites (now gneisses and schists; e.g., Hoosac Formation, Moretown Formation, and Rowe schist; Doll and others, 1961; Hatch and others, 1968). Structural relationships along the east flanks of these basement massifs are complex and may indicate considerable shortening by thrust imbrication. Nevertheless, the cover rocks for the massifs in a general way record a facies change from a shelf to a more off-shelf environment.

It may be that basement rocks of the Green Mountains, along with their sedimentary cover, were ramped upward from an original position somewhere near the transition between continental and oceanic crust. Numerous suggestions have been made to the effect that the edge of the early Paleozoic continent lay near the locus of presently exposed Grenville-type basement massifs. Rankin (1976) implied that these massifs (his Blue-Green-Long axis) marked the western edge of a zone of rifting related to the opening of the proto-Atlantic (Iapetus) Ocean. Rodgers (1968) noted that the transition from lower Paleozoic shallow water carbonates to deeper water clastics probably approximated the edge of continental crust and placed this line east of presently exposed Grenville basement massifs. If geometries of modern passive margins are indeed an analog to the ancient continental margin, the zone of transition between continental and oceanic crust is, we suggest, an extremely likely place for such ramp structures to develop. For example, Montadert and others (1979) have interpreted in a profile from the Bay of Biscay many listric faults within continental basement which appear to flatten into a zone of discontinuity within the crust. The tilted blocks within the attenuated continental crust have several kilometers of relief on them. Perhaps during subsequent shortening of such a margin, these weak zones would either be reactivated or facilitate basement-involved deformation. Such an implication has been made for the Green Mountains (Fig. 4, Rowley and Kidd, 1981).

The recent suggestion by Cook and Oliver (1981) that the Appalachian Bouguer gravity gradient extending from Alabama to Canada (see also Woollard and Joesting, 1964; Haworth and others, 1980) largely marks the edge of the late Precambrian–early Paleozoic continent has important implications. In the south, the gradient from low values on the west to high values on the east appears not to be related to the surface belts of rocks in part because its trend crosscuts the strike of the belts. A synthesis of available geologic and geophysical data indicated to Cook and Oliver (1981) that a major change in crustal density at depth is the main cause of the gravity gradient. The gradient is virtually continuous to the north where it bifurcates near the Connecticut-Massachusetts border (Haworth and others, 1980). From there, a zone of gravity highs continues along the Green Mountains of Vermont, the Sutton–Notre Dame Mountains of Québec, bends around the Gaspé Peninsula, and continues across the Gulf of St. Lawrence into western Newfoundland. A gravity gradient from low values on the west to higher values on the east extends from the area of bifurcation northeastward through eastern Massachusetts, southeastern New Hampshire, and eastern Maine.

The zone of gravity highs in the Gulf of St. Lawrence has been interpreted as the edge of the ancient North American continent by Haworth (1978). As discussed previously, however, gravity highs on the same trend farther south in Québec and New England have been interpreted in different ways. It is significant that in the Green Mountains (Bean, 1953; Diment, 1968) and the Sutton Mountains (Kumarapeli and others, 1981) a density contrast at depth, is required to satisfy the total Bouguer anomaly. In the Notre Dame Mountains (Seguin, 1982) this is apparently not so clear. Perhaps the potential field data are reflecting very different crustal properties in New England and Québec as compared to the central and southern Appalachians, or perhaps the density contrast is not entirely

due to near surface rocks in Québec. It is thus possible that the gravity data may be recording a fundamental change in crustal and/or upper mantle density along the entire Appalachian chain, and that this change occurs at depth beneath transported rocks which comprise the deformed mountain belt.

The seismic reflection data are critical in this regard. Cook and Oliver (1981) pointed out that the palinspastically restored position of the early Paleozoic carbonate bank edge was coincident (or nearly so) with the Appalachian gravity gradient and a zone of east-dipping reflections beneath the Inner Piedmont–Charlotte belt transition. As described by Cook and others (1979) and Cook and Oliver (1981), this zone (Fig. 7) may represent structural imbrication of off-shelf, more basinal facies sediments of the ancient continental margin, perhaps deposited near the transition from continental to oceanic crust. Other geophysical data (refraction, magnetics, seismic velocities) are consistent with this interpretation although do not uniquely constrain it. It is important to note also that in the south a zone of deep reflections (10.0 to 11.0 seconds), possibly representing the Moho, is present beneath and to the east of the zone of east-dipping events, whereas no reflections of this sort are seen to the west (Figs. 7, 8).

Speculatively, if the New England Appalachians have any geometric similarity to the southern Appalachians, one is tempted to regard the east-dipping events near the east flank of the Green Mountains and beneath the Bronson Hill anticlinorium and Merrimack Synclinorium (Fig. 3) as features similar to those beneath the Inner Piedmont–Charlotte belt to the south (Fig. 7). While in the south the reflections may lie beneath a 10 to 15-km-thick allochthon, in New England the dipping events project to the surface within rocks that mark a facies change from shelf to off-shelf, and occur slightly east of a gravity high which may represent a crustal density change at depth. One of the implications of Figure 3 is that there may have been a more extensive allochthon above the Green Mountains. This interpretation is reinforced by the seismic data from New Hampshire, which exhibit east-dipping events giving way eastward to flatter events and deep reflections beneath them becoming apparent. We believe that the subsurface reflection geometries of the New England and southern Appalachians show remarkable similarities, considering the differences observed in surface geology along strike (compare line drawings, Fig. 8).

In Québec, the seismic reflection data are not definitive in addressing this question and can perhaps be interpreted to argue against the preceding suggestion. The upper crust beneath the Notre Dame Mountains and eastward is regarded by many to be composed of a thick pile of transported off-shelf sediments containing some volcanics, and slices of oceanic and/or continental basement (St. Julien and Hubert, 1975; Ministère des Ri-

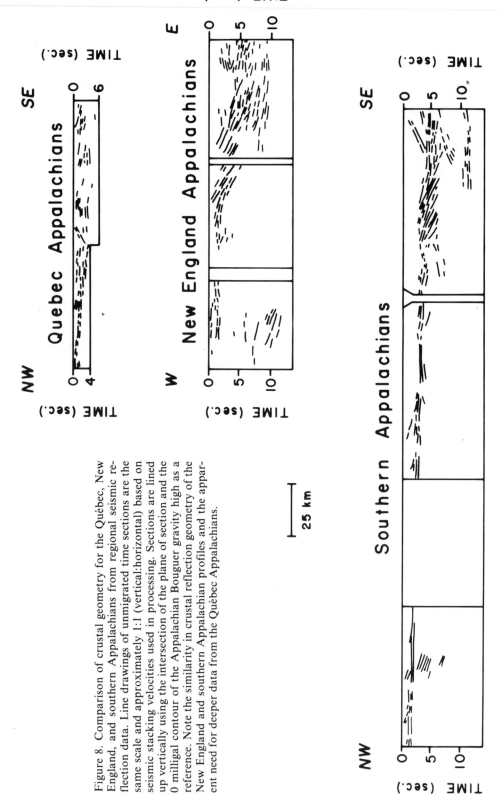

Figure 8. Comparison of crustal geometry for the Québec, New England, and southern Appalachians from regional seismic reflection data. Line drawings of unmigrated time sections are the same scale and approximately 1:1 (vertical:horizontal) based on seismic stacking velocities used in processing. Sections are lined up vertically using the intersection of the plane of section and the 0 milligal contour of the Appalachian Bouguer gravity high as a reference. Note the similarity in crustal reflection geometry of the New England and southern Appalachian profiles and the apparent need for deeper data from the Québec Appalachians.

chesses Naturelles, 1979b; Seguin, 1982). In this sense, the available data suggest proximity to a continent-ocean transition. There are few reflections on the Québec seismic line (Fig. 5; Ministère des Richesses Naturelles, 1979a) near the east flank of the Notre Dame Mountains which have the sort of east-dipping geometry we discussed for the southern and New England Appalachians. In addition, the zone of reflections marking the shelf sedimentary sequence overlying basement in Québec dips much more steeply than the zones in the New England and southern Appalachians (compare Figs. 3, 5, 7, 8).

In general, rocks in the Green Mountain anticlinorium are of higher metamorphic grade than those in the Notre Dame Mountains of Québec. Maps of metamorphic isograds (Thompson and Norton, 1968) and fossil isobaric surfaces based on calculated uplift rates (Doherty and Lyons, 1980) for New England suggest that a deeper erosion level is exposed in New England than in Québec. It may be, therefore, that the Green Mountains and related rocks represent a significant structural culmination along strike in the Appalachians and that any analogous structures in Québec should be at depth. Perhaps the structures we have discussed occur beneath the level of data collection in Québec (i.e., below 6.0 seconds), and the differences seen in the shallow parts of the seismic sections are a function of differences in erosion level. The answer, we suggest, awaits the acquisition of deeper seismic reflection data from the Québec Appalachians (see Fig. 8).

If the Appalachian gravity gradient does approximate the edge of the ancient North American continental margin (a suggestion made early on by Griscom in Zietz and Zen, 1973), an implication one couldmake is that allochthonous rocks have been transported considerably farther west in the southern as compared to the northern Appalachians. Our present interpretation is that this is the case for transported off-shelf and/or rift facies rocks (western Blue Ridge Ocoee and Chilhowee rocks in the south; basal Taconic sequence in New England; Charny Group in Québec). This seems reasonable in part because an estimated 100 to 130 km of transport of Valley and Ridge rocks took place during the Alleghanian orogenic event (Roeder and others, 1978; Harris and Bayer, 1979), whereas there is no definitive evidence for large magnitude Alleghanian movements in the western part of the northern Appalachians. We do not mean to imply, for example, that rock sequences carried in the upper plates of the Great Smoky and Giddings Brook faults (GSF, Fig. 7; GBF, Fig. 3) and those comprising the Chaudière nappe (Fig. 5) are correlative, nor do we want to imply that the faults themselves are correlative. However, in the sense that these basal faults juxtapose off-shelf or rift-related rocks above largely coeval shelf sediments in the three areas compared, they are geometrically similar. The patterns used in Figures 3, 5, and 7 are meant to convey this

tectonic relationship rather than correlations in a literal sense.

The question of whether Grenville basement has been transported farther in the southern as opposed to the northern Appalachians cannot be answered unequivocally at this time. It is clear that more deep seismic reflection profiling should be carried out over parts of the orogen where exposed Grenville rocks exist. Areas that we think are particularly critical are those in which stratigraphic relationships in metasediments overlying the basement are largely preserved. Possible targets for these studies include the Pine Mountain belt in Georgia (Schamel and Bauer, 1980) and the Baltimore gneiss domes in Maryland (Hopson, 1964; Tilton and others, 1970).

Perhaps some of these geometric similarities can be extended to include other mountain chains as well. For instance, recent COCORP data from the Ouachita Mountains of Arkansas (Nelson and others, 1983) show many similarities to seismic data from the Appalachians, in particular the Québec profile. In these areas one sees transported deep water facies sediments lying structurally atop largely coeval shelf rocks in a more external position and a major anticlinorial structure in a more internal position (Benton uplift in Arkansas; Notre Dame Mountains anticlinorium in Québec). Nelson and others (1983) suggest that the data, including the Bouguer gravity gradient from low values on the north to high values south of the Benton uplift are consistent with there being uplifted (fault imbricated?) continental crust beneath the Benton uplift along with a possible shallowing of the Moho at depth. Uplifted continental basement and thickening of a dense, intermediate crustal layer beneath the Ouachita-Marathon mountain system have been suggested by Nicholas and Rosendal (1975) to account for the gravity gradient there. These authors also noted similarities between the anomaly over the Ouachita foldbelt and the Appalachian orogen (Fig. 21, Nicholas and Rosendal, 1975).

The Ouachita Mountains and Québec Appalachians are also similar in that there are no large tracts of continental basement exposed at the surface and the deep water clastics are fault imbricated but more or less continuous across the axes of the uplifts. Perhaps due to differences in erosion level, rocks that core the anticlinorial uplifts in those areas are not exposed, whereas in the New England and southern Appalachians they are exposed. In New England, for example, the deeper water Taconic sequence is preserved in a regional synclinorium cratonward of the Green Mountain anticlinorium. It is clear at least in the case of the Green Mountains that the anticlinorium is cored by continental basement.

The geometric relationship of transported deeper water sediments over shelf rocks is certainly not an uncommon one. Other examples include the Jungbwa allochthon in the Himalayas (Gansser, 1964, 1974), the Hawasina allochthon in the Oman Mountains (Gealey, 1977; Bailey, 1981), the Humber Arm allochthon in the Newfoundland Appalachians (Bird and Dewey, 1970; Williams, 1975), and the Roberts and Golconda allochthons of the U.S. Cordillera (Burchfiel and Davis, 1972, 1975). In at least three of these cases (Himalayas, Oman, and Newfoundland) the deep water sediments are preserved in a synclinorial structure that is flanked in a more internal position by an anticlinorium known or inferred to be cored by continental basement.

One of the implications one can make from the Appalachian seismic data is that a considerable amount of underthrusting of continental crust can take place. An excellent modern analog of this exists in the Banda arc of Indonesia. There is compelling evidence that the Australian continental margin and its shelf sedimentary cover is being thrust beneath the Timor arc (Chamalaun and others, 1976; Hamilton, 1979). Furthermore, detailed geometric comparisons, both in style and scale, of the Banda arc region and the subsurface structure of the Appalachian orogen (Albaugh, 1981) have revealed remarkable similarities. In both the frontal part of the Appalachian deformed belt and the accretionary prism in the Timor region, the internal structure of the allochthon is complex and discordant with the largely undeformed, underlying (lower plate) shelf strata. Listric thrust faults are directed mostly toward the continent and flatten into a low-dipping zone of detachment. In the Banda arc a series of tectonic events from oceanic subduction, to incipient continental subduction, to an arc collision can be seen in the Java trench, Timor trough, and northern New Guinea margin, respectively. In view of the numerous suggestions that island arcs that collided with the ancient North American continent are still preserved in the Appalachians (e.g., Carolina slate belt in the south, Bronson Hill anticlinorium in New England, Ascot-Weedon volcanics in Québec), perhaps subsurface structures in the two regions would look very similar if the collisions currently underway in the Banda arc were carried to completion.

CONCLUSIONS

Deep seismic reflection profiling in the Appalachian orogen has provided new insights into the architecture of the crust beneath the deformed mountain chain. Not only has it been shown that very large horizontal movements of crystalline rocks have been accomplished, but also that involvement of the continental basement in deformation may have been a common ingredient in the evolution of the mountain belt. Significantly, the seismic studies appear to be suggesting that the present distribution of intensely deformed Appalachian rocks is confined to a relatively thin zone at high structural levels, and that the crust beneath the deformed belt, perhaps including an ancient

transition from continent to ocean, may lie largely preserved at depth. Corollaries that follow but need further testing are multifold: (1) the upper part of the continental crust was redistributed by thrust faulting and folding, while the lower part of the continental crust remained essentially rigid and undeformed during subduction; (2) the M discontinuity beneath the Appalachian orogen may in part be a relict oceanic feature; and (3) the accretion of some materials external to North America may have taken place in a "thin-skinned" mode. Maybe a similar case can be made for other mountain chains.

ACKNOWLEDGMENTS

As with all COCORP surveys, the conception, completion, and interpretational aspects of this study have greatly benefited from discussions with persons far too numerous to mention here. We are very grateful for the spirit of cooperative science which has been engendered by these discussions. The manuscript was reviewed by R. Hatcher, Jr., and H. Williams. COCORP field work was carried out by crew 6834 of the Petty-Ray Geophysical Division of Geosource, Inc. This research was supported by NSF Grant EAR-782367. Cornell Department of Geological Sciences contribution no. 709.

REFERENCES CITED

Albaugh, D. S., 1981, The Banda arc—A contemporary analog for subsurface structure of the Appalachian orogen [M.S. thesis]: Ithaca, Cornell University.

Bailey, E. H., 1981, Geologic map of Muscat-Ibra area, Sultanate of Oman: Journal of Geophysical Research, v. 86, pocket, scale 1:100,000.

Bean, R. J., 1953, Relation of gravity anomalies to the geology of central Vermont and New Hampshire: Geological Society of America Bulletin, v. 64, p. 509–538.

Bird, J. M., 1969, Middle Ordovician gravity sliding—Taconic region, *in* Kay, M., ed., North Atlantic—Geology and continental drift: American Association of Petroleum Geologists Memoir 12, p. 670–686.

Bird, J. M., and Dewey, J. F., 1970, Lithosphere plate–continental margin tectonics and the evolution of the Appalachian orogen: Geological Society of America Bulletin, v. 81, p. 1031–1060.

Brown, L. D., and others, 1983, Adirondack-Appalachian crustal structure: The COCORP northeast traverse: Geological Society of America Bulletin (in press).

Bryant, B., and Reed, J. C., Jr., 1970, Geology of the Grandfather Mountain window and vicinity, North Carolina and Tennessee: U.S. Geological Survey Professional Paper 615, 190 p.

Burchfiel, B. C., and Davis, G. A., 1971, Clark Mountain thrust complex in the Cordillera of southeastern California: Geologic summary and field trip guide: Geological Society of America Cordilleran Section Guidebook, p. 1–28.

——1972, Structural framework and evolution of the southern part of the Cordilleran orogen, western United States: American Journal of Science, v. 272, p. 97–118.

——1975, Nature and controls of Cordilleran orogenesis, western United States: Extensions of an earlier synthesis: American Journal of Science, v. 175-A, p. 363–396.

Cady, W. M., 1945, Stratigraphy and structure of west central Vermont: Geological Society of America Bulletin, v. 56, p. 515–558.

Chamalaun, F. H., Lockwood, K., and White, A., 1976, The Bouguer gravity field and crustal structure of eastern Timor: Tectonophysics, v. 30, p. 241–259.

Chapple, W. M., 1973, Taconic orogeny: Abortive subduction of the North American continental plate?: Geological Society of America Abstracts with Programs, v. 5, p. 573.

Clark, T. H., 1934, Structure and stratigraphy of southern Quebec: Geological Society of America Bulletin, v. 45, p. 1–20.

Coney, P. J., and others, 1972, The Champlain thrust and related features near Middlebury, Vermont, *in* Doolan, B. L., and Stanley, R. S., Guidebook for field trips in Vermont: New England Intercollegiate Geological Conference, 64th Annual Meeting Guidebook, Burlington, Vermont, University of Vermont, p. 97–116.

Cook, F. A., and Oliver, J. E., 1981, The early Paleozoic continental edge in the Appalachian orogen: American Journal of Science, v. 281, p. 993–1008.

Cook, F. A., and others, 1979, Thin-skinned tectonics in the crystalline southern Appalachians; COCORP seismic reflection profiling of the Blue Ridge and Piedmont: Geology, v. 7, p. 563–567.

——1981, COCORP seismic profiling of the Appalachian orogen beneath the Coastal Plain of Georgia: Geological Society of America Bulletin, Part I, v. 92, p. 738–748.

——1983, COCORP seismic reflection profiling of the southern Appalachians: American Association of Petroleum Geologists Studies in Geology (in press).

Diment, W. H., 1968, Gravity anomalies in northwestern New England, *in* Zen, E-an, White, W. S., Hadley, J. B., and Thompson, J. B., Jr., eds., Studies of Appalachian geology: Northern and maritime: New York, John Wiley and Sons, p. 399–413.

Doherty, J. T., and Lyons, J. B., 1980, Mesozoic erosion rates in northern New England: Geological Society of America Bulletin, Part I, v. 91, p. 16–20.

Doll, C. G., Cady, W. M., Thompson, J. B., Jr., and Billings, M. P., 1961, Centennial geologic map of Vermont: Vermont Geological Survey, scale 1:250,000.

Downie, E. A., 1980, Prograde and retrograde reaction sequence and conditions of metamorphism, north end of the Chester dome, southeastern Vermont: Geological Society of America Abstracts with Programs, v. 12, p. 415.

Drake, A. A., Jr., 1970, Structural geology of the Reading Prong, *in* Fisher, G. W., and others, eds., Studies of Appalachian geology: Central and southern: New York, John Wiley and Sons, p. 271–291.

Faul, H., Stern, T. W., Thomas, H. H., and Elmore, P.L.D., 1963, Ages of intrusion and metamorphism in the northern Appalachians: American Journal of Science, v. 261, p. 1–19.

Fisher, D. W., 1979, Folding in the foreland, middle Ordovician Dolgeville facies, Mohawk Valley, New York: Geology, v. 7, p. 455–459.

Fletcher, J. B., Sbar, M. L., and Sykes, L. R., 1978, Seismic trends and travel time residuals in eastern North America and their tectonic implications: Geological Society of America Bulletin, v. 89, p. 1656–1676.

Gansser, A., 1964, Geology of the Himalayas: London, Interscience.

——1974, Himalaya, *in* Spencer, A. M., ed., Mesozoic-Cenozoic orogenic belts—data for orogenic studies: Geological Society of London Special Publication no. 4, p. 267–278.

Gealey, W. K., 1977, Ophiolite obduction and geologic evolution of the Oman Mountains and adjacent areas: Geological Society of America Bulletin, v. 88, p. 1183–1191.

Gee, D. G., 1975, A tectonic model for the central part of the Scandinavian Caledonides: American Journal of Science, v. 175-A, p. 468–515.

Granger, B., St. Julien, P., and Slivitzky, A., 1980, A seismic profile across the southwestern part of the Québec Appalachians: Geological Society of America Abstracts with Programs, v. 12, p. 435.

Gwinn, V. E., 1964, Thin-skinned tectonics in the Plateau and northwestern Valley and Ridge provinces of the central Appalachians: Geological Society of America Bulletin, v. 75, p. 863–899.

Hamilton, W., 1979, Tectonics of the Indonesian region: U.S. Geological Survey Professional Paper 1078, 345 p.

Harper, C. T., 1967, Isotopic ages from the Appalachians and their tectonic significance: Canadian Journal of Earth Sciences, v. 5, p. 49–59.

Harris, L. D., 1976, Thin-skinned tectonics and potential hydrocarbon traps, illustrated by a seismic profile in the Valley and Ridge province of Tennessee: U.S. Geological Survey Journal of Research, v. 4, p. 379–386.

Harris, L. D., and Bayer, K. C., 1979, Sequential development of the Appalachian orogen above a master decollement—A hypothesis: Geology, v. 7, p. 568–572.

Harris, L. D., and others, 1981, Evaluation of southern eastern overthrust belt beneath Blue Ridge–Piedmont thrust: American Association of Petroleum Geologists Bulletin, v. 65, p. 2497–2505.

Harris, L. D., DeWitt, W. Jr., and Bayer, K. C., 1982, Seismic reflection data in the central Appalachians: Geological Society of America Abstracts with Programs, v. 14, p. 23.

Hatch, N. L., Jr., Schnabel, R. W., and Norton, S. A., 1968, Stratigraphy and correlation of the rocks on the east limb of the Berkshire anticlinorium in western Massachusetts and north-central Connecticut, *in* Zen, E-an, and others, eds., Studies of Appalachian geology: Northern and maritime: New York, John Wiley and Sons, p. 177–184.

Hatcher, R. D., Jr., 1972, Developmental model for the southern Appalachians: Geological Society of America Bulletin, v. 83, p. 1735–2760.

——1978, Tectonics of the western Piedmont and Blue Ridge: Review and speculation: American Journal of Science, v. 278, p. 276–304.

——1981, Thrusts and nappes in the North American Appalachian orogen, *in* McClay, K. R., and Price, N. J., eds., Thrust and nappe tectonics: Geological Society of London Special Publication no. 9, Oxford, Blackwell Scientific Publications, p. 491–499.

Hatcher, R. D., Jr., and Zietz, I., 1980, Tectonic implications of regional aeromagnetic and gravity data from the southern Appalachians, *in* Wones, D. R., ed., The Caledonides in the U.S.A.: International Geological Correlation Program Project 17, p. 235–244.

Haworth, R. T., 1978, Interpretation of geophysical data in the northern Gulf of St. Lawrence and its relevance to lower Paleozoic geology: Geological Society of America Bulletin, v. 89, p. 1091–1110.

Haworth, R. T., and others, 1980, Bouguer gravity anomaly map of the Appalachian orogen: Memorial University of Newfoundland map no. 3, scale 1:1,000,000.

Hiscott, R. N., 1978, Provenance of Ordovician deep water sandstones, Tourelle Formation, Québec and implications for initiation of the Taconic orogeny: Canadian Journal of Earth Sciences, v. 15, p. 1579–1597.

Hitchcock, C. H., 1883, The early history of the North-American continent: Science, v. 2, p. 293–297.

Hopson, C. A., 1964, The crystalline rocks of Howard and Montgomery Counties, *in* The geology of Howard and Montgomery Counties: Maryland Geological Survey, p. 27–215.

Karig, D. E., 1974, Evolution of arc systems in the western Pacific: Annual Review of Earth and Planetary Sciences, v. 2, p. 51–75.

Katz, S., 1955, Seismic study of crustal structure in Pennsylvania and New York: Bulletin of the Seismological Society of America, v. 45, p. 303–325.

Kay, M., 1951, North American geosynclines: Geological Society of America Memoir 48, 143 p.

Kumarapeli, P. S., Goodacre, A. K., and Thomas, M. D., 1981, Gravity and magnetic anomalies of the Sutton Mountains region, Québec and Vermont: Expressions of rift volcanics related to the opening of Iapetus: Canadian Journal of Earth Sciences, v. 18, p. 680–692.

Leet, D., 1941, Trial travel times for northeastern America: Bulletin of the Seismological Society of America, v. 31, p. 325–334.

Long, L., 1979, The Carolina slate belt—evidence of a continental rift zone: Geology, v. 7, p. 180–184.

Ministère des Richesses Naturelles du Québec, 1979a, Acquisition et traitement de données sismiques: Basses-Terres du St. Laurent; lignes sismiques 2001, 2002, et 2003, DP-665.

——1979b, Interpretation du profil sismique 2001 par SOQUIP, DP-721.

Montadert, L., and others, 1979, Rifting and subsidence of the northern continental margin of the Bay of Biscay: Initial Reports of the Deep Sea Drilling Project, v. 48, p. 1025–1060.

Nelson, K. D., and others, 1983, Results of COCORP seismic reflection profiling in the Ouachita Mountains, western Arkansas: Tectonics, v. 1, p. 413–430.

Nicholas, R. L., and Rozendal, R. A., 1975, Subsurface positive elements within the Ouachita foldbelt in Texas and their relation to Paleozoic cratonic margin: American Association of Petroleum Geologists Bulletin, v. 59, p. 193–216.

Nielson, D. L., and others, 1976, Gravity models and mode of emplacement of the New Hampshire plutonic series, in Lyons, P. C., and Brownlow, A. H., eds., Studies in New England geology: Geological Society of America Memoir 146, p. 301–318.

Nisbet, E., 1976, Structural studies in the northern Chester dome of east-central Vermont [Ph.D. thesis]: Albany, State University of New York, 167 p.

Odom, A. L., Russell, G. S., and Russell, C. W., 1976, Distribution and age of Precambrian basement in the southern Appalachians: Geological Society of America Abstracts with Programs, v. 8, p. 238.

Osberg, P. H., 1978, Synthesis of the geology of the northeastern Appalachians, U.S.A., in Caledonian-Appalachian orogen of the North Atlantic region: Geological Survey of Canada Paper 78-13, p. 137–148.

Oxburgh, E. R., 1968, An outline of the geology of the central eastern Alps: Geological Society of London Proceedings, v. 79, p. 1–46.

Rankin, D. W., 1976, Appalachian salients and recesses: Late Precambrian continental breakup and the opening of the Iapetus Ocean: Journal of Geophysical Research, v. 81, p. 5605–5619.

Rasetti, F., 1946, Cambrian and Early Ordovician stratigraphy of the lower St. Lawrence Valley: Geological Society of America Bulletin, v. 57, p. 687–706.

Ratcliffe, N. M., 1975, Cross section of the Berkshire massif at 42° N.: Profile of a basement reactivation zone, in Ratcliffe, N. M., ed.: New England Intercollegiate Geological Conference, 67th Annual Meeting Guidebook, p. 186–222.

——1979, Field guide to the Chatham and Greylock slices of the Taconic allochthon, and their relationship to the Hoosac-Rowe sequence, in Friedman, G. M., ed.: New York State Geological Association and New England Intercollegiate Geological Conference Guidebook, p. 388–425.

Ratcliffe, N. M., and Harwood, D. S., 1975, Blastomylonites associated with recumbent folds and overthrusts at the western edge of the Berkshire massif, Connecticut and Massachusetts—a preliminary report, in Tectonic studies of the Berkshire massif, western Massachusetts, Connecticut and Vermont: U.S. Geological Survey Professional Paper, 888-A, p. 1–19.

Ratcliffe, N. M., and Hatch, N. L., Jr., 1979, A traverse across the Taconide Zone in the area of the Berkshire massif, western Massachusetts, in Skehan, J. W., and Osberg, P. H., eds., The Caledonides in the U.S.A., Geological excursions in the northeast Appalachians, I.G.C.P. project 17: Weston, Massachusetts, Weston Observatory, p. 175–224.

Ratcliffe, N. M., and Mose, D. G., 1978, Probable Taconic age of the Middlefield thrust zone, eastern margin of the Berkshire massif,

Massachusetts, on the basis of Rb/Sr geochronology of intrusive granitic rocks: Geological Society of America Abstracts with Programs, v. 10, p. 81.

Ratcliffe, N. M., and Zartman, R. E., 1976, Stratigraphy, isotophic ages, and deformational history of basement and cover rocks of the Berkshire massif, southwestern Massachusetts, in Page, L. R., ed., Contributions to stratigraphy of New England: Geological Society of America Memoir 148, p. 373–411.

Rich, J., 1934, Mechanics of low angle overthrust faulting as illustrated by Cumberland overthrust block Virginia, Kentucky, and Tennessee: American Association of Petroleum Geologists Bulletin, v. 18, p. 1584–1596.

Robinson, P., and Hall, L. M., 1980, Tectonic synthesis of southern New England, in Wones, D. R., ed., The Caledonides in the U.S.A.: International Geological Correlations Program Project 17: Virginia Polytechnic Institute Memoir 2, p. 73–82.

Rodgers, J., 1949, Evolution of thought on structure of middle and southern Appalachians: American Association of Petroleum Geologists Bulletin, v. 33, p. 1643–1654.

——1968, The eastern edge of the North American continent during the Cambrian and Early Ordovician, in Zen, E-an, and others, eds., Studies of Appalachian geology: Northern and maritime: New York, John Wiley and Sons, p. 141–150.

——1970, The tectonics of the Appalachians: New York, Wiley-Interscience, 271 p.

Roeder, D., Gilbert, O., Jr., and Witherspoon, W., 1978, Evolution and macroscopic structure of the Valley and Ridge thrust belt, Tennessee and Virginia: University of Tennessee Studies in Geology 2, 25 p.

Rosenfeld, J. L., 1968, Garnet rotations due to major Paleozoic deformations in southeast Vermont, in Zen, E-an, White, W. S., Hadley, J. B., and Thompson, J. B., Jr., eds., Studies of Appalachian geology: Northern and maritime: New York, John Wiley and Sons, p. 185–222.

Rowley, D. B., and Kidd, W.S.F., 1981, Stratigraphic relationships and detrital composition of the Medial Ordovician flysch of western New England: implications for the tectonic evolution of the Taconic orogeny: Journal of Geology, v. 89, p. 199–218.

Rowley, D. B., Kidd, W.S.F., and Delano, L. L., 1979, Detailed stratigraphic and structural features of the Giddings Brook slice of the Taconic allochthon in the Granville area, in Friedman, G. M., ed.: New York State Geological Association and New England Intercollegiate Geological Conference Guidebook, p. 186–242.

Schamel, S., and Bauer, D., 1980, Remobilized Grenville basement in the Pine Mountain window, in Wones, D. R., ed., The Caledonides in the U.S.A.: International Geological Correlations Program Project 17, Virginia Polytechnic Institute Memoir 2, p. 313–316.

Schilt, S., and others, 1979, The heterogeneity of the continental crust: results from deep crustal seismic reflections profiling using the Vibroseis technique: Reviews of Geophysics and Space Physics, v. 17, p. 354–368.

Seely, D. R., Vail, P. R., and Walton, G. G., 1974, Trench slope model, in Burk, C. A., and Drake, C. L., eds., The geology of continental margins: New York, Springer-Verlag, p. 249–260.

Seguin, M. K., 1982, Geophysics of the Québec Appalachians: Tectonophysics v. 81, p. 1–50.

Stevens, R. K., 1970, Cambro-Ordovician flysch sedimentation and tectonics in western Newfoundland and their possible bearing on a proto-Atlantic, in Lajoie, J., ed., Flysch sedimentology in North America: Geological Association of Canada Special Paper 7, p. 165–178.

St. Julien, P., and Hubert, C., 1975, Evolution of the Taconian orogen in the Québec Appalachians: American Journal of Science, v. 275A, p. 337–362.

Taylor, S. R., and Toksöz, M. N., 1979, Three dimensional crust and upper mantle structure of the northeastern United States: Journal of

Geophysical Research, v. 84, p. 7627–7644.

Taylor, S. R., Toksöz, M. N., and Chaplin, M. P., 1980, Crustal structure of the northeastern United States: Contrasts between Grenville and Appalachian provinces: Science, v. 208, p. 595–597.

Thompson, J. B., Jr., 1950, A gneiss dome in southeastern Vermont [Ph.D. thesis]: Cambridge, Massachusetts Institute of Technology, 149 p.

——1967, Bedrock geology of the Pawlet quadrangle, Vermont, Part II eastern portion: Vermont Geological Society Bulletin 30, p. 65–98.

Thompson, J. B., Jr., and Norton, S. A., 1968, Paleozoic regional metamorphism in New England and adjacent areas, *in* Zen, E-an, and others, eds., Studies of Appalachian geology: Northern and maritime: New York, John Wiley and Sons, p. 319–328.

Thompson, J. B., Jr., and others, 1968, Nappes and gneiss domes in west-central New England, *in* Zen, E-an, and others, eds., Studies of Appalachian geology: Northern and maritime: New York, John Wiley and Sons, p. 203–218.

Tilton, G. R., and others, 1960, 1000 million-year-old minerals from the eastern United States and Canada: Journal of Geophysical Research, v. 65, p. 4173, 4179.

Tilton, G. R., Doe, B. R., and Hopson, C. A., 1970, Zircon age measurements in the Maryland Piedmont, with special reference to Baltimore gneiss problems, *in* Fisher, G. W., and others, eds., Studies of Appalachian geology: Central and southern: New York, John Wiley and Sons, p. 429–434.

Welby, C. W., 1961, Bedrock geology of the central Champlain Valley of Vermont: Vermont Geological Survey Bulletin 14, 296 p.

Williams, H., 1975, Structural succession, nomenclature and interpretation of transported rocks in western Newfoundland: Canadian Journal of Earth Sciences, v. 12, p. 1874–1894.

——1978, Tectonic lithofacies map of the Appalachian orogen: Memorial University of Newfoundland map no. 1, scale 1:1,000,000.

Wolff, J. E., 1891, On the lower Cambrian age of the Stockbridge limestone: Geological Society of America Bulletin, v. 2, p. 331–337.

Woollard, G. P., 1939, The geological significance of gravity investigations in Virginia: American Geophysical Union Transactions, 20th Annual Meeting, p. 317–323.

——1940, Gravitational determination of deep-seated crustal structure of continental borders: American Geophysical Union Transactions, 21st Annual Meeting, p. 808–815.

Woollard, G. P., and Joesting, H. R., 1964, Bouguer gravity anomaly map of the United States: United States Geological Survey, scale 1:2,500,000.

Zen, E-an, 1961, Stratigraphy and structure at the north end of the Taconic Range of west-central Vermont: Geological Society of America Bulletin, v. 72, p. 293–338.

——1967, Time and space relationships of the Taconic allochthon and autochthon: Geological Society of America Special Paper 97, 107 p.

——1968, Nature of the Ordovician orogeny in the Taconic area, *in* Zen, E-an, and others, eds., Studies of Appalachian geology: Northern and maritime: New York, John Wiley and Sons, p. 129–139.

——1972, Some revisions in the interpretation of the Taconic allochthon, west-central Vermont: Geological Society of America Bulletin, v. 83, p. 2573–2587.

Zietz, I., and Zen, E-an, 1973, Northern Appalachians: Geotimes, v. 18, p. 24–28.

Zietz, I., and others, 1980, Magnetic anomaly map of the Appalachian orogen: Memorial University of Newfoundland map no. 2, scale 1:1,000,000.

MANUSCRIPT ACCEPTED BY THE SOCIETY SEPTEMBER 10, 1982

Geological Society of America
Memoir 158
1983

A deep structural profile across the Appalachians of southern Quebec

Pierre St.-Julien
Department of Geology
Laval University
Quebec, Québec G1K 7P4
Canada

Anne Slivitsky
Department of Geology
Memorial University of Newfoundland
St. John's, Newfoundland A1B 3X5
Canada

Tomas Feininger
Department of Geology
Laval University
Quebec, Québec G1K 7P4
Canada

ABSTRACT

A 150-km-long seismic line was shot from a point on the St. Lawrence River 50 km southwest of Quebec City, southeastward to the U.S. border in 1979. The line crosses the autochthonous domain, the foreland thrust belt, and the allochthonous domain of the Humber Zone; it also crosses the Dunnage Zone and overlying rocks of the Connecticut Valley–Gaspé synclinorium. Reflectors on the derived seismic profile have been correlated with surface geology and the logs of four deep wells, and in turn used to construct a deep structural profile across the Appalachians of southern Quebec.

The principal conclusions drawn from the profile are: (A) Grenville basement occurs at depth under the Humber Zone, and along with cover rocks, it has been cut by southeast-dipping syndepositional normal faults in the authochthonous domain, the foreland thrust belt, and the northwestern part of the allochthonous domain. Several of the fault blocks were tilted northward. (B) Nappe emplacement took place during Middle Ordovician time. (C) Later Acadian(?) thrust faults in the Notre Dame anticlinorium may have utilized progressively deeper levels of detachment and at depth may involve Grenville basement. (D) Rocks of the Connecticut Valley–Gaspé synclinorium have been thrust over the Dunnage Zone, and along the seismic line they contain no granite plutons at depth.

INTRODUCTION

Early in 1979 the Geosource Company shot a seismic line across the southwestern part of the Quebec Appalachians from the St. Lawrence River at Pointe Platon to the U.S. border at the town of Audet, for the Provincial Department of Energy and Resources (Fig. 1). A preliminary geophysical and structural interpretation of the line was prepared by the Société Québécoise d'Initiative Pétrolière (SOQUIP). The goal of the present study is to correlate surface geology with seismic reflectors recorded along the line to construct a deep structural profile across the southwestern part of the Quebec Appalachians.

The seismic line crosses areas covered by geologic maps of varying detail. Our strip map (Fig. 2 in pocket inside back cover) is a compilation based on Clark and Globensky (1973), Benoît (1958), Charbonneau (1975), Cooke (1937), Riordon (1954), Blackburn (1975), Kelly (1975), Marleau (1958), and unpublished maps by Jacques Muller and Pierre St-Julien. In addition, regional studies by Bird and Dewey (1970), St-Julien and Hubert (1975), and Williams and St-Julien (1978) were used in synthesizing the evolution of the Taconic orogen in the Quebec Appalachians.

TECTONIC AND STRATIGRAPHIC CONTEXT

Williams (1978, 1979), based on earlier work in Newfoundland (Williams and others, 1972, 1974), subdivided the Appalachian orogen into five tectonostratigraphic zones, each characterized by Middle Ordovician or older rocks with unique stratigraphic and structural characteristics. From west to east, the zones are: Humber, Dunnage, Gander, Avalon, and Meguma.

Rocks of the Humber Zone trace the development and destruction of the continental margin of the Iapetus Ocean in early Paleozoic time (Rodgers, 1968; Williams and Stevens, 1974; Williams, 1979). This Atlantic-type margin lies on Grenville basement. The southeastern limit of the Humber Zone is the Baie Verte–Brompton line (St-Julien and others, 1976; Williams and St-Julien, 1978), which is interpreted to be the contact between lower Paleozoic rocks deposited on continental crust to the northwest and those deposited on an oceanic crust to the southeast (St-Julien and Hubert, 1975; St-Julien and others, 1976; Williams and St-Julien, 1978).

The Dunnage Zone is the vestige of an oceanic domain (Iapetus) and is composed principally of island arc sequences (Kean and Strong, 1975) and mélanges (Horne, 1969; St. Julien and Hubert, 1975; Kay, 1976; Hibbard and Williams, 1979), all laid down on oceanic crust (Upadhyay and others, 1971; Smitheringale, 1972; Kay, 1975; Laurent, 1975, 1977; Norman and Strong, 1975; Kidd, 1977; Williams, 1979). Important rock types include tho-

leiitic basalt, calc-alkalic andesite and rhyolite, pelagic and hemipelagic sediments, and turbidites. Rocks of Silurian and Devonian age of the Connecticut Valley–Gaspé synclinorium in part overlay the rocks of the Dunnage zone in the southeast.

Humber Zone

St-Julien and Hubert (1975) subdivided the Humber Zone of the southwestern part of the Quebec Appalachians into an autochthonous domain, the foreland thrust belt, and an allochthonous domain (Fig. 3 in pocket inside back cover).

The autochthonous domain. This domain is bounded to the north by the Grenville basement and to the south by the first thrust fault (Figs. 2, 3). The domain is composed of a platform sequence overlain by turbidites which in turn are covered by a regressive sequence. The rocks are relatively undeformed and range from Cambrian to Late Ordovician in age. Their stratigraphy has been studied by Logan (1863), Ells (1896), Parks (1930), Clark (1944, 1972), Houde and Clark (1962), Clark and Globensky (1973), and Clark and others (1979).

The Potsdam Group (upper Cambrian) constitutes the base of the autochthonous domain. In ascending order, the Potsdam Group is composed of variegated sandstone, conglomerate, and white orthoquartzite and has an aggregate thickness from 450 to 800 m. The Beekmantown Group of Early Ordovician age conformably overlies the Potsdam Group. The Beekmantown is composed of dolomite, dolomitic limestone, shale, and sandstone and has an aggregate thickness of 120 to 300 m. The conformably overlying Middle Ordovician Chazy Group is composed of alternating shale, siltstone, and sandstone, and there are horizons of limestone interstratified with shale at the top of the group. The mean thickness of the Chazy Group is 110 m. The Black River Group conformably overlies the Chazy Group. The Black River is made up of limestone and dolomitic limestone interbedded with shale. The thickness of the Black River Group is only about 8 m in the Quebec City area, although near Montreal it attains a thickness of 31 m. The overlying middle Ordovician Trenton Group is composed chiefly of calcilutite, nodular limestone, and crystalline limestone, all interlayered with shale. The mean thickness of the Trenton Group is 170 m. The Utica Shale, also of Middle Ordovician age, conformably overlies the Trenton Group. The Utica is made up of bituminous and locally limy black shale and thin beds of dolomite near the base. The thickness of the Utica Shale ranges from 90 to 120 m. The overlying turbiditic Lorraine Group is made up of more or less sandy argillites interbedded with thin limestones and sandstones. The thickness of the Lorraine Group is about 760 m. The unconformably overlying Richmond Group

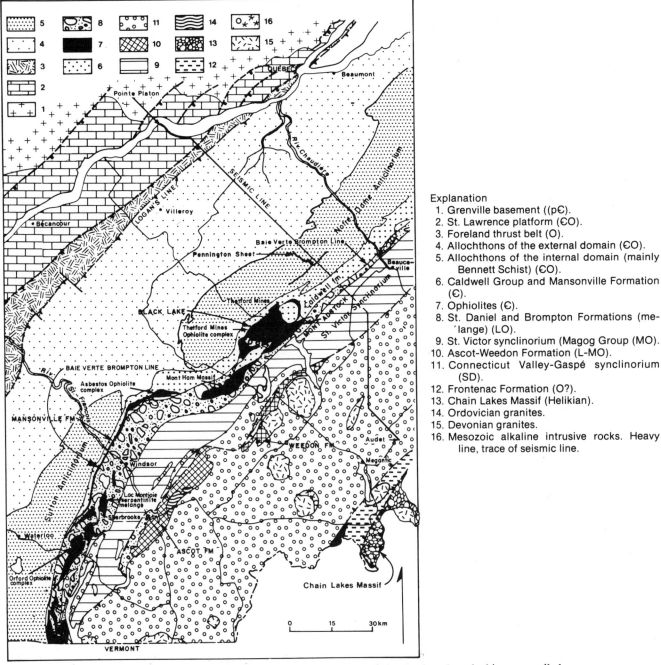

Figure 1. Geological map of the southwestern part of the Quebec Appalachians compiled from various sources by P. St-Julien.

Explanation
1. Grenville basement ((pC).
2. St. Lawrence platform (CO).
3. Foreland thrust belt (O).
4. Allochthons of the external domain (CO).
5. Allochthons of the internal domain (mainly Bennett Schist) (CO).
6. Caldwell Group and Mansonville Formation (C).
7. Ophiolites (C).
8. St. Daniel and Brompton Formations (me-´lange) (LO).
9. St. Victor synclinorium (Magog Group (MO).
10. Ascot-Weedon Formation (L-MO).
11. Connecticut Valley-Gaspé synclinorium (SD).
12. Frontenac Formation (O?).
13. Chain Lakes Massif (Helikian).
14. Ordovician granites.
15. Devonian granites.
16. Mesozoic alkaline intrusive rocks. Heavy line, trace of seismic line.

(Upper Ordovician) constitutes a regressive sequence composed of interstratified sandstone and limestone argillite and has a total thickness of 660 m.

In the vicinity of the seismic line, only the Black River and Trenton Groups, Utica Shale, and Lorraine Group are exposed. Deep wells, however, show that from northwest to southeast the sequence is progressively more nearly complete. For example, at the Imperial Lowlands no. 4 Lotbinière well (Fig. 3), rocks of the Black River Group unconformably overlie Grenville basement. The

Potsdam, Beekmantown, and Chazy Groups are missing. At the SOQUIP Shell Ste. Croix no. 1 well to the southeast, on the other hand, the complete sequence of the autochthonous domain is present with the exception of the Richmond Group.

The foreland thrust belt. This belt is composed of rock units like those found in the autochthonous domain with the exception of the Richmond Group, although their stratigraphic order is repeated many times over by a multitude of imbricated thrust faults (St-Julien and Hubert,

1975; St-Julien, 1979). The northern limit of the foreland thrust belt is the northernmost thrust fault and the southern limit is Logan's line (Figs. 2, 3).

The allochthonous domain. This domain is subdivided into the external nappe zone and the internal nappe zone. The external nappe zone is bordered to the northwest by Logan's line, and to the southeast by the Richardson fault (Figs. 2, 3). From northwest to southeast, the external nappe zone is made up of (1) the Promontoire de Québec nappe, (2) the St. Flavien slice, (3) the Rivière Etchemin olistostrome (formerly called the Etchemin River wildflysch by St-Julien and others, 1972; St-Julien and Hubert, 1975; and St-Julien, 1979), (4) the Rivière Chaudière nappe, (5) a repetition of the Rivière Etchemin olistostrome, (6) a sequence of red and green shales equivalent to the Pointe-de-Lévy slice as defined by St-Julien and others (1972), and (7) a sequence of black rhythmites and green, gray, and purple mudstones. The ages of the rocks range from Cambrian to Middle Ordovician. Ther rocks are faintly recrystallized and locally attain the prehnite-pumpellyite facies of regional metamorphism.

The internal nappe zone, limited to the northwest by the Richardson fault and to the southeast by the Baie Verte–Brompton line, is made up of rock sequences like those in the external nappe zone, although they are relatively more metamorphosed to the greenschist facies. The relatively intense metamorphism and complex deformation make it difficult to distinguish individual nappes in the zone.

The rocks of the allochthonous domain are interpreted to have been laid down on the continental rise (St-Julien and Hubert, 1975). The spatial distribution of facies on the rise is shown on a palinspastic section (Fig. 4 in pocket inside back cover).

Toward the northwest, the oldest rocks lying on the Grenville basement in the continental rise are the terrigenous rocks and limestone assemblage of Early Cambrian age. These rocks constitute the Oak Hill Group, and the Tibbit Hill Formation is at the base (Clark 1936). Rocks laterally equivalent to the Oak Hill Group to the southeast constitute the feldspathic sandstone-shale assemblage of the Charny, Armagh, and Caldwell Groups. The Charny Group is composed of multicolored pelitic schist with interlayers of siltstone and feldspathic sandstone (St-Julien and Hubert, 1975; St-Julien, 1979). The age of the Charny Group is Early Cambrian (Rasetti, 1946). The Lower Cambrian(?) Armagh Group was subdivided by Vallières (1971) in the St. Malachie area (30 km northeast of the seismic line) into a lower part composed of massive, green, feldspathic sandstone and green pelite, and an upper part composed of interbedded sandstone and red and green pelites. Along the seismic line, the Armagh Group is relatively more pelitic, and sandstone accounts for only about

20% of the group, as opposed to 80% in the St. Malachie area. The Lower or Middle Cambrian(?) Caldwell Group (St-Julien, 1972) is made up principally of feldspathic sandstone interbedded with multicolored phyllite. Dark gray tholeiitic metabasalt, locally porphyritic and with pillow structures, is preserved in some outcrops.

An assemblage of shale, limestone conglomerate, and orthoquartzite of probably Cambrian to Early Ordovician age overlies the feldspathic sandstone-shale assemblage of the Charny, Armagh, and Caldwell Groups and constitutes two nappes of the external nappe zone along the seismic line. The northwesternmost nappe is composed of argillite and green, gray, and red mudstone with intercalated calcarenite, calcisiltite, and limestone conglomerate. These rocks may be correlative with the Lower Ordovician rocks of the Pointe-de-Lévy slice as defined by St-Julien and others (1972) in the Quebec City area. To the southeast, a second nappe is composed of alternating black, pyrite-rich shale and siltstone containing two horizons of limestone conglomerate, mudstone, and green, gray, and purple slates. The rocks are correlative with those of the St. Hénédine nappe northeast of the seismic line (St-Julien and others, 1972; Vallières and others, 1978). The Rosaire Group (Béland, 1957; Benoît, 1958) is part of the shale-limestone conglomerate-orthoquartzite assemblage. Along the seismic line, the Rosaire consists of alternating gray and green phyllites and siltstone and orthoquartzite (St-Julien and Hubert, 1975, 1979). A sequence of red and green shales, lithologically similar to the Rivière Ouelle Formation (Hubert, 1965) in the internal nappe zone, here is interpreted stratigraphically to overlie the Rosaire Group. It seems likely that the red and green shales as well as the Rosaire Group are part of the shale-limestone conglomerate-orthoquartzite assemblage. If this view is correct, then the Rosaire Group lies on (Fig. 4) rather than under the Caldwell Group as previously interpreted (St-Julien and Hubert, 1975, p. 344).

A facies of argillaceous limestone and shale overlain by the Etchemin River olistostrome (St-Julien and others, 1972; St-Julien and Hubert, 1975; St-Julien, 1979) caps the rocks of the internal nappe zone. The olistostrome consists of an argillaceous matrix with scattered blocks of Lower or Middle Ordovician radiolarian chert, argillaceous limestone, limy slate, sandstone, and laminated limestone.

Dunnage Zone

The Dunnage Zone is the oceanic domain southeast of the Baie Verte–Brompton line. It is characterized by the following rocks in ascending order: ophiolite complexes (Laurent, 1975, 1977; St-Julien and Hubert, 1975); red and green argillite with polygenic conglomerate (Hébert, 1981); island-arc volcanic rocks (Laurent and others, 1979; Laurent, 1980); a shale olistostrome assemblage (previously called the St. Daniel mélange, St-Julien and Hubert, 1975); felsic tuff and pelagic and hemipelagic sediments of the Beauceville Formation; and the turbidite sequence of the St. Victor Formation. The last two formations constitute the Magog Group of Middle Ordovician age and form the St. Victor synclinorium. Along the seismic line, only the island-arc volcanic rocks and overlying formations crop out.

Calc-alkalic volcanic rocks of the Ascot-Weedon Formation crop out southeast of the Beauceville and St. Victor Formations. The Ascot-Weedon, also of Middle Ordovician age, represents the remains of a synchronous island arc southeast of the St. Victor synclinorium (Figs. 2, 4). It is exposed immediately west of the seismic line (Fig. 3).

Connecticut Valley–Gaspé Synclinorium

The Connecticut Valley–Gaspé synclinorium lies southeast of the Guadeloupe fault and is made up of rocks of the Silurian-Devonian St. Francis Group (Clark, 1937; Duquette, 1961). In ascending order, the St. Francis Group includes the Lambton, Ayers Cliff, and Compton Formations (St-Julien, 1970; Kelly, 1975). The Compton Formation, which makes up most of the synclinorium along the seismic line, is a monotonous turbidite sequence of alternating gray and black shale and fine grained laminated sandstone.

Terrigenous and metavolcanic rocks of the Frontenac Formation crop out in the extreme southeast (Fig. 2). Although considered to be early Devonian by Marleau (1958), recent studies suggest that the Frontenac Formation is Cambrian or Ordovician (Harron, 1976; S. R. Chevé, personal communication).

Several stocks of Late Devonian granite have been emplaced in the St. Francis Group, but only the Mont St. Sébastien Granite crops out near the seismic line (Fig. 2).

STRUCTURAL PROFILE

The structural profile (Fig. 2) is divided into five structural units. Beginning in the northwest, the units are the autochthonous domain, the foreland thrust belt, the allochthonous domain, the oceanic domain, and the Connecticut Valley–Gaspé synclinorium.

Autochthonous Domain

At the northwestern end of the seismic profile (Figs. 3, 5 in pocket inside back cover), the lowest reflector represents the unconformity between the Grenville basement and the Black River Group. The second reflector represents the contact between the top of the

Trenton Group and the base of the Utica Shale, and the highest reflector represents the top of the Utica Shale. To the southeast, another reflector appears at the top of the Potsdam Group. No reflectors separate the different limy formations owing to a lack of density contrasts; the deep wells, however, show that these formations are present (Fig. 3).

The platform rocks form the large, open Chambly-Fortierville syncline which is related to the thrusting of the Appalachians. En échelon normal faults with northeast strike and steep southeast dip affect the platform rocks. Geological observations, the seismic profile, and logs of the deep wells show that these faults were active from Precambrian to Late Ordovician time, the major displacements having occurred during deposition of the Trenton Group and Utica Shale (St-Julien and Hubert, 1975). The faults are largely obscured by thrust sheets of the foreland thrust belt and by nappes of the allochthonous domain. However, on aeromagnetic maps it is possible to follow the extension of some of these faults under the allochthons to the southwest. Vertical displacements measured on the seismic profile range from 230 to 1,080 m (Figs. 3, 5). Some of the blocks have undergone rotation and are tilted northward. The importance of normal faulting in the southward deepening of the platform is evident.

Foreland Thrust Belt

A series of southeast-dipping thrust faults imbricate the southeastern part of the platform (St-Julien and others, 1972; St-Julien, 1979). The faults involve progressively older rocks as the decollement surfaces cut to ever-deeper stratigraphic levels (Fig. 3). In outcrop, the thrusts appear to involve only the youngest rocks. However, toward the southeast, it is clear that thrust faults involve the entire platform sequence. This is confirmed by the two deep wells, SOQUIP and others St. Flavien nos. 3 and 4 (Fig. 3). Individual thrusts have displacements as great as 25 km (Fig. 3).

External Nappe Zone

This zone is composed of stacked nappes (St-Julien and others, 1972; Clark and Globensky, 1973; Muller, unpubl.). The Promontoire de Québec nappe (Fig. 3), composed of the Quebec City Formation, is the most northwesterly nappe. It is overlain by the Rivière Etchemin olistostrome, which in turn is overlain by the St. Flavien slice. This is succeeded by the Rivière Chaudière nappe, made up of rocks of the Charny Group repeated by a series of thrust faults (Figs. 2, 3). The Chaudière nappe is succeeded by "shale with blocks" (Muller, unpubl.), an olistostrome correlative with the Etchemin River olistostrome. This in turn is overlain by a nappe of Lower Ordovician rocks correlative with the Levis Formation of the Pointe-de-Levy slice in the Quebec City area (St-Julien and others, 1972; St-Julien, 1979).

The uppermost nappe along the seismic line is also made up of Lower Ordovician rocks, correlative with the pelites of the St. Hénédine Nappe (St-Julien and others, 1972; Vallières and others, 1978). A slice of limy rocks, equivalent to the Bulstrode Formation (St-Julien and Hubert, 1975; Globensky, 1978) separates the two uppermost nappes.

The rocks have undergone repeated deformation, and in the Quebec City area the orientation of structural elements differs from one nappe to another (St-Julien and others, 1972; St-Julien, 1979). The first phase of deformation is probably related to the emplacement of the nappes during Early and Middle Ordovician time. Cleavage is well developed only in the axial zone of folded ductile rocks. A second phase of deformation postdates nappe emplacement and is evident in the southeastern part of the external nappe zone. This phase has imposed a northeast-striking, steeply dipping cleavage. All rocks are weakly metamorphosed.

Internal Nappe Zone

The Richardson fault, which marks the northwestern boundary of the internal nappe zone, exhibits a wide range of dips. Northeast of the seismic line at St. Malachie (Vallières, 1971), the fault includes slivers of Precambrian rocks and dips southeastward. To the southwest, it steepens progressively, and at the seismic line it dips to the northwest. Southwest of the St. Malachie area, the fault occurs in a zone of intensely deformed rocks and is difficult to map. It may follow one of two traces. One trace follows the same stratigraphic level as in the St. Malachie area, between the sandstones of the Armagh Group on the southeast and the pelites of the St. Hénédine nappe on the northwest (Figs. 2, 3). A less likely trace, based on the interpretation of aeromagnetic maps, lies in the lower part of the Oak Hill Group.

Contacts between nappes in the internal nappe zone are blurred by metamorphism and intense deformation. Only two early faults are readily mappable: the Richardson fault and the thrust marked by the ultrabasic Pennington sheet. Accordingly, we shall here discuss stratigraphic rather than structural units, though even stratigraphic units are in places rendered obscure by deformation. For example, in the Notre Dame Mountains, the Rosaire, Caldwell, and Oak Hill Groups are lumped together as the Bennett Schist, and only the presence of the Pennington sheet allows a tentative separation of the Rosaire and Caldwell Groups.

The first stratigraphic unit in the northwest is the Armagh Group. This group has undergone two phases of deformation. The first phase produced folds with north-westerly axes, whereas the superimposition of the second phase of folding produced northwest-plunging reclined folds with an axial cleavage (S^2) that strikes to the northeast.

The Oak Hill Group southeast of the Armagh Group forms a complex syncline overturned toward the southeast that has undergone three phases of deformation (Charbonneau, 1975; Charbonneau and St-Julien, 1981). A stratigraphic unit equivalent to the Rivière Ouelle Formation crops out southeast of the Oak Hill Group. A northeast-striking S^2 cleavage that dips steeply toward the northwest is prominent. The folds resulting from the superposition of the two early phases of deformation are reclined and plunge toward the northwest.

The Rosaire and Caldwell Groups, separated by the Middle Cambrian Pennington sheet (Laurent and Vallerand, 1974), crop out southeast of the Armagh and Oak Hill Groups. The Pennington sheet has been affected by at least two phases of deformation (St-Julien and others, 1972; St-Julien and Hubert, 1975).

In the Bennett Schist, three phases of deformation can be recognized. The first, coeval with nappe emplacement, transposed bedding into parallelism with schistosity S^1. The second phase, probably the most intense, followed nappe emplacement and produced recumbent folds with penetrative axial plane schistosity (S^2) and northwest-bearing axes. Because the seismic line parallels the axes of the recumbent folds, the folds themselves are poorly expressed on the profile (Fig. 3). The third phase of deformation produced the Notre Dame anticlinorium. This open structure is prominent on the seismic profile (Fig. 5). The peak of regional metamorphism had passed prior to the third phase of deformation.

The numerous reflectors are interpreted to be ultrabasic rocks of the Pennington sheet, as well as metabasalts at the base of the feldspathic sandstone-shale assemblage, and volcanic rocks of the Tibbit Hill Formation laid down during a tensional phase in Early Cambrian time (Vallières 1971; St-Julien and Hubert, 1975). The repeated reflectors probably represent thrust faults, folded in the same manner that regional mapping has shown them to be folded at the surface. Late thrust faults may involve the Grenville basement at depth. The Notre Dame anticlinorium itself may have been produced by these late thrust faults having utilized progressively deeper levels of detachment (Fig. 6). The decrease in convexity of the reflectors with depth bears out this interpretation. The late thrust faults may be related to the Acadian orogeny, a view supported by analogy with the Guadeloupe fault which cuts Silurian and Devonian rocks to the southeast and forms the border of the Connecticut Valley–Gaspé synclinorium (see below).

Rocks of the Caldwell and Rosaire Groups crop out

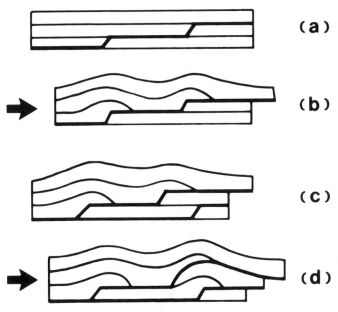

Figure 6. Development of stacked and folded thrust faults. (a) Initial decollement surface over which antiforms develop at thrust ramps (b) in response to tangential pressure. The process is repeated in response to continuing tangential pressure (c, d), older and higher thrust faults being progressively more intensely folded (modified from Jones, 1971).

along the seismic line southeast of the Notre Dame anticlinorium and form a recumbent fold that closes to the southeast and whose axis bears northeastward (Fig. 3). Only the lower, reversed flank of the fold crops out. The recumbent fold was subsequently folded, first about axes that plunge steeply to the north, and then about axes that plunge steeply to the northeast.

A late cleavage cuts all rocks of the allochthonous domain. Across the external nappe zone, the cleavage defines a regional fan with southeasterly dips in the northwest and northwesterly dips in the southeast. In the internal nappe zone, the cleavage defines the Notre Dame anticlinorium with dips to the northwest and to the southeast off a broad central area of subhorizontal dips. These relationships are apparent on the seismic profile (Fig. 5).

In summary, the internal nappe zone shows three phases of deformation. The first was coeval with nappe emplacement in Early and Middle Ordovician time; the second took place at the end of Ordovician time (St-Julien and Hubert, 1975); and the third, possibly coeval with the Acadian orogeny, may have involved the Grenville basement in thrust faulting under the Notre Dame anticlinorium.

Oceanic Domain

Rocks and structures southeast of the Baie Verte–Brompton line record the formation and destruction of oceanic crust and associated island arcs (St-Julien and others, 1976; Williams and St-Julien, 1978). The Baie Verte–Brompton line is marked by slivers of oceanic crust now represented by ophiolite complexes and by the Cambrian-Ordovician St. Daniel olistostrome to the southeast. The olistostrome is made up of unsorted angular fragments and blocks of green and gray shale, siltstone and dolomitic siltstone, feldspathic sandstone and quartzite, gabbro, volcanic rocks similar to those of the ophiolite complexes, and serpentinite all in a matrix of dark gray and green shale. Large blocks range from a few meters to more than 1 km in length.

The Beauceville and overlying St. Victor Formations of the Magog Group crop out southeast of the olistostrome. The Beauceville Formation is 600 m thick and is composed of alternating pelagic shale, felsic tuff, chert, and tuffaceous arenite. The St. Victor Formation is composed of turbidites with rare horizons of felsic tuff. The Magog Group forms the St. Victor synclinorium which at the seismic line plunges 20° to the southwest and is host to an axial-plane slaty cleavage.

The principal reflectors observed in the oceanic domain are from the Beauceville Formation and from felsic tuffs in the St. Victor Formation.

The Guadeloupe fault cuts across the southeastern part of the St. Victor synclinorium to constitute the northwestern border of the Connecticut Valley–Gaspé synclinorium (Fig. 2). The fault is pronounced on the seismic profile (Fig. 5). Reflectors along the Guadeloupe fault at depth may be calc-alkalic volcanic rocks of the Ascot-Weedon Formation which crop out 4 km southwest of the seismic line (Fig. 2). In places, the Ascot-Weedon Formation occurs as thin slices along the Guadeloupe fault.

Connecticut Valley–Gaspé Synclinorium

Along the seismic line the Connecticut Valley–Gaspé synclinorium is made up of a Silurian-Devonian turbidite sequence which has been thrust over the oceanic domain. The rocks are folded isoclinally with subvertical axial surfaces and horizontal plunges. The virtual absence of reflectors matches the monotonous homogeneity of the rocks observed in the field and suggests that no granite plutons are present at depth (Fig. 5).

CONCLUSIONS

1. Grenville basement is present under the autochthonous rocks and under the allochthons probably at least to the internal nappe zone.

2. Grenville basement and its cover of platform sedimentary rocks are affected by southeast-dipping normal faults in the autochthonous domain, the foreland thrust

belt, and the northwestern part of the allochthonous domain.

3. The normal faults were active during sedimentation, and several of the fault blocks have undergone rotation and are tilted northward.

4. The age of the olistostromes and olistoliths suggests that nappe emplacement took place during Middle Ordovician time.

5. Later Acadian(?) thrust faults in the Notre Dame anticlinorium may have taken progressively deeper levels of detachment.

6. Grenville basement may be affected by late thrust faults at depth in the core of the Notre Dame anticlinorium.

7. The Silurian-Devonian rocks of the Connecticut Valley–Gaspé synclinorium have been thrust over Middle Ordovician rocks of the St. Victor synclinorium.

8. Granite plutons are absent at depth along the seismic line in the Connecticut Valley–Gaspé synclinorium.

ACKNOWLEDGMENTS

We thank B. Granger and the Geophysics Department of SOQUIP for their help. The study was made possible by grants from the Quebec Department of Education (Formation de Chercheurs et d'Action Concertée).

REFERENCES CITED

Béland, J., 1957, St. Magloire and Rosaire–St-Pamphile areas, southern Quebec: Quebec Department of Mines, Geological Report 76, 49 p.

Benoît, F., 1958, Geology of the St-Sylvestre and St-Joseph West Half Area [Ph.D. thesis]: Laval University, 116 p.

Bird, J. M., and Dewey, J. F., 1970, Lithosphere plate-continental margin tectonics and the evolution of the Appalachian orogen: Geological Society of America Bulletin, v. 81, p. 1031–1060.

Blackburn, M., 1975, Analyse structurale des assises du Groupe de Caldwel à l'Est du complexe ophiolitique de Thetford-Mines [M.Sc. thesis]: Laval University, 61 p.

Charbonneau, J. M., 1975, Analyse structurale des tectonites metamorphiques du groupe de Oak Hill dans le région de Saint-Sylvestre, Appalaches du Québec [M.Sc. thesis]: Laval University, 65 p.

Charbonneau, J. M., and St-Julien, P., 1981, Analyse structurale et relations déformation-métamorphisme, Groupe d'Oak Hill, région du mont Sainte-Marguerite, Appalaches du Québec: Canadian Journal of Earth Sciences, v. 18, p. 1051–1064.

Clark, T. H., 1936, A Lower Cambrian series from southern Quebec: Royal Canadian Institute Transactions, v. 21, Part 1, p. 135–151.

——1937, Beauceville Series, St-Francis Series, and Lake Aylmer Series, *in* Cooke, H. C., ed.,: Geological Survey of Canada Memoir 211, p. 33–52.

——1944, Unfolded Paleozoic rocks of St. Lawrence lowlands, *in* Dresser, J. A., and Denis, T. C., The geology of Quebec, Vol. II: Descriptive Geology: Quebec Department of Mines, Geological Report 20, p. 250–291.

——1972, Montreal area: Quebec Department of Natural Resources, Geological Report 101, 244 p.

Clark, T. H., and Globensky, Y., 1973, Portneuf and parts of St. Raymond and Lyster map-areas: Quebec Department of Natural Resources, Geological Report 148, 110 p.

Clark, T. H., Globensky, Y., and Hofmann, H., 1979, Paleozoic stratigraphy of the Lowland of Quebec: Geological Association of Canada, Field Trip A-7, Laval University, 35 p.

Cooke, H. C., 1937, Thetford, Disraeli and eastern half of Warwick map-areas, Quebec: Geological Survey of Canada Memoir 211, 176 p.

Duquette, G., 1961, Geology of the Weedon Lake Area and its vicinity, Wolfe and Compton Counties [Ph.D. thesis]: Laval University, 308 p.

Ells, R. W., 1896, Report on a portion of the Province of Quebec comprised in the Southwest Sheet of the "Eastern Townships" map (Montreal Sheet): Geological Survey of Canada, Annual Report, v. 7, Part J., p. 1–92.

Globensky, Y., 1978, Drummondville area: Quebec Department of Natural Resources, Geological Report 192, 107 p.

Harron, G. A., 1976, Metallogeny of sulphide deposits in the Eastern Townships: Quebec Department of Natural Resources, ES-27, 42 p.

Hébert, R., 1981, Conglomérats polygéniques ophiolitiques: anciens éboulis de talus de fond océanique?: Canadian Journal of Earth Sciences, v. 18, p. 619–623.

Hibbard, J. P., and Williams, H., 1979, The regional setting of the Dunnage Mélange in the Newfoundland Appalachians: American Journal of Science, v. 279, p. 993–1021.

Horne, G. S., 1969, Early Ordovician chaotic deposits in the central volcanic belt of northeast Newfoundland: Geological Society of America Bulletin, v. 80, p. 2451–2464.

Houde, M., and Clark, T. H., 1962, Geological map of the St. Lawrence lowlands: Quebec Department of Natural Resources, Map no. 1407.

Hubert, Claude, 1965, Stratigraphy of the Quebec Complex in the l'Islet-Kamouraska area, Quebec [Ph.D. thesis]: McGill University, 192 p.

Jones, P. B., 1971, Folded faults and sequence of thrusting in Alberta foothills: American Association of Petroleum Geologists Bulletin, v. 55, no. 2, p. 292–306.

Kay, Marshall, 1975, Campbellton sequence, manganiferous beds adjoining the Dunnage Mélange, northern Newfoundland: Geological Society of America Bulletin, v. 86, p. 105–108.

——1976, Dunnage Mélange and subduction of the Protacadic Ocean, northeast Newfoundland: Geological Society of America Special Paper 175, 49 p.

Kean, B. F., and Strong, D. F., 1975, Geochemical evolution of an Ordovician island arc of the central Newfoundland Appalachians: American Journal of Science, v. 275, p. 97–118.

Kelly, R., 1975, Area of Mounts Sainte-Cécile and Saint-Sébastien: Quebec Department of Natural Resources, Geological Report 176, 30 p.

Kidd, W.S.F., 1977, The Baie Verte lineament, Newfoundland: Ophiolite complex floor and mafic volcanic fill of a small Ordovician marginal basin, *in* Talwani, M., and Pitman, W. C., eds., Island arcs, deep sea trenches and back-arc basins: American Geophysical Union, Maurice Ewing Series 1, p. 407–418.

Laurent, Roger, 1975, Occurrences and origin of the ophiolites of southern Quebec, northern Appalachians: Canadian Journal of Earth Sciences, v. 12, p. 443–455.

——1977, Ophiolite of the Quebec Appalachians, *in* Coleman, R. G., and Irwin, W. P., eds., North America ophiolites: Oregon Department of Geology and Mineral Industries Bulletin 95, p. 25–40.

——1980, Environment of formation, evolution and emplacement of the Appalachian ophiolites from Quebec: Extract from Ophiolites, Proceedings of International Ophiolite Symposium, Cyprus 1979: Cyprus Geological Survey Department, p. 628–636.

Laurent, Roger, and Vallerand, P., 1974, Ar^{40}/K^{40} isochron age for the amphibolites of the ophiolitic complexes of the Appalachian of Quebec: Geological, Association of Canada, Program and Abstracts, p. 53.

Laurent, Roger, Hébert, R., and Hébert, Y., 1979, Tectonic setting and petrological features of the Quebec Appalachian ophiolites, *in* Malpas, J., and Talkington, R. W., eds., Ophiolites of the Canadian Appalachians and Soviet Urals: Geology Department, Memorial University of Newfoundland, Report 8, p. 53–77.

Logan, W. E., 1863, Report on the geology of Canada: Geological Survey of Canada, Report of Progress from Commencement to 1863.

Marleau, R. A., 1958, Geology of the Woburn, the East-Megantic, and the Armstrong areas, Frontenac and Beauce Counties [Ph.D. thesis]: Laval University, 184 p.

Norman, R. E., and Strong, D. F., 1975, The geology and geochemistry of ophiolitic rocks exposed at Mings Bight, Newfoundland: Canadian Journal of Earth Sciences, v. 12, p. 777–797.

Parks, W. A., 1930, Report on the oil and gas resources of the Province of Quebec: Quebec Bureau of Mines, Annual Report 1929, Part B, p. 1–121.

Rasetti, F., 1946, Cambrian and Early Ordovician stratigraphy of the lower St. Lawrence Valley: Geological Society of America Bulletin, v. 57, p. 687–705.

Riordon, P. H., 1954, Thetford Mines–Black Lake areas: Quebec Department of Natural Resources, Preliminary Report 295.

Rodgers, John, 1968, The eastern edge of the North American continent during the Cambrian and Early Ordovician, *in* Zen, E-an and others, eds., Studies of Appalachian geology: Northern and maritime: New York, John Wiley and Sons, p. 141–150.

St-Julien, Pierre, 1970, Geology of Disraeli area (east-part): Quebec Department of Natural Resources, Preliminary Report 587, 22 p.

——1972, Appalachian tectonics in the Eastern Townships of Quebec: XXI International Geological Congress, Montréal, 1972 Guidebook B-21, 21 p.

——1979, Structure and stratigraphy of platform and Appalachian sequences near Quebec city: Geological Association of Canada, Field trip A-9, Laval University, 31 p.

St-Julien, Pierre, and Hubert, C., 1975, Evolution of the Taconian orogen in the Quebec Appalachians, *in* Tectonics and Mountain Ranges: American Journal of Science, v. 275-A, p. 337–362.

——1979, Structural setting of the Thetford Mines Ophiolite Complex: Geological Association of Canada, Field Trip B-10, Laval University, 27 p.

St-Julien, Pierre, Hubert, C., Skidmore, B., and Béland, Jacques, 1972, Appalachian structure and stratigraphy, Quebec: XXI International Geological Congress, Montréal, 1972 Guidebook A56-C56, 99 p.

St-Julien, Pierre, Hubert, C., and Williams, Harold, 1976, The Baie Verte–Brompton line and its possible tectonic significance in the northern Appalachians: Geological Society of America Abstracts with Programs, v. 8, no. 2, p. 259–260.

Smitheringale, W. G., 1972, Low potash Lushs Bight tholeiites: Ancient oceanic crust in Newfoundland: Canadian Journal of Earth Sciences, v. 9, p. 574–588.

Upadhyay, H. D., Dewey, J. F., and Neale, E.R.W., 1971, The Betts Cove ophiolite complex, Newfoundland: Appalachian oceanic crust and mantle: Geological Association of Canada Proceedings, v. 24, p. 27–34.

Vallières, A., 1971, Relations stratigraphiques et structurales du Super-Groupe de Québec dans la Région de Saint-Malachie ouest [M.Sc. thesis]: Montreal University, 100 p.

Vallières, A., Hubert, C., and Brooks, C., 1978, A slice of basement in the western margin of the Appalachian orogen, Saint-Malachie, Québec: Canadian Journal of Earth Sciences, v. 15, p. 1242–1249.

Williams, Harold, 1978, Tectonic lithofacies map of the Appalachian orogen: Memorial University of Newfoundland, Map. No. 1, 2 sheets.

Williams, Harold, 1979, Appalachian orogen in Canada: Canadian Journal of Earth Sciences, v. 12, p. 982–995.

Williams, Harold, and St-Julien, Pierre, 1978, The Baie-Verte–Brompton line in Newfoundland and regional correlations in the Canadian Appalachians, *in* Current research, Part A: Geological Survey of Canada Paper 78-1A, p. 225–229.

Williams, Harold, and Stevens, R. K., 1974, The ancient continental margin of eastern North America, *in* Burk, C. A., and Drake, C. L., eds., The Geology of Continental Margins: New York, Springer-Verlag, p. 781–796.

Williams, Harold, Kennedy, M. J., and Neale, E.R.W., 1972, The Appalachian structural province, *in* Price, R. A., and Douglas, R.J.W., eds., Variations in tectonic styles in Canada: Geological Association of Canada Special Paper 11, p. 181–261.

——1974, The northeastward termination of the Appalachian orogen, *in* Nairn, A.E.M., and Stehli, F. G., eds., The ocean basins and margins, Vol. 2: New York, Plenum Press, p. 79–123.

MANUSCRIPT ACCEPTED BY THE SOCIETY SEPTEMBER 10, 1982

Geological Society of America
Memoir 158
1983

Tectonic significance of paired gravity anomalies in the southern and central Appalachians

M. D. Thomas
Gravity, Geothermics, and Geodynamics Division
Earth Physics Branch
Department of Energy, Mines and Resources
Ottawa, Ontario K1A OY3
Canada

ABSTRACT

Extensive, positive-negative paired gravity anomalies occur along a number of Precambrian boundaries separating terranes with contrasting structural characteristics and radiometrically determined ages. Collective evidence from the boundaries supports an origin by plate collision following convergent plate movements operating in the style of modern day plate tectonics. The paleosubduction direction can be determined from the relative ages of the sutured terranes, the younger one being identified as a "reactivated" terrane formed in response to subduction beneath it. Because the positive-negative pattern of gravity anomalies is invariable with respect to the relative ages of the sutured terranes, the paleosubduction direction can be established with confidence on the basis of the gravity pattern alone; the latter also identifies the suture position.

In the southern and central Appalachians, such utility of the basement is prevented by a widely-preserved cover of supracrustal rocks. Geological indicators of paleosubduction direction and suturing are present in these rocks, but because of the determined or possible allochthonous nature of some of the critical terranes, locating deeper, more fundamental sections of suture zones is problematical. However, the presence of paired gravity anomalies, strikingly similar to Precambrian examples, affords a novel method for identifying the location of a deep suture and the associated paleosubduction direction. Studies of these anomalies lead to the conclusion that a plate carrying a proto-American block subducted southeastward, leading to collision with an "accreted" block, in agreement with the general consensus that such a collision occurred in the Ordovician.

Along the COCORP seismic profile, gravity modelling indicates that the suture dips southeastward beneath the Inner Piedmont and transects a master décollement outlined by the seismic studies. The presence of a suture in this locality suggests that any thin-skinned tectonic model for this part of the Appalachians should be restricted to the area northwest of the suture.

INTRODUCTION

Cook and others (1979) have interpreted COCORP seismic reflection data in the southern and central Appalachians in terms of a thin-skinned tectonic model. Harris and Bayer (1979) also favored a thin-skinned model and pointed to several seismic sections as supporting evidence. A fundamental, and controversial, feature of the COCORP model is a master décollement that extends approximately 330 km from the Valley and Ridge province southeast ard to the Carolina slate belt and above which crystalline rocks are thrust an estimated 260 km northwestward. The thin-skinned model and its implications for the tectonic evolution and hydrocarbon potential of the Appalachian orogen have become a focus for vigorous debate (chronologically: Ellwood and others, 1980a; Williams, 1980; Cook and others, 1980a; Harris and Bayer, 1980; Reed and Bryant, 1980; Cook and others, 1980b; Moench, 1980; Cook and others, 1980c; Friedman and Reeckmann, 1980; Ellwood and others, 1980b). Throughout the debate, the prominent positive-negative Bouguer gravity anomaly pair that extends the length of the southern and central Appalachians (Fig. 1a) has received little attention. Williams (1980) cited it as evidence against an extensive décollement; Cook and others (1980a) replied briefly that is presence does not invalidate the décollement hypothesis. Here, the possible tectonic significance of this intriguing anomaly pair and its consequences for the thin-skinned model are examined more closely. It is concluded that the belt of steep gradients separating relatively negative and positive regions of the pair may be related to a major collisional suture that separates crusts of contrasting density and thickness. A preferred model, interpreted from the gravity profile along the COCORP section, suggests that the suture dips southeastward beneath the Inner Piedmont and intersects the surface within the northwestern half of the Inner Piedmont. If this interpretation is correct, the presence of a crustal suture within the Inner Piedmont apparently is at variance with the idea of a subhorizontal décollement that is continuous from one side of the Inner Piedmont to the other (Cook and others, 1979). It is proposed, therefore, that the application of the thin-skinned model be limited to the Valley and Ridge, Blue Ridge, and a maximum of a few tens of kilometers of the Inner Piedmont immediately south of the Brevard Zone.

RATIONALE

The present interpretation of the Appalachian gravity anomalies utilizes Hutton's concept of uniformitarianism in a converse fashion, the more distant past being viewed as the key to the more recent past. In this case, the former is manifest as paired Bouguer gravity anomalies at Precambrian structural boundaries interpreted as collisional sutures formed by plate tectonics, and the latter takes the

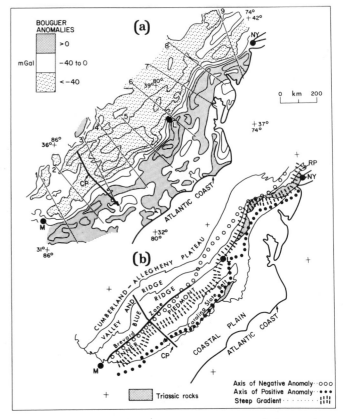

Figure 1. a. Simplified Bouguer anomaly map of the southern and central Appalachians after Woollard and Joesting (1964); contour interval, 20 mGal. L, Lynchburg; M, Montgomery; NY, New York. Positions of 9 stacked profiles (Fig. 2c) are indicated. CP, COCORP Profile. b. Simplified geological map of the southern and central Appalachians with principal axes of major gravity anomalies superimposed. L, M, NY, CP as in *a* above. RP, Reading Prong.

form of the paired anomalies of the southern and central Appalachians. Thomas and others (1980) have suggested that Precambrian paired gravity anomalies are collision-related phenomena reflecting a particular crustal configuration that is commonly developed at suture zones. Examples along orogenic belts ranging in age from 1800 to 600 Myr suggest that plate tectonics operated in a similar mode throughout most of Proterozoic time; the added example of the southern and central Appalachians indicates that the process remained unchanged to at least about 450 Myr B.P. The striking similarity between Precambrian and Appalachian paired anomalies and significant geological similarities between the respective associated orogens form the basis of an analogy that is used to compare tectonic developments of Precambrian and Appalachian orogenic belts.

Prerequisite to the success of the analogy is the operation of plate tectonics at the times of inferred suturing in the Precambrian. That this is a viable proposition is demonstrated by a variety of evidence from the eastern margin of the West African craton, a section of which coincides with paired gravity anomalies. Leblanc (1976) has described a typical ophiolite assemblage supposedly representing obducted Proterozoic lithosphere emplaced during the Pan African orogeny around 600 Myr B.P. Upper mantle peridotites, ultrabasic and basic cumulates, quartz diorite stocks, submarine lavas, spilites, keratophyres, greywackes, and jaspilites are all present. In addition, Black and others (1979) report high pressure—low temperature metamorphism (jadeitic pyroxene), an accretion zone suggestive of development in an island arc and marginal sea environment, and a calc-alkaline batholith in the reactivated Pan African terrane to the east. These and other features suggested to them that the West African craton, carrying a passive continental margin, collided with an active continental margin through eastward subduction. Ball (1980), following Tapponnier and Molnar's (1976) treatment of India-Eurasia collision, has demonstrated that the geometry of late Pan African brittle deformation may reflect the stress field operative during indentation of a "plastic" Pan African crust by a more rigid West African craton.

Other Precambrian regions yielding substantive evidence of collision include: the Arabian Shield, where an ophiolite has been mapped (Shanti and Roobol, 1979); the Gariep belt in southwestern Africa, where glaucophane-bearing schists and possible oceanic crust and trench mélange are present (Kröner, 1979); the Baltic Shield, where Krogh (1977) explains the formation of Norwegian gneiss eclogites by continent-continent collision; and the 3200 km long Circum-Superior geosyncline of the Canadian Shield proposed as a suture by Gibb and Walcott (1971) based on the interpretation of the tectonic emplacement of cherts, pillow basalts, and serpentinites typical of the plate accretion environment among coarse clastics of the plate consumption environment. Extensive sections of the latter suture are associated with paired gravity anomalies. Collectively, these various examples make a convincing case for the existence of plate tectonics in the Precambrian.

THE PRECAMBRIAN ANALOGUE

The Precambrian analogue incorporates (1) paired gravity anomalies at probable collision zones, (2) a crustal model derived from the anomalies, and (3) consistent polarity of depositional environments, metamorphic grades, and structure with respect to the relative ages of the sutured terranes. In cases of paired gravity anomalies in the Canadian Shield, the gravity field decreases gradually from a background level over an older structural province to a minimum near its boundary and then increases sharply to a maximum within the adjacent younger province (Fig. 2a). A simple "type" model (Gibb and Thomas, 1976) that explains these anomalies consists of two single-layered crustal blocks of different mean density and thick-

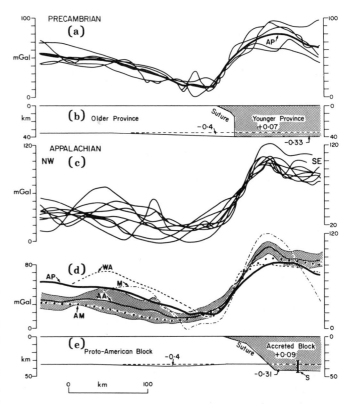

Figure 2. a. Five stacked gravity profiles selected across Precambrian boundaries in the Canadian Shield and an average Precambrian gravity profile (AP). Stacking was achieved by eye using the steepest gradients as references for horizontal control. b. A "type" crustal model derived from AP (after Gibb and Thomas, 1976). Density contrasts are in g/cm³; that above dashed line is relative to that of the standard crust of the older province, those below are relative to the density of the mantle. c. Nine stacked gravity profiles across the southern and central Appalachians. Stacking as in *a* above. Locations are shown in Fig. 1a. d. AA is an average Appalachian gravity profile obtained for the nine profiles in *c*; the shaded envelope about this curve is defined by plus and minus a standard deviation. AM is the curve corresponding to the "type" Appalachian crustal model shown in *e*. Comparative gravity profiles from Precambrian boundaries interpreted as sutures are: AP, average Canadian Shield profile; M, profile across Musgrave Block, Australia; WA, profile across eastern margin of West African craton. e. "Type" Appalachian crustal model. Vertical bar labelled S in the accreted block represents the range of seismic thicknesses under the positive gravity anomaly determined by James and others (1968) in the middle Atlantic states. Density contrasts are in g/cm³; that above dashed line is relative to that of the standard crust of the proto-American block, those below are relative to the density of the mantle.

ness in approximate relative isostatic equilibrium separated along a steeply dipping boundary, equated with a suture (Fig. 2b). According to the model, the younger block is thicker and denser, and a wedge of non-isostatic crust is present at the base of the older block. Seismic evidence, where available, supports the interpretation of thicker crust in the younger province (Mereu and Hunter, 1969; Berry and Fuchs, 1973). The physical development of this type of model may be compared with the "basement reactivation" model of Dewey and Burke (1973). In this model, when all the oceanic lithosphere between converging continents has been subducted, continued convergence is effected by thickening of continental crust that probably involves ductile creep at lower levels and fracture at higher levels and is probably concentrated in the overriding active plate margin. Thickening is accompanied by rising geotherms that induce partial melting of the lower crust, resulting in upward migration of granitic liquids and formation of a refractory lower crust characterized by granulites and rocks of the anorthosite-mangerite suite. Eventually, isostatic recovery and erosion might lead to the exposure of such lower crustal assemblages. The common occurrence of granulitic rocks in the terranes associated with the younger block of the gravity model lends substantial support to the Dewey and Burke (1973) model. Gravity models similar to the Canadian examples have been proposed also for the collisional eastern margin of the West African craton (Bayer and others, 1975; Louis, 1978) and for boundaries between Australian Precambrian blocks (Wellman, 1978), one of which has been described as a collisional suture (Davidson, 1973).

Large-scale geological features at the boundaries that have a consistent orientation with respect to the polarity of the older and younger provinces or blocks are (1) a change from miogeosynclinal to eugeosynclinal assemblages toward the younger province, (2) an increase in metamorphic grade in the same direction, and (3) thrusting directed toward and folds overturned toward the older province.

The juxtaposition of isotopically younger "reactivated" terranes and older "non-reactivated" crust at the boundaries and interpretation of the gravity anomalies in terms of two contrasting crustal blocks support a collision origin for the boundary zones. The direction of pre-collision subduction in these Precambrian examples is obvious, the plate carrying the older province must have subducted beneath the younger province to produce the observed effects of reactivation and reset radiometric clocks. In addition, because the polarity of the gravity anomalies is consistent with respect to the older-younger polarity of the provinces (negative anomaly within the older province or straddling boundary, positive anomaly within the younger province), the gravity signature alone is a reliable indicator of the direction of subduction.

In younger, Phanerozoic orogenic belts, the basement picture is often obscured by widely-preserved, commonly allochthonous, supracrustal rocks, making identification of sutures on the basis of distinguishing between reactivated and non-reactivated basements much more difficult. This is particularly true in trying to locate the deep crustal

segments of sutures. However, if paired gravity anomalies are present, they provide, via the Precambrian analogue, a remote sensor for defining cryptic sutures and paleosubduction directions.

APPLICATION TO THE SOUTHERN AND CENTRAL APPALACHIANS

The paired gravity anomalies of the southern and central Appalachians extend for about 1700 km (Fig. 1a), maintaining a fairly constant profile (Fig. 2c) that is similar to profiles across Precambrian collision zones (Fig. 2d). Correlations between the anomalies and surface geology are somewhat limited and rather broad-scale in nature (Fig. 1b). The negative anomaly, for example, overlies mainly the Valley and Ridge in the northeastern part of the orogen but migrates into the Blue Ridge and marginal region of the Piedmont in the southwestern part of the orogen. The presence of an isostatic component in this anomaly is indicated by the close correlation between the anomaly and the core of the Appalachian mountains along a significant section of the orogen. The positive anomaly exhibits a better relationship to the geology and lies almost entirely within the Piedmont, where its axis follows the Carolina slate belt for about 600 km. The belt of steep gradients separating the negative and positive anomalies cannot be correlated with any single geological feature and overlies the Blue Ridge northeast of Lynchburg and the Piedmont south of Lynchburg (Fig. 1b). The lack of a consistent relationship, throughout the orogen, between either anomaly and a singular geological feature suggests that the anomalies, in large part, are generated by large-scale buried features.

The idea of mass distributions deep within the crust as a source of Appalachian anomalies has long been favored by several workers (Woollard, 1939; Nettleton, 1941; Diment, 1968). In terms of the present interpretation, it is of historical interest that Woollard presented an island arc hypothesis to explain the negative anomaly as long ago as 1939, and the following quote from Nettleton (1941) has relevance: "However, it seems probable that the source of the primary gravity features is in mass distributions rather deep within the earth's crust, which must have their origin in the tectonic forces which caused the Appalachian uplift but are not superficially evident from the surface geology of the area." By virtue of the Precambrian analogue, it is proposed that those "tectonic forces" were a product of plate convergence and that the Appalachian paired gravity anomalies are a phenomenon created by the collision of two plates.

An average or "type" model for the southern and central Appalachians based on the collision concept, and similar to the Precambrian model (Fig. 2b), is shown in Fig. 2e. It consists of two single-layered crustal blocks in relative isostatic equilibrium separated by a suture dipping southeastward. The northwestern block is referred to as the proto-American block, and the denser and thicker southeastern block is called the accreted block; these correspond to the older and younger provinces, respectively, of the Canadian Precambrian model.

A description of the constraints and assumptions used to construct the model follows. A crustal thickness of 35 km, based on Warren and Healy's (1973) compilation of seismic thicknesses, was assigned to the northwestern margin of the proto-American block, a region where the gravity field is assumed to attain a background level or datum relative to the paired anomalies; the mean elevation for this region was estimated to be 390 m. Using these values, the crustal column in the region was adopted as a standard to be used in the interpretation of the average Appalachian gravity profile AA of Fig. 2d. Other values used in the gravity modelling and isostatic calculations were: 130 m for the mean elevation of the accreted block; 2.70 g/cm³ for the density of all crustal material above sea level, based on information provided by Watkins (1964) and Long (1974); a density contrast of 0.4 g/cm³ between the mantle and the crust, a value within the range of values discussed by Woollard (1968).

By assuming relative isostatic equilibrium, any segment of the gravity profile can be modelled as a crustal column with an assigned mean density and a calculated thickness relative to a standard crust. In the present case, one of the principal objectives of the gravity modelling was to determine the nature of the crust below the positive anomaly. This was accomplished by calculating the minimum positive density contrast, relative to the standard crust, required to reproduce the amplitude of the positive anomaly. For the accreted block, this minimum value was determined to be 0.09 g/cm³, for which the corresponding thickness is 43 km (Fig. 2e). With these values established, modelling proceeded by adjusting the shape of the contact between the proto-American and accreted blocks until the form of the steep gradient was reproduced. This was achieved for a contact dipping southeastward at about 20° from sea level to a depth of 10 km, and at about 40° at greater depths.

In the model, a slight thickening of the proto-American block occurs southeast of the region of standard crust toward the core of the Appalachian mountains, where the average elevation increases to about 460 m. The thickening is consistent with isostatic compensation. By comparison with the standard column, where the mean elevation is 390 m, the crust under the mountains would require the addition of a root about 0.5 km thick to maintain relative isostatic equilibrium. The maximum thickness of the root in the model is 2.5 km, which, given its generalized nature, is reasonable agreement. Noticeable mismatches between the average gravity profile (AA) and the

profile corresponding to the model (AM) (Fig. 2d) occur along the northwestern flank of the negative anomaly and in the region of the peak of the positive anomaly. These are a consequence of the average and simplified character of the model, in which no attempt has been made to model geological detail. The mismatch over the proto-American block relates to a number of separate positive gravity anomalies (Fig. 2c) in various parts of the orogen that were smoothed into a single positive feature during the process of averaging the profiles. The mismatch over the accreted block is associated with a gravity feature that is consistently present in all the individual profiles, namely the peak or axis of the positive anomaly. It has been noted that the Carolina slate belt correlates quite well with this axis, and this correlation may prove ultimately to have important significance for the collision model.

The only seismic constraint introduced in the gravity modelling was the 35 km crustal thickness estimated from Warren and Healy (1973) for the northwestern part of the proto-American block. A single-layered crustal model for the middle Atlantic states (James and others, 1968) provides seismic thicknesses for the region extending from the core of the mountains to the Atlantic coast, but was not used as a constraint in the gravity interpretation because exploratory calculations using mean crustal densities demonstrated that the Moho configuration generated gravity profiles that could not reasonably match observed profiles across the entire width of the orogen. The seismic model is basically symmetrical and produces symmetrical gravity profiles. In contrast, observed gravity profiles are markedly asymmetrical. The 15 km root under the mountains predicted from the seismic studies represents an enormous overcompensation for the mean elevation of the mountains when simple isostatic calculations show that compensation can be achieved by a root that is only 0.5 km thick. The 43 km thickness obtained for the accreted block in the gravity model compares with somewhat smaller seismic thicknesses ranging generally from 35 to 40 km, and exceptionally from 30 to 45 km (James and others, 1968) in the corresponding area of the orogen. The gravity model may also be compared with a two-layered seismic model reported by Warren (1968) along a profile crossing the southern fringe of the area examined by James and others (1968). In this model, the crust, unlike the crust in the gravity model (Fig. 2e), maintains a nearly constant thickness of 34 km across the orogen. On the other hand, an aspect of the seismic model that is relevant to the gravity model is an increase in thickness of the lower crustal layer from about 3 km under the negative anomaly to 14 km under and east of the positive anomaly, where the gravity model indicates a denser crust. Because the seismic models differ so radically in a region of common ground, their usefulness as comparative material for the gravity model is obviously limited, and any support for the latter implicit in these models must be regarded as tentative.

The Appalachian gravity signature and model indicate (1) a major collisional suture along the belt of steep gradients separating negative and positive anomalies, (2) crustal blocks of significantly different mean density, hence composition, on either side of the suture, and (3) that a plate carrying the northwestern or proto-American block was subducted southeastward beneath a plate carrying the southeastern or accreted block. Geological similarities with the Precambrian analogue that support these conclusions are (1) on a broad scale, a change from miogeosynclinal to eugeosynclinal rocks from the region of the negative anomaly toward that of the positive, though in some areas this general pattern is interrupted by allochthonous sheets, e.g., possible oceanic terrane in the Blue Ridge above the Hayesville-Fries fault (Hatcher, 1978a); (2) a general increase in metamorphic grade in the same direction; and (3) thrusting directed away from the positive anomaly and occurring mainly within the region of the negative anomaly. Furthermore, the proposed suture coincides approximately with the boundary between a structural domain to the northwest characterized by thrusting and one to the southeast, in which comparatively high angle faulting is predominant (Fig. 3). The latter domain covers largely the southeastern part of the Piedmont where the fault pattern has been likened to large strike-slip fault systems (Hatcher and others, 1977), though the sense of movement of the component faults is unknown (Hatcher, 1978b). The pattern of two structural domains separated along a suture zone is analogous to the situation produced by India-Eurasia collision (Molnar and Tapponnier, 1977) and is interpreted as additional evidence for southeastward subduction.

The southeastward subduction and the development of large-scale crustal structure in the southern and central Appalachians by collision tectonics, implicit in the gravity model, are supported by some previous plate tectonic models presented primarily on the strength of geological arguments. According to Odom and Fullagar (1973), during middle Cambrian times the Piedmont had already developed as an island arc system above a subduction zone which eventually consumed the oceanic crust between the Blue Ridge province and the Piedmont arc. A southeastward direction of subduction is suggested by Ordovician and older Paleozoic calc-alkaline magmatic activity within the Piedmont. In the resulting collision culminating in middle to late Ordovician times, a suture developed along the site of the Brevard Zone (Fig. 1b). Odom and Fullagar (1973) further proposed that, following collision, northwestward subduction was initiated beneath the Piedmont leading to the final closing of the proto-Atlantic. Hatcher (1978a) presented a similar model, with closure of a marginal sea between the North American continent and a rifted continental fragment (= Inner Piedmont) being effected by southeastward subduction. However, unlike Odom and Fullagar (1973), who regarded the Brevard Zone as a suture, Hatcher (1978a) proposed that it originated as a ductile root zone. Cook and others (1979) also postulated a collision involving southeastward

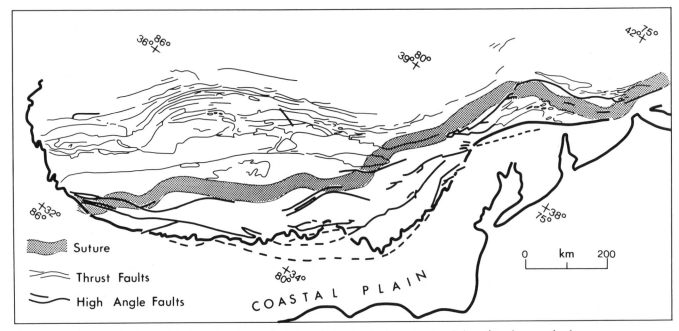

Figure 3. Relationship of proposed Appalachian suture to structural domains characterized by thrust faulting (to northwest of suture) and high angle faulting, possibly strike-slip in nature (to southeast). Faults after Hatcher (1978b) and Williams (1978).

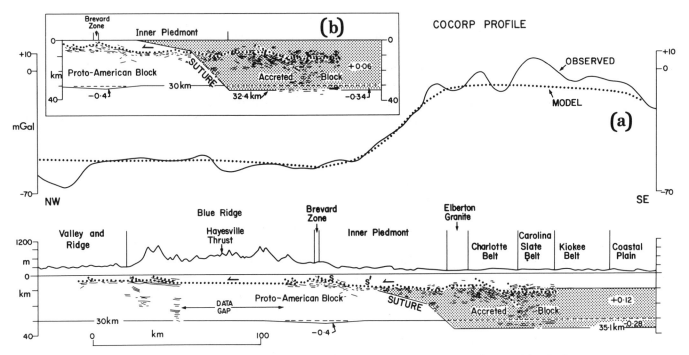

Figure 4. a. Observed and model gravity profiles along COCORP Profile (see Fig. 1a for location), elevation profile with main geological subdivisions indicated and the COCORP seismic section after Cook and others (1979) with gravity model superposed. In the CO-CORP section, reflectors are indicated by fine continuous lines and the master dècollement and subsidiary thrusts by heavier dotted lines; direction of thrusting indicated by arrows. Shaded area of gravity model represents the anomalously dense portion of the accreted block which is 0.12 g/cm³ more dense than crustal material in the proto-American block. Density contrasts in g/cm³; that above dashed line is relative to that of the standard crust of the proto-American block, those below are relative to the density of the mantle. Because the COCORP experiments were conducted along roads and the gravity profile, elevation profile and geology are taken along a profile consisting of straight segments (CP in Fig. 1), the COCORP data have been projected onto CP. This has resulted in "best fitting" the COCORP section to the geological boundaries on CP. Most of the adjustments were made within the data gap under the Blue Ridge and by closing a very small gap in the Piedmont. b. Part of COCORP section with superposed gravity model in which anomalously dense material (shaded area) of accreted block is distributed through the entire crust and is 0.06 g/cm³ more dense than the crust of the proto-American block. Density contrasts in g/cm³; that above dashed line is relative to that of the standard crust of the proto-American block, those below are relative to the density of the mantle.

subduction of a proto-North American continent beneath a Piedmont microcontinent in middle Ordovician to early Silurian times. The collision represented by the gravity model is equated with the Ordovician collision of these various models that followed the closure of the marginal sea northwest of the Piedmont. That it is not an earlier Precambrian event is ruled out by the fact that the geological criteria cited in support of the model involve rocks of Paleozoic age.

GRAVITY MODEL AND
COCORP SEISMIC SECTION

The COCORP seismic reflection profile (Cook and others, 1979) provides detailed crustal information across

the orogen from the Valley and Ridge to the Carolina slate belt (Fig. 4a). The proposed master dècollement extends across the entire section, increasing in depth gradually from about 3-4 km under the Valley and Ridge to about 12 km under the Carolina slate belt. Above it, crystalline Precambrian and Paleozoic rocks of the Blue Ridge, Inner Piedmont, Charlotte belt, and Carolina slate belt are believed to constitute an allochthonous sheet overlying relatively flat-lying autochthonous lower Paleozoic sedimentary rocks; the sheet is estimated to have been thrust at least 260 km to the northwest. Cook and others (1979) ascribe the development of the dècollement to westward thrusting produced by a succession of three separate collisions. Specific details on the mechanism of its growth are not described, but it seems that it propagated southeastward through successively accreted crustal units. The décollement originated in the first collision, between a proto-North American continent and a Piedmont microcontinent in the mid-Ordovician, as the Blue Ridge and part of the Piedmont were transported northwestward onto platform sedimentary assemblages of the Valley and Ridge. Northwestward subduction was then initiated along the southeastern edge of the now accreted Piedmont microcontinent, leading to collision with an island arc represented by the Carolina slate belt in the Devonian. Finally, northwestward subduction below the southeastern margin of the newly accreted Carolina slate belt led to collision between the enlarged proto-North American continent and African or South American plates in Permo-Carboniferous time.

Isostatic "collision-type" models for the gravity profile along the COCORP line, superimposed on a crustal section depicting seismic reflectors outlined by Cook and others (1979), are shown in Fig. 4a and 4b. In deriving the model in Fig. 4a, consideration was given to the major, subhorizontal reflection feature, preferentially interpreted as a décollement by Cook and others (1979); it was assumed, arbitrarily, that the gravity signature is produced by an abrupt, suture-related change in mean crustal density occurring below the décollement, and that the 10 km or so of crust above the décollement were of more or less uniform mean density across the entire section. The gravity model is restricted, therefore, to depths greater than 10 km, but this does not imply, necessarily, a buried suture, although the vertical change in density across the décollement, within the accreted block, could be explained as a buried feature. It has been noted previously that the gravity signature is unlikely to represent a (hidden) Precambrian suture. However, the overthrusting hypothesis of Cook and others (1979) does raise the possibility of a buried early Paleozoic suture.

As far as can be determined, detailed density data, which might substantiate the assumption of uniform mean crustal density above the décollement and could be critical in the gravity interpretation, are not available along the COCORP line. Limited information provided by Long (1974) indicates that in the Blue Ridge and Piedmont of Georgia, granitic and gneissic rocks which are ubiquitous (Williams, 1978) have densities typically in the range 2.6 to 2.7 g/cm^3, while Watkins (1964) indicates that the Valley and Ridge sedimentary section in adjacent Tennessee has an average density that is probably less than 2.7 g/cm^3; density variations in the vicinity of the COCORP line would appear, therefore, to lie within a relatively small 0.1 g/cm^3 range.

The thickness of the northwestern or proto-American block (Fig. 4a) was constrained by assuming that the lowest COCORP reflector below the Blue Ridge might represent the Moho, as comparatively deep reflectors under

the Piedmont are thought to do (Cook and others, 1979); it occurs at 10 seconds of two-way travel time, approximately equal to a depth of 30 km. The mean elevation of this block was estimated to be 500 m, and the crustal root assumed to compensate for this topography is included in the 30 km of crust below sea level. Other values used in modelling were: a mean elevation of 135 m for the accreted block; a density of 2.7 g/cm^3 for all crust above sea level; and a density contrast of 0.4 g/cm^3 between the mantle and crust. The model was derived using essentially the same procedure as that used to obtain the type model, with the proto-American block, 30 km thick below sea level and 0.5 km thick above, being used as a standard crust. One difference in the case of the COCORP section is that the whole width of the proto-American block is treated as standard crust, rather than just the northwestern portion. This is a consequence of the negative anomaly, in this part of the orogen, having so little amplitude that it appears quite flat in profile (Fig. 4a); it was, therefore, selected as a datum for modelling.

In the model (Fig. 4a), the accreted block below a depth of 10 km is more dense than the proto-American one by 0.12 g/cm^3; the total thickness of the accreted block is 35 km, which is in good agreement with the depth of the lowest reflectors in the COCORP section in the same area (Cook and others, 1979). The suture between the blocks was modelled as dipping at approximately 15° between the décollement and a depth of 20 km and at a much steeper 45° below a depth of 20 km. It separates a crust to the northwest that, below a depth of about 10 km, is conspicuously free from reflectors from crust to the southeast that contains abundant reflectors. This might be construed as additional evidence for the presence of two discrete crustal units, or it might be fortuitous.

The contact between the proto-American and accreted blocks in the uppermost 10 km of crust is not defined by a density boundary because it was assumed that the crust above the décollement was of uniform density. The identification of a suture in this segment of crust is based, therefore, largely on geological considerations. However, the geometry of the gravity model and its spatial relationship to selected features of the COCORP seismic section and surface geology play an important role in the interpretation and lead to interesting speculation regarding the course of the suture in the uppermost crust. Of central interest in the speculation is the Brevard Zone.

Several workers view the Brevard Zone as a suture, among them Odom and Fullagar (1973), who call it a "fossil subduction zone," and Rankin (1975), who describes it as a "transported suture." If it is a suture, then the link between the Brevard Zone and the deep suture defined by the gravity model (Fig. 4a) could be represented by the intervening section (S-S') of the décollement (Fig. 4a) as defined by Cook and others (1979). Under this interpretation, the sections of the décollement to either side of section S-S′ would bear no relationship to one another because they occur in separate blocks on opposite sides of a suture. The part of the décollement northwest of S-S′ can be fitted without difficulty into a model that has the Brevard Zone as a suture and be explained simply as a northwestward-transported tectonic slice possibly rooted in the suture zone. The part of the décollement within the accreted block is not so easily accomodated into the model, and, in addition, it is necessary to explain why it should be a density boundary. It could be argued that the décollement is post-suturing. If this were true, the configuration of the model suggests that very little differential horizontal movement has occurred between the Brevard Zone and the deeper part of the suture; the large change in density across the décollement in the accreted block remains a problem as far as its geological significance is concerned.

If Hatcher's (1978a) argument that the Brevard Zone is not a suture is accepted, a somewhat different interpretation is required. Hatcher proposed that the Brevard Zone originated as a ductile zone related to early thrusts formed in the unstable sea floor of the marginal sea between the North American continent and the Piedmont microcontinent. One of the thrusts developed into a Hayesville-Fries-Brevard fault during the Ordovician with the Hayesville-Fries fault, itself considered a suture by Hatcher (1978a), continuing to move, carrying later Precambrian rocks of the southeastern oceanic facies northwestward over those of the northwestern rifted margin facies. The Hayesville-Fries fault was rooted in the primordial Brevard Zone, which was reactivated much later in Carboniferous or Permian time and was ramped to the surface as a backlimb on the Blue Ridge thrust sheet. Following this interpretation, the question must be asked— where is the deep section of the suture formed by the closure of the marginal sea? Is it possible that the primordial Brevard Zone was itself "rooted" in the deeper parts of a suture? If the latter is feasible, then the tectonic development envisaged by Hatcher (1978a) is not contradicted by the gravity model (Fig. 4a).

Given the difficulties with explaining the décollement in the accreted block, an alternative model was constructed, in which anomalously dense material occupies the entire crustal column in the accreted block (Fig. 4b), and the suture is defined by a density boundary throughout the crust. The suture surfaces within the structurally complex Inner Piedmont a few tens of kilometers southeast of the Brevard Zone. The density of the accreted block in this model is only 0.06 g/cm^3 greater than that of the proto-American block, so it would require extremely detailed density studies to detect such a relatively small increase. The geometry of this model (Fig. 4b) is more in harmony with Hatcher's (1978a) concept of the tectonic

evolution of the area, with the Brevard Zone occurring within the same major block of crust and separate from the suture zone. The décollement (Cook and others, 1979) northwest of the suture can again be related to the suture zone as a rooted tectonic slice, but the section of the décollement in the accreted block is still a problem, though, in this instance, there is no density contrast associated with it. For these reasons, the model of Fig. 4b is preferred over that of Fig. 4a. The shallow dipping (14°) upper section of the suture is an interesting feature of the model since it reflects on a large scale the near-horizontal tectonics manifest in the large nappes and other allochthonous elements that characterize Inner Piedmont geology (Griffin, 1974a; Rankin, 1975; Hatcher, 1978a).

The presence of an Ordovician suture zone within the Inner Piedmont, as suggested by the gravity model (Fig. 4b), is inconsistent with the idea of a décollement that is continuous from the Valley and Ridge to the Carolina slate belt (Cook and others, 1979), notwithstanding the fact that Cook and others (1979) have extended their master décollement across several proposed sutures. Williams (1980) has already argued that "It seems incongruous . . . that such suture zones are crossed by a continuous subhorizontal sedimentary reflector". Tectonic and isostatic movements surely must have disrupted any décollement. Furthermore, there is evidence for such movements. Dallmeyer (1978), using ^{40}Ar/^{39}Ar ages reflecting dates of post metamorphic cooling, indicated that the Inner Piedmont underwent approximately 24 km of uplift between regional metamorphism at approximately 365 Myr B.P. and near exhumation of the present erosion level at about 220 Myr B.P.; the thermal-metamorphic peak was probably earlier, between about 420 and 380 Myr B.P. Dallmeyer's (1978) study did not include data from the Blue Ridge, so that the amount of relative movement between that area and the Inner Piedmont is indeterminate. Nevertheless, some differential uplift, that would probably offset any horizontal feature, is indicated by the variation in the metamorphic grades across these regions. The vertical movements would have been effected by the long history (Ordovician-Carboniferous) of faulting in the region (Hatcher and Odom, 1980). Griffin (1974b) also appealed to vertical en bloc uplift of the Inner Piedmont mobile thermal core by isostatic adjustment to better explain cataclastized portions of adjacent deformed belts. Milici (1975), to explain age relations of major structural blocks produced by Alleghanian deformation west of the Blue Ridge, proposed a thin-skinned gravity spreading and sliding model in which the driving force of deformation is gravitational combined with horizontal compression generated by a rising mobile thermal core in the Piedmont. Similar arguments have been advanced by Fullagar and Butler (1979).

Other evidence that militates against the décollement

continuing southeast of the suture is that there is little indication of Alleghanian activity in the Piedmont (Griffin,
1974b; Fullagar and Butler, 1979; Ellwood and others,
1980c); this weakens the case, implicit in Cook and others'
(1979) thesis, for linking Alleghanian deformation in the
Valley and Ridge to a Permo-Carboniferous collision east
of the Carolina slate belt via the décollement.

The configuration of the preferred gravity model
(Fig. 4b) is compatible with the picture of a décollement,
with underlying sedimentary rocks beneath the Blue
Ridge, extending some tens of kilometers southeastward
into the Inner Piedmont (Cook and others, 1979). The
exotic carbonates in the Brevard Zone (Hatcher, 1971)
testify that carbonates are present below the region at
least as far southeast as this zone. However, southeast of
the suture, in the accreted block, the presence of a
décollement, so problematical to the gravity model of
Fig. 4a, is questionable. If a décollement is present here, it
is very difficult to relate it to that northwest of the suture.
Consequently, horizontal and subhorizontal reflectors in
this region, rather than representing sedimentary rocks
continuous with sedimentary strata below the Blue Ridge
(Cook and others, 1979), may well represent foliated metamorphic and igneous rocks as suggested by Moench
(1980). The location of these reflectors within the accreted
block and the southeastward dip of many of them raise
the possibility that they are associated with a former subduction complex.

CONCLUSIONS

The paired gravity anomalies of the southern and
central Appalachians are interpreted to record a major
Ordovician collision between a proto-American plate and
an "accreted" plate resulting from subduction of the
former southeastward. The importance and magnitude of
the structure produced by this collision are perhaps reflected in the fact that the proposed suture, which underlies the belt of steep gradients separating positive and
negative anomalies, is more or less coincident with a
major boundary between stress provinces (Zoback and
Zoback, 1980). In the region of the COCORP profile, the
suture may surface, possibly at a very shallow angle, in the
highly metamorphic and structurally complex terrane of
the Inner Piedmont. To the northeast, approximately between Lynchburg and New York where the belt of steep
gradients overlies the Blue Ridge, exploratory gravity
models place the Blue Ridge within the "accreted" block.
This suggests that the provenance of the Blue Ridge is the
accreted block and that there has been increasing northwestward transport of segments of this block southwestward along the orogen. There may have been other
collisions in the Appalachian orogen, but the one inferred
from the gravity models appears to dominate as far as the
megatectonic structure of the region is concerned.

ACKNOWLEDGEMENTS

The ideas presented here on paired gravity anomalies
have evolved during several years of cooperative study
with Dr. R. A. Gibb, Earth Physics Branch; his contribution to the manuscript in the form of discussion and cri-
tique is gratefully acknowledged. My thanks for similar
contributions go also to Drs. A. K. Goodacre and J. F.
Sweeney, and Mr. M. R. Dence, Earth Physics Branch,
and to Mr. F. A. Cook, Cornell University. Special thanks
for comprehensive reviews of the manuscript are extended
to Dr. R. D. Hatcher, Jr., University of South Carolina,
who provided a deeper insight into aspects of the geology,
and to Dr. R. W. Simpson, United States Geological Survey, for extremely useful comments on the gravity interpretation. Notwithstanding various comments received,
the contents of this paper are the responsibility of the
author.

REFERENCES CITED

Ball, E., 1980, An example of very consistent brittle deformation over a
  wide intracontinental area: the late Pan-African fracture system of
  the Tuareg and Nigerian Shield: Tectonophysics, v. 61, p. 363–379.

Bayer, R., Black, R., Fabre, J., and Louis, P., 1975, Etude des anomalies
  gravimétriques au front de la chaine dahomeyenne (Pan-Africaine),
  in Rapport d'activité centre géologique et géophysique de Montpellier, p. 125.

Berry, M. J., and Fuchs, K., 1973, Crustal structure of the Superior and
  Grenville provinces of the northeastern Canadian Shield: Bulletin of
  the Seismological Society of America, v. 63, p. 1393–1432.

Black, R., Caby, R., Moussine-Pouchkine, A., Bayer, R., Bertrand,
  J. M., Boullier, A. M., Fabre, J., and Lesquer, A., 1979, Evidence
  for late Precambrian plate tectonics in West Africa: Nature, v. 278,
  p. 223–227.

Cook, F. A., Albaugh, D. S., Brown, L. D., Kaufman, S., Oliver, J. E.,
  and Hatcher, R. D., Jr., 1979, Thin-skinned tectonics in the crystalline southern Appalachians; COCORP seismic-reflection profiling of
  the Blue Ridge and Piedmont: Geology, v. 7, p. 563–567.

Cook, F. A., Albaugh, D. S., Brown, L. D., Kaufman, S., Oliver, J. E.,
  and Hatcher, R. D., Jr., 1980a, Reply on "Thin-skinned tectonics in the crystalline southern Appalachians; COCORP seismic-
  reflection profiling of the Blue Ridge and Piedmont": Geology, v. 8,
  p. 213–214.

Cook, F. A., Albaugh, D. S., Brown, L. D., Kaufman, S., Oliver, J. E.,
  and Hatcher, R. D., Jr., 1980b, Reply on "Thin-skinned tectonics in the crystalline southern Appalachians; COCORP seismic-
  reflection profiling of the Blue Ridge and Piedmont": Geology, v. 8,
  p. 215–216.

Cook, F. A., Albaugh, D. S., Brown, L. D., Kaufman, S., Oliver, J. E.,
  and Hatcher, R. D., Jr., 1980c, Reply on "Thin-skinned tectonics in the crystalline southern Appalachians; COCORP seismic-
  reflection profiling of the Blue Ridge and Piedmont": Geology, v. 8,
  p. 403–404.

Dallmeyer, R. D., 1978, ^{40}Ar/^{39}Ar incremental-release ages of hornblende and biotite across the Georgia Inner Piedmont: their bearing
  on late Paleozoic-early Mesozoic tectonothermal history: American
  Journal of Science, v. 278, p. 124–149.

Davidson, D., 1973, Plate tectonics model for the Musgrave Block-
  Amadeus Basin Complex of central Australia: Nature Physical
  Science, v. 245, p. 21–23.

Dewey, J. F., and Burke, K.C.A., 1973, Tibetan, Variscan, and Precambrian basement reactivation: products of continental collision: Journal of Geology, v. 81, p. 683–692.

Diment, W. H., 1968, Gravity anomalies in northwestern New England, *in* Zen, E-An, and others, eds., Studies of Appalachian Geology: Northern and Maritime: New York, Interscience Publishers, p. 399–413.

Ellwood, B. B., Stormer, J. C., Jr., Wenner, D. B., Whitney, J. A., and Reuter, J. H., 1980a, Discussion of the hydrocarbon potential of rocks underlying the southern Appalachian Piedmont allochthon: Geology, v. 8, p. 205–206.

Ellwood, B. B., Stormer, J. C., Jr., Wenner, D. B., Whitney, J. A., and Reuter, J. H., 1980b, Reply on "Discussion of the hydrocarbon potential beneath the southern Appalachian Piedmont": Geology, v. 8, p. 404–405.

Ellwood, B. B., Whitney, J. A., Wenner, D. B., Mose, D., and Amerigian, C., 1980c, Age, paleomagnetism, and tectonic significance of the Elberton granite, northeast Georgia Piedmont: Journal of Geophysical Research, v. 85, p. 6521–6533.

Friedman, G. M., and Reeckmann, S. A., 1980, Comment on 'Discussion of the hydrocarbon potential beneath the southern Appalachian Piedmont': Geology, v. 8, p. 404.

Fullagar, P. D., and Butler, J. R., 1979, 325 to 265 m.y.-old granitic plutons in the Piedmont of the southeastern Appalachians: American Journal of Science, v. 279, p. 161–185.

Gibb, R. A., and Thomas, M. D., 1976, Gravity signature of fossil plate boundaries in the Canadian Shield: Nature, v. 262, p. 199–200.

Gibb, R. A., and Walcott, R. I., 1971, A Precambrian suture in the Canadian Shield: Earth and Planetary Science Letters, v. 10, p. 417–422.

Griffin, V. S., Jr., 1974a, Analysis of the Piedmont in northwest South Carolina: Geological Society of America Bulletin, v. 85, p. 1123–1138.

Griffin, V. S., Jr., 1974b, Plate tectonics and the Ouachita System in Texas, Oklahoma, and Arkansas: Discussion: Geological Society of America Bulletin, v. 85, p. 145–146.

Harris, L. D., and Bayer, K. C., 1979, Sequential development of the Appalachian orogen above a master dècollement—a hypothesis: Geology, v. 7, p. 568–572.

Harris, L. D., and Bayer, K. C., 1980, Reply on "Sequential development of the Appalachian orogen above a master dècollement—a hypothesis": Geology, v. 8, p. 214.

Hatcher, R. D., Jr., 1971, Stratigraphic, petrologic, and structural evidence favoring a thrust solution to the Brevard problem: American Journal of Science, v. 270, p. 177–202.

Hatcher, R. D., Jr., 1978a, Tectonics of the western Piedmont and Blue Ridge, southern Appalachians: review and speculation: American Journal of Science, v. 278, p. 276–304.

Hatcher, R. D., Jr., 1978b, Synthesis of the southern and central Appalachians, U.S.A., *in* Caledonian-Appalachian orogen of the North Atlantic region: Geological Survey of Canada Paper 78-13, p. 149–157.

Hatcher, R. D., Jr., and Odom, A. L., 1980, Timing of thrusting in the southern Appalachians, USA: model for orogeny?: Journal of the Geological Society, v. 137, p. 321–327.

Hatcher, R. D., Jr., Howell, D. E., and Talwani, P., 1977, Eastern Piedmont fault system: speculations on its extent: Geology, v. 5, p. 636–640.

James, D. E., Jefferson Smith, T., and Steinhart, J. S., 1968, Crustal structure of the middle Atlantic states: Journal of Geophysical Research, v. 73, p. 1983–2007.

Krogh, E. J., 1977, Evidence of Precambrian continent-continent collision in western Norway: Nature, v. 267, p. 17–19.

Kröner, A., 1979, Pan-African mobile belts as evidence for a transitional tectonic regime from intraplate orogeny to plate margin orogeny, *in* Tahoun S. A., ed., Evolution and mineralization of the Arabian-

Nubian Shield: Volume 1: Oxford, Pergamon Press, p. 21–37.

Leblanc, M., 1976, Proterozoic oceanic crust at Bou Azzer: Nature, v. 261, p. 34–35.

Long, L. T., 1974, Bouguer gravity anomalies of Georgia, *in* Stafford, L. P., compiler, Symposium on the petroleum geology of the Georgia coastal plain: Georgia Geological Survey Bulletin 87, p. 141–166.

Louis, P., 1978, Gravimétrie et géologie en Afrique occidentale et centrale: Bureau de Recherches Géologiques et Minières Mémoire 91, p. 53–61.

Mereu, R. F., and Hunter, J. A., 1969, Crustal and upper mantle structure under the Canadian Shield from Project Early Rise data: Bulletin of the Seismological Society of America, v. 59, p. 147–165.

Milici, R. C., 1975, Structural patterns in the southern Appalachians: evidence for a gravity slide mechanism for Alleghanian deformation: Geological Society of America Bulletin, v. 86, p. 1316–1320.

Moench, R. H., 1980, Comment on "Thin-skinned tectonics in the crystalline southern Appalachians; COCORP seismic-reflection profiling of the Blue Ridge and Piedmont": Geology, v. 8, p. 402.

Molnar, P., and Tapponnier, P., 1977, The collision between India and Eurasia: Scientific American, v. 236, p. 30–41.

Nettleton, L. L., 1941, Relation of gravity to structure in the northern Appalachian area: Geophysics, v. 6, p. 270–286.

Odom, A. L., and Fullagar, P. D., 1973, Geochronologic and tectonic relationships between the Inner Piedmont, Brevard Zone, and Blue Ridge belts, North Carolina: American Journal of Science, v. 273A, p. 133–149.

Rankin, D. W., 1975, The continental margin of eastern North America in the southern Appalachians: the opening and closing of the Proto-Atlantic ocean: American Journal of Science, v. 275A, p. 298–336.

Reed, J. C., Jr., and Bryant, B., 1980, Comment on "Thin-skinned tectonics in the crystalline southern Appalachians: COCORP seismic-reflection profiling of the Blue Ridge and Piedmont" and "Sequential development of the Appalachian orogen above a master dècollement—a hypothesis": Geology, v. 8, p. 214–215.

Shanti, M., and Roobol, M. J., 1979, A late Proterozoic ophiolite complex at Jabal Ess in northern Saudi Arabia: Nature, v. 279, p. 488–491.

Tapponnier, P., and Molnar, P., 1976, Slip-line field theory and large-scale continental tectonics: Nature, v. 264, p. 319–324.

Thomas, M. D., Gibb, R. A., and Mukhopadhyay, M., 1980, Comment on "Evidence for late Precambrian plate tectonics in West Africa": Nature, v. 284, p. 192.

Warren, D. H., 1968, Transcontinental geophysical survey (35°—39° N) Seismic refraction profiles of the crust and upper mantle from 74° to 87° W longitude: U.S. Geological Survey Miscellaneous Geologic Investigations Map I-535-D.

Warren, D. H., and Healy, J. H., 1973, Structure of the crust in the conterminous United States: Tectonophysics, v. 20, p. 203–213.

Watkins, J. S., 1964, Regional geologic implications of the gravity and magnetic fields of a part of eastern Tennessee and southern Kentucky: U.S. Geological Survey Professional Paper 516-A.

Wellman, P., 1978, Gravity evidence for abrupt changes in mean crustal density at the junction of Australian crustal blocks: Bureau of Mineral Resources Journal of Australian Geology and Geophysics, v. 3, p. 153–162.

Williams, H., 1978, Tectonic lithofacies map of the Appalachian orogen: Memorial University of Newfoundland Map No. 1, Scale 1:1,000,000.

Williams, H., 1980, Comment on "Thin-skinned tectonics in the crystalline southern Appalachians; COCORP seismic-reflection profiling of the Blue Ridge and Piedmont" and "Sequential development of the Appalachian orogen above a master dècollement—a hypothesis": Geology, v. 8, p. 211–212.

Woollard, G. P., 1939, The geological significance of gravity investigations in Virginia: American Geophysical Union, Transactions of 20th Annual Meeting, p. 317–323.

Woollard, G. P., 1968, The interrelationship of the crust, the upper mantle, and isostatic gravity anomalies in the United States, *in* Knopoff, L., and others, eds., The crust and upper mantle of the Pacific area: Washington, D.C., AGU Geophysical Monograph 12, p. 312–341.

Woollard, G. P., and Joesting, H. R., 1964, Bouguer gravity anomaly map of the United States: Published by the American Geophysical Union.

Zoback, M. L., and Zoback, M., 1980, State of stress in the conterminous United States: Journal of Geophysical Research, v. 85, p. 6113–6156.

MANUSCRIPT ACCEPTED BY THE SOCIETY SEPTEMBER 10, 1982
CONTRIBUTION OF THE EARTH PHYSICS BRANCH NO. 988

Geological Society of America
Memoir 158
1983

Geologic interpretation of geophysical maps
of the pre-Cretaceous "basement" beneath the Coastal Plain
of the Southeastern United States

Michael W. Higgins
U.S. Geological Survey
6481 Peachtree Industrial Boulevard
Doraville, Georgia 30360

Isidore Zietz
Phoenix Corporation
1700 Old Meadow Road
McLean, Virginia 22102

ABSTRACT

Salient features of the new aeromagnetic map of the Southeastern United States (Zietz and Gilbert, 1980) are: (1) the Charleston magnetic terrane that is generally high magnetically and has numerous distinct, very high magnetic anomalies within it; (2) the northern Florida magnetic terrane that is virtually identical magnetically to the Charleston magnetic terrane; (3) a linear series of magnetic low anomalies within a continuous magnetic low anomaly, collectively called the Altamaha magnetic anomaly, that is more than 1,150 km long and that arcs across the Continental Shelf, from about 33°30′N., 76°30′W., to the Georgia coastline at the mouth of the Altamaha River and trends inland across southern Georgia and Alabama; (4) the southern end of the East Coast anomaly and its shoreward branch, the Brunswick anomaly, which is part of the northern Florida terrane; (5) the characteristic magnetic terranes of the Piedmont and Valley and Ridge provinces; (6) the southern end of the New York-Alabama lineament and the magnetically high terrane west of it; and (7) the lineament formed by the nearly straight northwestern margin of the Charleston magnetic terrane in South Carolina and Georgia, the northwestern margin of the Altamaha anomaly, and the southern margin of the magnetically high terrane northwest of the New York-Alabama lineament in Alabama.

A newly compiled gravity map of part of the Southeastern United States shows that the Charleston and northern Florida magnetic terranes have mixed gravity expression, with gravity high anomalies coinciding with the distinct, very high anomalies on the aeromagnetic map. In general, the trace of the Altamaha magnetic anomaly either coincides with or lies just south of gravity low anomalies that are linear and form a linear series along or closely parallel to the magnetic anomaly. Near its northeastern end, the Altamaha magnetic anomaly lies along a relatively steep, northwestward-sloping gravity gradient. The East Coast anomaly coincides with linear gravity high anomalies.

The Charleston and northern Florida magnetic terranes are interpreted as being virtually the same geologic terrane, a predominantly mafic terrane, intruded by mafic plutons of batholithic proportions, that, until late Paleozoic time, was part of the African or African/South American plate. The northwestern margin of the Charleston terrane is interpreted as the Alleghanian suture between Africa and North America, and also as a major strike-slip fault, the Carolina-Mississippi fault, that extends to the southwest along the northwestern border of the Altamaha anomaly and the southern border of the magnetically high terrane northwest of the New York-Alabama lineament. The Altahama anomaly is interpreted as being caused by a fault-bounded, sediment-filled trough, locally as deep as 6 km, that divides the Charleston-northern Florida terrane. The Carolina-Mississippi fault truncates the Charleston terrane, the Piedmont and Valley and Ridge provinces, the New York-Alabama lineament, and the magnetically high terrane northwest of the New York-Alabama lineament, and the absence on the southeastern side of the fault of magnetic terranes found on the northwestern side suggests right-lateral displacement.

INTRODUCTION

Beneath the Cretaceous and Cenozoic sediments and sedimentary rocks of the southern Atlantic and eastern Gulf Coastal Plain is a vast terrane of pre-Cretaceous "basement" rocks of various types and ages (Daniels and others, in press; Chowns and Williams, in press). Until recently, our only knowledge of these hidden rocks came from gravity maps, a few seismic lines, and scattered oil-well tests that generally penetrated less than a meter or so of the pre-Cretaceous rocks. In 1973, the Coastal Plains Regional Commission, the U.S. Geological Survey, and the State Geological Surveys along the East Coast joined in a cooperative program of aerogeophysical mapping of the southern Atlantic and eastern Gulf Coastal Plain. The mapping is now complete, and a compilation of the aeromagnetic map (including offshore data published elsewhere) is published (Zietz and Gilbert, 1980). The purpose of this paper is to interpret the aeromagnetic map (including more recent data in Alabama; Fig. 1 in pocket in back of book), in conjunction with a newly compiled gravity map of the same area, and to speculate about the origin of some of its salient features.

THE AEROMAGNETIC MAP

Because the sediments and sedimentary rocks of the Coastal Plain are essentially nonmagnetic, the anomalies on the aeromagnetic map (Fig. 1) must derive from magnetic crystalline "basement" rocks. The thickness of sediments and sedimentary rocks above the anomaly-causing rocks broadens the observed wavelengths of the magnetic anomalies by causing the magnetometer to be farther from the anomaly-causing rocks. Locally, nonmagnetic Triassic-Jurassic sedimentary sections within the "basement" add to this effect, as does depth of water offshore. Flight directions, altitudes, spacing of flight lines, and other details of the surveys can be found in Zietz and Gilbert (1980).

The magnetic anomalies (Fig. 1) do not, in general,

reflect only the rocks immediately beneath the Coastal Plain cover. Rather, they probably derive from a cumulative effect from a section through the magnetic "basement" rocks for a considerable depth (perhaps as much as several kilometers) beneath the top of the pre-Cretaceous "basement". This cumulative effect probably accounts for the general lack of *direct* correspondence between the aeromagnetic map and the maps of the pre-Cretaceous "basement" compiled by Daniels and others (in press) and Chowns and Williams (in press). Because the thickness of the cumulative section that contributes to an anomaly depends largely upon the distance of the top of that section from the magnetometer, correspondence between the aeromagnetic map and the rocks at the "basement" surface should be greater where the Coastal Plain cover is thin, and where there is no thick nonmagnetic Triassic-Jurassic sedimentary section.

One of the most significant features on the aeromagnetic map (Fig. 1) is a deep, linear magnetic low anomaly that arcs across the Continental Shelf, from about 33°30′N. by 76°30′W., to the coastline north of Brunswick, Georgia, and continues across Georgia into Alabama (A-A′ on Fig 1). This anomaly is here called the Altamaha anomaly, because it is coincident with the coastline approximately at the mouth of the Altamaha River. The Altamaha anomaly, never more than about 55 km wide, lies between two magnetic terranes characterized by broad wavelength magnetic highs and scattered, very high "bullseye-shaped" anomalies superimposed on the generally high background. Throughout much of Georgia (Fig. 1), the Altamaha anomaly is bounded on the northeast by a strip of intermediate magnetic intensity (600-800 gammas) about 40 km wide. The magnetically high terrane north and northwest of the Altamaha anomaly is here called the Charleston magnetic terrane (for Charleston, S.C.); the high terrane south and southeast of the anomaly is here called the northern Florida magnetic terrane (even though part of it is in Georgia). Overall, the magnetic character of the two terranes is very similar. The smaller amplitude, short-wavelength anomalies in parts of the northwestern part of the Charleston terrane are due to the fact that the nonmagnetic sedimentary cover is thinner there.

East of the Altamaha anomaly, offshore, is the East Coast anomaly (Drake and others, 1968; Taylor and others, 1968; Emery and others, 1970), a linear magnetic high anomaly (B-B' in Fig. 1) that follows the edge of the Continental Shelf for more than 3,000 km, from south of Newfoundland to east of Georgia. Off the Georgia coast, the East Coast anomaly bifurcates (Taylor and others, 1968), and the "inner branch" trends westward and breaks up into a series of discontinuous high anomalies that trend inland for about 90 km, parallel to the Altamaha anomaly (C-C' on Fig. 1). This series of magnetic highs within the northern Florida magnetic terrane has been informally called the Brunswick anomaly (Pickering and others, 1977).

Another important feature on the aeromagnetic map is the magnetically high area in northwestern Alabama, and particularly the nearly straight, northeast-trending southeastern border of this high area. This border is the southwestern end of the "New York-Alabama lineament" (King and Zietz, 1978) that extends northeastward more than 1,600 km and is a major feature of the crust of eastern North America.

Perhaps the most striking feature of the aeromagnetic map is the linearity of the northwestern margin of the Charleston magnetic terrane, the northwestern margin of the Altamaha anomaly in Alabama, and the southern margin of the high terrane northwest of the New York-Alabama lineament (D-D' on Fig. 3 in pocket in back of book). This lineament extends for more than 1,000 km across the Southeastern United States, marking the boundaries of five major magnetic terranes.

GRAVITY MAP

Figure 2 (in pocket in back of book) is a new compilation of gravity data for part of the Southeastern United States. In general, the trace of the Altamaha magnetic anomaly (A-A' on Fig. 2) either coincides with, or lies just south of, gravity low anomalies that in most places are linear, and form a linear series along, or closely parallel to, the Altamaha anomaly. Near its northeastern end, however, the Altamaha anomaly lies along a relatively steep, northwestward-sloping gravity gradient.

Both the Charleston and northern Florida magnetic terranes have mixed gravity expressions. Most of the prominent magnetic high anomalies in these terranes (Fig. 1) coincide with prominent gravity highs (Fig. 2). Gravity lows are also present in the Charleston and northern Florida terranes, but the dominant gravity expression is intermediate to high.

INTERPRETATIONS

As a rule, mafic rocks are generally more magnetic (have higher magnetic susceptibilities) and have higher specific gravities than felsic rocks. Magnetic highs accompanied by gravity highs are almost invariably caused by mafic rocks, and, by the same token, magnetic lows accompanied by gravity lows are generally caused by felsic igneous rocks or thick sequences of nonmagnetic sedimentary rocks or sediments. As noted above, the pre-Cretaceous "basement" beneath the southeastern Coastal Plain is composed of a wide variety of rock types of different ages that have been delineated on maps compiled on the basis of cuttings and a few short cores from scattered oilwell tests (Milton and Hurst, 1965; Daniels and others, in press; Chowns and Williams, in press) and preliminary aeromagnetic data (Daniels and others, in press). There is not a direct match between the geology at the top of the pre-Cretaceous "basement" and the salient features on the aeromagnetic and gravity maps. This lack of correspondence is due, in part, to the presence of extensive, thick Triassic-Jurassic nonmagnetic sedimentary sequences and, in part, to the cumulative magnetic effect described above. However, from the broad, regional view of plate tectonics, the distribution of rock types immediately beneath the Cretaceous sediments and sedimentary rocks in the southeastern Coastal Plain is not that important, because broad-wavelength magnetic and gravity features derive from deeper, primary features and from cumulative effects. In our opinion, the fundamental geologic terranes and linear features are reflected in the aeromagnetic and gravity maps and are shown in Figure 3.

We interpret the Charleston and northern Florida magnetic terranes as being virtually the same geologic terrane, composed at depth of the same general rock types, probably of the same general ages. On the basis of the geophysical maps, we interpret them as chiefly mafic terranes (because they are magnetically high overall) intruded by mafic plutons of batholithic proportions that cause the large (generally bullseye-shaped) magnetic and gravity high anomalies (Figs. 1 and 2). The two magnetic terranes are divided by the Altamaha anomaly.

In northern Florida, southern Georgia, and southern Alabama (south of the Altamaha anomaly), the rocks immediately beneath the Cretaceous Coastal Plain sedimentary rocks and sediments are unmetamorphosed or mildly metamorphosed Lower Ordovician to Middle Devonian sedimentary rocks (Applin, 1951; Bridge and Berdan, 1952; Pojeta and others, 1976; Chowns and Williams, in press; Daniels and others, in press) that have yielded faunas having European, North African, and South American affinities (Wilson, 1966; Pojeta and others, 1976, and references therein). It seems fairly certain that during the early Paleozoic these rocks and the magnetic rocks they must rest upon (the northern Florida magnetic terrane) were not attached to the North American plate. Bobyarchick (1980) and Chowns and Williams (in press) have recently suggested that the lower Paleozoic rocks in northern Florida may be correlative with West African sequences.

There is no paleontologic evidence to indicate the age of the rocks in the pre-Cretaceous "basement" north of the Altamaha anomaly. If rocks correlative with the lower Paleozoic rocks south of the anomaly are present north of the anomaly, they are covered by Triassic-Jurassic sedimentary sections or by felsic volcanic rocks of unknown age (Milton and Hurst, 1965; Daniels and others, in press; Chowns and Williams, in press). If our interpretation from the geophysical maps, that the Charleston and northern Florida magnetic terranes are essentially the same geologic terrane, is correct, then the Charleston terrane also was probably not attached to the North American plate during the early Paleozoic.

The interpretation that the Charleston and northern Florida terranes were not attached to the North American plate during the early Paleozoic makes the northwestern margin of the Charleston terrane (Figs. 1 and 3) especially important, for this margin might then be a suture zone, or more specifically, the Alleghanian suture zone between the North American and African (or African/South American) plates. Although only a few fossils have ever been found in the southeastern Piedmont south of Virginia, and paleobiogeographical affinities are indeterminable for the few known fossils (St. Jean, 1973; Cloud and others, 1976; Maher and others, 1981), there is evidence that the slate belt was attached to North America since the Ordovician (Hatcher, 1978; Brown and Barton, 1980, Van der Voo, 1980), thereby suggesting that all the Piedmont has also been part of North America since that time. We suggest that the northwestern boundary of the Charleston magnetic terrane (Fig. 3) is the Alleghanian suture between Africa or South America and North America. Hatcher (1978), Zietz and Higgins (1980), and Bobyarchick (1980) have suggested that the suture is somewhere in this general vicinity beneath the Coastal Plain.

In addition to the characteristics that suggest that the northwestern boundary of the Charleston terrane is the suture between Africa (or Africa/South America) and North America, the linearity of this boundary (Figs. 1 and 3) strongly suggests that it may also be a strike-slip fault.

Because the Altamaha anomaly is a low magnetic anomaly, it is probably caused either by felsic igneous rocks or by a thick section of nonmagnetic sediments or sedimentary rocks. The fact that the anomaly is more than

1,150 km long, and nowhere more than about 55 km wide, suggests that it is not caused by a felsic intrusion, or even by a series of felsic intrusions. As geologic maps of the pre-Cretaceous "basement" show (Milton and Hurst, 1965; Daniels and others, in press; Chowns and Williams, in press), felsic volcanic rocks dominate the "basement" surface in the vicinity of the Altamaha anomaly in southeastern Georgia. These volcanic rocks are probably not the cause of the anomaly, however, because they do not form a linear belt corresponding to the anomaly, and because they cover a large area away from the anomaly. Moreover, these same felsic volcanic rocks are present over the magnetic and gravity highs that almost certainly mark mafic igneous rocks in the northern Florida terrane, and there are no pronounced linear magnetic low anomalies like the Altamaha anomaly associated with other areas of felsic volcanic rocks beneath the southeastern Coastal Plain. The felsic volcanic rocks in southeastern Georgia probably do produce the intermediate magnetic area (600-800 gammas) just north of the Altamaha anomaly and perhaps contribute to some of the gravity lows in this area.

The fact that through much of its course the Altamaha anomaly is either coincident with, or just south of, gravity lows also suggests that it is caused either by felsic igneous rocks or by a thick nonmagnetic sedimentary section. The magnetic anomaly is located at the southern edge of many of the gravity lows. This is consistent with theory (Vacquier and others, 1963) and with observations that the peaks of total-intensity magnetic anomalies at these latitudes are generally located to the south of matching gravity lows.

Seismic lines across the Altamaha anomaly offshore suggest that it is caused by a trough filled with a thick sedimentary section (Klitgord and Behrendt, 1979). Klitgord and Behrendt (1979, p. 107–108) depicted the feature associated with the Altamaha anomaly (of this paper) offshore as a long narrow graben, or series of grabens, 3 to 6 km deep.

We interpret the Altamaha anomaly (offshore and onshore) as being caused by a fault-bounded trough filled with a thick nonmagnetic sedimentary section. Based on magnetic depth estimates, this trough may be locally as deep as 4 km beneath the "basement" surface. The Altamaha anomaly trough appears to have essentially divided the predominately mafic Charleston-northern Florida crust from about 33°30'N. lat. off the southern North Carolina coast, at least to southwestern Georgia (Fig. 3). The Charleston and northern Florida terranes appear to merge around the northeastern end of the trough.

A postulated strike-slip fault, here called the Carolina-Mississippi fault, seems to follow approximately the northwestern margin of the Charleston terrane through South Carolina and Georgia, continues to the southwest at least into southeastern Mississippi (Figs. 1 and 3), and appears to cut off the Piedmont province (including different magnetic terranes within the Piedmont), the Valley and Ridge province, the New York-Alabama lineament, and the magnetically high terrane northwest of the New York-Alabama lineament. Displacement along the Carolina-Mississippi fault is interpreted to be right-lateral because none of the magnetic terranes on the northwestern side of the fault can be identified on the southeastern side (Fig. 3).

The age of many of the features reflected in the aeromagnetic and gravity maps, and even the age of many of the rocks at the "basement" surface, is debatable. If our interpretations are correct, much of the strike-slip displacement along the Carolina-Mississippi fault must be younger than Pennsylvanian, because it cuts the Valley and Ridge province. Latest major displacement along the fault must be older than Cretaceous, and because there is strong evidence that continental drift had begun by about 180 m.y. ago (Pitman and Talwani, 1972; Vogt, 1973), thus placing eastern North America in a tensional tectonic regime at that time, latest major movement along the Carolina-Mississippi fault is probably older than about Late Triassic. The age of the Altamaha anomaly trough and the thick section of sedimentary rocks that we suggest fills it is obscure. The trough is probably younger than the large mafic plutons that have intruded the Charleston and northern Florida terranes, because none of the plutons appear to have intruded the trough, but the age of the plutons is unknown. The exact relationship between the Altamaha anomaly trough and the Carolina-Mississippi fault is also obscure. One interpretation would be that the trough is truncated by the fault in Alabama. This would mean that the trough is a Paleozoic feature transported into place along with the African (or African/South American) crust. However, an equally viable interpretation would be that the trough is a Mesozoic feature associated with the rifting stage of continental separation, and that the rifting at its northwestern border in Alabama followed the established crustal break along the Carolina-Mississippi fault. The solution of the age of the Altamaha anomaly trough must await determination of the age of the mafic plutons in the Charleston and northern Florida terranes and the felsic volcanic rocks in southeastern Georgia.

ACKNOWLEDGEMENTS

We are indebted to T. M. Chowns, D. L. Daniels, David Gottfried, L. D. Brown, and G. S. Gohn for helpful discussions of the geophysical maps and the pre-Cretaceous geology of the southeastern Coastal Plain, and for constructive reviews of the manuscript by Louis Pavlides, J. D. Phillips, G. S. Gohn, and R. D. Hatcher, Jr.

REFERENCES CITED

Applin, P. L., 1951, Preliminary report on buried pre-Mesozoic rocks in Florida and adjacent states: U.S. Geological Survey Circ, v. 91, 28 p.

Bobyarchick, A. R., 1980, The Eastern Piedmont fault system and its relationship to Alleghanian tectonics in the southern Appalachians: Jour. Geology, v. 89, p. 335–347.

Bridge, J., and Berdan, J. M., 1952, Preliminary correlation of the Paleozoic rocks from test wells in Florida and adjacent parts of Georgia and Alabama: Florida Geol. Survey Guidebook, Assoc. Am. State Geologists 44th Ann. Mtg. Field Trip, April 1952, p. 29–38.

Brown, L., and Barton, C., 1980, Paleomagnetism of some Paleozoic intrusive rocks in the southern Appalachian Piedmont (abs.): Geol. Soc. America Abs. with Programs, v. 12, no. 7, p. 393.

Chowns, T. M., and Williams, C. T., *in press*, Pre-Cretaceous rocks beneath the Georgia Coastal Plain—Regional implications, *in* Gohn, G. S., ed., Studies related to the Charleston, S. C., earthquake of 1886—Tectonics and seismicity: U.S. Geol. Survey Prof. Paper.

Cloud, P., Wright, J. E., and Glover, L., III, 1976, Traces of animal life from 620-million-year-old rocks in North Carolina: American Scientist, v. 64, p. 396–406.

Daniels, D. L., Zietz, I., and Popenoe, P., *in press*, Geologic interpretation of new aeromagnetic maps of the southeastern Coastal Plain, *in* Gohn, G. S., ed., Studies related to the Charleston, S.C., earthquake of 1886–Tectonics and seismicity: U.S. Geol. Survey Prof. Paper.

Drake, C. L., Ewing, J. I., and Stockard, H., 1968, The continental margin of the eastern United States: Canadian Jour. Earth Sci., v. 5, p. 993–1010.

Emery, K. O., Phillips, J. D., Bowin, C. O., Bunce, E. T., and Knott, S. T., 1970, Continental rise off eastern North America: Am. Assoc. Petroleum Geologists Bull., v. 54, p. 44–108.

Hatcher, R. D., Jr., 1978, Tectonics of the western Piedmont and Blue Ridge, southern Appalachians: Review and speculation: Am. Jour. Sci., v. 278, p. 276–304.

King, E. R., Jr., 1978, The New York-Alabama lineament: geophysical evidence for a major crustal break in the basement beneath the Appalachian basin: Geology, v. 6, no. 5, p. 312–318.

Klitgord, K. D., and Behrendt, J. C., 1979, Basin structure of the U.S. Atlantic margin, *in* Watkins, J. S., and others, eds., Geology and geophysics of continental margins: Am. Assoc. Petroleum Geologists Mem. 29, p. 85–112.

Maher, H. D., Palmer, A. R., Secor, D. T., and Snoke, A. W., 1981, New trilobite locally in the Piedmont of South Carolina, and its regional implications: Geology, v. 9, p. 34–36.

Milton, C., and Hurst, V. J., 1965, Subsurface "basement" rocks of Georgia: Georgia Geol. Survey Bull. 76, 56 p.

Pickering, S. M., Jr., Higgins, M. W., and Zietz, I., 1977, Relation between the southeast Georgia embayment and the onshore extent of the Brunswick anomaly (abs.): EOS, v. 58, p. 432.

Pitman, W. C., III, and Talwani, M., 1972, Sea-floor spreading in the North Atlantic: Geol. Soc. America Bull., v. 83, no. 3, p. 619–646.

Pojeta, J., Jr., Kriz, J., and Berdan, J. M., 1976, Silurian-Devonian pelecypods and Paleozoic stratigraphy of subsurface rocks in Florida and Georgia and related Silurian pelecypods from Bolivia and Turkey: U.S. Geol. Survey Prof. Paper 879, 32 p.

St. Jean, J., 1973, A new Cambrian trilobite from the Piedmont of North Carolina: Am. Jour. Sci., v. 273-A, p. 196–216.

Taylor, P. T., Zietz, I., and Dennis, L. S., 1968, Geologic implications of aeromagnetic data for the eastern continental margin of the United States: Geophysics, v. 33, no. 5, p. 755–780.

Van der Voo, R., 1980, The Paleozoic assembly of Pangea: A plate tectonic model for the Taconic, Acadian, and Appalachian orogenies (abs.): Geol. Soc. America Abs. with Programs, v. 12, no. 7, p. 539.

Vogt, P. R., 1973, Early events in the opening of the North Atlantic, *in* Tarling, D. H., and Runcorn, S. K., eds., Implications of continental drift to the earth sciences: New York, Academic Press, v. 2, p. 693–712.

Wilson, J. T., 1966, Did the Atlantic close and then reopen?: Nature, v. 201, no. 5050, p. 676–681.

Zietz, I., and Gilbert, F. P., 1980, Aeromagnetic map of part of the southeastern United States: U.S. Geol. Survey Geophys. Inv. Map GP 936, scale 1:2,000,000.

Zietz, I., and Higgins, M. W., 1980, Interpretation of a new aeromagnetic map of the southeastern Coastal Plain, U.S.A. (abs.): Geol. Soc. America Abs. with Programs, v. 12, no. 7, p. 554.

MANUSCRIPT ACCEPTED BY THE SOCIETY SEPTEMBER 10, 1982

Geological Society of America
Memoir 158
1983

An interpretation of the geology of the Mauritanides orogenic belt (West Africa) in the light of geophysical data

J. P. Lécorché
J. Roussel
J. Sougy

Laboratoire associé au CNRS n° 132 "Etudes géologiques ouest-africaines" Université d'Aix-Marseille III,
13397 Marseille Cedex 13, France

Z. Guetat
Centre Géologique et Géophysique, Université de Montpellier II, 34060 Montpellier Cedex, France

INTRODUCTION

The Mauritanides orogenic belt (Fig. 1), lying opposite the Appalachian belt across the Atlantic, is similar to the Appalachians in only being known in its external zone where it is in contact with the neighboring craton and its sedimentary cover (Taoudeni basin). For the Mauritanides, the craton lies to the east rather than the west, in contrast to the Appalachians. On the western (internal) margin of the Mauritanides belt, a thick coastal sedimentary basin, which formed after the opening of the Atlantic, masks the Mauritanides geology and complicates geophysical interpretation. By comparison with the Appalachian orogen, the Mauritanides do not enjoy the advantages of extensive exposure, nor the advantage of a large number of sophisticated geological studies. As late as 1960, it was still considered to be an integral part of the Precambrian basement beneath the Taoudeni basin. Notwithstanding much progress since that date, a great deal of work remains to be done, particularly in geochemistry and geochronology, before which time few of the proposed interpretations can go beyond the stage of working hypotheses. Lécorché and Sougy (1978) and Dia *et al.* (1979) have recently reviewed the evolution of geologic ideas in this region, and Lécorché (1980) has presented a new interpretation of the Mauritanides orogen.

This article seeks to establish the extent to which our geological understanding of the orogen (Plate 1: In pocket in back of book) is compatible with geophysical, mainly gravimetric, data (Plate 2: In pocket in back of book). These geophysical data impose a series of constraints upon geological interpretations. Certain conflicts of evidence, such as the apparent "thin-skinned" tectonic style of the chain associated with a major positive gravimetric anomaly, can only be resolved by deep seismic profiles such as have been undertaken in the Appalachian belt (Cook *et al.*, 1979, 1980; Hatcher, 1981).

OUTLINE OF THE GEOLOGY

The West African fold belt, or Mauritanides belt (Sougy, 1962b), comprises a folded and metamorphosed zone which has been very strongly eroded and does not currently form a mountain range. It is exposed (Fig. 1) between latitudes 12°N and 23°N as a long (1,300 km) and narrow (0-120 km) north-south belt interrupted only between 20°N and 21°N by the Reguibat uplift culmination. Southward, its natural prolongation seems to be the Rokelides belt of Sierra Leone—Liberia (Allen, 1969), although a second branch, just to the north of the Bové basin, diverges south-westward. Northward the Mesozoic deposits of the Aaiun basin cover the continuation of the Mauritanides belt, the folded foreland of which is observed in Zemmour (Tindouf basin).

The foreland of the Mauritanides is the West African Precambrian craton which crops out in the Reguibat uplift and in the Kayes and Eastern Senegal inliers (Plate 1: In pocket in back of book). This foreland is generally covered by horizontal Upper Proterozoic to Paleozoic sediments of the Taoudeni basin (Fig. 1).

Sediments of the Mesozoic-Cenozoic Senegal-Mauritanian basin, which overlie the western units of the Mauritanides belt, extend westward as far as the Atlantic coast and continental shelf, increasing considerably in thickness

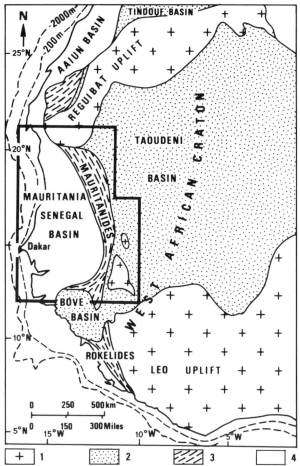

Figure 1: The Mauritanides in relation to the other major structural elements of North-West Africa. 1: Precambrian basement; 2: Upper Precambrian and Paleozoic cover; 3: Pan-African (Rokelides) and Caledonian-Hercynian (Mauritanides) fold belts; 4: Mesozoic-Cenozoic cover. The area of the gravity survey is marked.

westward. These are sediments deposited on the East Atlantic passive margin after opening of the Atlantic Ocean.

Three major tectonic elements can be identified in the area (Fig. 1): the craton, the orogen, and the coastal basin, all of which are heavily obscured in the north by active dune fields trending WSW (Azefal, Akchar, Amatlich, and Aouker: see Plate 2 in pocket in back of book).

In this section, we review in sequence: the western border of the West African craton and its epicontinental cover, the relations between the belt and the foreland, the orogenic belt proper in the area of its outcrop, the geological interpretations of the orogen, and the principal characteristics of the Senegal-Mauritanian coastal basin.

Foreland: The Western Margin of the West African Craton and Its Cover

The craton proper is composed of three components.

Folded and strongly metamorphosed and migmatized Archean rocks (Barrère, 1967), dated at about 2700 Ma, are found principally in the Reguibat uplift (Amsaga, Tijirit, Tasiast, Tiris, and Ghallaman) and in the western part of the Leo uplift (Guinea, Liberia) (Plate 1: In pocket in back of book). Birrimian rocks, folded and weakly metamorphosed during the Eburnean orogeny (2000–1800 Ma), make up the eastern part of the Reguibat uplift and the main part of the basement in the inliers of Eastern Senegal and Kayes and in the Leo uplift. Granites were emplaced between 2000 and 1600 Ma (Vachette *et al.*, 1975), by which time the cratonic character had been definitively acquired.

The epicontinental cover of the craton shows large scale homogeneity but small scale variability. The most recent and detailed study by Trompette (1973) in Mauritanian Adrar distinguishes four lithostratigraphic supergroups (Fig. 2).

Supergroup 1 ($\cong$1400 m), in unconformity upon basement, comprises alternations of quartzitic sandstones and sandstones or shales with stromatolitic limestones (particularly well-developed in the north). Supergroup 1, with an age between 1000 Ma and less than 700 Ma (Clauer, 1975), is not found at any point on the western margin of the basin, its most westerly extent being at Atar, in the Southwest of Kayes, and at Ségou.

Supergroup 2 ($\cong$1200 m) covers unconformably both basement and supergroup 1 (partially glacially eroded). It begins at the base by tillites (in the broad sense), the first term of a triad comprising also baryte-limestone and silexites. These are followed by shales and stromatolitic limestone horizons and then by muddy sandstones and very fine-grained sandstones ("red series"). At the top are quartzitic sandstones and fine-bedded marine sandstones with *Scolithus*. Supergroup 2 is dated between 650 Ma and Middle Ordovician. In contrast to supergroup 1, it is remarkably uniform on the scale of the basin and implies subsidence rates (15 m/Ma) which Bronner *et al.* (1980) have suggested are characteristic of sedimentation in a cratonic area. This led them to suggest that, before the deposition of supergroup 2, there was a temporary remobilization of the craton at about 650 Ma (Pan-African orogeny). The source of detrital material seems to have been from the north initially, and from the SSE during and after deposition of the "red series", perhaps because of a late Pan-African uplift which generated molasse.

Supergroup 3 ($\cong$200 m) lies with a glacial erosional disconformity upon the supergroup 2 partially eroded. It begins with a sandstone formation of glacial character (Upper Ordovician) followed by transgressive shales and siltstones with Silurian graptolite faunas. The base of supergroup 3 is the level of the glacial horizon known throughout West Africa (Sougy and Lécorché, 1963; Beuf *et al.*, 1971; Deynoux, 1980) and equated in Morocco with

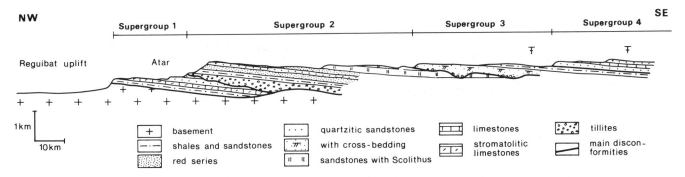

Figure 2: Lithostratigraphic ideal section of the Mauritanian Adrar.

the Upper Ashgillian (Destombes, 1968). The Silurian sediments are poorly developed. Thin and sandy in the south, they tend to thicken in their upper part in the NW of Adrar, where they have affinities with those of the Moroccan Anti-Atlas (Drot and Lécorché, 1971), in which they attain a thickness of 1000 m. Bronner *et al.* (1980) suggested that the slow contemporary subsidence rate may be due to isostatic uplift of the basement after decay of the Upper Ordovician ice sheet.

Supergroup 4 (>400 m), comprising sandstones, ferruginous siltstones and carbonates with Devonian faunas, lies with an erosional disconformity on the supergroup 3. The Devonian of supergroup 4 is only known, outside Zemmour and the Western Sahara, from Adrar, Tagant, and to the south of Assaba at Godiovol (Crévola *et al.*, 1974). It also reflects uniform epicontinental sedimentation.

Relations Between the Belt and the Foreland

The western margin of the foreland descends beneath the eastern border of the Mauritanides belt, and its sedimentary cover is commonly folded in this region. It presents varied characteristics, which are presented here from north to south.

In Zemmour (Plate 1: In pocket in back of book), in the south-west corner of the Tindouf basin, the Paleozoic cover becomes progressively more folded toward the west where eventually ESE directed overfolds and thrusts develop with a NNE-SSW strike (the "chain" of Dhlou, Dacheux, 1967).

In the southern part of the Western Sahara (currently the province of South Morocco), the major metamorphic units of the belt appear for the first time in outcrop. The basement rocks of the Reguibat uplift and a narrow discordant skin of Upper Ordovician and Siluro-Devonian cover rocks descend beneath allochthonous metamorphic formations (Sougy, 1962a). The tectonic contact is marked by mylonites. The Reguibat uplift is a major culmination of the cratonic surface, which extends far to the west near to the present coast at 16°W and interrupts the outcrop of the belt. On the southern margin of the Reguibat uplift,

the cover rocks are absent in the west, and the nappes rest there directly on basement. To the east and south-east, they rest on progressively younger beds, from the uppermost Proterozoic (supergroup 2) of western Adrar to the folded Devonian (Frasnian). The Upper Proterozoic rocks of Atar (supergroup 1) are never in contact with the belt.

From Iriji to south of Assaba, the folded rocks of supergroups 2, 3, and 4 crop out. They pass eastward continuously into the flat-lying strata of the Adrar, Tagant, and Assaba plateaus, which belong to the vast Taoudeni basin, in the center of which lie Carboniferous sediments unknown in the vicinity of the belt.

South of Assaba, the craton reappears in the Kayes and Eastern Senegal inliers. In the east, it is covered by the Upper Proterozoic sandstones of the great tabular plateaus of Afollé and Tambaoura (supergroup 1) and in the west by folded uppermost Proterozoic rocks of the Falémé series (Bassot, 1966) (supergroup 2). These latter are themselves discordantly overlain toward the south by flat-lying Upper Ordovician and Siluro-Devonian rocks in the Bové basin.

The Mauritanides Belt Proper

According to Lécorché's (1980) interpretation, the Mauritanides belt can be schematically divided into three great units from south to north (Figs. 1 and 3). *The folded autochthonous and parautochthonous formations* of Eastern Senegal disappear beneath the Upper Ordovician beds of the Bové basin and seem to extend beyond into Sierra Leone in the Rokelide chain. *The external nappes* extend from the south of the Reguibat uplift to the east of Akjoujt through Aftout Tagant and Assaba as far as the Bakel region. These nappes are not known to the north of the Reguibat uplift nor are the rocks of supergroup 2 of which they seem to be partly composed. To the south, they disappear beneath the coastal basin between Kidira and Goudiry, although they may occur in some allochthonous thrust masses in the Koulountou river area. *The internal nappes* of the Western Sahara and those of Akjoujt are separated probably as a result of recent erosion, by the westerly extension of the Reguibat uplift. Their extension

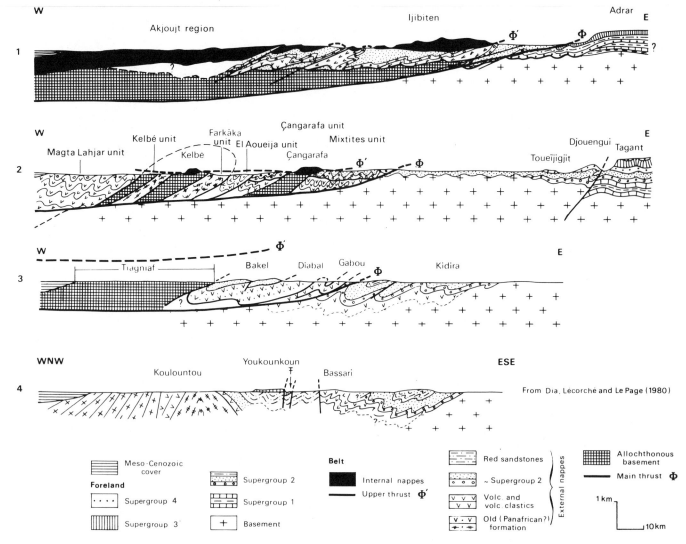

Figure 3: Schematic sections across the Mauritanides (from Lécorché, 1980). The locations of these sections are shown in Plate 1: In pocket in back of book.

toward the north is hidden beneath the Mesozoic rocks of the coastal basin, but presumed by the external folding of Zemmour. To the south, they are restricted to the Akjoujt region and to several klippen attributed to them to the west of Tagant.

The folded formations of Eastern Senegal. These unmetamorphosed and slightly metamorphosed autochthonous and parautochthonous formations, mainly attributable to supergroup 2, make up a great NNE-SSW striking synclinorium in the Kidira and Youkounkoun regions. This synclinorium is broken in its central region by a faulted anticlinal ridge known as the Bassari ridge (Fig. 3, cross section 4).

To the east, the glacial base of these folded formations, equivalent to the base of supergroup 2, rests directly on the Birrimian basement of Eastern Senegal, precisely as in W Adrar it rests on Archean basement of the Reguibat

uplift. On the other hand, in the Bassari ridge, a thick volcanic and volcanic-sedimentary substratum occurs beneath the glacial horizon and thickens considerably toward the south, where it is poly-deformed and metamorphosed (Villeneuve, 1980). In the deepest parts of the synclinorium, the cover is up to 3000-4000 m thick. The core of the synclinorium is occupied by extensive outcrops of red beds of molasse facies belonging to supergroup 2. The whole sequence is then discordantly overlain by horizontal Upper Ordovician sandstones (supergroup 3, Plate 1: In pocket in back of book) which are the basal beds of the Bové basin. Thrust sheets of granite (Niokolo-Koba) at the margin of the western anticlinal culmination of the Koulountou may belong to a SW extension of the external nappes or to the folded formations of Eastern Senegal, thus underlining their parautochthonous character. In summary, this southern zone appears to have behaved as a foreland for the belt, having had a stronger tectonic history than the foreland to the north, but only during one pre-Upper Ordovician period.

The external nappes. These nappes only appear to the south of the Reguibat uplift between Akjoujt and Iriji. In the region to the east of Akjoujt, they crop out in flat areas or depressions (areas of reg) which separate areas of rocky bluffs characteristic of the internal nappes from the western border of the craton and its folded cover. In Lécorché's (1980) interpretation, they constitute the major outcropping part of the belt in the south. They are locally, and sometimes over vast distances, covered by micaceous quartzites belonging to the sole of the internal nappes, which thus form klippen of thin allochthonous sheets. These klippen are numerous north of Aouker and increasingly rare toward the south.

The external nappes are composed of old migmatized basement, ultrabasites, volcanics, and acid and basic volcanoclastic rocks as well as of a little-altered sedimentary cover analogous to the lower half of the supergroup 2 cover on the craton (from the tillite to the red series).

The metamorphic grade is in the greenschist facies. In the area east of Akjoujt, the sedimentary cover is inverted over large distances, which is interpreted as evidence of large first generation recumbent folds (F1). These beds are re-folded by a second phase (F2) overturned toward the ENE, and by a third less intense phase (F3) in which folds, striking N-S, are overturned or merely asymmetric toward the east. From Adrar to the south of the Senegal River, these nappes (post F3 thrusting = Φ) overthrust rocks as young as Devonian.

To the south of Aouker, the folding phase F3 and the overthrusting phase Φ impose a strong N-S grain on the terrain. The old basement and the metavolcanics occupy the "median zone" which is flanked by units of sedimentary cover, the whole area reflecting a strongly thrusted anticlinal megastructure overturned toward the east. Thin granodioritic sheets, commonly showing thinning and mylonitic zones, are intercalated within these formations, generally to the west of the metavolcanics and the old basement (Fig. 3, cross section 2).

On the northern margin of the Aouker, basement of Archean character (Bou Naga), covered by a thin skin of very slightly metamorphosed phosphatic detrital sediments belonging to the basal part of supergroup 2, appears as a window in the external nappes. The units of this window display structures similar to those of the external nappes, and basement is possibly involved in the major overturned folds. The present position of this basement rock, at least 1200 m above the presumed basement of the foreland, can be used as evidence that it is not a simple autochthonous window. It seems once to have played this role, before being displaced to the NE into its present position, well onto the Taoudeni basin itself (Lécorché, 1980). Low-

angle tectonic contacts disappear beneath the coastal basin to the south-west of Kidira, from latitude 14° N (Fig. 3, cross sections 3-4).

The internal nappes. The internal nappes largely comprise volcanic and basic volcanoclastic sediments, together with ferruginous quartzites and micaschists. Spilites, gabbros, peridotites, and serpentinites are also present, but as separate units. True ophiolites have not been recognized. In the Akjoujt region, the upper unit comprises basement which is very similar to the migmatized Archean gneisses of the Reguibat uplift but has a mylonitized sole (Giraudon and Sougy, 1963). In Adrar Soutouf (Western Sahara), charnockites and basic rocks appear to cap the series.

In the Akjoujt region, the material of the internal nappes is metamorphosed up to the amphibolite grade. After acquisition of schistosity, probably associated with the first phase of isoclinal folding (F1), the rocks show at least two subsequent phases of deformation—sub-isoclinal folds (F2) with ENE-WSW axes and folds (F3) overturned toward the east with N-S axes—prior to the emplacement of the nappes along horizontal shear planes Φ' during phase Φ.

The folds in these nappes are truncated basally by a thrust plane, above which beds of quartzite and quartz-mica-schists frequently occur. These nappes lie on the external nappes or even directly upon the foreland, as happens around the southwestern extremity of the Reguibat uplift.

One hundred kilometers ESE of Akjoujt, the Ijibiten klippen with its quartzite sole provides the most easterly evidence of the extension of the internal nappes (Fig. 3, cross section 1). Lécorché (1980) made this the object of detailed study. The internal nappes, south of Aouker, only outcrop in progressively smaller klippen, disappearing at about latitude 17°N.

Interpretations and Conclusions on the Geology of the Belt

In contrast to the group of nappes which constitutes the main belt, the folded formations of Eastern Senegal belong to the folded foreland. The occurrence in the cores of these folds of volcanic-clastic rocks of orogenic character distinguishes them from those of the foreland farther north. This distinction is accentuated by the fact that they are co-linear with the Rokelide belt to the south of the discordant Bové basin: Eastern Senegal as well as Rokelides structures were acquired before the superimposition of the Upper Ordovician sediments of the basin.

The contact of the external nappes against the folded foreland, from the southern margin of the Reguibat uplift to Eastern Senegal, is characterized by the juxtaposition of the varied materials of the nappes against the whole range of formations of the craton and its sedimentary cover. In the absence of natural sections, the mapped form of this contact, which is sinuous on a small scale and extends for hundreds of kilometers, is interpreted as the trace of an enormous low-angle tectonic contact. Shear movement along this plane carried a previously deformed suite of rocks over the sediments of the Taoudeni basin (including rocks at least as young as the Frasnian) or directly over their cratonic substratum.

Similarly, the basal contact of the internal nappes upon the craton or its thin autochthonous cover to the north of the Reguibat uplift, and upon the external nappes to the south of the uplift, appears to be an extremely flat thrust plane. Quartzites frequently lie above the basal thrust plane of the nappes. As in the case of the external nappes, each nappe displays its own fold style, suggesting that these major late-stage, sub-horizontal shearing movements have truncated, moved, and brought together rock series which had previously evolved in different ways in different places.

Thus, it is suggested that there were initially two distinct belts brought together in post-Frasnian times to produce the current polyphase Mauritanides orogenic belt.

The first of these belts, represented by the external nappes, involves rocks of up to the Cambro-Ordovician boundary (upper part of supergroup 2). Study of angular discordances in the equivalent sedimentary cover of the foreland (Tagant: Dia *et al.,* 1969) shows that these occurred primarily during the Ordovician before the deposition of the glacial sandstones of the Upper Ordovician. We suggest that there was an intra-Ordovician or "Taconic" folding event which took place in a domain west of the area now occupied by the external nappes. The folded volcanic-sedimentary series prior to the Bové basin, to the south of Kidira, may be a contemporary autochthon.

The formation of the second belt, represented by the internal nappes, cannot currently be dated. However, the quartzites which are frequently found at the truncated bases of the internal nappes, and which in Aftout Tagant are attributed to the Upper Ordovician, can be used to suggest a post-Upper Ordovician age for the nappes. Their source cannot be determined, but the inclusion within them of basement comparable with that of the Reguibat uplift suggests a source far to the west, in the region of the Atlantic coast or farther. Moreover, their extension to the north, in contrast to that of the external nappes and of supergroup 2, as well as their disappearance to the south toward latitude 17°N, suggests a different latitudinal location of the source area compared with that of the first belt.

The geometry of tectonic contacts, particularly in the north, suggests a "thin-skinned" tectonic style with nappes resting on the craton and its sedimentary cover above roughly horizontal shear planes. We also suggest that erosion of the Rebuibat culmination has created a vast semi-

window in the internal nappes, producing an eroded E-W front of 250 km, allowing basal shear planes to be studied for almost the whole exposed width of the belt. We may have here a thin-skinned structure which is very similar to that of the southern Appalachians, as elucidated by the COCORP project (Cook *et al.,* 1979; Hatcher, 1981) by means of seismic reflection, where faults with a rectilinear surface trace, as in the Brevard zone, become horizontal at depth. The same may be true in the central, north-south section of the Mauritanides, where autochthonous (Chiron, 1973) and allochthonous interpretations (Dia *et al.,* 1980) are in conflict.

The Senegal-Mauritania Coastal Basin

This Mesozoic-Cenozoic basin occupies the whole area between the Atlantic Ocean and the Mauritanides belt, onto which it has transgressed. Its southern margin partially covers the Paleozoic Bové basin. In the north, it is continued beyond the Reguibat uplift by the Mesozoic-Cenozoic Aaiun basin, beneath which disappear the internal nappes of the Western Sahara and the folded Paleozoic formations of Zemmour.

Except for the Upper Cretaceous of the Cape Vert peninsula (Ndiass dome), only beds of Eocene and continental and marine Quaternary are exposed at the surface in the basin. The so-called "Continental Terminal" beds have been shown by Tessier *et al.* (1975) to contain weathered Cenozoic marine facies. The westernmost exposed rocks of the basin are the basic volcanics of the Dakar area. This thick, little deformed sequence cannot be easily studied from its surface geology because of the flatness of the terrain and the deep surface weathering.

Our knowledge of the sub-surface geology of the basin is derived primarily from the work of petroleum geologists (Maugis, 1955; Nettleton, 1962; Aymé, 1965; De Spengler *et al.,* 1966). It comprises Mesozoic and Cenozoic rocks dipping to the west at low angles. The top of the basement also dips gently from east to west as far as longitude 15°30'W, beyond which it dips more strongly (De Spengler *et al.,* 1966). There is strong subsidence accompanied by normal faults parallel to the coast west of longitude 15°30'W. The nature, age, and depth of the substratum west of this longitude are not generally known. Boreholes have reached Lower Cretaceous to Upper Jurassic sediments (Castelain, 1965). This post-Paleozoic cover probably reaches a thickness of 10,000 m or more in the Dakar region.

GEOPHYSICS

Because a large part of the Mauritanides is hidden beneath the coastal basin sediments, and because, in the absence of relief, we only have a two-dimensional picture of the belt, it is doubly important that our geological knowledge is reassessed in the light of geophysical data which may set bounds on geological hypotheses.

Gravity and magnetic surveys have been undertaken in the area shown in Fig. 1. The gravity data are mainly from regional surveys conducted by ORSTOM* (Crenn and Rechenmann, 1965). About 9000 gravity measurements have been made in Western Mauritania and Senegal. The station spacing is about 4-5 km along approximately SW-NE traverses separated by 10 to 20 km. The precision of measurements is generally of the order of 0.5 to 1 mgal, although in places it may reach only 2 or 3 mgal. West of 15° W in Senegal, Gambia, and Casamance, gravity data are from detailed oil exploration surveys (COPETAO, SAP, SPS, BRP).** Some magnetic measurements have also been made along ORSTOM'S profiles with vertical field variometers. The observations have not been corrected for the diurnal variations of the Earth's magnetic field, and the accuracy is of the order of 50%. Although appreciable disturbances from subsurface masses and laterites are evident on magnetic profiles, the correlation of the gravity and magnetic fields may be useful in some areas to gain an insight into the anomaly sources.

Plate 2 (In pocket in back of book) presents a Bouguer gravity anomaly map compiled from the different surveys with a contour interval of 5 mgal (Crenn and Rechenmann, 1965; Liger, 1980; Guetat, 1981).

The data from the Mauritania-Senegal continental shelf (Fig. 4) were collected by Uchupi *et al.* (1976) by means of a larger scale survey than used on land. Thus, the correlation between the marine and land data is not precise, but the similarity of the two patterns in the coastal zone suggests that they can be used together.

The general anomaly pattern (Fig. 4, Plate 2: In pocket in back of book) reflects three main domains. (i) In the central region, there is a prominent NNW-SSE trending belt of positive anomalies which parallels the main exposed segment of the Mauritanides fold belt, although the axis of the gravity high is slightly west of the axis of the outcrop and covered by the easternmost part of the Mauritania-Senegal basin. The so-called *Mauritanides anomaly* is a striking feature which extends approximately 700 km from south of the Reguibat uplift to Eastern Senegal. It probably marks a major crustal suture in the ancient West African cratonic margin and separates two crustal provinces. (ii) East of the Mauritanides anomaly, *a broad regional negative anomaly*, mainly characterized by NE-SW gravity trends, is associated with the western border of the Precambrian granitized West African craton

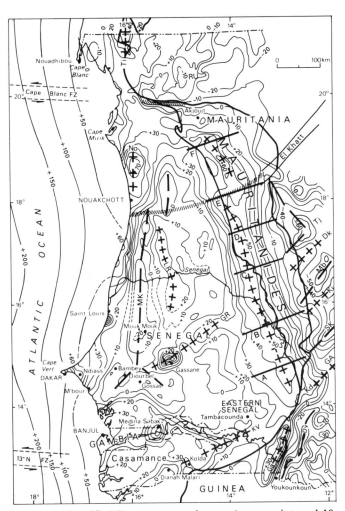

Figure 4: Simplified Bouguer anomaly map (contour interval 10 mgal) of Mauritania and Senegal, showing the principal gravimetric trends and also showing the principal geological subdivisions. The terrestrial data are from Crenn and Rechenmann (1965); the offshore data are based on the work of Uchupi *et al.* (1976). Lines of crosses: gravity highs; dashed lined: gravity lows; GA, SK, . . . :location of gravity anomalies discussed in text; full lines: location of gravimetric sections shown on Fig. 5; lines of oblique dashes: presumed fault zones.

and with its Upper Precambrian and Paleozoic cover (Taoudeni basin). (iii) West of the Mauritanides anomaly, *a generally positive Bouguer anomaly field* contrasts with the lows observed in the Taoudeni basin. It corresponds with the Mesozoic and Tertiary Mauritania-Senegal coastal basin and its basement.

In each of the three domains, the gravity field displays anomalies with different wavelengths, trends, shapes, and amplitudes that are associated mostly with density variations which are laterally and vertically extensive in the crust. These anomalies are interpreted and discussed in relation to regional tectonic and geological features which have been described in the first part of this paper.

In general, there is no direct correlation between sur-

*ORSTOM: Office de la Recherche Scientifique et Technique Outre-Mer.

**COPETAO: Compagnie des Pétroles Total d'Afrique de l'Ouest; SAP: Société Africaine des Pétroles; SPS: Société des Pétroles du Sénégal; BRP: Bureau de Recherches Pétrolières.

ficial geology and the gravity data which are related to deeper sources in the crust. For example, the Mesozoic-Tertiary basin does not correlate with the main positive anomaly (Fig. 4). We have used transformed maps, power spectrum analysis (Spector and Grant, 1970), and linear programming (Safon et al., 1977), which is an approach to the inverse problem (Sabatier, 1977), as aids to direct interpretation

Gravity Anomalies Associated with the Western Border of the West African Craton

Areas of basement outcrop. In the northern part of the study area, the southwestern part of the Reguibat uplift, comprising Lower Precambrian granites, migmatites, and metamorphic rocks (Tasiast, Tijirit, and Amsaga regions) is marked by negative anomalies (RU, on Plate 2: In pocket in back of book), the trend of which reflects the general structural grain of this part of the uplift. In the east, however, toward the Adrar region, slightly higher amplitude lows coincide with thickening of the Upper Precambrian and Paleozoic cover toward the Richat-Tagant trough (Bronner et al., 1980).

Roughly along latitude 20°N, there is a gravimetrically sharp boundary between the southwestern part of the Reguibat uplift and the northernmost extension of the main Mauritanides belt. Here, the Akjoujt segment of the belt turns toward the west. Although there is no geological evidence for vertical faulting along this boundary, its straight E-W trend and the profound change in gravity across the boundary suggest a major discontinuity. This gravimetric change may be related to differential warping or arching of the Reguibat uplift in late Proterozoic(?) or early Paleozoic(?) time (Bronner and Roussel, 1978). It is interesting to note that this geophysical discontinuity is co-linear with the continent-ward projection of the Cape Blanc sinistral fracture zone (Le Pichon et al., 1977).

On the western border of the Reguibat uplift, near the latitude of Nouadhibou, there is a major positive anomaly of more than 40 mgal (Ti, on Plate 2: In pocket in back of book) which has been incompletely mapped but which probably persists north of the Mauritanian border. This appears to coincide, in part at least, with the extent of Hercynian nappes of basement north of Tiferchaï (Sougy, 1962a). Extension of mapping farther north, into the Adrar Soutouf, would allow the positive anomaly relation to the northern end of the chain to be elucidated. The characteristics of the anomaly are similar to those (No, on Plate 2: In pocket in back of book) of the Nouakchott anomaly (Liger, 1980) and can be interpreted in the same way, as a dense, deep intrusion.

The two other areas of Precambrian basement outcrop are the inliers of Eastern Senegal and Kayes. Both areas are mainly characterized by SW-NE to SSW-NNE

trending gravity anomalies. Gravimetric models on negative gravity anomalies suggest that the sources, at 3 to 4 km depth, may be intrusive granites. The gravity pattern does not reflect generally the volcanic-clastic rocks, rich in mafic intrusions, described by Bassot (1966) as the Dialé and Mako series.

Anomalies associated with the foreland of the Mauritanides on the western border of the Taoudeni basin. South of latitude 15° in Eastern Senegal and in Mali, there is generally gravitational equilibrium in those areas covered by the sedimentary formations of the foreland. In Tambaoura and on the doleritic plateau of Yélimané, gravity variations are small, and there are no significant anomalies. It is interesting that the Kayes-Timbuktu lineament, known in parts to be a fracture zone (Simon et al., 1982), is not reflected by the gravity data.

To the north of the basement inliers, the central region east of the Mauritanides (the regions of Afollé, Assaba, and Tagant) is characterized by a series of well-defined negative anomalies, of medium and long wavelength, elongated in a SW-NE direction and separated by positive anomalies of similar trend. This anomaly pattern seems to be controlled by major tectonic lineaments in the Precambrian basement.

In southern Afollé, positive anomalies (GA, on Plate 2: In pocket in back of book), well-defined on residual anomaly map (Guetat, 1981), form a NE-SW belt, *the Godiovol-Afollé anomaly,* which extends to the southwest as far as the Godiovol region. The gravimetric models reveal the presence of a dense mass in the basement at between one and five kilometers depth, which we suggest to be a basic intrusion. These interpretations suggest an important NE-SW fracture in the basement (Godiovol-Afollé structure) which could have been the source of the dolerites described by Bense (1964). It is interesting that the major SW-NE structure (Kd, on Plate 2: In pocket in back of book) which terminates the major positive anomaly of the Mauritanides is co-linear with the Godiovol-Afollé structure. These observations, together with the relative westward curvature of the southern part of the Mauritanides belt and the NE-SW strike-slip faults in the intervening Kidira region (Le Page, 1978), suggest the existence of an important crustal structure which may have been a location of subsequent dextral slip during formation of the belt and which may have been an important determinant of its change of direction at the latitude of Kidira.

The Sélibabi-Kankossa negative anomaly (SK, on Plate 2: In pocket in back of book) is of large amplitude (−40 to −50 mgal) and occurs in a region where supergroup 2 is exposed. It has a NE-SW trend parallel to the Godiovol-Afollé structure and extends from near Tamchaket in the north-east, through Kankossa, to the external zone of the chain in the area of Sélibabi in the south-west. Gravimetric modelling (Guetat, 1981) suggests that it represents an elongated depression filled by more than 3000 m of sediment, which contrasts with the conclusion of 1000-2000 m of sediment drawn from the previous aeromagnetic survey (UNESCO-ASGA, 1968).

The Kiffa axis relatively positive anomaly (an anomaly culmination in a zone of negative anomalies, Ki, on Plate 2: In pocket in back of book) has a similar NE-SW trend and lies between the Sélibabi-Kankossa negative anomaly and the negative anomaly of Mbout. It is also characterized by a magnetic high of more than 200 γ. There is nothing in the exposed sediments of supergroup 2 which suggests an explanation for these anomalies. The anomaly can be explained by a model in which we assume it to be underlain by a rock with a density contrast of +0.1 g/cm^3 and a susceptibility of 0.01 uem/cm^3, which would correspond to a basaltic mass (Crenn and Rechenmann, 1965). However, in view of the series of sedimentary basins elongated NE-SW in this area, it seems most likely that it can be explained as an uplifted basement block with varying magnetic properties.

The Mbout negative anomaly (Mb, on Plate 2: In pocket in back of book) extends NE toward Assaba, between Diouk and Kiffa, an area covered by the unfolded sediments of supergroups 2 and 3. The southwestern extremity extends across structural units of the Mauritanides belt, in particular the zone interpreted by Chiron (1973) as an axial root zone. This view must now be untenable, as the hypothetical root zone is clearly cut by the NE-SW anomaly axis. The anomaly reflects the presence of a relatively deep and asymmetric sedimentary basin which deepens toward its southeastern margin, where the steepening of the anomaly suggests the presence of faults on the flanks of the neighboring horst-like Kiffa structure.

The Touijigjigt negative anomaly (Tj, on Plate 2: In pocket in back of book) is a well-defined and strong feature (−55 mgal) to the north of the weakly positive Diouk saddle (Dk, on Plate 2: In pocket in back of book) in Tagant and is associated with folded sediments of supergroups 2 to 4 in the foreland, but also with the eastern tectonic units of the Mauritanides belt (mixtite unit, the volcanic-sedimentary units of El Aoueija and Farkaka, and a unit of the quartzites of Sangarafa). The isobaths on magnetic basement show that sediment thicknesses may be greater than 3000 m in the region of the anomaly. The anomaly crosses the Mauritanides belt without being affected by density changes in the outcropping rocks, such as the dense Farkaka and Gadel units. Here again, the rocks of the belt cannot have local roots and can only represent a thin slice of rocks transported over the folded foreland.

In conclusion, the gravimetric anomalies of the western border of the Taoudeni basin, which formed the foreland of the Mauritanides, appear to be intimately related to the structure and surficial topographic form of the Precambrian basement. This is characterized by a series of horsts and grabens, predominantly aligned in a NE-SW direction, which seem to have controlled sedimentation in the Upper Precambrian and Paleozoic. Farther to the east, however, seismic profiles made by the petroleum company AGIP show the basement surface to be remarkably flat, except in the north-west (Tiris-Richat trough) and south (Nara trough), suggesting that the horsts and grabens only exist along the margin of the belt. Moreover, the gravity data show that *these structures extend beneath the eastern part of the Mauritanides belt,* which agrees with current interpretations (Lécorché and Sougy, 1978; Dia *et al.,* 1979; Lécorché, 1980) in which *the main part of the outcropping chain merely forms a thin allochthonous skin which has moved over the foreland,* exemplifying the style of "thin-skinned tectonics."

Gravity Anomalies Associated with the Senegal-Mauritania Coastal Basin Area

The area of the basin is gravimetrically a vast zone of generally positive anomalies of different wavelengths. West of the great positive anomaly of the Mauritanides, along the basin's eastern margin, anomalies in the basin appear to be elongated along N-S and SW-NE axes. There are also several strongly positive circular anomalies. Finally, in Gambia and Casamance, a complex positive anomaly is oriented roughly by E-W.

Gravimetric signatures in the basin east of 15° W. The two principal gravimetric axes, oriented SW-NE, are located to the east of a zone of N-S flexures and faults along longitude 15°30′W, where the depth of the substratum is less than 2,000 m.

A positive anomaly along the Kolda-Velingara axis (KV, on Plate 2: In pocket in back of book), of more than 20 mgal amplitude, is roughly parallel to the southwestern arm of the Mauritanides. Interpretation based on linear programming (Safon, 1977; Guetat, 1981) indicates a dense body with its base at about 17 km depth. This major crustal discontinuity may be related to the basement structures, such as the Godiovol-Afollé anomaly, which have been described above. To the west, the anomaly seems to be connected to the Gambia-Casamance positive area, marked by important crustal structures and basic intrusions (Crenn and Rechenmann, 1965; Liger and Roussel, 1979; Liger, 1980).

The Revane anomaly (GR, on Plate 2: In pocket in back of book) to the north is the second major positive axis in the area. It merges with the principal Mauritanides anomaly and extends in a NE-SW direction into central Senegal. It remains a significant feature on the anomaly map projected to 12,000 m altitude (Guetat, 1981), indicating the presence of a deep-seated structure in the basement. *The Gassane positive anomaly* is of elliptical form and appears to be a prolongation of the Revane axis. It is interpreted as a dense intrusion in the substratum with its top at about 2 km depth and its base at 14 km. This configuration suggests that the south-westerly termination of the Revane structure could have been reactivated during the emplacement of the Gassane body which took place prior to the deposition of the Cretaceous and probably Jurassic sedimentary cover (Liger, 1980).

Outside the areas of these major NE-SW structures, gravity values in this eastern part of the basin, between the Mauritanides anomaly and 15°30′W, lie between 0 and +10 mgal, indicating approximate isostatic equilibrium.

The positive anomaly of Lake Rkiz (LR, on Plate 2: In pocket in back of book) is the only north-south anomaly in this zone. It extends between 16° and 18°N and has a width of 30 km, in an area where the basement is at a depth of less than 1 km. Its form suggests deep-seated heterogeneity within the basement.

Thus, in the basement beneath the coastal basin, there appear to be a series of structures with a NE-SW orientation as in the cratonic zone to the east of the Mauritanides. The parallelism of the Kolda-Velingara and Gassane-Revane axes with the Godiovol-Afollé and Diouk axes suggests the possibility that these were continuous before the development of the Mauritanides fold belt.

Anomalies within the deep basin to the west of meridian 15°30′W. In the southern part of the basin, *the positive anomaly of Gambia-Casamance,* 200 km long by 100 km wide, is the only geophysical structure in the basin with an E-W elongation. It can only be explained by major dense plutonic masses derived from the mantle and may be related to the Casamance graben described by Burke (1976) and ascribed by him to an early stage in the opening of the Atlantic. It should be noted that this anomaly is aligned parallel to the 13°N east-west fracture zone located on the continental margin (Hayes and Rabinowitz, 1975; Liger and Roussel, 1979).

To the north of 15°N, the style of the anomalies changes. They become highly elongated in a north-south direction.

The Mouk-Mouk negative anomaly (MK, on Plate 2: In pocket in back of book) is the only important negative anomaly in the coastal sedimentary basin. It extends from 17°40′N southeast of Nouakchott, as far to the south as Gossas at the latitude of Dakar, and occurs to the west of meridian 15°30′, the approximate eastern limit of the deep basin (>2,000 m). The isobaths on the top of the magnetic basement indicate a depth of 3,000 m to the trough of the anomaly. Several interpretations have been proposed (Crenn and Rechenmann, 1965). Liger's (1980) explanation involves the combined effects of a thickening of the

sedimentary cover from east to west and a progressive rise in the Moho toward the west, beginning west of the meridian of Kebemer (16°20′). Its position between two positive anomalies which are elongated in the N-S direction and the thickness of the sedimentary cover suggest tectonic extension and the consequent development of a trough along the trough of the anomaly (Guetat, 1981).

The positive anomaly along the coast between Nouakchott and M'bour, to the west of the Mouk-Mouk anomaly, extends for nearly 400 km to the SE of Dakar. It is characterized by a steep seaward gradient of greater than 2 mgal/km, and a series of superimposed local anomalies clearly shown on the maps of residual anomalies and vertical gradient (Liger and Roussel, 1979). It is also associated with an important positive linear magnetic anomaly which appears to form an on-shore segment of the *West African coastal magnetic anomaly* (WACMA), which is the eastern boundary of the magnetic quiet zone (Liger, 1980; Roussel and Liger, 1981). Gravimetric models show that the coastal anomaly is associated with a significant shallowing of the Moho, reflecting a change in the nature of the crust along the line of the WACMA.

The positive anomaly north of Nouakchott (No, on Plate 2: In pocket in back of book) has a N-S elongation and shows a maximum value of 70 mgal. Its axis appears displaced to the east compared with the coastal anomaly. It is not unlikely that the two anomalies form part of the same axis which has suffered dextral displacement, as is suggested by the deflection of the isanomalies along the Nouakchott parallel (18°N). This explanation is also supported by the deflection of the Mauritanides anomaly in the region of Bir Allah, not far from El Khatt where NE-SW trending faults affect the sedimentary cover on the foreland up to and including the Devonian. A satisfactory gravimetric model of the Nouakchott anomaly suggests the presence of a dense intrusive body with its top at a depth of 2.5 km and its base at 10 km.

Thus, gravimetry suggests two principal groups of anomalies in the coastal basin, characterized by N-S and SW-NE major trends. To the east of 15°30′W, the dominant SW-NE anomaly trend is about the same as that observed in the foreland on the western border of the craton. To the west of this meridian, basement lineations seem to disappear, and gravimetry reveals only long N-S lineations which reflect the possibility of more recent *tensional structures,* which are connected with opening of the Atlantic. The coastal gradient anomaly reflects crustal thinning to the west, together with changes in crustal composition.

Thus, the Senegal-Mauritanian basin appears to rest on thinned continental crust. This crustal block (Guetat, 1981), structurally analogous to the West African craton, is distinguished by dense mantle injections, located principally in the coastal zone, which reflect the change toward a crust of oceanic type.

The Mauritanides Positive Gravity Anomaly

The Mauritanides positive anomaly is the most striking gravimetric anomaly on the western margin of the West African craton. It has an amplitude greater than 50 mgal and is elongated NNW-SSE for more than 700 km, more or less coincident with the eastern border of the Senegal-Mauritanian coastal basin. In fact, although its axis is displaced to the west of the outcrop of the Mauritanides belt, it remains closely parallel to the trend of the belt from Akjoujt in the north as far as the latitude of Bakel in Eastern Senegal. Its axis does not cross the Reguibat uplift to the north but appears to be deflected toward the west, as are the outcrops of the chain. South of 14°N, the Mauritanides anomaly becomes the much narrower *Gamon positive anomaly* (Ga, on Plate 2: In pocket in back of book) oriented NNE-SSW, which has a different form. This anomaly stretches for 150 km, nearly parallel to the south-eastern arm of the Mauritanides. It is bounded on the east by a pronounced elongate minimum of −35 mgal amplitude (DY, on Plate 2: In pocket in back of book).

The Mauritanides positive anomaly. The Mauritanides anomaly is slightly asymmetric along the whole of its length, especially in the south, with a steeper (>2 mgal/km) gradient along its eastern flank. In Aouker, north of Bir Allah, approximately on the line of projection of the El Khatt fractures, the anomaly is strongly deflected, possibly reflecting dextral slip of the upper part of the dense mass.

The Mauritanides anomaly is only slightly attenuated on upward continuation maps: at 12,000 m the amplitude is still greater than 40 mgal. The principal source of this anomaly must be a deep, dense, and widespread body. Spectral analysis of the anomaly projected to 12,000 m predicts a mean depth of 15 km for the deepest interface (Guetat, 1981). Interpretation of gravimetric traverses across the anomaly using linear programming (Fig. 5) clearly shows that the major dense unit, treated as a homogeneous body, is rooted, and that the body is situated at between 15 and 30 km depth and dips toward the west. Using these assumptions, models have been constructed using the direct method.

The models in Fig. 6 correspond to a profile at about 16°30′N on the map of isostatic anomalies (Crenn and Rechenmann, 1965), crossing the positive anomaly as well as the negative anomaly on the craton. This model (Guetat, 1981) suggests the hypothesis of a significant rise of the Moho from the compensation depth of 30 km. The undercompensated eastern part corresponds to a thickening of the sialic crust beneath the margin of the craton.

The models in Fig. 7, calculated from the Bouguer anomaly (profile at about 16°30′), suggest a deep, dense body of density contrast +0.25 g/cm^3 and 0.28 g/cm^3, respectively, dipping toward the west and imply a local intrusion of the upper mantle. This could be the result of compression directed towards the east during the Ordovician (Lécorché's "Taconic" event). The form of the dense anomalous mass suggests major thrusting of a western crustal block over the craton.

In summary, the Mauritanides anomaly can be interpreted as an eastwardly asymmetric mantle ridge with its crest at only 15 km depth and continuous for more than 700 km, an idea originally proposed by Crenn and Rechenmann (1965), among several alternatives.

The continuity of the Mauritanides anomaly is locally interrupted to the north of Bir Allah and to the west of El Khatt where a marked deflection of isanomalies seems to indicate a dextral W-E displacement of about 40 km. Unfortunately, the Aouker dune complex prevents correlation between surface geology and gravimetric data.

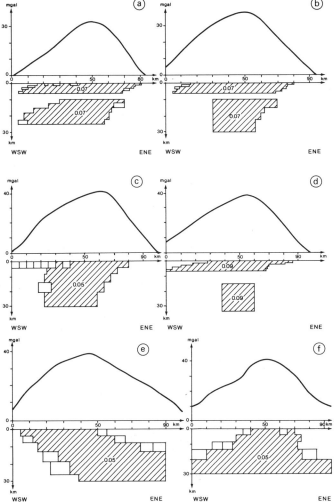

Figure 5: Interpretation of gravimetric profiles (residual anomaly) across the Mauritanides anomaly using the inverse approach and linear programming: ideal body and its density contrast in g/cm^3 (after Guetat, 1981). The locations of the profiles are shown on Fig. 4.

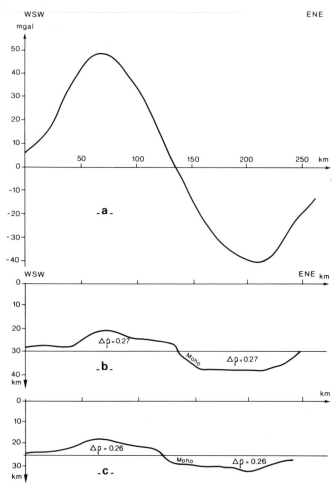

Figure 6: Interpretation of WSW-ENE gravimetric profile across the western margin of the West African craton from the coastal basin, through the Mauritanides and onto the craton and its cover. (a) profile of isostatic anomalies at about 16°30′N, after Guetat (1981); (b) calculated model assuming a compensation depth of 30 km; (c) modelling of Moho for a compensation level of 25 km.

However, the approximate co-linearity of the gravimetric structure and the major faults in the Khatt area which cut Devonian sediments suggest that the displacement was of post-Devonian age.

The transverse alignments of Nouakchott-Bir Allah -El Khatt and Kidira-Godiovol-Afollé mark the northern and southern boundaries, respectively, of both the principal deep-seated Mauritanides anomaly and the major NNW-SSE straight element of the exposed belt. These probably pre-existing major Birrimian structures were reactivated during the emplacement of the deep-seated mass and played an important role in the evolution of the central part of the belt. To the north, in the Akjoujt region, and to the south of Kidira, the structure of the chain appears to be different.

The Gamon positive anomaly (+40 mgal). *The Gamon positive anomaly* (Ga, on Plate 2: In pocket in back of

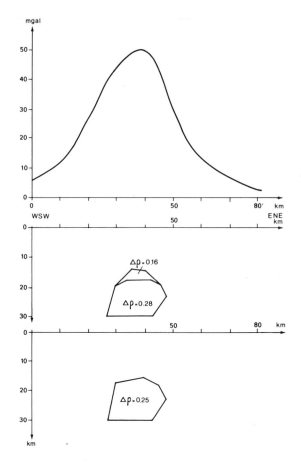

Figure 7: Interpretative models of a profile across the Mauritanides Bouguer anomaly at about 16°30′N from direct calculations.

book) is situated to the south of, but on line with, the Mauritanides anomaly. It is clearly distinguished from the latter by a different form and strike (NNE-SSW) and is separated from it by the Kidira-Godiovol-Afollé structure. It is flanked to the east by the *Dalafi negative anomaly* (DY, on Plate 2: In pocket in back of book) of similar size, and which coincides with the Falémé series trough, which forms part of the folded foreland.

The Gamon anomaly extends for about 150 km to the SSW as far as the Bové basin in Guinea at nearly 12°N. Passing just to the west of Youkounkoun, it clearly cuts the Koulountou structure, which is composed of granites and epimetamorphic schists. This structure has no influence on the deep anomaly, which suggests that it is made up of shallow thrust masses (Villeneuve, 1982) rather than being a sliced anticlinal rooted structure as Bassot (1966) proposed.

The vertical derivation amplifies the Gamon anomaly, and its eastern margin has a very steep gradient which is maintained on the high altitude anomaly maps. These strong gradients limit the number of possible hypotheses. Spectral analysis suggests that the upper discontinuity is situated at a depth of 2.5 km, possibly coinciding with an interface between the Youkounkoun sedimentary series and the roof of a dense mass whose base lies approximately at 9 km depth.

Gravimetric models employing direct calculation indicate a dense mass of density contrast +0.27 g/cm^3 which is highly asymmetric (with a dip of about 20° W on its western flank and close to 60° E on its eastern flank) and probably made up of dense, basic, or ultrabasic intrusive rocks emplaced, as indicated by the elongated form of the anomaly, along a deep-seated NNE-SSW fault structure.

From its style, amplitude, and length, the extension of the Gamon anomaly to the south in Guinea and Sierra Leone appears to be related to other well-marked positive anomalies. All these anomalies are similar to the positive gravimetric lineaments which define the suture zone between the eastern border of the craton and the Hoggar Dahomey Pan-African chain (Bayer and Lesquer, 1978; Black *et al.,* 1979), thus suggesting the possibility that the Gamon structure could be a link with the Rokelide belt in Sierra Leone (Allen, 1969).

The Dalafi-Youkounkoun negative anomaly. The northern part of this well-defined negative anomaly (DY, on Plate 2: In pocket in back of book) of about 40 mgal amplitude coincides with the area of the Falémé series, in the Dalafi area. In the south, at latitude 13° N, it curves toward the west, crossing the Bassari anticline, where a low-amplitude gravity maximum develops and then extends along the eastern section of the Youkounkoun basin, parallel to the Bassari ridge.

The northern part of the anomaly (*Dalafi anomaly*), where gravimetric analysis indicates a discontinuity at about 3.5 km depth, is interpreted as a major, deep but narrow, sedimentary trough occupied by detrital sediments of the Falémé series (supergroup 2). The rapid variations of mass suggest a NNE-SSW faulted structure at depth. Where the anomaly crosses the Niokolo-Koba River, gravimetric analysis suggests that the Falémé trough attains a depth of 4 to 5 km. This compares with a value of 2.4 km calculated from aeromagnetic data in the region of 13° N (Bassot, 1966). The difference could be explained by a mass of basic volcanics of a thickness greater than the kilometer estimated by Bassot.

After its deflection to the west, the anomaly extends to the SSW along the eastern side of the Youkounkoun basin (*Youkounkoun anomaly*). A strong gravimetric gradient existing along the whole length of the synclinorium separates it from the Gamon positive anomaly. Here again the sedimentary infill is estimated, from depth indices, to be greater than 4 km. It is noticeable that the vertical fault, which on all geological maps truncates the western margin of the anticlinal structure of the Bassari ridge, does not produce a significant gravimetric signal, suggesting that the structure only affects the sedimentary cover.

CONCLUSIONS

The foreland of the Mauritanides belt has a characteristic gravimetric signature (a strong mean negative anomaly within which occur minor troughs and culminations showing NE-SW axes) which confirms that it belongs to the West African craton. These NE-SW gravimetric trends, which reveal structures beneath a moderate thickness of sedimentary cover, are parallel to the structures which appear in basement windows. Geophysical studies suggest a series of horsts and grabens in a sedimentary cover of between 1000 and 3000 m thickness, and which follow the NE-SW structures in basement.

These basement structures clearly continue to the west for 30 to 50 km beyond the Mauritanides front (to Gadel, Mbout, Selibabi . . .). *This confirms the thin, allochthonous nature of the belt above a folded autochthonous sedimentary cover.*

In the N-S portion of the belt, the eastern structural units (the mixtite, El Aouija, and Farkaka units . . .), among which are basement units, thus appear to be nappes. They are not rooted elements of a Pan-African belt which would have served as a western limit of Paleozoic deposits, the hypothesis advanced by Chiron (1973).

The area to the west of the Mauritanides anomaly also has a characteristic gravity signature. It tends to be positive on the average, with anomalies oriented NE-SW and N-S. The gradient is high in the vicinity of the coast, with maximum gravity values beyond 60 mgal.

Several features are superimposed on those due to the substratum: the considerable thickening (10 km ?) of the coastal basin west of longitude 15° 30′ W; the existence of dense intrusive bodies, probably of basalt or dolerite; the existence of tensional structures oriented N-S probably related to the opening of the Atlantic Ocean; and westerly thinning of the continental crust marked by rise of the Moho. The Dakar region, west of the West-African coastal magnetic anomaly, may even rest on crust of oceanic character (Liger and Roussel, 1979; Roussel and Liger, 1981).

Putting aside these characteristics related to the Atlantic passive margin, it is evident that the structure of this region, particularly that east of longitude 15° 30′ W, suggests control by a basement very much like that of the foreland. We thus appear to have neighboring crustal blocks of similar character and orientation and must envisage a *coastal crustal block* very similar to the West African craton itself, but separated from it by a major intracontinental suture. To the west of longitude 15° 30′ W the basement thins, and the crust changes its character toward that of oceanic crust.

The positive anomaly of the Mauritanides is the gravimetric feature which dominates the whole of the area concerned, separating the craton from the *coastal block*.

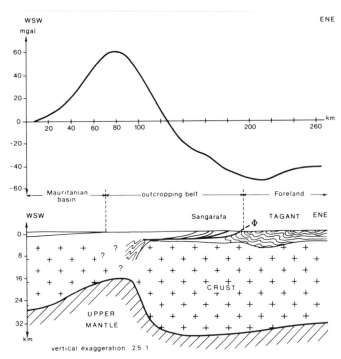

Figure 8: Gravimetric profile (Bouguer anomaly) across the western margin of the West African craton at the latitude of Sangarafa and a schematic geological interpretation of its significance.

The anomaly is clearly indirectly linked with the outcrop of the allochthonous rocks of the belt (Fig. 8). It is 700 km long and oriented NNW-SSE. Its axis is hidden beneath the thin eastern margin of the coastal basin, except in its northern prolongation where the trend of the vertically dipping volcanic-sedimentary rocks of the Agoualilet faithfully reflects the gravimetric trends, although the relationships of these to the allochthonous rocks of Akjoujt are poorly understood.

The Mauritanides anomaly reflects a dense mass along a major crustal discontinuity, rooted at between 15 and 30 km and dipping west, with the Moho rising to 15 km. It suggests a bulge of the mantle, asymmetric toward the east, and may reflect continued collision of two continental blocks after the closure of an inter-block trench rather than active margin collision with subduction as has been suggested for the eastern margin of this same cratonic block and the Pan-African belt (Black *et al.,* 1979), and in particular for the Dahomeyides (Crenn, 1957; Sagbohan, 1972; Trompette, 1979). Currently, this simple *model of intracontinental collision* is that which best explains the geological and geophysical data, although other interpretations have been proposed: basic intrusions, or folding of a basaltic layer (Blot *et al.,* 1962); bulging of the upper mantle and/or the effect of superficial rock series (Crenn and Rechenmann, 1965); a granodioritic horst (Chiron, 1973); subduction and remains of

oceanic crust (Dillon and Sougy, 1974); and existence of a late Pre-Cambrian fold belt of which the Agoualilet series could be a marginal representative (Lécorché and Sougy, 1978).

According to Lécorché's (1980) interpretation, this *Taconic suture* would have been discordantly overlain by subsequent Lower to Middle Paleozoic sediments (Upper Ordovician to Devonian), as it seems to be in Guinea, where the eastern folded arm of the Mauritanides passes beneath the Bové basin. However, farther north, post-Devonian tectonic movements have involved these rocks in the Hercynian nappes. The minor intra-Ordovician discontinuity observed in Tagant (Dia *et al.,* 1969) could be a result of this compressive phase in the foreland.

The NNE-SSW Gamon anomaly poses a problem. Although it lies along the prolongation of the Mauritanides, it has a different style, and its gradient is steeper. As it is prolonged by the Guinea-Sierra Leone anomalies, it may be related to an older, Pan-African suture, corresponding to the northern continuation of the Rokelide.

The Bassari fault has no gravimetric effect, thus confirming its superficial, non-crustal character.

The E-W Nouakchott-Bir Allah structure, revealed by displacement of several anomalies, suggests a dextral wrench movement across the basin, ending against the post-Devonian faults of El Khatt. Do we see here the terminus of a transform fault related to the opening of the Atlantic? The inferred dextral displacement of 40 km is not apparent in the surface geology.

To the north of this major displacement, the Mauritanides anomaly axis swings toward the west. Its trend reflects the trend of structures in the volcanic-sedimentary rocks of Agoualilet and parallels the external nappes of the foreland. The gravimetric gradient is less marked than in the central area of the belt. Further west, on the southwestern margin of the Reguibat uplift, a steeper gradient occurs along the prolongation of the Norfolk-Cape Blanc fracture suggested by Le Pichon *et al.* (1977). From a geological point of view, the external nappes disappear beneath the internal nappes and do not outcrop further along the northern flank of the belt. Thus, the limit of outcrop of the "Taconic" orogen chain appears to be intimately related to the westward swing of the belt. On the other hand, the internal nappes, whose "thin-skinned" tectonic style has been demonstrated by Bronner and Sougy (1969), lie directly on the foreland of the Reguibat uplift. Their northern limit is erosional, due to the culmination in the uplift region, suggesting that these nappes extended beyond the immediate foreland and joined those of South Morocco (Western Sahara) in covering the entire southwestern zone of the Reguibat uplift. The coincidence of this erosional limit with the steep E-W gravimetric gradient of the northern margin of the anomaly could reflect an isostatic re-equilibration which itself could be responsible for culmination of the Reguibat uplift and separation of Mauritanian and South Moroccan segments of the "Hercynian" orogen. The possible continuation of the Mauritanides anomaly, which emphasizes the "Taconic" axis, might be found farther west in the area of the Norfolk-Cape Blanc fracture zone.

In the absence of geochronological and geochemical data, a geodynamic evaluation of the belt is premature. There is no doubt that the Mauritanides is a complex mobile belt which has evolved on the western margin of the West African craton. The craton owes its structural format to the Eburnean orogeny, and it has behaved in a rigid fashion since that time. We suggest that a western block of the craton was moved away in the Upper Proterozoic, giving rise to a trench which filled with detrital volcanic-sedimentary materials. A first compressive phase (Pan-African orogen) took place at the end of the Proterozoic in the south, forming the Rokelide, followed by a second during the Ordovician with the resultant formation of the "Taconic" belt, developed particularly from Akjoujt to Kidira. A further phase of orogen development, at the end of the Devonian, occurred farther to the west in the region of the coastal anomalies or still farther west, but was thrust over the craton, particularly in the north. This phase also involved the preceding belt during a late stage of horizontal shearing.

The different models proposed for the formation of the Appalachians have not been taken into account in discussion of the Mauritanides. It now seems timely to coordinate our efforts in producing a coherent explanation of the evolution of both the North American and West African margins of the Atlantic. The existence of this western basement block between the presumed Proto-Atlantic and the West African craton could be of considerable importance in such an explanation.

ACKNOWLEDGEMENTS

We wish to thank the Centre National de la Recherche Scientifique, which has supported much of the work reported in this article. We thank Professor G. S. Boulton, who translated the text from the original French; Professor L. Glover, III, and S. Farrar for thorough reviewing; MM. R. Flicoteaux and M. Villeneuve for their constructive criticism; MM. Dassulle and Motte, who drew the diagrams; and Mme A. Grimaldi for typing the manuscript.

REFERENCES CITED

Allen, P. M., 1969, The geology of part of an orogenic belt in Western Sierra Leone, West Africa: Geologische Rundschau, v. 58, n. 2, p. 588–620.

Aymè, J. M., 1965, The Senegal salt basin, *in* Inst. Petroleum, ed., Salt basins around Africa: Elsevier, Amsterdam, p. 83–90.

Barrère, J., 1967, Le groupe précambrien de l'Amsaga entre Atar et Akjoujt (Mauritanie). Etude d'un métamorphisme profond et de ses relations avec la migmatisation: Mémoires du Bureau de Recherches Géologiques et Minièrs, n. 42, 275 p.

Bassot, J. P., 1966, Etude géologique du Sénégal oriental et de ses confins guinéo-maliens: Mémoires du Bureau de Recherches Géologiques et Minières, n. 40, 322 p.

Bayer, R., and Lesquer, A., 1978, Les anomalies gravimétriques de la bordure orientale du craton ouest-africain: géométrie d'une suture pan-africaine: Bulletin de la Société Géologique de France, t. 20, n. 6, p. 863–876.

Bense, C., 1964, Les formations sédimentaires de la Mauritanie méridionale et du Mali nord-occidental (Afrique de l'Ouest): Mémoires du Bureau de Recherches Géologiques et Minières, n. 20, 270 p.

Beuf, S., Biju-Duval, B., Charpal, O. de, Rognon, P., Gariel, O., and Bennacef, A., 1971, Les grès du Paléozoïque inférieur du Sahara. Sédimentation et discontinuités. Evolution structurale du craton: Technip ed., Paris, 480 p.

Black, R., Caby, R., Moussine-Pouchkine, A., Bayer, R., Bertrand, J. M., Boullier, A. M., Fabre, J., and Lesquer, A., 1979, Evidence for late Precambrian plate tectonics in West Africa: Nature, v. 278, n. 5701, p. 223–227.

Blot, C., Crenn, Y., and Rechenmann, J., 1962, Eléments apportés par la gravimétrie à la connaissance de la tectonique profonde du Sénégal: Comptes Rendus de l'Académie des Sciences, Paris, t. 254, p. 1131–1133.

Bronner, G., and Roussel, J., 1978, Données gravimétriques et structure de la dorsale Reguibat (Mauritanie): 6e Réunion Annuelle des Sciences de la Terre, Paris-Orsay, p. 72.

Bronner, G., Roussel, J., Trompette, R., and Clauer, N., 1980, Genesis and geodynamic evolution of the Taoudeni cratonic basin (Upper Precambrian and Paleozoic), Western Africa, *in* Bally, A. W., Bender, P. L., McGetchin, T. R., and Walcott, R. T., eds., Dynamic of Plate Interiors, Geodynamics series, v. 1: American Geophysical Union, Washington, p. 81–90.

Bronner, G., and Sougy, J., 1969, Etude structurale de la région de Tourarine (Mauritanides, NW d'Akjoujt, Rép. Islamique de Mauritanie): 5e Colloque de Géologie Africaine, Annales de la Faculté des Sciences de l'Université de Clermont-Ferrand, Géologie-Minéralogie, v. 41, n. 19, p. 77–78.

Burke, K., 1976, Development of graben associated with the initial rupture of the Atlantic Ocean: Tectonophysics, v. 36, n. 1-3, p. 93–112.

Carte Tectonique Internationale de l'Afrique au 1/5,000,000 1968: UNESCO/ASGA.

Castelain, J., 1965, Aperçu stratigraphique et micro-paléontologique du bassin du Sénégal. Historique de la découverte paléontologique: Mémoires du Bureau de Recherches Géologiques et Minières, n. 32, p. 135–156.

Chiron, J. C., 1973, Etude géologique de la chaîne des Mauritanides entre le parallèle de Moudjéria et le fleuve Sénégal (Mauritanie). Un exemple de ceinture plissée précambrienne reprise à l'Hercynien: Mémoires du Bureau de Recherches Géologiques et Minières, n. 84, 284 p.

Choubert, G., and Faure-Muret, A., 1969, Sur la série stratigraphique précambrienne de la partie sud-ouest du massif du Bas Dra (Tarfaya, Sud Marocain): Comptes Rendus de l'Académie des Sciences, Paris, v. 269, sér. D, p. 759–762.

Clauer, N., 1975, Dating of sedimentary minerals and rocks: possibilities of the Rb/Sr method and application to the Precambrian from the West African craton: Symposium Correlation of the Precambrian, Moscow, Abstracts of papers, p. 67–68.

Cook, F. A., Albaugh, D. S., Brown, L. D., Kaufman, S., Oliver, J. E., and Hatcher, R. D., 1979, Thin-skinned tectonics in the crystalline southern Appalachians; COCORP seismic-reflection profiling of the Blue Ridge and Piedmont: Geology, v. 7, p. 563–567.

Cook, F. A., Albaugh, D. S., Brown, L. D., Kaufman, S., Oliver, J. E., and Hatcher, R. D., 1980, Comment and reply *on* Thin-skinned tectonics in the crystalline southern Appalachians; COCORP seismic-reflection profiling of the Blue Ridge and Piedmont: Geology, v. 8, p. 403–404.

Crenn, Y., 1957, Mesures gravimétriques et magnétiques dans la partie centrale de l'A.O.F. Interprétations géologiques: Office de la Recherche Scientifique et Technique Outre-Mer éd., Paris, 39 p.

Crenn, Y., and Rechenmann, J., 1965, Mesures gravimétriques et magnétiques au Sénégal et en Mauritanie occidentale: Cahiers de l'Office de la Recherche Scientifique et Technique Outre-Mer, sér. Géophysique, n. 6, 59 p.

Crévola, G., Dars, R., Le Page, A., and Quin, J. P., 1974, Découverte de Dévonien fossilifère plissé à Godiovol (Guidimakha—République Islamique de Mauritanie): Compte Rendu sommaire de la Société Géologique de France, fasc. 2, p. 33–35.

Dacheux, A., 1967, Etude photogéologique de la chaîne de Dhlou (Zemmour—Mauritanie septentrionale): Rapports du Laboratoire de Géologie de l'Université de Dakar, n. 22, 45 p.

Destombes, J., 1968, Sur la nature glaciaire des sédiments du groupe du 2e Bani, Ashgill supérieur de l'Anti-Atlas, Maroc: Comptes Rendus de l'Académie des Sciences, Paris, v. 267, sér. D, p. 684–686.

Deynoux, M., 1980, Les formations glaciaires du Précambrien terminal et de la fin de l'Ordovicien en Afrique de l'Ouest. Deux exemples de glaciation d'inlandsis sur une plate-forme stable: Travaux des Laboratoires des Sciences de la Terre de St-Jérôme, Marseille, sér. B, n. 1, 554 p.

Dia, O., Lécorché, J. P., and Le Page, A., 1979, Trois événements orogé-niques dans les Mauritanides d'Afrique occidentale: Revue de Géologie Dynamique et de Géographie Physique, v. 21, fasc. 5, p. 403–409.

Dia, O., Sougy, J., and Trompette, R., 1969, Discordance de ravinement et discordance angulaire dans le 'Cambro-Ordovicien" de la région de Méjéria (Taganet occidental, Mauritanie): Bulletin de la Société Géologique de France, t. 7, n. 11, p. 207–221.

Dillon, W. P., and Sougy, J., 1974, Geology of West Africa and Canary and Cape Verde Islands, *in* Nairn, A. E., and Stehli, F. G., eds., The ocean basins and margins, v. 2: New York, Plen. Publish. Corp., p. 315–390.

Drot, J., and Lécorché, J. P., 1971, Sur la présence de *Diabolirhynchia hollardi* (Brachiopodes, Rhynchonellida) dans un niveau calcaire de l'Adrar mauritanien et ses conséquences sur la stratigraphie du Siluro-Dévonien de cette région: Annales de l'Université de Provence, Sciences, Marseille, v. 46, p. 181–188.

Giraudon, R., and Sougy, J., 1963, Position anormale du socle granitique des Hajar Dekhen sur la série d'Akjoujt et participation de ce socle à l'édification des Mauritanides hercyniennes (Mauritanie occidentale): Comptes Rendus de l'Académie des Sciences, Paris, v. 257, p. 937–940.

Guetat, Z., 1981, Etude gravimétrique de la bordure occidentale du craton ouest-africain: Thèse 3e cycle, Université des Sciences et Techniques du Languedoc, Montpellier, 185 p.

Hatcher, R. D., Jr., 1981, Thrusts and nappes in the North American Appalachian Orogen, *in* Pierce, N. J., and McClay, K. R., eds., Thrusts and nappe tectonics: Geological Society of London Publication, n. 9, p. 491–499.

Hayes, D. E., and Rabinowitz, P. D., 1975, Mesozoic magnetic lineations and the magnetic quiet zone off Northwest Africa: Earth Planetary Science Letters, v. 28, p. 105–115.

Lécorché, J. P., 1980, Les Mauritanides face au craton ouest-africain. Structure d'un secteur-clé: la région d'Ijibiten (Est d'Akjoujt, R. I. de Mauritanie): Thèse, Université d'Aix-Marseille III, 446 p.

Lécorché, J. P., and Sougy, J., 1978, Les Mauritanides, Afrique occidentale. Essai de synthèse, *in* IGCP project 27, contribution française n. 4, Caledonian-Appalachian Orogen of the North Atlantic Region:

Geological Survey of Canada, Paper 78-13, p. 231–239.

Le Page, A., 1978, Les unités structurales de la région de Bakel (Sénégal oriental). Leur place dans la chaîne des Mauritanides: Comptes Rendus de l'Académie des Sciences, Paris, t. 286, sér. D, p. 1853–1856.

Le Pichon, X., Sibuet, J. C., and Francheteau, J., 1977, The fit of the continents around the North-Atlantic Ocean: Tectonophysics, v. 38, p. 169–209.

Liger, J. L., 1980, Structure profonde du bassin côtier sénégalo-mauritanien. Interprétation de données gravimétriques et magnétiques: Travaux des Laboratoires des Sciences de la Terre de St-Jérôme, Marseille, sér. B, n. 16, 158 p.

Liger, J. L., and Roussel, J., 1979, Etude gravimétrique du bassin côtier profond sénégalais: Revue de Géologie Dynamique et de Géographie Physique, v. 21, fasc. 5, p. 419–427.

Maugis, P., 1955, Etudes de pré-reconnaissance pétrolière dans le bassin du Sénégal: Bulletin de la Direction Fédérale des Mines et de la Géologie de l'Afrique Occidentale Française, n. 19, p. 99–128.

Mazéas, J. P., and Pouit, G., 1968, Marques de mouvements hercyniens à composante tangentielle de grande amplitude dans la boutonnière précambrienne et infracambrienne du bas Oued Dra (Maroc méridional): Comptes Rendus de l'Académie des Sciences, Paris, v. 267, Sér. D, p. 1549–1552.

Nettleton, L., 1962, Gravity and magnetics for geologists and seismologists: American Association of Petroleum Geologists Bulletin, v. 46, n. 10, p. 1815–1838.

Roussel, J., and Liger, J. L., 1981, The boundary between continental and oceanic basement in Cape Vert area, West Africa: Geophysical arguments: 11th Colloquium of African Geology, Milton Keynes, U. K., abstracts, p. 18.

Sabatier, P., 1977, Positivity contraints in linear inverse problems: Geophysical Journal of the Royal Astronomical Society, v. 48, p. 415–469.

Safon, C., Vasseur, G., and Cuer, M., 1977, Some applications of linear programming to the inverse gravity problem: Geophysics, v. 4, p. 1215–1229.

Sagbohan, W., 1972, Contribution à la géologie du Dahomey par l'utilisation des mesures gravimétriques et magnétiques: Thèse de 3e cycle, mention Géophysique, Université de Strasbourg, 107 p.

Simon, B., Brisset, A., Roussel, J., and Sougy, J., 1982, Confrontation de la télédétection (analyse numérique et analogique, téléinterprétation à petite échelle) avec la cartographie géologique classique et les données gravimétriques du Mali sud-occidental (Afrique de l'Ouest): Bulletin de la Société Géologique de France, t. 24, n. 1, p. 13–22.

Sougy, J., 1962a, Contribution à l'étude géologique des guelbs Bou Leriah (région d'Aoucert, Sahara espagnol): Bulletin de la Société Géologique de France, t. 7, n. 4, p. 436–445.

Sougy, J., 1962b, West African fold belt: Geological Society of America Bulletin, v. 73, p. 871–876.

Sougy, J., and Lécorché, J. P., 1963, Sur la nature glaciaire de la base de la série de Garat el Hamouéid (Zemmour, Mauritanie septentrionale): Comptes Rendus de l'Académie des Sciences, Paris, t. 256, p. 4471–4474.

Spengler, A. de, Castelain, J., Cauvin, J., and Leroy, M., 1966, Le bassin secondaire-tertiaire du Sénégal, *in* D. Reyre ed., Bassins sédimentaires du littoral africain, 1ère partie: littoral atlantique: Association des Services Géologiques Africains, Paris, p. 80–94.

Tessier, F., Flicoteaux, R., Lappartient, J. R., and Triat, J. M., 1975, Réforme du concept de Continental terminal dans les bassins sédimentaires côtiers de l'Ouest-africain: 9e Congrès International de Sédimentologie, Nice, t. 1, p. 207–211.

Trompette, R., 1973, Le Précambrien supérieur et le Paléozoïque inférieur de l'Adrar de Mauritanie (bordure occidentale du bassin de Taoudeni, Afrique de l'Ouest). Un exemple de sédimentation de craton. Etude stratigraphique et sédimentologique. Thèse Université d'Aix-Marseille III: Travaux des Laboratoires des Sciences de la Terre de St-Jérôme, Marseille, sér. B, n. 7, 702 p.

Trompette, R., 1979, Les Dahomeyides au Bénin, Togo et Ghana: une chaîne de collision d'âge pan-africain: Revue de Géologie Dynamique et de Géographie Physique, v. 21, fasc. 5, p. 339–349.

Uchupi, E., Emery, K. O., Bowin, C. O., and Phillips, J. P., 1976, Continental margin off Western Africa: Senegal to Portugal: American Association of Petroleum Geologists Bulletin, v. 60, n. 5, p. 809–878.

Vachette, M., Rocci, G., Sougy, J., Caron, J.P.H., Marchand, J., Simon, B., and Tempier, C., 1975, Ages radiométriques Rb/Sr, de 2000 à 1700 MA de séries métamorphiques et granites intrusifs précam-

briens dans la partie N et NE de la dorsale Réguibat (Mauritanie septentrionale): 7ème Colloque International de Géologie Africaine, Florence, Italie, *in* Travaux des Laboratoires des Sciences de la Terre de St-Jérôme, Marseille, sér. B, n. 11, p. 142–143.

Villeneuve, M., 1980, Schéma géologique du Nord de la Guinée (Afrique de l'Ouest): Compte Rendu sommaire de la Société Géologique de France, fasc. 2, p. 54–57.

Villeneuve, M., 1982, Schéma lithostratigraphique des Mauritanides du Sud du Sénégal et au Nord de la Guinée d'après les données actuelles: Bulletin de la Société Géologique de France, t. 24, n. 2, p. 249–254.

MANUSCRIPT ACCEPTED BY THE SOCIETY SEPTEMBER 10, 1982

Printed in U.S.A.

Geological Society of America
Memoir 158
1983

Tectonic significance of similarities in the evolution of the Alabama-Pennsylvania Appalachians and the Alberta-British Columbia Canadian Cordillera

Raymond A. Price*
Department of Geological Sciences
Queen's University
Kingston, Ontario K7L 3N6
Canada

Robert D. Hatcher, Jr.
Department of Geology
University of South Carolina
Columbia, South Carolina 29208

ABSTRACT

Conspicuous similarities in character and relative time-space relationships of structures, metamorphism, magmatism, erosion, and sedimentation between the U.S. southern and central Appalachian (SCA) and the southern Canadian Cordillera (SCC) imply that the fundamental processes controlling orogenic evolution in each were similar. During the Taconic and Columbian orogenies (which affected the SCA and SCC, respectively), magmatic arcs converged with North America (NA), compressing, depressing, and metamorphosing the outboard part of miogeoclinal prisms which were displaced relatively short distances toward the NA craton. The Acadian orogeny in the SCA and the mid-Cretaceous interval in the SCC are characterized by widespread granitic intrusion. The former was accompanied by important compression, regional metamorphism, and foreland basin sedimentation locally, but the latter was an orogenic hiatus. During the Alleghanian (SCA) and Laramide (SCC) orogenies, the platformal cratonic cover and detrital outwash trapped in the foreland basins were scraped off the underriding NA craton and accreted to prograding wedges of imbricate thrust slices and décollement folds of previously deformed and metamorphosed miogeoclinal and accreted rocks. During later stages of the Laramide orogeny, external parts of the orogen were displaced northward on transform faults that sliced through the orogen. The Alleghanian orogeny terminated in the SCA by collision of Africa with eastern NA. In both orogens, the distance between the limit, toward the craton, of the transported miogeoclinal prism and a distinctive gravity gradient that appears to mark the external limit of intact NA continental crust defines the amount of relative displacement between the miogeocline and the NA craton. In both orogens, displacement decreases northward from several hundred km to less than 100 km. The similarities indicate that the results in NA of the Alleghanian collision between eastern NA and Africa are essentially the same as those of the oblique accretion of relatively small allochthonous terranes to the NA Cordillera.

*Present Address: Geological Survey of Canada, 601 Booth Street, Ottawa, Ontario K1A OE8, Canada.

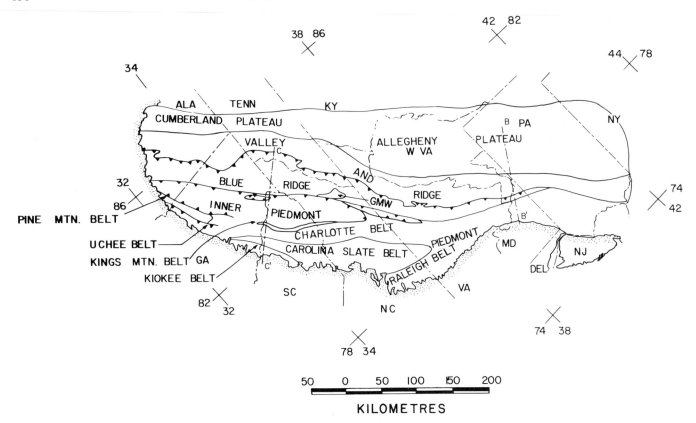

Figure 1. Index to principal structural subdivisions of the Alabama-Pennsylvanian segment
of the Appalachians. Triangles on hanging wall of thrust faults. See also Figure 2.

INTRODUCTION

The Paleozoic Appalachian orogenic belt and the Mesozoic-Cenozoic Cordilleran orogenic belt, which are symmetrically disposed on opposite sides of the North American craton, have in common many distinctive attributes of tectonic setting, tectonic style, and tectonic evolution. Some of these similarities were recognized long ago and provided the foundation upon which Marshall Kay's (1951) theory of geosynclines and mountain building was established. However, with the advent of plate tectonics and the demise of the geosynclinal theory, it has become fashionable to consider the Appalachian orogenic belt as fundamentally different from the Cordilleran orogenic belt. The Appalachian orogenic belt is viewed as a collisional mountain belt that is the product of the complete closure of an ocean basin and the ensuing continental collision between North America, on one hand, and Europe, Africa, and South America, on the other (Bird and Dewey, 1970; Hatcher, 1978; Cook and others, 1979); whereas, the Cordilleran orogenic belt is considered to be a continental margin mountain belt of Andean-type that has always been bordered by a large ocean basin and is the product of subduction of oceanic lithosphere beneath a continental margin (Hamilton, 1969; Monger and others, 1972; Dickinson, 1976; Coney, 1978). There has been a profound shift in the focus of attention from comparative tectonics, which attempts to identify apparent similarities between orogenic belts as a basis for developing models of mountain building, to the search for documentation of the differences between the two mountain belts that are implied by two contrasting plate tectonic models. A fundamental distinction between the Appalachians and the Cordillera, based on the application of contrasting simplistic plate tectonic models, warrants careful scrutiny in terms of what is actually known about the two orogenic belts, lest the nature and significance of any real similarities or differences between them be overlooked.

Our comparison of the setting, structural style, and tectonic evolution of the Alabama-Pennsylvania segment of the Appalachians (Figures 1 and 2) and the Alberta-British Columbia segment of the Cordillera (Figures 3 and 4), which is summarized in Table I, has identified enough fundamental similarities to convince us that both orogenic belts are products of the same basic processes. The same sequence of distinctive stages of deformation, metamorphism, and magmatism, superimposed upon the same general initial arrangement of supracrustal and basement rocks, has produced essentially the same results in each case. Both orogenic belts are the products of accretion of

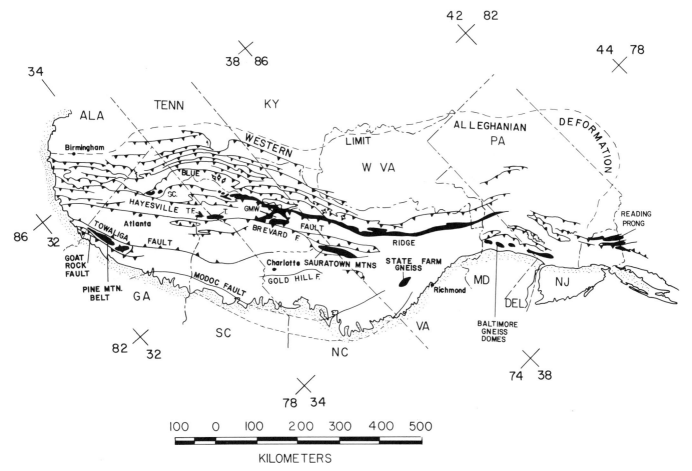

Figure 2. Simplified tectonic map of the Alabama-Pennsylvanian Appalachians (after Hatcher, 1981). Basement rocks shown in black. T.F.—Tallulah Falls dome; T.—Toxaway dome; GMW—Grandfather Mountain window; Triangles on hanging wall of thrust faults.

foreign masses of crustal rock to the margins of the North American Precambrian continental craton. In both cases, the accretion was a complex multistage process involving oblique convergence, the subduction of the basement of a continental terrace wedge which had accumulated outboard from the rifted margin of the North American Precambrian craton, and the juxtaposition of the detached continental terrace wedge over the adjacent part of the continental craton.

TECTONIC EVOLUTION COMPARED

The northeasterly trending early Proterozoic structures of the Churchill Province of the Canadian Shield, which had formed prior to about 1,800 Ma ago, were truncated by the initial rifting that defined the continental margin along which the Cordilleran orogenic belt formed. Deposition of a thick prism of middle Proterozoic (1.5-1.35 Ga) strata (Purcell Supergroup) athwart the early Proterozoic structures provided the earliest record of the existence of this rifted western margin of the North American Precambrian craton (Sears and Price, 1979). Later

rifting, recorded by the deposition of the late Proterozoic (850-600 Ma) Windermere Supergroup (Lis and Price, 1976), was apparently contemporaneous with the rifting that severed the middle Proterozoic (~1000 Ma) Grenvillian basement on the eastern side of the North American Precambrian craton and established the rifted margin along which the Appalachian continental terrace wedge accumulated (Stewart, 1976). The late Proterozoic deposits on opposite sides of the North American continental craton are remarkable for their similarity and for the fact that they are overlain by similar Eocambrian quartz arenites, marking the base of similar sequences of Cambro-Ordovician rocks that transgressed into the interior of the craton from both its Cordilleran and Appalachian margins.

The middle Ordovician Taconic orogeny, which marked the initial stage in the orogenic evolution of the Alabama-Pennsylvania segment of the Appalachian margin of North America, occurred in the outer parts of an early Paleozoic continental terrace wedge, which was still situated outboard from the rifted margin of the Precambrian craton. The Taconic orogeny was a collisional event.

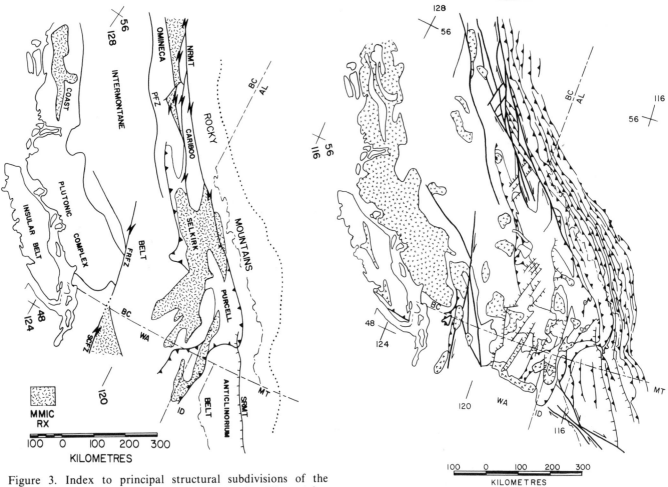

Figure 3. Index to principal structural subdivisions of the Alberta-British Columbia segment of the Cordillera (after Wheeler and Gabrielse, 1972; and Price, Monger, and Muller, 1981). FRFZ—Fraser River fault zone; NRMT—Northern Rocky Mountain Trench fault zone; SRMT—Southern Rocky Mountain Trench fault zone; PFZ—Pinchi fault zone; SCFZ—Straight Creek fault zone. See also Figure 4. Triangles on hanging wall of thrust faults; barbs on hanging wall of normal faults; half arrows show sense of strike-slip.

Figure 4. Tectonic map of the southeastern Canadian Cordillera (after Price, 1981; Price, Monger, and Muller, 1981; and Monger, Price, and Tempelman-Kluit, 1982). Granitic plutons shown by pattern; fault symbols as in Figure 3.

The outer part of the continental terrace wedge was partially overridden by a foreign terrane, comprising oceanic and continental rocks. These were accreted to the margin of North America when the intervening oceanic lithosphere sank into the mantle (Bird and Dewey, 1970; Hatcher, 1972, 1978; Hatcher and Odom, 1980). As the outer part of the continental terrace wedge was overridden by the foreign terrane and by sheets of ophiolite, it was deformed, subjected to intermediate-pressure regional metamorphism, and compressed against the cratonic interior. Clastic detritus shed from the foreign terrane and from the deformed part of the continental terrace wedge accumulated in a foreland basin that extended over the adjacent undeformed part of the continental terrace wedge and the neighboring parts of the continental craton (Hatcher, 1978; Hatcher and Odom, 1980).

The late Jurassic and early Cretaceous Columbian orogeny of the Alberta-British Columbia segment of the Canadian Cordillera is homologous with the Taconic orogeny. It marked the initial stage in the orogenic evolution of the Alberta-British Columbia segment of the Cordillera (Wheeler and Gabrielse, 1972). It also occurred in the outer part of the continental terrace wedge, while the continental terrace wedge still lay outboard from the rifted margin of the North American Precambrian craton (Price, 1981); it, too, was a collisional event, during which the outer part of the continental terrace wedge was partially overridden by a foreign terrane comprising oceanic and continental rocks that became accreted to the margin of North America. During the Columbian orogeny, the outer part of the Cordilleran continental terrace wedge, locally, was extensively overridden by parts of the foreign terrane and by sheets of ophiolite (Tempelman-Kluit, 1979), but elsewhere it seems to have been deformed, subjected to

TABLE 1

Similarities
Tectonic Evolution Compared

	Alabama-Pennsylvania Appalachians	Alberta-British Columbia Cordillera
continental basement	formed during Grenville orogeny (∿ 1000 Ma) structural trends are parallel with the Appalachians	formed during Hudsonian orogeny (∿ 1800 Ma) structural trends are perpendicular to the Cordillera
passive margin	established by Late Proterozoic (850-600 Ma) rifting and deposition of Great Smoky Supergroup Cambro-Ordovician rapid progradation of continental terrace wedge and onlap of cratonic interior	established by mid-Proterozoic rifting and deposition of Purcell Supergroup (> 1350 Ma) modified by Late Proterozoic (850-600 Ma) rifting and deposition of Windermere Supergroup Cambro-Ordovician rapid progradation of continental terrace wedge and onlap of cratonic interior Ordovician-Silurian slow subsidence of continental terrace wedge Early and Middle Devonian epeirogenic arching Upper Devonian to Middle Jurassic slow subsidence of continental terrace wedge
early collision	Taconic orogeny Middle Ordovician to Early Silurian outer part of continental terrace wedge was deformed and metamorphosed (during collision with accreted oceanic terrane) concurrent subsidence of foreland basin	Columbian orogeny Middle Jurassic to Early Cretaceous outer part of continental terrace wedge was deformed and metamorphosed (during collision with accreted arc and oceanic terranes) concurrent subsidence of foreland basin
intermediate stage	Acadian orogeny Middle and Upper Devonian widespread granitic magmatism in accreted terranes convergence (collision?), major folding, and subsidence of foreland basin in New England hiatus in convergence(?) and foreland basin subsidence to south	mid-Cretaceous widespread granitic magmatism in deformed part of continetal terrace wedge and accreted terranes hiatus in convergence and foreland basin subsidence
terminal collision	Alleghanian orogeny Late Carboniferous and Permian foreland thrust and fold belt developed as the continental terrace wedge (miogeocline) was detached from its basement and thrust across the ancient rifted margin of the craton south to north transition from thrusting to folding concurrent subsidence of the foreland basin concurrent left-hand strike-slip due to oblique collision with South America-Africa-Europe	Laramide orogeny Late Cretaceous and Paleocene foreland thrust and fold belt developed as the continental terrace wedge (miogeocline) was detached from its basement and thrust across the ancient rifted margin of the craton south to north transition from thrusting to folding concurrent subsidence of the foreland basin concurrent right-hand strike-slip due to oblique collision with accreted terranes
post-collisional extension	Late Triassic rifting and (?) left-hand strike-slip	Eocene crustal stretching and right-hand strike-slip

intermediate-pressure regional metamorphism, and displaced toward the cratonic interior without much overlap by the foreign terrane that become embedded in it (Monger and Price, 1979; Monger, Price, and Tempelman-Kuit, 1982). In the Alberta-British Columbia segment of the Cordillera, clastic detritus shed by the compressed, thickened, and displaced outer part of the continental terrace wedge accumulated in a foreland basin that extended over the adjacent undeformed part of the continental terrace wedge and the neighboring parts of the continental craton (Price, 1981).

The middle-late Ordovician Taconic orogeny of

the Alabama-Pennsylvanian Appalachians and the late Jurassic-early Cretaceous Columbian orogeny of the Alberta-British Columbia Cordillera are homologous; both display the same basic tectonic attributes and have the same origin, even though the Appalachian continental terrace wedge was a young feature (<500 Ma), and the Cordilleran continental terrace wedge was much older (>1000 Ma), at the time at which they were deformed.

The late Devonian Acadian orogeny of the Alabama-Pennsylvanian Appalachians and the mid-Cretaceous orogeny of the Alberta-British Columbia Cordillera also share many fundamental similarities. In contrast with the great horizontal convergence characteristic of the orogenic episodes that preceded and followed them, they both were primarily magmatic events, during which large volumes of granitic rocks intruded the deformed parts of the continental terrace wedges and the foreign terranes that had been accreted to them during the preceding collisional orogenies. The mid-Cretaceous granitic plutons of the eastern Canadian Cordillera are associated with high-temperature, low pressure, Buchan-type metamorphism (Gabrielse and Reesor, 1974; Monger and Hutchison, 1971). High-temperature, low-pressure, Buchan-type metamorphism was extensive in New England during the Acadian orogeny (Thompson and Norton, 1968); however, it was accompanied by horizontal compression of the accreted terranes against the ancient rifted margin of North America, and by attendant intermediate-pressure metamorphism, nappe formation, mountain building, and foreland basin sedimentation (Robinson and Hall, 1980). Moreover, it is unclear whether extensive deformation and metamorphism of this type occurred in the Alabama-Pennsylvanian segment of the Appalachian during the Acadian orogeny. Both the Acadian orogeny of the Alabama-Pennsylvanian Appalachians and the mid-Cretaceous orogeny of the Alberta-British Columbia Cordillera are characterized by a paucity of volcanic rocks. Acadian volcanic rocks (Traveler Rhyolite) occur in Maine (Rankin, 1968) but are unknown further south in the Appalachians. Mid-Cretaceous volcanic rocks are widespread in the western Canadian Cordillera (Monger and Price, 1979), which probably did not become accreted to North America until late Cretaceous and Tertiary time (Monger, Price, and Tempelman-Kluit, 1982); however, they are not common in the eastern Canadian Cordillera.

The Alabama-Pennsylvania segment of the Appalachians and and the Alberta-British Columbia segment of the Cordillera are probably best known for their well developed foreland thrust and fold belts. These zones of thin-skinned deformation occur along the cratonic margins of the orogenic belts and consist of platformal, miogeoclinal, and foreland basin sediments that were detached from their basement, horizontally compressed, and vertically thickened as they were displaced toward the interior of the adjacent continental craton. The foreland thrust and fold belts developed mainly during the terminal stages in the evolution of the orogenic belts: the Permian-Alleghanian orogeny of the Appalachians and the late Cretaceous-early Tertiary Laramide orogeny of the Cordillera. There was concurrent intense deformation, regional metamorphism, and magmatism on the opposite (outer) sides of both orogenic belts: in the Kiokee and Raleigh belts (Figure 1) of the Appalachians (Snoke and others, 1980) and in the Coast Plutonic Complex (Figure 3) of the Cordillera (Hutchison, 1970; Roddick and Hutchison, 1974; Woodsworth, 1979). This was associated with convergence and collision between North America (Laurasia) and Africa (Gondwanaland) in the case of the Appalachians (Hatcher, 1978) and between North America and an allochthonous composite accreted terrane in the case of the Cordillera (Monger, Price, and Tempelman-Kluit, 1982). In both cases, the continental terrace wedge (miogeocline) which had accumulated outboard from the rifted margin of the continent, on oceanic or tectonically attenuated continental crust, was detached from its basement and juxtaposed over the margin of the cratonic platform.

The style and the amount of tectonic shortening across the foreland thrust and fold belt vary significantly from south to north in the Alabama-Pennsylvania Appalachians and the Alberta-British Columbia Cordillera (Figures 5 and 6). In the southern Appalachians of Alabama, Tennessee, and Kentucky, the net shortening between the Blue Ridge and the undeformed foreland basin deposits of the Appalachian Plateau is about 200 km (Roeder, Gilbert, and Witherspoon, 1978; Hatcher and Zietz, 1978; Cook and others, 1979), and the structure is dominated by northwest-verging listric thrust faults with subordinate décollement folding; whereas, in the Pennsylvania Appalachians, where the net displacement across the foreland thrust and fold belt is less than 100 km, the structure is dominated by kink-type décollement folding with only minor listric thrust faulting above the throughgoing basal décollement zone (Gwinn, 1970; Faill, 1973). Likewise, in the Cordilleran foreland thrust and fold belt of southern Alberta and British Columbia, the net shortening between the Purcell Anticlinorium and the undeformed foreland basin deposits of the Alberta syncline is about 225 km; the structure is dominated by an array of overlapping and interfingering northeast-verging listric thrust faults, with only subordinate décollement folding (Bally and others, 1966; Price and Mountjoy, 1970; Price, 1981); whereas, in northeastern British Columbia, the net shortening across the same interval is on the order of 75 km, and the structure is dominated by kink-type folds with only subordinate thrust faulting above a throughgoing basal décollement (Thompson, 1979 and 1981; Gabrielse and Taylor, 1981).

During the Alleghanian and Laramide orogenies, the

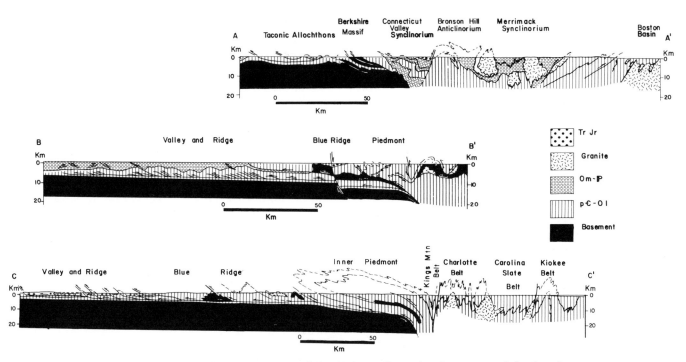

Figure 5. Three sections across parts of the Alabama-Pennsylvania segment of the Appalachians (after Hatcher, 1981). See Figure 9 for locations of lines at sections.

miogeoclines, which had developed outboard from the rifted margins of the North American Precambrian craton as oceanward-prograding continental terrace wedges and had been compressed and tectonically thickened during the preceding Taconic and Columbian orogenies and intruded by granitic plutons during the Acadian and mid-Cretaceous orogenies, were detached from their basement and displaced across the rifted continental margins onto the flank of the North American craton. The platformal deposits covering the craton, and the overlying foreland basin fill, were scraped off the flank of the craton and accreted to the overriding mass. Subsidence of the foreland basin can be attributed to isostatic flexure of the lithosphere in response to the load imposed upon it by the tectonic thickening of the supracrustal rocks and by the weight of the synorogenic detrital outwash from the

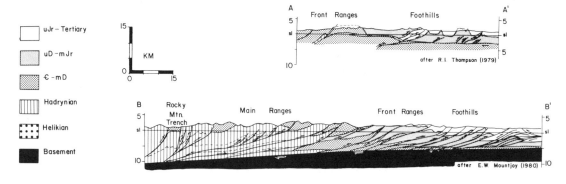

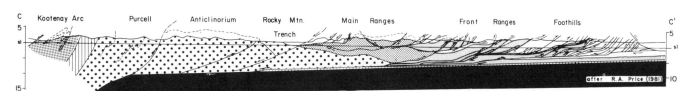

Figure 6. Three sections across parts of the Alberta-British Columbia segment of the Cordillera. See Figure 9 for locations of lines at section.

emerging thrust and fold structures that was trapped in this isostatically induced moat (Price, 1973; Beaumont, 1981). It is noteworthy that the thickest and most extensive part of the foreland basin fill in both the Alabama-Pennsylvania Appalachians and the Alberta-British Columbia Cordillera occurs in the southern part, where the amount of tectonic overlap between the miogeocline and the craton is greatest.

HOMOLOGOUS CRUSTAL STRUCTURE

There are significant similarities in gross crustal structure between the Alabama-Pennsylvania Appalachians and the Alberta-British Columbia Cordillera. Long-standing controversies about the deep structure along the foreland margin of the Appalachians and the Cordillera have been dissipated with the acquisition of new information from geophsyical investigations and deep drilling. Deep drilling and seismic reflection and refraction profiling in the Alberta-British Columbia segments of the foreland margin of the Cordillera showed that the deformation was thin skinned, at least as far west as the western Rocky Moun-

tains (Shaw, 1963; Keating, 1966; Bally and others, 1966). The lateral continuity of northeasterly trending high-amplitude, large-wavelength magnetic anomalies from the Churchill Province of the Canadian Shield to beneath the core of the Purcell Anticlinorium has shown that the Precambrian continental craton extends under virtually all the foreland thrust and fold belt without apparent disruption (Price, 1981). Deep reflection seismic profiling (Cook and others, 1979) has finally laid to rest the long-standing controversy over the existence and lateral extent of a basal décollement beneath the Appalachian foreland thrust and fold belt (Rodgers, 1964; Cooper, 1964); it has also confirmed the concept of a basal décollement extending under parts of the metamorphic core zone of the Appalachian Piedmont, as deduced from the analysis of near surface structures in the foreland thrust and fold belt (Hatcher, 1971 and 1981; Hatcher and Zietz, 1978). The magnetic anomalies associated with basement structure are less useful in establishing the internal limits of authochthonous basement beneath the Appalachians than beneath the southern Canadian Cordillera, because the magnetic anomalies in the Appalachians are associated with the tec-

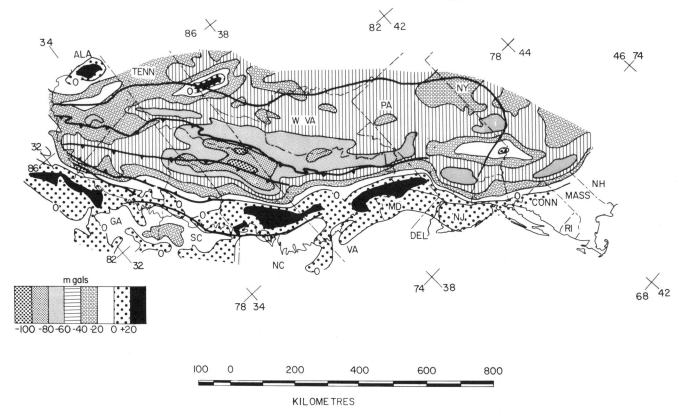

Figure 7. Bouguer gravity anomaly map of the United States Appalachians (after Woollard, and Joesting, 1964). A conspicuous zone of steep gradient in the Bouguer gravity anomaly field that extends from northeastern Connecticut (42°N; 74°W) through southeastern Pennsylvania to southern Alabama (32°N; 86°W) coincides with a change in structural level and/or a change from flat-lying to steeply dipping structures that marks locus of the edge of the Precambrian continental craton beneath the allochthonous rocks (see Figures 2, 5, and 9).

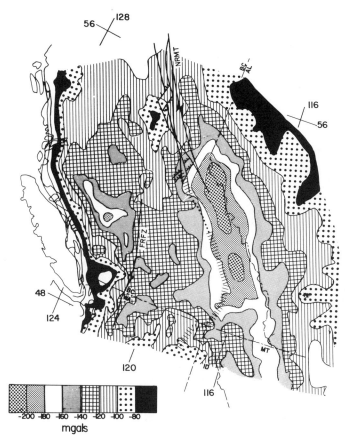

Figure 8. Bouguer gravity anomaly map of the southeastern Canadian Cordillera (after Earth Physics Branch, 1974). A conspicuous zone of steep gradient in the Bouguer gravity anomaly field that extends from the northeastern corner of Washington (WA) northwestward and then northward in alignment with the British Columbia (BC)-Alberta (AL) boundary marks the buried western edge of the Precambrian continental craton. The northwest-trending segment coincides with a change in structural level that results from the draping of allochthonous supracrustal rocks over the ancient rifted margin of North America (see Figures 4, 6, and 9). The north-trending segment is related to Late Cretaceous-Paleogene strike-slip faulting and crustal extension (Price, Monger, and Muller, 1981). Hachured line is western flank of Purcell-Selkirk Caribou Anticlinorium. FRFZ—Fraser River fault zone; NRMT—Northern Rocky Mountain Trench fault zone.

tonic fabric of the Grenvillian basement complex, which is subparallel rather than perpendicular, to the tectonic fabric of the overlying Appalachian orogen.

The locus of the ancient rifted margin of the North American Precambrian craton, which defined the hinge line separating the continental terrace wedge from the cratonic platform, can be identified, in both the Appalachians and the Cordillera, on the basis of relationships between the gross near-surface structure and the Bouguer gravity anomaly field (Figures 7 to 9). The locus of the ancient rifted continental margin, beneath the allochthonous supracrustal rocks, is expressed in the near-surface structure as a large regional monoclinal flexure that is superimposed upon the smaller scale structures. This regional monoclinal flexure occurs where the allochthonous supracrustal rocks are draped over the ramp formed by the rifted margin of the Precambrian basement complex. It coincides with a steep gradient in the Bouguer gravity anomaly field between the more negative anomalies beneath buried autochthonous continental craton and the less negative anomalies outboard from it (Figures 7 and 8).

In the southern British Columbia Cordillera, the regional monoclinal flexure is represented by the Kootenay Arc, which marks a change in structural level of about 15-20 km between middle Proterozoic strata in the deepest exposed levels in the Purcell Anticlinorium, on the continental side of the Kootenay Arc, and the middle Jurassic volcanic rocks on the opposite side (Figures 3 and 9). In the southern Appalachians, the regional monoclinal flexure marking the locus of the buried rifted margin of the continent follows the Kings Mountain belt in the Carolinas, which represents an abrupt change in structural level, between an extensive domain of relatively flat lying structures in the Inner Piedmont, Blue Ridge and Valley and Ridge belts, on the continental side, and the much more steeply dipping structures on the opposite side (Figures 1 and 9). The steep gradient in the Bouguer gravity anomaly field associated with both of these regional monoclinal flexures can be attributed to the change, beneath the allochthonous supracrustal rocks, from a thick slab of continental crust on the continental side, inboard from the ancient rifted continental margin, where the greatest negative Bouguer anomalies occur, to thin, tectonically attenuated continental crust, oceanic crust, or mixed crust that occurs beneath the allochthonous rocks outboard from the ancient rifted continental margin, where the less negative Bouguer gravity anomalies occur.

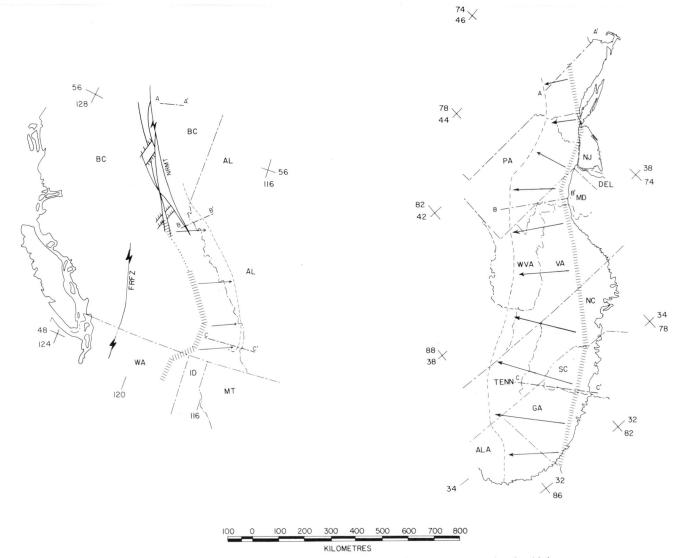

Figure 9. Right side: Buried edge of the Precambrian continental craton under the Alabama-Pennsylvania Appalachians (hachured line) as outlined by Bouguer gravity anomalies and regional geologic structure. Arrows show direction and amount of relative displacement of Precambrian basement slices and of thick continental terrace wedge deposits, which were deposited outboard from the Precambrian rifted continental margin. Dashed lines give locations of structure sections of Figure 5. Left side: Buried edge of the Precambrian continental craton under the Alberta-British Columbia segment of the Cordillera (hachured line) as outlined by Bouguer gravity anomalies and regional structure. Arrows show direction and amount of relative displacement of late Proterozoic and Early Paleozoic continental terrace wedge deposits which were deposited outboard from the Precambrian continental margin. Dashed lines give locations of structure sections of Figure 6.

CONCLUSIONS

The Alabama-Pennsylvania segment of the Paleozoic Appalachian orogenic belt and the Alberta-British Columbia segment of the Mesozoic-Cenozoic Cordilleran orogenic belt are remarkably similar in terms of their basic structure and the nature and sequence of the various stages in their tectonic evolution.

These similarities imply that the fundamental pro-

cesses controlling orogenic evolution in each were similar. Both orogenic belts are products of collisions between North America and other masses of buoyant crustal rocks.

ACKNOWLEDGMENTS

A previous draft of this paper was reviewed by H. Gabrielse,, M. Thomas, and H. Williams. We gratefully acknowledge their critical comments and suggestions for improving the presentation, but we assume sole responsibility for any errors or omissions in the paper

REFERENCES CITED

Bally, A. W., Gordy, P. L., and Stewart, G. A., 1966, Structure, seismic data, and orogenic evolution of southern Canadian Rockies: Canadian Petroleum Geology Bulletin, v. 14, p. 337–381..

Beaumont, C., 1981, Foreland basins: Geophysical Journal, Royal Astronomical Society, v. 65, p. 291–329.

Bird, J. M., and Dewey, J. F., 1970, Lithosphere plate-continental margin tectonics and the evolution of the Appalachian orogen: Geological Society of America Bulletin, v. 81, p. 1031–1060.

Coney, P. J., 1972, Cordilleran tectonics and North American plate motion: American Journal of Science, v. 272, p. 603–628.

Coney, P. J., 1978, Mesozoic-Cenozoic Cordilleran plate tectonics, *in* Smith, R. B., and Eaton, G. P., editors, Cenozoic tectonics and regional geophysics of the western Cordillera: Geological Society of America, Memoir 152, p. 33–50.

Cook, F. A., Albaugh, D. S., Brown, L. D., Kaufman, S., Oliver, J. E., and Hatcher, R. D., Jr., 1979, Thin-skinned tectonics in the crystalline southern Appalachians; COCORP seismic-reflection profiling of the Blue Ridge and Piedmont: Geology, v. 7, p. 563–567.

Cooper, B. N., 1964, Relation of stratigraphy to structure in the southern Appalachians, *in* Lowry, W. D., editor, Tectonics of the southern Appalachians: Virginia Polytechnic Institute Dept. of Geological Science, Memoir 1, p. 81–114.

Dickinson, W. R., 1976, Sedimentary basins developed during evolution of Mesozoic-Cenozoic arc-trench system in western North America: Canadian Journal of Earth Science, v. 13, p. 1268–1287.

Douglas, R.J.W., 1969, Geological Map of Canada: Geological Survey of Canada, Map 1250A, 1:5,000,000.

Earth Physics Branch, 1974, Bouguer anomaly map of Canada: Dept. of Energy Mines and Resources, Canada, Gravity Map Series, Map 74-1, 1:500,000.

Faill, R. T., 1973, Kink-band folding, Valley and Ridge Province, Pennsylvania: Geological Society of America Bulletin, v. 84, p. 1289–1314.

Gabrielse, H., and Reesor, J. E., 1974, The nature and setting of granitic plutons in the central and eastern parts of the Canadian Cordillera: Pacific Geology, v. 8, p. 109–138.

Gabrielse, H., and Taylor, G. C., 1981, Geological maps and cross-sections of the Cordillera from near Fort Nelson, British Columbia, to Gravina Island, southeastern Alaska: Geological Association of Canada, Abstracts, v. 6, p. A20.

Gwinn, V. E., 1970, Kinematic patterns and estimates of lateral shortening, Valley and Ridge and Great Valley Provinces, Central Appalachians, south-central Pennsylvania, *in* Fisher, G. W., Pettijohn, F. J., Reed, J. C., Jr., and Weaver, K. N., editors, Studies of Appalachian geology: central and southern: Interscience, New York, p. 127–146.

Hamilton, W., 1969, Mesozoic California and the underflow of the Pacific mantle: Geological Society of America Bulletin, v. 80, p. 2409–2430.

Harris, L. D., and Milici, R. C., 1979, Characteristics of thin-skinned style of deformation in the southern Appalachians, and potential hydrocarbon traps: U.S. Geological Survey Prof. Paper 1018, 40 p.

Hatcher, R. D., Jr., 1971, Structural, petrologic, and stratigraphic evidence favoring a thrust solution to the Brevard problem: American Journal of Science, v. 270, p. 177–202.

Hatcher, R. D., Jr., 1972, Development model for the southern Appalachians: Geological Society of America Bulletin, v. 83, p. 2735–2760.

Hatcher, R. D., Jr., 1978, Tectonics of the western Piedmont and Blue Ridge: Review and speculation: American Journal of Science, v. 278, p. 276–304.

Hatcher, R. D., Jr., 1981, Thrusts and nappes in the North American Appalachian Orogen, *in* McClay, K. R., and Price, N. J., editors, Thrust and nappe tectonics: Geological Society of London, Special Publication No. 9, p. 427–448.

Hatcher, R. D., Jr., and Odom, A. L., 1980, Timing of thrusting in the southern Appalachians, U.S.A.: Model for orogeny?: Journal, Geological Society of London, v. 137, p. 321–327.

Hatcher, R. D., Jr., and Zietz, I., 1978, Thin crystalline thrust sheets in the southern Appalachian Inner Piedmont and Blue Ridge, based on regional aeromagnetic data: Geological Society of America, Abstracts with Programs, v. 10, p. 417.

Hutchison, W. W., 1970, Metamorphic framework and plutonic styles in the Prince Rupert region of the central Coast Mountains, British Columbia: Canadian Journal of Earth Sciences, v. 7, p. 376–405.

Kay, G. M., 1951, North American geosynclines: Geological Society of America, Memoir 48, 143 p.

Keating, L. F., 1966, Exploration in the Canadian Rockies and Foothills: Canadian Journal of Sciences, v. 3, p. 713–723.

Lis, M. G., and Price, R. A., 1976, Large-scale block faulting during deposition of the Windermere Supergroup (Hadrynian) in southeastern British Columbia: Geological Survey of Canada, Paper v. 76-1A, p. 135–136.

Monger, J.W.H., and Hutchison, W. W., 1971, Metamorphic map of the Canadian Cordillera: Geological Survey of Canada, Paper 70-33.

Monger, J.W.H., and Price, R. A., 1979, Geodynamic evolution of the Canadian Cordillera—progress and problems: Canadian Journal of Earth Sciences, v. 16, p. 770–791.

Monger, J.W.H., Souther, J. G., and Gabrielse, H., 1972, Evolution of the Canadian Cordillera: a plate-tectonic model: American Journal of Science, v. 272, p. 577–602.

Monger, J.W.H., Price, R. A., and Tempelman-Kluit, D. J., 1982, Tectonic accretion and the origin of the two major metamorphic and plutonic welts in the Canadian Cordillera: Geology, v. 10, p. 70–75.

Mountjoy, E. W., 1980, Geology, Mount Robson, Alberta-British Columbia: Geological Survey of Canada Map 1499A.

Price, R. A., 1973, Large-scale gravitational flow of supracrustal rocks, southern Canadian Rockies: *in* De Jong, K. A., and Scholten, R., editors, Gravity and tectonics: Wiley, New York, p. 491–502.

Price, R. A., 1981, The Cordilleran foreland thrust and fold belt in the southern Canadian Rocky Mountains, *in* McClay, K. R., and Price, N. J., editors, Thrust and nappe tectonics: Geological Society of London, Special Publication No. 9, p. 427–448.

Price, R. A., Monger, J.W.H., and Muller, J. E., 1981, Cordilleran cross-section—Calgary to Vancouver; *in* Thompson, R. I., and Cook, D. G., editors, Field guides to geology and mineral deposits: Calgary '81 Annual Meeting, Geological Association of Canada, p. 261–334.

Price, R. A., and Mountjoy, E. W., 1970, Geologic structure of the Canadian Rocky Mountains between Bow and Athabasca Rivers—a progress report, *in* Wheeler, J. O., editor, Structure of the Southern Canadian Cordillera: Geological Association of Canada, Special Paper, v. 6, p. 7–25.

Rankin, D. W., 1968, Volcanism related to tectonism in the Piscataquis volcanic belt, an island arc of Early Devonian age in north-central Maine, *in* Zen, E., White, W. S., Hadley, J. B., and Thompson, J. B., Jr., editors, Studies of Appalachian geology: northern and maritime: Interscience, New York, p. 355–369.

Robinson, P., and Hall, L. M., 1980, Tectonic synthesis of southern New England, *in* Wones, D. R., editor, Proceedings: The Caledonides in the U.S.A., I.G.C.P. Project 27: Caledonide Orogen 1979 Meeting, Blacksburg, Virginia, Virginia Polytechnic Institute and State University, Memoir No. 2, p. 73–82.

Roddick, J. A., and Hutchison, W. W., 1974, Setting of the Coast Plutonic Complex, British Columbia: Pacific Geology, v. 8, p. 91–108.

Rodgers, J., 1964, Basement and no-basement hypotheses in the Jura and the Appalachian Valley and Ridge, in Lowry, W. D., editor, Tectonics of the Southern Appalachians: Virginia Polytechnic Institute, Dept. of Geological Sciences, Memoir 1, p. 71–80.

Roeder, D., Gilbert, O. E., Jr., and Witherspoon, W. D., 1978, Evolution and macroscopic structure of valley and ridge thrust belt, Tennessee and Virginia: University of Tennessee, Department of Geological Sciences, Studies in Geology 2, Knoxville, Tennessee.

Sears, J. W., and Price, R. A., 1978, The Siberian connection: A case for Precambrian separation of the North American and Siberian cratons: Geology, v. 6, p. 267–270.

Shaw, E. W., 1963, Canadian Rockies-orientation in time and space, in Childs, O. E., editor, Backbone of the Americas: American Association of Petroleum Geology, Memoir, v. 2, p. 231–242.

Snoke, A. W., Kish, S. A., and Secor, D. T., Jr., 1980, Deformed Hercynian granitic rocks from the Piedmont of South Carolina: American Journal of Science, v. 280, p. 1018–1034.

Stewart, J. H., 1976, Late Precambrian evolution of North America: plate tectonics implication: Geology, v. 4, p. 11–15.

Tempelman-Kluit, D. J., 1979, Transported cataclasite, ophiolite, and granodiorite in the Yukon: evidence of arc-continent collision: Geological Survey of Canada, Paper 79-14, 27 p.

Thompson, J. B., Jr., and Norton, S. A., 1968, Paleozoic regional metamorphism in New England and adjacent areas, in Zen, E., White, W. S., and Hadley, J. B., editors, Studies of Appalachian geology, northern and maritime: Interscience, New York, p. 319–327.

Thompson, R. I., 1979, A structural interpretation across part of the northern Rocky Mountains, British Columbia, Canada: Canadian Journal of Earth Sciences, v. 16, p. 1228–1241.

Thompson, R. I., 1981, The nature and significance of large 'blind' thrusts within the northern Rocky Mountains of Canada, in McClay, K. R., and Price, N. J., editors, Thrust and nappe tectonics: Geological Society of London, Special Publication No. 9, p. 449–462.

Tipper, H. W., Woodsworth, G. J., and Gabrielse, H., 1981, Tectonic assemblage map of the Canadian Cordillera: Geological Survey of Canada Map 1505A, scale 1:2,000,000.

Wheeler, J. O., and Gabrielse, H., 1972, The Cordilleran structural province, in Price, R. A., and Douglas, R.J.W., editors, Variations in tectonic styles in Canada: Geological Association of Canada, Special Paper, v. 11, p. 1–81.

Woodsworth, G. J., 1979, Metamorphism, deformation, and plutonism in the Mount Raleigh pendant, Coast Mountains, British Columbia: Geological Survey of Canada, Bulletin 295, 58 p.

Woollard, G. P., and Joesting, H. R., 1964, Bouguer gravity anomaly map of the United States: U.S. Geological Survey, scale 1/2,000.000.

MANUSCRIPT ACCEPTED BY THE SOCIETY SEPTEMBER 10, 1982

Geological Society of America
Memoir 158
1983

The distribution of layer parallel shortening fabrics in the Appalachian foreland of New York and Pennsylvania: Evidence for two non-coaxial phases of the Alleghanian orogeny

Peter Geiser
Department of Geology
University of Connecticut
Storrs, Connecticut 06268

Terry Engelder
Lamont-Doherty Geological Observatory
of Columbia University
Palisades, New York 10964

ABSTRACT

This paper presents a structural interpretation of a part of the central and northern Appalachian foreland using the correlation in orientation of such deformation features as mechanical twins, solution cleavage, crenulation cleavage, pencils, joints, and deformed fossils. Such a correlation suggests that, within the central Appalachians, the Alleghanian orogeny consists of two major phases: a deformation possibly as old as Pennsylvanian, herein called the Lackawanna phase, and a second deformation, termed the Main phase of Permian or younger age. Effects of the Lackawanna phase deformation are found mainly in the Hudson River Valley and Pocono plateau, while effects in the Main phase deformation are found throughout the Valley and Ridge and Alleghany Plateau. The Lackawanna phase is interpreted as the product of strike-slip motion, possibly between the Avalon microcontinent and North America. The Main phase may record the final convergence of Africa against North America and accreted terranes.

INTRODUCTION

The discovery of abundant evidence (deformed fossils) for layer parallel shortening in western New York (Engelder and Engelder, 1977) led us to analyze the kinematics and dynamics of the Alleghanian Orogeny in the central Appalachians (Engelder, 1979a, 1979b; Engelder and Geiser, 1979; Engelder and Geiser, 1980). In this paper, we present a compilation, correlation, and interpretation of structures indicative of layer parallel shortening in the central Appalachian structures. This compilation further supports Engelder and Geiser's (1980) interpretation that each of two separate and major Alleghanian oro-

genic events are recorded by structures in the central Appalachian foreland.

The region covered in our study includes the eastern portion of the Pennsylvania salient and the Delaware and Hudson Valleys from Stroudsburg, Pennsylvania, to Albany, New York (Figure 1). Detailed regional studies have concentrated on the New York and Pennsylvania plateaus, the Lackawanna syncline, and the Great Valley–Valley and Ridge transition of the Helderberg escarpment, New York. Reconnaissance work has been done throughout the Valley and Ridge of Pennsylvania and Maryland and in

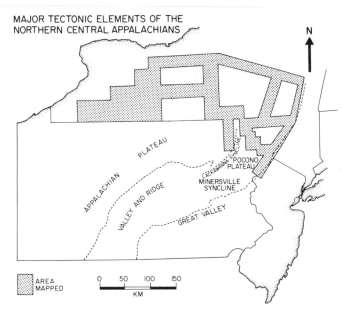

MAJOR TECTONIC ELEMENTS OF THE
NORTHERN CENTRAL APPALACHIANS

Figure 1. Major structural provinces of the northern Central Appalachians. Hatched areas are regions in which we have done detailed structuram mapping.

the Hudson River Valley from Newburgh to Albany, New York. Regional mapping utilized strips one to three quadrangles wide, with 5-10 stations per 7.5-minute quadrangle, at which structural data were gathered. The data were plotted using the existing geologic base provided by the state maps of New York (Fisher and others, 1970) and Pennsylvania (Gray and Sheps, 1964).

LAYER PARALLEL SHORTENING FABRIC

We use the term layer parallel shortening fabric (LPS fabric) to refer to the assemblage of structures produced during the process of layer parallel shortening. In the central Appalachians, these structures have been described by Nickelsen (1966, deformed fossils), Geiser (1970, 1974, solution cleavage, deformed fossils), Groshong (1971, 1975, mechanical twins, solution cleavage), Engelder and Engelder (1977, deformed fossils), Engelder (1979a, 1979b, mechanical twins, solution cleavage), and Engelder and Geiser (1979, pencils, solution cleavage, deformed fossils). Finite strain associated with layer parallel shortening is partitioned among these structures. Pressure solution is the dominant strain mechanism in many cases (Engelder, 1979a; Slaughter, 1980; Mitra, 1978) but not all (Spang and Groshong, 1981). Although Mitra (1978) has shown that partitioning in quartz between pressure solution and dislocation creep is a function of temperature, no such relationship has yet been found for strain partitioning between calcite twinning and pressure solution in limestones and calcareous siltstones of the New York plateau (Engelder, 1979a; Slaughter, 1980; Geiser, 1980). We also dis-

tinguish two types of crenulations: fold crenulations (Nickelsen, 1979, and Figure 2a) and cleavage crenulations (Figure 2b). Fold crenulations seem to be solely the product of microbuckles without any associated pressure solution, whereas cleavage crenulations are created by solution induced offsets of bedding or by the dissolution and removal of pre-existing fold limbs as described by Gray (1978).

The key structures related to the development of the LPS fabric in the central Appalachians are the major detachment faults associated with thin-skinned tectonics as described by Rich (1934), Rodgers (1953, 1970), Gwinn (1964, 1970), Harris and Milici (1977), and Perry (1978). The geometry of these faults consists of a series of ramps and flats with associated splays, duplexes, and zones of imbrication. In most instances, the major ramps and splays become progressively younger in the direction of propagation, with ramps climbing section in the direction of tectonic transport (Bally and others, 1966; Dahlstrom, 1970; Price and Mountjoy, 1970). In the central Appalachians, thrust faults ramp to the surface along portions of the Allegheny front and the Great Valley-Valley and Ridge transition (Rodgers, 1970). Otherwise, the detachments are buried, and the central Appalachians show little evidence of faulting at the surface (Rodgers, 1953; Gwinn, 1964, 1970; Wiltschko and Chapple, 1977; Perry, 1978).

Geiser (1977, 1980, 1982) has proposed that the regional development of LPS fabrics is related to movement on blind detachment faults by differential LPS. Thrusts formed by this mechanism have been termed LPS thrusts by Geiser (1982). LPS fabrics at the surface thus reflect the presence of deeper hidden or "blind" detachments, and, hence, these hidden detachments may be mapped from the distribution of the LPS fabrics. Successive deformations may cause the overprinting of structures formed during the propagation of an initial LPS thrust. An example of suchoverprinting is shown by Mitra and Elliott (1980) in their study of the deformation of the Blue Ridge, where cleavage overprinting is attributed to the progressive migration of a series of thrust sheets within the Blue Ridge. Tracing the fabrics to their highest stratigraphic level permits determination of the maximum age of the detachments and episodes of tectonic overprinting. The recognition of LPS fabrics associated with successive detachments is fundamental to our structural analysis and permits us to unravel the time and space history of the central and northern Appalachians.

Joints are also linked to a progressive deformation scheme for the development of detachments (Geiser, 1982). Some cross-strike joints may predate lithification and be part of an early lateral compaction of the sediments (Faill and Nickelsen, 1973; Nickelsen, 1979). Jointing is also closely associated with the formation of solution cleavage, as indicated by the cross-cutting rela-

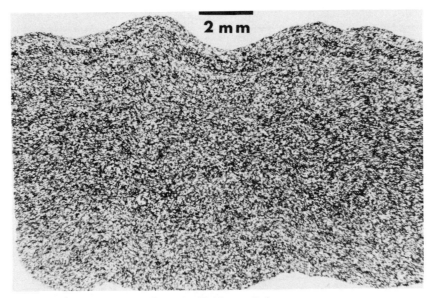

Figure 2a. Fold crenulations.

Figure 2b. Cleavage crenulations.

tionships between solution cleavage and calcite filled joints (Engelder and Geiser, 1980). Other cross-strike joints postdate lithification, as indicated by the presence of filled extension joints which break through grains and shell fragments (Engelder and Geiser, 1980). The synchronous development of LPS fabric and jointing indicates that some cross-strike jointing occurred during the thrust propagation process. Thus, the distribution of the jointing as well as LPS fabrics may both be used to delineate the extent and timing of movement on detachments and, hence, orogenic pulses.

COMPILATIONS

Distribution of Layer Parallel Shortening Fabric

LPS fabric data, collected by ourselves and students during seven field seasons from 1975 to 1981, cover the areas of New York and Pennsylvania as shown in Figure 1. A compilation of this data is shown on a trend-line map constructed by plotting the strike of either pencils, solution cleavage, crenulation planes, or the long axes of de-

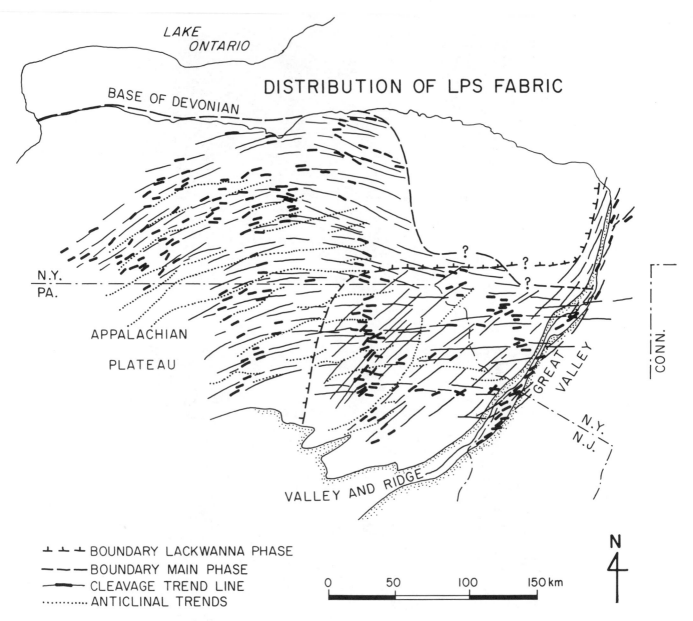

Figure 3. The distribution of layer parallel shortening fabrics across the Appalachian plateau to the Hudson Valley. The trend-line map was prepared by connecting data points (thick lines) with nearly parallel cleavage planes. The orientation of the cleavage planes is shown by a plot of the strike of cleavage planes.

formed fossils as measured in outcrop (Figure 3). Each outcrop where LPS fabrics were observed is represented by a short, thick line on Figure 3. Trend lines are then drawn to extrapolate between outcrop data. Part of the data shown on Figure 3 was published by Engelder and Engelder (1977) and Engelder and Geiser (1979) and reported by Geiser (1980), Slaughter (1980), and Washington (1980).

There exist two dominant sets of LPS fabrics, one with trend lines oriented at 080°-090° and the second with trend lines oriented at 060°-070°, which intersect in out-

crops within the region roughly defined by the Lacka-wanna syncline and the Pocono plateau (Figures 1 and 3). If the fabrics developed sequentially, the later fabric should overprint the earlier. Overprinting relations, how-ever, in outcrop and thin section are ambiguous (Figures 4 and 5). Although the two cleavage sets are found almost everywhere throughout the overprint region, they are not equally developed. On the Pocono plateau, the 080°-090° set seems most obvious in outcrop, while the 060°-070° set tends to stand out in outcrops in the Lackawanna syncline and Delaware Valley. This latter set, which parallels the

Figure 4. Photo of crossing crenulations, Route I-84 at intersection of Route PA-507, Pocono plateau. Scale is shown.

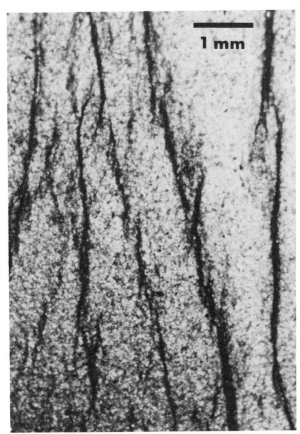

Figure 5. Photo micrograph of crossing sets of cleavage, same locality as Figure 4.

trend of the southern two-thirds of the Lackawanna syncline, is associated with the deformation we name the *Lackawanna phase,* while the 080°-090° set, which parallels the main fold trains of the Pennsylvania Appalachians, we name the *Main phase.* We have used a geographic name for the Lackawanna phase because it is geographically restricted relative to the Main phase. The overprinting takes the form of crossing sets of crenulations (Figure 4) or cleavages (Figure 5) or, in some cases, microfold interference patterns.

In addition to the two sets of LPS fabrics which are frequently found, three additional sets are sporadically developed and found from the eastern edge of the Pocono plateau westward. Members of each set (000°-010°, 320°-330°, and 350°) have been determined by using our trendline correlation. These sets appear in the form of crenulations (fold and cleavage) or solution cleavage. Where multiple sets overprint on the Pocono plateau, the rocks show a pronounced "sheen" in all argillaceous lithologies. The "sheen" is presumably due to the recrystallization of clays and micas, although it may also be related to the effects of multiple deformation (Beutner, 1982, personal communication). The 000°-010° set has been found from the northern Pocono plateau to the central Pennsyl-

vania plateau. Although fairly common on the Pocono plateau in central Pennsylvania, it seems to be restricted to north-south striking valleys (Pone, 1981). The 320°-330° set is restricted to the region extending from the central Pennsylvania plateau to the Lackawanna syncline. The 350° set occurs in a narrow belt extending from the western side of the Pocono plateau to the eastern limb of the Lackawanna syncline.

Distribution of Joints

Compilations of regional joint patterns in the Appalachian foreland include Parker (1942) in New York, Nickelsen and Hough (1967) in Pennsylvania, Dean and Kulander (1978) in West Virginia, and Engelder and Geiser (1980) in New York. Some general comments can be made about all the compilations from these regions.

1) All the major regional joint sets are mode I cracks propagating either at depth or near the surface. Hypothesized regionally developed shear joints, as, for example, discussed by Parker (1942), have not been supported by more recent studies (Nickelsen and Hough, 1967; Nickelsen, 1979; Kulander and Dean, 1978; and Engelder and Geiser, 1980).

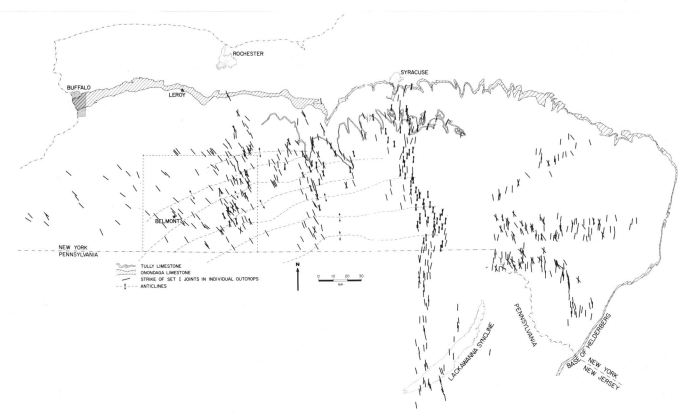

Figure 6a. Plot of strike of set I joints on Appalachian plateau. Each datum represents one or more set I joints within outcrops visited during our study.

2) The earliest joint sets predate finite amplitude folding and generally do not correlate with later Alleghanian deformations; these joints are found primarily as "cleating" in coal (Nickelsen and Hough, 1967; Nickensen, 1979; Kulander and Dean, 1978) and have been tied to the tectonic development of the Appalachian basin by Kulander and Dean (1978).

3) The presence of two or more joint sets is almost ubiquitous. Although the most common sets are approximately normal and parallel to the fold trends, some of these sets are not directly related to the folding process (Nickelsen and Hough, 1967; Kulander and others, 1979; Engelder and Geiser, 1980); however, others can be related (Nickelsen, 1979).

4) The Appalachian plateau of New York State has two well-developed cross-strike joint sets named set Ia and set Ib by Engelder and Geiser (1980) (Figure 6a). Set Ia is characterized by occasional calcite filling and has a marked western limit (Figure 6b), whereas set Ib has never been observed to be filled (Figure 6c). In the area between Binghamton and Syracuse, New York, set Ia parallels the compression direction indicated by finite strain and is contemporaneous with the development of solution cleavage, as indicated by the cross-cutting relationship between the cleavage and calcite-filled joints. To the east and west of this area, set Ia strikes about 10° clockwise from the com-

pression direction indicated by the finite strain. The difference in strike between set Ia and Ib is 15° to 30°, with set Ib counter-clockwise from Ia and never parallel to the compression direction indicated by the post-lithification solution cleavage. Engelder and Geiser (1980) conclude that set Ia and set Ib joints reflect different tectonic events for which joint set Ia formed after lithification and contemporaneously with the Main phase LPS fabrics. Engelder and Geiser (1980) hypothesize that the orientation of set Ib may be controlled by a prelithification tectonic event despite presenting evidence that formation of joint set Ib post dates joint set Ia.

ALLEGHANIAN DEFORMATIONS

Lackawanna Phase

The Lackawanna phase is the earliest of two major deformations that we have identified. The area affected by this deformation is recognized by an assemblage of structures including LPS fabrics, folds, thrusts, set Ib joints, and zones of fold terminations. The LPS fabrics associated with this event extend eastward from the area immediately west of the Lackawanna syncline where it is found as weakly developed cleavage and/or crenulation. Northwest of our boundary for the Lackawanna phase, a

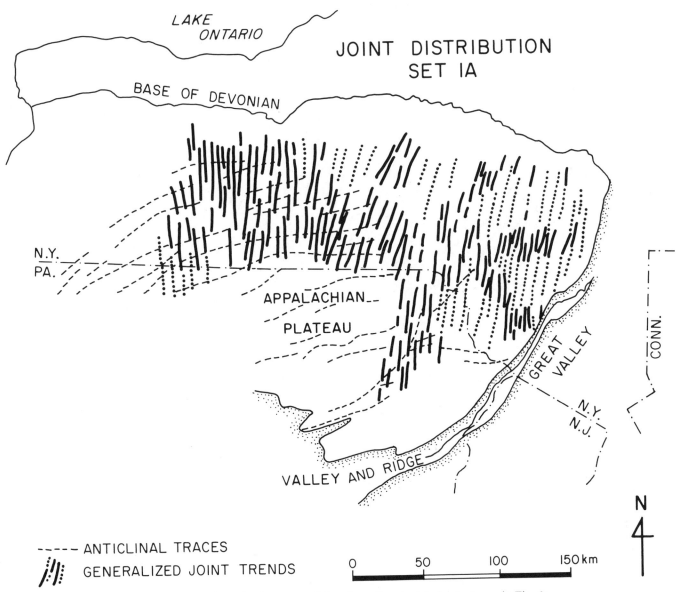

JOINT DISTRIBUTION
SET IA

----- ANTICLINAL TRACES
///::: GENERALIZED JOINT TRENDS

0   50   100   150 km

N

Figure 6b. Plot of trajectories drawn parallel to the strike of set Ia joints shown in Fig. 6a.

possible soft-sediment deformation and set Ib joints are the only structural elements which have an orientation compatible with the Lackawanna phase deformation. There is suggestive evidence for other folds on the Lackawanna trend in both the en echelon fold pattern in the Minersville synclinorium and the presence of low amplitude folds to the northeast of the Lackawanna syncline (Fletcher and Woodrow, 1970) (Figure 1). Other deformations overprint the Lackawanna trend throughout this region. Towards the north, the LPS fabric decreases in intensity and has not been found in the northern part, where the trend of the syncline bends around to about 020°. Presently, we have no explanation for the change in orientation of the northern tip of the Lackawanna syncline.

In the Bear Valley strip mine, located about 50 kms south of the Lackawanna syncline, Nickelsen (1979) has identified a set of structures almost identical to those we have described. In this region, Nickelsen recognizes six stages of deformation, the last five of which are associated with the Alleghanian Orogeny. Nickelsen's stages II (extension jointing), III (cleavage, small-scale folding), and IV (conjugate wrench and thrust faulting) are all associated with an early LPS event. The mean trend of bedding cleavage intersections is 068°, with associated extension joints at 337° (Nickelsen, 1979, Figure 4). The mean acute bisection of the conjugate wrench system is at 327°. This system of structures correlates almost precisely with our set Ib joints and the Lackawanna phase LPS fabric, which trends at 070°. Thus, the orientation of structures

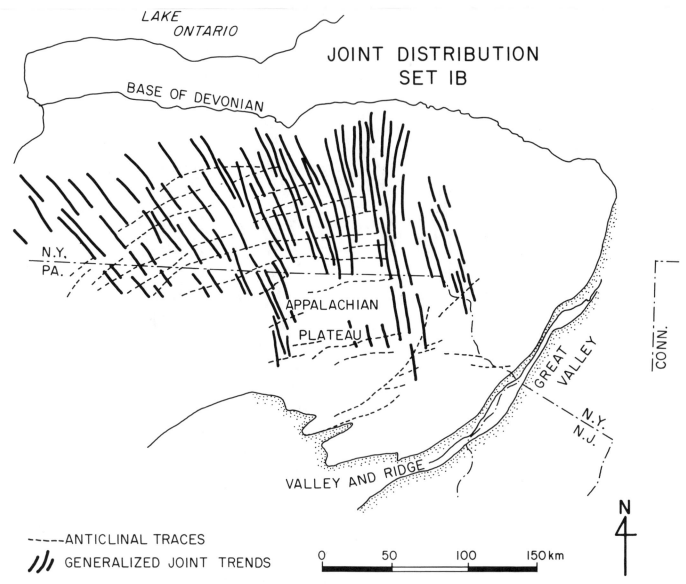

Figure 6c. Plot of trajectories drawn parallel to the strike of set Ib joints shown in Fig. 6a.

associated with Nickelsen's stages II-IV, the earliest Alleghanian events he finds, seems to be in agreement with the orientation of structures of proposed Lackawanna phase.

In the Lackawanna syncline, LPS fabrics parallel the 070° trend of the southern part of the Lackawanna syncline axis and become so well developed that they are the most obvious LPS fabric in this area. East of the Lackawanna syncline, the intensity of the 070° trend also diminishes, occurring only as scattered cleavage and fold crenulations. This relationship is found across the entire plateau to within 3-4 kilometers of the eastern edge of the plateau. As progressively lower parts of the section are exposed in crossing the Pocono plateau, the Lackawanna phase LPS fabrics become increasingly better developed so that, in the lower part of the Hamilton group, the

Lackawanna LPS fabrics are again the most strongly developed, with overprinting only sporadically and weakly developed.

The Lackawanna LPS fabrics can be mapped northward in the Helderberg and lower Hamilton Groups from the Delaware Valley into the Rondout and Hudson River Valleys. The LPS fabric in this region is almost exclusively a well developed solution cleavage. North of Orange County, New York, the solution cleavage is restricted to the interval between the Rondout Limestone and Ulster Group.

From Port Jervis northward, the trend of the Lackawanna phase cleavage gradually swings from 060°-070° to the 010° trends of the Helderberg escarpment. The cleavage can be traced continuously along the escarpment to the latitude of Albany, where the escarpment turns west.

From Albany, the cleavage can only be mapped along the escarpment 10 km to the west, where it dies out. As can be seen along the Rondout Valley and the Helderberg escarpment in Figure 3, the belt containing Lackawanna trends reflects the very narrow zone of foreland deformation which characterizes this region.

We recognize that the correlation of cleavage in the Hudson Valley with Alleghanian structures in the Lackawanna syncline is controversial. Our argument is based on the correlation of cleavage outcrop by outcrop southward down the Hudson and Delaware Valleys and across the Pocono plateau. Ratcliffe and others (1975) recognize the same cleavage and correlate it with an Acadian dynamothermal metamorphism to the east of the Hudson Valley. Their argument is that cleavage structures in the Hudson Valley, when traced eastward, can be shown by metamorphic inclusion textures to be syn- or pre-metamorphic with respect to probable Acadian metamorphism. However, at the present state of knowledge, our interpretation of an Alleghanian age for this change is based on our regional mapping and represents a more complete data base than that of Ratcliffe and others (1975), who only present structural data for the post-Taconic cleavage from the immediate vicinity of Mt. Ida. Moreover, we note that there is abundant evidence, in the form of post-metamorphic faulting, which suggests that both the Taconic and Acadian deformations to the east of the Hudson River Valley are themselves allochthonous.

Relationship among Lackawanna Phase LPS Fabrics, Thrusting, and Folding

A critical relationship among the various tectonic structures is seen along the Helderberg escarpment. This escarpment is characterized by a zone of imbricate thrusting involving all units from the Normanskill shale through the Helderberg group. The presence of cleavage in these structures, which predates thrusting and folding, indicates that the deformation initiated as an LPS thrust, was later broken into a series of imbricates (Geiser, 1980). It is this cleavage that we correlate with cleavage across the Pocono plateau and cleavage in the Lackawanna syncline. The relationship between cleavage and thrusting along the Helderberg escarpment is considered to support our interpretation that the Pocono plateau is a region of layer parallel shortening during the Lackawanna phase.

We suggest that the Lackawanna syncline is the surface manifestation of blind thrusting, with displacement approximately normal to the 070° trends of the Lackawanna phase LPS fabric and the Lackawanna syncline. Although Rodgers (1970) has hypothesized that basement must be involved in the formation of the Lackawanna synclines, as the Carboniferous rocks are almost a kilometer below the level they should be relative to the surrounding Devonian section, recent evidence from structure sections across this region fails to support this hypothesis (Elliott, 1980, personal communication).

The western border of the Lackawanna phase deformation is tentatively placed along the north-south trending zone of fold terminations and hinge trace offsets found to the west of the Lackawanna syncline (Figure 3). Cleavages parallel to the Lackawanna trend are only weakly and sporadically developed throughout this area and to the northwest. Consequently, the boundary of this deformation was drawn on the basis of the fold data rather than cleavages or jointing to the northwest.

Main Phase

The Main phase of the Alleghanian Orogeny in the central Appalachians is developed within both the New York and Pocono plateaus (Figure 3). Presently, its eastward extent is unknown. This event is the most widespread of the two phases which collectively form the Alleghanian Orogeny and is associated with the maximum deformation of the Appalachian foreland. LPS fabric for this phase extends northward at least to the zero isopach of the Silurian salts on the New York plateau and consists of deformed fossils, calcite twins, cleavage, and pencils (Engelder, 1979b). In Carboniferous rocks about 50 km north of the Allegheny front, pressure solution becomes a less important deformation mechanism, and finite strain is accommodated by folding crenulations with wavelengths of 1-2 cm (Figure 2a). The fold crenulations are apparently restricted to the upper Devonian and lower Mississippian units. South of the Allegheny front, where lower stratigraphic units are exposed again, solution cleavage reappears (Faill and Nickelsen, 1973; Geiser, 1974; Faill, 1979). On the Pocono plateau, solution cleavage sporadically appears in the Mississippian and Devonian sections where the best developed fabric in both Main and Lackawanna phases is a cleavage crenulation (Figure 2b).

Folding associated with the Main phase is most prominent west of the Lackawanna syncline. A few low amplitude, east-west trending folds have been recognized on the Pocono plateau (Fletcher and Woodrow, 1970). In addition Main phase folds refold the east limb of the Lackawanna syncline, thus unambiguously establishing that the Lackawanna phase pre-dates the Main phase.

Evidence for tectonic overprinting during the Alleghanian Orogeny has also been documented by Nickelsen's (1979) work. The last two structural stages (V and VI) at the Bear Valley strip mine, consisting of large scale folding and tightening of folds, deforms pre-existing structures along an 080° trend. This orientation correlates well with the Main phase structures to the north. An important question, not entirely resolved by Nickelsen's (1979) work, is whether the Bear Valley strip mine was affected by two separate and distinct tectonic events or by a simple, continuous event in which the associated stress field rotated incrementally 20° clockwise.

We believe that there are two factors that support the concept of two separate events rather than a single continuous event. Both our data and Nickelsen's (1979) show two distinct structural trends. Although Nickelsen has some evidence which suggests that the deformation associated with the wrench faulting can be interpreted in terms of a rotation, he concludes that the different orientations are due to local geometric effects on the stress field rather than a rotation in time. A second consideration arises from recent work by Pfiffner and Ramsey (1982), who point out that finite strain accumulations are nonlinear in behavior, thus leading rapidly to the accumulations of large strains. Consequently, the time required to produce the regionally developed strains of orogenic belts at strain rates between 10^{-13} and 10^{-15}/sec is quite small. For finite strain ratios associated with the deformation of the Appalachian orogen, $1.1 < 1+e_1/1+e_3 < 1.414$, the time required for deformation is less than 10 my and probably closer to 1 my. For example, Engelder and Geiser (1983) present evidence from *in situ* strain measurements that the deformation of the New York Plateau took an aggregate of 1 my. The implication of this is that the response of the orogen to stress loading is very rapid. Consequently, if the stress field was continuously rotating throughout the Alleghanian Orogeny, a rapid response time should generate sets of structures showing the entire range interval of orientations between the two major structural sets. This assumes that successive pulses were of roughly equivalent magnitude as would be required under the concept of a single orogenic event, and that the length of the Alleghanian (variously estimated to be between 60 and 120 my) is reasonably correct. These arguments, based on the data presented by Nickelsen (1979) and Engelder and Geiser (1983) and supported by the timing constraints indicated from the work of Pfiffner and Ramsey (1982), lead us to conclude that the Alleghanian Orogeny in the central Appalachians occurred as two separate events, each being associated with the development of blind thrusts at depth.

The initial deformation, the Lackawanna phase, is expressed by a northwest-directed detachment beneath the Pocono plateau. The age of this deformation is lower Upper Pennsylvanian or younger, as indicated by the youngest rocks affected by the deformation in the Lackawanna syncline (the Llewellyn Formation). The Main phase deformation is the product of a detachment whose displacement is directed north-south in eastern Pennsylvania but swings about the bend of the Pennsylvania salient. Its age, based on folded rocks on the Pennsylvania plateau, is early Permian or younger.

The origin of the three sporadically developed cleavage sets is presently not understood. There is some sugges-

tion from *in situ* strain data that the region was subject to a late E-W compression which might have generated the 000°-010° set (Engelder, 1980). However, this is speculative as we have not been able to relate these fabric directions to any other large-scale tectonic feature. Since we have been unable to determine the ages of the three sporadic sets relative to the principal deformations, the possibility remains that these fabrics represent minor Alleghanian deformational phases.

Other Evidence for Multiple Alleghanian Deformation

Scattered evidence for multiple tectonic events associated with the Alleghanian deformation has been found from as far north as the Narragansett Basin (Murray and Skehan, 1979; McMaster et al., 1981; Mosher, 1981) and as far south as southern West Virginia (Dean and Kulander, 1978). In the north, work on the Narragansett Basin indicates that throughout much of the Carboniferous the Narrangansett basin was the site of rapid deposition of non-marine clastics associated with a release type bend in a system of left-lateral strike slip faults. During the Permian, the basin was subjected to a major dynamothermal metamorphism which, according to McMaster et al. (1981) and Mosher (1981), is associated with a reversal of the strike slip motion so that the former release type bend became a restraining bend, resulting in a compressional event in the former basin.

In the Reading Prong of New Jersey, Drake and Lyttle (1980) have identified what they regard as two distinct episodes of Alleghanian deformation. Only a single Alleghanian event has so far been recognized in the region immediately south of the Reading Prong. Dean and Kulander (1977), however, have documented important evidence for at least two Alleghanian events on the folded Plateau of southern West Virginia. Here they find an early LPS event reflected in the formation of stylo-joints in which the axes of the stylolitic columns indicate that they were formed by a compression directed normal to **southern** Appalachian trends. This system of stylotized joints was subsequently folded about central Appalachian trends, thus clearly indicating two separate and distinct events. The region of overprinting extends for more than 100 kms along the margin of the plateau. In our interpretation, the change in the orogenic trends of the Roanoke Recess is the product of overprinting of Main phase structures on the Lackawanna trends, rather than either oroclinal bending or a relict of the original boundaries of the North American plate. Such an interpretation is consistent with the sedimentary history of the Roanoke region as discussed by Arkle (1974).

TECTONIC RECONSTRUCTION

In both the central and southern Appalachians, the

ALLEGHANIAN DISPLACEMENTS: APPALACHIAN FORELAND
AND ADJACENT STRIKE-SLIP TERRANE

① LACKAWANNA PHASE
② MAIN PHASE

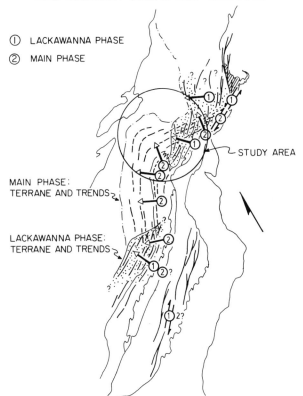

MAIN PHASE:
TERRANE AND TRENDS

LACKAWANNA PHASE:
TERRANE AND TRENDS

STUDY AREA

Figure 7. Trends of the Lackawanna and Main phase deformations currently known from the U.S. Appalachians.

foreland contains evidence for LPS fabrics from two phases of Alleghanian deformation (Figure. 7). We note that the evidence shown in Figure 7 has two characteristics: 1) Transport directions indicated for the Lackawanna phase are uniformly oriented NNW and independent of variation in the structural trends of the Appalachian Orogen and, therefore, presumably of the former boundaries of the North America Craton (Thomas, 1977). On the other hand, transport directions for the Main phase closely reflect the structural trends of the orogen. 2) Although the data are sparse, the sequence of overprinting is the same in all areas.

The two phases of Alleghanian deformation can be related to the sequence of events suggested by the paleomagnetic data of Kent and Opdyke (1978), as well as the more detailed tectonic synthesis suggested by LeFort and Van der Voo (1981) for the terminal Paleozoic orogeny of the Appalachian-Caledonide system. The data of Kent and Opdyke (1978) indicate in the Devonian that the Avalon Platform, consisting of the Canadian Maritime Provinces, eastern New England, and the British Isles, was about 15 degrees further south relative to its present position on the North American plate. In their view, during the Carbonif-

erous the Avalon Platform moved some 1500 km northward along a system of shear zones, finally "docking" some time in the Permian or later. LeFort and Van der Voo (1981), in a more elaborate synthesis, suggest a series of events analogous to the current collision between India and central Asia, in which a series of island arcs and microcontinents is collapsing between two older, more rigid plates (the Siberian and Indian platforms), the resulting deformation producing large-scale lateral motions within

ALLEGHANIAN OROGENY
LACKAWANNA PHASE
LATE DEVONIAN-POST LOWER PENNSYLVANIAN

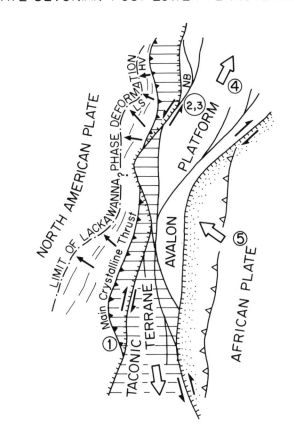

NB   Narragansett Basin
HV   Hudson Valley
LS   Lackawanna Syncline

Figure 8a. Tectonic sketch of Lackawanna phase of the Alleghanian Orogeny, showing relative displacement directions for the African plate and deforming Taconic and Avalon terrane. Displacement directions on the foreland are taken from compression directions as indicated by folds, faults, and LPS fabrics. Note that foreland displacements are independent of shape of North American plate margin. The numbers 1 to 5 indicate data from: (1) Cook et al. (1980); (2) Mosher (1981); (3) McMaster et al. (1980); (4) Kent and Opdyke (1978); (5) Le Fort and Van der Voo (1982).

the constricted terrane, as suggested by Molnar and Tapponnier (1978).

It is our hypothesis that the Lackawanna phase may be the product of either a similar initial period of lateral motion or one possibly associated with oblique subduction, during the Carboniferous. We envision the deformation to be similar to that presently occurring along the Naga-Arakan fold belt of Burma and the Sulaiman Range of Pakistan, where oblique convergence between India and Asia is forming a system of foreland fold-thrust belts on the same scale as the Appalachian foreland (Sarawar and DeJong, 1979).

For the initial Lackawanna phase of the Alleghanian orogeny, we follow the rigid indenter model of Lefort and Vander Voo (1981). In this model, the Avalon Platform is driven northward between the converging African and North American plates, producing the early left lateral motion and associated release bend formation of the Narragansett basin (McMaster et al., 1980). During this phase, a foreland fold thrust belt developed, driven by uniformly northwestward directed compression. Our present data suggest that much of the material within the Pennsylvania reentrant was little affected at this time.

Although a rigid indenter model can provide the necessary kinematics, an alternative to this which seems equally valid in light of present knowledge is a model involving oblique subduction and a form of large scale transpression (Dickinson and Yarborough, 1977). Such an interaction would not require a collision between the two rigid plates in the early phases of deformation; it would, however, seem to require that early stages of strike slip motion in the southern Appalachians be left lateral.

The Main phase of the Alleghanian is interpreted as the final closing and possible contact between the two rigid plates. One of the effects of this closure is to change the zone of faulting south of the Narragansett basin from a zone of simple strike slip motion into a transform between the African and North American plates, resulting in a reversal of the motion on these faults as the edges of the two plates make contact. In the foreland, the expulsion of material from the Pennsylvania reentrant provides the mass to form the body of the central Appalachians. The present curvature of the central Appalachians simply reflects the pre-existing geometry of the old North American plate, which established the geometric boundary conditions for this stage of the deformation. Deformation in the southern Appalachians presumably continues into and through this phase, during which the final assemblage of this part of the chain is completed.

1) Although we lack any sort of precise data on the original width of the Piedmont terrane, based on estimates of shortening within the Appalachians, it is reasonable to postulate that the total shortening is on the order of 100% or more. Given this width and a prograding suture

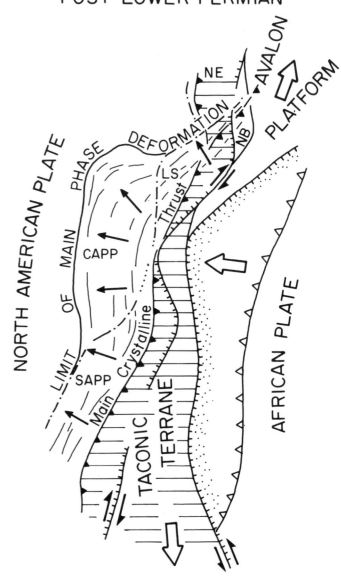

ALLEGHANIAN OROGENY
MAIN PHASE
POST LOWER PERMIAN

NB   Narragansett Basin
NE   New England
CAPP Central Appalachians
SAPP Southern Appalachians
LS   Lackawanna Syncline

Figure 8b. Tectonic sketch of Main phase of the Alleghanian Orogeny showing relative displacement directions for the African plate and deforming Taconic and Avalon terrane. Displacement directions on the foreland are taken from compression directions as indicated by folds, faults, and LPS fabrics. Note that, in contrast to Lackawanna phase, foreland displacement directions follow the shape of the North American plate margins.

(Roeder, 1979), the initial deformation would begin outboard and earlier than the events recorded by the foreland.

2) The rate at which thrusts are emplaced is clearly critical to questions of timing of the deformations. Here we note the evidence given by Pfiffner and Ramsey (1982), as well as our own data from the New York plateau [Engelder and Geiser, 1983], that the response of the upper crust to tectonic loadings is geologically instantaneous. Moreover, we note that the geometric requirements induced by a plate driven foreland deformation require that the displacement rates of thrust sheets be of the same order of magnitude as plate convergence (on the order of cms/yr).

3) The maximum age of the arrival of a deformation at any point is given by the youngest rocks affected by that event.

4) The Allegheny plateau in southwestern West Virginia shows two separate tectonic events recorded in the upper Mississippian Greenbrier limestone. An early LPS recorded by stylotized joints which parallel southern Appalachian trends is followed by a later refolding on central Appalachian trends (Dean and Kulander, 1978).

These observations and data suggest to us that, at a maximum, the Lackawanna phase may have begun no earlier than the late Mississippian in the southern part of the central Appalachians, reaching the Lackawanna area no earlier than early Pennsylvanian time. If these dates are correct, the initiation of the Alleghanian is somewhat older than is suggested by radiometric dates from the Narragansett basin, which indicate that the Alleghanian was a rather brief event in the Permian (Murray and Skehan, 1979).

However, the Mississippian to Pennsylvanian age for the deformation is more consistent with the 313-254 my age suggested by Snoke and others (1980) for the Kiokee belt. On the other hand, our suggestion that the Lackawanna phase represents a period of oblique subduction associated with large-scale strike-slip motion along the Appalachian orogen is also consistent with the Carboniferous history of rift type sedimentation of the Narragansett basin, which McMaster and others (1981) interpret as the product of a release type bend initiated as part of a strike-slip fault system.

The Main phase deformation then would represent the final closing between Africa with South America and North America. The complete suturing of continents drives the crystalline core zone westward along the entire length of the central Appalachians. The Lackawanna phase appears to have been restricted rather than distributed along the entire length with displacements whose orientation remains more or less uniformly directed toward the northwest. The age of the Main phase, which is the one originally associated with the Alleghanian and has

displacements whose orientation changes along strike (e.g., Rodgers, 1970), we interpret as early Permian or younger, and it may correlate with the early Permian deformation dated by the Narragansett Pier granite (Skehan and Murray, 1980).

Our current data indicate two discrete pulses during a sustained period of plate interactions. The pulses themselves are probably diachronous. Although we do see scattered evidence for other directions of translation, at this stage of investigation we cannot determine whether they are part of a continuous rotation of movement directions in which the Lackawanna phase and the Main phase were major pulses or whether they represent unique translations.

ACKNOWLEDGMENTS

Participants in the collection of data presented in this paper include Kathy Brockett, Stephanie Davis, Gail Moritz, Susan Randel, Jim Slaughter, David Spears, Pat Sullivan, and Paul Washington. National Science Foundation, Division of Earth Science, grants supporting the work include EAR 77-13000 (T.E.), EAR 77-14431 (P.G.), EAR 79-10849 (T.E.), and EAR 79-11085 (P.G.). Support also came from the Nuclear Regulatory Commission contract NRC-081-180. Early versions of this manuscript were reviewed by Dov Bahat, Ed Beutner, Roger Faill, Robert Hatcher, Steve Marshak, John Rodgers, and Don Secor.

REFERENCES CITED

Arkle, T., 1974, Stratigraphy of the Pennsylvanian and Permian Systems of the Central Appalachians, in Briggs, G., Ed., Carboniferous of the Southeastern United States: Geol. Soc. Am. Sp. Pap. 148, p. 5–29.

Bally, A. W., Gordy, P. L., and Stewart, G. A., 1966, Structure, seismic data, and orogenic evolution of southern Canadian Rockies: Bull. Can. Pet. Geol., 14, 337–381.

Cook, F. A., Albaugh, D. S., Brown, L. D., Kaufman, S., Oliver, J. E., and Hatcher, R. D., 1979, Thin-skinned tectonics in the crystalline southern Appalachians; COCORP seismic-reflection profiling of the Blue Ridge and Piedmont: Geology, v. 7, p. 563–567.

Dahlstrom, C.D.A., 1970, Structural geology in the eastern margin of the Canadian Rocky Mountains: Can. Petro. Geol. Bull., v. 18, p. 332–406.

Dean, S. L., and Kulander, B. R., 1978, Kinematic analysis of folding and pre-fold structures on the southwestern flank of the Williamsburg anticline, Greenbriar County, W. Virginia: Geol. Soc. Amer. Abs. with programs, v. 9, p. 132–133.

Dickinson, W. R., and Yarborough, H., 1977, Plate Tectonics and hydrocarbon accumulation: AAPG Cont. Ed. Course Note Series No. 1.

Drake, A. A., and Lyttle, P. T., 1980, Alleghanian thrust faults in the Kittatinny Valley, New Jersey, in Field Studies of New Jersey Geology and guide to Field trips: 52nd Annual Mtg. NYS Geol. Assoc., Manspiezer, W., ed., pp. 92–115.

Engelder, T., 1979a, Mechanisms for strain within the Upper Devonian clastic sequence of the Appalachian plateau, Western New York:

Am. Jour. Sci., v. 279, p. 527–542.

Engelder, T., 1979b, The nature of deformation within the outer limits of the central Appalachian foreland fold and thrust belt in New York State: Tectonophysics, v. 55, p. 289–310.

Engelder, T., 1980, Evidence from strain relaxation tests for the exchange of principal stress axes, *in* Hanks, T., and Raleigh, B., eds., Proc. Conf. IX—Magnitude of Deviatoric Stresses in the Earth's Crust and Upper Mantle: USGS Open File Report No. 80-625, p. 444–461, U.S. Dept. of Interior Geological Survey, Menlo Park, Ca. 94025.

Engelder, T., and Engelder, R., 1977, Fossil distortion and decollement tectonics on the Appalachian Plateau: Geology, v. 5, p. 457–460.

Engelder, T., and Geiser, P., 1979, The relationship between pencil cleavage and lateral shortening within the Devonian section of the Appalachian Plateau, New York: Geology, v. 7, p. 460–464.

Engelder, T., and Geiser, P., 1980, On the use of regional joint sets as trajectories of paleostress fields during the development of the Appalachian Plateau, New York: J. Geophys. Res., 85, no. B11, p. 6319–6341.

Engelder, T., and Geiser, P., 1983, Residual stress in the Tully Limestone, Appalachian Plateau, New York: J. Geophys. Res. (submitted).

Faill, R. T., 1979, Geology and mineral resources of The Montoursville South and Muncy Quadrangles and part of the Hughesville Quadrangle, Lycoming, Northcumberland and Montour Counties, Pennsylvania: Pennsylvania Dept. of Environ. Resources, Bureau of Topographic and Geologic Survey, Atlas 144ab., p. 114.

Faill, R. T., and Nickelsen, R. P., 1973, Structural geology, *in* Faill, R., ed., 38th Annu. Field Conf. of Pa. Geol., p. 9–38.

Fisher, D. W., Isachsen, Y. W., and Rickard, L. V., 1970, Geologic map of New York: New York State Museum and Science Service Map and Chart Series No. 15.

Fletcher, F. W., and Woodrow, D. L., 1970, Geology of Milford and Port Jervis quadrangles: Geol. Atlas A-223, Penn. Geol. Surv., Harpsburg, Penn.

Geiser, P. A., 1970, Deformation of the Bloomsburg Formation, Cacapon Mountain Anticline, Hancock, Md.: (Ph.D. dissertation), Johns Hopkins Univ., Baltimore, 128 p.

Geiser, P. A., 1974, Cleavage in some sedimentary rocks of the central Valley and Ridge province, Maryland: Geol. Soc. Am. Bull., v. 85, p. 1399–1412.

Geiser, P. A., 1977, Early deformation structures in the central Appalachians: a model and its implications: Geol. Soc. Amer. Abst. with Programs, N.E. section.

Geiser, P. A., 1980, Cleavage in Lower and Middle Devonian Rocks of the Hudson and Delaware River Valleys; Its implications for Appalachian tectonics: N.E. Sect. GSA, 15th annual Mtg., Abst., with programs.

Geiser, P. A., 1982, An examination of some models of thrust propagation and their use in the structural analysis of overthrust terranes: submitted to AAPG.

Gray, C., and Shepps, V. C., 1964, Geological map of Pennsylvania: Penn. Geol. Surv. 4th Series.

Gray, D. R., 1978, Microstructure of crenulation cleavages: an indicator of cleavage origin: Am. Jour. Sci., v. 279, p. 97–128.

Groshong, R. H., 1971, Strain in minor folds, Valley and Ridge province, Pennsylvania: (unpubl. Ph.D. dissertation), Brown Univ., Providence, R. I., 223 p.

Groshong, R. H., 1975, Strain, fractures, and pressure solution in natural single layer folds: Geol. Soc. Am. Bull., v. 86, p. 1363–1376.

Gwinn, V. E., 1964, Thin-skinned tectonics in the plateau and northwestern Valley and Ridge Provinces of the Central Appalachians: Geol. Soc. Am. Bull., v. 75, p. 863–900.

Gwinn, V. E., 1970, Kinematic patterns and estimates of lateral shortening, Valley and Ridge and Great Valley Provinces, Central Appalachians, south-central Pennsylvania: *in* Fisher, G. W., Pettijohn, F.

J., Reed, J. C., and Weaver, K. N., eds., Studies of Appalachian Geology: Central and Southern (Cloos Vol.)., p. 127–146.

Harris, L. D., and Milici, R. C., 1977, Characteristics of thin-skinned style of deformation in the southern Appalachians, and potential hydrocarbon traps: Geol. Surv. Prof. Paper 1018.

Kent, D. V., and Opdyke, N. D., 1978, Paleomagnetism of the Devonian Catskill red beds: Evidence for motion of the coastal New England-Canadian Maritime region relative to cratonic North America: J. Geophys. Res., 83, p. 4441–4450.

Kulander, B. R., Barton, C. C., and Dean, S. L., 1979, The application of fractography to core and outcrop fracture investigations: Report to U.S.D.O.E., Morgantown Energy Technology Center, METC/SP-79/3, p. 173.

Kulander, B. R., and Dean, S. L., 1978, Gravity, magnetics and structure, Alleghany Plateau/Western Valley and Ridge in West Virginia and adjacent states: West Va. Geol. and Economic Survey, Rept. of Investi. RI-27.

Lefort, J., and Van der Voo, R., 1981, A kinematic model for the collision and complete suturing between Gondwanaland and Laurusia in the Carboniferous, J. of Geol., v. 89, p. 537–550.

McMaster, R. L., deBoer, J., and Barclay, P. C., 1980, Tectonic development of Southern Narragansett Bay and offshore Rhode Island: Geol., v. 8, no. 10, p. 496–500.

Mitra, G., 1978, Ductile deformation zones and mylonites: The mechanical processes involved in the deformation of crystalline basement rocks: Am. Jour. Sci., v. 278, p. 1057–1084.

Mitra, G., and Elliot, D., 1980, Deformation of the Basement in the Blue Ridge and the development of the South Mountain cleavage: *in* Wones, D. R., ed., Proceedings, The Caledonides in the USA, VPI and SU Dept. of Geol. Sci., memoir no. 2, pp 307–311.

Molnar, P., and Tapponnier, P., 1977, Relation of the tectonics of eastern China to the India-Eurasian collision: application of slip-line field theory to large scale continental tectonics: Geology, v. 5, p. 212–216.

Mosher, S., 1981, Late Paleozoic deformation of the Narragansett Basin, Rhode Island: Geol. Soc. Am. Abst. with Program, v. 13, p. 515.

Murray, D. P., and Skehan, S. J., J. W., 1979, A traverse across the eastern margin of the Appalachian-Caledonide orogen, Southeastern New England: *in* Skehan, S. J., J. W., and Osberg, P. H., eds., The Caledonides in the U.S.A.: Geological excursions in the Northeast Appalachians, Weston Obsv., p. 1–35.

Nickelsen, R. P., 1966, Fossil distortion and penetrative rock deformation in the Appalachian plateau, Pennsylvania: Jour. Geology, v. 74, p. 924–931.

Nickelsen, R. P., 1979, Sequence of structural stages of the Allegheny orogeny at the Bear Valley Strip Mine, Shamokin, Pennsylvania: Am. Jour. Sci., v. 279, p. 225–271.

Nickelsen, R. P., and Hough, V. D., 1967, Jointing in the Appalachian Plateau of Pennsylvania: Geol. Soc. Am. Bull., v. 78, p. 609–630.

Parker, J. M., 1942, Regional systematic jointing in slightly deformed sedimentary rocks: Geol. Soc. Am. Bull., v. 53, p. 381–408.

Perry, W. J., 1978, Sequential deformation in the central Appalachians: Am. Jour. Sci., v. 278, p. 518–542.

Pfiffner, O. A., and Ramsay, J. G., 1982, Constraints on geological strain rates: Arguments from finite strain rates of naturally deformed rocks: J. Geophys. Res., v. 87, p. 311–321.

Pone, H. A., 1981, Joint spacing as a method of locating faults: Geol., v. 9, p. 258–261.

Price, R. A., and Mountjoy, E. W., 1970, Geologic structure of the Canadian Rocky Mountains between Bow and Athabasca Rivers—A progress report, *in* Wheeler, J. O., ed., Structure of the Southern Canadian Cordillera: Geol. Assoc. Can. Spec. Paper no. 6, p. 8–25.

Ratcliffe, N. M., Bird, J. M., and Bahrami, B., 1973, Structural and stratigraphic chronology of the Taconide and Acadian Polydeformational Belt of the central Taconics of NY State and Mass., *in* Ratcliffe, N. M., ed., Guidebook for field trips in western Mass., northern Conn. and adjacent areas of New York: N.E.I.G.C. 67th annu. Meet., City Col. of CUNY.

Rich, J. L., 1934, Mechanics of low-angle overthrusting faulting as illustrated by the Cumberland overthrust block: Am. Ass. Pet. Geol. Bull., v. 18, p. 1584–1596.

Rodgers, J., 1953, The folds and faults of the Appalachian Valley and Ridge Province: *in* McGrain, Preston, et. al., Ky. Geol. Surv. Spec. Publ. 1, p. 150–166.

Rodgers, J., 1970, The tectonics of the Appalachians: John Wiley and sons, New York, 271 pp.

Roeder, D., 1979, Continental collisions: Rev. Geophys. Space Phys., v. 17, p. 1098–1109, U.S. Nat. Rpt. I.U.G.G.

Sarawar, G., and Dejong, K. A., 1979, Arcs, oroclines, syntaxes: the curvatures of mountain belts in Pakistan, *in* Farah, A., and DeJong, K. A., eds., Geodynamics of Pakistan: Geol. Surv. of Pakistan, Quetta, p. 341–350.

Skehan, J. W., and Murray, D. P., 1980, A model for the evolution of the Eastern Margin (EM) of the Northern Appalachians: *in* Proceedings The Caledonides in the USA, IGCP, project 27, p. 67–72.

Slaughter, J., 1980, Strain and strain partitioning in Middle Devonian rocks of eastern New York Plateau: Geol. Soc. Am. Abst. with Prog., v. 12, p. 83.

Snoke, A. W., Kish, S. A., and Secor, D. T., 1980, Deformed Hercynian granite rocks from the Piedmont of South Carolina; Am. J. Sci., v. 280, p. 1018–1034.

Spang, J. H., and Groshong, R. H., 1981, Deformation mechanisms and strain history of a minor fold from the Appalachian Valley and Ridge Province: Tectonophysics, v. 72, p. 323–342.

Thomas, W. A., 1977, Evolution of Appalachian-Ouachita salients and recesses from reentrants and promontories in the continental margin: Am. Jour. Sci., v. 277, p. 1233–1278.

Washington, P., 1980, Evidence for multiple generations of cleavage in the Lackawanna syncline and Pocono plateau, their possible tectonic significance: NE section GSA, Abst. with programs, p. 88.

Wiltschko, D. V., and Chapple, W. M., 1977, Flow of weak rocks in Appalachian Plateau folds: Am. Ass. Pet. Geol. Bull., v. 61, p. 653–670.

Manuscript Accepted by the Society September 10, 1982
Lamont-Doherty Geological Observatory Contribution No. 3429.

Geological Society of America
Memoir 158
1983

Role of basement warps and
faults in localizing thrust fault ramps

David Wiltschko
Daniel Eastman
Department of Geological Sciences
The University of Michigan
Ann Arbor, Michigan 48109

ABSTRACT

Foreland thrust belts are regions where the stratigraphic section has failed. The close association in the field of thrust ramps and other structures suggests that this failure may not be haphazard. In this paper, we investigate two of these field associations—pre-existing basement warps and faults—and find that they both play a dual role in controlling the locations of thrust ramps. Two-layer, two-dimensional, photoelastic models show that pre-existing gentle basement warps primarily deflect faults by offering a rigid surface which causes the regional principal stress trajectories to bend; the highest stress concentration is about 1½. While also disturbing the regional stress trajectories, the main effect of pre-existing basement faults is to concentrate stress and, thereby, facilitate failure. The strength of the stress concentration above basement faults depends upon the fault angle and may be as high as 2 ½. Although not directly investigated, these results have three-dimensional implications. First, since failure takes place somewhere within the section above basement faults, faults must propagate *down* to join the sole fault as well as up to the surface for significant motion to take place, an intuition first arrived at by Kehle (written communication). Second, these results suggest that, once started, a thrust fault may propagate along strike away from these stress concentrations into regions where there is no apparent mechanical cause for the initial break. Consequently, only a few stress concentrations may control the gross architecture of an entire thrust belt since, once started, thrust faults presumably propagate on the strength of their own fault-tip singularity.

INTRODUCTION

If one wanted to make only one characterization of thrust belts, it would be that they are regions where the stratigraphic section has failed along spaced, curvilinear thrust fault zones. It is a reflection of the poor state of knowledge of thrust mechanics that even the first-order reason why thrust faults are where they are has not been adequately explained. Perhaps, this is because the formation of ramps may, at first, appear to be a nearly random process. However, in this paper we would like to show that the localization of ramps is not a random phenomenon and that, in fact, it may be controlled by only a few processes. The bases for this confidence are several relatively recently published seismic studies showing a close association between thrust ramps and basement structures and some mechanical arguments developed below which show that these associations may be causal.

First we discuss recognized regional stress concentration mechanisms, describe some photoelastic models which attach a mechanical significance to a few of them, and then apply these results to the evolution of the Idaho-Wyoming segment of the Western Overthrust Belt.

Previous Work

Field Associations. Many field studies and more recent reflection seismic studies suggest that regional stress concentration mechanisms exist. For instance, thrust ramps appear to be closely associated with other features (Fig. 1), one of the most commonly cited examples being pre-existing folds. As one example, Miller and Fuller (1954) propose the Pine Mountain fault underlying the Pine Mountain block of the southern Appalachians (Fig. 2) ramped from the Rome formation (Cambrian) to the Chattanooga Shale (Devonian/Mississippian) as a result of the resistance to further propagation offered by folding. In their view, the fault propagates into the fold "until it confronts a downward flexure where the fault can no longer follow the incompetent units. Once the cross-cutting has begun, many or most overthrust faults continue to break across the formations, competent and incompetent alike" (Miller and Fuller, 1954, p. 258–259). Another view is that the fault is a result, not the cause, of failure and that failure of the section takes place when the strongest unit can no longer support the stress applied to it. In the parlance of fold mechanics, the fold either "locks up" or reaches such a configuration that shortening can only continue by failure and subsequent motion on the fault. One mechanisms of lock up may be the increased difficulty of moving material into a fold core with increased fold amplitude (Wiltschko and Chapple, 1977). In any case, failure occurs at locations of high curvature for buckle folds and high shear for flexural slip folds. Any fold of finite amplitude may produce stress concentrations or local stresses higher than the applied load.

Unfortunately, it is difficult to judge how important this mechanism is. It is common for thrusts to terminate in folds. Does slip on the fault produce the fold which eventually fails, or does the folding develop to the point where failure takes place? The first is a result of fault slip (Gardner and Spang, 1973), whereas the other is a finite amplitude consequence of the folding process. While mechanically appealing, recognition of pre-existing folds is not sufficiently precise to evaluate their importance in most thrust belts. We will not examine them further.

Stratigraphic inhomogeneities have also been observed to be closely associated with fault ramps. Harris (1970) accounts for the location of the Jacksboro fault, the southwestern boundary of the Pine Mountain block, by thinning of the Chattanooga Shale. This shale, which contains the Pine Mountain fault over about one-half of the block's extent (Miller, 1973), is about 150 m thick just to the northeast of the Jacksboro fault (Ellen Meredity #1

Regional stress concentration mechanisms

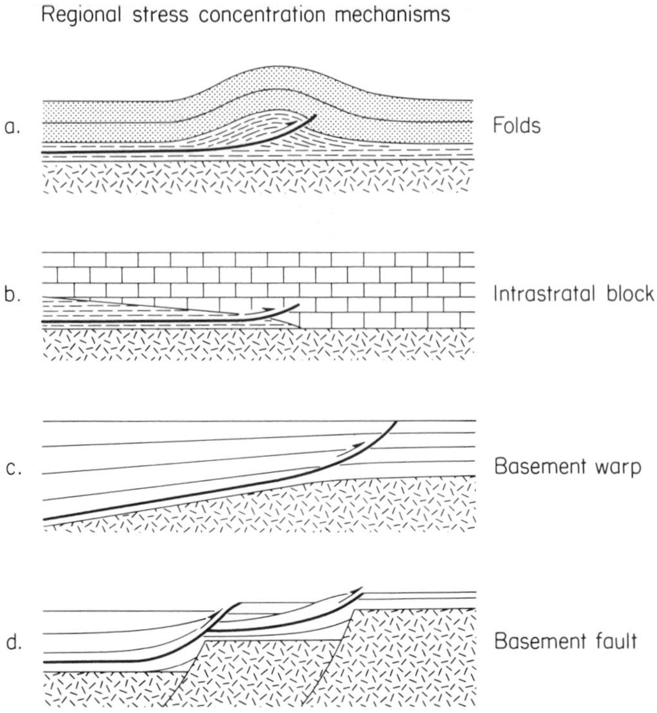

Figure 1: Four regional stress concentration mechanisms leading to thrust ramps.

well) but only 14 m thick to the southwest of the fault (John Lee West #6 well) (Fig. 2). Along the outcrop of the Pine Mountain fault, the Pine Mountain fault steps down stratigraphically from the Devonian/Mississippian Chattanooga to the Silurian Rockwood as the former thins from northeast to southwest. Apparently, there may be a minimum shale thickness below which motion on the fault becomes more difficult than breaking the overlying sheet.

These stratigraphic inhomogeneities are almost certainly much more prevalent on a local scale, especially in rocks where units are more discontinuous. The weak and strong units alike thin and thicken and, when stressed, support these stresses in a non-uniform manner. It is not difficult to imagine that in compression the feather ends of the strong units will create stress concentrations; in shear, the pinch outs of the weaker rocks such as shales will act as a stress concentration as more of the load is transferred to the surrounding stronger units. Bedding surfaces, with their natural bedding undulations, would also be expected to stress non-uniformly in shear. If the topography of these undulations is high, the difficulty of movement on these warps may cause large stress concentration.

The last class of regional stress concentration mechanisms is basement surface irregularities. Two subclasses have been recognized: (1) basement warps, such as the Moxa Arch in the Idaho-Wyoming thrust belt, and (2) normal faults, such as those found on most passive continental margins (Roberts, 1974; Sheridan, 1974, for

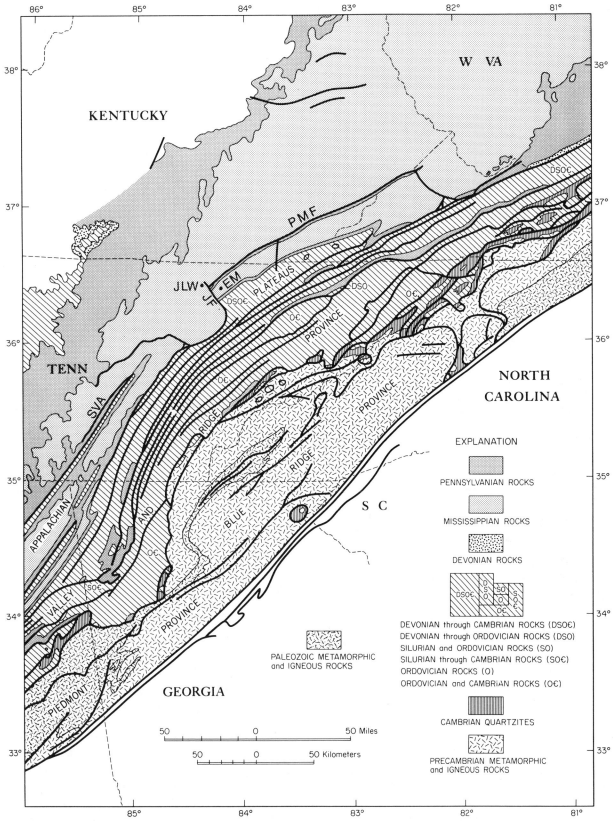

Figure 2: Pine Mountain block and environs, southern Appalachians. The Pine Mountain fault (PMF) underlies the Pine Mountain block and forms its northwestern border. The Jacksboro fault (JF)—a transverse ramps or tear fault forming the southwestern boundary of the block—is located where the Devonian Chattanooga shale thins from about 150 m in the Ellen Meredith #6 well (EM) to 14 m in the John Lee West #1 well (JLW). The Sequatchie Valley anticline is denoted by SVA.

instance). The Moxa Arch, a broad basement warp, lies both east of and beneath the thrust belt in eastern Idaho and western Wyoming (Fig. 3). Its development predates the ramping of the last two major thrusts (Darby and Prospect thrusts). These ramps are closely associated with the crest of the Arch and may be caused by it (Wach, 1977; Blackstone, 1979, p. 27-29; Dorr and Gingerich, 1980, p. 113). Similarly, in the southern Appalachians, Harris and Milici (1977) propose that a few of the major ramps may be caused by warps in the basement. In their opinion, a propagating thrust fault follows the sediment-basement interface and deflects upward where the basement shallows abruptly. Normal faults are commonly reported within the basement and sediments of rifted continental margins of many ages (Roberts, 1974; Sheridan, 1974) and may be common toward the craton. Jacobeen and Kanes (1974, 1975), for instance, interpret basement reflections in this manner beneath Broadtop Synclinorium in the central Appalachians. Here also, perhaps not by chance, the Broadtop thrust ramps from the Lower Cambrian to the Upper Ordovician. More recently, Thomas has documented the close associations between Birmingham anticlinorium—a large thrust anticline in the Valley and Ridge province of Alabama—and growth faulting in basement (Thomas, 1983). The thrust ramp above which the anticlinorium formed developed as the last event in a protracted history that is mostly characterized by normal faulting. In Thomas' view, the location of the thrust ramp is controlled by preexisting normal faults in basement. The recent SOQUIP seismic section through southeastern Quebec also documents a similar association between high-angle basement faults and ramps of thrust faults. Because of their inaccessibility to observation and the difficulties in interpreting basement reflections in complexly deformed terranes, this association has not been described in many other mountain belts.

Theoretical and Experimental Work. Theoretical work to date has not addressed the problem of stress concentration separate from the propagation of thrust faults. Hafner (1951) computed principal stress trajectories from polynomial stress functions for an end loaded sliding block. This much quoted model predicts the generally concave upward aspect of many thrust surfaces. Some of these models were subsequently investigated by Hubbert (1951) through non-scaled experiments with sand as the deforming medium. Sanford (1959) conducted a similar study for regions that experience displacements on their bottom surfaces.

More recently, Gallagher and Rizer (1977) and Rodgers and Rizer (1980) have investigated the effects of edge slits and cracks, respectively, in modifying an otherwise uniform field. Gallagher and Rizer (1977) model propagating faults as ½" (1.3 cm) wide slots machined into the edge of rectangular photoelastic material. They show

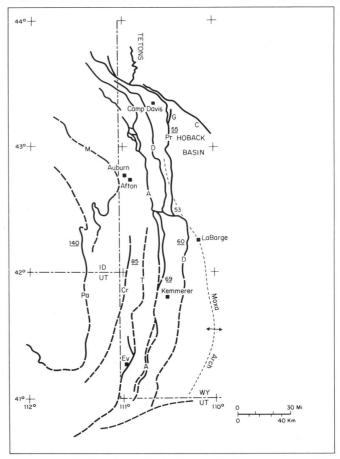

Figure 3: Idaho-Wyoming-Utah thrust belt, the Overthrust Belt. Symbols: Pa, Paris thrust; M, Meade thrust; Cr, Crawford thrust; T, Tunp thrust; A, Absaroka thrust; D, Darby thrust; Pr, Prospect thrust; G, Game Hill fault; C, Cache Creek fault; Ev, Evanston, Wyoming. Underlined numbers are dates on the adjacent thrust, in millions of years before present.

that, if the angle the slot makes with the compression direction is low, then the fracture could propagate by shear failure. Moreover, the orientation of the fracture would remain more or less parallel to that of the slot as long as the boundary conditions remain the same. The two sides of the slots do not touch, so the flaw is unrealistically frictionless. However, Rodgers and Rizer (1980) examine the stresses around a crack oriented at 30° to the surface, yet not having reached it, and overlain in some cases by a higher modulus layer. They conclude on the basis of photoelastic and dislocation studies that the fault will extend more or less with constant dip to the surface, unless the upper material is stronger, in which case the fault may tend to flatten toward the interface between the two different materials.

The theoretical models of Hafner (1951) assume that no pre-existing flaws are present, whereas Gallagher and Rizer (1977) and Rodgers and Rizer (1980) do. The models to be described next fall between these two sets of studies; we will investigate the reasons for stress concentrations within the regional fields described by Hafner (1951) which give rise to the fractures described by Gallagher and Rizer (1977) and Rodgers and Rizer (1980).

PHOTOELASTIC MODELS

Background

Stress concentrations can occur in several ways. They occur at internal boundaries such as cracks, holes, or hard inclusions or at external boundaries such as edge slots, reentrants, or warps where there is a change in curvature of the boundary and, nearly by definition, a mismatch of stresses across that boundary. In the case of the circular hole, the stresses radial to the hole's center are completely unsupported at the hole's edge; the same is true for the crack at its tip. In the former case, a well-known solution from elasticity theory shows that the stress concentration factor—the local stress divided by applied stress at infinity—is as high as 3. The stress concentration at the crack tip is theoretically infinite, though in real materials ductile processes decrease the sharpness of the real crack tip.

Stress concentrations are present in all stressed brittle rocks in one form or another. Incompletely cemented sedimentary rocks display large concentrations at grain contacts (Gallagher and others, 1974; Sutton and Wiltschko, 1982). Undulatory or discontinuous bedding produces stress concentrations as described before. In what follows, we will be examining the mechanisms of stress concentration on the scale of kilometers, however. Further, failure is never achieved in our models and as a result the propagation of fractures is not investigated directly, though potential fault orientations may be drawn. The question to be addressed is where are thrust ramps most likely to occur and how does this likelihood increase or decrease from situation to situation?

The photoelastic technique is a powerful way to investigate geometrically complex problems (Frocht, 1962; Dally and Riley, 1978). It relies on the fact that some high polymer plastics are optically anisotropic when stressed, the anisotropy being linearly proportional to the level of stress. These materials are linearly elastic if the duration of loading is not long. As a result, it is possible to build geometrically similar (Hubbert, 1937) scaled models of much larger geologic structures in order to investigate the effect of their geometry on the elastic stresses that may have existed.

As discussed more fully in the Appendix, all of our models are constructed from ¼" (6.4 mm) sheets of homogeneous epoxy plastic and consequently do not allow for the effects of layering or gravity.

RESULTS

Basement Warps

Figure 4a shows the configuration of a geometrically similar scale model of the Moxa Arch at the latitude of Afton, Wyoming (Fig. 3). It was constructed by casting Photolastic Corporation's PL-8 liquid epoxy plastic edgewise onto a ¼" (6.3 mm) plexiglass base which was previously machined to the proportions of the Moxa Arch shown in Plate IV of Royse and others (1975).

The stress intensities are greatest at the surface just past the crest of the Arch on the side away from the load and least also on the side away from the load at the model basement-sediment contact (Fig. 4b). These stresses are not great relative to the load, indicating that gentle basement arches are not particularly strong stress concentrators. However, the principal stress directions and potential fault orientations (Figs. 4c, d) indicate that the Moxa Arch at least does have an influence on the stress trajectories and, therefore, fault angles. Faults which sole both at the basement-sediment contact and further toward the crest of the Arch would be more horizontal. The curvature of these faults is independent of the role of gravity (compare Hafner, 1951, Fig. 6, which includes gravity).

Figures 4b and c taken together indicate that the first thrust to form over the arch would be that farthest from the load since the stresses are higher there. Furthermore, this fault may propagate from over the crest of the Arch *back* toward the level of detachment further west, a process others have suspected is true for all thrust faults (Kehle, 1978, written communication). In addition, no faults would disturb the rocks on the fixed side of the Arch below its crest; the stresses are very low there.

Basement Faults

Basement faults, however, are relatively strong stress concentrators. In Fig. 5a is the configuration for a normal fault with a dip of 45°, and in Fig. 5b the model stress magnitudes appear. Since the model is loaded to 0.65 order and the highest stress is 1.5 order, the stress concentration is 2.3.

Somewhat like the basement warp model, the maximum principal stress trajectories steepen toward the basement high and intersect the face of it toward the load at a relatively high angle. The area of disturbed stress trajectories is large and extends to the top surface of this model.

Unlike the warp model, however, the principal stress trajectories shallow and then steepen beyond the top corner of the basement fault (Figs. 5c and d). This behavior gives rise to unusual-looking potential fault orientations which shallow and then steepen in a similar manner.

Basement warp

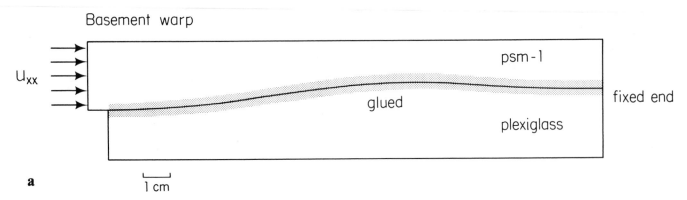

a

├─── 1 cm

Basement warp: magnitudes

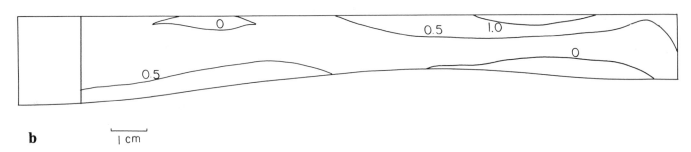

b

├─── 1 cm

Figure 4: Basement warp model. (a) Configuration of model materials and type of joins. Refer to the Appendix for construction details. U_{xx} is a uniform displacement, applied by a riding plunger to the side shown. (b) Stress magnitudes plotted as fringe orders. In this and the 45° normal fault model, the load is to 0.65 order. (c) Principal stress directions. (d) Potential fault orientations drawn under the assumptions that (1) the faults make an angle of 30° to the maximum principal stress direction, (2) propagation is instantaneous and, therefore, not affected by motion on the superincumbent sheet, (3) a fault does not alter the stress

Movement on faults with such topography is no doubt difficult if not improbable.

Interestingly, the stress concentraiton above a vertical fault is not as localized as that above the 45° normal fault; there are, in fact, two areas of high stress (Fig. 6). One area of high stress is at the sharp upper corner, like in the 45° normal fault model, but the other stress concentration is in front of the steep model fault face. These two areas of stress concentration lead to more gentle potential fault orientations. In addition, there is a dead zone where motion is unlikely due to the proximity to unyielding basement. Therefore, while the region just in front of the model fault may fracture, motion will only take place on higher level faults; the two lowest potential fault surfaces in Fig. 6d will most likely not develop.

Another peculiarity of this model is the fact that there is a stress gradient on the loaded end, unlike other models presented. A partial explanation for this is that this model, like the other models, was loaded with a plunger which applied a constant displacement (see Appendix). This gives rise to non-constant stresses within this model, even along the edge where the displacement is applied. Since the entire model is equally compressed, the shorter seg-

ment (between the face of the fault and the loaded end) must absorb the same displacement over a shorter distance than the long segment (between the fixed and loaded end). Since the strain is length change normalized to original length, shorter segments will have higher strains. This effect is masked in the 45° normal fault model by a lower load and higher stress concentration.

DISCUSSION

Summary of Modeling

All of the models investigated concentrate stress to a greater or lesser extent. In the case of the basement arch model, this concentration takes place near the crest where the section is thinnest. In the basement fault models, the highest stresses are found at the upper corner of the fault face or, in the case of the vertical fault, also in front of the fault face.

All the models also deflect principal stress directions in such a way as to suggest that potential shear fractures would shallow at least in the vicinity of the highest stress

Basement warp

Principal stress directions

——— σ_1
------- σ_3

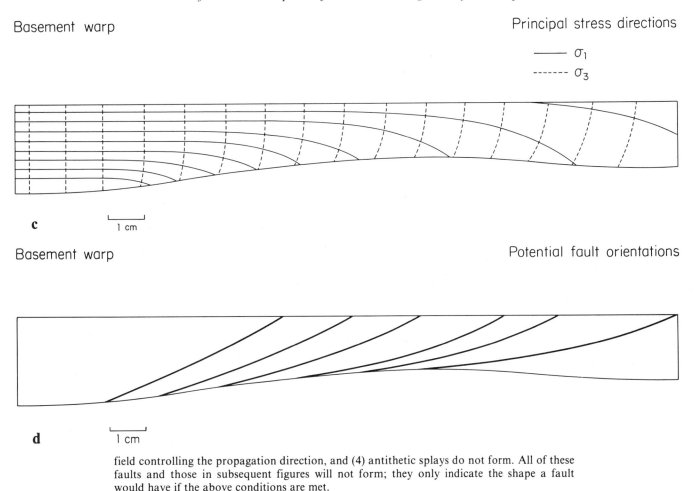

c   1 cm

Basement warp

Potential fault orientations

d   1 cm

field controlling the propagation direction, and (4) antithetic splays do not form. All of these faults and those in subsequent figures will not form; they only indicate the shape a fault would have if the above conditions are met.

concentration and, in the case of the basement faults, steepen beyond the model faults in the basement.

Three-Dimensional Implications

The nature of these stress concentrations suggests that failure of the section and subsequent initiation of a ramp may occur locally over basement warps and faults. It seems unlikely, however, that every thrust ramp must be explained in this way in every cross section. There are two reasons for this: (1) Thrust ramps will be transported away from their initial positions by motion on younger, deeper faults and, therefore, will no longer be near what caused them. The only exceptions are those thrusts which are the most cratonward and, therefore, have not been affected by other major thrusts (e.g., the Darby and Prospect thrusts of the Idaho-Wyoming thrust belt, see below). (2) The thrust fault surface will propagate along strike on the basis of the singularity at its tip into areas where there is no other mechanical cause for failure. Therefore, only a few stress concentrating mechanisms may account for the few major thrusts in a thrust belt, thus explaining why such areas of initial failure, or break points, are difficult to

find. In order to locate break points, it is necessary to have detailed timing evidence that shows which part of a thrust is oldest, a situation that rarely exists. The farthest moved part of a thrust may coincide with the oldest part.

CASE HISTORY: EVOLUTION OF THE IDAHO-WYOMING THRUST BELT

The Idaho-Wyoming thrust belt is understood better than most foreland fold and thrust belts for two reasons: (1) A relatively large amount of timing evidence has been worked out for most of the major thrusts (summarized in Dorr, 1981; Wiltschko and Dorr, in press). (2) This new timing evidence and a series of high resolution reflection seismic studies have allowed careful reconstruction of thrust-belt kinematics. These seismic studies show what has been known to explorationists for years, that there is a high in the basement in the eastern portion of the thrust belt, the Moxa Arch, which has apparently had an effect on the overlying thrust-faulted sedimentary cover. In addition, several large faults in the basements have led to wholesale uplift of large Precambrian masses. It will be suggested that, even though all of these did not exist in

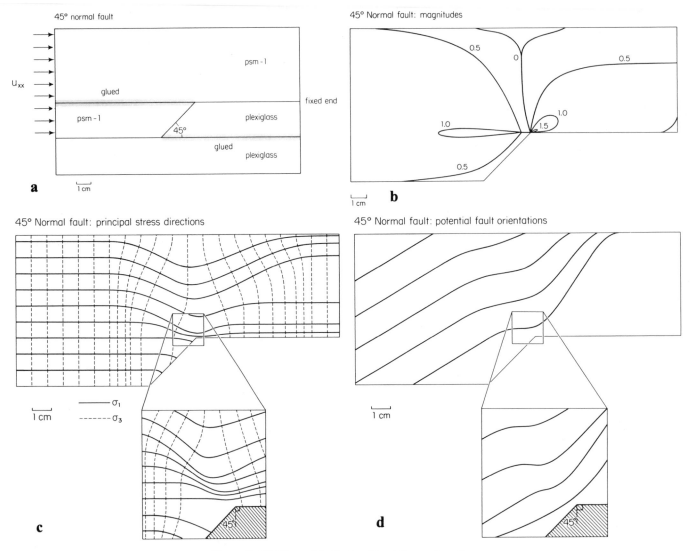

Figure 5: 45° Normal fault. See Fig. 4 for explanation.

every case before thrusting as assumed in the previous photoelastic models, they seem to have controlled the localization, and certainly have controlled the motion, of major portions of the thrust belt.

Basement Warps as Represented by the Moxa Arch

Geology. The Moxa Arch (= La Barge Platform) is a broad basement warp extending at least from Bridger Lake, Utah, to about 40 km east of Afton, Wyoming (Fig. 3). The eastern flank at the latitude of Afton dips about 3° to the east, and the western flank dips at 2° to the west (Royse and others, 1975, Plate IV). Near La Barge, Wyoming, its western flank dips as much as 10° to 15° (Blackstone, 1979, p. 27; compare his section B-B', Plate 5; see Fig. 8). Stratigraphic analysis indicates that the Arch grew primarily in the middle Upper Cretaceous since two formations of that age (Rock Springs and Blair,

which together are Adaville equivalents) are not present on its crest (Wach, 1977). In the sequence of events described by Royse and others (1975), based on restored seismically controlled sections, the Arch developed primarily during motion on the Absaroka fault but before formation of the Darby and Prospect thrust surfaces. The scenario preferred by Royse and others (1975) is adopted here.

The origin of the Moxa Arch is not known. Because of its proximity to the thrust belt on the west and the Wind River uplift on the east, it may to some degree be an isostatic response to crustal loading on both its flanks (Schedl and Wiltschko, 1980); the age of the initiation of Wind River range uplift seems to coincide with the formation of the Moxa Arch (Royse and others, 1975). However, this fact has also led Blackstone to speculate that it may be an early stage of what led further east to the development of the Wind River thrust (Blackstone, 1979;

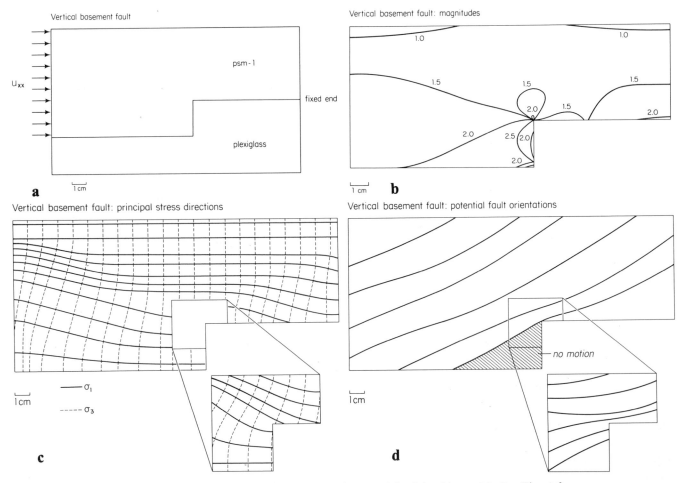

Figure 6: Vertical basement fault. Note the increased load in this model. See Fig. 4 for further explanation.

the western flank is known to be locally faulted (Dixon, 1982). These two possibilities cannot be tested at this time.

Despite its poorly understood origin, it is quite clear that the Arch has had a profound effect on thrust sheet geometry. At the Utah-Wyoming border, the crest lies about 31 km est of the most easterly thrust (Blackstone, 1980) and continues northward, staying 22 to 30 km east of the most easterly outcropping thrust trace without apparently affecting structures to the west. However, 22 km south of La Barge, Wyoming, the crest of the Arch turns westward to intersect the thrust belt about 9 km north of La Barge. Here, the trace of the Darby thrust, which tends generally north-south to the north of this area, turns abruptly eastward and trends about S 70° E for 30 km before apparently rather abruptly again resuming a north-south trend (Fig. 7; Rubey and others, 190; Rubey, 1973). The trace of the Absaroka thrust fault, as well as the stratigraphy in both the Darby and Absaroka plates, shows a similar change in trend, though less dramatically. In addition, the Darby thrust surface ramps in this area, shallows beyond the top of this ramp (see Blackstone, 1979, section C-C), and is torn by the Thompson fault

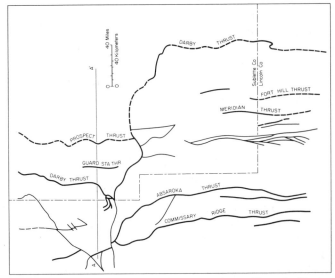

Figure 7: Area of termination of Prospect thrust. Here the Darby swings abruptly eastward in going from north to south, as does, to a lesser extent, the Absaroka thrust. Prospect thrust terminates in the subsurface about 9 km south of its disappearance beneath the Darby plate. Section A-A′ is shown in Fig. 8. After Blackstone, 1979, Plate 1.

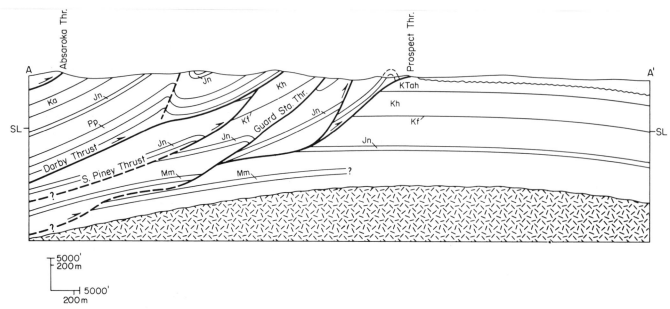

Figure 8: Cross section across the Moxa Arch, after Blackstone, 1979, Plate 5, section B-B'.
Both the Darby and Prospect thrusts ramp to the surface near the crest of the Moxa Arch.
The Fort Hill thrust is only seen in the subsurface. Hatched pattern is basement.
Symbols: Mm, Madison Limestone; Pp, Top of Phosphoria Formation; Jn, Nugget Sandstone; Kf,
Top of first Frontier Sandstone; Kh, Hilliard Shale; KTAH, Tertiary Hoback Formation
and Cretaceous Adaville Formation, undivided; Ka, Aspen Shale.

(Blackstone, 1979, Fig. 4). Finally, the Prospect thrust, a
major thrust which trends along the western flank of
Hoback Basin (Dorr and others, 1977) and then past the
southwestern termination of the Tetons, appears from
beneath the Darby thrust sheet in this locality. Blackstone
(1979) infers that the Prospect thrust's southern termination lies about 9 km south of the east-west trend of the
Darby thrust trace (Fig. 7), although Royse and others
(1975) believe the Prospect thrust surface joins with the
Hogsback thrust. The close association of structural
changes—ramping, shallowing, tearing, and termination—
in one or more thrust sheets is perhaps the most salient aspect of the geology of the central western Wyoming thrust
belt.

The Moxa Arch has been extended to the north by
several workers. By reverse logic, Wach (1977) claims that,
since there are closely spaced thrust ramps just southwest
of the Tetons, this is evidence for the Moxa Arch's presence there. We will interpret this in another way below.
Blackstone (1979) notes that the abrupt swing in the Sheep
Mountain thrust toward the south to the northwest of
Afton, Wyoming, the appearance of a major tear fault
south of this same town, and the offset of the Swan valley
graben to the east of Afton all argue for the northwestern
continuation of the Arch. Royse and others (1975) found
the crest of the Arch seismically, however, about 40 km
east of Afton, though the base of the ramps in the Darby
and Prospect plates lies beneath Afton.

Mechanics

Much of the behavior of the Darby and perhaps the
Absaroka thrusts can be explained by the results of the
photoelastic models described before (Fig. 4). As near La
Barge, the model fault surfaces shallow over the basement
warp and, perhaps, localize there as well. However, since
the Moxa Arch seems to be such a weak stress concentrator, its primary role most likely is that of a fault deflector.
This may explain why no thrusts which are clearly linked
to thrusts to the west are found now on the Wind River
side of the Arch. The position of the Moxa Arch, therefore, explains the ramping of thrusts on the western flank
of the Arch, the shallowing of the Darby to the east, and
the fact that few, if any, thrusts ramp east of its crest.

It is difficult to judge the Arch's effect on other areas.
Until it is found to the northwest of Jackson, it is not
possible to conclusively connect it to structures in the
overlying sedimentary rocks as has been done by Wach
(1977).

Other Basement Highs

The areas to the north and east of the Idaho-
Wyoming thrust belt have had a long history of vertical
motion. Beginning in late Cretaceous, an uplift termed the
Targhee uplift by Love (1973) rose, eroded to basement,

and shed coarse Precambrian gold-bearing quartzite clasts. This uplift existed for 35 million years into the middle Eocene. During this time, a southeastward trending prong known as the ancestral Teton-Gros Ventre uplift also grew along a northeast-dipping reverse fault. The uplift of this area was less than that of the Targhee uplift, not exposing Precambrian basement until the Eocene. Although the western part of the Targhee uplift subsided after mid-Eocene, the Tetons, Gros Ventres, and Wind River Mountains still remain of this area, estimated by Love (1973) to have once exposed 100 mi^2 (about 2590^2) of Precambrian rock to erosion.

These uplifts are, in part, synchronous with events in the thrust belt, and in a few cases they demonstrably affected those events. Dorr and others (1977) show that the Paleocene-Eocene Prospect (= Cliff Creek = Jackson) thrust ran up against a high-angle reverse fault, the Game Hill fault, during the last portion of the former's movement history. Grubbs and Van der Voo (1976), in addition, show that the frontal thrusts of the thrust belt were rotated as they moved into the pocket formed by the uplift of the Gros Ventres along the Cache fault to the north and east and the Game Hill fault to the east. These uplifts acted as buttresses to further motion.

The Targhee uplift was a large, high-standing area during the time that all but the oldest thrusts were moving. The nature of the faults along which uplift took place is not known. However, two largely speculative arguments suggest that the notion that it played a role in localizing thrust ramps is not farfetched. First, the thrust belt is very complicated just to the south and west of the Tetons today. The Prospect, Darby, Absaroka, and perhaps the St. John thrusts pass within 13 km of the southern end of the Tetons (Schroeder, 1969). In addition, this is an area of extreme imbrication, 14 minor splays being mapped in a 1 km traverse south of Teton pass. The rotations found by Grubbs and Van der Voo (1976) are consistent with northeastward motion being inhibited in this region but not to the south, resulting in the counterclockwise rotation seen in the area of Camp Davis. Both the imbrication and rotation could be caused by a buttressing effect.

Reconstructions

The following reconstructions are a schematic representation of how thrust localization and propagation could have taken place in a major thrust belt. They are based on (1) the timing evidence worked out by many people (summarized most recently in Dorr, 1981; Wiltschko and Dorr, in press), (2) the seismically controlled reconstructions of Royse and others (1975), and (3) the results of previous sections. The base is drawn as if present political and geographic boundaries are etched on postthrusting basement. No allowance for body strains has

been made, even though these are in places large (Eastman and Wiltschko, in prep.). Shown at each time are formed ramps, forming ramps, and inferred directions of propagating thrust faults. The latter are highly speculative since no thrust fault to date has been closely dated in more than one place along its length. Therefore, the following reconstruction should be viewed as partially fact and part fantasy to illustrate the propagation ideas developed above.

Meade Thrust Time. (Fig. 9) The Paris thrust had formed by this time, shedding the Ephraim conglomerate of the Gannett group westward (Armstrong and Cressman, 1963) during latest Jurassic and earliest Cretaceous. Nothing is known of the Paris thrust's three-dimensional origin, so we have shown it as formed. The Meade followed the Paris and is dated with the Crawford as mid-late Cretaceous. Perhaps also at this time the Absaroka had begun to propagate away from a hypothetical break point at the base of the Targhee uplift. The only dates for the Absaroka are further south (Fig. 3).

Absaroka Time. (Fig. 10) The Absaroka thrust must have reached the vicinity of Ryckman Creek by about Santonian where the Little Muddy Creek conglomerate

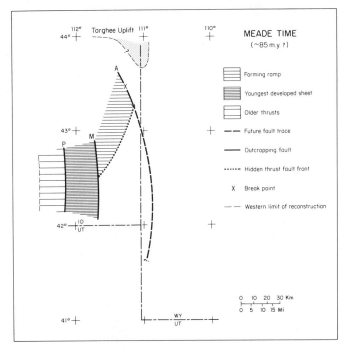

Figure 9: Evolution of the Idaho-Wyoming thrust belt: Time of major motion on the Meade thrust. Shown are older, formed thrust ramps (Older thrusts), the ramps currently most active (Youngest developed sheet), and forming ramps (Forming ramp). Lines labeled "hidden thrust fault front" are buried propagating thrust faults; these are propagating along strike as well as ramping toward the surface. Break points are highly speculative locations where the thrust fault may have first broken through the section. Symbols: P, Paris Willard thrust system; M, Meade thrust; A, Absaroka thrust. Locations of thrusts are restored using the reconstruction of Royse and others, 1975. Base is present political boundaries.

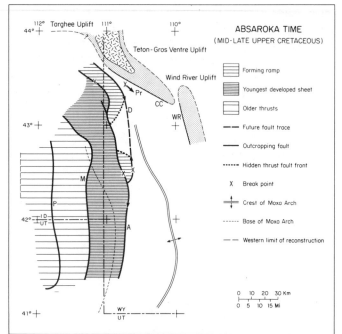

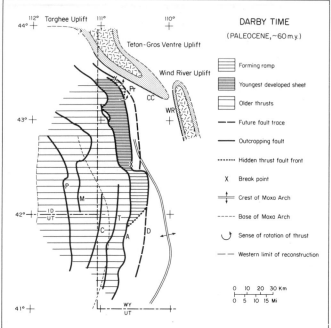

Figure 10: Evolution of the Idaho-Wyoming thrust belt: Time of major motion of the Absaroka thrust. By this time the Moxa Arch had largely formed, the Targhee Uplift-Ancestral Teton-Gros Ventre Uplift were well developed, and motion on the Wind River fault had commenced. Symbols as before plus: D, Darby thrust; Pr, Prospect; CC, Cache Creek fault; WR, Wind River fault. The Prospect may have started to develop at this time.

Figure 11: Evolution of the Idaho-Wyoming thrust belt: Time of major motion on the Darby thrust. During this time the Darby had ramped over the Moxa Arch, and the Prospect was about to move into the area where it has been dated (see Fig. 3). In addition, rotation of thrusts such as the Darby and possibly the Prospect is taking place next to the foreland uplifts to the northeast. See Figs. 9 and 10 for symbols.

was shed during an episode of early minor movement (Royse and others, 1975). The Paris and Meade thrusts were carried along as also was another undated thrust, the Tunp. At this time we speculate that the Darby broke in the vicinity of the Targhee uplift and perhaps also near the crest of the Moxa Arch. These two areas joined at the later time.

Darby Time. (Fig. 11) The only date on the Darby thrust comes from Hogsback Ridge nearly due west of La Barge, Wyoming. We have two previous segments joined and the thrust propagating southward past Hogsback Ridge at this time. Rotation of the Darby near Hoback canyon, as well as initial formation of the Prospect thrust, has started next to the Targhee uplift. The Prospect's future location is controlled by the configuration of the Moxa Arch, which is well developed by this time. Imbrication of the Darby plate is taking place as it runs into the Targhee uplift.

Prospect Time. (Fig. 12) The Targhee uplift, still a high area during the Paleocene-Eocene transition, continues to cause rotations of those thrusts near it. The Game Hill fault has formed, acting as a buttress to the eastward moving Prospect thrust and causing rotation of the rocks caught in the pocket between the Gros Ventres uplift and the Game Hill fault. The Prospect has propa-

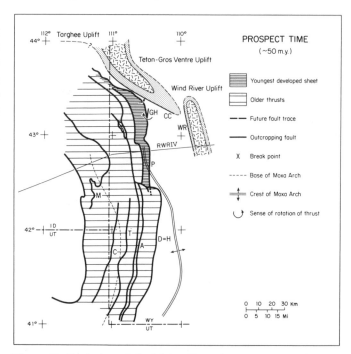

Figure 12: Evolution of the Idaho-Wyoming thrust belt: Time of major motion of the Prospect thrust. The Game Hill fault (GH) acts as a buttress which further rotates Prospect thrust. Rotations from Grubbs and Van der Voo, 1976. RWRIV is section line from Royse and others, 1975, Plate IV.

gated down into the La Barge area but has not cut up through the Darby plate in this interpretation.

Later Events. As described before, the Targhee uplift subsided in mid-Eocene, and the Teton uplift developed to its present spectacular topography in Pliocene-Pleistocene. The Teton fault is currently active.

ACKNOWLEDGEMENTS

The funding of the photoelastic lab was assembled from several sources. Major support came from the University of Michigan: The F. Scott Turner Bequest, Rackham Faculty Research grant, and a Preliminary Research grant from the Division of Research Development and Administration. Supplementary funds for the polariscope and other expenses were supported through the National Science Foundation grant EAR-7815477. It is a pleasure to thank these agencies and their respective officers for support.

Some of the initial ideas for this project were refined through correspondence with Ralph Kehle. We thank him for his patient help. Bill Rizer of Cities Service provided much initial help in setting up the photoelastic lab. Discussions with Rich Fortmann of Champlin Oil helped clarify the regional relations of the Moxa Arch. Craig Johnson helped supervise the construction of the loading apparatus, and Derwin Bell drafted the figures.

APPENDIX

Assumptions

In order to apply the photoelastic results to the field, it is necessary to know what is being modeled and what is not. The models were cut from ¼" (6.3 mm) photoelastic plastic and confined between two effectively rigid plates when deformed and analyzed so we are investigating what happens in a cross section under plane strain conditions; by implication, we can model only those real situations deformed in plane strain as well. Since the sheets are, in addition, homogeneous, it is not possible to investigate the role of layering. Finally, since the strength to weight ratio of these materials is large, gravity is not scaled either. What *is* being modeled, then, are the stresses which result from the geometries of interest, and they may be applied to the field both if these geometries are correctly inferred from the subsurface and if the rheology is significantly elastic over the fracture (as opposed to motion) portion of the structure's history.

Procedures

The photoelastic models used in our experiments were constructed in two ways: either by machining ¼" plexiglass and PSM-1 (from Photolastic Corp.) model plastic or by casting photoelastic liquid plastic type PLM-9 from Photolastic Corp. These specific plastics were chosen to provide a balance between the proper strength difference necessary to model basement sediment interaction and ease of machining.

Moxa Arch. The Moxa Arch model was created by casting. A piece of plexiglass roughly 1¼" x 7" was cut on a high speed vertical mill into a curved shape similar to that of the Moxa Arch. A mold was then fashioned using the cut piece of plexiglass as the template. Glass covered with mineral oil to prevent liquid plastic adhesion was clamped to the plexiglass, and clay was used to seal either end of the model. PLM-9 resin and hardener were then mixed following the directions of Photolastic Inc. Bulletin 1-205A.

Care must be taken not to introduce bubbles during the mixing and pouring processes. This can be minimized by preheating the mold to the temperature of the liquid plastic on pouring (49°C). The mixed PLM-9 is poured into the open end of the mold very slowly. It is almost impossible to totally avoid introducing bubbles, but it was found that, as long as they were relatively small and away from the interface, no stress concentration was created.

After hardening for two days, the two pieces were removed and machined on a mill so that the fitted model's exterior edges are square.

Basement Fault Models. Construction of the basement fault models was done using PSM-1 plastic sheets. Because PSM-1 is softer than plexiglass, it must be handled much more carefully. A nick or dent on any surface will act as a stress concentrator. Since the basement fault models involve only straight edges, they need only to be cut out and milled. Small edge effects, permanent strain, may appear after the milling process if the operator is too eager or uses a dull mill. These will usually disappear after several hours due to the plastic's viscoelastic memory properties, or they may be filed away. It is best, however, to always cut with a sharp end-mill, trying to remove less than 0.02" (0.5 mm) at a pass.

It is important that the two pieces of the model fit as perfectly as possible so that stress concentrations are not introduced. This was accomplished by cutting each model in four pieces; two 2" x 7" (5 x 13 cm) rectangles, one each of PSM-1 and plexiglass, and two trapezoids one inch wide, again one each of PSM-1 and plexiglass, but with shape dependent on the given model. After all of these pieces have been cut out, they are fitted together, and the model's exterior edges are squared on the mill. The two trapezoids were glued to the larger rectangule of the same plastic using a glue with the same strength as PSM-1. Once the models had been machined and glued, the edges and interfaces were carefully sanded to remove any larger nicks or burrs that may have been created. Sanding must be kept to a minimum, though, because sanding too long may cause an imperfect fit between the two plastics and, therefore, result in unwanted stress concentrations on the interfaces.

The model was analyzed in a transparent biaxial loading device consisting of two ½" x 8" x 12" (1.3 x 20.3 x 30.5 cm) plexiglass plates, bolted on two long sides and one short side to 9/32" thick and 1" (2.5 cm) wide steel plates. The viewing area is approximately 7" x 11" (17.8 x 27.9 cm). Provision was made for applying pressure to the top and bottom of models through two ¼" x 1" x 7½" (0.6 x 2.5 x 17.1 cm) steel plates inside the loading box and connecting by thumb screws to the steel plates sandwiched between the plexiglass windows.

In preparation for loading, thin rubber strips were placed on all outer edges of the model, further insuring that no stress concentrations are created by surface irregularities either in the plastic or the steel plates on the end, top, and bottom of the model when it is loaded up. With the top and bottom (the long dimension) confined with the internal steel plates, but not under pressure, the models were loaded on the free end with a plunger. The

190

D. Wiltschko and D. Eastman

plunger is connected to a large screw press built into the straining frame of the polariscope on which the loading box is resting. Our polariscope is a Photolastic Model 061 12" (30.5 cm) machine with diffused white light source. Each model was analyzed using standard photoelastic techniques.

REFERENCES CITED

Armstrong, F. C., and Cressman, E. R., 1963, The Bannock thrust zone, southeastern Idaho: U.S. Geol. Surv. Prof. Paper 374-J.

Blackstone, D. L., Jr., 1979, Geometry of the Prospect-Darby and La Barge faults at their junction with the La Barge Platform, Lincoln and Sublette Counties, Wyoming: Geol. Surv. Wyoming Rept. Inv. 18, 34 p.

Blackstone, D. L., Jr., 1980, Tectonic map of the overthrust belt, western Wyoming, southeastern Idaho, and northeastern Utah: Geol. Surv. of Wyoming.

Dahlstrom, C.D.A., 1970, Structural geology in the eastern margin of the Canadian Rocky Mountains: Bull. Can. Petrol. Geol., v. 18, p. 332–406.

Dally, J. W., and Riley, W. F., 1978, Experimental stress analysis: New York: McGraw-Hill, 571 pp.

Dixon, J., in press, Regional structural synthesis, Wyoming salient of Western overthrust belt: Amer. Assoc. Petroleum Geol. Bull., v. 66, p. 1560–1580.

Dorr, J. A., Jr., 1981, Timing of tectonic activity in the overthrust belt, western Wyoming and southeastern Idaho: Second Wyoming Conference, Univ. of Wyoming, Laramie, WY.

Dorr, J. A., Jr., and Gingerich, P. D., 1980, Early Cenozoic mammalian paleontology, geologic structure, and tectonic history in the overthrust belt near La Barge, western Wyoming: Contr. Geol., Univ. of Wyoming, v. 18, p. 101–115.

Dorr, J. A., Jr., Spearing, D. R., and Steidtmann, J. R., 1977, Deformation and deposition between a foreland uplift and an impinging thrust belt, Hoback Basin, Wyoming: Geol. Soc. America Spec. Pap. 177, 82 pp.

Dorr, J. A., Jr., and Wiltschko, D. V., in press, Mechanical evolution of the Idaho-Wyoming thrust belt, Amer. Assoc. Petrol. Geol. Bull.

Eastman, D. B., and Wiltschko, D. V., ms., Rock response to thrusting in the northern portion of the Western Overthrust Belt, western Wyoming.

Frocht, M. M., 1962, Photoelasticity, Vol. I: New York: John Wiley and Sons, 411 pp.

Gallagher, J. J., Friedman, M., Handin, J., and Sowers, G. M., 1974, Experimental studies relating to microfracture in sandstone: Tecton, v. 21, p. 203–247.

Gallagher, J. J., and Rizer, W. D., 1977, Photoelastic model studies of thrust fault initiation: Wyoming Geol. Assoc. Guidebook, 29th Annual Field Conf., p. 441–448.

Gardner, D.A.C., and Spang, J. H., 1973, Model studies of the displacement transfer associated with overthrust faulting: Bull. Can. Petrol. Geol., v. 21, p. 534–552.

Grubbs, K. L., and Van der Voo, R., 1976, Structural deformation of the Idaho-Wyoming overthrust belt (U.S.A.), as determined by Triassic paleomagnetism: Tecton., v. 33, p. 321–336.

Hafner, W., 1951, Stress distributions and faulting: Geol. Soc. America Bull., v. 62, p. 373–398.

Harris, L. D., 1970, Details of thin-skinned tectonics in parts of Valley and Ridge and Cumberland Plateau provinces of the southern Appalachians: in Fisher et al., eds., Studies in Appalachians' geology-central and southern: New York, Interscience, p. 161–173.

Harris, L. D., and Milici, R. C., 1977, Characteristics of thin-skinned

style of deformation in the southern Appalachians, and potential hydrocarbon traps: U.S. Geol. Surv. Prof. Pap. 1018, 40 pp.

Hubbert, M. K., 1937, Theory of scale models as applied to the study of geologic structures: Geol. Soc. America Bull., v. 48, p. 1459–1520.

Hubbert, M. K., 1951, Mechanical basis for certain familiar geologic structures: Geol. Soc. America Bull., v. 62, p. 355–372.

Jacobeen, F., Jr., and Kanes, W. H., 1974, Structure of the Broadtop synclinorium and its implications for Appalachian structural style: Amer. Assoc. Petrol. Geol. Bull., v. 58, p. 362–375.

Jacobeen, F., Jr., and Kanes, W. H., 1975, Structure of the Broadtop synclinorium, Wills Mountain anticlinorium, and Allegheny frontal zone: Amer. Assoc. Petrol. Geol. Bull., v. 59, p. 1136–1150.

Love, J. D., 1973, Harebell Formation (Upper Cretaceous) and Pinyon Conglomerate (uppermost Cretaceous and Paleocene), northwestern Wyoming: U.S. Geol. Surv. Prof. Pap. 734-A, 54 pp.

Miller, R. L., 1973, Where and why of Pine Mountain and other major fault planes, Va., Ky., and Tenn.: Amer. J. Sci., v. 273-A, p. 353–371.

Miller, R. L., and Fuller, J. O., 1954, Geology and oil resources of the Rose Hill district—the fenster area of the Cumberland overthrust block—Lee County, Virginia: Va. Geol. Surv. Bull., v. 71, 383 pp.

Roberts, D. G., 1974, Structural development of the British Isles, the continental margin, and the Rockall Plateau, in Burk, C. A., and Drake, C. L., eds., The geology of continental margins: New York, Springer-Verlag, p. 343–359.

Rodgers, D. A., and Rizer, W. D., 1980, Deformation and secondary faulting near the leading edge of a thrust fault, in McClay, K. R., and Price, N. J., eds., Thrust and nappe tectonics: Oxford, Blackwell Scientific Publications, Ltd., p. 65–77.

Royse, F., Jr., Warner, M. A., and Reese, D. L., 1975, Thrust belt structural geometry and related stratigraphic problems, Wyoming-Idaho-Northern Utah, in Boyland, D. W., ed., Deep drilling frontiers of the central Rocky Mountains: Denver, Rocky Mountain Assoc. Geologists, p. 41–54.

Rubey, W. W., 1973, Geologic map of the Afton Quadrangle and part of the Big Piney Quadrangle, Lincoln and Sublette Counties, Wyoming: U.S. Geol. Surv. Misc. Geol. Inv. Map I-686.

Rubey, W. W., Oriel, S. S., Tracey, J. I., Jr., 1980, Geologic map and structure sections of the Cokeville 30-minute quadrangle, Lincoln and Sublette Counties, Wyoming: U.S. Geol. Surv. Misc. Inv. Map I-1129.

Sanford, A. R., 1959, Analytical and experimental study of simple geological structures: Geol. Soc. America Bull., v. 70, p. 19–52.

Schedl, A., and Wiltschko, D. V., 1980, Isostatic effects of a moving thrust sheet: EOS, v. 61, p. 360.

Schroeder, M. L., 1969, Geologic maps of the Teton Pass Quadrangle, Teton County, Wyoming: U.S. Geol. Surv. Map GQ-793.

Sheridan, R. F., 1974, Atlantic continental margin of North America, in The geology of continental margins: New York, Springer-Verlag, p. 391–407.

Sutton, S. J., and Wiltschko, D. V., 1982, Deformation by overburden of a coarse quartzite conglomerate: J. Geol., v. 90, p. 725–733.

Thomas, W. A., in review, Synsedimentary structures in the Appalachian fold and thrust belt: Lowry Volume, Virginia Polytechnic Institute & State College.

Wach, P. H, 1977, The Moxa Arch an overthrust model?: Wyoming Geol. Assoc. Guidebook, 29th Annual Field Conf., p. 651–664.

Wiltschko, D. V., and Chapple, W. M., 1977, Flow of weak rocks in Appalachian Plateau folds: Amer. Assoc. Petrol. Geol. Bull., v. 61, p. 653–670.

Printed in U.S.A.

Geological Society of America
Memoir 158
1983

Detachment, shear, and compression in the central Alps

H. P. Laubscher

Geologisch-Palaeontologisches Institut der Universität Basel
Bernoullistrasse 32
Basel CH-4056
Switzerland

ABSTRACT

Alpine cover nappes are usually characterized by both folding and stretching, suggesting simple shear between two comparatively rigid plates: subducted basement below and an "orogenic lid" above with its frontal wedges. The lid consists of thrust masses piled up in earlier stages which, being cooler and stronger due to previous deformation, constitute a comparatively rigid body. Basement nappes are formed in a variety of modes. They may emerge as steeply dipping lobes into the shear zone and there flatten out; in this case, they develop from highly "viscous" masses at elevated temperature in a sort of distributed ramp under oblique compression. In other cases, they are sheared off from their crustal underpinnings and move as rigid bodies: a famous example is the Austroalpine Silvretta nappe. At its base, widespread mylonites are in some places interrupted by pseudotachylites. These are interpreted as due to stress concentration followed by explosive failure in patches that resisted creep. In the Early Tertiary, nappes generally moved north with respect to Europe, but at a late stage there was considerable backflow toward Africa. This may be due to arrival of the North Penninic subplate boundary in the subduction zone.

INTRODUCTION

The widely accepted convection model of plate tectonics implies a balance of material moving down and material moving up in the earth's gravity field. The geologist is mostly concerned with those near-surface aspects of the system visible in plate boundary zones. A sub-system with material balance problems of its own here plays a dominant role. Along divergent plate boundaries, near-surface masses move down on normal faults, while deep-seated masses move up to fill the developing gap. The two oppositely moving masses must be separated by a zone of disharmony, of detachment, and this is generally depicted as the sole for listric faults (for a review, see Bally and others, 1981). In convergent boundary zones, on the contrary, shallow masses move up to form the nappes, thrust sheets, and folds of Alpine type mountain ranges, whereas the more deep-seated masses move down—they are subducted. Again, there is a zone of disharmony, of detachment, between them, and it is this zone of detachment that

is the focus of this article. I shall first present some concepts useful for the examination of the problem, and then apply them to the analysis of a number of structures in the Alps.

THE OROGENIC LID AND ITS FRONTAL WEDGE (Fig. 1)

In the Alps, the obliquely convergent Africa-Europa plate boundary seems to have been under compression throughout the Tertiary. When the general situation is considered (Fig. 1; compare Laubscher, 1978), it may be concluded that the cool shallow masses consisting of all the tectonic slivers that have been detached from the subducted lithosphere act as a stress guide transmitting compression between the converging plates, much more so than the hot masses below, particularly more so than those in amphibolite facies conditions and hotter. The cool stress guide, or "orogenic lid", as it is a sort of lid on

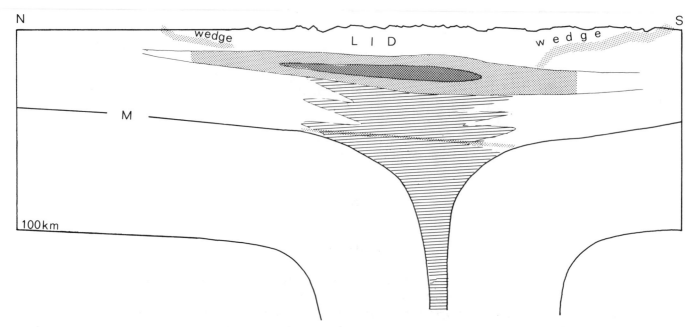

Figure 1: The lid of the continental collision zone (orogen) and its frontal wedges. This generalized cross-section is based on Angenheister and others (1972), Miller and others (1982), Panza and Müller (1979), and Panza and others (1980). Essential points are (1) the presence of velocity inversions, particularly a low velocity channel (shaded; dark shading with v_p less than 5.6 km/sec), and (2) two subducted slabs with possibly in between a funnel of detached middle and lower crustal material (ruled) that ordinarily does not enter the nappe edifice of the Alps (compare Laubscher, 1970, 1977). Usually the M-discontinuity of the two plates is shown as connected across these sub-lid masses (stippled band), but this connection can hardly be a crust-mantle boundary in the ordinary sense. All these sub-lid masses are believed to be mechanically weak, as evidenced by their observable fossil counterparts. The subducted slabs are possibly not in contact, in which case they would not act as a stress guide between the converging plates. Such decoupling of plates is evident in some arc-back-arc basin complexes such as the Aegean, where the hinge of the subducted African plate apparently moves away from Europe considerably faster than the African plate converges with it (Le Pichon and Angelier, 1979). The most effective stress guide of the system as shown is the lid. As plate convergence continues it will be stressed beyond its strength; experience shows that it gives way mostly at the frontal wedges (N or S) where composite shear zones (shear-induced folds, thrusts, decollements) develop. It is observations from the lower parts of such wedges this article is concerned with.

a cooking pot, is separated from the subducted material by a detachment zone that becomes more clearly defined as it approaches the foreland where it emerges at the surface. This frontal part of the orogenic lid has the shape of a wedge (frontal wedge). As a rule, the front of the lid is the place where material is scraped off the subducted lithosphere, or where "flaking" takes place, a process permitting obduction (Oxburgh, 1972; see also Laubscher, 1970, and Armstrong and Dick, 1974). However, the lid may sometimes be deformed behind instead of at its frontal parts, or on one side the wedge may be inactivated while its counterpart facing the other plate accommodates the whole plate convergence. A scenario for such developments may occur when pre-existing obstacles and irregularities, such as fracture zones or mountain ranges, move from the foreland into the subduction zone. Accumulation of mobile sub-lid masses by continued plate convergence

will superpose isostatic uplift of the lid; its upper parts will be eroded, and a corresponding portion of the hot underlying mass will cool and be incorporated into the lid; e.g., the Lepontine nappes of the central Alps, which underwent amphibolite facies metamorphism in the Paleogene, are now part of the orogenic lid after an uplift of perhaps 20 km and the corresponding erosion. In the following sections, some examples will be presented that document the sort of processes taking place at the base of the orogenic lid and its frontal wedge.

EXAMPLES FROM THE ALPS

Depending on various parameters, and particularly on the distribution of rock types and temperature, the detachment zone may assume different forms. Two contrasting examples will be discussed. The first is the Doldenhorn

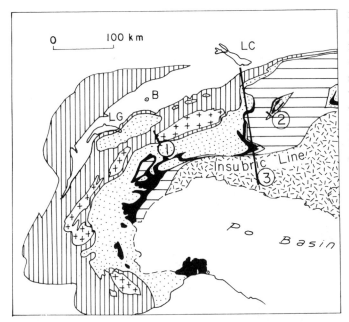

Figure 2: Location map showing the areas (cross-sections) discussed (numbers in circles): 1—Doldenhorn nappe complex, 2—Base of Silvretta nappe, Val Tasna, Lower Engadine, 3—Cross-section Fig. 16. The very generalized tectonic units are: vertically ruled—Helvetic and Ultra-Helvetic nappes and Jura; crosses—external crystalline massifs; dotted—Penninic nappes; black—ophiolite nappe; horizontally ruled—Austroalpine nappes; random dashes—southern Alps. LG = Lake Geneva, LC = Lake Constance, B = Berne.

nappe system, which illustrates detachment dominated by distributed shear, albeit with discontinuities and steep shearing gradients in places. The second is the Silvretta nappe, which has a very sharp lower boundary overlying a number of smaller nappes that were sheared off, dilacerated and dismembered, refolded, backfolded, and quite generally badly messed up; surprisingly, there seem to be vestiges of initial phases of intracrustal detachment that survived all this. While as a rule only large-scale aspects are discussed, these relict structures, as well as other information on the processes of detachment, require attention to smaller-scale phenomena.

The Doldenhorn nappe system

Two cross-sections through the Doldenhorn nappe complex by Lugeon (1914) are shown in Fig. 3. Exposures here are so good that a minimum of extrapolation and projection is necessary. These sections have been improved by later workers, e.g., Schläppi (1980) and Masson and others (1980), but the essence remains unchanged. Both the basement and the Mesozoic-Tertiary sediments have been deformed but with extreme disharmony. The frontal part of the nappe is a recumbent fold composed of a pile of smaller recumbent folds that, according to Schläppi (1980; see also his contribution in Laubscher and Ber-

noulli, 1980), are accentuated by thrusts. The inverse limb of the main recumbent fold consists of a marble which is a recrystallized mylonite of Upper Jurassic limestone. It lies on pre-Mesozoic basement and the basal Triassic sandstones, both of which are but little affected by tectonization. The entire rest of the original cover, depositional and tectonic, probably 10-15 km before nappe emplacement, is missing. This cannot be due to erosion, as the emplacement of the nappe took place under lower greenschist conditions. One is forced to accept the notion that the original cover was pushed away during nappe emplacement and was substituted by the nappe and its overlying orogenic lid ("substitution of cover" of Ellenberger, 1958). In the rear part of the nappe, the sediments, though intensely folded, are in an upright position again, and there is no inverse limb of mylonitic Upper Jurassic: the sediments are apparently "autochthonous", in stratigraphic continuity on top of the Variscan basement of the Aar massif, itself traditionally labeled "autochthonous". This basement, however, is severely tectonized and deformed into lobes, more rarely into thin slivers. An exploration of the dynamics and kinematics of Doldenhorn nappe development is attempted by means of the schematic Figures 4-6. Deformation apparently took place about 10 my ago at 300°-400°C (Frank and Stettler, 1979). The impression is that it affected a sequence with variable "viscosity". This term, of course, is but a collective description of all the individual mineral deformation mechanisms that contribute to the overall rheology of a rock. The viscosity of shales and fine-grained limestones was particularly low: the fine grain-size accelerates grain boundary processes such as pressure solution. Dolomites were very strong and commonly formed boudins. The basement lobes evoke the picture of a highly viscous material. Deformation here is apparently due to a variety of processes (Voll, 1980). The quartz is the weakest member and is subject to dislocation glide, the development of subgrains, deformation bands, deformation lamellae, Böhm lamellae, and pressure solution. The reduction of grain size again assists grain boundary processes, and grain size reduction is enhanced by cataclastic disintegration of feldspars and other minerals. Grain boundary migration and recrystallization gain in importance as temperature increases.

Figure 3 (see also the simplified Fig. 6) suggests an overall scenario in which these deformations took place. Between the orogenic lid and the highly viscous basement, the sediments were caught in a situation approximating simple shear. The basement itself, being less simply layered, and with a south-north viscosity gradient due to temperature variation and variations of weakening by grain-size reduction, is affected more by horizontal compression between the rigid foreland and high viscosity masses pushing from the rear. However, the steep lobes tend to flatten upward and merge into the simple shear

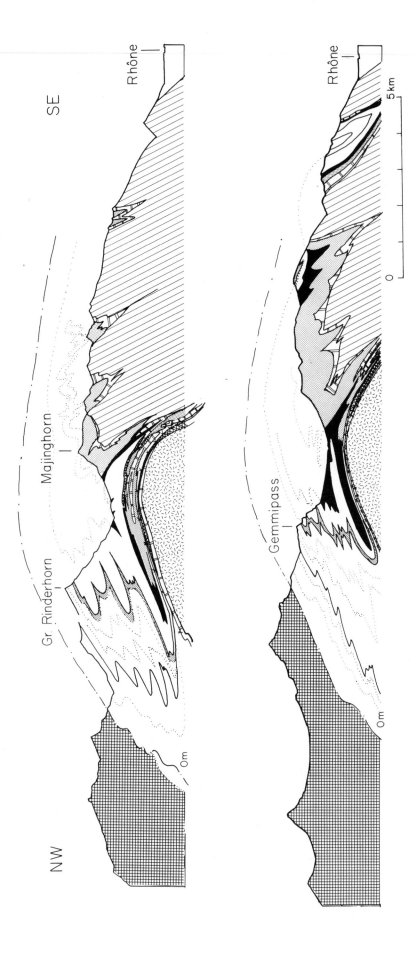

Figure 3: The Doldenhorn nappe complex, after Lugeon (1914), slightly simplified. Although there are a number of modern reinvestigations, the essential picture has not been changed. This classical representation documents the reliability of tectonic notions in this area. Cross-ruled—higher Helvetic nappes; dotted band—base of Upper Jurassic; black—Aalenian shales; shaded—Lower Jurassic; band with double lines—Triassic; irregular dashes—Gastern massif; obliquely ruled—basement lobes of the Aar massif; cross-hatched—thin basement slivers; crosses—base of the stretched and mylonitic inverse limb of the Doldenhorn nappe.

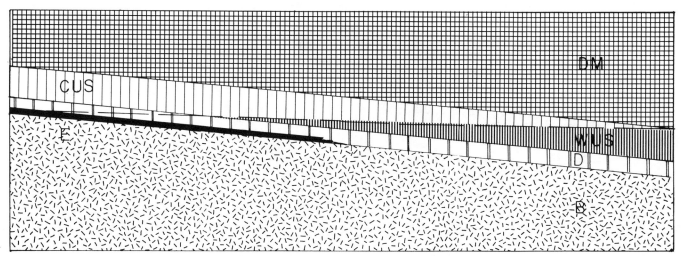

Figure 4: The distribution of material properties in the Helvetic nappe complex, at the beginning of Doldenhorn development. The present distribution of metamorphism shows greenschist facies for most of the Doldenhorn nappe with probable T of 300° to 400°C, increasing from front to rear (compare Frey and others, 1980; Masson and others, 1980, Fig. 10). These temperatures seem to correspond to those at the time of intensive deformation 10 my ago and probably imply an overburden ("orogenic lid") of 10-15 km. This "orogenic lid" consisted of fold and thrust masses of earlier phases. Inasmuch as they became progressively cooler upward, they also became more competent. Even those masses immediately overlying the Doldenhorn sediments, though comparatively warm, probably were stronger because planar layering had been destroyed. Although this is a gross oversimplification, the orogenic lid is represented in Figs. 3-5 as an essentially stiff board that undergoes gentle bending but is otherwise undeformed. For simplification, isotherms are assumed to be horizontal and to divide sharply the undeformed sediments (vertically ruled) between the basement (random dashes, B) and the deformed masses (DM) in the orogenic lid (cross-ruled) into a warm (narrow ruling = warm undeformed sediments = WUS) ductile and a cool (wide ruling = cool undeformed sediments = CUS) competent part. Band with double lines are competent beds, particularly dolomites (D); black are evaporites (E; very weak). Not to scale.

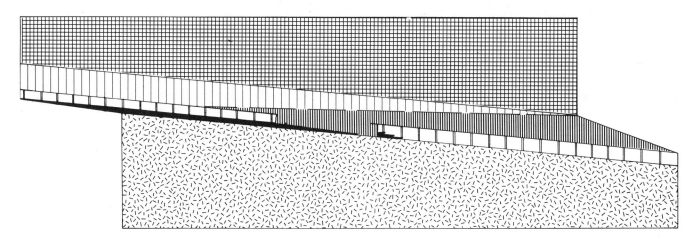

Figure 5: Simple shear displacement of the orogenic lid with respect to autochthonous basement. The interlayer between the two rigid masses consists of rheologically heterogeneous material (symbols and distribution as in Fig. 3). There is a downstep of the detachment level at the beginning of the evaporites, with a pull-apart (boudinage) of the competent rocks (dolomites). The gap is filled by flow of the incompetent rocks.

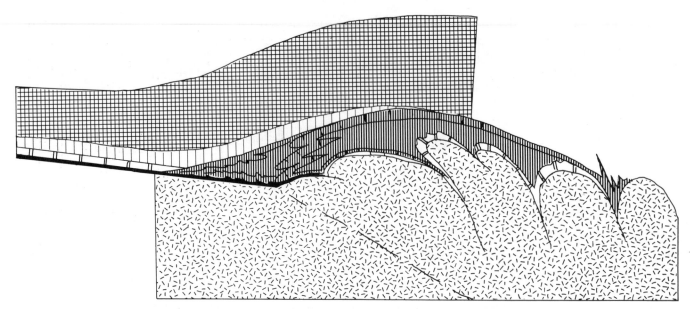

Figure 6: Diffuse ramping and squeezing in the southern, warmer part of the basement in addition to the quasi-simple shear of Fig. 4. The result resembles Fig. 2 and is a simplified version of the Doldenhorn nappe system. It leaves out such features as the thin basement slivers, apparently due to shear, as seen in Fig. 2, and internal deformation of the lid. This two-dimensional picture does not take into account three-dimensional aspects such as an important zone of distributed dextral shear beginning at the right end of the figure and extending to the south (Dolivo, 1980; Steck, 1980) and a possibly complementary zone of distributed sinistral shear in the Lötschenpass area (Schläppi, 1980). On the left side, the detachment plane must ramp somewhere to the surface.

regime of the sediments. The different modes of deformation are active simultaneously, with the more viscous basement lagging behind. Note that this situation does not require large basement thrusts: its ductile behavior sharply contrasts with such structures as the Wind River thrust (Smithson and others, 1978) or the Silvretta nappe (p. 8).

The development of the Doldenhorn nappe complex according to this scenario may be depicted schematically as shown in Figs. 4 to 6. A strong upper plate, the lid, is displaced to the north (left) by plate convergence with respect to a strong lower plate that is rigid in the north and highly viscous in the south. The sheared interval is heterogeneous and consists of the weak intervals WUS and E and the strong interval D. The situation that develops may be likened to boudinage which is typical for the dolomites: they break where the yielding zones WUS and E overlap. The frontal segment of D with its cover moves away to the north on the extremely weak evaporites, and the pull-apart gap is filled from above by the yielding masses WUS similarly to what happens on a smaller scale in boudinage. Generally, the break will not be as clean as shown, and a number of dolomite fragments will be left in the gap, as actually observed below the Doldenhorn nappe. Somewhere in the north (not shown in the figure), the shear zone must ramp and emerge at the surface. This could have happened in various places, e.g., in the Jura mountains (Laubscher, 1973; Laubscher and Bernoulli, 1980).

In Fig. 6, the situation is developed further to include "highly viscous" basement deformation in the southern, warmer, and more highly stressed part, and some details of deformation within the WUS zone. Basement deformation is represented as a sort of diffuse ramp with a considerable component of subhorizontal compression—the situation of squeezing between vise rather than the simple shear situation in the sediments—in accordance with the scenario sketched above. This figure already bears a reasonable resemblance to Fig. 3. It pinpoints some important particulars typical for many Alpine structures:

1. In the shear zone, accumulation of matter in local sinks (imbrication, folding: particularly the frontal folds of the Doldenhorn nappe) and stretching, moving away of matter from local sources as indicated by stretching lineations perpendicular to the strike of the nappe (Schläppi, 1980; Steck, 1980) and missing members of the original stratigraphic sequence, particularly in the southern domain, both occur together and are complementary; the Doldenhorn nappe has many elements of a shear-produced fold such as the experimental sheath folds of Cobbold and Quinquis (1980). The stretching is not a reliable symptom either of gravity sliding or of gravity spreading.

2. The structures of the different parts of the nappe are strongly dependent on the boundary conditions imposed by the whole shear system of the orogenic lid. These, in turn, are dependent on the initial conditions and

evolve in time: the boudinage gap in the north, essential for the formation of the frontal part of the fold, developed from the initial distribution of material properties.

3. Substitution of the original sedimentary cover by allochthonous masses is one of the important local or regional source-sink couples: the "boudin gap" is, at the same time, the source for material transport in the direction of lid movement and the sink for the substituting material.

To summarize, the Doldenhorn nappe was not an independently moving unit but rather a part of the shear zone at the base of the orogenic lid.

THE SILVRETTA NAPPE

An entirely different story is exhibited by the Austroalpine Silvretta nappe (Fig. 9). Its base and the underlying masses are being studied by my colleagues and myself in Val Tasna (see Fig. 2).

Though much that is new has been learned since the studies by Streckeisen (1928), Bearth (1932), Spaenhauer (1932), and Wenk (1934) of the crystalline part of the nappe in Switzerland, their work and that of Cadisch on the sediments (Cadisch and others, 1941, 1968) is still useful for a general introduction to the problem. Figure 8 is from Cadisch and others (1941), somewhat modified as sequences once considered in stratigraphic continuity have since been recognized as imbricated, folded, and refolded tectonic slivers or parts of nappes (Gürler, 1982). Of central importance for the theme of this article is the tectonic disharmony between the Silvretta nappe and the underlying units: over large distances, the contact is very sharp—see Figs. 9 and 10—although locally it may be somewhat faulted and imbricated, and it has been deformed into gentle folds of a few km wavelength. The Silvretta basement nappe here consists of amphibolites and gneisses and owes its internal structure to Paleozoic deformation under amphibolite facies conditions (for a review, see Scharbert and Schönlaub, 1980). During Alpine orogeny, it was deformed in the brittle field by discrete shear surfaces and fractures and, of particular importance, by the development of an extensive network of pseudotachylite veins (Hammer, 1930; Bearth, 1933; Masch, 1974) of possibly Middle to Late Cretaceous age (Thöni, 1981). In other areas there is widespread mylonitization (Streckeisen, 1928; Bearth, 1932; Wenk, 1934), and this has been dated as Middle Cretaceous farther east (Thöni, 1980).

Many aspects of the Silvretta nappe resemble the Blue Ridge thrust mass in the southern Appalachians (Cook and others, 1979), particularly in its being bounded by a sharp thrust and in its lack of internal deformation related to the thrusts that bound it. Interestingly, the sediments underlying it, though badly deformed, often show a tendency to arrange themselves subparallel to the thrust.

One can but wonder what kind of reflections would result on a COCORP profile.

The units underlying the Silvretta nappe consist mostly of slices of sedimentary cover from a variety of paleogeographic affinities, ranging to the Eocene (Rudolph, 1982), thus dating the emplacement of the nappe as Tertiary. In addition, there is a train of thin rolled out ophiolites and associated deep-sea sediments, and the complexly imbricated and multiply folded continental basement part of the Tasna nappe. At a late stage, these early north-vergent sub-Silvretta slices were folded back with a southeastern to southwestern vergence (Gürler, 1982).

The partial problems to be discussed in this section are: (1) How did the Silvretta basement get detached as an upward moving mass from its downward moving substrate in the Cretaceous? (2) How did its Tertiary movement as part of an orogenic lid interact with the underlying sequences?

Detachment of the Silvretta nappe from its original substrate

The Silvretta nappe acquired its present shape and large-scale features mostly during the Tertiary; however, documents of original detachment may still be found in some relict structures, including small-scale features, that survived subsequent motions over great distances; there are reasons to believe that the extensive network of mylonites and pseudotachylites are such relict structures (Thöni, 1981). They deserve particular attention as practically nothing is known about the processes of initial intracrustal detachment, in spite of its fundamental importance in collision tectonics. For this reason, some new information on the pseudotachylites that abound in the area is presented, although it is still incomplete.

The Silvretta-Oetztal nappe in western Austria and adjacent Switzerland underwent Mid-Cretaceous greenschist facies metamorphism, including the mylonites at its base (Thöni, 1980, 1981) and the sediments still covering it in a few places. It must have formed at the base of a mid-Cretaceous orogenic lid, under a cover of perhaps 10-15 km, but, considering the large-scale subsequent Africa-Europa movements, at a place very distant from its present position and in a very different tectonic context (Fig. 7; compare Laubscher and Bernoulli, 1982). Metamorphic grade decreases westward where the sediments are only anchimetamorphic (Dunoyer and Bernoulli, 1976). The pseudotachylites in Val Tasna itself have not been dated, but since they are cut off sharply by the basal thrust and are mylonitized in some places near the thrust, they may be assumed of pre-Tertiary origin, and the general scenario makes it likely that they are local deviations from the more widespread Cretaceous mylonites. Recently, Thöni

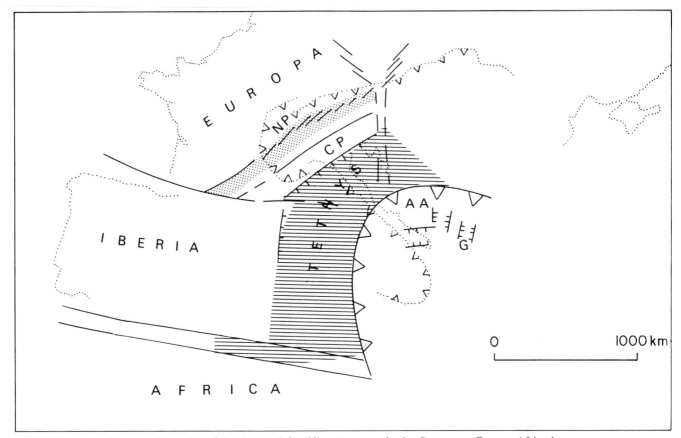

Figure 7: Situation of the Austroalpine Silvretta nappe in the Cretaceous Europa-Africa boundary zone. Dots—coastlines for reference. Dots with triangles—present position of Alpine frontal thrusts. Solid lines—tectonic boundaries in the Late Cretaceous. Iberia has been rotated counterclockwise since the Late Albian along the Pyrenean oblique belt. One branch of this belt joined the North-Penninic fracture zone (NP), whereas the main branch continued directly into Tethys and somehow joined the Austroalpine (AA) subduction zone. G is the Gosau grabens suggestive of Cretaceous back-arc spreading. CP = Central Penninic high zone.

(1981) published some radiometric (K-Ar) information on the age of the neighboring Jamtal pseudotachylites. Apparent ages scatter rather badly, but Thoeni thinks a Mid- to early Late Cretaceous age is most probable.

As a sample of the outcrop-scale geometry of the extensive pseudotachylite complex and their possible significance for the detachment problem, some results of my own field work in the area are presented in Figs. 11-14 (a more extensive study by H. U. Schmutz is nearing completion).

Figure 11 shows the main elements of the vein complex, which at first sight seem absolutely chaotic and provide evidence of order only after repeated attempts at analysis. There are two general dominating trends that cut layering and anastomose and a third important set of veins which parallels layering.

Figures 12-14 show some aspects of their very complex structure; they are sometimes dark colored, sometimes light gray veins of a homogeneous submicroscopically fine-grained material which, because of its isotropic

nature, has been called a pseudotachylite (Shand, 1917), the rheological state of which at the time of vein-filling is still debated (fine-grained, solid material vs molten rock; Hammer, 1930; Bearth, 1933; Sibson, 1975; Masch, 1974; Wenk, 1978). Certainly a large part of it was fragmented host-rock as manifest in many dykes where it varies from submicroscopic up to boulder size fragments of wall material (compare Bearth, 1933). Other parts of the host rock are invaded by an irregular network of ever thinner pseudotachylite veins, leading in many places to complete disintegration into a breccia. Rock fragments and host-rock masses between veins are commonly rotated, implying considerable dilation to provide space for rigid rotation. Dilation, of course, is also implied by the veins themselves and, in addition, by the displacement of pre-existing reference structures as shown in Figs. 12-14. Indeed, if one superposes the different motions documented by these various dilational features, one arrives at the conclusion represented schematically in Fig. 15—the rock mass expanded in a dominantly east-west (present geographic po-

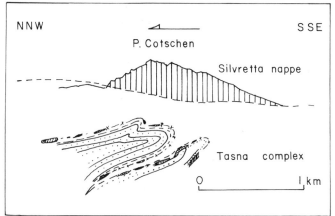

Figure 8: The relation between the Silvretta basement nappe (Austroalpine) and the underlying Penninic nappes in Val Tasna (see Fig. 2), after Cadisch and others (1941), simplified and slightly modified. Particularly conspicuous and intriguing at the same time are the southeastern vergent backfolds in the Middle Cretaceous sandstones (dotted) of the Tasna nappe complex. They are enveloped by a discontinuous train of basement slivers (cross-hatched and crosses) that are believed to be a badly sheared and stretched independent tectonic unit originally formed under the north-moving *traîneau écraseur* of the Silvretta nappe. With the other units they were involved in later backflow to the southeast. The Silvretta nappe is not visibly affected by the backflow; it apparently was a rather rigid boundary.

sition!) and upward direction. So far, this applies only to this particular outcrop. It should also be pointed out that in some loose boulders compressional elements (thrusts) associated with pseudotachylites have been found, though dilation clearly predominates. Vein quartz is often asso-

ciated with the pseudotachylites, but the exact relation remains to be worked out.

In view of the dilational nature of the pseudotachylite complex, the question may be asked whether it could not be the product of an extensional phase rather than of delamination due to plate convergence. Although no definitive answer is possible at this time, circumstantial evidence supports association with a subhorizontal detachment and shear zone: the pseudotachylite complex has a horizontal rather than vertical extension that is approximately parallel to the thrust, and no large-scale normal faulting has been discovered.

Although fragmentation played a large role, pseudotachylites are different from normal cataclastic rocks. The fragments are intruded as a mobile clastic mass with reduced intergranular friction into open fissures. Where they follow zones of evident shearing displacement in the host rock, as in Figs. 12-14, they are intrusive into gaping fractures that opened in the shear zone and are themselves sheared only weakly if at all (compare Grocott, 1981).

The brittle nature of the fragmentation and the unordered helter-skelter appearance of the intrusion phenomena suggest a sudden, explosive event, and I agree with those who propose that pseudotachylites are fossil earthquakes (Sibson, 1975). The exact rheology of the pseudotachylites at the time of emplacement is open to speculation. I think that participation of melt at some stages has been convincingly demonstrated. However, the explosive, very rapid event raises the question of a possibly dominant role of unstable mixtures in extreme pressure gradients

Figure 9: The base of the Silvretta basement nappe (-x-) in Val Urschai, a branch of Val Tasna, as seen from the southeast. The rectangle shows the location of Fig. 10. Its base is at 2500 m, and the dominant peak is about 3000 m. The thrustplane separates a Lower Paleozoic gneiss-amphibolite sequence (above) from a complex zone of dismembered, sheared, stretched, and multiply folded nappes, mostly sediments, including small relics of the ophiolitic Arosa zone and flysch masses of controversial origin, all weakly metamorphosed.

Figure 10: Small part of the basal Silvretta nappe containing those pseudotachylite veins illustrated in Figs. 11-14. The small rectangles show the location of Fig. 12 (right) and Fig. 13 (left). The sharp contact with the Arosa complex is marked by x. For a scale see Fig. 11.

with near vacuum in instantly opening gashes: a tiny fraction of gas and minute droplets of melt admixed to a suitable grain-size distribution of rock fragments (including dust) might conceivably act as carrier phase for the intrusions.

It is worthwhile to explore how this fits into the problem of how the Silvretta nappe got detached from its original underpinnings. The information, while too meager and disconnected for safe conclusions, still is apt to evoke what to me seems a plausible scenario—see Fig. 15. Open space for intrusion in a detachment and thrust situation develops where the thrust plane steps down in the direction of motion of the upper plate. Stress concentration for explosive release as an earthquake takes place where shear is obstructed by an obstacle, e.g., where the shearing surface is discontinuous. These two apparent conditions for the generation of the Silvretta pseudotachylites are met during initial detachment, when localized patches of yielding are nucleated according to a haphazard distribution of strength. These patches are on different levels and still separated by islands of strong rock. When these finally fail, first probably slowly with the opening of en echelon fissures filled with quartz, then in an accelerated way leading to explosion, shear patches of different levels may connect, as suggested in Fig. 15.

The pseudotachylites occur up to several hundred meters above the basal thrust plane, and the mylonites are found in various levels within the nappe. If interpreted as due to initial detachment of the nappe, this would mean that in the beginning a network of shear and shattering in a considerable volume of rock was formed instead of a narrow shear zone. This would not be surprising, as laboratory experiments show scattering of initial failure within an extensive volume rather than in a narrowly defined shear zone. Although it is not certain that the pseudotachylites formed at the very beginning of detachment, it would at least seem plausible that the conditions for resistance to shear and pseudotachylite formation were best as long as the sliding was intracrystalline and became less favorable when the nappe moved onto sediments and volcanics.

The plate-tectonic situation envisaged for the detachment process is shown in Fig. 7; Fig. 16b illustrates the probable relation of the obducted Austro-alpine nappes and their subducted African lithosphere, but after considerable movement.

Reactivation of the Cretaceous Silvretta unit in the Tertiary and the complex deformation in its substrate

The Silvretta nappe, and the Austroalpine nappes generally, in the Tertiary moved west and north over the Pennine realm (Figs. 16 a, b) as what has been termed the *traîneau écraseur* by Termier (1903), a "crushing sledge"

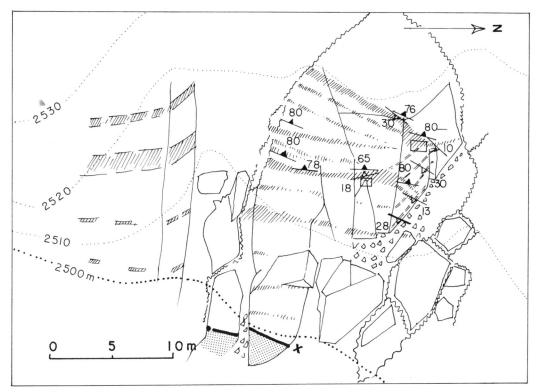

Figure 11: Sketch-map of the main pseudotachylite elements (cross-hatched) in the area of Fig. 10. An attempt is made to use a blown-up portion of the topographic map (dotted contours) for a vertical projection of the rather steep outcrop. Some topograhic features as seen on Fig. 8 in a very different perspective are roughly sketched in for orientation. The heavy line (x) marks the thrust plane, the two small rectangles indicate the location of Fig. 12 (right) and Fig. 13 (left). The attitude of the main pseudotachylite veins (a selection) is shown by the usual symbols, with full triangles the steeply west-dipping ones, with open triangles the moderately, mostly east-dipping ones. Positions of streams are suggested by wavy lines.

which overrode, crushed, and sheared all that was in its way. In our own terminology, the *traîneau écraseur* is the lid, cool and strong, and particularly so when at its sole there is a basement complex such as the Silvretta nappe. It is not surprising that the underlying Penninic masses are utterly dilacerated, consisting of detached slices that at a given time were imbricated and folded in one place and stretched, torn apart, and boudined in another. The situation is the same as that for the Doldenhorn nappe (Figs. 4-6), except that here there is a pronounced rheological discontinuity which exacerbates disharmony and shearing phenomena.

The Penninic nappes, like the Doldenhorn nappe, are shear structures at the base of the lid consisting of the higher nappes. For example, consider the Central Penninic Falknis and Sulzfluh nappes of the Swiss-Austrian border region. They form a discontinuous train of paleogeographically related sediments (e.g., Trümpy, 1980, Profile 1), sheared off their depositional basement and dragged to the north (relative to the subducted European plate), at the base of the moving lid. The sediments are stretched, discontinuous, and locally have accumulated

into a pile of folds (e.g., in the Falknis area, F in Fig. 16c)—likewise found to be typical for the Doldenhorn nappe and indeed generally for shear structures at the base of an orogenic lid. Mobilization of basement into lobes, here now often in a subhorizontal position (Fig. 16c), appears sluggish, and the basement is generally highly viscous, containing zones of largely diffuse (cataclastic to ductile) shear anastomosing around masses of little deformation (Milnes and Schmutz, 1978, Fig. 3; compare Bearth, 1952; Ramsay and Allison, 1979).

Backflow in a detachment scenario

Adding to the confusion there is the striking phenomenon of backfolding and backthrusting, or "backflow". As it raises important questions about the intracrustal detachment process, it will be examined in some detail. It is evident in the lower Engadine (Fig. 8; compare Gürler, 1982) but particularly striking farther west, in the Schams-Avers area (Fig. 17) in a similar tectonic position, where its significance has been hotly debated for many decades (e.g., Streiff, 1962; Milnes and Schmutz, 1978; Milnes and

Figure 12: Moderately east-dipping pseudotachylite veins with large shearing displacements within a subhorizontal major pseudotachylite zone (between the dashed lines), looking south. The scale bar measures 10 cm. The extreme stretching in this zone is made visible by the correlatable amphibolite band marked A: shearing segments are stretched out across the entire figure. Within the band, shearing and stretching are concentrated, but there are numerous pseudotachylite veins in the surrounding host rock.

Pfiffner, 1980). It is for this latter area that the following argumentation has been devised. Backfolding here may be seen as a particular example of regional backfolding affecting the generally north-vergent Penninic nappe system from the Engadine to the Mediterranean. Wherever stratigraphic evidence is available it implies Eocene sediments, in contradiction to Milnes and Schmutz (1978) and Milnes and Pfiffner (1980), who for the Avers place it into the Cretaceous.

Argand (1916) had ascribed backfolding to late thrusting of the African crust into the Alpine edifice in the Neogene Insubric phase, whereas Roeder (1973) considered the changing angle of subduction to have been of paramount importance. Without denying that the subduction complex as a whole may play a role, one may argue that backfolding is more immediately a part of the detachment process, and that its causes should first be looked for within the crust. The key question then is: which changing crustal conditions are associated with the change of vergence in the Tertiary? Two main possibilities exist, but they may actually have worked together: in the front, subduction of a pre-existing crustal structure that was an obstacle for the smooth continuation of crustal delamination; in the rear, a weakening of the orogenic lid permit-

ting easy escape of mobile delaminated crust and sediments.

As to the first possibility, backthrusting in the central Alps is indeed associated with an important inhomogeneity that was subducted into the path of the overriding lid: in the Eocene, subduction eventually reached the pre-existing intracontinental transpressive North-Penninic belt (Figs. 7, 16b), the beginnings of which have been traced to the Jurassic, with important compressive phases particularly in the Middle and Late Cretaceous. Geographic propinquity intimates its being a branch of the Pyrenean boundary, and general plate kinematics as well as the discontinuous nature of its manifestation suggest its having acted as an oblique sinistral, first divergent, then convergent, boundary zone throughout much of its Mesozoic history (compare Choukroune and others, 1973; Laubscher, 1975; Laubscher and Bernoulli, 1977, 1982). Its existence must be inferred from indirect evidence. Its schematic structure in Fig. 16 is adopted from well known obliquely convergent tectonics (Harding and Lowell, 1976, Fig. 6: "flower structure"; Laubscher, 1977, Fig. 2).

The effects of this new boundary on the further development of the orogenic lid and its base are shown in Fig. 16. First, the "flower", which had its own foredeeps

Figure 13: Steeply west-dipping pseudotachylite veins with shear displacement, looking north. The piece of tape is 3.8 cm. Between the dashed lines—badly fragmented host rock soaked with pseudotachylites.

(compare sections across the Pyrenees or the Venezuelan Andes, Bonini and others, 1977), is submerged into the advancing subduction zone which facilitates forward passage of the frontal wedge of the orogenic lid. The main difficulty must arise when the moving front of mobilization of basement (Fig. 6) reaches the obstacle. Several things may happen for which information is lacking or debatable. One piece of information that may have a bearing on the problem is the backfolding of the southern St. Gotthard massif (G in Fig. 16c) and of the Lepontine basement nappes impinging on it. The St. Gotthard massif is usually regarded as a part of the Ultrahelvetic basement (Trümpy, 1980), and particularly its southern portion may have been a member of the North-Penninic transpressive belt. In the Paleogene phase of compression, it was heated

to about 500°C under a tectonic cover of maybe 15 km (Frey and others, 1974, 1980) which acted as the orogenic lid. Classically the backfolding in the area has been described as the Lepontine nappes (and in particular the Lucomagno nappe) "boring into" the St. Gotthard massif. This "boring" would correspond, in our terminology, to the very common "wedge into split-apart" structures where an originally continuous sequence is forced apart by tectonically mobilized masses, the wedge (similar to the intrusion of a sill), with the upper uplifted split being basally bounded by a "back thrust" (compare Habicht, 1945; Laubscher, 1977; Price, 1981; Laubscher and Bernoulli, 1982). This possibility is depicted in Figs. 16c and 17. The deepseated back thrust, with much ductile deformation because of the elevated temperature, in this view climbs

Figure 14: Combination of pseudotachylites parallel to layering and in shear zones. The resulting irregular pseudotachylite body is outlined in dashes (only main features shown, the surrounding host rock is full of small additional veinlets and pockets). The tip of the pencil is 6 cm.

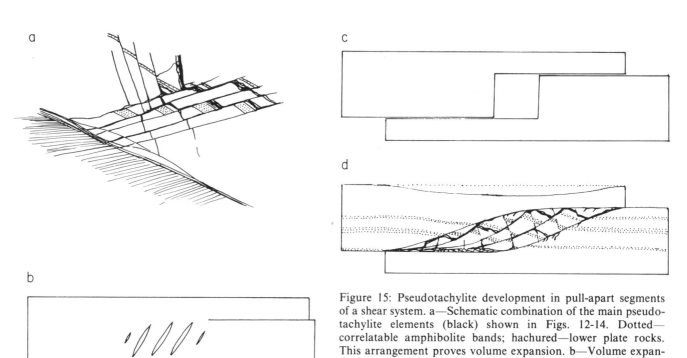

Figure 15: Pseudotachylite development in pull-apart segments of a shear system. a—Schematic combination of the main pseudotachylite elements (black) shown in Figs. 12-14. Dotted—correlatable amphibolite bands; hachured—lower plate rocks. This arrangement proves volume expansion. b—Volume expansion by en échelon gashes. c—Volume expansion by discrete pull-apart. d—Material balance requires a corresponding loss of volume somewhere else, e.g., by subhorizontal shear-stretching at the thrust of subsidiary shear planes, here suggested by the correlatable dotted bands. Volume expansion is compensated by a distributed sag in the upper plate (below the dotted line).

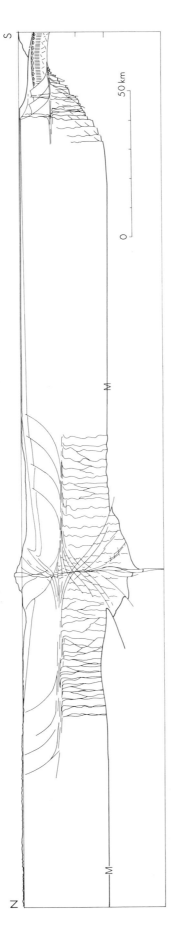

Figure 16a: The role of the north-Penninic subplate boundary in Alpine subduction (compare Fig. 7). Situation in the Late Cretaceous. The detachment zone in the middle crust had been activated in the extensional-sinistral phase in the Jurassic-Early Cretaceous, with listric normal faults above in the upper crust, and stretching with basaltic intrusions in the lower crust, (model INT of Lachenbruch and Sass, 1978, Fig. 9-8 c). Note that the detachment surface separates down-moving and up-moving masses. It is shown reactivated during oblique convergent movements in the later Cretaceous which resulted in the production of en échelon flower structures. Notice that the detachment zone now separates upward moving masses (above) from downward moving masses (below). The southern continental margin of the Europa plate, which was oblique-divergent, is shown on the right, with subduction symbolically suggested at the right margin in order to indicate that at that time it was far from the North-Penninic subplate boundary.

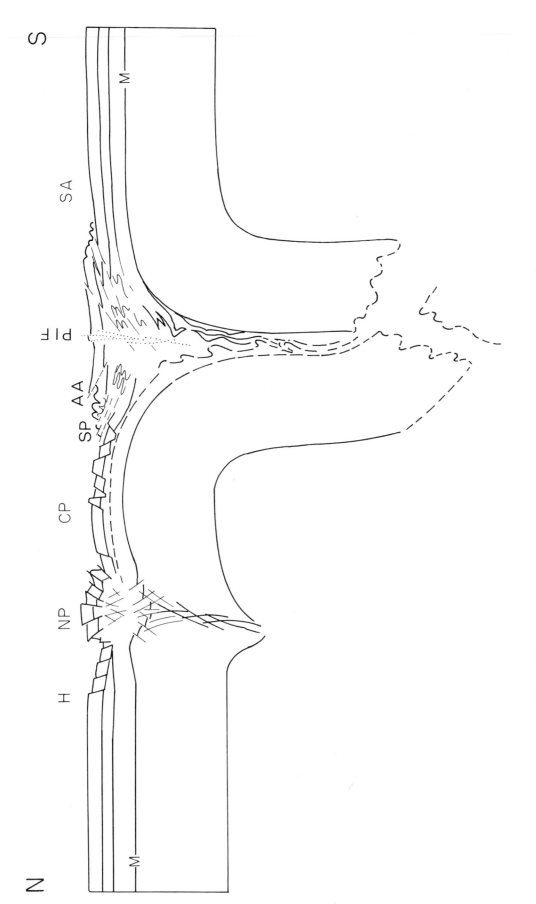

Figure 16b: Early Eocene situation, very schematic. Domains: H = Helvetic, NP = North Penninic-Ultrahelvetic; CP = Central Penninic (Briançonnais); SP = South Penninic; AA = Austroalpine, SA = South Alpine. The South-Penninic domain at this time was completely involved in the collision tectonics, its underpinnings were subducted while the surficial masses were detached and transformed into the ophiolite and associated nappes. PIF = Paleo-Insubric fault zone, a postulated precursor of the Miocene Insubric fault zone that particularly since Middle Cretaceous times is thought to have accommodated lateral displacements between the Africa and Europa plates. Its position is quite speculative, but it too, might conceivably have influenced the detachment process. By the Late Eocene, subduction from the north conveyed the North Penninic transpressive belt into the zone of detachment. The southern subduction zone is postulated because the Austroalpine nappes (AA) had been part of the Africa plate: their substrate had to be subducted somehow ("flaking").

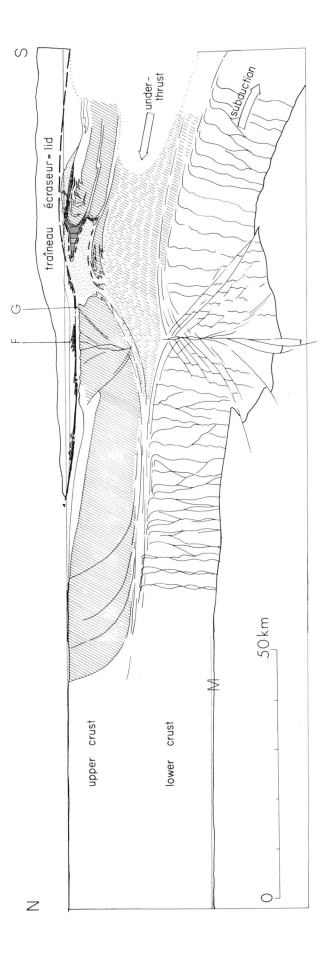

Figure 16c: Late Eocene situation. The detachment zone in the middle crust is reactivated as the North-Penninic subplate boundary enters the subduction zone. This time, upper and lower crust are split apart as high-T mobile masses (dashes) are wedged into the opening gap: the lower crust is bent down into the subduction zone. Widely ruled: upper crustal masses detached from lower crust. Narrowly ruled: Central-Penninic cover masses. Dotted: North-Penninic sediments. En échelon flower structures may be of highly variable structural relief. For reasons purely of illustration, very high relief and subsequent erosion are shown. The heavy interrupted line marks the base of the formerly north-moving orogenic lid at the left and the approximate base of backflow phenomena on the right. These are believed to be due to underthrusting from the right which is suggested symbolically by the termination of the signatures. This underthrust bears some resemblance to Argand's famed "Insubric phase" (1916, plate 3, Fig. 13).

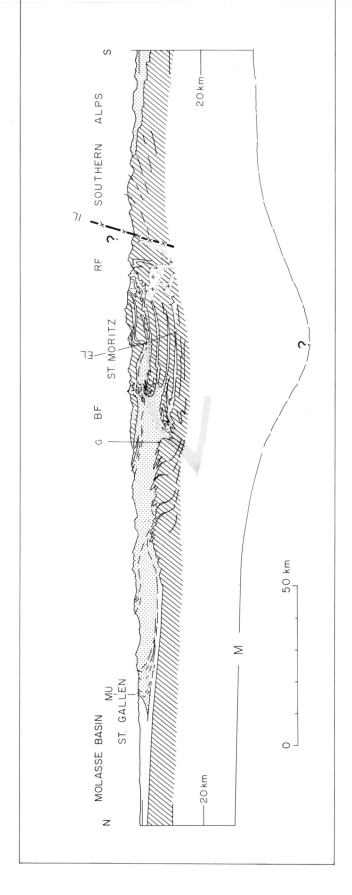

Figure 17: Simplified cross-section through the eastern part of the central Alps, after Geologische Generalkarte der Schweiz, 1:200,000. Ruled—upper crust, basement rocks; dotted—sediments involved in Alpine deformation; shaded—main zone of backflow (BF), corresponding to Fig. 16. MU—Frontal molasse underthrust; EL—Engadine line; RF—root fold north of the Insubric line (IL).

towards the south, where it first causes the backflow in the Penninic substrate of the orogenic lid and finally must ramp to the surface or end blindly by some broad deformation of the lid. Turning first to backflow in the Penninic domain, we note that it implied masses of a very heterogeneous rheology and that consequently the new stress gradients provoking backflow affected them variously, and in a qualitative way, I should like to compare the resulting flow field with some of those which Ramberg (1981, e.g., Figs. 15.4 and 15.5) produced in his centrifuge. The most mobile substance seems to have been the Prättigau flysch, which after backflow now is found in the imposing masses of the Oberhalbstein flysch (Streiff, 1962; for a divergent opinion, see Thum and Nabholz, 1972). The already existing little shear nappes of the Central Penninic cover were also brushed back sharply, while the basement lobes and slices of the Suretta nappe behaved in a more viscous manner as behooves basement (p. 13 and Figs. 16, 17). Between the two, steep shearing gradients caused sharp tectonic discontinuities.

As to the associated deformation in the orogenic lid, particularly southvergent thrusting, it would have to be looked for in the Austroalpine nappes of southern Graubünden and adjacent Italy, and even in the southern Alps beyond the Insubric line; see Fig. 2. There is much room in this zone for deformation of the Eocene orogenic lid, but the kinematics remain to be worked out.

After this back thrusting to the south, northward movement resumed and resulted in the formation of the Helvetic nappes, e.g., the Doldenhorn nappe. The exact manner in which the Gotthard obstacle was overcome remains to be solved. Some think that the "root zone" of the Helvetic nappes north of the Gotthard is the expression of a new subduction zone that jumped into that position from a more southerly location (e.g., Trümpy, 1980, p. 92). I prefer the solution intimated by the Doldenhorn development (Fig. 5): the Gotthard massif eventually was scraped off by the north-moving orogenic lid and the pressure of the mobilized sub-lid masses and incorporated into its basal shear-and-squeeze zone.

CONCLUSIONS

Alpine nappes formed at the sole of the frontal part of an orogenic lid, a surficial, cool stress-guide that connected the converging Africa and Europa plates. This sole emerges frontally by a system of decollement-ramp segments; in some places, it ends, temporarily or permanently, in a wedge-into-split-apart structure (or blind underthrust). Where the sole of the lid reaches depths with temperatures appropriate for ductile rock deformation, decollement degenerates into shear zones, where stretching and accumulation of matter in shear-induced folds take place, and into diffuse ramps with the formation of steeply

dipping basement lobes. The two types of deformation are simultaneous, and the steep lobes merge into the subhorizontal shear zones. Depending on the inherited and developing distribution of rheologies, a great variety of structures can be formed. Substitution of the original cover of a basement domain by allochthonous masses is frequent. Strong basement slices may be sheared off their underpinnings by creep in patches of mylonites, separated by competent islands which eventually break explosively in the cataclastic mode. In such places, pseudotachylites may be formed and may be interpreted as fossil witnesses to earthquakes. Severe pre-existing structures, when subducted, may affect sole deformation and in certain cases seem to have provoked underthrusting and backflow of material.

ACKNOWLEDGEMENTS

Exchange of views with a number of colleagues, particularly D. Bernoulli, B. Gürler, E. Schläppi, and H. U. Schmutz, is gratefully acknowledged. Work on the base of the Silvretta nappe and the underlying units is supported by the Swiss National Science Foundation, Project Nr. 2.940-0.77. R. D. Hatcher and S. Schamel have reviewed the paper and contributed to its clarification.

REFERENCES CITED

Angenheister, G., Bögel, H., Gebrande, H., Giese, P., Schmidt-Thomé, P., Zeil, W., 1972, Recent investigations of surficial and deeper crustal structures of the Eastern and Southern Alps: Geologische Rundschau, v. 61, p. 349–395.

Argand, E., 1916, Sur l'arc des Alpes Occidentales: Eclogae geologicae Helvetiae, v. 14, p. 145–191.

Armstrong, R. L., and Dick, H.J.B., 1974, A model for the development of thin overthrust sheets of crystalline rock: Geology, v. 2, p. 35–40.

Bally, A. W., Bernoulli, D., Davis, G. A., and Montadert, L., 1981, Listric normal faults in: 26ᵉ Congrès géologique international, Colloque C3, Géologie des Marges Continentales, Oceanologica Acta, p. 87–101.

Bearth, P., 1932, Geologie und Petrographie der Keschgruppe: Schweizerische Mineralogische und Petrographische Mitteilungen, v. 12, p. 256–279.

Bearth, P., 1933, Ueber Gangmylonite der Silvretta: Schweizerische Mineralogische und Petrographische Mitteilungen, v. 13, p. 347–355.

Bearth, P., 1952, Geologie und Petrographie des Monte Rosa: Beiträge zur Geologischen Karte der Schweiz, N.F. 96., 94 p.

Bonini, W., Pimstein de Gaete, C., and Graterol, V., 1977, Mapa de anomalías gravimétricas de Bouguer de la parte norte de Venezuela y areas vecinas, 1:100 000: República de Venezuela, Ministerio de Energía y Minas, Dirección de Geología, Caracas.

Cadisch, J., Bearth, P., and Spaenhauer, F., 1941, Erläuterungen zu Blatt Ardez (14): Geologischer Atlas der Schweiz, 51 p.

Cadisch, J., Eugster, H., and Wenk, E., 1968, Erläuterungen zu Blatt Scuol-Schuls-Tarasp (44): Geologischer Atlas der Schweiz, 68 p.

Choukroune, P., Le Pichon, X., Seguret, M., and Sibuet, J. C., 1973, Bay of Biscay and Pyrenees: Earth and Planetary Science Letters, v. 18, p. 110–118.

Cobbold, P. R., and Quinquis, H., 1981, Development of sheath folds in shear regimes: Journal of Structural Geology, v. 2, p. 119–126.

Cook, F. A., Albaugh, D., Brown, L., Kaufman, S., Oliver, J., and Hatcher, R., 1979, Thinskinned tectonics in the crystalline southern Appalachians: Geology, v. 7, . 563–567.

Dolivo, E., 1980, Nouvelles observations structurales au SW du Massif de l'Aar entre Visp et Gampel (Ph.D. thesis): Lausanne, Switzerland, University of Lausanne, 73 p.

Dunoyer de Segonzac, G., and Bernoulli, D., 1976, Diagenèse et métamorphisme des argiles dans le Rhétien Sud-alpin et Austro-alpin (Lombardie et Grisons): Bulletin de la Société géologique de France, série 7, v. 18, p. 1283–1293.

Ellenberger, F., 1958, Etude géologique du pays de Vanoise: Mémoires pour sevir à l'explication de la Carte géologique détaillée de la France, 561 p.

Frank, E., and Stettler, A., 1979, K-Ar and ^{39}Ar-^{40}Ar systematics of white k-mica from an Alpine metamorphic profile in the Swiss Alps: Schweizerische Mineralogische und Petrographische Mitteilungen, v. 59, p. 375–394.

Frey, M., Hunziker, J. C., Frank, W., Bocquet, J., Dal Piaz, G. V., Jäger, E., Niggli, E., 1974, Alpine Metamorphism of the Alps: Schweiz. Mineralogische und Petrographische Mitteilungen, v. 54, p. 247–290.

Frey, M., Teichmüller, M., Teichmüller, R., Mullis, J., Künzi, B., Breitschmid, A., Gruner, U., and Schwizer, B., 1980, Very low-grade metamorphism in external parts of the Central Alps: Illite crystallinity, coal rank and fluid inclusion data: Eclogae geologicae Helvetiae, v. 73, p. 173–203.

Grocott, J., 1981, Fracture geometry of pseudotachylite generation zones: a study of shear fractures formed during seismic events: Journal of Structural Geology, v. 3, p. 169–178.

Gürler, B., 1982, Geologie des Val Tasna und Umgebung (Ph.D. thesis): Basel, Switzerland, University of Basel, 189 p.

Habicht, K., 1945, Geologische Untersuchungen im südlichen sanktgallisch-appenzellischen Molassegebiet: Beiträge zur Geologischen Karte der Schweiz, N.F. 83., 166 p.

Hammer, W., 1930, Ueber Pseudotachylit in den Ostalpen: Jahrbuch der Geologischen Bundesanstalt, v. 80, p. 571–585.

Harding, T. P., and Lowell, J. D., 1979, Structure styles, their plate-tectonics habitats, and hydrocarbon traps in petroleum provinces: American Association of Petroleum Geologists Bulletin, v. 63, p. 1016–1058.

Lachenbruch, A. H., and Sass, J. H., 1978, Models of an extending lithosphere and heat flow in the Basin and Range province, in Smith, R. B., and Eaton, G. P., eds., Cenozoic tectonics and regional geophysics of the western Cordillera: Geological Society of America Memoir 152, p. 209–250.

Laubscher, H.P., 1970, Bewegung und Wärme in der alpinen Orogenese: Schweizerische Mineralogische und Petrographische Mitteilungen, v. 5, p. 565–596.

Laubscher, H. P., 1973, Jura Mountains, in de Jong, A., and Scholten, R., eds., Gravity and tectonics: New York, J. Wiley & Sons, Inc., p. 217–227.

Laubscher, H. P., 1975, Plate boundaries and microplates in Alpine history: American Journal of Science, v. 275, p. 865–876.

Laubscher, H. P., 1977, The tectonics of subduction in the Alpine System: Memorie della Società Geologica Italiana, v. 13, suppl. 2, p. 275–283.

Laubscher, H. P., 1978, Foreland folding: Tectonophysics, v. 47, p. 325–337.

Laubscher, H. P., and Bernoulli, D., 1977, Mediterranean and Tethys, in Nairn, A.E.M., and others, eds., The ocean basins and margins, v. 4A: Plenum Press, New York p. 1–28.

Laubscher, H. P., and Bernoulli, D., 1980, Cross-section from the Rhine Graben to the Po Plain, Excursion No. III, in Schweizerische Geologische Kommission, ed., Geology of Switzerland, a guide-book: Basel, New York, Wepf & Co., p. 183–209.

Laubscher, H. P., and Bernouli, D., 1982, History and deformation of the Alps, in Hsü, K. J., ed., Mountain building: London, Academic Press, p. 169–180.

Le Pichon, X., and Angelier, J., 1979, The Hellenic arc and trench system: a key to the neotectonic evolution of the eastern Mediterranean area: Tectonophysics, v. 60, p. 1–42.

Lugeon, M., 1914, Les Hautes Alpes Calcaires entre la Lizerne et la Kander (Wildhorn, Wildstrubel, Balmhorn et Torrenthorn): Matériaux pour la Carte géologique de la Suisse, N.S.30, v. 1/2, 206 p.

Masch, L., 1974, Untersuchung der Aufschmelzung und Deformation der Pseudotachylite der Silvretta (Oesterreich, Schweiz): Neues Jahrbuch für Mineralogie, Monatshefte, 1973, v. 11, p. 485–509.

Masson, H., Herb, R, and Steck, A., 1980, Helvetic Alps of Western Switzerland, Excursion No. 1, in Schweizerische Geologische Kommission, ed., Geology of Switzerland, a guide-book: Basel, New York, Wepf & Co., p. 109–153.

Miller, H., Müller, St., and Perrier, G., 1982, Structure and dynamics of the Alps—a geophysical inventory: Geodynamics Series, Alpine-Mediterranean Geodynamics American Geophysical Union, v. 7, p. 175–204.

Milnes, A. G., and Pfiffner, O. A., 1980, Tectonic evolution of the Central Alps in the cross section St. Gallen-Como: Eclogae geologicae Helvetiae, v. 73, p. 619–633.

Milnes, A. G., and Schmutz, H. U., 1978, Structure and history of the Suretta nappe (Pennine zone, Central Alps)—a field study: Eclogae geologicae Helvetiae, v. 71, p. 19–34.

Oxburgh, E. R., 1972, Flake tectonics and continental collision: Nature, v. 239, p. 202–204.

Panza, G. F., and Müller, St., 1979, The plate boundary between Eurasia and Africa in the Alpine area: Memorie di Scienze Geologiche, v. 33, p. 43–50.

Price, R. A., 1981, The Cordilleran foreland thrust and fold belt in the southern Canadian Rocky Mountains, in McClay, K. R., and Price, N. J., eds., Thrust and nappe tectonics: Blackwell Scientific Publications, Oxford, London, p. 427–448.

Ramberg, H., 1981, Gravity, deformation, and the earth's crust (second edition): London, Academic Press, 452 p.

Ramsay, J. G., and Allison, I., 1979, Structural analysis of shear zones in an alpinized Hercynian granite (Maggia Lappen, Pennine Zone, Central Alps): Schweizerische Mineralogische und Petrographische Mitteilungen, v. 59, p. 251–279.

Rudolph, J., 1982, Tieferes Tertiär im oberen Fimbertal, Unterengadiner Fenster: Neues Jahrbuch für Geologie und Paläontologie, Monatshefte, v. 3, p. 181–183.

Scharbert, S., and Schönlaub, H. P., 1980, Das Prävariszikum und Variszikum (die geologische Entwicklung vom Beginn der Ueberlieferung durch das Paläozoikum bis zum Ende der variszischen Zeit im Oberkarbon), in Oberhauser, R., ed., Der geologische Aufbau Oesterreichs, Wien, New York, Springer-Verlag, p. 3–20.

Schläppi, E., 1980, Geologische und tektonische Entwicklung der Doldenhorndecke und zugehöriger Elemente, (Ph.D. thesis), Bern, Switzerland, University of Bern, 154 p.

Shand, S. J., 1917, The pseudotachylite of Parijs (Orange Free State) and its relation to "trapshotten Gneis" and "flinty crush rock": Quarterly Journal of the Geological Society of London, v. 72, p. 198–221.

Sibson, R. H., 1975, Generation of pseudotachylite by ancient seismic faulting: Geophysical Journal, Royal Astronomical Society, v. 43, p. 775–794.

Smithson, S. B., Brewer, J., Kaufman, S., and Oliver, J., 1978, Nature of the Wind River thrust, Wyoming, from COCORP deep-reflection data and from gravity data: Geology, v. 6, p. 648–652.

Spaenhauer, F., 1932, Petrographie und Geologie der Grialetsch-Vadret-

Sursura-Gruppe (Graubünden): Schweizerische Mineralogische und Petrographische Mitteilungen, v. 12, p. 27–146.

Steck, A., 1980, Deux directions principales de flux synmétamorphiques dans les Alpes centrales: Bulletin de la Société vaudoise des Sciences naturelles, v. 75, p. 141–149.

Streckeisen, A., 1928, Geologie und Petrographie der Flüelagruppe (Graubünden): Schweizerische Mineralogische und Petrographische Mitteilungen, v. 8, p. 87–239.

Streiff, V., 1962, Zur östlichen Beheimatung der Klippendecken: Eclogae geologicae Helvetiae, v. 55, p. 77–132.

Termier, P., 1903, Les nappes des Alpes orientales et la synthèse des Alpes: Bulletin de la Société Géologique de la France, série 4, v. 3, p. 711–765.

Thöni, M., 1980, Zur Westbewegung der Oetztaler Masse. Räumliche und zeitliche Fragen an der Schlinigüberschiebung: Mitteilungen der Gesellschaft der Geologie- und Bergbaustudenten in Oesterreich, v. 26, p. 247–275.

Thöni, M., 1981, Arbeiten im Ostalpin W des Tauernfensters: Die frühalpine Geschichte der Ostalpen (Hochschulschwerpunkt S 15), Jahresbericht 1980, v. 2, Montanuniversität Leoben, p. 21–36.

Thum, I., and Nabholz, W., 1972, Zur Sedimentologie und Metamorphose der penninischen Flysch- und Schieferabfolgen im Gebiet Prättigau-Lenzerheide-Oberhalbstein: Beiträge zur Geologischen Karte der Schweiz, N.F. 144., 55 p.

Trümpy, R., 1980, An outline of the geology of Switzerland, *in* Schweizerische Geologische Kommission, ed., Switzerland, a guidebook: 26th International Geological Congress, Wepf & Co., Basel, New York, p. 1–104.

Voll, G., 1980, Ein Querprofil durch die Schweizer Alpen vom Vierwaldstätter See zur Wurzelzone—Strukturen und ihre Entwicklung durch Deformationsmechanismen wichtiger Minerale: Neues Jahrbuch für Geologie und Paläontologie, Abhandlungen, v. 160, p. 321–335.

Wenk, E., 1934, Beiträge zur Petrographie und Geologie des Silvrettakristallins: Schweizerische Mineralogische und Petrographische Mitteilungen, v. 14, p. 196–278.

Wenk, H. R., 1978, Are pseudotachylites products of fracture or fusion?: Geology, v. 6, p. 507–511.

MANUSCRIPT ACCEPTED BY THE SOCIETY SEPTEMBER 10, 1982

Printed in U.S.A.

Geological Society of America
Memoir 158
1983

Cover and basement: A contrast in style and fabrics

P. A. Rathbone*
Jane Herdman Laboratories of Geology
University of Liverpool
Liverpool, England

M. P. Coward
Department of Earth Sciences
University of Leeds
Leeds, England

A. L. Harris
Jane Herdman Laboratories of Geology
University of Liverpool
Liverpool, England

ABSTRACT

This paper speculates on the extent to which the "thin-skinned" tectonic model which has been proposed for the Appalachians may apply to the Scottish part of the Caledonide/Appalachian orogen. The Moine thrust zone in NW Scotland separates the Moine rocks of the orthotectonic zone of the Scottish Caledonides from the foreland Archean rocks with their late Proterozoic and Cambro-Ordovician cover sequence. It consists of a series of easterly dipping thrusts, decreasing in age downward and westward, and is characterized by cataclasite (later) and mylonite (earlier), reflecting decreasing ductility with time. The Sgurr Beag thrust (slide) separates two major divisions (Glenfinnan and Morar) in the Proterozoic Moine rocks above and to the east of the Moine thrust zone. Although now almost everywhere steeply inclined, the Sgurr Beag thrust is interpreted as having originally been shallowly inclined and subsequently modified by Caledonian folding and passive rotation during later deformation in the orthotectonic zone. Observations along the Sgurr Beag thrust show that, over a zone several hundred meters thick, there has been grain-size reduction, obliteration of minor folds, development of an intense parallel flaggy foliation, and the interleaving with the Moine cover of thin persistent slices of Archean gneisses. The metamorphic grade of the Moine rocks suggests that the displacement on the Sgurr Beag thrust was highly ductile, occurring at much higher temperatures and pressures than those in the Moine thrust zone. It is likely that the Sgurr Beag thrust is the within-basement extension of a thrust higher than, but analogous to, the Moine thrust.

INTRODUCTION

Work in the Appalachians (Harris and Bayer, 1979; Cook *et al.,* 1979) has sought to trace, by seismic reflection profiling, the eastward extension of thrusts which crop out in the Cumberland Plateau and Valley and Ridge

(Hatcher, 1981) in the western part of the southern Appalachians. Across Georgia, North Carolina, and Tennessee, interpretation of seismic reflection profiling has suggested that crystalline rocks are underlain by a basal decoupling zone, have been carried westward some 260 km, and now overlie Lower Paleozoic sedimentary rocks 1-5 km thick

---

*Present address: Geological Survey, Botswana.

(Cook *et al.,* op. cit.). This paper speculates on the extent to which this model may apply to the Scottish part of the Caledonide/Appalachian orogen but more particularly to the structural and textural phenomena which may accompany such thrusts where they pass through crystalline basement.

THE MOINE THRUST ZONE

The rocks of the Hebridean craton (Watson, 1975) in NW Scotland are separated from the Metamorphic Caledonides (Read, 1961) by the NNE-trending and easterly dipping Moine thrust zone (Peach *et al.,* 1907). The craton consists of late Archean (<2900 Ma) basement gneisses partly reworked during middle Proterozoic (Laxfordian) tectonic activity (1800 Ma) (cf. Watson, 1975). These are overlain by late Proterozoic (Torridonian) clastic sequences which were overstepped by Cambro-Ordovician quartzite and carbonate shelf sediments, some 700 m thick.

The Moine thrust zone consists of a series of thrusts, of which the Moine thrust (*sensu stricto*) is considered to be the oldest (Elliott and Johnson, 1980). It is the highest and outcrops furthest to the east. The lower and successively younger thrusts crop out successively westwards each carrying a slice of rock or nappe which is named after the thrust on which it has ridden. Thus, in Assynt (Fig. 1), where a culmination or bulge of the highest thrust is produced above a major duplex structure, a sequence of nappes, each successively younger and lower, can be distinguished—the Ben More, Glencoul, and Sole nappes. Similarly, in Eriboll on the northern coast of Scotland (Fig. 1), there is a westward sequence of Upper Arnaboll, Arnaboll, and Sole nappes. The general tectonic transport direction is WNW—approximately 290–300°. This is parallel to the elongation lineation in the more deformed rocks and normal to the general trend of the imbricates. In southern Assynt, the Borolan igneous complex postdates early thrust movements but predates the late movement. It has yielded an age of ~430 Ma, thus dating some of the movement in the Moine thrust zone (van Breemen *et al.,* 1979).

At levels seen at the present day in the Moine thrust zone, the thrusts expose cataclastic and mylonitic rocks, the nature of which depends on the depth at which they formed and the strain rate at which they were created. Textures, deformation styles, and intensities vary across the thrust zone, from sharp fault breaks in the lower thrusts in the west to thick mylonite zones in the east.

The Sole nappe consists essentially of Cambrian sediments. In the west, where the Sole lies in middle Cambrian heterogeneous lithologies and carbonate rocks, the Sole nappe contains many closely spaced reverse faults which curve in listric form off the Sole thrust (Peach *et al.,*

1907; Coward and Kim, 1981). There is no mylonitization, although carbonate rocks near the faults locally carry a few millimeters of silicification, suggesting the presence of some fluids. There are generally no slickensides or fibers along the faults. To the east, where the Sole thrust lies in basal Cambrian quartzites, the whole Cambro-Ordovician sedimentary sequence is imbricated. Here the quartzites show some evidence of shearing parallel to bedding; pipes (worm tubes of genus Skolithos) (Hallam and Swett, 1966) in the quartzite are locally sheared through shear strains of γ greater than 2 (where $\gamma = \tan 4$ and is the change in angle made by a line normal to the shear plane). The shear zones are narrow, a few centimeters to a meter wide, and are spaced about 10 m apart, although they become more closely spaced, and the shear strain increases toward the overlying thrust. Locally, these shears climb through the bedding and themselves become small thrusts. Within the shear zone and close to the thrusts, there has been localized grainsize reduction with sub-grain and new-grain formation and in the more intensely deformed rocks there are narrow quartz-ribbon mylonites. White (1979a) used recrystallized grain size in a quartz mylonite from one such shear zone at Ben Heilam, in the north of the Eriboll district, as a paleopiezometer. He estimated a differential stress of 0.37–1.38 kbar for the mylonite formation, although White (1979b) recognized that there are problems in using grain size as a paleo-piezometer. Between the shear zones, the grains maintain their original shape with only slight sub-grain formation.

The quartzite beds have also suffered up to 20–30% layer-parallel shortening parallel to the transport direction (Coward and Kim, 1981). This shortening of the beds is most pronounced close to thrust ramps and is probably related to sticking or drag of the thrust. This led to differential movement of the thrust, local thickening, and also to folding of several meters to hundreds of meters wavelength (cf. Berger and Johnson, 1980). The folds or ramps are generally overturned with high flexural shear strains in the overturned limbs. Folds produced on lower thrust ramps deform higher level folds and thrusts so that many generations of folds were produced, while rock textures are the product of several deformation phases.

To the east, the lowermost thrust lies in basement gneiss so that shear zones and their associated folds affect both basement and cover (Fig. 2). In the Eriboll area (Fig. 2), the basement gneiss has been strongly affected by Laxfordian reworking (Watson, 1975), and where unaffected by Caledonian deformation they show a characteristic Laxfordian NW-SE trending fabric formed by gneissic banding with generally concordant, but locally discordant, Laxfordian granites and pegmatites. In these gneisses, middle Proterozoic basic intrusions (Scourie dykes) had been sheared into concordance with the gneissic banding and subsequently folded around NW-trending,

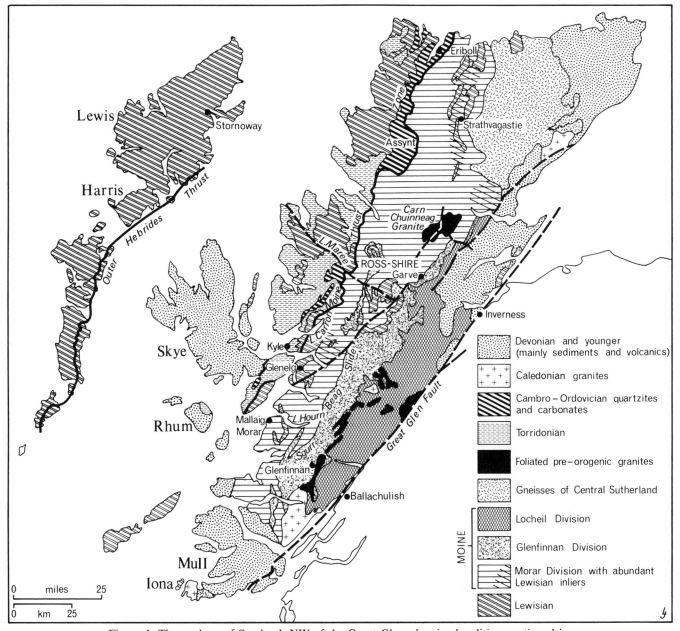

Figure 1. The geology of Scotland, NW of the Great Glen, showing localities mentioned in the text. Note that the separation of the Moines into separate divisions does not necessarily follow stratigraphic boundaries; the separation is largely used to facilitate structural and lithological description.

tight-to-isoclinal upright folds. In Fig. 2, the gneisses show some of those structures; the gneiss of Arnaboll Hill lies across the hinge zone of a large-scale, late-Laxfordian antiform.

These gneisses show the effects of Caledonian deformation along the major thrust zone where, within 1 to 2 m of the thrust, the Laxfordian structures are sheared into concordance with the Caledonian fabric. The Lewisian minerals show cataclastic textures but also a new syntectonic growth of chlorite, mica, and epidote. Where the thrusts climb from Lewisian gneiss to Cambrian quartzite

there are large-scale overturned folds on hanging-wall and footwall (see the Tioraidh fault on Fig. 2 and Fig. 3, section B). On the inverted fold limbs, the Lewisian rocks are smashed by closely spaced, steeply, though irregularly, dipping fractures coated by chlorite and epidote. Slickensides of quartz and chlorite form on small shears and generally plunge to the ESE, normal to the fold hinge.

The main thrust zones and shear zones in the Lewisian basement are shown in Fig. 2. The lowermost thrust that affects the gneisses is termed the Arnaboll thrust, although this is only one of many, and to the south and west

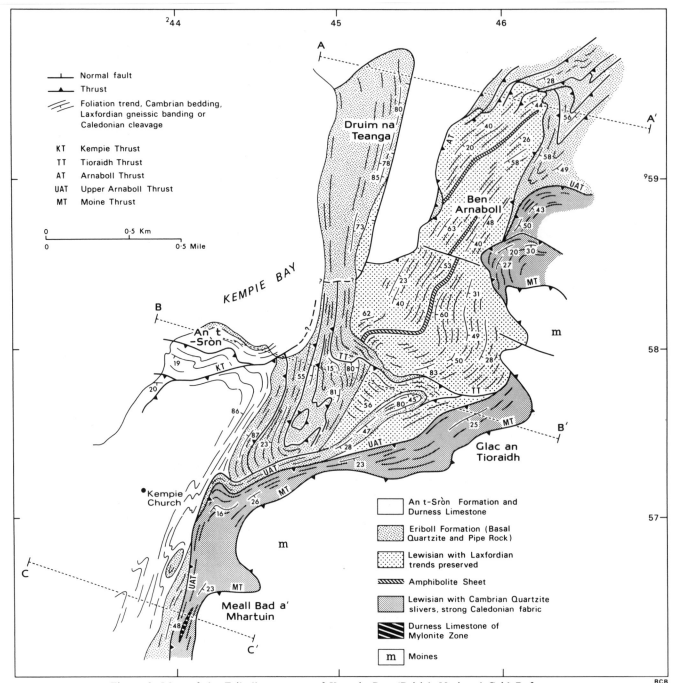

Figure 2. Map of the Eriboll area, east of Kempie Bay (British National Grid References given), showing the major thrusts and shears affecting the Lewisian rocks and Cambrian succession (Eriboll, An t-Sron and Durness Limestone formations).

it climbs to Upper Cambrian quartzites and limestones to become the Kempie thrust of Fig. 2. On Arnaboll Hill, the Arnaboll thrust is cut by the reverse faults and folded by the structures generated within or beneath the Lower Sole nappe. Where these later faults cut the gneiss, they generally form discrete fault planes, with no mylonitization and little to no alteration.

In the east of the Eriboll district, the Upper Arnaboll thrust carried mylonitic Lewisian gneiss together with slices of Cambrian quartzite, only a few meters thick, over the Arnaboll thrust. It was previously considered (Coward, 1980) that the Upper Arnaboll thrust moved first and then lower structures such as the Arnaboll thrust branched off and carried the whole package in "piggyback" fashion westward over the Cambrian. However, recent work in the Kempie area has shown that a thrust in

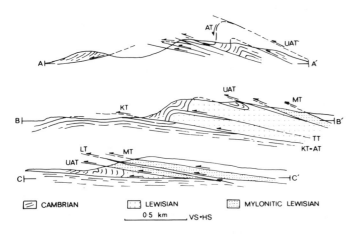

Figure 3. Cross sections through the Eriboll area, for locations see Fig. 2. AT = Arnaboll thrust, KT = Kempie thrust, MT = Moine thrust, TT = Tioraidh thrust, UAT = Upper Arnaboll thrust, LT = Late thrust carrying slice of Durness Limestone into the Upper Arnaboll nappe.

the Upper Arnaboll nappe must also have moved late in the thrust sequence because the nappe carries a fault-bounded block or horse of Cambrian limestone, presumably plucked from the underlying Cambrian imbricate zone. Thus, the thrust sequence must be: a) Upper Arnaboll nappe of mylonite Lewisian carried over less mylonitic Lewisian. b) Arnaboll thrust and others carry the Lewisian over Cambrian rocks. c) Differential movement of the back part of this thrust causes the Upper Arnaboll nappe to be carried further over the Arnaboll Lewisian, carrying with it a packet of underlying Cambrian sediments.

There are similar anomalous slices of Upper Cambrian limestone within the mylonitic Lewisian and Lower Cambrian quartzites at Glencoul in the Assynt area (Fig. 4), again suggesting late movement of an eastern thrust carrying up a pocket of limestone from beneath the main Ben More and Glencoul thrusts.

The eastern thrusts of Lewisian rock contain wide, low-angle zones of intense Caledonian deformation. Above the Upper Arnaboll thrusts the mylonitic Lewisian rocks are some 200–300 m wide and 50 m thick. On Creag na Faolinn, south of Loch Eriboll, the Caledonized Lewisian rocks are some 300 m thick and outcrop as a large, fault-bounded lens or horse, some 3 km by 1.5 km. Within these gneisses, it is still possible to recognize original Lewisian rock types, but here all the Laxfordian granites and pegmatites are concordant to the main schistosity which trends NE-SW with a gentle dip to the SE. There is a pronounced mineral lineation formed by broken and drawn out Lewisian minerals and fibrous trails of Caledonian quartz, feldspar, chlorite, and mica. Chlorite and epidote locally define a platy schistosity as well as coating later fracture surfaces. There are several generations of small-scale folds which deform the Caledonian schistosity. The

early phases are tight structures and have hinges which plunge to the ESE parallel to the mineral lineation, while later fold phases have a more varied orientation. Many of the folds have curvilinear hinges, suggesting a sheath-like form (Cobbold and Quinquis, 1980) where the hinges have been sheared almost into parallelism with the shear direction.

At Eriboll, the Moine nappe overlies the sheared Lewisian of the Upper Arnaboll nappe, although to the south in the Assynt district, it overrides the lower thrust zone, locally coming to rest directly on Cambrian sediments of the foreland. Above the Moine thrust, there is a broad zone of intensely deformed Proterozoic (Moine) psammites and pelites carrying slices of Lewisian basement. These Lewisian rocks are intensely deformed in the Caledonian and show few or no Lewisian structures and few Lewisian minerals. The origin of these slices is unknown—they may be horses or tight fold keels. Near the Moine thrust, there is locally up to 50 meters of mylonitic psammite, with a pronounced quartz ribbon fabric and a well-developed lineation plunging gently to the ESE. Christie (1963) reported elongate ribbons of quartz with ratios of 100:10:1 for the mylonites of the Stack of Glencoul. Most of the original clastic grains have been rendered into a mass of subgrains and new grains. The feldspar grains deformed principally by cataclasis, giving rise to fractured feldspar augen in a fine quartz matrix.

There are at least two phases of post mylonitic folding; the early folds are often sheath-like with hinges parallel to the transport direction. Mylonitic Moines commonly exhibit low-angle conjugate crenulation-like foliations

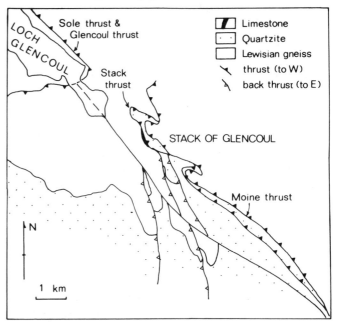

Figure 4. Highly simplified map of the thrust zone at the Stack of Glencoul in northern Assynt showing the position of a sliver of Durness Limestone caught beneath the Stack thrust.

which deform the main foliation. Some of these are thought to be a "shear band" cleavage which results from progressive large strains (White *et al.*, 1980). They indicate that the mylonites have suffered layer parallel extension.

There are also late cataclastic rocks and fault breccias. Elliott and Johnson (1980) suggested that the tectonic layering made by the mylonitic fabric may be used in the staircase trajectories of later faults. The brittle deformation in the mylonites may be the products of late displacements along the thrusts, the more brittle being produced as the mylonites are carried "piggy back" onto the foreland and as erosion cuts down on the thrust mass.

Thus, in summary, the sequence of thrusts in the Moine thrust zone is from east to west, as lower western thrusts fold or re-thrust upper eastern structures. However, locally the lower thrusts stick, and eastern thrusts form or reactivate to over-ride the lower thrusts. This confirms the general pattern of thrust propagation as outlined by Elliott and Johnson (1980) for the Moine thrust, where the structures tend to propagate towards the foreland, but illustrates that in detail the process is more complex, and several thrusts may form out of sequence. The early formed eastern thrusts produced wide zones of mylonite with a pronounced Caledonian tectonic foliation and lineation. As these thrusts were carried westward by successively lower structures and material was removed by erosion, deformation changed from ductile to brittle, and the width of affected rock narrowed so that the latest fault planes are discrete.

This change in rock type along a thrust, from ductile to brittle, is similar to that described by Sibson (1977) for the Outer Isles thrust in NW Scotland and by Sibson *et al.* (1981) for the Alpine fault of New Zealand. It can be argued that a passage across a fault zone from cataclastic to intensely deformed schist reflects an original distribution of fault rock types with increasing depth. Uplift in the faults juxtaposes the fault rocks formed at different depths, and as the rocks are carried upward and overburden removed by erosion, the type of fault rock will change on an individual fault. Thus, in the Moine thrust zone, the early fault rocks tend to be ductile mylonites, while the later movements which cut these or reactivate these tend to be cataclasite bearing or even clean-cut faults.

THE MOINE NAPPE: WEST OF THE SGURR BEAG SLIDE

The structures and textures within the Moine nappe are the product of polyphase deformation and metamorphism. The zone immediately to the east of the Moine thrust is made up of rocks of the Morar Division (Johnstone *et al.*, 1969). Within this division, the pelite, semipelite, and psammite formations can be read in terms of a general lithostratigraphy which is based on well-preserved sedimentary structures and which is refined by the vertical distribution of minor occurrences of calc-silicate as lenses and heavy mineral laminae (Johnstone *et al.*, 1969, table 1). The oldest lithostratigraphic formations within the Morar Division commonly lie adjacent to slices of Lewisian (Archean) basement which occupy the core of early isoclinal folds and which have clearly suffered a much more prolonged and complex thermal history than the Moines in the fold envelope (e.g., Ramsay, 1958).

Although K-Ar derived cooling ages of biotite and muscovite (Dewey and Pankhurst, 1970) and metamorphosed late-orogenic minor intrusions of late Ordovician/-Silurian age indicate that Caledonian deformation and metamorphism occurred, there is strong isotopic evidence that the rocks of the Morar Division had suffered Precambrian orogenesis. Mica schists and foliated granite have yielded isotopic ages in excess of 1000 Ma (Brook *et al.*, 1977), while pegmatites, now strongly foliated, give mineral ages which suggest emplacement about 750 Ma ago (van Breemen *et al.*, 1974). Most workers now agree that Caledonian polyphase deformation was imposed on already crystalline Morar Division rocks, and although metamorphic grade probably locally increased again to amphibolite facies (Powell, 1974; Smith, 1979), the Caledonian deformation was in many places accompanied by retrograde metamorphism.

The Carn Chuinneag granite, emplaced in already folded rocks 560 ± 10 Ma ago (Pidgeon and Johnson, 1974), suffered the Caledonian deformation, which rendered the alkali-feldspar megacrysts into augen which are wrapped by quartz ribbons and micas and extended generally southeast (Wilson and Shepherd, 1979). Fabrics of comparable orientation are recorded in the mylonites of the Moine thrust zone, and because these have been imposed on the Cambro-Ordovician sediments as well as on the Lewisian gneisses and Torridonian sediments, these fabrics too must be Caledonian in age.

It is concluded that the rocks of the Moine nappe were crystallized pelitic and psammitic schists already interleaved with Lewisian slices which occupy the major fold cores in Morar and Glenelg before the Caledonian orogenesis. They suffered several Caledonian deformations, including the ductile thrusting (slides) referred to below. The effects of reworking the already crystalline rocks are to some extent obscured by the recrystallization during Caledonian metamorphism which also effected the grain growth and the crystallization of new strain-free phases in the blastomylonites of the southern part of the thrust zone (Johnson, 1961).

THE SGURR BEAG SLIDE

The Morar Division rocks are limited, upward and to

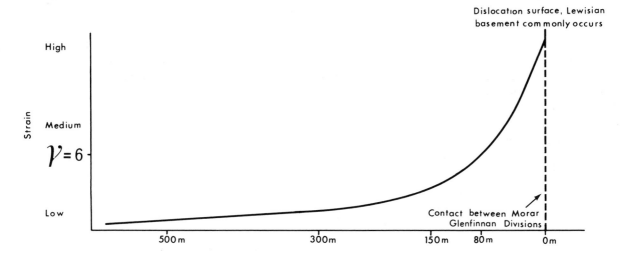

Associated features

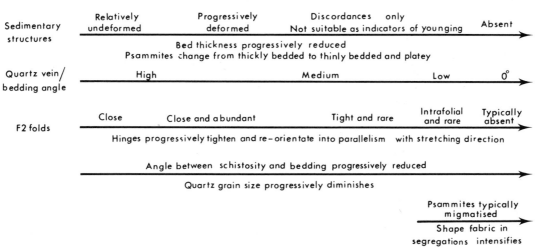

Figure 5. Postulated strain variation toward the Sgurr Beag Slide and a summary of the associated features.

the east, by the Sgurr Beag slide (Tanner, 1970; Tanner *et al.,* 1980; Rathbone and Harris, 1979). This is a ductile thrust of regional extent and has brought pelitic and psammitic gneisses of the Glenfinnan Division against the Morar Division rocks. The course of the slide is marked in many places by slices of Lewisian basement which, even where only a few meters thick, can often be traced along strike for distances the order of kilometers. The Lewisian slices are thick (2–3 km) in the Monar and Orrin areas (Ramsay, 1958 and 1963; Tobisch *et al.,* 1970), but, southward, individual slices are thinner and less abundant; eventually they die out at Kinlochourn (Fig. 1), while the slide, following the Morar-Glenfinnan boundary, can be traced with some confidence nearly as far as the Great Glen fault where the fault passes to the south of Mull (Fig. 1).

The structural and textural phenomena associated

with the Sgurr Beag slide have recently been established by Rathbone (1980) and Rathbone and Harris (1979). These can be summarized (Fig. 5) as follows:

a) Traverses in many places from west to east have revealed that, west of the slide, some 750 m from the contact between Glenfinnan and Morar Divisions or where the Lewisian slice crops out, the Morar Division psammites contain abundant sedimentary structures. From these, the original way-up of the strata can easily be read; the rocks have suffered polyphase deformation as shown by superimposed cleavages in pelitic bands, but the degree of deformation in the psammites is sufficiently mild as to preserve the cross-bedding. At this distance from the Morar-Glenfinnan contact, tectonic minor folds are normally of shallow plunge, and hinges, if curvilinear, are only slightly so.

b) With decreasing distance to the contact, minor

folds become tighter and more sheath-like as their hinges approach the down-dip extension lineation which is inclined eastward. Angles of cross-bedding within psammitic layers progressively decrease as strain increases and a critical point is reached, normally within 500 m of the Morar-Glenfinnan contact at which sedimentary structures cannot be reliably interpreted.

c) A further decrease in distance to the contact results in the disappearance of all significant angles between laminations in the psammites, minor folds become rare or absent, and within 80 m of the contact, all fabric elements are brought into absolute parallelism. Thus, the rocks take on an intense flaggy or platy appearance, normally with a marked down-dip lineation defined by grain-aggregate shapes. Sparse folds are intrafolial or rootless isoclines, or folds are entirely absent. These characteristics persist as far as the contact zone with the Glenfinnan Division. It is estimated that a shear strain of $\gamma = 6$ exists in the rocks 80 m from the contact, and it is likely that strain increases towards the contact (Fig. 5).

d) The Lewisian slices, where present in the slide zone, normally consist of hornblende-bearing feldspathic gneisses carrying small pods of almost monomineralic hornblende. Diopsidic marble, quartzo-feldspathic augen gneiss, serpentinite, and quartzite are other minor Lewisian lithologies recorded in the slide zone. Often very narrow, 1-2 m thick slices of Lewisian, interpreted as thin thrust slices of basement, are extremely persistent laterally and presumably in depth. It would be normal for a slice 1-2 m thick to be traceable for circa 1-2 km. Flaggy or platy fabrics are a feature of the Lewisian rocks with the competent hornblendite and quartzo-feldspathic aggregates augened and wrapped by the intense fabric.

e) Although exceptions do exist, notably in the Morar area, where Caledonian thermal overprinting was probably locally important, there is, on a regional scale, an apparent break in metamorphic grade across the contact between Morar and Glenfinnan Divisions. The Glenfinnan rocks were already gneissose before the thrusting and mineral assemblages recorded in pelitic, calcareous, and metabasic rocks indicate middle-to-upper amphibolite facies. Deformation in the Sgurr Beag slide zone has disrupted the gneissic foliation in the pelitic gneisses to the east of the contact for many tens of meters. It is likely that the abundant mica in the Glenfinnan pelites causes these rocks to behave in a different way to the predominant psammites of the Morar Division. Nevertheless, the pelites often show zones of intense granulation and grain size reduction.

f) In addition to features *a* to *e* described above, which are recognizable in the field, Rathbone (1980) and Rathbone and Harris (1979) have described textural changes recognizable in thin section. Recognition of these depends to a great extent on the degree to which subse-

quent recrystallization has modified the deformation textures in individual grains and the extent to which grain growth has taken place within the slide zone. In Glen Shiel (Fig. 1), it is clear that grain growth has modified the original slide fabrics. However, the original variable grain-size distribution, an original, largely sedimentary feature characteristic of the weakly deformed Morar psammites, has been eliminated and a uniform, much smaller grain size affirmed (Fig. 6). Evidence for progressively increasing grain-size reduction, produced by increasing strain, is seen at Garve (Fig. 1), where significant Caledonian recrystallization did not occur, and features associated with deformation predominate: undulose extinction, deformation bands, sub-grains, and new grains (cf. White, 1973, and

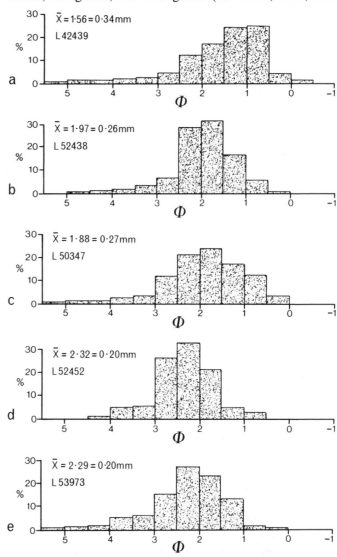

Figure 6. Graphs of frequency against quartz grain size, demonstrating grain size reduction toward the Lewisian. Distances from Lewisian: 450m, 225m, 170m, 50m, and 5m, respectively. Number of grains counted: 292, 274, 257, 258, and 334, respectively. L numbers refer to University of Liverpool sliced specimen numbers.

1976). These features are absent at Glen Shiel where Caledonian recrystallization occurred.

In summary, we conclude that the Sgurr Beag slide is a major zone of displacement and not just a discontinuity. There is evidence for a zone of simple shear which increases in intensity upward in the Morar Division, reaches a maximum intensity in the contact zone with the Glenfinnan Division where the Lewisian slices occur, and decreases in intensity upward into the Glenfinnan Division. Associated with the slide zone is a progressive break-down of grain size and an imposition of uniformity of grain size. Thus, the slide created in the Moines—which were already crystalline, but heterogeneous in terms of deformation and metamorphic grade—a zone of flaggy or platy rocks of remarkable along-strike persistence. Although closely studied in the Sgurr Beag slide zone, these features are not by any means unique to this slide zone and are a common feature of the Moine outcrop, both Glenfinnan and Morar, suggesting that Caledonian reworking of this type was widespread.

The Sgurr Beag slide zone is also of considerable cross-strike persistence. In the south, a series of south-plunging Caledonian folds carry the trace of the slide westward almost as far as the supposed outcrop of the Moine thrust between Mull and Iona (Fig. 1). In the north, the slide with its attendant Lewisian inliers is repeated to the west by folding around the Sguman Choinnich fold in Kintail and its extension northward into Ross-shire. This lateral persistence, allowing for the unrolling of the structures which fold the slide, is in the order of 25–50 km. It is significant, therefore, that the metamorphic grade of the Glenfinnan rocks, largely established before the Caledonian thrust sliding, is always more or less the same adjacent to the slide, i.e., mid-upper amphibolitic facies. The slide does not bring up lower crustal rocks. Thus, we conclude that the Sgurr Beag slide made a remarkably shallow cut through the crust, that is, it followed a "flat" rather than a thrust "ramp" structure. It owes its present almost invariable steep attitude to a combination of Caledonian post-slide folding and to passive rotation during Caledonian post-slide crustal shortening. The conclusion that the original eastward dip of the slide was shallow, but that there is a contrast in pre-slide metamorphic grade across it, is a strong indication that the displacement across the slide was large. It carries high grade rocks of the Glenfinnan Division as well as Lewisian gneiss onto rocks of the Morar Division, that is, it carries what were probably deeper level rocks onto higher level rocks. We conclude, therefore, that it has the geometry of a low angle thrust.

THE RELATIONSHIP BETWEEN THE MOINE THRUST AND SGURR BEAG SLIDE ZONES

The total displacement at the Moine nappe is unknown. However, the lower nappes of the Moine thrust zone contain Lewisian structures which possibly correlate with Lewisian structures on the foreland. Coward et al. (1980) and Elliott and Johnson (1980) have estimated a displacement of over 20–25 km from the Glencoul thrust in Assynt, from a correlation of Laxfordian structures. In the southern part of the Moine thrust zone, the correlation of Lewisian amphibolites from the foreland near Loch Maree with amphibolites from the thrust zone near Loch Carron suggests a displacement of about 45 km for the Kinlochewe-Kishorn thrust (Peach et al., 1907; Coward et al., 1980). Using the occurrence of Laxfordian granites in mylonites immediately beneath the Moine thrust zone, Elliott and Johnson (1980) suggest a displacement of at least 77 km for the zone. They consider this to be a lower estimate; a more realistic distance may be in the order of 100 km.

Where exposed, the Moine thrust is only gently dipping and locally dips gently westward where folded by underlying horse accretion. In the south, the Moine schists above the thrust are in greenschist facies. Nowhere in the Moine nappe are the rocks higher than amphibolite facies. Thus, there is no metamorphic evidence that the Moine thrust increases in dip to the east; 70 km (+) displacement on a steeply dipping or even moderately inclined thrust should carry up rocks of high metamorphic grade. Similarly, the geophysical data based on seismic refraction profile (the LISPB profile of Bamford et al., 1978) do not indicate any crustal thickening beneath the Moines or any offset of refracting horizons. Displacements of the Moine thrust zone cannot be taken up by shortening the whole crust NW of the Great Glen. We conclude, therefore, that the Moine thrust zone either maintains a constant gentle dip to the ESE or may flatten out. Elliott and Johnson (1980) note that, some 25 km east of the Moine thrust at Strath Vagastie, post-orogenic lamporphyres contain xenoliths resembling the acid gneiss of the Hebridean craton (Read and others, 1926), raising the possibility that this far east, at least, Moine rocks rest on a thrust whose footwall is similar to the Lewisian basement of the foreland. This will probably only be resolved by seismic reflection profiling.

In our view, the Sgurr Beag slide zone is likely to be the within-basement extension of a thrust (zone) analogous to the Moine thrust. The Sgurr Beag nappe, i.e., the thrust slice above the slide, probably carried Moine rocks far to the WNW at a level high above that now cut by erosion into the Hebridean craton. The folds of the Sgurr Beag slide presumably originated from a lower level displacement zone in a similar way that the folds of the Ben Arnaboll thrust originated from imbricates generated in the lower Sole nappe. It is to be expected that early shear zones will have a complex geometry with highly variable strikes and dips, while later shear zones which were generated at a lower structural level should be more uniform in orientation.

This raises the problem as to the origin of low angle fault zones in basement rocks. Some faults, such as the Wind River structure (Brewer *et al.,* 1980), maintain a constant dip of about 30° for over 25 km into the crust. Some faults, such as the southern Himalayan thrusts, form ramps dipping at about 30° in the basement but flatten to form bedding parallel detachment faults in the cover (Seeber *et al.,* 1981). In Scotland, however, there is evidence that the faults do not climb steep ramps in the Lewisian basement. The thickness of the Lewisian rocks above the Glencoul and Arnaboll thrust sheets is never more than one kilometer, and yet these blocks have been displaced for over 25 km, an average angle of climb of less than 2.5°. Moreover, at Assynt, these basement thrust sheets can be traced back across section for more than 5 km, and yet their coating of Cambrian rocks has a sheet dip parallel to that of the foreland; there is no indication of a general thickening of the sheets toward the hinterland as would be expected if the faults climbed steeply. Similarly, the Sgurr Beag slide zone appears to have followed a flat rather than a ramp while slicing through metamorphosed Moines.

We suggest, therefore, that the major thrust faults in NW Scotland have a staircase trajectory similar to those in foreland thrust belts but that the steps may be larger and further apart. The reason why the thrusts follow flats in the basement is still unknown. They may follow some initial anisotropy in the basement rocks, possibly formed by earlier deformation phases. In the more homogeneous Lewisian gneiss, the flats may follow zones of metamorphic phase change or metamorphic breakdown of specific minerals. Voll (1976) likewise suggests that the nearly constant thickness of many of the Alpine basement masses is due to their development on faults at approximately the same depth and that this was controlled by metamorphic mineral breakdown. According to Voll, the Helvetic basement masses formed at depths governed by the ease of quartz deformation, while the Pennine basement sheets formed at depths governed by the breakdown of feldspar.

One purpose of this paper is to draw attention to the striking possibility that major, well-defined zones of heterogeneity may well exist in the crust where thrust zones extend down into the basement. The superficial, rather easily recognized symptoms of high-level thrusts, brecciation, clean-cut thrust plates, and zones of fault-clay gouge, are thought to pass down with increasing confining pressure into finely banded mylonites. Both ductile mylonites and brittle cataclasites are seen in the Moine thrust zone, although, where found together, the ductile mylonites always formed before the brecciation. It is in the extension of these structures into more ductile, deeper parts of the crust, producing the Sgurr Beag slide features, that the de-

formation phenomena are less easily recognizable. Deformation at lower levels was accompanied by recrystallization and commonly followed by some grain growth; uniform fabrics of intense preferred orientation, both dimensional and crystallographic, are created.

It is interesting to speculate on the geophysical properties of these zones. To what extent, for example, would the thick zone of flaggy rocks along a ductile thrust produce a reflecting surface? If so, is the flaggy or platy nature sufficient alone; i.e., would the crystallization and grain growth, as it eliminated or diminished the preferred crystallographic and dimensional orientation of the slide fabrics, also diminish the geophysically identifiable properties of the zone? These problems are not yet answered; such problems as the relationship between seismic anisotropy and strain and the effect of later recrystallization are now being tackled at Leeds University. There is the probability that shallowly inclined seismic reflective zones, identified by geophysical prospecting and major COCORP type projects, may be merely structurally developed zones within the basement. They may not be zones of strong lithological contrast.

ACKNOWLEDGMENTS

P. A. Rathbone and A. L. Harris acknowledge discussion of the problems of ductile thrusting with Dr. J. S. Watterson. M. P. Coward's work is supported by NERC Grant GR/4100 (Moine Thrust). A. L. Harris' work is supported by NERC Grant GR3/3998.

REFERENCES CITED

Bamford, D., Nunn, D., Prodehl, C., and Jacob, B., 1978, LISPB IV. Crustal structure of northern Britain: Geophysical Journal of the Royal astronomical Society, v. 54, p. 43–60.

Berger, P., and Johnson, A. M., 1980, First-order analysis of deformation of a thrust sheet moving over a ramp: Tectonophysics, v. 70, T9–T24.

Brewer, J. A., Smithson, S. B., Oliver, J. E., Kaufman, S., and Brown, L. D., 1980, The Laramide Orogeny: Evidence from COCORP deep crustal seismic reflection profiles in the Wind River Mountains, Wyoming: Tectonophysics, v. 62, p. 165–189.

Brook, M., Brewer, M., and Powell, D., 1977, Grenville events in the Moine rocks of the northern Highlands, Scotland: Journal of the Geological Society of London, v. 133, p. 489–496.

Christie, J. M., 1963, The Moine Thrust Zone in the Assynt Region, N. W. Scotland: University of California Publications in Geological Sciences, v. 40, p. 345–419.

Cobbold, P. R., and Quinquis, H., 1980, Development of sheath folds in shear regimes: Journal of Structural Geology, v. 2, p. 119–126.

Cook, F. A., Albaugh, D. S., Brown, L. D., Kaufmann, S., Oliver, J. E., and Hatcher, R. D., 1979, Thin-skinned tectonics in the crystalline southern Appalachians; COCORP seismic-reflection profiling of the Blue Ridge at Piedmont: Geology, v. 7, p. 563–567.

Coward, M. P., 1980, The Caledonian thrusts and shear zones of NW Scotland: Journal of Structural Geology, v. 2, p. 11–17.

Coward, M. P., and Kim, J. H., 1981, Strain within thrust sheets, *in*

McClay, K. R. and Price, N. J. (Eds.), Thrust and nappe tectonics: Special Publication of the Geological Society of London, no. 9, p. 275–292.

Coward, M. P., Kim, J. H., and Parke, J., 1980, The Lewisian structure within the Moine thrust zone: Proceedings of the Geologists Association, v. 91, 327–337.

Dewey, J. F., and Pankhurst, R. J., 1970, The evolution of the Scottish Caledonides in relationship to their isotopic age pattern: Transactions of the Royal Society of Edinburgh, v. 68, 361–389.

Elliott, D., and Johnson, M.R.W., 1980, Structural evolution in the northern part of the Moine thrust belt, NW Scotland: Transactions of the Royal Society of Edinburgh, v. 71, p. 69–96.

Hallam, A., and Swett, K., 1966, Trace fossils from the lower Cambrian Pipe Rock of the north-west Highlands: Scottish Journal of Geology, v. 2, p. 101–106.

Harris, L. D., and Bayer, K. C., 1979, Sequential development of the Appalachian orogen above a master décollement—a hypothesis: Geology, v. 7, p. 568–572.

Hatcher, R. D., 1981, Thrusts and nappes in the North American Appalachian Orogen, *in* McClay, K. R., and Price, N. J. (eds.), Thrust and nappe tectonics: Special Publication of the Geological Society of London, no. 9, p. 491–499.

Johnson, M.R.W., 1961, Polymetamorphism in movement zones in the Caledonian thrust belt of north-west Scotland: Journal of Geology, v. 69, p. 417–432.

Johnstone, G. S., Smith, D. I., and Harris, A. L., 1969, The Moinian assemblage of Scotland: Memoir of the American Association of Petroleum Geologists, no. 12, p. 159–180.

Peach, B. N., Horne, J., Gunn, W., Clough, C. T., Hinxman, L. W., and Teall, J.J.H., 1907, The geological structure of the NW Highlands of Scotland: Memoir of the Geological Survey of the United Kingdom.

Pidgeon, T. R., and Johnson, M.R.W., 1974, A comparison of zircon U-Pb and whole rock Rb-Sr systems in three phases of the Carn Chuinneag Granite, NW Scotland: Earth and Planetary Science Letters, v. 24, p. 105–112.

Powell, D., 1974, Stratigraphy and structure of the western Moine and the problems of Moine orogenesis: Journal of the Geological Society of London, v. 130, p. 575–593.

Ramsay, J. G., 1958, Moine-Lewisian relations at Glenelg, Inverness-shire: Quarterly Journal of the Geological Society of London, v. 113, p. 487–520.

Ramsay, J. G., 1963, Structures and metamorphism of the Moine and Lewisian rocks, of the Northwest Caledonides, *in* Johnson, M.R.W., and Stewart, E. H., (Eds.), The British Caledonides: Oliver and Boyd, Edinburgh, p. 143–175.

Rathbone, P. A., 1980, Basement/cover relationships in the Moine Series of Scotland, with particular reference to the Sgurr Beag slide. Ph.D. thesis (University of Liverpool) Unpublished.

Rathbone, P. A., and Harris, A. L., 1979, Basement-cover relationships at Lewisian inliers in the Moine rocks, *in* Harris, A. L., *et al.*, (Eds.), The Caledonides of the British Isles—reviewed: Special Publication of the Geological Society of London, v. 8, p. 101–107.

Read, H. H., 1961, Aspects of the Caledonian magmatism in Britain: Proceedings of the Liverpool and Manchester Geological Society, v. 2, p. 653–683.

Read, H. H., Phemister, J., and Ross, G., 1926, The geology of Strath Oykel and Lower Loch Shin: Memoir of the Geological Survey of Scotland.

Seeber, L., Armbruster, J. and Quittmayer, R. C., 1981, Seismicity and continental subduction in the Himalayan Arc, *in* Zagros, Hindukush, Himalaya, geodynamic evolution (edited by Gupta, H. K. and Delany, F. M.) Geodynamics Series 3, American Geophysical Union, Washington, p. 215–242.

Sibson, R. H., 1977, Fault rocks and fault mechanics: Journal of the Geological Society of London, v. 133, 191–213.

Sibson, R. H., White, S. H., and Atkinson, B. K., 1981, Structure and distribution of fault rocks in the Alpine Fault Zone, New Zealand, *in* McClay, K. R., and Price, N. J., (Eds.), Thrust and nappe tectonics: Special Publication of the Geological Society of London, no. 9, p. 197–210.

Smith, D. I., 1979, Caledonian minor intrusions of the N. Highlands of Scotland, *in* Harris, A. L., et al., (eds.), The Caledonides of the British Isles—reviewed: Special Publication of the Geological Society of London, no. 8, p. 682–698.

Tanner, P.W.G., 1970, The Sgurr Beag Slide—a major tectonic break within the Moinian of the western Highlands of Scotland: Quarterly Journal of the Geological Society of London, v. 126, p. 435–463.

Tanner, P.W.G., Johnstone, G. S., Smith, D. I., and Harris, A. L., 1970, Moine stratigraphy and the problem of the Central Ross-shire inliers: Bulletin of the Geological Society of America, v. 81, p. 299–306.

Tobisch, O., Fleuty, M. J., Merh, S. S., Mukhopadhyay, D., and Ramsay, J. G., 1970, Deformational and metamorphic history of Moinian and Lewisian rocks between Strathconnon and Glen Affric: Scottish Journal of Geology, v. 6, p. 243–265.

van Breemen, O., Pidgeon, R. T., and Johnson, M.R.W., 1974, Precambrian and Palaeozoic pegmatites in the Moines of northern Sutherland: Journal of the Geological Society of London, v. 130, p. 493–507.

van Breemen, O., Aftalion, M., and Johnson, M.R.W., 1979, Age of the Borrolan complex, Assynt and late movements on the Moine thrust: Journal of the Geological Society of London, v. 136, p. 489–496.

Voll, G., 1976. Recrystallisation of quartz, biotite and feldspars from Erstfeld to the Leventina nappe, Swiss Alps, and its geological significance. Schweizerische Mineralogische und Petrographische Mitteilungen, v. 56, p. 641–647.

Watson, J. V., 1975, The Lewisian Complex, *in* Harris, A. L., et al., (Eds.), A correlation of Precambrian rocks in the British Isles: Special Report of the Geological Society of London, no. 6, p. 15–29.

White, S. H., 1973, Syntectonic recrystallisation and texture development in quartz: Nature, London, v. 244, p. 276–278.

White, S. H., 1976, The effects of strain on the microstructure, fabrics and deformation mechanisms in quartzites: Philosophical Transactions of the Royal Society of London, v. 283A, p. 69–86.

White, S. H., 1979a, Grain size and sub-grain size variation across a mylonite zone: Contributions to Mineralogy and Petrology, v. 70, p. 193–202.

White, S. H., 1979b, Difficulties associated with palaeostress estimates: Bulletin of Mineralogy, v. 102, p. 210–215.

White, S. H., Burrows, S., Carreras, J., Shaw, N., and Humphreys, J., 1980, On mylonites in ductile shear zones: Journal of Structural Geology, v. 2, p. 175–187.

Wilson, D., and Shepherd, J., 1979, The Carn Chuinneag granite and its aureole, *in* Harris, A. L., et al., (Eds.), The Caledonides of the British Isles—reviewed: Special Publication of the Geological Society of London, no. 8, p. 669–675.

MANUSCRIPT ACCEPTED BY THE SOCIETY SEPTEMBER 10, 1982

Typeset by WESType Publishing Services, Inc., Boulder, Colorado
Printed in U.S.A. by Malloy Lithographing, Inc., Ann Arbor, Michigan

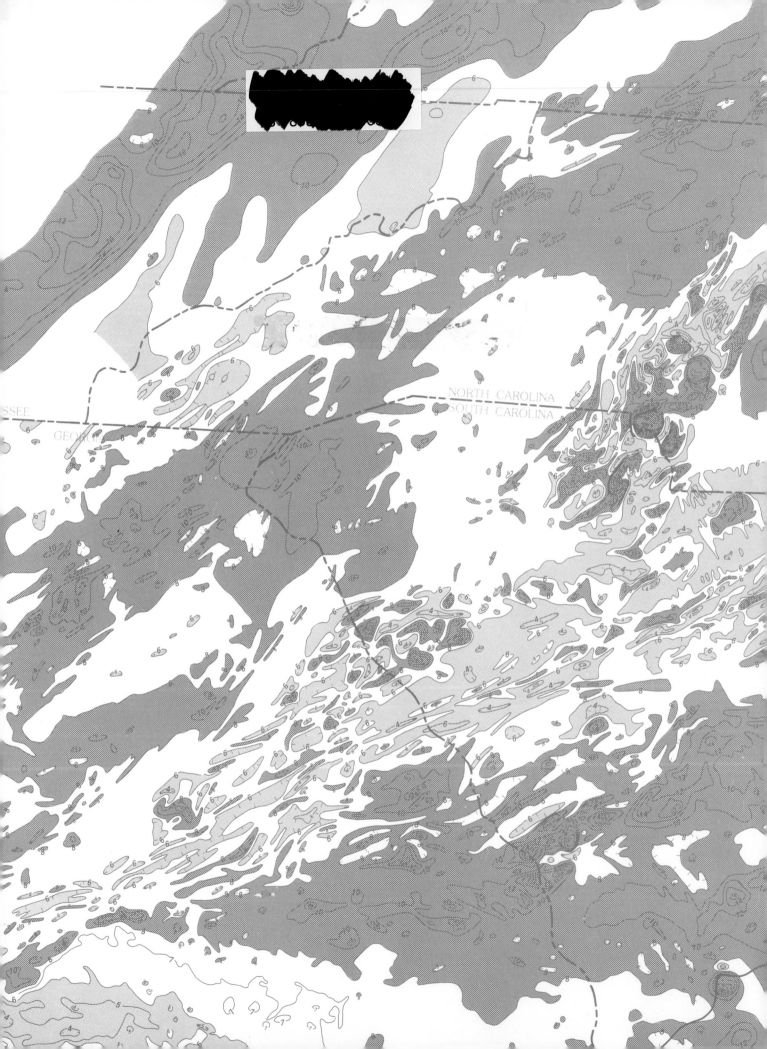

NORTH CAROLINA
SOUTH CAROLINA

GEORGIA